Langenscheidt Universal Spanish Dictionary

Spanish – English
English – Spanish

completely revised edition

edited by the
Langenscheidt editorial staff

New York · Berlin · Munich · Vienna · Zurich

Based on Langenscheidt's Pocket Spanish Dictionary
compiled by LEXUS.
Basado en el Diccionario Báscio Inglés de Langenscheidt
redactado por el equipo LEXUS.

2. 3. 4. 5. 09 08 07 06

Printed in Germany – Impreso en Alemania
ISBN 1-58573-492-6 (USA)
ISBN 0-88729-168-6 (Estados Unidos)
ISBN 3-468-96183-9 (España)

Contents
Índice

Abbreviations / Abreviaturas 4
La pronunciación del inglés 8
Spanish-English / Español-Inglés 11
English-Spanish / Inglés-Español 273
Los verbos irregulares ingleses 570
Numbers / Numerales 573

Abbreviations
Abreviaturas

stands for the headword	~	sustituye la voz-guía
and	&	y
see	☞	véase
registered trademark	®	marca registrada
adjective	*adj*	adjetivo
adverb	*adv*	adverbio
agriculture	AGR	agricultura
anatomy	ANAT	anatomía
Argentina	*Arg*	Argentina
architecture	ARQUI	arquitectura
article	*art*	artículo
astronomy	AST	astronomía
astrology	ASTR	astrología
attributive	*atr*	atributivo
motoring	AUTO	automóvil
aviation	AVIA	aviación
biology	BIO	biología
Bolivia	*Bol*	Bolivia
botany	BOT	botánica
British English	*Br*	inglés británico
Central America	*C.Am.*	América central
Chile	*Chi*	Chile
Colombia	*Col*	Colombia
commerce, business	COM	comercio
computers, IT term	COMPUT	informática
conjunction	*conj*	conjunción
Southern Cone	*CSur*	Cono Sur
sports	DEP	deporte
contemptuous	*desp*	despectivo

education (schools, universities)	EDU	educación, enseñanza (sistema escolar y universitario)
electronics, electronic engineering	ELEC	electrónica, electrotecnia
Spain	*Esp*	España
familiar, colloquial	F	familiar
feminine	*f*	femenino
feminine noun and adjective	*f/adj*	sustantivo femenino y adjetivo
railroad	FERR	ferrocarriles
figurative	*fig*	figurativo
financial	FIN	finanzas
physics	FÍS	física
formal	*fml*	formal
photography	FOT	fotografía
feminine plural	*fpl*	femenino plural
feminine singular	*fsg*	femenino singular
gastronomy	GASTR	gastronomía
geography	GEOG	geografía
geology	GEOL	geología
grammatical	GRAM	gramática
historical	HIST	histórico
IT term	INFOR	informática
interjection	*int*	interjección
interrogative	*interr*	interrogativo
invariable	*inv*	invariable
law	JUR	jurisprudencia
Latin America	*L.Am.*	América Latina
law	LAW	jurisprudencia
masculine	*m*	masculino
masculine noun and adjective	*m/adj*	sustantivo masculino y adjetivo
nautical	MAR	navegación, marina

mathematics	MAT	matemáticas
mathematics	MATH	matemáticas
medicine	MED	medicina
meteorology	METEO	meteorología
Mexico	*Mex*	México
Mexico	*Méx*	México
masculine and feminine	*m/f*	masculino y femenino
masculine and feminine plural	*m/fpl*	masculino y femenino plural
military	MIL	militar
mineralogy	MIN	mineralogía
motoring	MOT	automóvil
masculine plural	*mpl*	masculino al plural
music	MUS	música
music	MÚS	música
noun	*n*	sustantivo
nautical	NAUT	navegación, náutica
negative	*neg*	negativo
noun plural	*npl*	sustantivo al plural
noun singular	*nsg*	sustantivo al singular
oneself	o.s.	sí mismo
popular, slang	P	popular
past participle	*part*	participio (del pasado)
Peru	*Pe*	Perú
pejorative	*pej*	peyorativo
photography	PHOT	fotografía
physics	PHYS	física
painting	PINT	pintura
plural	*pl*	plural
politics	POL	política
preposition	*prep*	preposición
pronoun	*pron*	pronombre
preposition	*prp*	preposición

psychology	PSI	psicología
psychology	PSYCH	psicología
chemistry	QUÍM	química
radio	RAD	radio
railroad	RAIL	ferrocarriles
relative	*rel*	relativo
religion	REL	religión
River Plate	*Rpl*	Río de la Plata
South America	*S.Am.*	América del Sur
singular	*sg*	singular
someone	s.o.	alguien
sports	SP	deporte
Spain	*Span*	España
something	*sth*	algo, alguna cosa
subjunctive	*subj*	subjuntivo
bullfighting	TAUR	tauromaquia
also	*tb*	también
theater, theatre	TEA	teatro
technology	TÉC	técnica, tecnología
technology	TECH	técnica, tecnología
telecommunications	TELEC	telecomunicaciones
theater, theatre	THEA	teatro
typography, typesetting	TIP	tipografía
transportation	TRANSP	transportes
television	TV	televisión
vulgar	V	vulgar
auxiliary verb	*v/aux*	verbo auxiliar
verb	*vb*	verbo
Venezuela	*Ven*	Venezuela
intransitive verb	*v/i*	verbo intransitivo
impersonal verb	*v/impers*	verbo impersonal
transitive verb	*v/t*	verbo transitivo
West Indies	*W.I.*	Antillas
zoology	ZO	zoología

La pronunciación del inglés

A. Vocales y diptongos

[ɑ:] sonido largo parecido al de *a* en *raro*: *far* [fɑ:r].

[ʌ] *a* abierta, breve y oscura, que se pronuncia en la parte anterior de la boca sin redondear los labios: *butter* ['bʌtər], *come* [kʌm], *blood* [blʌd].

[æ] sonido breve, bastante abierto y distinto, algo parecido al de *a* en *parra*: *fat* [fæt], *ran* [ræn].

[ɒ:] vocal larga, bastante cerrada, entre *a* y *o*; más cercana a la *a* que a la *o*: *fall* [fɒ:l], *fault* [fɒ:lt].

[e] sonido breve, medio abierto, parecido al de *e* en *perro*: *bed* [bed], *less* [les], *hairy* ['herɪ].

[aɪ] sonido parecido al de *ai* en *estáis*, *baile*: *I* [aɪ], *lie* [laɪ], *dry* [draɪ].

[aʊ] sonido parecido al de *au* en *causa*, *sauce*: *house* [haʊs], *now* [naʊ].

[eɪ] *e* medio abierta, pero más cerrada que la *e* de *hablé*; suena como si la siguiese una [ɪ] débil, sobre todo en sílaba acentuada: *date* [deɪt], *play* [pleɪ].

[ə] 'vocal neutra', siempre átona; parecida al sonido de la *a* final de *cada*: *about* [ə'baʊt], *connect* [kə'nekt].

[i:] sonido largo, parecido al de *i* en *misa*, *vino*: *scene* [si:n], *sea* [si:], *feet* [fi:t], *ceiling* ['si:lɪŋ].

[ɪ] sonido breve, abierto, parecido al de *i* en *silba*, *tirria*, pero más abierto: *big* [bɪg], *city* ['sɪtɪ].

[oʊ] *o* larga, más bien cerrada, sin redondear los labios ni levantar la lengua: *note* [noʊt], *boat* [boʊt], *below* [bɪ'loʊ].

[ɔː] vocal larga, bastante cerrada; es algo parecida a la *o* de *por*: *abnormal* [æb'nɔːrml], *before* [bɪ'fɔːr].

[ɔɪ] diptongo cuyo primer elemento es una *o* abierta, seguido de una *i* abierta pero débil; parecido al sonido de *oy* en *doy*: *voice* [vɔɪs], *boy* [bɔɪ].

[ɜː] forma larga de la 'vocal neutra' [ə], algo parecida al sonido de *eu* en la palabra francesa *leur*: *word* [wɜːrd], *girl* [gɜːrl].

[uː] sonido largo, parecido al de *u* en *cuna*, *duda*: *fool* [fuːl], *shoe* [ʃuː], *you* [juː], *rule* [ruːl].

[ʊ] *u* pura pero muy rápida, más cerrada que la *u* de *burra*: *put* [pʊt], *look* [lʊk].

B. Consonantes

[b] como la *b* de *cambiar*: *bay* [beɪ], *brave* [breɪv].

[d] como la *d* de *andar*: *did* [dɪd], *ladder* ['lædər].

[f] como la *f* de *filo*: *face* [feɪs], *baffle* ['bæfl].

[g] como la *g* de *golpe*: *go* [goʊ], *haggle* ['hægl].

[h] se pronuncia con aspiración fuerte, sin la aspereza gutural de la *j* en *Gijón*: *who* [huː], *ahead* [ə'hed].

[j] como la *y* de *cuyo*: *you* [juː], *million* ['mɪljən].

[k] como la *c* de *casa*: *cat* [kæt], *kill* [kɪl].

[l] como la *l* de *loco*: *love* [lʌv], *goal* [goʊl].

[m] como la *m* de *madre*: *mouth* [maʊθ], *come* [kʌm].

[n] como la *n* de *nada*: *not* [nɑːt], *banner* ['bænər].

[p] como la *p* de *padre*: *pot* [pɑːt], *top* [tɑːp].

[r] Cuando se pronuncia, es un sonido muy débil, más bien semivocal, que no tiene nada de la vibración fuerte que caracteriza la *r* española; se articula elevando la punta de la lengua hacia el

paladar duro: *rose* [roʊz], *pride* [praɪd], *there* [ðer].

[s] como la *s* de *casa*: *sit* [sɪt], *scent* [sent].

[t] como la *t* de *pata*: *take* [teɪk], *patter* ['pætər].

[v] inexistente en español; a diferencia de *b*, *v* en español, se pronuncia juntando el labio inferior con los dientes superiores: *vein* [veɪn], *velvet* ['velvɪt].

[w] como la *u* de *huevo*: *water* ['wɒːtər], *will* [wɪl].

[z] como la *s* de *mismo*: *zeal* [ziːl], *hers* [hɜːrz].

[ʒ] inexistente en español; como la *j* en la palabra francesa *jour*: *measure* ['meʒər], *leisure* ['liːʒər]. Aparece a menudo en el grupo [dʒ], que se pronuncia como el grupo *dj* de la palabra francesa *adjacent*: *edge* [edʒ], *gem* [dʒem].

[ʃ] inexistente en español; como *ch* en la palabra francesa *chose*: *shake* [ʃeɪk], *washing* ['wɑːʃɪŋ]. Aparece a menudo en el grupo [ʧ], que se pronuncia como la *ch* en *mucho*: *match* [mæʧ], *natural* ['næʧrəl].

[θ] como la *z* de *zapato* en castellano: *thin* [θɪn], *path* [pæθ].

[ð] forma sonorizada del anterior, algo como la *d* de *todo*: *there* [ðer], *breathe* [briːð].

[ŋ] como la *n* de *banco*: *singer* ['sɪŋər], *tinker* ['tɪŋkər].

A

a ◇ *dirección* to; **al este de** to the east of; **ir ~ la cama / al cine** go to bed / to the movies ◇ *situación* at; **al sol** in the sun; **está ~ cinco kilómetros** it is five kilometers away ◇ *tiempo*: **~ las tres** at three o'clock; **estamos ~ quince de febrero** it's February fifteenth; **~ los treinta años** at the age of thirty ◇ *modo*: **~ la española** the Spanish way; **~ mano** by hand; **~ pie** on foot; **~ 50 kilómetros por hora** at fifty kilometers an hour ◇ *precio*: **¿~ cómo** *o* **cuánto está?** how much is it? ◇ *objeto indirecto*: **dáselo ~ tu hermano** give it to your brother ◇ *objeto directo*: **vi ~ mi padre** I saw my father ◇ *para introducir pregunta*: **¿~ que no lo sabes?** I bet you don't know; **~ ver...** OK ...

abad *m* abbot

abajo 1 *adv* ◇ *situación* below, underneath; *en edificio* downstairs; **ponlo ahí ~** put it down there; **el cajón de ~** *siguiente* the drawer below; *último* the bottom drawer ◇ *dirección* down; *en edificio* downstairs; **empuja hacia ~** push down ◇ *con cantidades*: **de diez para ~** ten or under **2** *int*: **¡~ los traidores!** down with the traitors!

abalanzarse rush *o* surge forward; **~ sobre algo / alguien** pounce on sth / s.o.

abandonar *lugar* leave; *objeto, a alguien* abandon; *a esposa, hijos* desert; *idea, actividad* give up; **abandonarse** let o.s. go; **~ a** abandon o.s. to; **abandono** *m* abandonment; DEP *de carrera* retirement; **en un estado de ~** in a state of neglect

abanicar fan; **abanicarse** fan o.s.; **abanico** *m* fan; *fig* range

abaratar reduce the price of; *precio* reduce

abarcar cover; *L.Am.* (*acaparar*) hoard; **~ con la vista** take in

abarrotado packed; **abarrotes** *mpl L.Am.* groceries; (**tienda de**) **~** grocery store, *Br* grocer's

abastecer supply (**de** with); **abastecimiento** *m* supply

abatible collapsible, folding *atr*; **abatimiento** *m* gloom; **abatir** *edificio* knock down; *árbol* cut down; AVIA shoot *o* bring down; *fig* kill; (*deprimir*) depress

abdicación *f* abdication; **abdicar** abdicate

abecé *m fig* ABCs *pl*, *Br* ABC
abedul *m* birch
abeja *f* ZO bee; **abejorro** *m* bumblebee
abertura *f* opening
abeto *m* fir (tree)
abierto 1 *part* ☞ ***abrir* 2** *adj* open
abismo *m* abyss; *fig* gulf
ablandar *tb fig* soften
abnegación *f* self-denial; **abnegado** selfless
abogado *m*, **-a** *f* lawyer; *en tribunal superior* attorney, *Br* barrister; ***no le faltaron ~s*** *fig* there were plenty of people who defended him; **abogar:** **~ *por alguien*** defend; *algo* advocate
abolición *f* abolition; **abolir** abolish
abollado dented; **abolladura** *f* dent
abominable abominable; **abominar** detest, loathe
abonable COM payable; **abonado** *m*, **-a** *f* subscriber; *a teléfono*, *gas*, *electricidad* customer; *a ópera*, *teatro* season-ticket holder; **abonar** COM pay; AGR fertilize; *Méx* pay on account; **~ *el terreno*** *fig* sow the seeds; **abonarse** *a espectáculo* buy a season ticket (***a*** for); *a revista* take out a subscription (***a*** to); **abono** *m* COM payment; AGR fertilizer; *para espectáculo*, *transporte* season ticket
abordar MAR board; *tema*, *asunto* broach, raise; *problema* tackle, deal with; *a una persona* approach
aborigen 1 *adj* native, indigenous **2** *m/f* native
aborrecer loathe, detest; **aborrecimiento** *m* loathing
abortar 1 *v/i* MED miscarry; *de forma provocada* have an abortion **2** *v/t plan* foil; **aborto** *m* miscarriage; *provocado* abortion; *fig* F freak F
abotonar button up
abrasar 1 *v/t* burn **2** *v/i del sol* burn; *de bebida*, *comida* be boiling hot; **abrasarse:** ***~ de sed*** F be parched F; ***~ de calor*** F be sweltering F
abrazar hug; **abrazarse** embrace; **abrazo** *m* hug; ***un ~*** *en carta* best wishes; *más íntimo* love
abrelatas *m inv* can opener, *Br tb* tin opener
abreviar shorten; *palabra* abbreviate; *texto* abridge; **abreviatura** *f* abbreviation
abridor *m* bottle opener
abrigar wrap up; *esperanzas* hold out; *duda* entertain; **abrigarse** wrap up warm; **abrigo** *m* coat; (*protección*) shelter; ***ropa de ~*** warm clothes; ***al ~ de*** in the shelter of
abril *m* April
abrir 1 *v/t* open; *túnel* dig; *grifo* turn on **2** *v/i de persona* open up; *de ventana*, *puerta* open; ***en un ~ y cerrar de ojos***

in the twinkling of an eye
abrochar, abrocharse do up; *cinturón de seguridad* fasten
abrumar overwhelm (***con*** *o* ***de*** with)
abrupto *terreno* rough; *pendiente* steep; *tono, respuesta* abrupt; *cambio* sudden
absolución *f* absolution
absolutamente absolutely; ***no entendió ~ nada*** he didn't understand a thing; **absoluto** absolute; ***en ~*** not at all
absolver JUR acquit; REL absolve
absorber absorb; (*consumir*) take; COM take over; **absorción** *f* absorption; COM takeover
abstemio 1 *adj* teetotal **2** *m*, **-a** *f* teetotaler, *Br* teetotaller
abstención *f* abstention; **abstenerse** refrain (***de*** from); POL abstain; **abstinencia** *f* abstinence; ***síndrome de ~*** MED withdrawal symptoms *pl*
abstracción *f* abstraction; ***hacer ~ de*** exclude; **abstracto** abstract; **abstraer** abstract; **abstraerse** shut o.s. off (***de*** from); **abstraído 1** *adj* preoccupied; ***~ en algo*** engrossed in sth **2** *part* ☞ ***abstraer***
absurdo 1 *adj* absurd **2** *m*: ***es un ~ que*** it's absurd that
abuchear boo
abuela *f* grandmother; **abuelo** *m* grandfather; ***~s*** grandparents
abultar be bulky; ***no abulta casi nada*** it takes up almost no room at all
abundancia *f* abundance; ***comida en ~*** plenty of food; **abundante** plentiful, abundant; **abundar** be plentiful *o* abundant
aburrido (*que aburre*) boring; (*que se aburre*) bored (***de*** with); **aburrimiento** *m* boredom; **aburrir** bore; **aburrirse** get bored (***de*** with)
abusar: ***~ de*** abuse; *persona* take advantage of; ***~ sexualmente de*** sexually abuse; **abuso** *m* abuse; ***~s deshonestos*** indecent assault
a.C. (= ***antes de Cristo***) BC (= before Christ)
acá here; ***de ~ para allá*** from here to there; ***de entonces para ~*** since then
acabado *m* finish; **acabar** finish; ***acabé haciéndolo yo*** I finished up *o* ended up doing it myself; ***~ con*** put an end to; *caramelos* finish off; *persona* destroy; ***~ de hacer algo*** have just done sth; ***va a ~ mal*** F *persona* he'll come to no good; ***esto va a ~ mal*** F this is going to end badly; **acabarse** *de actividad* finish, end; *de pan, dinero* run out; ***se nos ha acabado el azúcar*** we've run out of sugar; ***¡se acabó!*** that's that!
academia *f* academy; ***~ de idiomas*** language school

acallar *tb fig* silence
acalorado *fig* heated; ***estar ~*** be agitated; **acalorar** *fig* inflame; **acalorarse** (*enfadarse*) get worked up; (*sofocarse*) get embarrassed
acampada *f* camp; ***ir de ~*** go camping; **acampar** camp
acantilado *m* cliff
acaparar hoard, stockpile; *tiempo* take up; *interés* capture; (*monopolizar*) monopolize
acariciar caress; *perro* stroke; *idea* toy with
acarrear carry; *fig* give rise to, cause; **acarreo** *m* transportation
acaso perhaps; ***por si ~*** just in case
acatamiento *m* compliance (***de*** with); **acatar** comply with, obey
acatarrarse catch a cold
acaudalado wealthy, well-off
acceder (*ceder*) agree (***a*** to), accede (***a*** to) *fml*; ***~ a*** *lugar* gain access to; *cargo* accede to *fml*
accesible accessible; **acceso** *m tb* INFOR access; *de fiebre* attack; *de tos* fit; ***de difícil ~*** inaccessible; **accesorio 1** *adj* incidental **2** *m* accessory
accidentado 1 *adj terreno* rough; *viaje* eventful **2** *m*, **-a** *f* casualty; **accidental** (*no esencial*) incidental; (*casual*) chance *atr*; **accidente** *m* accident; (*casualidad*) chance; GEOG feature; ***~ de tráfico*** *o* ***de circulación*** road traffic accident; ***~ laboral*** industrial accident
acción *f* action; ***acciones*** COM stock, shares; ***poner en ~*** put into action; **accionar** activate; **accionista** *m/f* stockholder, shareholder
acebo *m* holly
aceite *m* oil; ***~ de girasol / oliva*** sunflower / olive oil; **aceitera** *f* TÉC oilcan; GASTR cruet; **aceituna** *f* olive
aceleración *f* acceleration; **acelerador** *m* accelerator; **acelerar 1** *v/t motor* rev up; *fig* speed up; ***aceleró el coche*** she accelerated **2** *v/i* accelerate
acelgas *fpl* BOT Swiss chard
acento *m* accent; (*énfasis*) stress, emphasis; **acentuar** stress; *fig* accentuate, emphasize
aceptable acceptable; **aceptación** *f* acceptance; (*éxito*) success; **aceptar** accept
acequia *f* irrigation ditch
acera *f* sidewalk, *Br* pavement; ***ser de la otra ~*** F be gay
acerbo sharp
acerca: *~ de* about
acercar bring closer; ***~ a alguien a un lugar*** give s.o. a ride *o Br* lift somewhere; **acercarse** approach; (*ir*) go; *de grupos, países* come closer together; *de fecha* draw near; ***¡acércate!*** come

closer
acero *m* steel; **~ *inoxidable*** stainless steel
acertado *comentario* apt; *elección* good, wise; ***estar muy ~*** be dead right; **acertante** *m/f de apuesta* winner; **acertar 1** *v/t respuesta* get right; *al hacer una conjetura* guess **2** *v/i* be right; **acertijo** *m* riddle, puzzle
achacar attribute (***a*** to)
achaque *m* ailment
achicar make smaller; MAR bail out; **achicarse** get smaller; *fig* feel intimidated
acidez *f* acidity; **~ *de estómago*** heartburn; **ácido 1** *adj tb fig* sour, acid **2** *m* acid
acierto *m idea* good idea; *respuesta* correct answer; *habilidad* skill
aclamación *f* acclaim; **aclamar** acclaim
aclarar 1 *v/t problema* clarify, clear up; *ropa, vajilla* rinse **2** *v/i de día* break; *del tiempo* clear up; **aclararse: ~ *la voz*** clear one's throat; ***no me aclaro*** F I don't understand; *por cansancio etc* I can't think straight
aclimatarse acclimatize, become acclimatized
acné *m* acne
acobardar daunt; **acobardarse** get frightened
acogedor welcoming; *lugar* cozy, *Br* cosy; **acoger** receive; *en casa* take in; **acogerse: ~ *a algo*** have recourse to sth; **acogida** *f* reception
acolchar quilt, pad
acometer 1 *v/t* attack; *tarea* tackle **2** *v/i* attack; **~ *contra algo*** attack sth
acomodado well-off; **acomodador** *m* usher; **acomodar** adapt; *a alguien* accommodate
acompañamiento *m* accompaniment; **acompañante** *m/f* companion; MÚS accompanist; **acompañar** *(ir con)* go with, accompany *fml*; *(permanecer con)* keep company; MÚS, GASTR accompany
acondicionador *m* conditioner; **acondicionar** *un lugar* equip, fit out; *pelo* condition
acongojar grieve, distress
aconsejable advisable; **aconsejar** advise
acontecer take place, occur; **acontecimiento** *m* event
acoplar *piezas* fit together
acorazado armored, *Br* armoured; **acorazar** armor-plate, *Br* armour-plate; **acorazarse** *fig* protect o.s.
acordar agree; **acordarse** remember; ***¿te acuerdas de él?*** do you remember him?; **acorde 1** *adj*: **~ *con*** in keeping with **2** *m* MÚS chord
acordeón *m* accordion
acordonar cordon off
acortar 1 *v/t* shorten **2** *v/i* take

a short cut
acosar hound, pursue; *con preguntas* bombard; **acoso** *m fig* hounding, harassment; ***~ sexual*** sexual harassment
acostar put to bed; **acostarse** go to bed; (*tumbarse*) lie down; ***~ con alguien*** go to bed with s.o.
acostumbrado (*habitual*) usual; ***estar ~ a algo*** be used to sth; **acostumbrar 1** *v/t* get used (***a*** to) **2** *v/i*: ***acostumbraba a venir*** he used to come; **acostumbrarse** get used (***a*** to)
acotar *terreno* fence off; *texto* annotate
acrecentar increase
acreditado well-known, reputable; **acreditar** *diplomático etc* accredit (***como*** as); (*avalar*) prove; **acreditarse** get a good reputation
acreedor *m*, **~a** *f* creditor; **acreencia** *f L.Am.* credit
acróbata *m/f* acrobat
acta(s) *f(pl)* minutes *pl*
actitud *f* (*disposición*) attitude; (*posición*) position
activar activate; (*estimular*) stimulate; **actividad** *f* activity; **activo 1** *adj* active; ***en ~*** on active service **2** *m* COM assets *pl*
acto *m* (*acción*), TEA act; *ceremonia* ceremony; ***~ seguido*** immediately afterward; ***en el ~*** instantly
actor *m* actor; **actriz** *f* actress
actuación *f* TEA performance; (*intervención*) intervention; **actual** present, current; ***un tema muy ~*** a very topical issue; **actualidad** *f* current situation; ***en la ~*** at present, presently; (*hoy en día*) nowadays; ***~es*** current affairs; **actualizar** bring up to date, update; **actualmente** currently
actuar (*obrar, ejercer*), TEA act; MED work, act
acuarela *f* watercolor, *Br* watercolour
acuario *m* aquarium
Acuario *m/f inv* ASTR Aquarius
acuático aquatic; ***deporte ~*** water sport
acuchillar stab
acudir come; ***~ a alguien*** turn to s.o.; ***~ a las urnas*** go to the polls
acueducto *m* aqueduct
acuerdo *m* agreement; ***estar de ~ con*** agree with; ***llegar a un ~, ponerse de ~*** come to *o* reach an agreement; ***de ~ con algo*** in accordance with sth; ***¡de ~!*** alright!, OK!
acumulador *m* ELEC accumulator, storage battery; **acumular, acumularse** accumulate
acuñar *monedas* mint; *expresión* coin
acuoso watery
acupuntura *f* acupuncture
acusación *f* accusation; **acu-**

sado *m*, **-a** *f* defendant; **acusar** accuse (***de*** of); JUR charge (***de*** with); (*manifestar*) show; ***~ recibo de*** acknowledge receipt of; **acuse** *m*: ***~ de recibo*** acknowledg(e)ment
acústico acoustic
adaptación *f* adaptation; ***~ cinematográfica*** movie version; **adaptador** *m* adaptor; **adaptar, adaptarse** adapt (***a*** to)
adecuado suitable, appropriate
adelantado advanced; ***por ~*** in advance; ***ir ~*** *de un reloj* be fast; **adelantamiento** *m* AUTO passing maneuver, *Br* overtaking manoeuvre; **adelantar 1** *v/t mover* move forward; *reloj* put forward; AUTO pass, *Br* overtake; *dinero* advance; (*conseguir*) achieve, gain **2** *v/i de un reloj* be fast; (*avanzar*) make progress; AUTO pass, *Br* overtake; **adelantarse** *mover* move forward; (*ir delante*) go on ahead; *de estación, cosecha* be early; *de un reloj* gain; ***se me adelantó*** she got there first; **adelante** *en espacio* forward; ***seguir ~*** carry on, keep going; ***¡~!*** come in; ***más ~*** *en tiempo* later on; ***de ahora en ~*** from now on; ***salir ~*** *fig*: *de persona* succeed; *de proyecto* go ahead; **adelanto** *m tb* COM advance
adelfa *f* BOT oleander
adelgazar 1 *v/t* lose **2** *v/i* lose weight
ademán *m* gesture; ***hacer ~ de*** make as if to
además 1 *adv* as well, besides **2** *prp*: ***~ de*** as well as
adentro 1 *adv* inside; ***mar ~*** out to sea; ***~ de*** *L.Am.* inside **2** *mpl*: ***para sus ~s*** to oneself
aderezar *con especias* season; *ensalada* dress; *fig* liven up; **aderezo** *m* GASTR seasoning; *para ensalada* dressing
adeudado in debt; **adeudar** owe; ***~ en cuenta*** debit an account; **adeudarse** get into debt
adherir stick; **adherirse** *a superficie* stick (***a*** to), adhere (***a*** to) *fml*; ***~ a una organización*** become a member of *o* join an organization; ***~ a una idea*** support an idea; **adhesión** *f* adhesion; **adhesivo** *m/adj* adhesive
adicción *f* addiction; ***~ a las drogas*** drug addiction
adición *f* MAT addition; *Rpl en restaurante* check, *Br* bill; **adicional** additional; **adicionar** MAT add, add up
adicto 1 *adj* addicted (***a*** to); ***ser ~ al régimen*** be a supporter of the regime **2** *m*, **-a** *f* addict
adiestrar train
adinerado wealthy
adiós 1 *int* goodbye, bye; *al cruzarse* hello **2** *m* goodbye;

decir ~ say goodbye (***a*** to)
aditivo *m* additive
adivinar guess; *de adivino* foretell; **adivino** *m* fortune teller
adjetivo *m* adjective
adjudicar award
adjunto 1 *adj* deputy *atr*; ***profesor ~*** assistant teacher; *en universidad* associate professor, *Br* lecturer **2** *m*, **-a** *f* assistant **3** *adv*: ***~ le remitimos*** please find enclosed
administración *f* administration; *de empresa etc* management; ***~ pública*** civil service; **administrador** *m*, **~a** *f* administrator; *de empresa etc* manager; **administrar** *medicamento* administer, give; *empresa* run, manage; *bienes* manage; **administrativo 1** *adj* administrative **2** *m*, **-a** *f* administrative assistant
admirable admirable; **admiración** *f* admiration; ***signo de ~*** exclamation mark; **admirador** *m*, **~a** *f* admirer; **admirar** admire; (*asombrar*) amaze; **admirarse** be amazed (***de*** at *o* by)
admisible admissible; **admisión** *f* admission; **admitir** (*aceptar*) accept; (*reconocer*) admit
ADN (= ***ácido desoxirribonucleico***) DNA (= deoxyribonucleic acid)
adobar GASTR marinate
adobe *m* adobe
adolescencia *f* adolescence; **adolescente** *m/f* adolescent
adonde where
adónde where
adopción *f* adoption; **adoptar** adopt; **adoptivo** *padres* adoptive; *hijo* adopted
adoquín *m* paving stone
adorable lovable, adorable; **adorar** love, adore; REL worship
adormecedor soporific; **adormecerse** doze off
adormidera *f* BOT poppy
adornar decorate; **adorno** *m* ornament; *de Navidad* decoration
adquirir acquire; (*comprar*) buy; **adquisición** *f* acquisition; ***hacer una buena ~*** make a good purchase; **adquisitivo: *poder ~*** purchasing power
adrede on purpose, deliberately
adrenalina *f* adrenaline
aduana *f* customs; **aduanero 1** *adj* customs *atr* **2** *m*, **-a** *f* customs officer
aducir *argumentos* give, put forward; (*alegar*) claim
adueñarse: *~ de* take possession of
adulación *f* flattery; **adulador** flattering *atr*; **adular** flatter
adultera *f* adulteress; **adulterar** adulterate; **adulterio** *m* adultery; **adúltero 1** *adj* adulterous **2** *m* adulterer
adulto 1 *adj* adult; ***edad -a*** adulthood **2** *m*, **-a** *f* adult

adverbio *m* adverb
adversario *m*, **-a** *f* adversary, opponent; **adverso** adverse; **adversidad** *f* adversity, hard times *pl*
advertencia *f* warning; **advertir** warn (***de*** about); (*notar*) notice
adviento *m* REL Advent
adyacente adjacent
aéreo air *atr*; *vista, fotografía* aerial; ***compañía -a*** airline
aerodeslizador *m* hovercraft; **aerodinámico** aerodynamic; **aeródromo** *m* airfield, aerodrome; **aerograma** *m* air mail letter; **aeromozo** *m*, **-a** *f* *L.Am.* flight attendant; **aeronáutica** *f* aeronautics; **aeronave** *f* airplane, *Br* aeroplane; **aeropuerto** *m* airport; **aerosol** *m* aerosol; **aerotaxi** *m* air taxi
afable pleasant, affable
afamado famous
afán *m* (*esfuerzo*) effort; (*deseo*) eagerness; ***sin ~ de lucro*** *organización* not-for-profit; **afanarse** make an effort
afear: ***~ algo / a alguien*** make sth / s.o. look ugly
afección *f* MED complaint, condition; **afectado** (*afligido*) upset (***por*** by); (*amanerado*) affected; **afectar** affect; (*conmover*) upset, affect; (*fingir*) feign; **afectivo** emotional; **afecto** *m* affection; ***tener ~ a alguien*** be fond of s.o.; **afectuoso** affectionate
afeitado *m* shave; **afeitadora** *f* electric razor; **afeitar** shave; *barba* shave off; **afeitarse** shave, have a shave
afeminado effeminate
aferrado stubborn
afición *f* love (***por*** of); (*pasatiempo*) pastime, hobby; ***la ~*** DEP the fans; **aficionado 1** *adj*: ***ser ~ a*** be interested in **2** *m*, **-a** *f* enthusiast; *no profesional* amateur; **aficionarse** become interested (***a*** in)
afilado sharp; **afilador** *m* sharpener; **afilar** sharpen; *L.Am.* F (*halagar*) butter up F; *S.Am.* (*seducir*) seduce
afiliación *f* affiliation (***a*** to), becoming a member (***a*** to); **afiliado** *m* member; **afiliarse:** ***~ a*** become a member of, join
afinar MÚS tune; *punta* sharpen; *fig* fine-tune
afinidad *f* affinity
afirmación *f* statement; *declaración positiva* affirmation; **afirmar** state, declare; **afirmativo** affirmative
aflicción *f* grief, sorrow
afligir afflict; (*apenar*) upset; *L.Am.* F (*golpear*) beat up; **afligirse** get upset
aflojar 1 *v/t nudo* loosen; F *dinero* hand over **2** *v/i de tormenta* abate; *de viento, fiebre* drop
afluencia *f* *fig* influx, flow;

horas de ~ peak times; **afluente** *m* tributary; **afluir** flock, flow
afónico: *está ~* he has lost his voice
afortunadamente fortunately, luckily; **afortunado** lucky, fortunate
afrenta *f* insult, affront; **afrentar** insult, affront
África Africa; **africano 1** *adj* African **2** *m*, **-a** *f* African; **afroamericano 1** *adj* African-American **2** *m*, **-a** *f* African-American; **afroantillano, afrocaribeño 1** *adj* Afro-Caribbean **2** *m*, **-a** *f* Afro-Caribbean
afrontar face (up to)
afuera outside; **afueras** *fpl* outskirts
agacharse bend down; (*acuclillarse*) crouch down; *L.Am.* (*rendirse*) give in
agalla *f* ZO gill; ***tener ~s*** F have guts F
agarradera *f L.Am.* handle
agarrado *fig* F mean, stingy F; **agarrar 1** *v/t* (*asir*) grab; *L.Am.* (*tomar*) take; *L.Am.* (*atrapar, pescar*), *resfriado* catch; *L.Am. velocidad* pick up; ***~ una calle*** *L.Am.* go along a street **2** *v/i* (*asirse*) hold on; *de planta* take root; *L.Am. por un lugar* go; ***agarró y se fue*** he upped and went; **agarrarse** (*asirse*) hold on; *L.Am. a golpes* get into a fight
agasajar fête
agencia *f* agency; ***~ inmobiliaria*** real estate office, *Br* estate agency; ***~ de viajes*** travel agency
agenda *f diario* diary; *programa* schedule; *de mitin* agenda
agente *m/f* agent; ***~ de cambio y bolsa*** stockbroker; ***~ de policía*** police officer
ágil agile
agitación *f* POL unrest; **agitar** shake; *brazos, pañuelo* wave; *fig* stir up
aglomeración *f de gente* crowd; **aglomerar** pile up
agobiado *fig* stressed out; ***~ de trabajo*** snowed under with work; **agobiante** oppressive
agolparse crowd together
agonía *f* agony; **agonizante** dying; **agonizar** *de persona* be dying; *de régimen* be crumbling
agosto *m* August
agotado exhausted (*vendido*) sold out; **agotador** exhausting; **agotamiento** *m* exhaustion; **agotar** exhaust; **agotarse** (*cansarse*) exhaust o.s.; (*terminarse*) run out; (*venderse*) sell out
agraciado *persona* attractive
agradable pleasant, nice; **agradar: *me agrada la idea*** *fml* I like the idea; ***nos ~ía mucho que…*** *fml* we would be delighted if …
agradecer: *~ algo a alguien* thank s.o. for sth; ***te lo agra-***

dezco I appreciate it; **agradecido** grateful, appreciative; **agradecimiento** *m* appreciation; **agrado** *m*: ***ser del ~ de alguien*** be to s.o.'s liking
agrandar make bigger
agrario land *atr*, agrarian; *política* agricultural
agravante 1 *adj* JUR aggravating *atr* **2** *f* aggravating factor; **agravar** make worse, aggravate; **agravarse** get worse, deteriorate
agraviar offend, affront; **agravio** *m* offense, *Br* offence
agregado *m*, **-a** *f en universidad* senior lecturer; *en colegio* senior teacher; POL attaché; ***~ cultural*** cultural attaché
agregar add
agresión *f* aggression; **agresividad** *f* aggression; **agresivo** aggressive; **agresor** *m*, **~a** *f* aggressor
agriarse *de vino* go sour; *de carácter* become bitter
agrícola agricultural, farming *atr*; **agricultor** *m*, **~a** *f* farmer; **agricultura** *f* agriculture
agridulce bittersweet
agrietarse crack; *de manos, labios* chap
agrio *fruta* sour; *disputa, carácter* bitter
agrios *mpl* BOT citrus fruit
agrónomo: ***ingeniero ~*** agriculture specialist, agronomist
agrupar group, put into groups
agua *f* water; ***~ corriente*** running water; ***~ dulce*** fresh water; ***~ mineral*** mineral water; ***~ oxigenada*** (hydrogen) peroxide; ***~ potable*** drinking water; ***es ~ pasada*** it's water under the bridge; ***se me hace la boca ~*** it makes my mouth water; ***~s residuales*** effluent, sewage
aguacate *m* BOT avocado
aguacero *m* downpour
aguafiestas *m/f inv* party pooper F
aguafuerte *m* etching
aguamarina *f* aquamarine
aguantar 1 *v/t un peso* bear, support; *respiración* hold; (*soportar*) put up with; ***no lo puedo ~*** I can't stand *o* bear it **2** *v/i* hang on; **aguantarse** *contenerse* keep quiet; ***me tuve que aguantar*** *conformarme* I had to put up with it; **aguante** *m* patience; *física* stamina
aguar *fiesta* spoil
aguardar 1 *v/t* wait for **2** *v/i* wait
aguardiente *m fruit-based alcoholic spirit*
aguarrás *m* turpentine
agudeza *f de sonido* high pitch; MED intensity; (*perspicacia*) sharpness; ***~ visual*** sharp-sightedness; **agudo** acute; (*afilado*) sharp; *sonido* high-pitched; (*perspicaz*)

sharp
aguijón *m* ZO sting; *fig* spur
águila *f* eagle; ***¿~ o sol?*** *Méx* heads or tails?
aguja *f* needle; *de reloj* hand
agujerear make holes in; **agujero** *m* hole
agujetas *fpl* stiffness; ***tener ~*** be stiff
aguzar sharpen; ***~ el oído*** prick up one's ears
ahí there; ***está por ~*** it's (somewhere) over there; *dando direcciones* it's that way
ahijada *f* goddaughter; **ahijado** *m* godson
ahínco *m* effort; ***trabajar con ~*** work hard
ahogado *en agua* drowned; **ahogar** (*asfixiar*) suffocate; *en agua* drown; AUTO flood; *protestas* stifle; **ahogarse** choke; (*asfixiarse*) suffocate; *en agua* drown; AUTO flood; **ahogo** *m* breathlessness
ahondar: ***~ en algo*** go into sth in depth
ahora now; (*pronto*) in a moment; ***~ mismo*** right now; ***por ~*** for the time being; ***~ bien*** however; ***desde ~, de ~ en adelante*** from now on; ***¡hasta ~!*** see you soon
ahorcar hang; **ahorcarse** hang o.s.
ahorrador 1 *adj* thrifty **2** *m*, **~a** *f* saver, investor; **ahorrar 1** *v/t* save; ***~ algo a alguien*** save s.o. sth **2** *v/i* save (up); **ahorro** *m* saving; ***~s*** savings; ***caja de ~s*** savings bank
ahumado smoked; ***cristal ~*** tinted glass; **ahumar** smoke
airado angry
airbag *m* AUTO airbag; **airbus** *m* AVIA airbus
aire *m* air; ***~ acondicionado*** air-conditioning; ***al ~ libre*** in the open air; ***a mi ~*** in my own way; ***hace mucho ~*** it is very windy; **airear** *tb fig* air
airoso: ***salir ~ de algo*** do well in sth
aislado isolated; **aislante 1** *adj* insulating **2** *m* insulator; **aislar** isolate; ELEC insulate; **aislador** *m* insulator; **aislamiento** *m* TÉC, ELEC insulation; *fig* isolation
ajado *flores* withered; (*desgastado*) worn
ajedrez *m* chess
ajeno *propiedad, problemas etc* someone else's; ***me era totalmente ~*** it was completely alien to me; ***estar ~ a*** be unaware of; ***por razones -as a nuestra voluntad*** for reasons beyond our control
ajetrearse F get het up; **ajetreo** *m* bustle
ajo *m* BOT garlic; ***estar en el ~*** F be in the know F
ajuar *m de novia* trousseau
ajustable adjustable; **ajustado** tight; **ajustar 1** *v/t máquina etc* adjust; *tornillo* tighten; *precio* set; ***~ cuentas*** *fig* settle a score **2** *v/i* fit; **ajuste** *m*:

~ *de cuentas* settling of scores
ajusticiar execute
al *prp* ***a*** *y art* ***el***; **~ *entrar*** on coming in, when we / they *etc* came in
ala *f* wing; MIL flank; **~ *delta*** hang glider
alabanza *f* acclaim; **alabar** praise, acclaim
alabastro *m* alabaster
alacena *f* larder
alacrán *m* ZO scorpion
alado winged
alambique *m* still
alambrado *m* wire netting
alambre *m* wire; **~ *de espino*** *o* ***de púas*** barbed wire
alameda *f* boulevard; *de álamos* poplar grove; **álamo** *m* BOT poplar; **~ *temblón*** aspen
alarde *m* show, display
alargador *m* TÉC extension cord, *Br* extension lead; **alargar** lengthen; *prenda* let down; *en tiempo* prolong; *mano, brazo* stretch out; **alargarse** *de sombra, día* get longer
alarido *m* shriek
alarma *f* alarm; ***dar la voz de* ~** raise the alarm; **alarmar** alarm; **alarmarse** become alarmed
alba *f* dawn
albahaca *f* BOT basil
albañil *m* bricklayer
albarán *m* delivery note
albaricoque *m* BOT apricot; **albaricoquero** *m* apricot tree
albergue *m* refuge, shelter; **~ *juvenil*** youth hostel
albóndiga *f* meatball
albornoz *m* bathrobe
alborotador *m*, **~a** *f* rioter; **alborotar 1** *v/t* stir up; (*desordenar*) disturb **2** *v/i* make a racket; **alboroto** *m* commotion
albufera *f* lagoon
álbum *m* album
alcachofa *f* BOT artichoke; *de ducha* shower head
alcahuete *m*, **-a** *f* go-between; *Rpl* (*chivato*) telltale F; *entre delincuentes* grass F
alcalde *m*, **-esa** *f* mayor; **alcaldía** *f* mayor's office, city hall
alcance *m* reach; *de arma etc* range; *de medida* scope; *de tragedia* extent, scale; ***al* ~ *de la mano*** within reach; ***dar* ~ *a alguien*** catch up with s.o.
alcanfor *m* camphor
alcantarillado *m* sewer system; *de sumideros* drainage system
alcanzar 1 *v/t* reach; *a alguien* catch up with; *cantidad* amount to **2** *v/i en altura* reach; *en cantidad* be enough; **~ *a oír*** manage to hear
alcaparra *f* BOT caper
alcázar *m* fortress
alcoba *f S.Am.* bedroom
alcohol *m* alcohol; **~ *de quemar*** denatured alcohol, *Br*

methylated spirits *sg*; **alcoholemia** *f* blood alcohol level; ***prueba de ~*** drunkometer test, *Br* Breathalyzer® test; **alcohólico 1** *adj* alcoholic **2** *m*, **-a** *f* alcoholic; **alcoholismo** *m* alcoholism
alcornoque *m* BOT cork oak; ***pedazo de ~*** F blockhead F
aldaba *f* doorknocker
aldea *f* (small) village
aleación *f* alloy
alegar 1 *v/t motivo* cite; ***~ que*** claim that **2** *v/i L.Am.* (*discutir*) argue; (*quejarse*) moan; **alegato** *m* JUR *fig* speech; *Andes* argument
alegoría *f* allegory
alegrar make happy; (*animar*) cheer up; **alegrarse** cheer up; F *bebiendo* get tipsy; ***~ por alguien*** be pleased for s.o. (***de*** about); **alegre** happy; F *bebido* tipsy; **alegría** *f* happiness
alejamiento *m* removal, separation; *fig* distancing
alemán 1 *m/adj* German **2** *m*, **-ana** *f persona* German; **3** *m idioma* German; **Alemania** Germany
alentar (*animar*) encourage; *esperanzas* cherish
alergia *f* allergy; **alérgico** allergic (***a*** to)
alerta 1 *adv*: ***estar ~*** be on the alert **2** *f* alert; ***dar la ~*** raise the alarm; ***poner en ~*** alert
aleta *f* ZO fin; *de buzo* flipper; *de la nariz* wing
aletear flap its wings
alevosía *f* treachery
alfabético alphabetical; **alfabeto** *m* alphabet
alfalfa *f* BOT alfalfa
alfarería *f* pottery; **alfarero** *m*, **-a** *f* potter
alféizar *m* sill, windowsill
alférez *m* second lieutenant
alfil *m* bishop
alfiler *m* pin; ***~ de gancho*** *Arg* safety pin
alfombra *f* carpet; *más pequeña* rug; **alfombrado** *m L.Am.* carpeting, carpets *pl*; **alfombrilla** *f* mouse mat
alga *f* BOT alga; *marina* seaweed
algarroba *f* BOT carob, carob bean; **algarrobo** *m* BOT carob, carob tree
álgebra *f* algebra
álgido *fig* decisive
algo 1 *pron* something; *en frases interrogativas o condicionales* anything; ***~ es ~*** it's something, it's better than nothing **2** *adv* rather, somewhat
algodón *m* cotton
alguacil *m*, **~esa** *f* bailiff
alguien somebody, someone; *en frases interrogativas o condicionales* anybody, anyone
algún *en frases* some; *en frases interrogativas o condicionales* any; ***~ día*** some day
alguno 1 *adj* some; *en frases interrogativas o condicionales* any; ***no la influyó de modo ~*** it didn't influence her in any way; ***¿has estado algu-***

na vez en…? have you ever been to …? **2** *pron*: *persona* someone, somebody; ***~s opinan que…*** some people think that …; ***~ se podrá usar*** *objeto* we'll be able to use some of them

alhaja *f* piece of jewelry *o Br* jewellery; *fig* gem; ***~s*** jewelry

aliado *m*, **-a** *f* ally; **alianza** *f* POL alliance; (*anillo*) wedding ring; **aliarse** form an alliance

alias *m inv* alias

alicatado *m* tiling, tiles *pl*

alicates *mpl* pliers

aliciente *m* (*estímulo*) incentive; (*atractivo*) attraction

aliento *m* breath; *fig* encouragement

aligerar *carga* lighten; ***~ el paso*** quicken one's pace

alijo *m* MAR consignment

alimentación *f* (*dieta*) diet; *acción* feeding; ELEC power supply; **alimentar 1** *v/t* feed; ELEC power **2** *v/i* be nourishing; **alimento** *m* (*comida*) food; ***tiene poco ~*** it has little nutritional value; **alimentario, alimenticio** food *atr*; ***industria -a*** food industry; ***producto ~*** foodstuff

alinear align

aliñar dress

alisar smooth

alistar MIL draft; **alistarse** enlist; *L.Am.* (*prepararse*) get ready

aliviar alleviate, relieve; **alivio** *m* relief

aljibe *m* cistern, tank

allá *de lugar* (over) there; ***~ por los años veinte*** back in the twenties; ***más ~*** further on; ***más ~ de*** beyond; ***el más ~*** the hereafter; ***~ ella*** F that's up to her

allanar (*alisar*) smooth; (*aplanar*) level (out); *obstáculos* overcome

allegado *m*, **-a** *f* relation, relative

allí there; ***por ~*** over there; *dando direcciones* that way; ***¡~ está!*** there it is!

alma *f* soul

almacén *m* warehouse; (*tienda*) store, shop; ***grandes almacenes*** department store; **almacenar** *tb* INFOR store

almanaque *m* almanac

almeja *f* ZO clam

almendra *f* almond; **almendro** *m* almond tree

almíbar *m* syrup

almidón *m* starch; **almidonar** starch

almirante *m* admiral

almohada *f* pillow; ***consultarlo con la ~*** sleep on it; **almohadilla** *f* small cushion; TÉC pad

almorranas *fpl* piles

almorzar *al mediodía* have lunch; *a media mañana* have a mid-morning snack; **almuerzo** *m al mediodía* lunch; *a media mañana* mid-morning snack; ***~ de trabajo*** working lunch

alojamiento *m* accommodations *pl*, *Br* accommodation; **alojar** accommodate; **alojarse** stay
alondra *f* ZO lark
alpargata *f Esp* espadrille
alpinismo *m* mountaineering; **alpinista** *m/f* mountaineer, climber
alquilar *de usuario* rent; *de dueño* rent out; **alquiler** *m acción: de coche etc* rental; *de casa* renting; *dinero* rental, *Br tb* rent; ***~ de coches*** car rental, *Br tb* car hire
alquitrán *m* tar
alrededor 1 *adv* around **2** *prp*: ***~ de*** around; **alrededores** *mpl* surrounding area
alta *f* MED discharge; ***darse de ~*** *en organismo* register
altanería *f* arrogance, disdain; **altanero** arrogant
altar *m* altar
altavoz *m* loudspeaker
alteración *f* alteration; **alterado** *persona* upset; ***~ genéticamente*** genetically altered *o* modified; **alterar** alter; *a alguien* upset; ***~ el orden público*** cause a breach of the peace; **alterarse** get upset (***por*** because of)
altercado *m* argument
alternar 1 *v/t* alternate **2** *v/i* mix; **alternativa** *f* alternative; **alternativo** alternative; **alterno** alternate; ***corriente -a*** ELEC alternating current
alterne *m* F hospitality *in hostess bars*; ***bar de ~*** hostess bar; ***chica de ~*** hostess
altiplanicie *f*, **altiplano** *m* high plateau; ***El Altiplano*** the Bolivian plateau, the Bolivian Altiplano
altisonante high-flown
altitud *f* altitude
altivo haughty
alto[1] 1 *adj persona* tall; *precio, número, montaña* high; ***-as presiones*** high pressure; ***~ horno*** blast furnace; ***clase -a*** high class; ***en -a mar*** on the high seas; ***en voz -a*** out loud **2** *adv volar, saltar* high; ***hablar ~*** speak loudly; ***pasar por ~*** overlook; ***poner más ~*** TV, RAD turn up **3** *m* (*altura*) height; *Chi* pile
alto[2] *m* halt; (*pausa*) pause; ***hacer un ~*** stop; ***~ el fuego*** ceasefire
altoparlante *m L.Am.* loudspeaker
altramuz *m* lupin
altura *f* MAT height; MÚS pitch; AVIA altitude, height; GEOG latitude; ***a estas ~s*** by this time; ***estar a la ~ de algo*** be up to sth
alubia *f* BOT kidney bean
alucinar 1 *v/i* hallucinate **2** *v/t* F amaze; **alucine** *m*: ***de ~*** F amazing; **alucinógeno** *m* hallucinogen
alud *m* avalanche
aludir: ***~ a*** allude to
alumbrado 1 *adj* lit **2** *m* lighting; **alumbramiento** *m* birth; **alumbrar 1** *v/t* (*dar luz a*) light (up) **2** *v/i* give

off light
aluminio *m* aluminum, *Br* aluminium; ***papel de ~*** aluminum foil
alumno *m*, **-a** *f* student
alunizar land on the moon
alusión *f* allusion (***a*** to)
alza *f* rise; ***en ~*** *en bolsa* rising; **alzamiento** *m* MIL, POL uprising; **alzar** *barrera*, *brazo* lift, raise; *precios* raise
ama *f* (*dueña*) owner; ***~ de casa*** housewife; ***~ de llaves*** housekeeper
amabilidad *f* kindness; **amable** kind (***con*** to)
amaestrar train
amago *m* threat; ***hizo ~ de levantarse*** she made as if to get up; ***~ de infarto*** minor heart attack
amainar *de lluvia* ease up
amamantar *bebé* breastfeed; *cría* feed
amanecer 1 *v/i* get light; *de persona* wake up **2** *m* dawn
amansar break in, tame; **amansarse** become tame, become quieter
amante 1 *adj* loving; ***es ~ de …*** he's fond of … **2** *m/f* lover
amapola *f* BOT poppy
amar love
amaraje *m* AVIA landing *on water*; **amarar** AVIA land *on water*
amargar *ocasión* spoil; ***~ a alguien*** make s.o. bitter; **amargo** *tb fig* bitter; **amargura** *f tb fig* bitterness
amarillento yellowish; **amarillo** *m/adj* yellow
amarra *f* MAR mooring rope; ***tener buenas ~s*** *fig* have contacts; **amarrar** *L.Am.* (*atar*) tie; **amarre** *m* MAR mooring, berth
amasar *pan* knead; *fortuna* amass
amazona *f* horsewoman
Amazonas: *el ~* the Amazon
ambages *mpl*: ***decirlo sin ~*** say it straight out
ámbar *m* amber; ***el semáforo está en ~*** the lights are yellow, *Br* the lights are at amber
ambición *f* ambition; **ambicionar** aspire to; **ambicioso** ambitious
ambientador *m* air freshener; **ambiental** environmental; **ambiente 1** *adj*: ***medio ~*** environment; ***temperatura ~*** room temperature **2** *m* (*entorno*) environment; (*situación*) atmosphere
ambigú *m* buffet
ambigüedad *f* ambiguity; **ambiguo** ambiguous
ámbito *m* area; (*límite*) scope
ambos, ambas 1 *adj* both **2** *pron* both (of us / you / them)
ambulancia *f* ambulance; **ambulante 1** *adj* traveling, *Br* travelling **2** *m/f L.Am.* (*vendedor*) street seller; **ambulatorio 1** *adj* MED out-patient *atr* **2** *m* out-patient clinic
amén 1 *m* amen **2** *prp*: ***~ de*** as

well as

amenaza *f* threat; **~ *de bomba*** bomb scare; **amenazador** threatening; **amenazante** threatening; **amenazar 1** *v/t* threaten (***con***, ***de*** with) **2** *v/i*: **~ *con*** threaten to

ameno enjoyable

América America; **América Central** Central America; **América Latina** Latin America; **América del Norte** North America; **América del Sur** South America; **americana** *f* American (woman); *prenda* jacket; **americano** *m/adj* American

ametralladora *f* machine gun

amianto *m* asbestos

amiba *f* ameba, *Br* amoeba

amígdala *f* tonsil; **amigdalitis** *f* tonsillitis

amigo 1 *adj* friendly; ***ser* ~ *de algo*** be fond of sth **2** *m*, **-a** *f* friend; ***hacerse* ~*s*** make friends

aminorar reduce; **~ *la marcha*** slow down

amistad *f* friendship; **~*es*** friends; **amistoso** friendly; ***partido* ~** DEP friendly (game)

amnistía *f* amnesty

amo *m* (*dueño*) owner; HIST master

amodorramiento *m* drowsiness

amoldar adapt (***a*** to); **amoldarse** adapt (***a*** to)

amonestación *f* warning; DEP caution; **amonestar** reprimand; DEP caution

amoníaco, amoniaco *m* ammonia

amontonar pile up; **amontonarse** pile up; *de gente* crowd together

amor *m* love; **~ *mío*** my love, darling; **~ *propio*** self-respect; ***hacer el* ~** make love; **amoroso** amorous

amortiguador *m* AUTO shock absorber; **amortiguar** *impacto* cushion; *sonido* muffle

amortización *f* repayment, redemption; **amortizar** pay off

amparar protect; (*ayudar*) help; **amparo** *m* protection; (*cobijo*) shelter; ***al* ~ *de*** under the protection of

amperio *m* ampere, amp

ampliación *f de casa*, *carretera* extension; FOT enlargement; **ampliar** *plantilla* increase; *negocio* expand; *plazo*, *edificio* extend; FOT enlarge; **amplificación** *f* amplification; **amplificador** *m* amplifier; **amplificar** amplify; **amplio** *casa* spacious; *gama*, *margen* wide; *falda* full; **amplitud** *f* breadth

ampolla *f* MED blister; (*botellita*) vial, *Br* phial

amputar amputate

amueblar furnish

amuleto *m* charm

analfabeto 1 *adj* illiterate **2** *m*, **-a** *f* illiterate

analgésico 1 *adj* painkilling,

analgesic **2** *m* painkiller, analgesic
análisis *m inv* analysis; **~ *de mercado*** market research; **~ *de sangre*** blood test; **analista** *m/f* analyst; **analizar** analyze
analogía *f* analogy; **analógico** analog, *Br* analogue; **análogo** analogous
ananá(s) *m S.Am.* pineapple
anaquel *m* shelf
anarquía *f* anarchy
anatomía *f* anatomy
anca *f* haunch; **~*s de rana*** frogs' legs
ancho 1 *adj* wide, broad; ***a sus -as*** at ease, relaxed **2** *m* width; **~ *de vía*** FERR gauge; ***dos metros de ~*** two meters wide
anchoa *f* anchovy
anchura *f* width
anciana *f* old woman; **ancianidad** *f* old age; **anciano 1** *adj* old **2** *m* old man
ancla *f* anchor; **anclar** anchor
andamio *m* scaffolding
andar 1 *v/i* (*caminar*) walk; (*funcionar*) work; ***andando*** on foot; **~ *bien* / *mal*** *fig* go well / badly; **~ *con cuidado*** be careful; **~ *en algo*** (*buscar*) rummage in sth; **~ *haciendo algo*** be doing sth; ***¡anda!*** come on! **2** *v/t* walk
andén *m* platform; *L.Am.* sidewalk, *Br* pavement
Andes *mpl* Andes; **andinismo** *m L.Am.* mountaineering, climbing; **andinista** *m/f L.Am.* mountaineer, climber; **andino** Andean
andrajoso ragged
anécdota *f* anecdote
anejo 1 *adj* attached **2** *m* annex, *Br* annexe
anemia *f* anemia, *Br* anaemia; **anémico** anemic, *Br* anaemic
anestesia *f* anesthesia *Br* anaesthesia
anexión *f* POL annexation; **anexionar** POL annex; **anexo 1** *adj* attached **2** *m edificio* annex, *Br* annexe
anfiteatro *m* amphitheater, *Br* amphitheatre; *de teatro* dress circle
anfitrión *m* host; **anfitriona** *f* hostess
ánfora *f L.Am.* POL ballot box; HIST amphora
ángel *m* angel; **~ *custodio*** guardian angel
angina *f*: **~*s*** sore throat, strep throat; **~ *de pecho*** angina
angosto narrow
angostura *f* angostura
anguila *f* eel; **angula** *f* elver
angular 1 *adj* angular; ***piedra ~*** cornerstone **2** *m* TÉC angle iron; ***gran ~*** FOT wide-angle lens *sg*; **ángulo** *m* MAT, *fig* angle; **anguloso** angular
angustia *f* anguish; **angustiar** distress; **angustiarse** agonize (***por*** over); **angustioso** agonizing
anhelar long for; **anhelo** *m* longing, desire (***de*** for)
anidar nest

anilla *f* ring; ***cuaderno de ~s*** ring binder
anillo *m* ring
ánima *f* REL soul; TÉC bore
animación *f* liveliness; *en películas* animation; ***hay mucha ~*** it's very lively; **animado** lively; **animador** *m* host; ***~ turístico*** events organizer; **animadora** *f* hostess; DEP cheerleader
animal 1 *adj* animal *atr*; *fig* stupid **2** *m tb fig* animal; ***~ doméstico*** *mascota* pet; *de granja* domestic animal
animar cheer up; (*alentar*) encourage; **animarse** cheer up
ánimo *m* spirit; (*coraje*) encouragement; ***estado de ~*** state of mind; ***con ~ de*** with the intention of; ***¡~!*** cheer up!
animosidad *f* animosity
animoso spirited
aniquilar annihilate
anís *m* BOT aniseed; *bebida* anisette
aniversario *m* anniversary
ano *m* ANAT anus
anoche last night; ***antes de ~*** the night before last; **anochecer 1** *v/i* get dark **2** *m* dusk
anomalía *f* anomaly; **anómalo** anomalous
anónimo 1 *adj* anonymous **2** *m* poison pen letter
anorak *m* anorak
anormal abnormal
anotar note down
ansia *f* yearning; (*inquietud*) anxiousness; **ansiar** yearn for, long for; **ansiedad** *f* anxiety; **ansioso** anxious; ***está ~ por verlos*** he's longing to see them
ante[1] *m* suede; ZO moose; *Méx* (*postre*) *egg and coconut dessert*
ante[2] *prp posición* before; *dificultad* faced with; ***~ todo*** above all
anteanoche the night before last
anteayer the day before yesterday
antebrazo *m* forearm
antecedente *m* precedent; ***~s penales*** previous convictions; ***poner a alguien en ~s*** put s.o. in the picture; **anteceder** precede, come before; **antecesor** *m*, **~a** *f* predecessor
antelación *f*: ***con ~*** in advance
antemano: ***de ~*** beforehand
antena *f de radio, televisión* antenna, *Br* aerial; ZO antenna; ***~ parabólica*** satellite dish
anteojos *mpl* binoculars
antepasado *m*, **-a** *f* ancestor
antepecho *m de ventana* sill; (*barandilla*) parapet
anteponer: ***~ algo a algo*** put sth before sth
anterior previous, former; **anterioridad** *f*: ***con ~*** before, previously; ***con ~ a*** before
antes 1 *adv* before; ***cuanto ~, lo ~ posible*** as soon as pos-

sible; ***poco ~*** shortly before; ***~ que nada*** first of all **2** *prp*: ***~ de*** before
antesala *f* lobby
antibala(s) bulletproof
antibiótico *m* antibiotic
anticiclón *m* anticyclone
anticipación *f* anticipation; ***con ~*** in advance; **anticipado** *pago* advance *atr*; *elecciones* early; ***por ~*** in advance; **anticipar** *sueldo* advance; *fecha*, *viaje* move up, *Br* bring forward; *información* give a preview of
anticonceptivo *m* contraceptive
anticongelante *m* antifreeze
anticuado antiquated; **anticuario** *m* antique dealer
antideslizante non-slip
antídoto *m* MED antidote; *fig* cure
antifaz *m* mask
antigüedad *f* age; *en el trabajo* length of service; ***~es*** antiques; **antiguo** old; *del pasado remoto* ancient
antipatía *f* antipathy, dislike; **antipático** disagreeable, unpleasant
antirrobo *m* AUTO antitheft device
antiséptico *m/adj* antiseptic
antiterrorista *brigada* antiterrorist *atr*; ***la lucha ~*** the fight against terrorism
antojarse: ***se le antojó salir*** he felt like going out; ***se me antoja que...*** it seems to me that ...; **antojo** *m* whim; *de embarazada* craving; ***a mi ~*** as I please
antología *f* anthology; ***de ~*** *fig* F incredible F
antorcha *f* torch
antro *m* F dive F, dump F
antropófago *m*, **-a** *f* cannibal
anual annual; **anualidad** *f* annual payment
anuario *m* yearbook
anublarse cloud over
anudar knot
anular[1] cancel; *matrimonio* annul; *gol* disallow
anular[2] *adj* ring-shaped; ***dedo ~*** ring finger
anunciar announce; COM advertise; **anuncio** *m* announcement; (*presagio*) sign; COM advertisement; ***~ luminoso*** illuminated sign; ***~s por palabras, pequeños ~s*** classified advertisements
anverso *m* obverse
añadidura *f*: ***por ~*** in addition; **añadir** add
añejo mature
año *m* year; ***~ bisiesto*** leap year; ***~ fiscal*** fiscal year, *Br* financial year; ***~ luz*** light year; ***~ nuevo*** New Year; ***¿cuándo cumples ~s?*** when's your birthday?; ***¿cuántos ~s tienes?*** how old are you?; ***a los diez ~s*** at the age of ten; ***los ~s veinte*** the twenties
añoranza *f* yearning (***de*** for); **añorar** miss
apacible mild-mannered
apaciguar pacify, calm down

apadrinar be godparent to; *político* support, back; *artista etc* sponsor; ***~ a la novia*** give the bride away
apagado *fuego* out; *luz* off; *persona* dull; *color* subdued; **apagar** *televisor, luz* turn off; *fuego* put out; **apagarse** *de luz* go off; *de fuego* go out; **apagón** *m* blackout
apalear beat
apañado F resourceful; **apañarse** manage; ***apañárselas*** manage, get by
aparador *m* sideboard; *Méx* (*escaparate*) shop window
aparato *m* piece of equipment; *doméstico* appliance; BIO, ANAT system; *de partido político* machine; ***al ~*** TELEC speaking; **aparatoso** spectacular
aparcamiento *m* parking lot, *Br* car park; ***~ subterráneo*** underground parking garage, *Br* underground car park; **aparcar 1** *v/t* park; *proyecto* shelve **2** *v/i* park
aparecer appear
aparejador *m*, **~a** *f architectural technician*, *Br* quantity surveyor; **aparejo** *m*: ***~s de pesca*** fishing gear; **aparejar** prepare; *caballo* saddle; MAR rig; ***traer aparejado*** entail, bring with it
aparentar pretend; ***no aparenta la edad que tiene*** she doesn't look her age; **aparente** (*evidente*) apparent; *L.Am.* (*fingido*) feigned;
aparición *f* appearance; (*fantasma*) apparition; **apariencia** *f* appearance; ***en ~*** outwardly
apartado *m* section; ***~ de correos*** PO box; **apartamento** *m* apartment, *Br* flat; **apartamiento** *m* separation; *L.Am.* (*apartamento*) apartment, *Br* flat; **apartar** separate; *para después* set aside; *de un sitio* move away (***de*** from); ***~ a alguien de hacer algo*** dissuade s.o. from doing sth; **apartarse** move aside (***de*** from); ***~ del tema*** stray from the subject; **aparte** to one side; (*por separado*) separately; ***~ de*** aside from, *Br* apart from; ***punto y ~*** new paragraph
apasionado 1 *adj* passionate **2** *m/f* enthusiast; **apasionar** fascinate; **apasionarse** develop a passion (***por*** for)
apatía *f* apathy; **apático** apathetic
apearse get off, alight *fml*
apedrear throw stones at; *matar* stone
apego *m* attachment
apelación *f* JUR appeal; **apelar** *tb* JUR appeal (***a*** to)
apellido *m* surname; ***~ de soltera*** maiden name
apenar sadden
apenas 1 *adv* hardly, scarcely **2** *conj* as soon as
apéndice *m* appendix; **apendicitis** *f* appendicitis
aperitivo *m comida* appetizer;

bebida aperitif
apero *m utensilio* implement; *L.Am.* (*arneses*) harness
apertura *f* opening; FOT aperture; POL opening up
apestar 1 *v/t* stink out F **2** *v/i* reek (***a*** of)
apetecer: ***¿qué te apetece?*** what do you feel like?; **apetecible** appetizing
apetito *m* appetite; **apetitoso** appetizing
ápice *m*: ***ni un ~*** *fig* not an ounce; ***no ceder ni un ~*** *fig* not give an inch
apicultura *f* beekeeping
apilar pile up
apio *m* BOT celery
apisonadora *f* steamroller; **apisonar** roll
aplacar *hambre* satisfy; *sed* quench; *a alguien* calm down
aplanar level, flatten; ***~ las calles*** *C.Am., Pe* hang around the streets; **aplanarse** *fig* (*descorazonarse*) lose heart
aplastar *tb fig* crush
aplaudir 1 *v/i* applaud, clap **2** *v/t tb fig* applaud; **aplauso** *m* round of applause
aplazar *visita* put off, postpone; *Arg* fail
aplicable applicable; **aplicación** *f* application; **aplicar** apply
aplique *m* wall light
apoderado *m* COM agent; **apoderar** authorize; **apoderarse** take possession *o* control (***de*** of)
apodo *m* nickname
apoplejía *f* apoplexy; ***ataque de ~*** stroke
aportar contribute; ***~ pruebas*** JUR provide evidence
apostar 1 *v/t* bet (***por*** on) **2** *v/i* bet; ***~ por algo*** opt for sth
apóstol *m* apostle
apoyar lean (***en*** against), rest (***en*** against); (*respaldar, confirmar*) support; **apoyo** *m fig* support
apreciable (*visible*) appreciable, noticeable; (*considerable*) considerable, substantial; **apreciación** *f* appreciation; **apreciado** valued; **apreciar** appreciate; (*sentir afecto por*) be fond of; **aprecio** *m* respect
apremio *m* pressure
aprender, aprenderse learn; **aprendiz** *m*, **~a** *f* apprentice, trainee; **aprendizaje** *m* apprenticeship
aprestar, aprestarse get ready
apresurar hurry; **apresurarse** hurry up; ***~ a hacer algo*** hurry *o* rush to do sth
apretado tight; **apretar 1** *v/t botón* press; (*pellizcar, pinzar*) squeeze; *tuerca* tighten; ***~ el paso*** quicken one's pace; ***~ los puños*** clench one's fists **2** *v/i de ropa, zapato* be too tight
aprieto *m* predicament
aprisa quickly
aprisionar *fig* trap
aprobación *f* approval; *de ley*

passing; **aprobado** *m* EDU pass; **aprobar** approve; *comportamiento*, *idea* approve of; *examen* pass
apropiación *f* appropriation
apropiado appropriate, suitable; **apropiarse:** *~ de algo* take sth
aprovechable usable; **aprovechado 1** *adj desp* opportunistic **2** *m*, **-a** *f desp* opportunist; **aprovechamiento** *m* exploitation, use; ***~ de residuos*** use of waste material; **aprovechar 1** *v/t* take advantage of; *tiempo*, *espacio* make good use of **2** *v/i* take the opportunity (***para*** to); ***¡que aproveche!*** enjoy your meal!
aprovisionamiento *m* provisioning, supply; **aprovisionar** provision, supply; **aprovisionarse** stock up (***de*** on)
aproximación *f* approximation; (*acercamiento*) approach; *en lotería* consolation prize; **aproximadamente** approximately; **aproximado** approximate; **aproximar** bring closer; **aproximarse** approach; **aproximativo** approximate, rough
aptitud *f* aptitude (***para*** for), flair (***para*** for); **apto** suitable (***para*** for); *para servicio militar* fit; EDU pass
apuesta *f* bet
apuntado pointed
apuntador *m*, **~a** *f* TEA prompter
apuntalar *edificio* shore up; *fig* prop up
apuntar 1 *v/t* (*escribir*) note down; TEA prompt; *en curso etc* put down (***en***, ***a*** on; ***para*** for); ***~ con el dedo*** point at *o* to **2** *v/i con arma* aim; **apunte** *m* note
apuñalar stab
apurado *L.Am.* (*con prisa*) in a hurry; (*pobre*) short (of cash); **apurar 1** *v/t vaso* finish off; *a alguien* pressure **2** *v/i Chi*: ***no me apura*** I'm not in a hurry for it; **apurarse** worry; *L.Am.* (*darse prisa*) hurry (up); **apuro** *m* predicament; *vergüenza* embarrassment; *L.Am.* rush; ***me da ~*** I'm embarrassed
aquejado: ***estar ~ de*** be suffering from
aquel, aquella, aquellos, aquellas that; *pl* those
aquél, aquélla, aquéllos, aquéllas that (one); *pl* those (ones)
aquello that
aquí here; *en el tiempo* now; ***desde ~*** from here; ***por ~*** here
árabe 1 *m/f & adj* Arab **2** *m idioma* Arabic
Arabia Saudí Saudi Arabia
arado *m* plow, *Br* plough
arancel *m* tariff; **arancelario** tariff *atr*
arándano *m* blueberry
araña *f* ZO spider; *lámpara* chandelier
arañar scratch; **arañazo** *m*

scratch
arar plow, *Br* plough
arbitraje *m* arbitration; **arbitrar** *en fútbol, boxeo* referee; *en tenis, béisbol* umpire; *en conflicto* arbitrate; **arbitrario** arbitrary; **árbitro** *m en fútbol, boxeo* referee; *en tenis, béisbol* umpire; *en conflicto* arbitrator
árbol *m* tree; ~ ***genealógico*** family tree
arbusto *m* shrub, bush
arca *f* chest; ~ ***de Noé*** Noah's Ark
arcada *f* MED: ***me provocó ~s*** it made me retch
arcaico archaic
arcángel *m* archangel
arce *m* BOT maple
arcén *m* shoulder, *Br* hard shoulder
archifamoso very famous
archipiélago *m* archipelago
archivador *m* file cabinet, *Br* filing cabinet; **archivar** *documentos* file; *asunto* shelve; **archivo** *m* archive; INFOR file
arcilla *f* clay
arco *m* ARQUI arch; MÚS bow; *L.Am.* DEP goal; ~ ***iris*** rainbow
arder burn; *estar muy caliente* be very hot; **ardiente** *persona, amor* passionate; *defensor* ardent; *bebida* scalding
ardilla *f* squirrel
ardor *m entusiasmo* fervor, *Br* fervour; ~ ***de estómago*** heartburn
arduo arduous
área *f* area; DEP ~ ***de castigo*** *o* ***de penalty*** penalty area; ~ ***de servicio*** service area
arena *f* sand; ***~s movedizas*** quicksand; **arenoso** sandy
arenque *m* herring
arete *m L.Am. joya* earring
Argel Algiers; **Argelia** Algeria; **argelino 1** *adj* Algerian **2** *m*, **-a** *f* Algerian
Argentina Argentina; **argentino 1** *adj* Argentinian **2** *m*, **-a** *f* Argentinian
argolla *f L.Am.* ring
argucia *f* clever argument; **argüir** argue; **argumentación** *f* argumentation; **argumentar** argue; **argumento** *m razón* argument; *de libro etc* plot
aria *f* aria
aridez *f* aridity, dryness; **árido** arid, dry; *fig* dry
Aries *m/f inv* ASTR Aries
arisco unfriendly
arista *f* MAT edge; BOT beard
aristocracia *f* aristocracy; **aristocrático** aristocratic
arma *f* weapon; ~ ***blanca*** knife; ~ ***de fuego*** firearm; ***alzarse en ~s*** rise up in arms; **armada** *f* navy; **armadura** *f* armor, *Br* armour; **armamento** *m* armaments *pl*; **armar** MIL arm; TÉC assemble; ~ ***un escándalo*** F make a scene
armario *m* closet, *Br* wardrobe; *de cocina* cabinet, *Br* cupboard

armazón *f* skeleton, framework
armería *f* gunstore
armiño *m* ZO stoat; *piel* ermine
armisticio *m* armistice
armonía *f* harmony; **armónica** *f* harmonica, mouth organ; **armónico** *m/adj* harmonic
arnés *m* harness; *para niños* leading strings *pl*, *Br* leading reins *pl*
aro *m* hoop; *L.Am.* (*pendiente*) earring
aroma *m* aroma; *de flor* scent; **aromático** aromatic
arpa *f* harp; **arpista** *m/f* harpist
arpón *m* harpoon
arquear *espalda* arch; *cejas* raise
arqueo *m* MAR capacity; COM: **~** (***de caja***) cashing up
arqueología *f* archeology, *Br* archaeology
arquitecto *m*, **-a** *f* architect; **arquitectura** *f* architecture
arrabal *m* poor outlying area
arraigado entrenched
arrancar 1 *v/t planta*, *página* pull out; *vehículo* start (up); (*quitar*) snatch **2** *v/i de vehículo*, *máquina* start (up); INFOR boot (up); *Chi* (*huir*) run away; **arranque** *m* AUTO starter; (*energía*) drive; (*ataque*) fit
arrastrar 1 *v/t por el suelo*, INFOR drag (***por*** along); (*llevarse*) carry away **2** *v/i por el suelo* trail on the ground; **arrastrarse** crawl; *fig* (*humillarse*) grovel (***delante de*** to);
arrastre *m*: ***estar para el ~*** *fig* F be fit to drop F
arrebatador breathtaking; **arrebatar** snatch (***a*** from); **arrebatarse** get excited; **arrebato** *m* fit
arrecife *m* reef
arredrarse be intimidated (***ante*** by)
arreglado neat; ***si empieza a llover estamos ~s*** if it starts to rain, that'll be just dandy; **arreglar** (*reparar*) fix, repair; (*ordenar*) tidy (up); (*solucionar*) sort out; MÚS arrange; **~ *cuentas*** settle up; *fig* settle scores; **arreglarse** get ready; *de problema* get sorted out; (*apañarse*) manage; ***arreglárselas*** manage; **arreglo** *m* (*reparación*) repair; (*solución*) solution; (*acuerdo*), MÚS arrangement; ***~ de cuentas*** settling of scores; ***con ~ a*** in accordance with
arremeter: *~ contra* charge (at); *fig* (*criticar*) attack
arrendamiento *m* renting; **arrendar** *L.Am.* (*dar en alquiler*) rent (out); (*tomar en alquiler*) rent; ***se arrenda*** for rent; **arrendatario** *m*, **-a** *f* tenant
arrepentirse be sorry; (*cambiar de opinión*) change one's mind; ***~ de algo*** regret sth
arrestar arrest; **arresto** *m* ar-

rest
arriba 1 *adv* up; *en edificio* upstairs; ***el cajón de ~ siguiente*** the next drawer up, the drawer above; *último* the top drawer; ***~ del todo*** right at the top; ***sigan hacia ~*** keep going up; ***me miró de ~ abajo*** *fig* she looked me up and down; ***de diez para ~*** ten or above **2** *int* long live
arribada *f*, **arribaje** *m* MAR arrival; **arribar** MAR arrive, put in
arribista *m/f* social climber
arriesgar risk
arrimar move closer
arrinconar (*acorralar*) corner; *libros etc* put away; *persona* cold-shoulder
arroba *f* INFOR "at" symbol
arrodillarse kneel (down)
arrogancia *f* arrogance; **arrogante** arrogant
arrojar throw; *resultado* produce; (*vomitar*) throw up; **arrojarse** throw o.s.; **arrojo** *m* bravery
arrollador overwhelming; **arrollar** AUTO run over; *fig* crush
arropar wrap up; *fig* protect
arroyo *m* stream; ***sacar a alguien del ~*** *fig* lift s.o. out of the gutter
arroz *m* rice; ***~ con leche*** rice pudding
arruga *f* wrinkle; **arrugar** wrinkle
arruinar ruin
arsenal *m* arsenal
arsénico *m* arsenic
arte *m* (*pl f*) art; ***~ dramático*** dramatic art; ***bellas ~s*** fine art; ***malas ~s*** guile
artefacto *m* (*dispositivo*) device
arteria *f* artery
arterio(e)sclerosis *f* arteriosclerosis
artesa *f* trough
artesana *f* craftswoman; **artesanía** *f* (handi)crafts *pl*; **artesano** *m* craftsman
articulación *f* ANAT, TÉC joint; *de sonidos* articulation; **articulado** articulated; **articular** articulate
artículo *m* article; COM product, item
artífice *m* author
artificial artificial
artificio *m* trick; (*artefacto*) device; **artificioso** sly; (*falto de naturalidad*) affected
artillería *f* artillery
artista *m/f* artist; **artístico** artistic
artritis *f* arthritis
artrosis *f* rheumatoid arthritis
arveja *f Rpl, Chi, Pe* pea
arzobispo *m* archbishop
as *m tb fig* ace
asa *f* handle
asado *m/adj* roast
asalariado *m*, **-a** *f* wage earner; *de empresa* employee
asaltar attack; *banco* rob; **asalto** *m* attack (***a*** on); *robo* robbery, raid; *en boxeo* round

asamblea *f reunión* meeting; *ente* assembly
asar roast; **~ *a la parrilla*** broil, *Br* grill
ascendente 1 *adj* rising, upward **2** *m* ASTR ascendant; **ascender 1** *v/t a empleado* promote **2** *v/i de temperatura etc* rise; *de montañero* climb; DEP, *en trabajo* be promoted (***a*** to); **ascendiente** *m* ancestor; **ascensión** *f* ascent; **ascenso** *m de temperatura, precios* rise (***de*** in); *de montaña* ascent; DEP, *en trabajo* promotion; **ascensor** *m* elevator, *Br* lift; **ascensorista** *m/f* elevator operator
asceta *m/f* ascetic; **ascético** ascetic
asco *m* disgust; ***me da ~*** I find it disgusting; ***¡qué ~!*** how disgusting!
ascua *f* ember; ***estar en*** *o* ***sobre ~s*** be on tenterhooks
asediar *tb fig* besiege
asegurado 1 *adj* insured **2** *m*, **-a** *f* insured; **aseguradora** *f* insurance company; **asegurar** (*afianzar*) secure; (*prometer*) assure; (*garantizar*) guarantee; COM insure; **asegurarse** make sure
asemejarse: **~ *a*** look like
asentimiento *m* approval, agreement; **asentir** agree (***a*** to); *con la cabeza* nod
aseo *m* cleanliness; (*baño*) restroom, toilet
asequible *precio* affordable; *obra* accessible
asesinar murder; POL assassinate; **asesinato** *m* murder; POL assassination; **asesino** *m*, **-a** *f* murderer; POL assassin
asesor *m*, **~a** *f* consultant, advisor, *Br* adviser; **~ *de imagen*** public relations consultant
asesoramiento *m* advice; **asesorar** advise; **asesoría** *f* consultancy
asfalto *m* asphalt
asfixia *f* asphyxiation; **asfixiar, asfixiarse** asphyxiate, suffocate
así 1 *adv* (*de este modo*) like this; (*de ese modo*) like that; **~ *no más*** *S.Am.* just like that; **~ *pues*** so; **~ *que*** so; **~ *de grande*** this big; **~ ~** so so **2** *conj*: **~ *como*** *al igual que* while, whereas
Asia Asia; **asiático 1** *adj* Asian **2** *m*, **-a** *f* Asian
asiduidad *f* frequency; ***con ~*** *con frecuencia* regularly; **asiduo** regular
asiento *m* seat; ***tomar ~*** take a seat
asignar allocate; *persona, papel* assign; **asignatura** *f* subject
asilado *m*, **-a** *f* POL asylum seeker; **asilo** *m* home, institution; POL asylum; **~ *de ancianos*** old people's home
asimilar assimilate
asimismo (*también*) also; (*igualmente*) likewise
asistencia *f* (*ayuda*) assist-

ance; *a lugar* attendance (***a*** at); ***~ en carretera*** AUTO roadside assistance; ***~ médica*** medical care; **asistenta** *f* cleaner; **asistente** *m/f* (*ayudante*) assistant; ***~ social*** social worker; ***los ~s*** those present; **asistir 1** *v/t* help, assist **2** *v/i* be present

asma *f* asthma; **asmático** asthmatic

asno *m* ZO donkey; *persona* idiot

asociación *f* association; **asociar** associate

asomarse lean out (***por*** of)

asombrar amaze, astonish; **asombro** *m* amazement, astonishment; **asombroso** amazing, astonishing

asomo *m*: ***ni por ~*** no way

aspecto *m de persona, cosa* look, appearance; (*faceta*) aspect; ***tener buen ~*** look good

aspereza *f* roughness; **áspero** *superficie* rough; *sonido* harsh; *persona* abrupt

aspiraciones *fpl* aspirations

aspirador *m*, **~a** *f* vacuum cleaner; **aspirante** *m/f a cargo* candidate (***a*** for); *a título* contender (***a*** for); **aspirar 1** *v/t* suck up; *al respirar* inhale, breathe in **2** *v/i*: ***~ a*** aspire to

aspirina *f* aspirin

asquear disgust; **asqueroso 1** *adj* (*sucio*) filthy; (*repugnante*) revolting, disgusting **2** *m*, **-a** *f* creep

asta *f* flagpole; (*pitón*) horn

asterisco *m* asterisk

astilla *f* splinter; ***~s para fuego*** kindling; ***hacer ~s algo*** *fig* smash sth to pieces

astillero *m* shipyard

astracán *m* astrakhan

astro *m* AST, *fig* star; **astrología** *f* astrology; **astrólogo** *m*, **-a** *f* astrologer; **astronauta** *m/f* astronaut; **astronave** *f* spaceship; **astronomía** *f* astronomy

astucia *f* shrewdness, astuteness; **astuto** shrewd, astute

asumir assume; (*aceptar*) accept, come to terms with

asunto *m* matter; F (*relación*) affair; ***~s exteriores*** foreign affairs; ***no es ~ tuyo*** it's none of your business

asustar frighten, scare

atacar attack

atajar 1 *v/t* check the spread of, contain; *L.Am. pelota* catch **2** *v/i* take a short cut; **atajo** *m L.Am.* short cut

atalaya 1 *f* watchtower **2** *m/f* sentinel

ataque *m* (*agresión*) attack; (*acceso*) fit; ***~ cardíaco*** *o* ***al corazón*** heart attack; ***le dio un ~ de risa*** she burst out laughing

atar tie (up); *fig* tie down

atardecer 1 *v/i* get dark **2** *m* dusk

atareado busy

atasco *m* traffic jam

ataúd *m* coffin, casket

ate *m Méx* quince jelly

atención *f* attention; (*corte-*

sía) courtesy; ***¡~!*** your attention, please!; ***llamar la ~ a alguien*** *reñir* tell s.o. off; *por ser llamativo* attract s.o.'s attention; ***prestar ~*** pay attention (***a*** to)
atender 1 *v/t a enfermo* look after; *en tienda* attend to **2** *v/i* pay attention (***a*** to)
atenerse: **~ *a*** *normas* abide by; *consecuencias* accept; ***saber a qué ~*** know where one stands
atentado *m* attack (***contra***, ***a*** on); ***~ terrorista*** terrorist attack
atento attentive; ***estar ~ a*** pay attention to
atenuante JUR extenuating; **atenuar** lessen, reduce
ateo 1 *adj* atheistic **2** *m*, **-a** *f* atheist
aterrizaje *m* AVIA landing; ***~ forzoso*** *o* ***de emergencia*** emergency landing; **aterrizar** land
aterrorizar terrify; *(amenazar)* terrorize
atestado overcrowded
atestiguar JUR testify; *fig* bear witness to
ático *m piso* top floor; *apartamento* top floor apartment *o Br* flat; *(desván)* attic
atizar *fuego* poke; *pasiones* stir up; ***le atizó un golpe*** she hit him
atleta *m/f* athlete; **atletismo** *m* athletics
atmósfera *f* atmosphere
atolondrado scatterbrained
atómico atomic; **átomo** *m* atom; ***ni un ~ de*** *fig* not an iota of
atónito astonished, amazed
atontado dazed, stunned
atormentar torment
atornillar screw on
atosigar pester
atracadero *m* MAR mooring; **atracar 1** *v/t banco* hold up; *a alguien* mug; *Chi* F make out with F **2** *v/i* MAR dock
atracción *f* attraction
atraco *m* robbery; *de persona* mugging
atractivo 1 *adj* attractive **2** *m* appeal, attraction; **atraer** attract
atrapar catch, trap
atrás *posición* at the back, behind; *movimiento* back; ***años ~*** years ago *o* back; ***hacia ~*** back, backward; ***quedarse ~*** get left behind; **atrasado** *en estudios*, *pago* behind (***en*** in *o* with); *reloj* slow; *pueblo* backward; ***ir ~ de un reloj*** be slow; **atrasar 1** *v/t reloj* put back; *fecha* postpone, put back **2** *v/i de reloj* lose time; **atraso** *m* backwardness; COM ***~s*** arrears
atravesar cross; *(perforar)*, *crisis* go through
atrevido daring; **atreverse** dare
atribuir attribute (***a*** to); **atributo** *m* attribute
atril *m* lectern

atrocidad *f* atrocity
atropellado in a rush; **atropellar** knock down; **atropello** *m* running over; *escándalo* outrage
atroz appalling, atrocious
ATS (= ***ayudante técnico sanitario***) registered nurse
atún *m* tuna (fish)
aturdido in a daze
audacia *f* audacity; **audaz** bold, audacious
audible audible
audición *f* TEA audition; JUR hearing
audiencia *f* audience; JUR court; ***índice de ~*** TV ratings *pl*
audífono *m* hearing aid; **audiovisual** audiovisual
auditivo auditory; *problema* hearing *atr*
auditor *m*, **~a** *f* auditor; **auditorio** *m* (*público*) audience; *sala* auditorium
aula *f* classroom; *en universidad* lecture hall, *Br* lecture theatre
aumentar 1 *v/t* increase **2** *v/i* increase, go up; **aumento** *m* increase (***de*** in); *de sueldo* raise, *Br* rise; ***ir en ~*** be increasing
aun even; ***~ así*** even so
aún still; *en oraciones negativas* yet; *en comparaciones* even; ***~ no*** not yet
aunque although, even though; + *subj* even if
aureola *f* halo
auricular *m de teléfono* receiver; ***~es*** headphones, earphones
auscultar: ***~ a alguien*** listen to s.o.'s chest
ausencia *f de persona* absence; *no existencia* lack (***de*** of); **ausentarse** leave, go away; **ausente** absent
austeridad *f* austerity; **austero** austere
austral southern
Australia Australia; **australiano 1** *adj* Australian **2** *m*, **-a** *f* Australian
Austria Austria; **austriano 1** *adj* Austrian **2** *m*, **-a** *f* Austrian
auténtico authentic
autismo *m* autism
auto *m* JUR order; *L.Am.* AUTO car
autoadhesivo self-adhesive
autobanco *m* ATM, cash machine
autobiografía *f* autobiography
autobús *m* bus
autocar *m* bus
autocaravana *f* camper van
autocine *m* drive-in movie theater
autodefensa *f* self-defense, *Br* self-defence
autodisparador *m* FOT automatic shutter release
autoescuela *f* driving school
autógrafo *m* autograph
automático automatic
automóvil *m* car, automobile; **automovilismo** *m* driving; **automovilista** *m/f* motorist

autonomía *f* autonomy; *en España* automous region
autopista *f* freeway, *Br* motorway
autopsia *f* autopsy
autor *m*, **~a** *f* author; *de crimen* perpetrator
autoridad *f* authority; **autorización** *f* authority; **autorizar** authorize; **autorizado** (*permitido*) authorized; (*respetado*) authoritative
autorradio *m* car radio
autoservicio *m* supermarket; *restaurante* self-service restaurant
autostop *m* hitchhiking; ***hacer ~*** hitchhike; **autostopista** *m/f* hitchhiker
autovía *f* divided highway, *Br* dual carriageway
auxiliar 1 *adj* auxiliary; *profesor* assistant **2** *m/f* assistant; **~** *f* ***de vuelo*** stewardess, flight attendant **3** help; **auxilio** *m* help; ***primeros ~s*** first aid
aval *m* guarantee
avalancha *f* avalanche
avance *m* advance
avanzar advance, move forward; MIL advance (***hacia*** on)
avaricia *f* avarice; **avaro 1** *adj* miserly **2** *m*, **-a** *f* miser
ave *f* bird; *S.Am.* (*pollo*) chicken; **~ *de presa*** *o* ***de rapiña*** bird of prey
avellana *f* hazelnut
avena *f* oats *pl*
avenencia *f* agreement
avenida *f* avenue
aventura *f* adventure; *riesgo* venture; *amorosa* affair; **aventurar** risk; *opinión* venture; **aventurero** adventurous
avergonzar (*aborchornar*) embarrass; ***le avergüenza*** *algo reprensible* she's ashamed of it; **avergonzarse** be ashamed (***de*** of)
avería *f* TÉC fault; AUTO breakdown; **averiado** broken down
averiguar find out
aversión *f* aversion
avestruz *m* ostrich
aviación *f* aviation; MIL air force; **aviador** *m*, **-a** *f* pilot, aviator
avicultura *f* poultry farming
avidez *f* eagerness; **ávido** eager (***de*** for), avid (***de*** for)
avión *m* plane; ***por ~*** *mandar una carta* (by) airmail; **avioneta** *f* light aircraft
avisador *m* warning light; *sonoro* alarm; *L.Am.* (*anunciante*) advertiser; **avisar** *notificar* let know, tell; *de peligro* warn; (*llamar*) send for; **aviso** *m* notice; (*advertencia*) warning; *L.Am.* (*anuncio*) advertisement; ***hasta nuevo ~*** until further notice; ***sin previo ~*** without any warning
avispa *f* wasp
avispado bright, sharp
axila *f* armpit
ay ow!, ouch!; *de susto* oh!
ayer yesterday; **~ *por la ma-***

ñana yesterday morning
ayuda *f* help, assistance; **ayudante** *m/f* assistant; **ayudar** help
ayunar fast; **ayunas:** ***estoy en ~*** I haven't eaten anything
ayuntamiento *m* city council, town council; *edificio* city hall
azafata *f* flight attendant; ***~ de congresos*** hostess
azafrán *m* saffron
azahar *m* orange / lemon blossom
azotea *f* flat roof
azúcar *m* (*also f*) sugar; ***~ glas*** confectioner's sugar, *Br* icing sugar
azufre *m* sulfur, *Br* sulphur
azul 1 *adj* blue; ***~ celeste*** sky-blue; ***~ marino*** navy(-blue) **2** *m* blue
azulejo *m* tile

B

B.A. (= ***Buenos Aires***) Buenos Aires
babero *m* bib
babor *m* MAR port
baca *f* AUTO roof rack
bacalao *m* cod
bache *m* pothole; *fig* rough patch
bachiller *m/f* high school graduate; **bachillerato** *m* *Esp high school leaver's certificate*
bacteria *f* bacteria
bagatela *f* trinket
bahía *f* bay
bailador 1 adj: ***ser muy ~*** love dancing **2** *m*, **~a** *f* dancer; **bailaor** *m*, **~a** *f* flamenco dancer; **bailar** dance; **bailarín** *m*, **-ina** *f* dancer; **baile** *m* dance; *fiesta formal* ball; ***~ de salón*** ballroom dancing
baja *f* fall, drop; ***estar de ~*** (***por enfermedad***) be off sick; ***~s*** MIL casualties; **bajada** *f* fall; **bajar 1** *v/t voz, precio* lower; *escalera* go down; ***~ algo*** *de arriba* get sth down **2** *v/i* go down; *de intereses* fall, drop
bajeza *f* (*calidad*) baseness; (*acto*) despicable thing to do
bajo 1 *adj* low; *persona* short; ***por lo ~*** at least **2** *m* MÚS bass; *piso* first floor, *Br* ground floor **3** *adv cantar, hablar* quietly, softly; *volar* low **4** *prp* under; ***tres grados ~ cero*** three degrees below zero
bala *f* bullet; ***ni a ~*** *L.Am.* F no way
balance *m* COM balance; **balancear** *caderas* swing; **balancearse** swing, sway; MAR rock; **balancín** *m* TÉC rocker; (*mecedora*) rocking chair; **balanza** *f* scales *pl*; ***~ comercial*** balance of trade;

~ de pagos balance of payments

balbucear, balbucir stammer; *de niño* babble

balcón *m* balcony

balde: *de ~* for nothing; *en ~* in vain

baldío 1 *adj* uncultivated; *fig* useless **2** *m* uncultivated land

baldosa *f* floor tile

Baleares *fpl* Balearics; **baleárico** Balearic

baliza *f* MAR buoy

ballena *f* ZO whale

ballet *m* ballet

balneario *m* spa

balón *m* ball; **baloncesto** *m* basketball; **balonmano** *m* handball; **balonvolea** *m* volleyball

balsa *f* raft

bálsamo *m* balsam

baluarte *m* stronghold; *persona* pillar, stalwart

bambú *m* bamboo

banal banal

banana *f L.Am., Rpl, Pe, Bol* banana

banca *f actividad* banking; *conjunto de bancos* banks *pl*; *en juego* bank; DEP, *Méx* (*asiento*) bench; *~ electrónica* on-line banking

banco *m* COM bank; *para sentarse* bench; *~ de arena* sand bank; *~ de datos* data bank

banda *f* MÚS, (*grupo*) band; *de delincuentes* gang; (*cinta*) sash; *en fútbol* touchline; *~ sonora* soundtrack

bandeja *f* tray

bandera *f* flag; **banderilla** *f* TAUR banderilla (*dart stuck into bull's neck during bullfight*); **banderola** *f* flag

bandido *m*, **-a** *f* bandit

bandolero *m*, **-a** *f* bandit

banquero *m*, **-a** *f* banker

banqueta *f L.Am.* stool; *L.Am.* (*acera*) sidewalk, *Br* pavement; *~ trasera* AUTO back seat

banquete *m* banquet; *~ de bodas* wedding reception

banquillo *m* JUR dock; DEP bench

bañador *m* swimsuit; **bañar** bathe; **bañarse** have a bath; *en el mar* go for a swim; **bañera** *f* (bath)tub, bath; **bañera de hidromasaje** whirlpool, Jacuzzi®; **baño** *m en la bañera* bath; *en el mar* swim; *esp L.Am.* bathroom; (*ducha*) shower; **baño de sangre** blood bath; **baño de sol** sunbathing session; **baños de sol** sunbathing

baqueta *f* MÚS drumstick

bar *m* bar

baraja *f* deck of cards

barajar 1 *v/t naipes* shuffle; *fig* consider **2** *v/i* quarrel

baranda *f en billar* cushion

barandilla *f* handrail, banister

baratear sell off

baratija *f* trinket

baratillo *m tienda* cut-price store; (*mercadillo*) street

market
barato cheap
barba *f* beard
barbacoa *f* barbecue
barbaridad *f* barbarity; ***costar una ~*** cost a fortune; ***¡qué ~!*** what a thing to say / do!; **bárbaro 1** *adj* F tremendous, awesome F; ***¡qué ~!*** amazing! F **2** *m*, **-a** *f* F punk F
barbero *m* barber
barbilla *f* chin
barbudo bearded
barca *f* boat; **barcaza** *f* barge; **barco** *m* boat; *más grande* ship; ***~ de vela*** sailing ship
barítono *m* baritone
barman *m* bartender, *Br* barman
barniz *m* varnish; **barnizar** varnish
barómetro *m* barometer
barquero *m* boatman
barquillo *m* wafer; *Méx, C.Am.* ice-cream cone
barra *f de metal, en bar* bar; *de cortinas* rod; ***~ de labios*** lipstick; ***~ de pan*** baguette; ***~ espaciadora*** space-bar; ***~ de herramientas*** INFOR tool bar; ***~ invertida*** backslash
barraca *f* (*chabola*) shack; *de tiro* stand; *de feria* stall; *L.Am.* (*deposito*) shed; ***~s*** *L.Am.* shanty town
barranco *m* ravine
barredera 1 *f* street sweeper **2** *adj*: ***red ~*** trawl net
barrena *f* gimlet; AVIA: ***entrar en ~*** go into a spin
barrera *f* barrier; ***~ del sonido*** sound barrier
barricada *f* barricade
barriga *f* belly; ***rascarse la ~*** *fig* F sit on one's butt F
barril *m* barrel
barrio *m* neighborhood, *Br* neighbourhood, area; ***~ de chabolas*** *Esp* shanty town
barro *m* mud
barroco *m/adj* baroque
barruntar suspect
barullo *m* uproar, racket
basar base (***en*** on)
báscula *f* scales
base *f* QUÍM, MAT, MIL base; ***~ de datos*** INFOR database; ***~s*** *de concurso etc* conditions; ***a ~ de*** by dint of; **básico** basic
basílica *f* basilica
básquetbol *m L.Am.* basketball
bastante 1 *adj* enough; *número o cantidad considerable* plenty of; **2** *adv* quite, fairly; ***bebe ~*** she drinks quite a lot; **bastar** be enough; ***basta con uno*** one is enough; ***¡basta!*** that's enough!
bastos *mpl suit in Spanish deck of cards*
basura *f tb fig* trash, *Br* rubbish; ***cubo de la ~*** trash can, *Br* rubbish bin; **basurero** *m* garbage collector, *Br* dustman
bata *f* robe, *Br* dressing gown; MED (white) coat; TÉC lab coat
batalla *f* battle; **batallón** *m*

battalion
batata *f* BOT sweet potato
batería *f* MIL, ELEC, AUTO battery; MÚS drums, drum kit; ***~ de cocina*** set of pans; ***aparcar en ~*** AUTO parallel park
batida *f de caza* beating; *de policía* search
batido 1 *adj camino* well-trodden **2** *m* GASTR milkshake; **batidora** *f* mixer
batiente *m* jamb
batir beat; *nata* whip; *récord* break
batuta *f* MÚS baton; ***llevar la ~*** *fig* F be the boss F
baúl *m* chest, trunk; *L.Am.* AUTO trunk, *Br* boot
bautismo *m* baptism, christening; **bautizar** baptize, christen; *barco* name; *vino* F water down; **bautizo** *m* baptism, christening
baya *f* berry
bayeta *f* cloth
baza *f en naipes* trick; *fig* trump card
bazar *m* hardware and fancy goods store; *mercado* bazaar
bazo *m* ANAT spleen
beatificar REL beatify; **beatitud** *f* beatitude; **beato 1** *adj desp* overpious **2** *m*, **-a** *f desp* over-pious person
bebé *m* baby
bebedor *m*, **~a** *f* drinker; **beber** drink; **bebida** *f* drink
beca *f* scholarship, grant
béchamel *f* béchamel (sauce)
beige beige
béisbol *m* baseball
belén *m* nativity scene
belga *m/f & adj* Belgian; **Bélgica** Belgium
Belice Belize; **beliceño 1** *adj* Belizean **2** *m*, **-a** *f* Belizean
bélico war *atr*; **belicoso** warlike, bellicose; *fig persona* belligerent
belleza *f* beauty; **bello** beautiful
bellota *f* BOT acorn
bemol *m* MÚS flat
bencina *f* benzine; *Pe, Bol* (*gasolina*) gas, *Br* petrol
bendecir bless
beneficencia *f* charity; **beneficiar** benefit; *Rpl ganado* slaughter; **beneficiarse** benefit (***de***, ***con*** from); **beneficio** *m* benefit; COM profit; *Rpl* slaughterhouse; *C.Am.* coffee-processing plant; ***en ~ de*** in aid of; **beneficioso** beneficial; **benéfico** charity *atr*
benévolo benevolent, kind; (*indulgente*) lenient
benigno MED benign
berberecho *m* ZO cockle
berenjena *f* egg plant, *Br* aubergine
bermudas *mpl*, *fpl* Bermuda shorts
berro *m* BOT watercress
berza *f* BOT cabbage
besar kiss; **beso** *m* kiss
bestia 1 *f* beast **2** *m/f fig* F brute F; *mujer* bitch F; **bestial** F tremendous F; **bestialidad** *f* act of cruelty

besugo *m* ZO bream; *fig* F idiot
besuquear F smother with kisses
betún *m* shoe polish
biberón *m* baby's bottle
Biblia *f* Bible; **bíblico** biblical
biblioteca *f* library; *mueble* bookcase; **bibliotecario** *m*, **-a** *f* librarian
bicarbonato *m*: ~ **(de sodio)** bicarbonate of soda
bicho *m* bug; (*animal*) creature; *fig* F *persona* nasty piece of work; **~s** vermin; **¿qué ~ te ha picado?** what's eating you?
bici *f* F bike; **bicicleta** *f* bicycle; **ir** *o* **montar en ~** go cycling; **~ de montaña** mountain bike
bidé *m* bidet
bidón *m* drum
biela *f* TÉC connecting rod
bien 1 *m* good; **~es** goods, property; **~es de consumo** consumer goods; **~es inmuebles** real estate **2** *adv* well; (*muy*) very; **más ~** rather; **o ~... o...** either … or …; **¡está~!** it's OK!, it's alright!; **¡~ hecho!** well done!
bienal 1 *adj* biennial **2** *f* biennial event
bienaventurado REL blessed; **bienestar** *m* well-being; **bienhechor 1** *adj* beneficent **2** *m* benefactor; **bienvenida** *f* welcome; **dar la ~ a alguien** welcome s.o.; **bienvenido** welcome
bife *m* *Rpl* steak
biftec *m* steak
bifurcarse fork
bigamia *f* bigamy
bigote *m* mustache, *Br* moustache; **~s** *de gato etc* whiskers
bigudí *m* hair curler
bikini *m* bikini
bilateral bilateral
bilingüe bilingual
bilis *f* bile; *fig* F bad mood
billar *m* billiards; **~ americano** pool
billete *m* ticket; **~ abierto** open ticket; **~ de autobús** bus ticket; **~ de banco** bill, *Br* banknote; **~ de ida, ~ sencillo** one-way ticket, *Br* single (ticket); **~ de ida y vuelta** round-trip ticket, *Br* return (ticket); **billetero** *m* billfold, *Br* wallet
billón *m* trillion
bimensual twice-monthly
bimotor 1 *adj* twin-engined **2** *m* twin-engined plane
biodegradable biodegradable
biografía *f* biography; **biográfico** biographical
biología *f* biology; **biológico** biological; AGR organic
biombo *m* folding screen
biopsia *f* MED biopsy
biquini *m* bikini
birria *f* F piece of junk F; **va hecha una ~** F she looks a real mess
bis *m* encore; **9 ~** 9A
bisabuela *f* great-grand-

mother; **bisabuelo** *m* great-grandfather
bisagra *f* hinge
bisiesto: ***año ~*** leap year
bisnieta *f* great-granddaughter; **bisnieto** *m* great-grandson
bisoñé *m* hairpiece, toupee
bisté, bistec *m* steak
bisturí *m* MED scalpel
bisutería *f* costume jewelry *o Br* jewellery
bizco cross-eyed
bizcocho *m* sponge (cake)
blanca *f persona* white; MÚS half-note, *Br* minim; ***estar sin ~*** *fig* F be broke F; **blanco 1** *adj* white; (*sin escrito*) blank; ***arma -a*** knife **2** *m persona* white; (*diana*), *fig* target; ***dar en el ~*** hit the nail on the head; **Blancanieves** *f* Snow White; **blancura** *f* whiteness
blando soft; **blandura** *f* softness
blanquear whiten; *pared* whitewash; *dinero* launder
blasfemar curse, swear; REL blaspheme; **blasfemia** *f* REL blasphemy
blindado armored, *Br* armoured; *puerta* reinforced; ELEC shielded; **blindaje** *m de vehículo* armor *o Br* armour plating
bloc *m* pad
bloque *m* block; POL bloc; ***~ de apartamentos*** apartment building, *Br* block of flats; ***en ~*** en masse; **bloquear** block; DEP obstruct; (*atascar*) jam; MIL blockade; COM freeze; **bloqueo** *m* blockade
blusa *f* blouse
boa *f* boa constrictor
boato *m* ostentation
bobada *f* piece of nonsense
bobina *f* bobbin; FOT reel, spool; ELEC coil
bobo 1 *adj* silly, foolish **2** *m*, **-a** *f* fool
boca *f* mouth; ***~ a ~*** mouth to mouth; ***~ de metro*** subway entrance; ***~ abajo*** face down; ***~ arriba*** face up; ***se me hace la ~ agua*** my mouth is watering; **bocacalle** *f* side street; **bocadillo** *m* sandwich; **bocado** *m* mouthful, bite; **bocajarro:** ***a ~*** at point-blank range; *fig decir* point-blank; **bocazas** *m/f inv* F loudmouth F
boceto *m* sketch
bochorno *m* sultry weather; *fig* embarrassment; **bochornoso** *tiempo* sultry; *fig* embarrassing
bocina *f* MAR, AUTO horn
bocio *m* MED goiter, *Br* goitre
boda *f* wedding
bodega *f* wine cellar; MAR, AVIA hold; *L.Am.* bar; *C.Am., Pe, Bol* grocery store
bodegón *m* PINT still life
bofetada *f* slap
boga *f*: ***estar en ~*** *fig* be in fashion
boicot *m* boycott; **boicotear** boycott

boina *f* beret
boj *m* BOT box
bola *f* ball; TÉC ball bearing; *de helado* scoop; F (*mentira*) fib F; **~ *de nieve*** snowball
bolera *f* bowling alley
bolero 1 *m* MÚS bolero **2** *m/f Méx* F bootblack
boleta *f L.Am.* ticket; (*pase*) passt; (*voto*) ballot paper; **boletería** *f L.Am.* ticket office; *en cine, teatro* box office; **boletero** *m*, **-a** *f L.Am.* ticket clerk; *en cine, teatro* box office employee
boletín *m* bulletin, report; **~ *de evaluación*** report card; **~ *meteorológico*** weather report; **boleto** *m L.Am.* ticket; **~ *de autobús*** *L.Am.* bus ticket; **~ *de ida y vuelta*** *L.Am.*, **~ *redondo*** *Méx* round-trip ticket, *Br* return
bólido *m fig* racing car
bolígrafo *m* ball-point pen
Bolivia Bolivia; **boliviano 1** *adj* Bolivian **2** *m*, **-a** *f* Bolivian
bollería *f* bakery
bollo *m* bun; (*abolladura*) bump
bolo *m* pin; *C.Am.*, *Méx* christening present; **bolos** *mpl* bowling
bolsa *f* bag; COM stock exchange; *L.Am.* (*bolsillo*) pocket; **~ *de agua caliente*** hot-water bottle
bolsillo *m* pocket; ***meterse a alguien en el* ~** F win s.o. over; **bolso** *m* purse, *Br* handbag
bomba *f* bomb; TÉC pump; *S.Am.* gas station; **~ *de relojería*** time bomb; ***caer como una* ~** *fig* F come as a bombshell; ***pasarlo* ~** F have a great time; **bombardear** bomb; **bombardero** *m* bomber; **bombear** *líquido* pump; *balón* lob
bombero *m*, **-a** *f* firefighter
bombilla *f* light bulb; *Rpl metal straw for the mate gourd*
bombo *m* MÚS bass drum; TÉC drum
bombón *m* chocolate; *fig* F babe F; **bombona** *f* cylinder; **bombonería** *f* candy store, *Br* sweet shop
bonachón good-natured
bonaerense 1 *adj* of Buenos Aires, Buenos Aires *atr* **2** *m/f* native of Buenos Aires
bondad *f* goodness, kindness; ***tenga la* ~ *de*** please be so kind as to; **bondadoso** caring
boniato *m* sweet potato
bonificación *f* (*gratificación*) bonus; (*descuento*) discount; **bonificar** (*gratificar*) give a bonus to; (*descontar*) give a discount of
bonito 1 *adj* pretty **2** *m* ZO tuna
bono *m* voucher; COM bond
boquerón *m* anchovy
boquiabierto *fig* F speechless
boquilla *f* MÚS mouthpiece; *de manguera* nozzle

borbotar bubble
borda *f* MAR gunwale; ***echar por la ~*** throw overboard
bordado **1** *adj* embroidered **2** *m* embroidery; **bordar** embroider; **~ *algo*** *fig* do sth brilliantly
borde *m* edge; ***al ~ de*** *fig* on the verge *o* brink of
bordillo *m* curb, *Br* kerb
bordo *m*: ***a ~*** on board
borla *f* tassel
borrachera *f* drunkenness; ***agarrar una ~*** get drunk; **borracho** **1** *adj* drunk **2** *m*, **-a** *f* drunk
borrador *m* eraser; *de texto* draft; (*boceto*) sketch; **borrar** erase; INFOR *tb* delete; *pizarra* clean; *recuerdo* blot out
borrasca *f* area of low pressure
borrego *m* lamb
borrón *m* blot; *mancha extendida* smudge; ***hacer ~ y cuenta nueva*** *fig* wipe the slate clean; **borroso** blurred, fuzzy
bosque *m* wood; *grande* forest
bosquejar *dibujo* sketch; *fig plan* outline; **bosquejo** *m* sketch; *fig* outline
bostezar yawn; **bostezo** *m* yawn
bota *f* boot; ***~ de montar*** riding boot
botadura *f* MAR launch
botánica *f* botany; **botánico** **1** *adj* botanical **2** *m*, **-a** *f* botanist
botar **1** *v/t* MAR launch; *pelota* bounce; *L.Am.* (*echar*) throw; *L.Am.* (*desechar*) throw out; *L.Am.* (*despedir*) fire **2** *v/i de pelota* bounce
bote *m* (*barco*) boat; *L.Am.* (*lata*) can; (*tarro*) jar; ***~ de la basura*** *Méx* trash can, *Br* rubbish bin; ***~ salvavidas*** lifeboat; ***de ~ en ~*** packed out
botella *f* bottle
botellero *m* wine rack
botica *f* pharmacy, *Br tb* chemist's (shop); **boticario** *m*, **-a** *f* pharmacist, *Br tb* chemist
botijo *m container with a spout for drinking from*
botín *m* loot; *calzado* ankle boot
botiquín *m* medicine chest; *estuche* first-aid kit
botón *m* button; BOT bud; **botones** *m inv* bellhop, bellboy
bóveda *f* vault
bovino bovine
boxeador *m*, **~a** *f* boxer; **boxear** box; **boxeo** *m* boxing
boya *f* buoy; *de caña* float; **boyante** *fig* buoyant
bozal *m para perro* muzzle
bracero *m*, **-a** *f* agricultural laborer *o Br* labourer; ***de ~*** arm in arm
bragas *fpl* panties
bragueta *f* fly
bramar roar; *del viento* howl; **bramido** *m* roar
brandy *m* brandy

branquia *f* ZO gill
brasa *f* ember; ***a la ~*** GASTR char-broiled, *Br* char-grilled; **brasero** *m* brazier; *eléctrico* electric heater
Brasil Brazil; **brasileño 1** *adj* Brazilian **2** *m*, **-a** *f* Brazilian
bravo *animal* fierce; *mar* rough; *persona* brave; *L.Am.* (*furioso*) angry; ***¡~!*** well done!; *en concierto etc* bravo!; **bravura** *f de animal* ferocity; *de persona* bravery
braza *f* breaststroke; **brazalete** *m* bracelet; (*banda*) armband; **brazo** *m* arm; ***con los ~s abiertos*** with open arms
brea *f* tar, pitch
brecha *f* breach; *fig* F gap; MED gash F
bregar struggle; *trabajar* work hard
breve brief; ***en ~*** shortly; **brevedad** *f* briefness, brevity
brezo *m* BOT heather
bribón *m*, **-ona** *f* rascal
bricolaje *m* do-it-yourself, DIY
brida *f de caballo* bridle; TÉC clamp; ***a toda ~*** at top speed
brillante 1 *adj* bright; *fig* brilliant **2** *m* diamond; **brillar** *fig* shine; **brillo** *m* shine; *de estrella, luz* brightness; ***dar*** *o* ***sacar ~ a algo*** polish sth; **brillantez** *f* brilliance
brincar jump up and down; **brinco** *m* F leap, bound; ***dar ~s*** jump
brindar 1 *v/t* offer **2** *v/i* drink a toast (***por*** to); **brindis** *m inv* toast
brío *m fig* F verve, spirit; **brioso** F spirited, lively
brisa *f* MAR breeze
británico 1 *adj* British **2** *m*, **-a** *f* Briton, Brit F
broca *f* TÉC drill bit
brocado *m* brocade
brocha *f* brush
broche *m* broach, *Br* brooch; (*cierre*) fastener; *L.Am.* (*pinza*) clothes pin
broma *f* joke; ***en ~*** as a joke; ***gastar ~s*** play jokes; **bromear** joke; **bromista** *m/f* joker
bronca *f* F telling off F; *Méx* P fight
bronce *m* bronze; **bronceado 1** *adj* tanned **2** *m* suntan; **bronceador** *m* suntan lotion; **broncearse** get a tan
bronco *voz* harsh, gruff
bronquial bronchial; **bronquios** *mpl* bronchial tubes; **bronquitis** *f* bronchitis
brotar BOT sprout, bud; *fig* appear, arise; **brote** *m* BOT shoot; MED, *fig* outbreak; ***~s de bambú*** bamboo shoots; ***~s de soja*** beansprouts
bruja *f* witch; **brujo** *m* wizard; **brujería** *f* witchcraft
brújula *f* compass
bruma *f* mist; **brumoso** misty
brusco sharp, abrupt
brutal brutal; P *fiesta* incredible F; **brutalidad** *f* brutality;
bruto 1 *adj* brutish; (*inculto*)

ignorant; (*torpe*) clumsy; COM gross **2** *m*, **-a** *f* brute, animal
bucal oral
buceador *m*, **~a** *f* diver; **bucear** dive; *fig* delve (***en*** into)
buche *m de ave* crop; *de persona* F belly F
bucle *m* (*rizo*) curl; INFOR loop
budín *m* pudding
budismo *m* Buddhism
buenaventura *f* fortune
bueno good; (*bondadoso*) kind; (*sabroso*) nice; ***por las -as*** willingly; ***de -as a primeras*** without warning; ***ponerse ~*** get well; ***¡~!*** well!; ***¿~?*** *Méx* hello; ***-a voluntad*** goodwill; ***¡-as!*** hello!; ***~s días*** good morning; ***-as noches*** good evening; ***-as tardes*** good evening
buey *m* ox
búfalo *m* buffalo
bufanda *f* scarf; *fig* F perk
bufete *m* lawyer's office
buhardilla *f* attic
búho *m* owl
buitre *m* vulture
bujía *f* AUTO spark plug
bulbo *m* bulb
Bulgaria Bulgaria; **búlgaro 1** *adj* Bulgarian **2** *m*, **-a** *f* Bulgarian **3** *m idioma* Bulgarian
bullicio *m* din; (*actividad*) bustle; **bullir** boil; *de lugar* swarm (***de*** with)
bulo *m* F rumor, *Br* rumour
bulto *m* package; MED lump; *en superficie* bulge; (*silueta*) vague shape; (*pieza de equipaje*) piece of baggage
buñuelo *m Esp* fritter
buque *m* ship; ***~ de guerra*** warship
burbuja *f* bubble
burdel *m* brothel
burdo rough
burgués 1 *adj* middle-class, bourgeois **2** *m*, **-esa** *f* member of the bourgeoisie; **burguesía** *f* middle class, bourgeoisie
burla *f* joke; (*engaño*) trick; ***hacer ~ de alguien*** F make fun of s.o.; **burlar** F get around; **burlarse** make fun (***de*** of); **burlesco** *tono* joking; *gesto* rude
burlón 1 *adj* mocking **2** *m*, **-ona** *f* mocker
burocracia *f* bureaucracy; **burócrata** *m/f* bureaucrat; **burocrático** bureaucratic
burro *m* donkey
bus *m* bus
busca 1 *f* search; ***en ~ de*** in search of **2** *m* F pager; **buscar** search for, look for; **búsqueda** *f* search
busto *m* bust
butaca *f* armchair; TEA seat
butano *m* butane
butifarra *f type of sausage*
buzo *m* diver
buzón *m* mailbox, *Br* postbox; INFOR mailbox; ***~ de voz*** TELEC voice mail; **buzoneo** *m* direct mailing

C

C (= ***Centígrado***) C (= Centigrade); (= ***compañía***) Co. (= Company); c (= ***calle***) St. (= Street)
cabal: ***no estar en sus ~es*** not be in one's right mind
cabalgadura *f* mount; **cabalgar** ride; **cabalgata** *f* procession
caballa *f* ZO mackerel
caballería *f* MIL cavalry; (*caballo*) horse
caballería *f* MIL cavalry; (*caballo*) horse
caballero 1 *adj* gentlemanly **2** *m* gentleman; HIST knight; *trato* sir; (***servicio de***) ***~s*** men's room, gents; *en tienda de ropa* menswear; **caballeroso** gentlemanly
caballete *m* PINT easel; TÉC trestle
caballo *m* horse; *en ajedrez* knight; ***~ balancín*** rocking horse; ***a ~ entre*** halfway between; ***montar*** *o* ***andar*** *Rpl* ***a ~*** ride (a horse); ***ir a ~*** go on horseback
cabaña *f* cabin
cabaret *m* cabaret
cabecear 1 *v/i* nod **2** *v/t el balón* head; **cabecera** *f* head; *de periódico* masthead; *de texto* top
cabecilla *m/f* ringleader
cabellera *f* hair; *de cometa* tail
cabello *m* hair; **cabelludo** hairy
caber fit; ***caben tres litros*** it holds three liters; ***cabemos todos*** there's room for all of us; ***no cabe duda*** *fig* there's no doubt
cabestrillo *m* MED sling
cabestro *m* halter
cabeza 1 *f* head; ***~ de ajo*** bulb of garlic; ***~*** (***de ganado***) head (of cattle); ***~ nuclear*** nuclear warhead; ***el equipo a la ~*** *o* ***en ~*** the team at the top **2** *m/f*: ***~ de familia*** head of the family; ***~ de turco*** scapegoat; ***~ rapada*** skinhead
cabezota pig-headed
cabida *f* capacity; ***dar ~ a*** hold
cabina *f* cabin; ***~ telefónica*** phone booth
cabizbajo dejected
cable *m* ELEC cable; MAR line, rope; ***echar un ~ a alguien*** give s.o. a hand; **cablear** wire up
cabo *m* end; GEOG cape; MAR rope; MIL corporal; ***al ~ de*** after; ***de ~ a rabo*** F from start to finish; ***llevar a ~*** carry out
cabra *f* goat; ***estar como una ~*** F be nuts F; **cabrearse** P get mad F; **cabritilla** *f* kid (skin)
cabrón *m* V bastard P, son of a bitch V

cacahuate *m Méx* peanut
cacahuete *m* peanut
cacao *m* cocoa; *de labios* lip salve
cacarear 1 *v/i de gallo* crow; *de gallina* cluck **2** *v/t* F crow about F
cacería *f* hunt
cacerola *f* pan
cacharro *m* pot; *Méx*, *C.Am.* F (*trasto*) piece of junk; *Méx*, *C.Am.* F *coche* junkheap; ***lavar los ~s*** *Méx*, *C.Am.* wash the dishes
cachear frisk; **cacheo** *m* frisk
cachete *m* cheek
cacho *m* F bit; *Rpl* (*cuerno*) horn; *Ven*, *Col* F (*marijuana*) joint F; ***jugar al ~*** *Bol*, *Pe* play dice
cachondeo *m*: ***estar de ~*** F be joking; ***tomar a ~*** F take as a joke; **cachondo** F (*caliente*) horny F; (*gracioso*) funny
cachorro *m* pup
cacique *m* chief; POL *local political boss*; *fig* F tyrant
caco *m* F thief
cactus *m inv* cactus
cada each; *con énfasis en la totalidad* every; ***~ uno, ~ cual*** each one; ***~ vez*** every time, each time; ***~ vez más*** more and more; ***~ tres días*** every three days; ***uno de ~ tres*** one out of every three
cadáver *m* (dead) body, corpse
cadena *f* chain; *de perro* leash; TV channel; ***~ perpetua*** life sentence
cadencia *f* MÚS rhythm
cadera *f* hip
cadete *m* MIL cadet; *Rpl*, *Chi* office junior, errand boy
caducar expire; **caducidad** *f*: ***fecha de ~*** expiration date, *Br* expiry date; *de alimentos*, *medicinas* use-by date; **caduco** BOT deciduous; *persona* senile; *belleza* faded
caer fall; ***me cae bien / mal*** *fig* I like / don't like him; ***dejar ~ algo*** drop sth; ***estar al ~*** be about to arrive; ***~ enfermo*** fall ill
café *m* coffee; (*bar*) café; ***~ instantáneo*** instant coffee; ***~ solo*** black coffee; **cafeína** *f* caffeine; **cafetera** *f* coffee maker; *para servir* coffee pot; **cafetería** *f* coffee shop
cagar V have a shit P; **cagarse** shit o.s. P
caída *f* fall
caído 1 *adj* fallen; *hombros* sagging; ***~ de ánimo*** downhearted **2** *mpl*: ***los ~s*** MIL the fallen
caimán *m* ZO alligator; *Méx*, *C.Am. útil* monkey wrench
caja *f* box; *de reloj*, *ordenador* case; COM cash desk; *en supermercado* checkout; ***~ de ahorros*** savings bank; ***~ de cambios*** gearbox; ***~ de caudales, ~ fuerte*** safe; ***~ de cerillas*** matchbox; ***~ de música*** music box; ***~ postal*** post office savings bank; ***~ registradora*** cash register; **cajero**

m, -a *f* cashier; *de banco* teller; **~ *automático*** ATM
cajón *m* drawer; *L.Am.* casket, coffin
cal *f* lime
cala *f* cove
calabacín *m* zucchini, *Br* courgette; **calabaza** *f* pumpkin
calabozo *m* cell
calado soaked
calamar *m* squid
calambre *m* ELEC shock; MED cramp
calamidad *f* calamity
calar 1 *v/t* (*mojar*) soak; *persona, conjura* see through **2** *v/i de zapato* leak; *de ideas* take root; **~ *hondo en*** make a big impression on; **calarse** *de motor* stall; **~ *hasta los huesos*** get soaked to the skin
calavera *f* skull
calcar trace
calceta *f*: ***hacer* ~** knit; **calcetín** *m* sock
calcio *m* calcium
calco *m* tracing; *fig* copy
calcomanía *f* decal, *Br* transfer
calculable calculable; **calculadora** *f* calculator; **calcular** *tb fig* calculate; **cálculo** *m* calculation; MED stone; **~ *biliar*** gallstone; **~ *renal*** kidney stone
caldear warm up; *ánimos* inflame
caldera *f* boiler; *Rpl*, *Chi* kettle; **calderilla** *f* small change
calderón *m* MÚS *tb signo* pause
caldo *m* GASTR stock; **~ *de cultivo*** *fig* breeding ground
calefacción *f* heating; **~ *central*** central heating; **calefactor** *m* heater
calendario *m* calendar; (*programa*) schedule
calentador *m* heater; **~ *de agua*** water heater; **calentamiento** *m*: **~ *global*** global warming; **calentar** heat (up); **~ *a alguien*** *fig* provoke s.o.; **calentura** *f* fever
calidad *f* quality; ***en* ~ *de médico*** as a doctor
cálido *tb fig* warm
caliente hot; F (*cachondo*) horny F; ***en* ~** in the heat of the moment
calificación *f* description; EDU grade, *Br* mark; **calificado** qualified; *trabajador* skilled; **calificar** describe (***de*** as); EDU grade, *Br* mark; **calificativo 1** *adj* qualifying **2** *m* description
callado quiet; **callar 1** *v/i* go quiet; (*guardar silencio*) be quiet; ***¡calla!*** be quiet!, shut up! **2** *v/t* silence
calle *f* street; DEP lane; **callejón** *m* alley; **~ *sin salida*** blind alley; *fig* dead end; **callejear** stroll (around the streets); **callejero 1** *adj* street *atr* **2** *m* street directory
callista *m/f* podiatrist, *Br* chiropodist
callo *m* callus; **~s** GASTR tripe
calma *f* calm; **calmante 1** *adj*

soothing **2** *m* MED sedative; **calmar** calm (down)
calor *m* heat; *fig* warmth; ***hace mucho ~*** it's very hot; ***tengo ~*** I'm hot; **caloría** *f* calorie
calumnia *f oral* slander; *por escrito* libel; **calumniar** *oralmente* slander; *por escrito* libel; **calumnioso** *oral* slanderous; *por escrito* libelous, *Br* libellous
caluroso hot; *fig* warm
calva *f* bald patch
calvicie *f* baldness; **calvo 1** *adj* bald **2** *m* bald man
calzada *f* road (surface); **calzado** *m* footwear; **calzador** *m* shoe horn
calzón *m* DEP shorts *pl*; *L.Am. de hombre* shorts *pl*, *Br* (under)pants *pl*; *L.Am. de mujer* panties *pl*
calzoncillos *mpl* shorts, *Br* (under)pants
cama *f* bed; ***~ de matrimonio*** double bed; ***irse a la ~*** go to bed
camaleón *m* chameleon
cámara *f* FOT, TV camera; (*sala*) chamber; ***~ de comercio e industria*** chamber of commerce and industry; ***a ~ lenta*** in slow motion; ***~ de vídeo*** video camera
camarada *m/f* comrade; *de trabajo* colleague, co-worker
camarera *f* waitress; **camarero** *m* waiter
camarón *m L.Am.* shrimp, *Br* prawn
camarote *m* MAR cabin
cambiable changeable; **cambiante** changing; *tiempo* changeable; **cambiar 1** *v/t* change (***por*** for); *compra* exchange (***por*** for) **2** *v/i* change; ***~ de lugar*** change places; ***~ de marcha*** AUTO shift gear, *Br* change gear; **cambiarse** change; ***~ de ropa*** change (one's clothes);
cambio *m* change; COM exchange rate; ***~ de marchas*** AUTO gear shift, *Br tb* gear change; ***~ de sentido*** U-turn; ***a ~ de*** in exchange for; ***en ~*** on the other hand
camello 1 *m* ZO camel **2** *m/f* F (*vendedor de drogas*) dealer
camerino *m* TEA dressing room
camilla *f* stretcher
caminar walk; *fig* move; ***caminando*** on foot; **camino** *m* (*senda*) path; (*ruta*) way; ***a medio ~*** halfway; ***de ~ a*** on the way to; ***por el ~*** on the way; ***abrirse ~*** *fig* make one's way; ***ir por buen / mal ~*** *fig* be on the right / wrong track; ***ponerse en ~*** set out
camión *m* truck, *Br tb* lorry; *Méx* bus; **camionero** *m*, **-a** *f* truck driver, *Br tb* lorry driver; *Méx* bus driver; **camioneta** *f* van
camisa *f* shirt; **camiseta** *f* T-shirt; **camisón** *m* nightdress
camorra *f* F fight; ***armar ~*** F cause trouble
campamento *m* camp

campana *f* bell; **~ *extractora*** extractor hood; **campanada** *f* chime; **campanario** *m* bell tower
campaña *f* campaign
campechano down-to-earth
campeón *m*, **-ona** *f* champion; **campeonato** *m* championship; ***de ~*** F terrific F
campesino 1 *adj* rural, country *atr* **2** *m*, **-a** *f* farmer; *muy pobre* peasant; **campestre** rural, country *atr*
camping *m* campground, *Br tb* campsite
campista *m/f* camper
campo *m* field; DEP field, *Br tb* pitch; (*estadio*) stadium, *Br tb* ground; ***el ~*** (*área rural*) the country; **~ *de batalla*** battlefield; **~ *de golf*** golf course; **~ *visual*** MED field of vision; ***a ~ traviesa, ~ a través*** cross-country
camposanto *m* cemetery
camuflaje *m* camouflage; **camuflar** camouflage
cana *f* gray *o Br* grey hair
Canadá Canada; **canadiense** *m/f & adj* Canadian
canal *m* channel; TRANSP canal; **canalizar** channel
canalla *m* swine F, rat F
canalón *m* gutter
Canarias *fpl* Canaries; ***Islas ~*** Canary Islands
canario 1 *adj* Canary *atr* **2** *m* ZO canary
canasta *f* basket; *juego* canasta; **canasto** *m* basket
cancelar cancel; *deuda, cuenta* settle, pay
cáncer *m* cancer; **Cáncer** *m/f inv* ASTR Cancer
cancha *f* DEP court; *L.Am. de fútbol* field, *Br tb* pitch; **~ *de tenis*** tennis court; ***¡~!*** *Rpl* F gangway! F
canciller *m* Chancellor; *S.Am. de asuntos exteriores* Secretary of State, *Br* Foreign Minister
canción *f* song; ***siempre la misma ~*** F the same old story F
candado *m* padlock
candela *f* *L.Am.* fire; ***¿me das ~?*** have you got a light?
candelero *m*: ***estar en el ~*** be in the limelight
candidato *m*, **-a** *f* candidate; **candidatura** *f* candidacy
cándido naive
canela *f* cinnamon
cangrejo *m* crab
canguro 1 *m* ZO kangaroo **2** *m/f* F baby-sitter
canica *f* marble
canilla *f L.Am.* faucet, *Br* tap
canje *m* exchange; **canjear** exchange (***por*** for)
canoa *f* canoe
canonizar canonize
cansado tired; **cansar** tire; (*aburrir*) bore; **cansarse** get tired; (*aburrirse*) get bored; **~ *de algo*** get tired of sth
cantábrico: (*mar*) *Cantábrico* Bay of Biscay
cantante *m/f* singer; **cantar 1** *v/t & v/i* sing **2** *m*: ***ése es otro***

~ *fig* F that's a different story
cántaro *m* pitcher; ***llover a ~s*** F pour down
cantautor *m*, **~a** *f* singer-songwriter
cantera *f* quarry
cantidad *f* quantity, amount; ***había ~ de*** there was (*pl* were) a lot of
cantimplora *f* water bottle
cantina *f* canteen
canto[1] *m* singing; *de pájaro* song
canto[2] *m* edge; (*roca*) stone; ~ ***rodado*** boulder
cantor 1 *adj* singing; ***niño ~*** choirboy; ***pájaro ~*** songbird **2** *m*, **~a** *f* singer
caña *f* BOT reed; (*tallo*) stalk; *cerveza* small glass of beer; *L.Am.* straw; ***muebles de ~*** cane furniture; ***~ de azúcar*** sugar cane; ***~ de pescar*** fishing rod
cáñamo *m* hemp; *L.Am.* marijuana plant
cañería *f* pipe
caño *m* pipe; *de fuente* spout
cañón 1 *m* cannon; *antiaéreo, antitanque etc* gun; *de fusil* barrel; GEOG canyon **2** *adj* F fantastic F
caoba *f* mahogany
caos *m* chaos; **caótico** chaotic
capa *f* layer; *prenda* cloak; ***~ de ozono*** ozone layer; ***~ de pintura*** coat of paint
capacidad *f* capacity; (*aptitud*) competence
capataz *m* foreman; **capataza** *f* forewoman
capaz able (**de** to); ***ser ~ de*** be capable of
capilar capillary *atr*; *loción* hair *atr*
capilla *f* chapel; ***~ ardiente*** chapel of rest
capital 1 *adj importancia* prime; ***pena ~*** capital punishment **2** *f de país* capital **3** *m* COM capital; **capitalismo** *m* capitalism; **capitalista 1** *adj* capitalist **2** *m/f* capitalist
capitán *m* captain; **capitanear** captain
capitulación *f* capitulation, surrender; (*pacto*) agreement; **capitular** surrender, capitulate
capítulo *m* chapter
capó *m* AUTO hood, *Br* bonnet
capota *f* AUTO top, *Br* hood
capricho *m* whim; **caprichoso** capricious
Capricornio *m/f inv* ASTR Capricorn
cápsula *f* capsule; ***~ espacial*** space capsule
captar understand; RAD pick up; *negocio* take; **captura** *f* capture; *en pesca* catch; ***tasa de ~s*** fishing quota; **capturar** capture
cara *f* face; (*expresión*) look; *fig* nerve; ***~ a algo*** facing sth; ***~ a ~*** face to face; ***de ~ a*** facing; *fig* with regard to; ***dar la ~*** face the consequences; ***echar algo en ~ a***

alguien remind s.o. of sth; ***tener buena / mala ~*** *de comida* look good / bad; *de persona* look well / sick; ***~ o cruz*** heads or tails
caracol *m* snail; ***¡~es!*** wow! F; *enfado* damn! F
carácter *m* character; **característica** *f* characteristic; **característico** characteristic (**de** of); **caracterizar** characterize; TEA play
caradura *m/f* F guy / woman with a nerve, *Br* cheeky devil F
carajillo *m coffee with a shot of liquor*
caramba wow!; *enfado* damn! F
caramelo *m dulce* candy, *Br* sweet; (*azúcar derretida*) caramel
carátula *f de disco* jacket; *L.Am. de reloj* face
caravana *f* (*remolque*) trailer, *Br* caravan; *de tráfico* traffic jam; *Méx* (*reverencia*) bow
caray F wow! F; *enfado* damn! F
carbohidrato *m* carbohydrate
carbón *m* coal; **carbonizar** char; **carbono** *m* carbon
carburador *m* AUTO carburetor, *Br* carburettor; **carburante** *m* fuel
carcajada *f* laugh, guffaw; ***reír a ~s*** roar with laughter
cárcel *f* prison; **carcelero** *m*, **-a** *f* warder, jailer
carcoma *f* woodworm
cardenal *m* REL cardinal; (*hematoma*) bruise
cardíaco, cardiaco cardiac; **cardiólogo** *m*, **-a** *f* cardiologist
cardo *m* BOT thistle
carecer: ***~ de algo*** lack sth; **carencia** *f* lack (**de** of)
careo *m* confrontation
carestía *f* high cost
careta *f* mask
carga *f* load; *de buque* cargo; MIL, ELEC charge; (*responsabilidad*) burden; ***~ fiscal*** *o* ***impositiva*** tax burden; ***ser una ~ para alguien*** be a burden to s.o.; **cargado** loaded (**de** with); *aire* stuffy; *ambiente* tense; *café* strong; **cargamento** *m* load; **cargar 1** *v/t arma, camión* load; *batería, acusado* charge; COM charge (**en** to); *L.Am.* (*traer*) carry; ***esto me carga*** *L.Am.* P I can't stand this **2** *v/i* (*apoyarse*) rest (**sobre** on); (*fastidiar*) be annoying; ***~ con algo*** carry sth; **cagarse** *con peso, responsabilidad* weigh o.s. down; F (*matar*) bump off F; F (*romper*) wreck F
cargo *m* position; JUR charge; ***alto ~*** *persona* high-ranking official; ***está a ~ de Gómez*** Gómez is in charge of it; ***hacerse ~ de algo*** take charge of sth
Caribe *m* Caribbean; **caribeño** Caribbean
caricatura *f* caricature
caricia *f* caress

caridad *f* charity
caries *f* MED caries
cariño *m* affection, fondness; ***hacer ~ a alguien*** *L.Am.* (*acariciar*) caress s.o.; (*abrazar*) hug s.o.; ***¡~!*** darling!; ***con ~*** with love; **cariñoso** affectionate
carioca of / from Rio de Janeiro
caritativo charitable
carlinga *f* cockpit
carnaval *m* carnival
carne *f* meat; *de persona* flesh; ***~ de gallina*** *fig* goose bumps *pl*; ***~ picada*** ground meat, *Br* mince
carnero *m* ram
carnet *m* card; ***~ de conducir*** driver's license, *Br* driving licence; ***~ de identidad*** identity card
carnicería *f* butcher's; *fig* carnage; **carnicero** *m*, **-a** *f* butcher
caro expensive, dear; ***costar ~*** *fig* cost dear
carpa *f de circo* big top; ZO carp; *L.Am. para acampar* tent; *L.Am. de mercado* stall
carpeta *f* file
carpintería *f* carpentry; *de obra* joinery; **carpintero** *m* carpenter; *de obra* joiner
carrera *f* race; EDU degree course; *profesional* career; ***a las ~s*** at top speed; ***~s de coches*** motor racing
carreta *f* cart; **carrete** *m* FOT (roll of) film; ***~ de hilo*** reel of thread
carretera *f* highway, (main) road; ***~ de circunvalación*** beltway, *Br* ring road; **carretilla** *f* wheelbarrow
carril *m* lane; ***~-bici*** cycle lane; ***~-bus*** bus lane
carrito *m* cart, *Br* trolley; ***~ de bebé*** buggy; **carro** *m* cart; *L.Am.* car; *L.Am.* (*taxi*) taxi, cab; ***~ de combate*** tank; ***~-patrulla*** *L.Am.* patrol car
carrocería *f* AUTO bodywork
carta *f* letter; GASTR menu; (*naipe*) (playing) card; (*mapa*) chart; ***~ certificada*** *o* ***registrada*** registered letter; ***~ urgente*** special-delivery letter; ***a la ~*** a la carte; ***dar ~ blanca a alguien*** give s.o. carte blanche; ***poner las ~s boca arriba*** *fig* put one's cards on the table; **cartabomba** *f* letter bomb; **cartabón** *m* set square
cartel *m* poster; ***estar en ~*** *de película* be on
cartelera *f* billboard; *de periódico* listings *pl*
cartera *f* wallet; (*maletín*) briefcase; COM, POL portfolio; *de colegio* knapsack, *Br* satchel; *L.Am.* purse, *Br* handbag; *mujer* mailwoman, *Br* postwoman; **cartero** *m* mailman, *Br* postman
cartón *m* cardboard; *de tabaco* carton; ***~ piedra*** pap(i)er-mâché
cartucho *m de arma* cartridge
cartuja *f* monastery
casa *f* house; (*hogar*) home;

en ~ at home; *a casa* home; *voy a casa de Marta* I'm going to Marta's (house); *~ cuna* children's home; *~ de huéspedes* rooming house, *Br* boarding house; *~ matriz* head office; *~ de socorro* first aid post
casado married; **casamiento** *m* marriage; **casar** *fig* match (up); *~ con* go with; **casarse** get married; *~ con alguien* marry s.o.
cascada *f* waterfall
cascanueces *m inv* nutcrackers
cascar crack; *algo quebradizo* break; *fig* F whack F; *~la* peg out F
cáscara *f de huevo* shell; *de naranja, limón* peel
casco *m* helmet; *de barco* hull; (*botella vacía*) empty (bottle); *edificio* empty building; *de caballo* hoof; *de vasija* fragment; *~s* (*auriculares*) headphones; *~ urbano* urban area; *~s azules* MIL blue berets, UN peacekeeping troops
casera *f* landlady; **casero 1** *adj* home-made; *comida -a* home cooking **2** *m* landlord
caseta *f* hut; *de feria* stall
casete *m* (*also f*) cassette
casi almost, nearly; *en frases negativas* hardly
casilla *f en formulario* box; *en tablero* square; *de correspondencia* pigeon hole; *S.Am.* post office box
casino *m* casino
caso *m* case; *en ~ de que, ~ de* in the event that, in case of; *hacer ~* take notice; *en todo ~* in any case, in any event; *en el peor de los ~s* if the worst comes to the worst; *en último ~* as a last resort
caspa *f* dandruff
cassette *m* (*also f*) cassette
casta *f* caste
castaña *f* chestnut; **castaño 1** *adj color* chestnut, brown **2** *m* chestnut (tree); *color* chestnut, brown; **castañuela** *f* castanet; *estar como unas ~s* F be over the moon F
castellano 1 *adj* Castilian **2** *m*, **-a** *f* Castilian **3** *m* (Castilian) Spanish
castidad *f* chastity
castigar punish; **castigo** *m* punishment
castillo *m* castle; *~ de fuegos artificiales* firework display
castizo pure
casto chaste
castor *m* beaver
castrar castrate; *fig* emasculate
casual chance *atr*; **casualidad** *f* chance, coincidence; *por o de ~* by chance
catalán 1 *adj* Catalan **2** *m*, **-ana** *f* Catalan **3** *m idioma* Catalan
catalizador *m* catalyst; AUTO catalytic converter
catálogo *m* catalog, *Br* cata-

logue
catar taste
catarata *f* GEOG waterfall; MED cataract
catarro *m* cold; *inflamación* catarrh
catástrofe *f* catastrophe
catear F flunk F
cátedra *f* EDU chair
catedral *f* cathedral
catedrático *m*, **-a** *f* EDU head of department
categoría *f* category; *social, de local, restaurante* class; (*estatus*) standing; ***actor de primera ~*** first-rate actor; **categórico** categorical
catolicismo *m* (Roman) Catholicism; **católico 1** *adj* (Roman) Catholic **2** *m*, **-a** *f* (Roman) Catholic
catorce fourteen
catre *m* bed
caucho *m* rubber; *L.Am.* (*neumático*) tire, *Br* tyre
caución *f* guarantee, security
caudal *m de río* volume of flow; *fig* wealth
caudillo *m* leader
causa *f* cause; (*motivo*) reason; JUR lawsuit; ***a ~ de*** because of; **causar** cause
cáustico *tb fig* caustic
cautela *f* caution; **cauteloso** cautious
cautivar *fig* captivate; **cautiverio** *m*, **cautividad** *f* captivity; **cautivo 1** *adj* captive **2** *m*, **-a** *f* captive
cauto cautious
cava *m* cava, *sparkling wine*
cavar dig
caverna *f* cavern
caviar *m* caviar
cavidad *f* cavity
caza 1 *f* hunt; *actividad* hunting; ***~ mayor / menor*** big / small game; ***andar a la ~ de algo / alguien*** be after sth / s.o. **2** *m* AVIA fighter; **cazador** *m* hunter; **cazadora** *f* hunter; *prenda* jacket;
cazar 1 *v/t animal* hunt; *fig: información* track down; (*pillar, captar*) catch; ***~ un buen trabajo*** get o.s. a good job **2** *v/i* hunt; ***ir a ~*** go hunting
cazo *m* saucepan
cazuela *f* pan; *de barro, vidrio* casserole
c/c (= ***cuenta corriente***) C/A (= checking account)
CD *m* (= ***disco compacto***) CD; *reproductor* CD-player;
CD-ROM *m* CD-ROM
cebada *f* barley
cebar fatten; *anzuelo* bait; *L.Am. mate* prepare; **cebo** *m* bait
cebolla *f* onion; **cebolleta** *f*, **cebollino** *m planta* scallion, *Br* spring onion
cebra *f* zebra; ***paso de ~*** crosswalk, *Br* zebra crossing
cecear *en acento regional* pronounce Spanish “s” as “th”; *como defecto* lisp
ceder 1 *v/t* give up; (*traspasar*) transfer, cede; ***~ el paso*** AUTO yield, *Br* give way **2** *v/i* give way, yield; *de viento, lluvia* ease off

cedro *m* cedar
cédula *f L.Am.* identity document
cegar blind; *tubería* block; **ceguera** *f tb fig* blindness
ceja *f* eyebrow
cejar give up
celador *m*, **~a** *f* orderly; *de cárcel* guard; *de museo* attendant
celda *f* cell
celebración *f* celebration; **celebrar** *misa* celebrate; *reunión, fiesta* have, hold; **célebre** famous; **celebridad** *f* fame; *persona* celebrity
celeste light blue, sky blue; **celestial** celestial; *fig* heavenly
celibato *m* celibacy; **célibe** *m/f & adj* celibate
celo *m* zeal; (*cinta adhesiva*) Scotch® tape, *Br* Sellotape®; ***en ~*** ZO in heat; ***~s*** jealousy; ***tener ~s de*** be jealous of ; **celoso** jealous
célula *f* cell; **celular** cellular; **celulitis** *f* cellulite; **celulosa** *f* cellulose
cementerio *m* cemetery
cemento *m* cement
cena *f* dinner
cenar 1 *v/t*: ***~ algo*** have sth for dinner **2** *v/i* have dinner
cenicero *m* ashtray
Cenicienta *f* Cinderella
ceniza *f* ash; ***~s*** ashes
censo *m* census; ***~ electoral*** voting register, electoral roll; **censor** *m*, **~a** *f* censor; **censura** *f* censorship; **censurar** censor; *tratamiento* condemn
cent (= ***céntimo***) cent
centavo *m* cent
centella *f* spark; (*rayo*) flash of lightning
centenario 1 *adj* hundred-year-old *atr* **2** *m* centennial, *Br* centenary
centeno *m* BOT rye
centésimo 1 *adj* hundredth **2** *m*, **-a** *f* hundredth
centígrado centigrade; **centímetro** *m* centimeter, *Br* centimetre
céntimo *m* cent; ***estar sin un ~*** not have a red cent F
centinela *m/f* sentry; *de banda criminal* lookout
centolla *f*, **centollo** *m* ZO spider crab
central 1 *adj* central **2** *f* head office; ***~ atómica*** *o* ***nuclear*** nuclear power station; ***~ eléctrica*** power station; ***~ telefónica*** telephone exchange; ***~ térmica*** thermal power station; **centralita** *f* TELEC switchboard; **centralizar** centralize; **centrar** *tb* DEP center, *Br* centre; *esfuerzos* focus (***en*** on); **centrarse** concentrate (***en*** on); **céntrico** central; **centrifugadora** *f* centrifuge; *para ropa* spin-dryer; **centrifugar** spin; **centro** *m* center, *Br* centre; ***~ comercial*** (shopping) mall, *Br tb* shopping centre; ***~ urbano*** *en señal* town center;
Centroamérica Central

America; **centroamericano** Central American
ceñido tight; **ceñirse:** *~ a algo fig* stick to sth
cepa *f de vid* stock
cepillar brush; **cepillo** *m* brush; *~ de dientes* toothbrush
cepo *m* trap; AUTO Denver boot, *Br* (wheel) clamp
cera *f* wax
cerámica *f* ceramics
cerca[1] *f* fence
cerca[2] *adv* near, close; ***de ~*** close up; ***~ de*** near, close to; (*casi*) nearly
cercado *m* fence
cercanía *f*: ***tren de ~s*** suburban train; **cercano** nearby; ***~ a*** close to, near to; **cercar** surround; *con valla* fence in
cerciorarse make sure (***de*** of)
cerco *m* ring; *de puerta* frame; *L.Am.* fence; ***poner ~ a*** lay siege to
cerda *f animal* sow; *fig* F *persona* pig F; *de brocha* bristle; **cerdo** *m* hog, *Br* pig; *fig* F *persona* pig F
cereal *m* cereal; ***~es*** (breakfast) cereal
cerebelo *m* ANAT cerebellum; **cerebral** cerebral; **cerebro** *m* ANAT brain; *fig*: *persona* brains *sg*
ceremonia *f* ceremony; **ceremonial** *m/adj* ceremonial; **ceremonioso** ceremonious
cereza *f* cherry; **cerezo** *m* cherry (tree)
cerilla *f* match
cero *m* zero, *Br tb* nought; *en fútbol etc* zero, *Br* nil; *en tenis* love; ***bajo / sobre ~*** below / above zero; ***empezar desde ~*** *fig* start from scratch
cerrado closed; *persona* narrow-minded; (*tímido*) introverted; *cielo* overcast; ***curva -a*** tight curve; **cerradura** *f* lock; **cerrajero** *m*, **-a** *f* locksmith; **cerrar 1** *v/t* close; *tubería* block; *grifo* turn off; ***~ con llave*** lock **2** *v/i* close
cerro *m* hill
cerrojo *m* bolt; ***echar el ~*** bolt the door
certamen *m* competition
certero accurate
certeza *f* certainty
certidumbre *f* certainty
certificado 1 *adj carta* registered **2** *m* certificate; **certificar** certify; *carta* register
cervecería *f* bar
cerveza *f* beer; ***~ de barril*** *o* ***de presión*** draft, *Br* draught (beer); ***fábrica de ~*** brewery
cesación *f* cessation; **cesar** stop; ***no ~ de hacer algo*** keep on doing sth; ***sin ~*** non-stop
cesárea *f* MED Cesarean, *Br* Caesarean
cese *m* cessation
cesión *f* transfer
césped *m* lawn
cesta *f* basket; ***~ de la compra*** shopping basket; **cesto** *m* large basket

chabacano vulgar, tacky F
chabola *f* shack; ***barrio de ~s*** shanty town
chacal *m* jackal
chacha *f* F maid
cháchara *f* chatter
chafar squash; *cosa erguida* flatten; F *planes etc* ruin
chaflán *m* corner
chal *m* shawl
chalado F crazy F (***por*** about)
chalet *m* chalet; ***~ adosado*** *house sharing one or more walls with other houses*; ***~ pareado*** duplex, *Br* semi-detached house
chalupa *f* MAR small boat; *Méx* stuffed tortilla
chamaca *f C.Am., Méx* girl; **chamaco** *m C.Am., Méx* boy
chamba *f Méx* F job
champán *m*, **champaña** *m* champagne
champiñón *m* mushroom
champú *m* shampoo
chamuscar scorch; *pelo* singe
chance 1 *m L.Am.* chance; ***dame ~*** let me have a try **2** *conj Méx* perhaps
chancho *m L.Am.* hog, *Br* pig; *carne* pork
chanchullo *m* F trick, scam F
chancleta *f* thong; *S.Am.* F baby girl
chándal *m* sweats *pl*, *Br* tracksuit
chantaje *m* blackmail; **chantajear** blackmail
chanza *f* wisecrack
chapa *f* (*tapón*) cap; (*plancha*) sheet (of metal); (*insignia*) badge; AUTO bodywork;
chapado plated; ***~ a la antigua*** old-fashioned
chaparro *Méx* small
chaparrón *m* downpour; *fig* F *de insultos* barrage
chapistería *f* AUTO body shop
chapotear splash
chapucear botch
chapucero 1 *adj* shoddy **2** *m*, **-a** *f* shoddy worker
chapurrear: ***~ el francés*** speak poor French
chapuza *f* shoddy piece of work; (*trabajo menor*) odd job
chapuzar duck; **chapuzarse** dive in; **chapuzón** *m* dip; ***darse un ~*** go for a dip
chaqué *m* morning coat; **chaqueta** *f* jacket; ***~ de punto*** cardigan; **chaquetón** *m* three-quarter length coat
charanga *f* brass band
charca *f* pond; **charco** *m* puddle
charcutería *f* delicatessen
charla *f* chat; *organizada* talk; **charlar** chat
charnela *f* hinge
charol *m* patent leather
chárter charter *atr*
chasco *m* joke; ***llevarse un ~*** be disappointed
chasis *m inv* AUTO chassis
chasquear click; *látigo* crack
chatarra *f* scrap; **chatarrero** *m*, **-a** *f* scrap merchant
chato *nariz* snub; *L.Am. nivel*

low
chaval *m* F kid F, boy; **chavala** *f* F kid F, girl
chaveta *f* TÉC (cotter) pin; ***estar*** **~** F be nuts F; ***perder la*** **~** F go off one's rocker F
checo 1 *adj* Czech **2** *m*, **-a** *f* Czech **3** *m idioma* Czech
cheque *m* check, *Br* cheque; **~ *sin fondos*** bad check (*Br* cheque); **~ *de viaje*** traveler's check, *Br* traveller's cheque; **chequear** check; **chequeo** *m* MED check-up; **chequera** *f* checkbook, *Br* chequebook
chic *m/adj* chic
chica *f* girl
chicharrones *mpl* cracklings, *Br* pork scratchings
chichón *m* bump
chicle *m* chewing gum
chico 1 *adj* small, little **2** *m* boy
chiflado F crazy F (***por*** about)
Chile Chile; **chileno 1** *adj* Chilean **2** *m*, **-a** *f* Chilean
chillar shriek; *de cerdo* squeal; **chillón 1** *adj voz* shrill; *color* loud **2** *m*, **-ona** *f* loudmouth
chimenea *f* chimney; *de salón* fireplace
chimpancé *m* chimpanzee
China China; **china** *f* Chinese woman; *Rpl* serving girl; *Rpl* (*niñera*) nursemaid
chinche *f* ZO bedbug; *L.Am.* (*chincheta*) thumbtack, *Br* drawing pin
chincheta *f* thumbtack, *Br* drawing pin
chinela *f* slipper
chinesco Chinese; **chino 1** *adj* Chinese **2** *m* Chinese man; *idioma* Chinese; ***trabajo de ~s*** F hard work
chip *m* INFOR chip
chipirón *m* baby squid
chiquilla *f* girl, kid F; **chiquillo** *m* boy, kid F; **chiquillada** *f* childish trick
chirimoya *f* custard apple
chirona *f*: ***en*** **~** F in the can F, inside F
chirriar squeak; **chirrido** *m* squeak
chisme *m* F bit of gossip; *objeto* doodad F, *Br* doodah F; **chismorrear** F gossip; **chismoso 1** *adj* gossipy **2** *m*, **-a** *f* F gossip
chispa *f* spark; (*cantidad pequeña*) spot; *fig* F wit; **chispear** spark; *fig* sparkle; *de lluvia* spit
chisporrotear *de leña* crackle; *de aceite* spit
chiste *m* joke
chistera *f* top hat
chistoso funny
chivarse F rat F (***a*** to); **chivato** *m*, **-a** *f* F stool pigeon F
chivo *m* ZO kid; *C.Am., Méx* wages *pl*
chocante startling; *que ofende* shocking; (*extraño*) odd; *L.Am.* (*antipático*) unpleasant; **chocar** crash (***con, contra*** into); ***~le a alguien*** surprise s.o.; (*ofender*) shock s.o.; **~ *con un problema***

come up against a problem
chocho F senile; ***estar ~ con*** dote on
chocolate *m* chocolate; F (*hachís*) hash F
chófer *L.Am.*, **chofer** *m* driver
chollo *m* F bargain
chopo *m* BOT poplar
choque *m* collision, crash; DEP, MIL clash; MED shock
chorizo *m* chorizo (*spicy cured sausage*); F thief; *Rpl* (*filete*) rump steak
chorrear gush out, stream; (*gotear*) drip; **chorro** *m líquido* jet, stream; *fig* stream; *C.Am.* faucet, *Br* tap
choza *f* hut
christmas *m* Christmas card
chubasco *m* shower
chuchería *f* knick-knack; (*golosina*) candy, *Br* sweet
chufa *f* BOT tiger nut
chuleta *f* GASTR chop
chulo F fantastic F; *Méx* (*guapo*) attractive; (*presuntuoso*) cocky F
chumbera *f C.Am.* prickly pear
chupada *f* suck; *de cigarrillo* puff; **chupado** F (*delgado*) skinny; F (*fácil*) dead easy F; *L.Am.* F drunk; **chupar** suck; (*absorber*) soak up; **chupete** *m de bebé* pacifier, *Br* dummy; (*sorbete*) Popsicle®, *Br* ice lolly
chupi F great F, fantastic F
churrasco *m Rpl* steak
churro *m* fritter; (*chapuza*) botched job
chusco **1** *adj* funny **2** *m* piece of bread
chusma *f desp* rabble *desp*
chutar DEP shoot;; **chutarse** F *con drogas* shoot up F
Cía. (= ***Compañía***) Co. (= Company)
ciática *f* MED sciatica
ciber... cyber...
cicatriz *f* scar; **cicatrizar** scar
ciclismo *m* cycling; **ciclista** *m/f* cyclist; **ciclo** *m* cycle; *de cine* season; **ciclomotor** *m* moped
ciclón *m* cyclone
cicuta *f* BOT hemlock
ciega *f* blind woman; **ciego** **1** *adj* blind; ***a -as*** blindly **2** *m* blind man
cielo *m* sky; REL heaven; ***ser un ~*** F be an angel F; ***~ raso*** ceiling
cien a *o* one hundred
ciencia *f* science; ***~ ficción*** science fiction; ***a ~ cierta*** for certain, for sure; **científico** **1** *adj* scientific **2** *m*, **-a** *f* scientist
cieno *m* silt
ciento a *o* one hundred; ***el cinco por ~*** five percent
cierre *m* fastener; *de negocio* closure; ***~ centralizado*** AUTO central locking; ***~ relámpago*** *L.Am.* zipper, *Br* zip
cierto certain; ***es ~*** it's true; ***~ día*** one day; ***por ~*** incidentally; ***estar en lo ~*** be right
ciervo *m* deer; ***~ volante*** stag beetle

cifra *f* figure; **cifrar** write in code; **~ *su esperanza en*** pin one's hopes on; **cifrarse: ~ *en*** amount to
cigala *f* ZO crayfish
cigarra *f* ZO cicada
cigarrillo *m* cigarette; **cigarro** *m* cigar; *L.Am.* cigarette
cigüeña *f* ZO stork
cigüeñal *m* AUTO crankshaft
cilindrada *f* AUTO cubic capacity; **cilíndrico** cylindrical; **cilindro** *m* cylinder
cima *f* summit; *fig* peak
cimentar lay the foundations of; *fig* base (***en*** on); **cimientos** *mpl* foundations
cinc *m* zinc
cincel *m* chisel; **cincelar** *metal* engrave; *piedra* chisel
cinco five; **cincuenta** fifty
cine *m* movies *pl*, cinema; **cineasta** *m/f* film-maker
cínico 1 *adj* cynical **2** *m*, **-a** *f* cynic; **cinismo** *m* cynicism
cinta *f* ribbon; *de música, vídeo* tape; **~ *adhesiva*** adhesive tape; **~ *aislante*** friction tape, *Br* insulating tape; **~ *métrica*** tape measure; **~ *de vídeo*** video tape
cintura *f* waist; **cinturón** *m* belt; **~ *de seguridad*** AUTO seatbelt
ciprés *m* BOT cypress
circo *m* circus
circuito *m* circuit; ***corto ~*** ELEC short circuit; **circulación** *f* movement; FIN, MED circulation; AUTO traffic; **circular 1** *adj* circular **2** *v/i* circulate; AUTO drive, travel; *de persona* move (along); **círculo** *m* circle; **~ *vicioso*** vicious circle
circunferencia *f* circumference
circunscribir limit (***a*** to)
circunspecto circumspect, cautious
circunstancia *f* circumstance
circunvalación *f*: (***carretera de***) **~** beltway, *Br* ring-road
ciruela *f* plum; **~ *pasa*** prune
cirugía *f* surgery; **~ *estética*** cosmetic surgery; **cirujano** *m*, **-a** *f* surgeon
cisne *m* ZO swan
cisterna *f de WC* cistern
cita *f* appointment; *de texto* quote, quotation; **citar** *a reunión* arrange to meet; *a juicio* summon; (*mencionar*) mention; *de texto* quote; **citarse** arrange to meet; **citación** *f* JUR summons *sg*, subpoena
cítrico *m* citrus fruit
ciudad *f* town; *más grande* city; ***Ciudad de México*** Mexico City; **~ *universitaria*** university campus; **ciudadano** *m*, **-a** *f* citizen; **ciudadanía** *f* citizenship; **ciudadela** *f* citadel
cívico civic; **civil** civil; ***casarse por lo ~*** have a civil wedding; **civilización** *f* civilization; **civilizado** civilized; **civilizar** civilize; **civilizarse** become civilized
clamar: ~ *por algo* clamor *o* *Br* clamour for sth; **clamor**

m roar; *fig* clamor, *Br* clamour
clandestino POL clandestine, underground
claqué *m* tap-dancing
clara *f de huevo* white; *bebida* shandy-gaff, *Br* shandy
claraboya *f* skylight
claridad *f* light; *fig* clarity; **clarificar** clarify
clarín *m* bugle
clarinete *m* clarinet
claro *tb fig* clear; *color* light; (*luminoso*) bright; *salsa* thin; *¡~!* of course!; ***hablar ~*** speak plainly
clase *f* class; (*variedad*) kind, sort; ***~ particular*** private class; ***dar ~*** (***s***) teach
clásico classical
clasificación *f* DEP league table; **clasificar** classify; **clasificarse** DEP qualify; ***~ tercero*** come in third
claudicar give in
claustro *m* ARQUI cloister
cláusula *f* clause
clausura *f de acto* closing ceremony; *de bar, local* closure; REL cloister; **clausurar** *acto oficial* close; *por orden oficial* close down
clavar stick (***en*** into); *clavos* drive (***en*** into); *uñas* sink (***en*** into); ***~ a alguien por algo*** F overcharge s.o. for sth
clave 1 *f* key; ***en ~*** in code **2** *adj* (*importante*) key
clavel *m* BOT carnation
clavícula *f* ANAT collarbone
clavija *f* ELEC pin
clavo *m de metal* nail; GASTR clove; *CSur* F *persona* dead loss F; ***dar en el ~*** hit the nail on the head
claxon *m* AUTO horn
clemencia *f* clemency, mercy; **clemente** clement, merciful
clérigo *m* priest, clergyman
clic *m* INFOR click; ***hacer ~ en*** click on
clienta, cliente *m/f de tienda* customer; *de empresa* client; **clientela** *f* clientele, customers *pl*
clima *m* climate; **climatizador** *m* air conditioner
clínica *f* clinic
clip *m para papeles* paperclip; *para el pelo* bobby pin, *Br* hairgrip
cloaca *f tb fig* sewer
clon *m* clone; **clonación** *f*; **clonar** clone
cloro *m* chlorine
cloroformo *m* chloroform
club *m* club; ***~ náutico*** yacht club
clueca *f* broody hen
coagularse coagulate; *de sangre* clot
coalición *f* coalition
coartada *f* JUR alibi
cobarde 1 *adj* cowardly **2** *m/f* coward; **cobardía** *f* cowardice
cobaya *m/f* guinea pig
cobertizo *m* shed; **cobertura** *f* cover; TV *etc* coverage
cobra *f* cobra
cobrador *m*, *~a f a domicilio*

collector; **cobrar** **1** *v/t* charge; *subsidio, pensión* receive; *deuda* collect; *cheque* cash; *salud, fuerzas* recover; *importancia* acquire **2** *v/i* be paid, get paid
cobre *m* copper
cobro *m* charging; *de subsidio* receipt; *de deuda* collection; *de cheque* cashing
cocaína *f* cocaine; **cocainómano** *m*, **-a** *f* cocaine addict
cocer cook; *en agua* boil; *al horno* bake
coche *m* car; *Méx* (*taxi*) cab, taxi; **~ de caballos** horse-drawn carriage; **~ cama** sleeping car; **~ comedor** *L.Am.* dining car; **~ de línea** (long-distance) bus; **cochecito** *m*: **~ de niño** stroller, *Br* pushchair; **coche-bomba** *m* car bomb; **cochecito** *m*: **~ de niño** stroller, *Br* pushchair; **coche-literas** *m* sleeping car; **coche-restaurante** *m* restaurant car
cochina *f* sow; F *persona* pig F; **cochino** **1** *adj fig* filthy, dirty; (*asqueroso*) disgusting **2** *m* hog, *Br* pig; F *persona* pig F ; **cochinillo** *m* suck(l)ing pig
cocido **1** *adj* boiled **2** *m* stew
cocina *f habitación* kitchen; *aparato* cooker, stove; *actividad* cooking; **cocinar** cook; **cocinero** *m*, **-a** *f* cook
coco *m* BOT coconut; *monstruo* bogeyman F
cocodrilo *m* crocodile
cocotero *m* coconut palm
cóctel *m* cocktail
codicia *f* greed; **codiciar** covet; **codicioso** greedy
código *m* code; **~ de barras** barcode; **~ postal** zip code, *Br* postcode
codo *m* elbow; **~ con ~** *fig* F side by side; **hablar por los ~s** F talk nineteen to the dozen F
codorniz *f* quail
cofre *m de tesoro* chest; *para alhajas* jewelry *o Br* jewellery box
coger **1** *v/t* (*asir*) take (hold of); *del suelo* pick up; *ladrón, enfermedad* catch; TRANSP catch, take; (*entender*) get; *L.Am.* V screw V **2** *v/i en un espacio* fit; *L.Am.* V screw V; **~ por la primera a la derecha** take the first right
cogida *f* TAUR goring
coherencia *f* coherence; **coherente** coherent; **ser ~ con** be consistent with
cohete *m* rocket
coincidencia *f* coincidence; **coincidir** coincide
coito *m* intercourse
cojear *de persona* limp, hobble; *de mesa* wobble
cojín *m* cushion; **cojinete** *m* TÉC bearing
cojo lame; *mesa* wobbly
col *f* cabbage; **~ de Bruselas** Brussels sprout
cola[1] *f* (*pegamento*) glue
cola[2] *f* (*de animal*) tail; *de gente* line, *Br* queue; *L.Am.* F *de*

persona butt F; ***hacer ~*** stand in line, *Br* queue

colaboración *f* collaboration; **colaborador** *m*, **~a** *f* collaborator; *en periódico* contributor; **colaborar** collaborate

colación *f*: ***traer*** *o* ***sacar a ~*** bring up

colador *m* colander; *para té etc* strainer

colapsar paralyze; *tráfico* bring to a standstill; **colapso** *m* collapse; ***provocar un ~ en la ciudad*** bring the city to a standstill

colarse F *en un lugar* get in; *en una fiesta* gatecrash; *en una cola* cut in line, *Br* push in

colcha *f L.Am.* bedspread; **colchón** *m* mattress; *fig* buffer

colección *f* collection; **coleccionar** collect; **coleccionista** *m/f* collector; **colecta** *f* collection; **colectivo 1** *adj* collective **2** *m L.Am.* bus; *Méx, C.Am.* taxi

colega *m/f* colleague; F pal

colegiado *m*, **-a** *f* DEP referee

colegio *m* school; ***~ profesional*** professional institute

cólera 1 *f* anger; ***montar en ~*** get into a rage **2** *m* MED cholera

colgador *m L.Am.* hanger; **colgar 1** *v/t* hang; TELEC put down **2** *v/i* hang (***de*** from); TELEC hang up; **colgarse** hang o.s.; INFOR F lock up; ***~ de algo*** hang from sth; ***~ de alguien*** hang onto s.o.

colibrí *m* hummingbird

cólico *m* colic

coliflor *f* cauliflower

colilla *f* cigarette end

colina *f* hill

colindante adjoining

colisión *f* collision; *fig* clash; **colisionar** collide (***con*** with)

collar *m* necklace; *para animal* collar

colmena *f* beehive

colmillo *m* eye tooth; *de perro* fang; *de elefante* tusk

colmo *m*: ***¡es el ~!*** this is the last straw!; ***para ~*** to cap it all

colocación *f* positioning, placing; (*trabajo*) position; **colocar** put, place; ***~ a alguien en un trabajo*** get s.o. a job

Colombia Colombia; **colombiano 1** *adj* Colombian **2** *m*, **-a** *f* Colombian

Colón Columbus

colonia *f* colony; *perfume* cologne; ***~ de verano*** summer camp; **colonizar** colonize

color *m* color, *Br* colour; ***~ café*** coffee-colored; *L.Am.* brown; ***televisión en ~*** color TV; **colorado** red; **colorear** color, *Br* colour

colosal colossal

columna *f* column; ***~ vertebral*** ANAT spinal column

columpio *m* swing

coma 1 *f* GRAM comma **2** *m* MED coma
comadre *f L.Am.* godmother;
comadrona *f* midwife
comandancia *f distrito* command; (*cuartel*) command headquarters *sg o pl*; *Méx* police station; **comandante** *m* MIL commander; *rango* major; AVIA captain
comarca *f* area
combate *m* combat; MIL engagement; DEP fight; ***fuera de ~*** out of action; **combatir** fight
combinación *f* combination; *prenda* slip; ***hacer ~*** TRANSP change; **combinado** *m* cocktail; **combinar** combine
combustible *m* fuel; **combustión** *f* combustion
comedia *f* comedy; **comediante** *m* actor
comedor *m* dining room
comentar comment on
comenzar begin
comer 1 *v/t* eat; *a mediodía* have for lunch **2** *v/i* eat; *a mediodía* have lunch; ***dar de ~ a alguien*** feed s.o.
comercial 1 *adj* commercial; *de negocios* business *atr*; ***el déficit ~*** the trade deficit **2** *m/f* representative; **comercializar** market, sell; *desp* commercialize; **comerciante** *m/f* trader; ***~ al por menor*** retailer; **comerciar** trade, do business; **comercio** *m* trade; *local* store, shop
comestible 1 *adj* eatable, edible **2** *m* foodstuff; ***~s*** food
cometa 1 *m* comet **2** *f* kite
cometer commit; *error* make;
cometido *m* task
cómic *m* comic; **cómico 1** *adj* comical **2** *m*, **-a** *f* comedian
comida *f* (*comestibles*) food; *ocasión* meal
comienzo *m* beginning
comillas *fpl* quotation marks
comino *m* BOT cumin
comisaría *f* precinct, *Br* police station; **comisario** *m* commissioner; *de policía* captain, *Br* superintendent;
comisión *f* committee; *de gobierno*, (*recompensa*) commission
comité *m* committee
como 1 *adv* as; ***así ~*** as well as; ***había ~ cincuenta*** there were about fifty **2** *conj* if; ***~ si*** as if; ***~ no llegó, me fui solo*** as *o* since she didn't arrive, I went by myself
cómo how; ***¡~ me gusta!*** I really like it; ***¿~ dice?*** what did you say?; ***¡~ no!*** *Méx* of course!
comodidad *f* comfort
comodín *m en naipes* joker
cómodo comfortable
compacto compact
compadecer feel sorry for
compañero *m*, **-a** *f* companion; *en una relación, un juego* partner; ***~ de trabajo*** coworker, colleague; ***~ de clase*** classmate; **compañía** *f* company; ***hacer ~ a alguien*** keep s.o. company

comparable comparable; **comparación** *f* comparison; **comparar** compare

comparecer appear

comparsa 1 *f* TEA: ***la ~*** the extras *pl* **2** *m/f* TEA extra; *fig* rank outsider

compartimento *m* FERR car, *Br* compartment

compartir share (***con*** with)

compás *m* MAT compass; MÚS rhythm; ***al ~*** to the beat

compasión *f* compassion; **compasivo** compassionate

compatible INFOR compatible

compatriota *m/f* compatriot

compendio *m* summary

compensación *f* compensation; **compensar 1** *v/t* compensate (***por*** for) **2** *v/i fig* be worthwhile

competencia *f* (*habilidad*) competence; *entre rivales* competition; (*incumbencia*) area of responsibility; ***~ desleal*** unfair competition; **competente** competent

competición *f* DEP competition; **competidor 1** *adj* rival **2** *m*, **~a** *f* competitor; **competir** compete (***con*** with); **competitivo** competitive

complaciente obliging, helpful

complejo 1 *adj* complex **2** *m* PSI complex; ***~ de inferioridad*** inferiority complex

complementario complementary; **complemento** *m* complement; ***~s de moda*** fashion accessories

completar complete; **completo** complete; *autobús*, *teatro* full; ***por ~*** completely

complicación *f* complication; **complicar** complicate

cómplice *m/f* accomplice; **complicidad** *f* complicity

componente *m* component; **componer** make up, comprise; *sinfonía, poema etc* compose; *algo roto* fix; **componerse** be made up (***de*** of); *L.Am.* MED get better

comportamiento *m* behavior, *Br* behaviour; **comportar** involve, entail; **comportarse** behave

composición *f* composition; **compositor** *m*, **~a** *f* composer

compota *f* compote

compra *f* purchase; ***ir de ~s*** go shopping; ***~s online*** online shopping; **comprador** *m*, **~a** *f* buyer, purchaser; **comprar** buy, purchase; **compraventa** *f* buying and selling

comprender understand; (*abarcar*) include; **comprensible** understandable; **comprensión** *f* understanding; *de texto*, *auditiva* comprehension; **comprensivo** understanding

compresa *f* sanitary napkin, *Br* sanitary towel; **compresión** *f tb* INFOR compression; **compresor** *m* compressor; **comprimido** *m* MED pill;

comprimir compress

comprobación *f* check; **comprobante** *m* proof; (*recibo*) receipt; **comprobar** check; (*darse cuenta de*) realize

comprometer compromise; (*obligar*) commit; **comprometerse** promise (***a*** to); *a una causa* commit o.s.; *de novios* get engaged; **compromiso** *m* commitment; (*obligación*) obligation; (*acuerdo*) agreement; (*apuro*) awkward situation

computadora *f L.Am.* computer; ***~ de escritorio*** desktop (computer); ***~ personal*** personal computer; ***~ portátil*** laptop; **computar** count; (*calcular*) calculate

común common; ***por lo ~*** generally; **comunal** communal; ***elecciones ~es*** *L.Am.* municipal elections

comunicación *f* communication; TRANSP link; **comunicar 1** *v/t* TRANSP connect, link; ***~ algo a alguien*** inform s.o. of sth **2** *v/i* communicate; TELEC be busy

comunidad *f* community; ***~ autónoma*** autonomous region

comunión *f* REL communion

comunismo *m* Communism; **comunista** *m/f & adj* Communist

con with; ***pan ~ mantequilla*** bread and butter; ***~ todo eso*** in spite of all that; ***~ tal de que*** provided that, as long as; ***~ hacer eso*** by doing that

cóncavo concave

concebir conceive

conceder concede; *entrevista, permiso* give; *premio* award

concejal *m*, **~a** *f* councilor, *Br* councillor; **concejo** *m* council

concentración *f* concentration; *de personas* gathering; **concentrar** concentrate

concepción *f* BIO, *fig* conception; ***la Inmaculada Concepción*** REL the Immaculate Conception; **concepto** *m* concept; ***en ~ de algo*** COM (in payment) for sth; ***bajo ningún ~*** on no account

concerniente: ***~ a*** concerning, regarding; ***en lo ~ a*** with regard to; **concernir** concern; ***en lo que concierne a...*** as far as ... is concerned

concertar *cita* arrange; *precio* agree; *esfuerzos* coordinate

concertino *m/f* MÚS concertmaster, *Br* leader (of the orchestra)

concesión *f* concession; COM dealership; **concesionario** *m* dealer

concha *f* ZO shell

conciencia *f* conscience; ***a ~*** conscientiously; ***con plena ~ de*** fully conscious of; **concienzudo** conscientious

concierto *m* MÚS concert; *fig* agreement

conciliación *f* JUR reconciliation; **conciliar** reconcile; **~ el sueño** get to sleep
concilio *m* council
conciso concise
concluir conclude; **conclusión** *f* conclusion; **en ~** in short; **concluyente** conclusive
concordar 1 *v/t* reconcile **2** *v/i* agree (**con** with)
concretar specify; (*hacer concreto*) realize; **concretarse** materialize; *de esperanzas* be fulfilled; **concreto 1** *adj* specific; (*no abstracto*) concrete; **en ~** specifically **2** *m* *L.Am.* concrete
concurrencia *f* audience; *de circunstancias* combination; **concurrido** crowded; **concursante** *m/f* competitor; **concursar** compete; **concurso** *m* competition; COM tender
concurrir: ~ a attend
conde *m* count
condecoración *f* decoration; **condecorar** decorate
condena *f* JUR sentence; (*desaprobación*) condemnation; **condenar** JUR sentence (**a** to); (*desaprobar*) condemn
condensador *m* condenser; **condensar** condense; *libro* abridge
condesa *f* countess
condescendiente *actitud* accommodating; *desp* condescending
condición *f* condition; **a ~ de que** on condition that; **estar en condiciones de** be in a position to; **condicional** *m/adj* conditional; **condicionar: ~ algo en** make sth conditional on
condimentar flavor, *Br* flavour; **condimento** *m* seasoning
condiscípulo *m*, **-a** *f* *en universidad* fellow student; *en colegio* fellow student, *Br* fellow pupil
condón *m* condom
conducción *f* AUTO driving; *de calor, electricidad* conduction; (*tuberías*) piping; (*cables*) cables *pl*
conducir 1 *v/t* *vehículo* drive; (*dirigir*) lead (**a** to); ELEC, TÉC conduct **2** *v/i* drive; *de camino* lead (**a** to); **conducta** *f* conduct; **conducto** *m* pipe; *fig* channel; **por ~ de** through; **conductor** *m*, **~a** *f* driver; **~ de orquesta** *L.Am.* conductor
conectar connect
conejillo *m*: **~ de Indias** *tb fig* guinea pig; **conejo** *m* rabbit
conexión *f* connection
confección *f* making; *de vestidos* dressmaking; *de trajes* tailoring; **confeccionar** make
confederación *f* confederation
conferencia *f* lecture; (*reunión*) conference; TELEC long-distance call; **conferenciante** *m/f* lectur-

er; **conferir** award

confesar 1 *v/t* REL confess; *delito* confess to, admit **2** *v/i* JUR confess; **confesarse** confess; (*declararse*) admit to being; **confesión** *f* confession; **confesionario** *m* confessional; **confeso** self-confessed; **confesor** *m* REL confessor

confiado trusting; **confianza** *f* confidence; **~ *en sí mismo*** self-confidence; ***de ~*** *persona* trustworthy; ***amigo de ~*** close friend; **confiar 1** *v/t secreto* confide (***a*** to); **~ *algo a alguien*** entrust s.o. with sth, entrust sth to s.o. **2** *v/i* trust (***en*** in); (*estar seguro*) be confident (***en*** of); **confidencia** *f* confidence; **confidencial** confidential; **confidente 1** *m* (*soplón*) informer; (*amigo*) confidant **2** *f* (*soplón*) informer; (*amiga*) confidante

configuración *f* configuration; **configurar** shape; INFOR set up, configure

confirmación *f* confirmation; **confirmar** confirm

confiscación *f* confiscation; **confiscar** confiscate

confitar crystallize

confitería *f* candy store, *Br* confectioner's

confitura *f* preserve

conflictivo *época, zona* troubled; *persona* troublesome; **conflicto** *m* conflict

confluencia *f de ríos* confluence; *de calles* junction; **confluir** meet, converge

conformar 1 *v/t* (*constituir*) make up; (*dar forma a*) shape **2** *v/i* agree (***con*** with); **conformarse** make do (***con*** with); **conforme 1** *adj* satisfied (***con*** with) **2** *prp*: **~ *a*** in accordance with; **conformidad** *f* (*acuerdo*) agreement; (*consentimiento*) consent; ***de*** *o* ***en ~ con*** in accordance with

confort *m* comfort; **confortable** comfortable; **confortar**: **~ *a*** comfort

confrontación *f* confrontation; **confrontar** compare; *a personas* bring face to face; *peligro, desafío* face up to; **confrontarse: ~ *con*** face up to

confundir confuse; (*equivocar*) mistake (***con*** for); **confundirse** make a mistake; **~ *de calle*** get the wrong street; **confusión** *f* confusion; **confuso** confused

congelación *f* freezing; **~ *de precios*** price freeze; **congelado** frozen; **congelador** *m* freezer; **congelar** freeze

congeniar get on well (***con*** with)

congénito congenital

congestión *f* MED congestion; **~ *del tráfico*** traffic congestion

congoja *f* anguish

congraciarse ingratiate o.s. (***con*** with)

congratulaciones *fpl* con-

gratulations; **congratular** congratulate; **congratularse:** *~ de o por algo* congratulate o.s. on sth
congregar bring together; **congresista** *m/f* conference *o* convention delegate, conventioneer; **congreso** *m* conference, convention; ***Congreso*** *en EE.UU.* Congress; ***~ de los diputados*** *lower house of Spanish parliament*
congruencia *f* consistency; MAT congruence
cónico conical
conífera *f* BOT conifer
conjetura *f* conjecture
conjugación *f* GRAM conjugation; *fig* combination; **conjugar** GRAM conjugate; *fig* combine
conjunción *f* GRAM conjunction; **conjuntivitis** *f* MED conjunctivitis; **conjunto 1** *adj* joint **2** *m de personas, objetos* collection; *de prendas* outfit; MAT set; ***en ~*** as a whole
conjuración *f* plot, conspiracy
conllevar entail
conmemoración *f* commemoration; **conmemorar** commemorate
conmigo with me
conmoción *f* shock; (*agitación*) upheaval; **conmocionar** shock; **conmocionarse** be moved; **conmovedor** moving; **conmover** move
conmutador *m* ELEC switch; *L.Am.* TELEC switchboard
cono *m* cone
conocer know; *por primera vez* meet; (*reconocer*) recognize; ***dar a ~*** make known; **conocerse** know one another; *por primera vez* meet (one another); *a sí mismo* know o.s.; ***se conoce que*** it seems that; **conocido 1** *adj* well-known **2** *m*, **-a** *f* acquaintance; **conocimiento** *m* knowledge; MED consciousness; ***perder el ~*** lose consciousness
conque so
conquista *f* conquest; **conquistador** *m* conqueror; **conquistar** conquer; *persona* win over
consabido usual
consagrar REL consecrate; (*hacer famoso*) make famous; *vida* devote
consciente MED conscious; ***~ de*** aware of, conscious of
consecuencia *f* consequence; ***a ~ de*** as a result *o* consequence of; ***en ~*** consequently; **consecuente** consistent; **consecutivo** consecutive; ***tres años ~s*** three years in a row; **conseguir** get; *objetivo* achieve
consejero *m*, **-a** *f* adviser; COM director; ***~ delegado*** CEO, chief executive officer; **consejo** *m* piece of advice; ***~ de administración*** board of directors; ***~ de mi-***

nistros *grupo* cabinet; *reunión* cabinet meeting
consentimiento *m* consent; **consentir 1** *v/t* allow; *a niño* indulge **2** *v/i*: **~ en algo** agree to sth
conserje *m/f* superintendent, *Br* caretaker
conserva *f*: **en ~** canned, *Br tb* tinned; **~s** canned food; **conservador** conservative; **conservante** *m* preservative; **conservar** conserve; *alimento* preserve; **conservatorio** *m* conservatory
considerable considerable; **consideración** *f* consideration; **considerar** consider
consigna *f* order; *de equipaje* baggage room, *Br* left luggage
consigo with him / her; (*con usted, con ustedes*) with you; (*con uno*) with you, with one *fml*
consiguiente consequent; **por ~** and so, therefore
consistencia *f* consistency; **consistente** consistent; (*sólido*) solid; **consistir** consist (**en** of)
consolar console
consolidar consolidate
consomé *m* consommé
consonancia *f*: **en ~ con** in keeping with; **consonante** *f* consonant
consorcio *m* consortium
conspiración *f* conspiracy; **conspirar** conspire; **conspirador** *m*, **~a** *f* conspirator
constancia *f* constancy; **dejar ~ de** leave a record of; **constante** constant; **constar** be recorded; **~ de** consist of
constatación *f* verification; **constatar** verify
consternado dismayed
constipado 1 *adj*: **estar ~** have a cold **2** *m* cold; **constiparse** get a cold
constitución *f* constitution; **constitucional** constitutional; **constituir** constitute, make up; *empresa, organismo* set up
construcción *f* construction; (*edificio*) building; **constructor** *m*, **~a** *f* builder; **construir** build, construct
consuelo *m* consolation
cónsul *m/f* consul; **consulado** *m* consulate
consulta *f* consultation; MED *local* office, *Br* surgery; **consultar** consult; **consultorio** *m* MED office, *Br* surgery
consumar complete, finish; *crimen* carry out; *matrimonio* consummate; **consumición** *f* consumption; **ya pago yo la ~** *en bar* I'll pay; **consumidor** *m*, **~a** *f* COM consumer; **consumir** consume; **consumo** *m* consumption; **de bajo ~** economical
contabilidad *f* accountancy; **llevar la ~** do the accounts; **contable** *m/f* accountant
contactar: **~ con alguien**

contact s.o.; **contacto** *m* contact; AUTO ignition; ***ponerse en ~*** get in touch (***con*** with)

contado: ***al ~*** in cash; **contador 1** *m* meter **2** *m*, **~a** *f L.Am.* accountant; **contaduría** *f L.Am.* accountancy

contagiar *infect*; ***~ la gripe a alguien*** give s.o. the flu; **contagiarse** get infected; **contagio** *m* contagion; **contagioso** contagious

contaminación *f* contamination; *de río, medio ambiente* pollution; **contaminante 1** *adj* polluting **2** *m* pollutant; **contaminar** contaminate; *río, medio ambiente* pollute

contar 1 *v/t* count; (*narrar*) tell **2** *v/i* count; ***~ con*** count on

contemplación *f*: ***sin contemplaciones*** without ceremony; **contemplar** look at

contemporáneo 1 *adj* contemporary **2** *m*, **-a** *f* contemporary

contenedor *m* TRANSP container; ***~ de basura*** dumpster, *Br* skip; ***~ de vidrio*** bottle bank; **contener** contain; *respiración* hold; *muchedumbre* hold back; **contenerse** control o.s.; **contenido** *m* content

contentar please; **contentarse** be satisfied (***con*** with); **contento** (*satisfecho*) pleased; (*feliz*) happy

contestación *f* answer; **contestador** *m*: ***~ automático*** answer machine; **contestar 1** *v/t* answer, reply to **2** *v/i* reply (***a*** to), answer (***a*** sth); *de forma insolente* answer back

contexto *m* context

contienda *f* conflict; DEP contest

contigo with you

contiguo adjoining, adjacent

continencia *f* continence

continental continental; **continente** *m* continent

continuación *f* continuation; ***a ~*** (*ahora*) now; (*después*) then; **continuar** continue; **continuo** (*sin parar*) continuous; (*frecuente*) continual

contorno *m* outline

contorsión *f* contortion

contra against; ***en ~ de*** against

contraataque *m* counterattack

contrabajo *m* double bass

contrabandista *m/f* smuggler; **contrabando** *m* contraband, smuggled goods *pl*; *acción* smuggling; ***hacer ~*** smuggle; ***pasar algo de ~*** smuggle sth in

contracción *f* contraction

contracepción *f* contraception; **contraceptivo** *m/adj* contraceptive

contradecir contradict; **contradicción** *f* contradiction; **contradictorio** contradictory

contraer contract; ***~ matrimonio*** marry

contralto MÚS **1** *m* countertenor **2** *f* contralto
contraluz *f*: ***a ~*** against the light
contramedida *f* countermeasure
contraorden *f* countermand
contrapartida *f* COM contra-entry; ***como ~*** *fig* in contrast
contraproducente counterproductive
contrario 1 *adj* contrary; *sentido* opposite; *equipo* opposing; ***al ~, por el ~*** on the contrary; ***de lo ~*** otherwise; ***ser ~ a algo*** be opposed to sth **2** *m*, **-a** *f* adversary, opponent
contrasentido *m* contradiction
contraseña *f* password
contrastar contrast; **contraste** *m* contrast
contratación *f de trabajadores* hiring, recruitment; ***~ bursátil*** trading; **contratar** contract; *trabajadores* hire
contratiempo *m* setback
contratista *m/f* contractor; ***~ de obras*** main contractor
contrato *m* contract
contravención *f* contravention; **contravenir** contravene
contraventana *f* shutter
contribución *f* contribution; (*impuesto*) tax; **contribuir** contribute (***a*** to); **contribuyente** *m/f* taxpayer
control *m* control; (*inspección*) check; ***~ remoto*** remote control; **controlador** *m*, **~a** *f*: ***~ aéreo*** air traffic controller; **controlar** control; (*vigilar*) check; **controlarse** control o.s.
controversia *f* controversy; **controvertido** controversial
contumaz obstinate
contusión *f* bruise
convalecencia *f* convalescence; **convalecer** convalesce; ***~ de*** recover from
convencer convince; **convencimiento** *m* conviction
convención *f* convention; **convencional** conventional
conveniencia *f de hacer algo* advisability; ***hacer algo por ~*** do sth in one's own interest; **conveniente** convenient; (*útil*) useful; (*aconsejable*) advisable; **convenio** *m* agreement; **convenir 1** *v/t* agree **2** *v/i* be advisable; ***no te conviene*** it's not in your interest
convento *m de monjes* monastery; *de monjas* convent
conversación *f* conversation; **conversar** make conversation
conversión *f* conversion; **convertible 1** *adj* COM convertible **2** *m L.Am.* convertible; **convertir** convert; **convertirse: *~ en algo*** turn into sth
convexo convex
convicción *f* conviction; **convicto** JUR convicted
convidado *m*, **-a** *f* guest; **convidar** invite (***a*** to)

convincente convincing
convivencia *f* living together
convocar summon; *huelga* call; *oposiciones* organize; **convocatoria** *f* announcement; *de huelga* call
convoy *m* convoy
convulsión *f* convulsion; *fig* upheaval; **convulsivo** convulsive
conyugal conjugal; **cónyuge** *m/f* spouse
coñac *m* (*pl* ~s) brandy, cognac
cooperación *f* cooperation; **cooperar** cooperate; **cooperativa** *f* cooperative; **cooperar** cooperate
coordinación *f* coordination; **coordinar** coordinate
copa *f de vino etc* glass; DEP cup; ***tomar una*** ~ have a drink; **~s** *(en naipes) suit in Spanish deck of cards*
copia *f* copy; **copiadora** *f* (photo)copier; **copiar** copy
copiloto *m/f* copilot
copioso copious
copla *f* verse; (*canción*) popular song
copo *m* flake; ***~ de nieve*** snowflake; ***~s de maíz*** cornflakes
coque *m* coke
coquetear flirt
coraje *m* courage; ***me da*** ~ *fig* F it makes me mad F
coral[1] *m* ZO coral
coral[2] *f* MÚS choir
Corán *m* Koran
corazón *m* heart; *de fruta* core; **corazonada** *f* hunch
corbata *f* tie
corchea *f* MÚS eighth note, *Br* quaver
corchete *m* hook and eye; *Chi* (*grapa*) staple; **~s** TIP square brackets
corcho *m* cork
corcova *f* hump(back), hunchback; **corcovado** humpbacked, hunchbacked
cordel *m* string
cordero *m* lamb
cordial cordial; **cordialidad** *f* cordiality
cordillera *f* mountain range
cordón *m* cord; *de zapato* shoelace; ***~ umbilical*** umbilical cord
cordura *f* sanity; (*prudencia*) good sense
Corea Korea; **coreano 1** *adj* Korean **2** *m*, **-a** *f* Korean **3** *m idioma* Korean
coreografía *f* choreography; **coreógrafo** *m*, **-a** *f* choreographer
cornada *f* TAUR goring
córnea *f* cornea
corneja *f* ZO crow
córner *m en fútbol* corner (kick)
corneta *f* MIL bugle
cornudo 1 *adj* horned **2** *m* cuckold
coro *m* MÚS choir; *de espectáculo, pieza musical* chorus; ***a*** ~ together, in chorus
corona *f* crown; ***~ de flores*** garland; **coronación** *f* coronation; **coronar** crown

coronel *m* MIL colonel

coronilla *f* ANAT crown; ***estoy hasta la ~*** F I've had it up to here F

corpiño *m* bodice; *Arg* (*sujetador*) bra

corporación *f* corporation; **corporal** *placer*, *estética* physical; *fluido* body *atr*; **corpulento** solidly built

Corpus (Christi) *m* Corpus Christi

corral *m* farmyard

correa *f* lead; *de reloj* strap

corrección *f* correction; *en el trato* correctness; **correcto** correct; (*educado*) polite; **corrector 1** *adj* correcting *atr* **2** *m*, **~a** *f*: **~ (*de pruebas*)** proofreader

corredor 1 *m*, **~a** *f* DEP runner; COM agent; ***~ de bolsa*** stockbroker **2** *m* ARQUI corridor

corregir correct

correo *m* mail, *Br tb* post; ***~s*** post office; ***~ aéreo*** airmail; ***~ electrónico*** e-mail; ***~ de voz*** voicemail; ***por ~*** by mail; ***echar al ~*** mail, *Br tb* post

correr 1 *v/i* run; (*apresurarse*) rush; *de tiempo* pass; ***~ con los gastos*** pay the expenses; ***a todo ~*** at top speed **2** *v/t* run; *cortinas* draw; *mueble* slide

correspondencia *f* correspondence; FERR connection; **corresponder: *~ a alguien*** *de bienes* be for s.o., be due to s.o.; *de responsabilidad* be up to s.o.; *de asunto* concern s.o.; *a un favor* repay s.o.; ***actuar como corresponde*** do the right thing; **correspondiente** corresponding; **corresponsal** *m/f* correspondent

corretaje *m* brokerage

corrida *f*: ***~ de toros*** bullfight

corriente 1 *adj* (*actual*) current; (*común*) ordinary; ***estar al ~*** be up to date **2** *f* ELEC, *de agua* current; ***~ de aire*** draft, *Br* draught

corroborar corroborate

corroer corrode; *fig* eat up

corromper corrupt

corrosión *f* corrosion; **corrosivo** corrosive; *fig* caustic

corrupción *f* decay; *fig* corruption; **corrupto** corrupt

corsario *m* corsair, privateer

corsé *m* corset

cortacésped *m* lawnmower

cortado 1 *adj* cut; *calle* closed; *leche* curdled; *persona* shy; ***quedarse ~*** be embarrassed **2** *m* coffee with a dash of milk; **cortar 1** *v/t* cut; *electricidad* cut off; *calle* close **2** *v/i* cut; **cortarse** cut o.s.; *fig* F get embarrassed; ***~ el pelo*** have one's hair cut; **cortaúñas** *m inv* nail clippers *pl*

corte[1] *m* cut; ***~ de luz*** power outage, *Br* power cut; ***~ de pelo*** haircut; ***~ de tráfico*** F road closure; ***me da ~*** F I'm embarrassed

corte[2] *f* court; *L.Am.* JUR (law) court; ***las Cortes***

Spanish parliament
cortejo *m* entourage
cortés courteous; **cortesía** *f* courtesy
corteza *f de árbol* bark; *de pan* crust; *de queso* rind
cortijo *m* farmhouse
cortina *f* curtain
corto short; ***~ de vista*** near-sighted; ***quedarse ~*** fall short; **cortocircuito** *m* ELEC short circuit; **cortometraje** *m* short (movie)
corva *f* back of the knee
corzo *m* ZO roe deer
cosa *f* thing; ***como si tal ~*** as if nothing had happened; ***decir a alguien cuatro ~s*** give s.o. a piece of one's mind; ***eso es otra ~*** that's something else; ***¿qué pasa? – poca ~*** what's new? - nothing much; ***son ~s de la vida*** that's life
cosecha *f* harvest; **cosechar** harvest; *fig* gain, win
coser sew; ***ser ~ y cantar*** F be dead easy F
cosmética *f* cosmetics; **cosmético** *m/adj* cosmetic
cosquillas *fpl*: ***hacer ~ a alguien*** tickle s.o.; ***tener ~*** be ticklish; **cosquilloso** ticklish; *fig* touchy
Costa Rica Costa Rica; **costarricense** *m/f & adj* Costa Rican
costa[1] *f*: ***a ~ de*** at the expense of; ***a toda ~*** at all costs
costa[2] *f* GEOG coast
costado *m* side; ***por los cuatro ~s*** *fig* throughout
costar 1 *v/t* cost; *trabajo, esfuerzo etc* take **2** *v/i en dinero* cost; ***me costó*** it was hard work; ***cueste lo que cueste*** at all costs; ***~ caro*** *fig* cost dear
coste *m* ☞ ***costo***
costear pay for
costilla *f* ANAT rib; GASTR sparerib
costo *m* cost; ***~ de la vida*** cost of living; **costoso** costly
costra *f* MED scab
costumbre *f* custom; *de una persona* habit; ***de ~*** usual
costura *f* sewing; **costurera** *f* seamstress; **costurero** *m* sewing box
cotejar compare; **cotejo** *m* comparison
cotidiano daily
cotización *f* (*precio*) price; (*cuota*) contribution; (*valor*) value; **cotizar** *de trabajador* pay social security, *Br* pay National Insurance; *de acciones, bonos* be listed
coto *m*: ***~ de caza*** hunting reserve; ***poner ~ a algo*** *fig* put a stop to sth
coyuntura *f* situation; ANAT joint
C.P. (= ***código postal***) zip code, *Br* post code
cráneo *m* ANAT skull, cranium
cráter *m* crater
creación *f* creation; **creador** *m*, **~a** *f* creator; **crear** create; *empresa* set up; **creativo** cre-

ative

crecer grow; **crecida** *f* rise in river level; (*inundación*) flooding; **creciente** growing; *luna* waxing; **crecimiento** *m* growth

crédito *m* COM credit; ***a ~*** on credit; ***no dar ~ a sus oídos / ojos*** F not believe one's ears / eyes

crédulo credulous

creencia *f* belief; **creer 1** *v/i* believe (***en*** in) **2** *v/t* think; (*dar por cierto*) believe; ***¡ya lo creo!*** F you bet! F; **creerse: *~ que…*** believe that …; ***se cree muy lista*** she thinks she's very clever; **creíble** credible

crema *f* GASTR cream

cremación *f* cremation

cremallera *f* zipper, *Br* zip; TÉC rack

crepitar crackle

crepúsculo *m tb fig* twilight

crespo curly

cresta *f* crest

creyente 1 *adj*: ***ser ~*** REL believe in God **2** *m* REL believer

cría *f acción* breeding; *de zorro, león* cub; *de perro* puppy; *de gato* kitten; *de oveja* lamb; ***sus ~s*** her young; **criada** *f* maid; **criadero** *m de animales* breeding establishment; *de ratas* breeding ground; *de plantas* nursery; **criado** *m* servant; **criador** *m*, **~a** *f* breeder; **criar** *niños* raise, bring up; *animales* breed; **criarse** grow up; **criatura** *f* creature; F (*niño*) baby, child

criba *f* sieve; **cribar** sift, sieve; *fig* select

crimen *m* crime; **criminal** *m/f* & *adj* criminal; **criminalidad** *f* crime

crío *m*, **-a** *f* F kid F

criollo 1 *adj* Creole **2** *m*, **-a** *f* Creole

crisantemo *m* BOT chrysanthemum

crisis *f inv* crisis

crispado irritated

cristal *m* crystal; (*vidrio*) glass; (*lente*) lens; *de ventana* pane; ***~ líquido*** liquid crystal; **cristalería** *f fábrica* glassworks *sg*; *objetos* glassware

cristiandad *f* Christendom; **cristianismo** *m* Christianity; **cristiano 1** *adj* Christian **2** *m*, **-a** *f* Christian; **Cristo** Christ

criterio *m* criterion; (*juicio*) judg(e)ment

crítica *f* criticism; ***muchas ~s*** a lot of criticism; **criticar** criticize; **crítico 1** *adj* critical **2** *m*, **-a** *f* critic

Croacia Croatia; **croata 1** *adj* Croatian **2** *m/f* Croat(ian); **3** *m idioma* Croat(ian)

cromo *m* QUÍM chrome; (*estampa*) picture card

crónica *f* chronicle; *en periódico* report

crónico MED chronic

cronista *m/f* reporter

cronológico chronological

cronometrar DEP time; **cronómetro** *m* stopwatch
croqueta *f* croquette
croquis *m inv* sketch
cruce *m* cross; *de carreteras* crossroads *sg*; ***~ en las líneas*** TELEC crossed line
crucero *m* cruise
crucial crucial
crucificar crucify; **crucifijo** *m* crucifix; **crucigrama** *m* crossword
crudeza *f* harshness; *de enfrentamiento* severity; *de lenguaje, imágenes* crudeness;
crudo **1** *adj alimento* raw; *fig* harsh; *lenguaje, imágenes* crude **2** *m* crude (oil)
cruel cruel; **crueldad** *f* cruelty
crujiente GASTR crunchy;
crujir creak; *al arder* crackle; *de grava* crunch
cruz *f* cross; ***Cruz Roja*** Red Cross; **cruzar** cross; **cruzarse** pass one another; ***~ de brazos*** cross one's arms; ***~ con alguien*** pass s.o.
cuaderno *m* notebook; EDU exercise book
cuadra *f* stable; *L.Am.* (*manzana*) block; **cuadrado** *m/adj* square; ***al ~*** squared
cuadrilla *f* squad, team
cuadro *m* painting; (*grabado*) picture; (*tabla*) table; DEP team; ***~ de mandos*** *o* ***de instrumentos*** AUTO dashboard; ***de*** *o* ***a ~s*** checked
cuádruple, cuadruplo *m* quadruple
cuajada *f* GASTR curd; **cuajar** *de nieve* settle; *fig*: *de idea, proyecto etc* come together, jell F; **cuajarse** *de leche* curdle; *de nieve* settle
cual **1** *pron rel*: ***el ~, la ~*** *etc cosa* which; *persona* who; ***por lo ~*** (and) so **2** *adv* like
cualidad *f* quality
cualquier any; ***~ cosa*** anything; ***de ~ modo*** *o* ***forma*** anyway; **cualquiera** *persona* anyone, anybody; *cosa* any (one); ***un ~*** a nobody; ***¡~ lo comprende!*** nobody can understand it!
cuando **1** *conj* when; *condicional* if **2** *adv* when; ***de ~ en ~*** from time to time; ***~ menos*** at least
cuándo when
cuantía *f* amount, quantity; *fig* importance; **cuantioso** substantial
cuanto **1** *adj*: ***~ dinero quieras*** as much money as you want; ***unos ~s chavales*** a few boys **2** *pron* all, everything; ***unas -as*** a few; ***todo ~*** everything **3** *adv*: ***~ antes, mejor*** the sooner the better; ***en ~*** as soon as; ***en ~ a*** as for
cuánto **1** *interr* how much; *pl* how many; ***¿a ~ están?*** how much are they?; ***¿a ~s estamos?*** what's the date today? **2** *exclamaciones*: ***¡~ gente había!*** there were so many people!; ***¡~ me alegro!*** I'm so pleased!
cuarenta forty

cuarentena *f* quarantine; ***una ~*** a quarantine period
Cuaresma *f* Lent
cuartel *m* barracks *pl*; ***~ general*** headquarters *pl*
cuarteto *m* MÚS quartet; ***~ de cuerda*** string quartet
cuarto 1 *adj* fourth **2** *m* (*habitación*) room; (*parte*) quarter; ***~ de baño*** bathroom; ***~ de estar*** living room; ***~ de hora*** quarter of an hour; ***de tres al ~*** F third-rate; ***las diez y ~*** quarter after ten, *Br* quarter past ten; ***las tres menos ~*** a quarter to *o* of three
cuarzo *m* quartz
cuatro four
Cuba Cuba; **cubano 1** *adj* Cuban **2** *m*, **-a** *f* Cuban
cuba *f*: ***estar como una ~*** F be plastered F
cúbico cubic
cubierta *f* MAR deck; AUTO tire, *Br* tyre; **cubierto 1** *part* ☞ ***cubrir*** **2** *m*; *en la mesa* place setting; ***~s*** flatware, *Br* cutlery
cubilete *m* cup (*for dice*)
cubitera *f bandeja* ice tray; (*cubo*) ice bucket
cubito *m*: ***~ de hielo*** ice cube
cubo *m* cube; *recipiente* bucket; ***~ de la basura*** garbage can, *Br* rubbish bin
cubrir cover (***de*** with); **cubrirse** cover o.s.
cucaracha *f* cockroach
cuchara *f* spoon; ***meter su ~*** *L.Am.* F stick one's oar in F; **cucharada** *f* spoonful; **cucharilla** *f* teaspoon; **cucharón** *m* ladle
cuchichear whisper
cuchilla *f* razor blade; **cuchillo** *m* knife
cuclillas: *en ~* squatting
cuco 1 *m* cuckoo; ***reloj de ~*** cuckoo clock **2** *adj* (*astuto*) sharp
cucurucho *m de papel etc* cone; *sombrero* pointed hat
cuello *m* ANAT neck; *de camisa etc* collar
cuenca *f* GEOG basin; **cuenco** *m* bowl
cuenta *f* (*cálculo*) sum; *de restaurante* check, *Br* bill; COM account; ***~ atrás*** countdown; ***~ bancaria*** bank account; ***~ corriente*** checking account, *Br* current account; ***más de la ~*** too much; ***darse ~ de algo*** realize sth; ***pedir ~s a alguien*** ask s.o. for an explanation; ***perder la ~*** lose count; ***tener*** *o* ***tomar en ~*** take into account
cuentagotas *m inv* dropper
cuentakilómetros *m inv* odometer, *Br* mileometer
cuento *m* (short) story; (*pretexto*) excuse; ***~ chino*** F tall story F; ***venir a ~*** be relevant
cuerda *f* rope; *de guitarra, violín* string; ***~s vocales*** ANAT vocal chords
cuerdo sane; (*sensato*) sensible
cuerno *m* horn; *de caracol* feeler; ***irse al ~*** F fall through, be wrecked; ***poner***

los ~s a alguien F be unfaithful to s.o.

cuero *m* leather; *Rpl* (*fuete*) whip; ***en ~s*** F naked

cuerpo *m* body; *de policía* force; ***~ diplomático*** diplomatic corps

cuervo *m* ZO raven, crow

cuesta *f* slope; ***~ abajo*** downhill; ***~ arriba*** uphill; ***a ~s*** on one's back

cuestión *f* question; ***en ~ de...*** in a matter of …; **cuestionar** question; **cuestionario** *m* questionnaire

cueva *f* cave

cuidado *m* care; ***¡~!*** look out!; ***andar con ~*** tread carefully; ***me tiene sin ~*** I couldn't care less; ***tener ~*** be careful; **cuidadora** *f Méx* nursemaid; **cuidadoso** careful; **cuidar 1** *v/t* look after, take care of **2** *v/i*: ***~ de*** look after, take care of; **cuidarse** look after o.s., take care of o.s.; ***~ de hacer algo*** take care to do sth

culata *f* butt

culebra *f* ZO snake

culebrón *m* TV soap

culminante: ***punto ~*** peak, climax

culo *m* V ass V, *Br* arse V; F butt F, *Br tb* bum F

culpa *f* fault; ***ser por ~ de alguien*** be s.o.'s fault; ***tener la ~*** be to blame (***de*** for); **culpable 1** *adj* guilty **2** *m/f* culprit; **culpar:** ***~ a alguien de algo*** blame s.o. for sth

cultivador *m* grower; **cultivar** AGR grow; *tierra* farm; *fig* cultivate; **cultivo** *m* AGR crop; BIO culture; **culto 1** *adj* educated **2** *m* worship; **cultura** *f* culture; **cultural** cultural; **culturismo** *m* bodybuilding

cumbre *f tb* POL summit

cumpleaños *m inv* birthday

cumplido *m* compliment; ***no andarse con ~s*** not stand on ceremony; **cumplidor** reliable

cumplimentar *trámite* carry out; **cumplimiento** *m de promesa* fulfillment, *Br* fulfilment; *de ley* compliance (***de*** with); **cumplir 1** *v/t orden* carry out; *promesa* fulfill, *Br* fulfil; *condena* serve; ***~ diez años*** reach the age of ten **2** *v/i*: ***~ con algo*** carry sth out; ***~ con su deber*** do one's duty

cuna *f tb fig* cradle

cuneta *f* ditch

cuña *f* wedge

cuñada *f* sister-in-law; **cuñado** *m* brother-in-law

cuota *f* share; *de club*, *asociación* fee

cupo *m* quota

cupón *m* coupon

cúpula *f* dome; *esp* POL leadership

cura 1 *m* priest **2** *f* cure; (*tratamiento*) treatment; *Méx*, *C.Am.* F hangover; **curable** curable; **curación** *f* (*recuperación*) recovery; (*tratamiento*) treatment; **curar 1** *v/t tb*

GASTR cure; (*tratar*) treat; *herida* dress; *pieles* tan **2** *v/i* MED recover (**de** from); **curarse** MED recover; *Méx, C.Am.* F get drunk
curiosidad *f* curiosity; **curioso 1** *adj* curious **2** *m*, **-a** *f* onlooker
curita *f L.Am.* Band-Aid®, *Br* Elastoplast®
cursar *carrera* take; *orden, fax* send; *instancia* deal with
cursi F *persona* affected; **cursilería** *f* affectation
cursillista *m/f* course participant; **cursillo** *m* short course
cursiva *f* italics *pl*
curso *m* course; **en el ~ de** in the course of
cursor *m* INFOR cursor
curtido 1 *adj* weather-beaten **2** *m* tanning; **~s** tanned hides; **curtir** tan; *fig* harden
curva *f* curve; **curvo** curved
custodia *f* JUR custody; **custodiar** guard
cutáneo skin *atr*; **cutis** *m* skin
cuyo, -a whose

D

daltónico color-blind, *Br* colour-blind; **daltonismo** *m* color-blindness, *Br* colour-blindness
dama *f* lady; **~ de honor** bridesmaid; **(juego de) ~s** checkers *sg*, *Br* draughts *sg*
damasco *m* damask; *L.Am. fruta* apricot
damnificado 1 *adj* affected **2** *m*, **-a** *f* victim
danés 1 *adj* Danish **2** *m*, **-esa** *f* Dane **3** *m idioma* Danish
danza *f* dance; **danzar** dance
dañar harm; *cosa* damage; **dañarse** harm o.s.; *de un objeto* get damaged; **dañino** harmful; *fig* malicious; **daño** *m* harm; *a un objeto* damage; **hacer ~** hurt; **~s** damage; **~s y perjuicios** damages
dar 1 *v/t* give; *beneficio* yield **2** *v/i*: **dame** give it to me, give me it; **~ a** *de ventana* look onto; **~ con algo** come across sth; **~ de sí** *de material* stretch, give; **¡qué más da!** what does it matter!; **da igual** it doesn't matter
dardo *m* dart
darse *de una situación* arise
dársena *f* dock
datar: ~ de date from
dátil *m* BOT date
dato *m* piece of information; **~s** information, data *sg*; **~s personales** personal details
D.C. (= **después de Cristo**) AD (= Anno Domini)
de ◇ *origen* from; **~... a** from … to ◇ *posesión* of; **el coche ~ mi amigo** my friend's car ◇ *material* (made) of; **un anillo ~ oro** a gold ring

◊ *contenido* of; ***un vaso ~ agua*** a glass of water ◊ *cualidad*: ***una mujer ~ 20 años*** a 20 year old woman ◊ *causa* with; ***temblaba ~ miedo*** she was shaking with fear ◊ *hora*: ***~ noche*** at night, by night; ***~ día*** by day ◊ *en calidad de* as; ***trabajar ~ albañil*** work as a bricklayer ◊ *agente* by; ***~ Goya*** by Goya ◊ *condición* if; ***~ haberlo sabido*** if I'd known

deambular wander around

debacle *f* debacle

debajo 1 *adv* underneath **2** *prp*: (***por***) ***~ de*** under, below

debate *m* debate, discussion; **debatir 1** *v/t* debate, discuss **2** *v/i* struggle

deber 1 *m* duty; ***~es*** homework **2** *v/t* owe **3** *v/i en presente* must, have to; *en pretérito* should have; *en futuro* (will) have to; *en condicional* should; ***debe de tener quince años*** he must be about 15; **debido 1** *part* ☞ ***deber*** **2** *adj*: ***como es ~*** properly; ***~ a*** owing to

débil weak; **debilitar** weaken; **debilidad** *f*

débito *m* COM debit

debut *m* début; **debutar** make one's début

década *f* decade

decadencia *f* decadence; *de un imperio* decline; **decadente** decadent; **decaer** *tb fig* decline; *de salud* deteriorate; **decaído 1** *part* ☞ ***decaer*** **2** *adj fig* depressed, down F; **decaimiento** *m* decline; *de salud* deterioration

decapitar behead, decapitate

decatlón *m* DEP decathlon

decena *f*: ***una ~ de*** about ten

decencia *f* decency

decenio *m* decade

decente decent

decepción *f* disappointment; **decepcionar** disappoint

decidido 1 *part* ☞ ***decidir*** **2** *adj* decisive; ***estar ~*** be determined (***a*** to); **decidir** decide; **decidirse** make up one's mind, decide

décima *f* tenth; ***tener ~s*** MED have a slight fever

decimal decimal *atr*; **décimo 1** *adj* tenth **2** *m de lotería share of a lottery ticket*

decir 1 *v/t* say; (*contar*) tell; ***querer ~*** mean; ***~ que sí*** say yes; ***es ~*** in other words; ***¡no me digas!*** you're kidding!; ***¡quién lo diría!*** who would believe it!; ***se dice que...*** they say that ..., it's said that ... **2** *v/i*: ***¡diga!, ¡dígame!*** *Esp* TELEC hello

decisión *f* decision; *fig* decisiveness; **decisivo** decisive

declamar declaim

declaración *f* declaration; ***~ de la renta*** *o* ***de impuestos*** tax return; ***prestar ~*** JUR testify, give evidence; **declarar 1** *v/t* state; *bienes* declare; ***~ culpable*** find guilty **2** *v/i* JUR give evidence; **declararse** declare o.s.; *de incendio*

break out; ~ ***a alguien*** declare one's love for s.o.
declinar decline
declive *m fig* decline
decodificador *m* ☞ ***descodificador***
decoración *f* decoration; **decorado** *m* TEA set; **decorar** decorate
decrecer decrease, diminish
decrépito decrepit; **decrepitud** *f* decrepitude
decretar order, decree; **decreto** *m* decree
dedal *m* thimble
dedicación *f* dedication; **dedicar** dedicate; *esfuerzo* devote; **dedicatoria** *f* dedication
dedo *m* finger; ~ ***del pie*** toe; ~ ***gordo*** thumb; ~ ***índice*** forefinger
deducción *f* deduction; **deducir** deduce; COM deduct
defecto *m* defect; *moral* fault; INFOR default; **defectuoso** defective, faulty
defender defend
defensa 1 *f* JUR, DEP defense, *Br* defence; *L.Am.* AUTO fender, *Br* wing **2** *m/f* DEP defender; **defensivo** defensive; **defensor** *m*, **~a** *f* defender, champion; JUR defense counsel, *Br* defending counsel; ~ ***del pueblo*** *en España* ombudsman
deficiencia *f* deficiency; ***con ~ auditiva*** with a hearing problem; **deficiente 1** *adj* deficient; (*insatisfactorio*) inadequate **2** *m/f* handicapped person; **déficit** *m* deficit
definición *f* definition; **definir** define; **definitivo** definitive; *respuesta* definite; ***en -a*** all in all
deforestación *f* deforestation; **deforestar** deforest
deformar distort; MED deform; **deforme** deformed
defraudación *f* fraud; **defraudar** disappoint; (*estafar*) defraud; ~ ***a Hacienda*** evade taxes
defunción *f* death, demise *fml*
degenerar degenerate (***en*** into)
degradación *f* degradation; MIL demotion
degustación *f* tasting; **degustar** taste
dehesa *f* meadow
dejadez *f* slovenliness; (*negligencia*) neglect
dejado 1 *part* ☞ ***dejar* 2** *adj* slovenly
dejar 1 *v/t* leave; (*permitir*) let, allow; (*prestar*) lend; *beneficios* yield; ***déjame en la esquina*** drop me at the corner **2** *v/i*: ~ ***de hacer algo*** (*parar*) stop doing sth; ***no deja de fastidiarme*** he keeps (on) annoying me; **dejarse** let o.s. go
delantal *m* apron
delante in front; (*más avanzado*) ahead; (*enfrente*) opposite; ***por ~*** ahead; ~ ***de*** in

front of; ***el asiento de ~*** the front seat; **delantera** *f* DEP forward line; ***llevar la ~*** lead; **delantero** *m*, **-a** *f* DEP forward
delatar: ***~ a alguien*** inform on s.o.; *fig* give s.o. away; **delator** *m*, **~a** *f* informer
delegación *f* delegation; (*oficina*) local office; ***~ de Hacienda*** tax office; **delegado** *m*, **-a** *f* delegate; COM representative
deleitar delight; **deleite** *m* delight
deletrear spell
delfín *m* ZO dolphin
delgadez *f de cuerpo* slimness; (*esbeltez*) thinness; **delgado** slim; *lámina, placa* thin
deliberación *f* deliberation; **deliberar** deliberate (***sobre*** on)
delicadeza *f* gentleness; *de acabado, tallado* delicacy; (*tacto*) tact; **delicado** delicate
delicia *f* delight; **delicioso** delightful; *comida* delicious
delimitar delimit
delincuencia *f* crime; **delincuente** *m/f* criminal
delineante *m/f* draftsman, *Br* draughtsman; *mujer* draftswoman, *Br* draughtswoman; **delinear** draft; *fig* draw up
delirante delirious; *fig*: *idea* crazy; **delirar** be delirious; ***¡tú deliras!*** *fig* you must be crazy!; **delirio** *m* MED delirium; ***tener ~ por el fútbol*** be mad about soccer; ***~s de grandeza*** delusions of grandeur
delito *m* offense, *Br* offence
demanda *f* demand (***de*** for); JUR lawsuit, claim; **demandado** *m*, **-a** *f* JUR defendant; **demandante** *m/f* JUR plaintiff; **demandar** JUR sue
demarcación *f* demarcation; **demarcar** demarcate
demás 1 *adj* remaining **2** *adv*: ***lo ~*** the rest; ***los ~*** the rest, the others; ***por lo ~*** apart from that; **demasiado 1** *adj* too much; *antes de pl* too many **2** *adv antes de adj, adv* too; *con verbo* too much
demencia *f* MED dementia; *fig* madness; **demente 1** *adj* demented, crazy **2** *m/f* mad person
democracia *f* democracy; **demócrata 1** *adj* democratic **2** *m/f* democrat; **democrático** democratic
demoler demolish; **demolición** *f* demolition
demonio *m* demon; ***¡~s!*** F hell! F, damn! F
demora *f* delay; **demorar 1** *v/i* stay on; *L.Am.* (*tardar*) be late; ***no demores*** don't be long **2** *v/t* delay
demostración *f* proof; *de método* demonstration; *de fuerza, sentimiento* show; **demostrar** prove; (*enseñar*) demonstrate; (*mostrar*) show; **demostrativo** demon-

strative
denegar refuse
denigrar degrade; (*criticar*) denigrate
denominación *f* name; **~ de origen** *guarantee of quality of a wine*; **denominador** *m*: **~ común** *tb fig* common denominator; **denominar** designate
denotar show, indicate
densidad *f* density; **denso** *bosque* dense; *fig* weighty
dentadura *f*: **~ postiza** false teeth *pl*, dentures *pl*; **dentífrico** *m* toothpaste; **dentista** *m/f* dentist; **dentición** *f* teething; (*dientes*) teeth *pl*
dentro 1 *adv* inside; **por ~** inside **2 ~ de** *en espacio* in, inside; *en tiempo* in, within
denuncia *f* report; **poner una ~** make a formal complaint; **denunciante** *m/f person who reports a crime*; **denunciar** report; *fig* condemn, denounce
departamento *m* department; *L.Am.* (*apartamento*) apartment, *Br* flat
dependencia *f* dependence (**de** on); COM department; **depender** depend (**de** on); **~ de alguien** *en una jerarquía* report to s.o.; **eso depende** that all depends; **dependiente 1** *adj* dependent **2** *m*, **-a** *f* sales clerk, *Br* shop assistant
depilar *con cera* wax; *con pinzas* pluck; **depilatorio** *m* depilatory
deplorable deplorable; **deplorar** deplore
deporte *m* sport; **deportista** *m/f* sportsman; *mujer* sportswoman; **deportivo** sports *atr*, *actitud* sporting
deposición *f* deposition; **depositar** *tb fig* put, place; *dinero* deposit (**en** in); **depósito** *m* COM deposit; (*almacén*) store; *de agua*, AUTO tank; **~ de cadáveres** morgue, *Br* mortuary
depravado depraved; **depravar** deprave
depreciación *f* depreciation; **depreciar** lower the value of; **depreciarse** depreciate, lose value
depresión *f* depression; **deprimido** depressed; **deprimir** depress
depuración *f* purification; POL purge; **depuradora** *f* purifier; **depurar** purify; *agua* treat; POL purge
derecha *f tb* POL right; **a la ~** *posición* on the right; *dirección* to the right
derecho 1 *adj lado* right; (*recto*) straight; *C.Am. fig* straight, honest **2** *adv* straight **3** *m* (*privilegio*) right; JUR law; **del ~** on the right side; **~ de asilo** right to asylum; **~s de autor** royalties; **~s humanos** human rights; **no hay ~** it's not fair, it's not right; **tener ~ a** have a right to **4** *mpl*: **~s** fees

derivación *f* derivation; **derivar** derive (***de*** from); *de barco* drift

dermatólogo *m*, **-a** *f* dermatologist

derramar spill; *luz*, *sangre* shed; (*esparcir*) scatter; **derramarse** spill; *de gente* scatter; **derrame** *m* MED: ***~ cerebral*** stroke

derrapar AUTO skid

derretir melt; **derretirse** melt; *fig* be besotted (***por*** with)

derribar *edificio*, *persona* knock down, demolish; *avión* shoot down; POL bring down; **derribo** *m de edificio* demolition; *de persona* knocking down; *de avión* shooting down; POL overthrow

derrocar POL overthrow

derrochador *m*, **~a** *f* spendthrift; **derrochar** waste; *salud*, *felicidad* burst with; **derroche** *m* waste

derrota *f* defeat; **derrotar** MIL defeat; DEP beat, defeat

derrumbamiento *m accidental* collapse; *intencionado* demolition; **derrumbarse** collapse, fall down; *de una persona* go to pieces

desabrido (*soso*) tasteless; *persona* surly; *tiempo* unpleasant

desabrochar undo, unfasten

desacatar *orden* disobey; *ley*, *regla* break; **desacato** *m* JUR contempt

desacertar be wrong; **desacierto** *m* mistake

desaconsejar advise against

desacoplar uncouple

desacostumbrar: ***~ a alguien de algo*** get s.o. out of the habit of sth; **desacostumbrarse:** ***~ a algo*** get out of the habit of sth

desacreditar discredit

desacuerdo *m* disagreement; ***estar en ~ con*** disagree with

desafiar challenge; *peligro* defy

desafinado out of tune; **desafinar** be out of tune

desafío *m* challenge; *al peligro* defiance

desafortunadamente unfortunately; **desafortunado** unfortunate

desagradable unpleasant, disagreeable; **desagradecido** ungrateful; *tarea* thankless; **desagrado** *m* displeasure

desagüe *m* drain; *acción* drainage; (*cañería*) drainpipe

desahogado spacious; **desahogarse** *fig* F let off steam F

desahuciar: ***~ a alguien*** declare s.o. terminally ill; (*inquilino*) evict s.o.; **desahucio** *m* JUR eviction; ***demanda de ~*** eviction order

desairar snub; **desaire** *m* snub

desalentar discourage; **desaliento** *m* discouragement

desalinización *f* desalination
desaliñado slovenly
desalmado 1 *adj* heartless **2** *m*, **-a** *f* heartless person
desalojar *ante peligro* evacuate; (*desahuciar*) evict; (*vaciar*) vacate
desamparado defenseless, *Br* defenceless; **desamparo** *m* neglect
desangrarse bleed to death
desanimado discouraged, disheartened; **desanimar** discourage, dishearten; **desanimarse** become discouraged *o* disheartened
desapacible nasty, unpleasant
desaparecer 1 *v/i* disappear, vanish **2** *v/t L.Am.* disappear F; **desaparición** *f* disappearance
desapercibido unnoticed
desaprensivo unscrupulous
desaprobación *f* disapproval; **desaprobar** disapprove of
desaprovechado wasted; **desaprovechar** *oportunidad* waste
desarmar MIL disarm; TÉC take to pieces, dismantle; **desarme** *m* MIL disarmament
desarraigar *tb fig* uproot; **desarraigo** *m fig* rootlessness
desarreglar make untidy; *horario* disrupt; **desarreglo** *m* disorder; *de horarios* disruption
desarrollar develop; *tema* explain; *trabajo* carry out; **desarrollarse** develop, evolve; (*ocurrir*) take place; **desarrollo** *m* development; ***país en vías de ~*** developing country
desaseado F scruffy
desasosegar make uneasy; **desasosegarse** become uneasy; **desasosiego** *m* disquiet, unease
desastre *m tb fig* disaster; **desastroso** disastrous
desatar untie; *fig* unleash
desatención *f* lack of attention, inattention; **desatender** neglect; (*ignorar*) ignore; **desatento** (*desconsiderado*) discourteous; (*distraído*) inattentive
desatinado foolish; **desatinar** (*actuando*) act foolishly; (*hablando*) talk nonsense; **desatino** *m* mistake
desatornillar unscrew
desavenencia *f* disagreement
desaventajado unfavorable, *Br* unfavourable
desayunar 1 *v/i* have breakfast **2** *v/t*: ***~ algo*** have sth for breakfast; **desayuno** *m* breakfast
desbancar *fig* displace, take the place of
desbarajuste *m* mess
desbloquear *carretera* clear; *mecanismo* free up, unjam; *cuenta bancaria* unfreeze
desbordar 1 *v/t de un río*

overflow, burst; *de un multitud* break through; *de un acontecimiento* overwhelm; *fig* exceed **2** *v/i* overflow; **desbordarse** *de un río* burst its banks; *fig* get out of control

descabellado: ***idea -a*** F hare-brained idea

descafeinado decaffeinated; *fig* watered-down

descalabro *m* calamity

descalificación *f* disqualification; **descalificar** disqualify

descalzo barefoot

descansar rest, have a rest; ***¡que descanses!*** sleep well; **descanso** *m* rest; DEP half time; TEA interval; ***sin ~*** without a break

descapotable *m* AUTO convertible

descarado rude, impertinent

descarga *f* ELEC, MIL discharge; *de mercancías* unloading; INFOR download; **descargar** *arma*, ELEC discharge; *fig*: *ira etc* take out (**en, sobre** on); *mercancías* unload; INFOR download; *de responsabilidad, culpa* clear (**de** of); **descargo** *m* defense, *Br* defence

descaro *m* nerve

descarrilamiento *m* FERR derailment; **descarrilar** derail

descartar rule out

descendencia *f* descendants *pl*; **descendente** downward; *escala* descending; **descender 1** *v/i* go down, descend; *para indicar acercamiento* come down, descend; *fig* go down, decrease; **~ de** descend from **2** *v/t escalera* go down; *para indicar acercamiento* come down; **descendiente 1** *adj* descended **2** *m/f* descendant; **descenso** *m de precio etc* drop; *de montaña*, AVIA descent; DEP relegation

descentralizar decentralize

descifrar decipher; *fig* work out

descodificador *m* decoder; **descodificar** decode

descolgar take down; *teléfono* pick up

descolorar bleach; **descolorarse** fade; **descolorido** faded; *fig* colorless, *Br* colourless

descomedido immoderate; (*descortés*) rude

descomponer (*dividir*) break down; (*pudrir*) cause to decompose; *L.Am.* (*romper*) break; **descomponerse** (*pudrirse*) decompose, rot; TÉC break down; *Rpl* (*emocionarse*) break down (in tears); ***se le descompuso la cara*** he turned pale; **descomposición** *f* breaking down; *putrefacción* decomposition; (*diarrea*) diarrhea, *Br* diarrhoea; **descompuesto 1** *part* ☞ ***descomponer*** **2** *adj alimento* rotten; *cadá-*

ver decomposed; *persona* upset; *L.Am.* tipsy; *L.Am. máquina* broken down
descomunal enormous
desconcertado disconcerted; **desconcertar** *a persona* disconcert; **desconcertarse** be disconcerted, be taken aback
desconectar 1 *v/t* ELEC disconnect **2** *v/i fig* switch off
desconfiado mistrustful, suspicious; **desconfianza** *f* mistrust, suspicion; **desconfiar** be mistrustful, be suspicious (**de** of)
descongelar *comida* thaw, defrost; *refrigerador* defrost; *precios* unfreeze
descongestionar MED clear; *tráfico* relieve
desconocer not know; **desconocido 1** *adj* unknown **2** *m*, **-a** *f* stranger; **desconocimiento** *m* ignorance
desconsiderado inconsiderate
desconsolado inconsolable; **desconsuelo** *m* grief; **desconsolar** distress
descontar COM deduct, take off; *fig* exclude
descontento 1 *adj* dissatisfied **2** *m* dissatisfaction
desconvocar call off
descorchador *m Rpl* corkscrew; **descorchar** *botella* uncork
descortés impolite, rude; **descortesía** *f* discourtesy, impoliteness
descoser *costura* unpick; **descoserse** *de dobladillo etc* come unstitched; *de prenda* come apart at the seams
descrédito *m* discredit; ***caer en ~*** be discredited
describir describe; **descripción** *f* description
descubierto 1 *part* ☞ ***descubrir*** **2** *adj* uncovered; *persona* bareheaded; *cielos* clear; *piscina* open-air; ***al ~*** in the open; ***quedar al ~*** be exposed **3** *m* COM overdraft;
descubrimiento *m* discovery; (*revelación*) revelation;
descubrir discover; *poner de manifiesto* uncover, reveal; *estatua* unveil
descuento *m* discount; DEP stoppage time
descuidado careless; **descuidar 1** *v/t* neglect **2** *v/i*: **¡descuida!** don't worry!; **descuidarse** get careless; *en cuanto al aseo* let o.s. go; (*despistarse*) let one's concentration drop; **descuido** *m* carelessness; (*error*) mistake; (*omisión*) oversight; ***en un ~*** *L.Am.* in a moment of carelessness
desde 1 *prp en el tiempo* since; *en el espacio*, *en escala* from; ***~ 1993*** since 1993; ***~ hace tres días*** for three days; ***~... hasta...*** from … to … **2** *adv*: ***~ luego*** of course; ***~ ya*** *Rpl* right away
desdén *m* disdain, contempt; **desdeñar** scorn; **desdeño-**

so disdainful, contemptuous
desdicha *f* (*desgracia*) misfortune; (*infelicidad*) unhappiness; **desdichado 1** *adj* unhappy; (*sin suerte*) unlucky **2** *m*, **-a** *f* poor soul
deseable desirable; **desear** wish for; *suerte etc* wish; ***¿qué desea?*** what would you like?
desecar dry
desechable disposable; **desechar** (*tirar*) throw away; (*rechazar*) reject; **desechos** *mpl* waste
desembalar unpack
desembarcar disembark; **desembarco** *m*, **desembarque** *m de personas* disembarkation; *de mercancías* landing
desembocadura *f* mouth; **desembocar** flow (***en*** into); *de calle* come out (***en*** into); *de situación* end (***en*** in)
desembolsar pay out; **desembolso** *m* expenditure
desembragar 1 *v/t embrague* release **2** *v/i* release the clutch, declutch; **desembrague** *m* declutching
desempaquetar unwrap
desempate *m* POL: ***una votación de ~*** a vote to decide the winner; (***partido de***) **~** DEP decider, deciding game
desempeñar *tarea* carry out; *cargo* hold; *papel* play; **desempeño** *m de tarea*, *papel* performance
desempleo *m* unemployment
desempolvar *v/t* dust; *fig* dust off; *conocimientos teóricos* brush up
desencadenar *fig* trigger; **desencadenarse** *fig* be triggered
desencantar *fig* disillusion, disenchant; **desencanto** *m fig* disillusionment
desenchufar ELEC unplug
desenfadado self-assured; *programa* light, undemanding; **desenfado** *m* ease
desenfrenado frenzied, hectic; **desenfreno** *m* frenzy
desenganchar *caballo* unhitch; *carro* uncouple; **desengancharse** get loose; *fig* F kick the habit F
desengañar disillusion; **desengañarse** become disillusioned (***de*** with); (*dejar de engañarse*) stop kidding o.s.; **desengaño** *m* disappointment
desenlace *m* outcome
desenmascarar *fig* unmask, expose
desenredar untangle; *situación confusa* straighten out, sort out
desenvoltura *f* ease; **desenvuelto 1** *part* ☞ ***desenvolver* 2** *adj* self-confident
desenvolver unwrap; **desenvolverse** *fig* cope
deseo *m* wish; **deseoso: *~ de hacer algo*** eager to do sth
desequilibrado 1 *adj* unbal-

anced **2** *m*, **-a** *f*: ***ser un ~ mental*** be mentally unbalanced; **desequilibrar** unbalance; ***~ a alguien*** throw s.o. off balance
deserción *f* desertion; **desertar** MIL desert; **desertor** *m*, **~ora** *f* deserter
desescombro *m* clearing (up), removal
desesperación *f* despair; **desesperado** in despair; **desesperar 1** *v/t* infuriate, exasperate **2** *v/i* despair (***de*** of); **desesperarse** get exasperated
desestabilizar POL destabilize
desestimar *queja* reject
desfachatez *f* impertinence
desfalco *m* embezzlement
desfallecer faint; **desfallecimiento** *m* (*debilidad*) weakness; (*desmayo*) fainting fit
desfase *m* gap; ***~ horario*** jet lag
desfavorable unfavorable, *Br* unfavourable
desfigurar disfigure
desfilar parade; **desfile** *m* parade; ***~ de modelos*** *o* ***de modas*** fashion show
desgana *f* loss of appetite; ***con ~*** *fig* half-heartedly
desgarrador heartrending; **desgarrar** tear up; *corazón* break; **desgarro** *m* MED tear
desgastado worn out; **desgastar** wear out; *defensas* wear down; **desgaste** *m* wear (and tear)
desglose *m* breakdown, itemization
desgracia *f* misfortune; *suceso* accident; ***por ~*** unfortunately; **desgraciado 1** *adj* unfortunate; (*miserable*) wretched **2** *m*, **-a** *f* wretch; (*sinvergüenza*) swine F
desgravar 1 *v/t* deduct **2** *v/i* be tax-deductible
desgreñar dishevel
desguazar scrap
deshabitado uninhabited
deshacer undo; *maleta* unpack; *planes* wreck; (*suspender*) cancel; **deshacerse** *de nudo de corbata, lazo etc* come undone; *de hielo* melt; ***~ de*** get rid of; **deshecho 1** *part* ☞ ***deshacer* 2** *adj* F *anímicamente* devastated F; *de cansancio* beat F
deshelar, deshelarse thaw
desheredar disinherit
deshielo *m* thaw
deshonesto dishonest; **deshonra** *f* dishonor, *Br* dishonour; **deshonrar** dishonor, *Br* dishonour
deshora *f*: ***a ~ (s)*** at the wrong time
desierto 1 *adj* empty, deserted; ***isla -a*** desert island **2** *m* desert
designación *f* appointment, naming; *de lugar* selection; *de candidato* designation; **designar** appoint, name; *lugar* select
desigual unequal; *terreno* uneven; **desigualdad** *f* ine-

quality
desilusión *f* disappointment; **desilusionar** disappoint; (*quitar la ilusión*) disillusion
desinfección *f* disinfection; **desinfectante** *m* disinfectant; **desinfectar** disinfect
desintegración *f tb* FÍS disintegration; **desintegrarse** disintegrate; *de grupo de gente* break up
desinterés *m* lack of interest; (*generosidad*) unselfishness; **desinteresado** unselfish
desintoxicación *f* detoxification
desistir give up, stop
desleal disloyal
desleír dissolve; **desleírse** dissolve
deslenguado 1 *adj* foul-mouthed **2** *m*, **-a** *f* foul-mouthed person
desligar separate (***de*** from); *fig*: *persona* cut off (***de*** from)
desliz *m fig* F slip-up F; **deslizar 1** *v/t* slide, run (***por*** along); *idea*, *frase* slip in **2** *v/i* slide; **deslizarse** slide
deslucido tarnished; *colores* dull, drab; **deslucir** tarnish; *fig* spoil; **deslucirse** *de colores* fade; *de persona* be discredited
deslumbrar *fig* dazzle
desmán *m* outrage
desmantelar dismantle
desmaquillar remove make-up from; **desmaquillarse** take one's make-up off
desmarcarse DEP lose one's marker; ~ ***de*** distance o.s. from
desmayado *persona* unconscious; *voz* weak; *color* pale; **desmayarse** faint; **desmayo** *m* fainting fit; ***sin*** ~ without flagging
desmedido excessive
desmejorar 1 *v/t* spoil **2** *v/i* MED get worse, go downhill; **desmejorarse** MED get worse, go downhill; (*perder esplendor*) lose one's looks
desmentido *m* denial; **desmentir** deny; *a alguien* contradict
desmenuzar crumble up; *fig* break down
desmesurado excessive
desmontable easily dismantled; **desmontar 1** *v/t* dismantle, take apart; *tienda de campaña* take down **2** *v/i* dismount
desmoronarse *tb fig* collapse
desnivel *m* unevenness; *entre personas* disparity
desnudar undress; *fig* fleece; **desnudarse** undress; **desnudez** *f* nudity; *fig* nakedness; **desnudismo** *m* nudism; **desnudo 1** *adj* naked; (*sin decoración*) bare **2** *m* PINT nude
desobedecer disobey; **desobediencia** *f* disobedience; **desobediente** disobedient
desocupación *f L.Am.* unemployment; **desocupado 1** *adj apartamento* empty; *L.Am. sin trabajo* unem-

ployed **2** *mpl*: ***los ~s*** the unemployed; **desocupar** vacate
desodorante *m* deodorant
desolación *f* desolation; **desolado** desolate; *fig* devastated; **desolador** devastating; **desolar** *tb fig* devastate
desorden *m* disorder; **desordenado** untidy, messy; *fig* disorganized; **desordenar** make untidy
desorganización *f* lack of organization; **desorganizado** disorganized
desorientarse get disoriented, lose one's bearings; *fig* get confused
despachar 1 *v/t a persona, cliente* attend to; *problema* sort out; (*vender*) sell; (*enviar*) send, dispatch **2** *v/i* meet (***con*** with); **despacho** *m* office; *diplomático* dispatch; ***~ de billetes*** ticket office
despacio slowly; *L.Am.* (*en voz baja*) in a low voice
desparramar scatter; *líquido* spill; *dinero* squander; **desparramarse** spill; *fig* scatter
despectivo contemptuous; GRAM pejorative
despedazar tear apart
despedida *f* farewell; ***~ de soltero*** stag party; ***~ de soltera*** hen party; **despedir** see off; *empleado* dismiss; *perfume* give off; *de jinete* throw; **despedirse** say goodbye (***de*** to)
despegar 1 *v/t* remove, peel off **2** *v/i* AVIA, *fig* take off; **despegue** *m* AVIA, *fig* take-off
despejado *cielo, cabeza* clear; **despejar** clear; *persona* wake up; **despejarse** *de cielo* clear up; *fig* wake o.s. up
despensa *f* larder
desperdicio *m* waste; ***~s*** waste; ***no tener ~*** be worthwhile
desperfecto *m* (*defecto*) flaw; (*daño*) damage
despertador *m* alarm (clock); **despertar 1** *v/t* wake; *apetito* whet; *sospecha* arouse; *recuerdo* reawaken **2** *v/i* wake up; **despertarse** wake (up)
despido *m* dismissal
despierto awake; *fig* bright
despilfarrar squander
despistado scatterbrained
desplazamiento *m* trip; (*movimiento*) movement; **desplazar** move; (*suplantar*) take over from; **desplazarse** travel
desplegar unfold, open out; MIL deploy
desplomarse collapse
despoblar depopulate; **despoblarse** become depopulated o deserted
despojar strip (***de*** of)
despreciar look down on; *propuesta* reject; **desprecio** *m* contempt; (*indiferencia*) disregard; *acto* slight
desprender detach, separate;

olor give off; **desprenderse** come off; **~ *de*** *fig* part with; *de estudio* emerge; **desprendimiento** *m* detachment

despreocupado (*descuidado*) careless; (*sin preocupaciones*) carefree

desprevenido unprepared; ***pillar*** *o L.Am.* ***agarrar ~*** catch unawares

después (*más tarde*) afterward, later; *seguido en orden* next; *en el espacio* after; ***yo voy ~*** I'm next; **~ *de*** after; **~ *de que se vaya*** after he's gone

desquite *m* compensation; ***tomarse el ~*** F get one's own back

destacado outstanding; **destacar** stand out

destajo *m*: ***a ~*** piecework

destapar open, take the lid off; *fig* uncover

desterrar exile; **destierro** *m* exile

destilación *f* distillation; **destilar** distill; *fig* exude

destinar *fondos* allocate (***para*** for); *a persona* post (***a*** to); **destinatario** *m*, **-a** *f* addressee; **destino** *m* fate; *de viaje etc* destination; *en el ejército etc* posting

destituir dismiss

destornillador *m* screwdriver; **destornillar** unscrew

destreza *f* skill

destrozar destroy; *emocionalmente* shatter, devastate

destrucción *f* destruction; **destructor 1** *adj* destructive; ***máquina ~a de documentos*** document shredder **2** *m barco* destroyer; **destruir** destroy; (*estropear*) ruin, wreck

desunión *f* lack of unity

desusado obsolete

desvalijar rob; *apartamento* burglarize, burgle

desván *m* attic

desvelar keep awake; *secreto* reveal; **desvelo** *m* sleeplessness; ***~s*** efforts

desventaja *f* disadvantage; **desventajoso** disadvantageous

desventura *f* misfortune; **desventurado 1** *adj* unfortunate **2** *m*, **-a** *f* unfortunate

desvergonzado shameless

desviación *f* diversion; **desviar** *golpe* deflect; *tráfico, río* divert; **~ *la conversación*** change the subject; **~ *la mirada*** look away; **~ *a alguien del buen camino*** lead s.o. astray; **desvío** *m* diversion

detallado detailed; **detalle** *m* detail; *fig* thoughtful gesture; ***al ~*** retail; **detallista** *m/f* COM retailer

detectar detect; **detective** *m/f* detective; **~ *privado*** private detective

detención *f* detention; ***orden de ~*** arrest warrant; **detener** stop; *de policía* arrest, detain; **detenerse** stop

detergente *m* detergent

deteriorar damage
determinación *f* (*intrepidez*) determination; (*decisión*) decision; **determinado** certain; **determinar** determine; **determinarse** decide (***a*** to)
detestar detest
detrás behind; ***por ~*** at the back; *fig* behind your / his etc back; ***~ de*** behind; ***uno ~ de otro*** one after the other; ***estar ~ de algo*** *fig* be behind sth
detrimento *m*: ***en ~ de*** to the detriment of
deuda *f* debt; ***estar en ~ con alguien*** *fig* be in s.o.'s debt; **deudor** *m*, **~a** *f* debtor
devaluación *f* devaluation; **devaluar** devalue
devastar devastate
devoción *f tb fig* devotion
devolución *f* return; *de dinero* refund; **devolver** give back, return; *fig*: *visita, saludo* return; F (*vomitar*) throw up F; **devolverse** *L.Am.* go back
devorar devour
devoto 1 *adj* devout **2** *m*, **-a** *f* devotee
DF (= ***Distrito Federal***) Mexico City
día *m* day; ***~ de fiesta*** holiday; ***~ festivo*** holiday; ***~ hábil*** *o* ***laborable*** work day; ***poner al ~*** update, bring up to date; ***a los pocos ~s*** a few days later; ***algún ~, un ~*** some day, one day; ***de ~*** by day; ***ya es de ~*** it's light already; ***el ~ menos pensado*** when you least expect it; ***hace mal ~*** *tiempo* it's a nasty day; ***hoy en ~*** nowadays; ***todos los ~s*** every day; ***un ~ sí y otro no*** every other day; ***¡buenos ~s!*** good morning
diabetes *f* diabetes; **diabético 1** *adj* diabetic **2** *m*, **-a** *f* diabetic
diablo *m* devil; ***mandar a alguien al ~*** tell s.o. to go to hell
diafragma *m* diaphragm
diagnóstico 1 *adj* diagnostic **2** *m* diagnosis
diagonal 1 *adj* diagonal **2** *f* diagonal (line)
diagrama *m* diagram
dialecto *m* dialect
diálogo *m* dialog, *Br* dialogue
diamante *m* diamond
diámetro *m* diameter
diapositiva *f* FOT slide, transparency
diario 1 *adj* daily **2** *m* diary; (*periódico*) newspaper; ***a ~*** daily
diarrea *f* MED diarrhea, *Br* diarrhoea
dibujante *m/f* draftsman, *Br* draughtsman; *mujer* draftswoman, *Br* draughtswoman; *de viñetas* cartoonist; **dibujar** draw; *fig* describe; **dibujo** *m* drawing; *estampado* pattern; ***~s animados*** cartoons; ***película de ~s animados*** animation
diccionario *m* dictionary

dicha *f* (*felicidad*) happiness; (*suerte*) good luck

dicho 1 *part* ☞ **decir 2** *adj* said; **~ y hecho** no sooner said than done; **mejor ~** or rather **3** *m* saying

dichoso happy; F (*maldito*) damn F

diciembre *m* December

dictado *m* dictation; **dictador** *m*, **~a** *f* dictator

dictamen *m* (*informe*) report; (*opinión*) opinion; **emitir un ~** make out a report; **dictaminar** state

dictar dictate; *ley* announce; **~ sentencia** JUR pass sentence

diecinueve nineteen; **dieciocho** eighteen; **dieciséis** sixteen; **diecisiete** seventeen

diente *m* tooth; **~ de ajo** clove of garlic; **~ de león** BOT dandelion; **poner los ~s largos a alguien** make s.o. jealous

diesel *m* diesel

diestro 1 *adj*: **a ~ y siniestro** *fig* F left and right **2** *m* TAUR bullfighter

dieta *f* diet; **estar a ~** be on a diet; **~s** traveling *o Br* travelling expenses

diez ten

difamación *f* defamation; *de palabra* slander; *por escrito* libel; **difamar** slander, defame; *por escrito* libel

diferencia *f* difference; **a ~ de** unlike; **con ~** *fig* by a long way; **diferencial** *m* differential; **diferenciar** differentiate; **diferente** different

diferido TV: **en ~** prerecorded;

diferir 1 *v/t* postpone **2** *v/i* differ (**de** from)

difícil difficult; **dificultad** *f* difficulty; **poner ~es** make it difficult

dificultar hinder

difteria *f* MED diphtheria

difundir spread; (*programa*) broadcast; **difundirse** spread

difunto 1 *adj* late **2** *m*, **-a** *f* deceased

digerir digest; **digestible** digestible; **digestión** *f* digestion; **digestivo** digestive

digital digital

dignarse deign; **dignidad** *f* dignity; **dignatario** *m*, **-a** *f* dignitary; **digno** worthy; *trabajo* decent

dilapidar waste

dilatación *f* dilation; **dilatar 1** *v/t* dilate; (*prolongar*) prolong; (*aplazar*) postpone **2** *v/i Méx* (*tardar*) be late; **no me dilato** I won't be long

dilema *m* dilemma

diligencia *f* diligence; *vehículo* stagecoach; **~s** JUR procedures, formalities; **diligente** diligent

diluir dilute

diluvio *m* downpour; *fig* deluge

dimensión *f* dimension; *fig* size, scale; **dimensiones** measurements

diminuto tiny, diminutive

dimisión *f* resignation; **dimitir** resign
Dinamarca Denmark
dinamita *f* dynamite
dínamo, dinamo *f o L.Am. m* dynamo
dinero *m* money; **~ *en efectivo*, ~ *en metálico*** cash
dinosaurio *m* dinosaur
Dios *m* God; **¡~ *mío!*** my God!; **¡*por* ~!** for God's sake!
diosa *f* goddess
diploma *m* diploma; **diplomacia** *f* diplomacy; **diplomático 1** *adj* diplomatic **2** *m*, **-a** *f* diplomat
diputación *f* deputation; **diputado** *m*, **-a** *f* representative, *Br* Member of Parliament
dique *m* dike, *Br* dyke
dirección *f tb* TEA, *de película* direction; COM management; POL leadership; *de coche* steering; *en carta* address; ***en aquella* ~** that way; **~ *asistida*** AUTO power steering; **~ *de correo electrónico*** e-mail address; **directivo 1** *adj* governing; COM managing **2** *m*, **-a** *f* COM manager; **directo** direct; ***en* ~** TV, RAD live; **director 1** *adj* leading **2** *m*, **~a** *f* manager; EDU principal, *Br* head (teacher); TEA, *de película* director; **~ *de orquesta*** conductor; **directorio** *m tb* INFOR directory; **directriz** *f* guideline
dirigir TEA, *película* direct; COM manage, run; MÚS conduct; **~ *una carta a*** address a letter to; **~ *una pregunta a*** direct a question to; **dirigirse** make, head (***a*, *hacia*** for)
discapacidad *f* disability; **discapacitado 1** *adj* disabled **2** *m*, **-a** *f* disabled person
disciplina *f* discipline; **discípulo** *m*, **-a** *f* REL, *fig* disciple
disco *m* disk, *Br* disc; MÚS record; (*discoteca*) disco; DEP discus; **~ *compacto*** compact disc; **~ *duro*, *L.Am.* ~ *rígido*** INFOR hard disk
discordia *f* discord; (*colección de discos*) record collection
discoteca *f* disco
discreción *f* discretion; ***a* ~** *disparar* at will; ***a* ~ *de*** at the discretion of
discrepancia *f* discrepancy; (*desacuerdo*) disagreement; **discrepar** disagree
discreto discreet
discriminar discriminate against; (*diferenciar*) differentiate
disculpa *f* apology; **disculpar** excuse
discurso *m* speech; *de tiempo* passage, passing
discusión *f* discussion; (*disputa*) argument; **discutir 1** *v/t* discuss **2** *v/i* argue (***sobre*** about)
disentería *f* MED dysentery
diseñador *m*, **~a** *f* designer;

diseñar design; **diseño** *m* design; ~ ***gráfico*** graphic design

disfraz *m para ocultar* disguise; *para fiestas* costume, fancy dress; **disfrazarse** *para ocultarse* disguise o.s. (***de*** as); *para divertirse* dress up (***de*** as)

disfrutar 1 *v/t* enjoy **2** *v/i* have fun, enjoy o.s.; ~ ***de buena salud*** be in *o* enjoy good health

disgustado upset (***con*** with); **disgustar** upset; **disgustarse** get upset; **disgusto** *m*: ***me causó un gran*** ~ I was very upset; ***llevarse un*** ~ get upset; ***a*** ~ unwillingly

disidente *m/f* dissident

disimular 1 *v/t* disguise **2** *v/i* pretend

disipar *duda* dispel

diskette *m* diskette, floppy (disk)

dislexia *f* dyslexia; **disléxico 1** *adj* dyslexic **2** *m*, **-a** *f* dyslexic

dislocación *f* MED dislocation; *fig* distortion

disminución *f* decrease; **disminuido 1** *adj* handicapped **2** *m*, **-a** *f* handicapped person; **disminuir 1** *v/t gastos, costos* reduce, cut; *velocidad* reduce **2** *v/i* decrease, diminish

disolución *f* dissolution; **disolver** dissolve; *manifestación* break up

disparador *m* FOT shutter release; **disparar 1** *v/t tiro, arma* fire; *foto* take; *precios* send up **2** *v/i* shoot, fire; **dispararse** *de arma, alarma* go off; *de precios* shoot up, rocket F

disparate *m* F piece of nonsense; ***es un*** ~ ***hacer eso*** it's crazy to do that

disparo *m* shot

dispensar dispense; *recibimiento* give; (*eximir*) excuse (***de*** from)

dispersar disperse

disponer 1 *v/t* (*arreglar*) arrange; (*preparar*) prepare; (*ordenar*) stipulate **2** *v/i*: ~ ***de algo*** have sth at one's disposal; **disponible** available; **disposición** *f* disposition; *de objetos* arrangement; ~ ***de ánimo*** state of mind; ***estar a*** ~ ***de alguien*** be at s.o.'s disposal

dispositivo *m* device

dispuesto 1 *part* ☞ ***disponer*** **2** *adj* ready (***a*** to)

disputar 1 *v/t* dispute; *partido* play **2** *v/i* argue (***sobre*** about)

disquete *m* INFOR diskette, floppy (disk)

distancia *f tb fig* distance; **distante** *tb fig* distant

distensión *f* MED strain; *fig*: *de ambiente* easing; POL détente

distinción *f* distinction; ***a*** ~ ***de*** unlike; **distinguido** distinguished; **distinguir** distinguish (***de*** from); (*divisar*)

make out; *con un premio* honor, *Br* honour; **distintivo** *m* emblem; MIL insignia; **distinto** different; **~s** (*varios*) several
distorsión *f* distortion
distracción *f* distraction; (*descuido*) absent-mindedness; (*diversión*) entertainment; (*pasatiempo*) pastime; **distraer** distract; ***la radio la distrae*** she enjoys listening to the radio; **distraído 1** *part* ☞ ***distraer* 2** *adj* absent-minded; *temporalmente* distracted
distribución *f* distribution; **distribuidor** *m* distributor; **distribuir** distribute; *beneficio* share out
distrito *m* district
disturbio *m* disturbance
disuadir dissuade; POL deter; ***~ a alguien de hacer algo*** dissuade s.o. from doing sth
diurno day *atr*
divagar digress
diversidad *f* diversity
diversión *f* fun; (*pasatiempo*) pastime; ***aquí no hay muchas diversiones*** there's not much to do around here; **diverso** diverse; **~s** several, various
divertido funny; (*entretenido*) entertaining; **divertir** entertain; **divertirse** have fun, enjoy o.s.
dividir divide
divino *tb fig* divine
divisa *f* currency; **~s** foreign currency
división *f* division
divorciado 1 *adj* divorced **2** *m*, **-a** *f* divorcee; **divorciarse** get divorced; **divorcio** *m* divorce
divulgar spread
doblar 1 *v/t* fold; *cantidad* double; *película* dub; MAR round; *pierna*, *brazo* bend; *en una carrera* pass, *Br* overtake; ***~ la esquina*** go around *o* turn the corner **2** *v/i* turn; **doble 1** *adj* double; *nacionalidad* dual; ***~ clic*** *m* double click; ***hacer ~ clic en*** double click on **2** *m*: ***el ~*** twice as much (***de*** as); ***el ~ de gente*** twice as many people; **~s** *tenis* doubles **3** *m/f en película* double
doce twelve; **docena** *f* dozen
dócil docile
doctor *m*, **~a** *f* doctor
documentación *f* documentation; *de una persona* papers; **documental** *m* documentary; **documentar** document; **documentarse** do research; **documento** *m* document; ***~ nacional de identidad*** national identity card
dogma *m* dogma
dogo *m* ZO mastiff
dólar *m* dollar
dolencia *f* ailment; **doler** *tb fig* hurt; ***me duele el brazo*** my arm hurts; **dolido** *fig* hurt; **dolor** *m tb fig* pain; ***~ de cabeza*** headache; ***~ de***

estómago stomach-ache; ***~ de muelas*** toothache; **doloroso** *tb fig* painful
domador *m*, **~a** *f* tamer; **domar** *tb tb fig* tame; *caballo* break in
doméstico 1 *adj* domestic, household *atr* **2** *m*, **-a** *f* servant
domiciliado resident; **domiciliar** *pago* pay by direct billing, *Br* pay by direct debit; **domicilio** *m* address; ***repartir a ~*** do home deliveries
dominación *f* domination; **dominante** dominant; *desp* domineering; **dominar** dominate; *idioma* have a good command of
domingo *m* Sunday; ***~ de Ramos*** Palm Sunday
dominicano 1 *adj* Dominican **2** *m*, **-a** *f* Dominican
dominio *m* control; *fig* command; ***ser del ~ público*** be in the public domain
don[1] *m* gift; ***~ de gentes*** way with people
don[2] *m* Mr; ***~ Enrique*** Mr Sanchez *English uses the surname while Spanish uses the first name*
donación *f* donation; ***~ de órganos*** organ donation; **donar** donate; **donativo** *m* donation
donde 1 *adv* where **2** *prp esp L.Am.*: ***fui ~ el médico*** I went to the doctor
dónde *interr* where; ***¿de ~ eres?*** where are you from?; ***¿hacia ~ vas?*** where are you going?
doña *f* Mrs; ***~ Estela*** Mrs Sanchez *English uses the surname while Spanish uses the first name*
dopaje, doping *m* doping; **dopar** dope; **doparse** take drugs
dorada *f* ZO gilthead
dorado gold; *montura* gilt
dormido asleep; ***quedarse ~*** fall asleep; **dormilón** *m*, **-ona** *f* F sleepyhead F; **dormir 1** *v/i* sleep; (*estar dormido*) be asleep **2** *v/t* put to sleep; ***~ a alguien*** MED give s.o. a general anesthetic *o Br* anaesthetic; **dormirse** go to sleep; (*quedarse dormido*) fall asleep; (*no despertarse*) oversleep; **dormitorio** *m* bedroom
dorsal 1 *adj* dorsal **2** *m* DEP number; **dorso** *m* back
dos two; ***de ~ en ~*** in twos; ***los ~*** both; ***cada ~ por tres*** all the time
dosis *f inv* dose
dotar equip (**de** with); *fondos* provide (**de** with); *cualidades* endow (**de** with); **dote** *f a novia* dowry; ***tener ~s para algo*** have a gift for sth
draga *f máquina* dredge; *barco* dredger; **dragar** dredge
drama *m* drama; **dramatizar** dramatize; **dramaturgo** *m*, **-a** *f* playwright, dramatist
drástico drastic

drenaje *m* drainage; **drenar** drain
droga *f* drug; **~ *de diseño*** designer drug; **drogadicto 1** *adj* addicted to drugs **2** *m*, **-a** *f* drug addict; **drogarse** take drugs; **drogodependencia** *f* drug dependency
droguería *f store selling cleaning and household products*
ducha *f* shower; **ducharse** have a shower, shower
duda *f* doubt; **dudar 1** *v/t* doubt **2** *v/i* hesitate (***en*** to); **dudoso** doubtful; (*indeciso*) hesitant
duelo *m* grief; (*combate*) duel
duende *m* imp
dueño *m*, **-a** *f* owner
dulce 1 *adj* sweet; *fig* gentle **2** *m* candy, *Br* sweet; **dulzura** *f tb fig* sweetness
duna *f* dune
dúplex *m* duplex (apartment)
duplicado *m/adj* duplicate; **duplicar** duplicate
duque *m* duke; **duquesa** *f* duchess
duración *f* duration; **duradero** lasting; *ropa, calzado* hard-wearing; **durante** *indicando duración* during; *indicando período* for; ***~ seis meses*** for six months; **durar** last
durazno *m L.Am.* BOT peach
Durex® *m Méx* Scotch tape®, *Br* Sellotape®
dureza *f de material* hardness; *de carne* toughness; *de clima, fig* harshness; **duro 1** *adj* hard; *carne* tough; *clima, fig* harsh; ***~ de oído*** F hard of hearing **2** *adv* hard **3** *m* five peseta coin
DVD *m* (= ***disco de video digital***) DVD

E

e *conj* (*instead of* ***y*** *before words starting with* ***i, hi***) and
ebanista *m* cabinetmaker; **ébano** *m* ebony; **ebanistería** *f* cabinetmaking
ebrio drunk
ebullición *f*: ***punto de ~*** boiling point
echar 1 *v/t* (*lanzar*) throw; (*poner*) put; *de un lugar* throw out; *humo* give off; *carta* mail, *Br tb* post; ***~ a alguien del trabajo*** fire s.o.; ***~ abajo*** pull down, destroy; ***~ la culpa a alguien*** put the blame on s.o.; ***me echó 40 años*** he thought I was 40 **2** *v/i*: ***~ a*** start to, begin to; ***~ a correr*** start *o* begin to run, start running; **echarse** (*tirarse*) throw o.s.; (*tumbarse*) lie down; (*ponerse*) put on; ***~ a llorar*** start *o* begin to cry, start crying
eclesiástico ecclesiastical, church *atr*

eclipse *m* eclipse
eco *m* echo; ***tener ~*** *fig* make an impact
ecografía *f* (ultrasound) scan
ecología *f* ecology; **ecológico** ecological; *alimentos* organic; (*que no daña el medio ambiente*) environmentally friendly; **ecologista** *m/f* ecologist
economía *f* economy; *ciencia* economics *sg*; ***~ de mercado*** market economy; ***~ sumergida*** black economy; **económico** economic; (*barato*) economical; **economista** *m/f* economist; **economizar** economize on, save
Ecuador Ecuador
ecuador *m* equator
ecuatorial equatorial
ecuatoriano 1 *adj* Ecuadorean **2** *m*, **-a** *f* Ecuadorean
eczema *m* eczema
edad *f* age; ***la Edad Media*** the Middle Ages *pl*; ***la tercera ~*** the over 60s; ***a la ~ de*** at the age of; ***¿qué ~ tienes?*** how old are you?, what age are you?
edición *f* edition
edicto *m* edict
edificación *f* construction, building; **edificar** construct, build; **edificio** *m* building
editar edit; (*publicar*) publish; **editor** *m*, **~a** *f* editor; **editorial 1** *m* editorial, leading article **2** *f* publishing company, publisher
edredón *m* eiderdown
educación *f* (*crianza*) upbringing; (*modales*) manners *pl*; ***~ física*** physical education, PE; **educado** polite; ***mal ~*** rude; **educativo** educational; **educar** educate; (*criar*) bring up; *voz* train
EE.UU. (= ***Estados Unidos***) US(A) (= United States (of America))
efectivo 1 *adj* effective; ***hacer ~*** COM cash **2** *m*: ***en ~*** (in) cash; **efecto** *m* effect; ***~ invernadero*** greenhouse effect; ***~s secundarios*** side effects; ***en ~*** indeed; ***surtir ~*** take effect, work; **efectuar** carry out
eficacia *f* efficiency; **eficaz** (*efectivo*) effective; (*eficiente*) efficient; **eficiencia** *f* efficiency; **eficiente** efficient
efusivo effusive
egipcio 1 *adj* Egyptian **2** *m*, **-a** *f* Egyptian; **Egipto** Egypt
egoísmo *m* selfishness, egoism; **egoísta 1** *adj* selfish, egoistic **2** *m/f* egoist
eje *m* axis; *de auto* axle; *fig* linchpin
ejecución *f* (*realización*) implementation, carrying out; *de condenado* execution; MÚS performance; **ejecutar** (*realizar*) carry out, implement; *condenado* execute; INFOR run, execute; MÚS play, perform; **ejecutiva** *f* executive; **ejecutivo 1** *adj* executive; ***el poder ~*** POL the executive **2** *m* executive;

el Ejecutivo the government

ejemplar 1 *adj alumno etc* model *atr*, exemplary **2** *m de libro* copy; *de revista* issue; *animal, planta* specimen; **ejemplo** *m* example; ***dar buen ~*** set a good example; ***por ~*** for example

ejercer 1 *v/t cargo* practice, *Br* practise; *influencia* exert **2** *v/i de profesional* practice, *Br* practise; **ejercicio** *m* exercise; COM fiscal year, *Br* financial year; ***hacer ~*** exercise; **ejercitar** *músculo, derecho* exercise; **ejercitarse** train; ***~ en*** practice, *Br* practise

ejército *m* army

el 1 *art* the **2** *pron*: ***~ de...*** that of ...; ***~ de Juan*** Juan's; ***~ que está...*** the one who is ...

él *sujeto* he; *cosa* it; *complemento* him; *cosa* it; ***de ~*** his; ***es ~*** it's him

elaborar produce, make; *metal etc* work; *plan* devise, draw up

elasticidad *f* elasticity; **elástico 1** *adj* elastic **2** *m* elastic; (*goma*) elastic band

elección *f* choice; **electo** elect; **elector** *m* voter; **electoral** election *atr*, electoral

electricidad *f* electricity; **electricista** *m/f* electrician; **eléctrico** *luz, motor* electric; *aparato* electrical; **electrizar** *tb fig* electrify

electrodoméstico *m* electrical appliance

electrónica *f* electronics; **electrónico** electronic; ***libro ~*** e-book, electronic book; ***comercio ~*** e-business;

electrotecnia *f* electrical engineering

elefante *m* elephant; ***~ marino*** elephant seal, sea elephant

elegancia *f* elegance; **elegante** elegant

elegir choose; *por votación* elect

elemental (*esencial*) fundamental, essential; (*básico*) elementary, basic; **elemento** *m* element

elepé *m* LP, album

elevación *f* elevation; **elevado** high; *fig* elevated; **elevador** *m* hoist; *L.Am.* elevator, *Br* lift; **elevar** raise; **elevarse** rise; *de monumento* stand

eliminar eliminate; *desperdicios* dispose of; **eliminatoria** *f* DEP qualifying round, heat

élite *f* elite

ella *sujeto* she; *cosa* it; *complemento* her; *cosa* it; ***de ~*** her; ***es de ~*** it's hers; ***es ~*** it's her

ellas *sujeto* they; *complemento* them; ***de ~*** their; ***es de ~*** it's theirs; ***son ~*** it's them

ello it

ellos *sujeto* they; *complemento* them; ***de ~*** their; ***es de ~*** it's theirs; ***son ~*** it's them

elocuencia *f* eloquence; **elocuente** eloquent

elogiar praise; **elogio** *m* praise; **elogioso** full of praise, highly complimentary

El Salvador El Salvador

eludir evade, avoid

emanar 1 *v/i fml* emanate (***de*** from) *fml*; *fig* stem (***de*** from) **2** *v/t* exude, emit

emancipación *f* emancipation; **emanciparse** become emancipated

embadurnar smear (***de*** with)

embajada *f* embassy; **embajador** *m*, **~a** *f* ambassador

embalaje *m* packing; *paquete* packaging; **embalar** pack

embalse *m* reservoir

embarazada 1 *adj* pregnant **2** *f* pregnant woman; **embarazo** *m* pregnancy; ***interrupción del ~*** termination, abortion; **embarazoso** awkward, embarrassing

embarcación *f* vessel, craft; **embarcadero** *m* wharf; **embarcar 1** *v/t pasajeros* board, embark; *mercancías* load **2** *v/i* board, embark; **embarcarse** *en barco* board, embark; *en avión* board; ***~ en*** *fig* embark on; **embarco** *m* embarkation

embargar JUR seize; *fig* overwhelm; **embargo** *m* embargo; JUR seizure; ***sin ~*** however

embarque *m* boarding; *de mercancías* loading

embaucar trick, deceive

embelesar captivate

embellecer make more beautiful; **embellecerse** grow more beautiful

embestir charge (***contra*** at)

emblema *m* emblem; **emblemático** emblematic

embolia *f* MED embolism

émbolo *m* TÉC piston

embolsar, embolsarse pocket

emborrachar make drunk, get drunk; **emborracharse** get drunk

emboscada *f* ambush

embotellamiento *m* traffic jam; **embotellar** bottle

embragar AUTO **1** *v/t* engage **2** *v/i* engage the clutch; **embrague** *m* AUTO clutch

embriagar *fig* intoxicate; **embriaguez** *f* intoxication

embrión *m* embryo; **embrionario** embryonic

embrollar muddle, mix up; **embrollarse** get complicated; *de hilos* get tangled up; **embrollo** *m* tangle; *fig* mess, muddle

embromar *Rpl* F (*molestar*) annoy

embrujar *tb fig* bewitch

embudo *m* funnel

embuste *m* lie; **embustero 1** *adj* deceitful **2** *m*, **-a** *f* liar

emergencia *f* emergency

emerger emerge

emigración *f* emigration; **emigrante** *m* emigrant; **emigrar** emigrate; ZO migrate

eminente eminent

emisión *f* emission; COM is-

sue; RAD, TV broadcast; **emisora** *f* radio station; **emitir** *calor, sonido* give out, emit; *moneda* issue; *opinión* express, give; *veredicto* deliver; RAD, TV broadcast; *voto* cast
emoción *f* emotion; ***¡qué ~!*** how exciting!; **emocionado** excited; **emocionante** (*excitante*) exciting; (*conmovedor*) moving; **emocionar** excite; (*conmover*) move; **emocionarse** get excited; (*conmoverse*) be moved
emotivo emotional; (*conmovedor*) moving
empalagoso sickly; *fig* sickly sweet
empalmar 1 *v/t* connect, join **2** *v/i* connect, join up (***con*** with); *de idea, conversación* follow on (***con*** from); **empalme** *m* TÉC connection; *de carreteras* intersection, *Br* junction
empanada *f* pie; **empanar** coat in breadcrumbs
empapado soaked; **empapar** soak; (*absorber*) soak up
empapelar wallpaper
empaquetar pack
emparedado *m* sandwich
empastar *muela* fill; *libro* bind; **empaste** *m* filling
empatar tie, *Br* draw; (*igualar*) tie the game, *Br* equalize; **empate** *m* tie, draw; ***gol del ~*** *en fútbol* equalizer
empedernido inveterate, confirmed
empedrado *m* paving; **empedrar** pave
empeine *m* instep
empeñar pawn; **empeñarse** (*endeudarse*) get into debt; (*esforzarse*) make an effort (***en*** to); ***~ en hacer*** *obstinarse* insist on doing, be determined to do
empeño *m* (*obstinación*) determination; (*esfuerzo*) effort; *Méx lugar* pawn shop
empeoramiento *m* deterioration, worsening; **empeorar 1** *v/t* make worse **2** *v/i* deteriorate, get worse
emperador *m* emperor; *pez* swordfish; **emperatriz** *f* empress
empezar start, begin; ***~ a hacer algo*** start to do sth, start doing sth; ***~ por hacer algo*** start *o* begin by doing sth; **empiezo** *m S.Am.* start, beginning
empinado steep
emplasto *m* MED poultice; *fig* soggy mess
emplazamiento *m* site, location; JUR subpena, *Br* subpœna
empleado 1 *adj*: ***le está bien ~*** it serves him right **2** *m*, **-a** *f* employee; ***-a de hogar*** maid; **emplear** (*usar*) use; *persona* employ; **empleo** *m* employment; (*puesto*) job; (*uso*) use; ***modo de ~*** instructions *pl* for use
empobrecerse become impoverished, become poor; **empobrecimiento** *m* im-

poverishment
empollar F cram F, *Br* swot F; **empollón** *m* F grind F, *Br* swot F
empotrado built-in, fitted
emprendedor enterprising; **emprender** embark on, undertake; **~*la con alguien*** F take it out on s.o.
empresa *f* company; *fig* venture, undertaking; **empresaria** *f* businesswoman; **empresarial** business *atr*; ***ciencias ~es*** business studies; **empresario** *m* businessman
empujar push; *fig* urge on; **empujón** *m* push, shove; **empuje** *m* push; *fig* drive
empuñar grasp
en (*dentro de*) in; (*sobre*) on; ***~ inglés*** in English; ***~ la calle*** on the street, *Br tb* in the street; ***~ casa*** at home; ***~ coche / tren*** by car / train
enagua(s) *f(pl)* petticoat
enajenar JUR transfer; (*trastornar*) drive insane
enamorado in love (***de*** with); **enamorarse** fall in love (***de*** with)
enano 1 *adj* tiny; *perro, árbol* miniature, dwarf *atr* **2** *m* dwarf
encabezamiento *m* heading; **encabezar** head; *movimiento* lead
encadenar chain (up); *fig* link together
encajar 1 *v/t piezas* fit; *golpe* take **2** *v/i* fit (***en*** in; ***con*** with); **encaje** *m* lace
encalar whitewash
encallar MAR run aground
encantado (*contento*) delighted; *castillo* enchanted; ***¡~!*** nice to meet you; **encantador** charming; **encantar:** ***me / le encanta*** I love / he loves it; **encanto** *m* (*atractivo*) charm; ***como por ~*** as if by magic; ***eres un ~*** you're an angel
encarcelar put in prison, imprison
encarecer put up the price of; **encarecerse** become more expensive; *de precios* increase, rise; **encarecidamente:** ***le ruego ~ que...*** I beg you to ... ; **encarecimiento** *m de precios* increase, rise; (*alabanza*) (exaggerated) praise; (*empeño*) insistence
encargado *m*, **-a** *f* person in charge; *de un negocio* manager; **encargar** (*pedir*) order; ***le encargé que me trajera...*** I asked him to bring me ...; **encargarse** (*tener responsibilidad*) be in charge; ***yo me encargo de la comida*** I'll take care of the food; **encargo** *m* job, errand; COM order; ***¿te puedo hacer un ~?*** can I ask you to do something for me?; ***hecho por ~*** made to order
encarnado red; **encarnar** *cualidad etc* embody; TEA play
encéfalo *m* brain

encendedor *m* lighter; **encender 1** *v/t fuego* light; *luz, televisión* switch on, turn on; *fig* inflame, arouse; **encendido 1** *adj luz, televisión* (switched) on; *fuego* lit; *cara* red **2** *m* AUTO ignition
encerar polish, wax
encerrar lock up, shut up; (*contener*) contain
enchufar ELEC plug in; **enchufe** *m* ELEC *macho* plug; *hembra* outlet, *Br* socket; ***tener ~*** *fig* F have connections
encía *f* gum
enciclopedia *f* encyclopedia
encierro *m protesta* sit-in; *de toros* bull running
encima on top; ***~ de*** on top of, on; ***por ~ de*** over, above; ***por ~ de todo*** above all; ***hacer algo muy por ~*** do sth very quickly; ***no lo llevo ~*** I haven't got it on me; ***ponerse algo ~*** put sth on; **encimera** *f sábana* top sheet; *Esp mostrador* worktop
encina *f* holm oak
encinta pregnant
encogerse *de material* shrink; *fig*: *de persona* be intimidated, cower; ***~ de hombros*** shrug (one's shoulders)
encolerizarse get angry
encomendar entrust (***a*** to); **encomendarse** commend o.s. (***a*** to)
encomienda *f L.Am.* HIST *grant of land and labor by colonial authorities after the Conquest*
encontrar find; **encontrarse** (*reunirse*) meet; (*estar*) be; ***~ con alguien*** meet s.o., run into s.o.; ***me encuentro bien*** I'm fine
encorvado *persona, espalda* stooped
encorvar hunch; *estantería* buckle
encuadernación *f* binding; **encuadernar** bind
encubridor *m*, **~a** *f* accessory after the fact; **encubrir** *delincuente* harbor, *Br* harbour; *delito* cover up
encuentro *m* meeting, encounter; DEP game; ***salir o ir al ~ de alguien*** meet s.o.; ***~s online*** online dating
encuesta *f* survey; (*sondeo*) (opinion) poll
encurtidos *mpl* pickles
endeble weak, feeble
enderezar straighten out; **enderezarse** straighten up; *fig* straighten o.s. out, sort o.s out
endeudarse get into debt
endibia *f* BOT endive
endosar COM endorse; ***me lo endosó a mí*** F she landed me with it F
endrina *f* BOT sloe
endulzar sweeten; (*suavizar*) soften
endurecer harden; *fig* toughen up; **endurecerse** harden, become harder; *fig* become harder, toughen up
enebro *m* BOT juniper
eneldo *m* BOT dill

enema *m* MED enema
enemigo 1 *adj* enemy *atr* **2** *m* enemy; ***ser ~ de*** *fig* be opposed to, be against; **enemistad** *f* enmity; **enemistarse** fall out
energético *crisis* energy *atr*; *alimento* energy-giving; **energía** *f* energy; ***~ solar*** solar power, solar energy; **enérgico** energetic; *fig* forceful, strong
enero *m* January
enfadado annoyed (***con*** with); (*encolerizado*) angry (***con*** with); **enfadar** (*molestar*) annoy; (*encolerizar*) make angry, anger; **enfadarse** (*molestarse*) get annoyed (***con*** with); (*encolerizarse*) get angry (***con*** with); **enfado** *m* (*molestia*) annoyance; (*cólera*) anger
énfasis *m* emphasis; ***poner ~ en*** emphasize, stress; **enfático** emphatic
enfermar 1 *v/t* drive crazy **2** *v/i* get sick, *Br tb* get ill; **enfermedad** *f* illness, disease; **enfermería** *f sala* infirmary, sickbay; *carrera* nursing; **enfermero** *m*, **-a** *f* nurse; **enfermizo** unhealthy; **enfermo 1** *adj* sick, ill **2** *m*, **-a** *f* sick person
enfilar *camino* take; *perlas* string
enfocar *cámara* focus; *imagen* get in focus; *fig*: *asunto* look at; **enfoque** *m fig* approach
enfrentamiento *m* clash, confrontation; **enfrentar** confront, face up to; **enfrentarse** DEP meet; ***~ con alguien*** confront s.o.; ***~ a algo*** face (up to) sth
enfrente opposite; ***~ de*** opposite
enfriar *vino* chill; *algo caliente* cool (down); *fig* cool; **enfriarse** (*perder calor*) cool down; (*perder demasiado calor*) get cold, go cold; *fig* cool, cool off; MED catch a cold
enfurecerse get furious
enganchar hook; F *novia, trabajo* land F; **engancharse** get caught (***en*** on); MIL sign up, enlist; ***~ a la droga*** F get hooked on drugs F
engañar 1 *v/t* deceive, cheat; (*ser infiel a*) cheat on; **engaño** *m* (*mentira*) deception, deceit; (*ardid*) trick; **engañoso** *persona* deceitful; *apariencias* deceptive
engatusar F sweet-talk F
engendrar father; *fig* breed, engender *fml*
englobar include, embrace
engordar 1 *v/t* put on, gain **2** *v/i de persona* put on weight; *de comida* be fattening; **engorde** *m* fattening (up)
engorroso tricky
engranaje *m* TÉC gears *pl*; *fig* machinery; **engranar** mesh, engage
engrandecer enlarge; (*ensalzar*) praise; **engrandecerse** grow in stature

engrasar grease, lubricate; **engrase** *m* greasing, lubrication
engreído conceited
engrosar 1 *v/t* swell, increase **2** *v/i* put on weight
engullir bolt (down)
enhorabuena *f* congratulations *pl*; ***dar la ~*** congratulate (***por*** on)
enigma *m* enigma; **enigmático** enigmatic
enjabonar soap
enjambre *m tb fig* swarm
enjaular cage; *fig* jail, lock up
enjuagar rinse; **enjuague** *m acto* rinsing; *líquido* mouthwash
enjugar *deuda etc* wipe out; *líquido* mop up; *lágrimas* wipe away
enjuto lean, thin
enlace *m* link, connection; ***~ matrimonial*** marriage
enlazar 1 *v/t* link (up), connect; *L.Am. con cuerda* rope, lasso **2** *v/i de carretera* link up; AVIA, FERR connect
enloquecer 1 *v/t* drive crazy *o* mad **2** *v/i* go crazy *o* mad
enlutar plunge into mourning; **enlutarse** go into mourning
enmarañar *pelo* tangle; *asunto* complicate, muddle
enmascarar hide, disguise
enmendar *asunto* rectify, put right; JUR, POL amend; ***~le la plana a alguien*** find fault with what s.o. has done; **enmienda** *f* POL amendment
enmohecerse go moldy *o Br* mouldy; *de metal* rust
enmudecer 1 *v/t* silence **2** *v/i* fall silent
enojar (*molestar*) annoy; *L.Am.* (*encolerizar*) make angry; **enojarse** *L.Am.* (*molestarse*) get annoyed; (*encolerizarse*) get angry; **enojo** *m L.Am.* anger; **enojoso** (*delicado*) awkward; (*aburrido*) tedious, tiresome
enorgullecerse be proud (***de*** of)
enorme enormous, huge
enredadera *f* BOT creeper, climbing plant
enredar 1 *v/t* tangle, get tangled; *fig* complicate **2** *v/i* make trouble; **enredo** *m* tangle; (*confusión*) mess, confusion; (*intriga*) intrigue; *amoroso* affair
enrejar *ventana* put bars on
enriquecer make rich; *fig* enrich; **enriquecerse** get rich; *fig* be enriched
enrojecer 1 *v/t* turn red **2** *v/i* blush, go red; **enrojecerse** go red
enrollar roll up; *cable* coil; *hilo* wind; ***me enrolla*** F I like it, I think it's great
ensaimada *f* GASTR *pastry in the form of a spiral*
ensalada *f* GASTR salad
ensalzar extol, praise
ensamblar assemble
ensanchar widen; *prenda* let out; **ensanche** *m de carretera* widening; *de ciudad* new

suburb
ensañarse show no mercy (***con*** to)
ensayar test, try (out); TEA rehearse; **ensayo** *m* TEA rehearsal; *escrito* essay; ***~ general*** dress rehearsal
enseguida immediately, right away
ensenada *f* inlet, cove
enseñanza *f* teaching; ***~ primaria*** elementary education, *Br* primary education; ***~ secundaria*** *o* ***media*** secondary education; ***~ superior*** higher education; **enseñar** (*dar clases*) teach; (*mostrar*) show
ensillar saddle
ensimismado deep in thought
ensordecedor deafening; **ensordecer 1** *v/t* deafen **2** *v/i* go deaf
ensuciar (get) dirty; *fig* tarnish; **ensuciarse** get dirty; *fig* get one's hands dirty
ensueño *m*: ***de ~*** *fig* fairy-tale *atr*, dream *atr*
entablar strike up, start
entallado tailored, fitted
entarimado *m* (*suelo*) floorboards *pl*; (*plataforma*) stage, platform; **entarimar** floor
ente *m* (*ser*) being, entity; F (*persona rara*) oddball F; (*organización*) body
entender understand; ***~ de algo*** know about sth; **entenderse** communicate; ***a ver si nos entendemos*** let's get this straight; ***yo me entiendo*** I know what I'm doing; ***~ con alguien*** get along with s.o.; **entendido 1** *adj* understood; ***tengo ~ que*** I understand that **2** *m*, **-a** *f* expert, authority; **entendimiento** *m* understanding; (*inteligencia*) mind
enterado knowledgeable, well-informed; ***estar ~ de*** know about; ***darse por ~*** get the message; **enterarse** find out, hear (***de*** about); ***¡para que te enteres!*** F so there! F; ***¡se va a enterar!*** F he's in for it! F
enteramente entirely
entereza *f* fortitude
entero 1 *adj* whole, entire; (*no roto*) intact; ***por ~*** completely, entirely **2** *m* (*punto*) point
enterrador *m*, **~a** *f* gravedigger; **enterramiento** *m* burial; **enterrar** bury; ***~ a todos*** outlive everybody
entibiar, entibiarse *tb fig* cool down
entidad *f* entity, body
entierro *m* burial; (*funeral*) funeral
entoldado *m de tienda* awning; *para fiesta* tent, *Br* marquee
entonación *f* intonation; **entonar 1** *v/t* intone, sing; *fig* F perk up **2** *v/i* sing in tune
entonces then; ***por ~, en aquel ~*** in those days, at that

time

entorno *m* environment

entorpecer hold up, hinder; *paso* obstruct; *entendimiento* dull

entrada *f acción* entry; *lugar* entrance; *localidad* ticket; *pago* deposit; *de comida* starter; ***de ~*** from the outset; **entradas** *fpl* receding hairline; **entrante 1** *adj mes etc* next, coming **2** *m* GASTR starter

entrañas *fpl* entrails

entrar 1 *v/i para indicar acercamiento* come in, enter; *para indicar alejamiento* go in, enter; *caber* fit; INFOR log on *o* in; ***me entró frío / sueño*** I got cold / sleepy, I began to feel cold / sleepy; ***este tipo no me entra*** I don't like the look of the guy **2** *v/t para indicar acercamiento* bring in; *para indicar alejamiento* take in

entre *dos cosas, personas* between; *más de dos* among(st); *expresando cooperación* between; ***la relación ~ ellos*** the relationship between them

entreabierto half-open

entreacto *m* TEA interval

entrecortado *habla* halting; *respiración* difficult, labored, *Br* laboured

entredicho *m*: ***poner en ~*** call into question, question

entrega *f* handing over; *de mercancías* delivery; (*dedicación*) dedication; ***~ a domicilio*** (home) delivery; ***~ de premios*** prize-giving; ***hacer ~ de algo a alguien*** present s.o. with sth; **entregar** give, hand over; *trabajo, deberes* hand in; *mercancías* deliver; *premio* present; **entregarse** give o.s. up; ***~ a*** *fig* dedicate o.s. to

entrelazar interweave

entremeses *mpl* GASTR appetizers, hors d'oeuvres

entremeter insert

entrenador *m*, **~a** *f* coach; **entrenamiento** *m* coaching; **entrenar, entrenarse** train

entresuelo *m* mezzanine; TEA dress circle

entretanto meanwhile, in the meantime

entretener 1 *v/t* (*divertir*) entertain, amuse; (*retrasar*) detain; (*distraer*) distract **2** *v/i* be entertaining; **entretenerse** (*divertirse*) amuse o.s.; (*distraerse*) keep o.s. busy; (*retrasarse*) linger; **entretenido** (*divertido*) entertaining, enjoyable; ***estar ~*** *ocupado* be busy; **entretenimiento** *m* entertainment, amusement

entretiempo *m*: ***de ~*** *ropa* mid-season; *CSur* DEP half time

entrever make out, see

entrevista *f* interview; **entrevistar** interview; **entrevistarse: *~ con alguien*** meet (with) s.o.

entristecer sadden
entrometerse meddle (**en** in); **entrometido 1** *part* ☞ ***entrometerse* 2** *adj* meddling *atr*, interfering **3** *m* meddler, busybody
entumecerse go numb, get stiff
enturbiar *tb fig* cloud
entusiasmado excited; **entusiasmar** excite, make enthusiastic; **entusiasmarse** get excited, get enthusiastic (**con** about); **entusiasmo** *m* enthusiasm; **entusiasta 1** *adj* enthusiastic **2** *m/f* enthusiast
enumerar list, enumerate
enunciar state
envasar *en botella* bottle; *en lata* can; *en paquete* pack; **envase** *m* container; *botella* (empty) bottle; ***~ de cartón*** carton
envejecer age
envenenar *tb fig* poison
envergadura *f* AVIA wingspan; MAR breadth; *fig* magnitude, importance; ***de gran o mucha ~*** *fig* of great importance
enviado *m*, **-a** *f* POL envoy; *de un periódico* reporter, correspondent; **enviar** send
envidia *f* envy, jealousy; ***me da ~*** I'm envious *o* jealous; ***tener ~ a alguien de algo*** envy s.o. sth; **envidiar** envy; ***~ a alguien por algo*** envy s.o. sth; **envidioso** envious, jealous; **envidiable** enviable
envío *m* shipment
envoltorio *m* wrapper; **envoltura** *f* cover, covering; *de regalo* wrapping; *de caramelo* wrapper
envolver wrap (up); (*rodear*) surround; (*involucrar*) involve; ***~ a alguien en algo*** involve s.o. in sth
enyesar *pared* plaster; MED put in plaster
enzima *f o m* BIO enzyme
eólico wind *atr*; ***parque ~*** wind farm
epidemia *f* epidemic
epilepsia *f* MED epilepsy; **epiléptico 1** *adj* epileptic **2** *m*, **-a** *f* epileptic
epílogo *m* epilog, *Br* epilogue
episcopal episcopal
episodio *m* episode
época *f* time, period; *parte del año* time of year; GEOL epoch; ***hacer ~*** be epoch-making
equilibrado well-balanced; **equilibrar** balance; **equilibrio** *m* balance; FÍS equilibrium; **equilibrista** *m/f* acrobat; *con cuerda* tightrope walker
equinoccio *m* equinox
equipaje *m* baggage, luggage; ***~ de mano*** hand baggage
equipamiento *m*: ***~ de serie*** AUTO standard features *pl*; **equipar** equip (**con** with)
equiparar put on a level (***a o con*** with); ***~ algo con algo*** *fig* compare sth to sth
equipo *m* DEP team; *acceso-*

rios equipment; *~ de música o de sonido* sound system
equitación *f* riding
equitativo fair, equitable
equivalente *m/adj* equivalent; **equivaler** be equivalent (**a** to)
equivocación *f* mistake; ***por ~*** by mistake; **equivocado** wrong; **equivocar:** ***~ a alguien*** make s.o. make a mistake; **equivocarse** make a mistake; ***te has equivocado*** you are wrong *o* mistaken; ***~ de número*** TELEC get the wrong number; **equívoco 1** *adj* ambiguous, equivocal **2** *m* misunderstanding; (*error*) mistake
era *f* era
erección *f* erection; **erecto** erect
erguir raise, lift; (*poner derecho*) straighten; **erguirse** *de persona* stand up, rise; *de edificio* rise
erial *m* uncultivated land
erigir erect
erizado bristling (**de** with); **erizarse** *de pelo* stand on end; **erizo** *m* ZO hedgehog; ***~ de mar*** ZO sea urchin
ermita *f* chapel; **ermitaño 1** *m* ZO hermit crab **2** *m*, **-a** *f* hermit
erosión *f* erosion
erótico erotic; **erotismo** *m* eroticism
erradicar eradicate, wipe out
errante wandering; **errar 1** *v/t* miss; ***~ el tiro*** miss **2** *v/i* miss; ***~ es humano*** to err is human; **errata** *f* mistake, error; *de imprenta* misprint, typo
erróneo wrong, erroneous *fml*; **error** *m* mistake, error; ***~ de cálculo*** error of judg(e)ment
eructar belch F, burp F
erudito 1 *adj* learned, erudite **2** *m* scholar
erupción *f* GEOL eruption; MED rash
esa ☞ ***ese***
ésa ☞ ***ése***
esbeltez *f* slimness; **esbelto** slim
esbozar sketch; *proyecto etc* outline; **esbozo** *m* sketch; *de proyecto etc* outline
escabeche *m type of marinade*
escabroso rough; *problema* tricky; *relato* indecent
escabullirse escape, slip away
escafandra *f* diving suit; AST space suit
escala *f tb* MÚS scale; AVIA stopover; ***~ de cuerda*** rope ladder; ***~ de valores*** scale of values; ***a ~*** to scale, life-sized
escalada *f* DEP climb, ascent; ***~ de los precios*** increase in prices; **escalador** *m*, **~a** *f* climber; **escalar** climb
escaldar GASTR blanch; *manos* scald
escalera *f* stairs *pl*, staircase; ***~ de caracol*** spiral staircase; ***~ de incendios*** fire escape;

~ de mano ladder; ***~ mecánica*** escalator; **escalerilla** *f de avión* steps *pl*; *en barco* gangway
escalofriante horrifying; **escalofrío** *m* shiver
escalón *m* step; *de escalera de mano* rung
escalope *m* escalope
escama *f* ZO scale; *de jabón, piel* flake; **escamar** scale; *fig* make suspicious
escamotear (*ocultar*) hide, conceal; (*negar*) withhold
escandalizar shock, scandalize; **escandalizarse** be shocked; **escándalo** *m* scandal; (*jaleo*) racket, ruckus; ***armar un ~*** make a scene; **escandaloso** scandalous; (*ruidoso*) noisy, rowdy
escandinavo 1 *adj* Scandinavian **2** *m*, **-a** *f* Scandinavian
escanear scan; **escáner** *m* scan
escaño *m* POL seat
escapada *f* escape; **escapar** escape (***de*** from); ***dejar ~*** *oportunidad* pass up; *suspiro* let out, give; **escaparse** (*huir*) escape (***de*** from); *de casa* run away (***de*** from); ***~ de*** *situación* get out of
escaparate *m* store window
escape *m de gas* leak; AUTO exhaust; ***salir a ~*** rush out
escarabajo *m* ZO beetle
escarbar 1 *v/i tb fig* dig around (***en*** in) **2** *v/t* dig around in
escarcha *f* frost
escardar hoe
escarlata *m/adj inv* scarlet
escarmentar 1 *v/t* teach a lesson to **2** *v/i* learn one's lesson
escarnecer deride; **escarnio** *m* derision
escarpado sheer, steep
escasear be scarce; **escasez** *f* shortage, scarcity; **escaso** *recursos* limited; ***andar ~ de algo*** *falto* be short of sth; ***-as posibilidades de*** not much chance of; ***falta un mes ~*** it's barely a month away
escatimar be mean with; ***no ~ esfuerzos*** spare no effort
escayola *f* (plaster) cast; **escayolar** put in a (plaster) cast
escena *f* scene; *escenario* stage; ***entrar en ~*** come on stage; ***hacer una ~*** *fig* make a scene; **escenario** *m* stage; *fig* scene; **escenificar** stage; **escenografía** *f arte* set design; (*decorados*) scenery
escepticismo *m* skepticism, *Br* scepticism; **escéptico 1** *adj* skeptical, *Br* sceptical **2** *m*, **-a** *f* skeptic, *Br* sceptic
esclarecer throw *o* shed light on; *misterio* clear up
esclavitud *f* slavery; **esclavo** *m* slave
esclusa *f* lock
escoba *f* broom; **escobilla** *f* small brush; AUTO wiper blade
escocer sting, smart

escocés 1 *adj* Scottish **2** *m* Scot, Scotsman; **escocesa** *f* Scot, Scotswoman; **Escocia** Scotland
escoger choose, select
escolar 1 *adj* school *atr* **2** *m/f* student; **escolarización** *f* education, schooling; **escolarizar** educate
escollo *m* MAR reef; (*obstáculo*) hurdle, obstacle
escolta 1 *f* escort **2** *m/f motorista* outrider; (*guardaespaldas*) bodyguard; **escoltar** escort
escombros *mpl* rubble
esconder hide, conceal; **esconderse** hide; **escondidas** *fpl S.Am.* hide-and-seek; ***a ~*** in secret; **escondite** *m* hiding place; *juego* hide-and--seek; **escondrijo** *m* hiding place
escopeta *f* shotgun; ***~ de aire comprimido*** air gun, air rifle
escoria *f* slag; *desp* dregs *pl*
Escorpio *m/f inv* ASTR Scorpio; **escorpión** *m* ZO scorpion
escotado low-cut; **escote** *m* neckline; *de mujer* cleavage
escotilla *f* MAR hatch
escozor *m* burning sensation, stinging; *fig* bitterness
escribir write; (*deletrear*) spell; ***~ a máquina*** type; **escrito 1** *part* ☞ ***escribir*** **2** *adj* written; ***por ~*** in writing **3** *m* document; ***~s*** writings; **escritor** *m*, **~a** *f* writer; **escritorio** *m* desk; ***artículos de ~*** stationery; **escritura** *f* writing; JUR deed; ***Sagradas Escrituras*** Holy Scripture
escrúpulo *m* scruple; ***sin ~s*** unscrupulous; **escrupuloso** (*cuidadoso*) meticulous; (*honrado*) scrupulous; (*aprensivo*) fastidious
escrutar scrutinize; *votos* count
escuadra *f* MAT set square; *de carpintero* square; MIL squad; MAR squadron; DEP *de portería* top corner
escuchar 1 *v/t* listen to; *L.Am.* (*oír*) hear **2** *v/i* listen
escudo *m arma* shield; *insignia* badge; *moneda* escudo; ***~ de armas*** coat of arms
escuela *f* school; ***~ de comercio*** business school; ***~ de idiomas*** language school; ***~ primaria*** elementary school, *Br* primary school
escueto succinct, concise
escultor *m*, **~a** *f* sculptor; **escultura** *f* sculpture
escupir 1 *v/i* spit **2** *v/t* spit out
escurridizo slippery; *fig* evasive; **escurrir 1** *v/t ropa* wring out; *platos, verduras* drain **2** *v/i de platos* drain; *de ropa* drip-dry; **escurrirse** *de líquido* drain away; (*deslizarse*) slip; (*escaparse*) slip away
ese, esa, esos, esas that; *pl* those
ése, ésa, ésos, ésas *pron singular* that (one); *pl* those

(ones)
esencia *f* essence; **esencial** essential
esfera *f* sphere; **esférico 1** *adj* spherical **2** *m* DEP F ball
esforzar strain; **esforzarse** make an effort, try hard; **esfuerzo** *m* effort; ***sin ~*** effortlessly
esfumarse F *tb fig* disappear
esgrima *f* fencing; **esgrimir** *arma* wield; *fig*: *argumento* put forward
esguince *m* sprain
eslabón *m* link; ***el ~ perdido*** the missing link
eslogan *m* slogan
eslovaco 1 *adj* Slovak(ian) **2** *m*, **-a** *f* Slovak **3** *m idioma* Slovak; **Eslovaquia** Slovakia
Eslovenia Slovenia; **esloveno 1** *adj* Slovene, Slovenian **2** *m*, **-a** *f* Slovene, Slovenian **3** *m idioma* Slovene
esmaltar enamel; ***~ las uñas*** put nail polish on; **esmalte** *m* enamel; ***~ de uñas*** nail polish, nail varnish
esmerado meticulous
esmeralda *f* emerald
esmerarse take great care (***en*** over)
esmerilar grind
esmero *m* care
esnob 1 *adj* snobbish **2** *m* snob; **esnobismo** *m* snobbishness
eso that; ***en ~*** just then; ***~ mismo, ~ es*** that's it, that's the way; ***a ~ de las dos*** at around two; ***por ~*** that's why; ***¿y ~?*** why's that?
esófago *m* ANAT esophagus, *Br* oesophagus
espabilado (*listo*) bright, smart; (*vivo*) sharp
espacial *cohete*, *viaje* space *atr*; FÍS, MAT spatial; **espacio** *m* space; TV program, *Br* programme; ***~ de tiempo*** space of time; ***~ vital*** living space; **espacioso** spacious, roomy
espada *f* sword; ***~s*** (*en naipes*) *suit in Spanish deck of cards*
espaguetis *mpl* spaghetti *sg*
espalda *f* back; ***a ~s de alguien*** behind s.o.'s back; ***de ~s a*** with one's back to; ***por la ~*** from behind; ***nadar a ~*** swim backstroke
espantajo *m* scarecrow; *fig* sight; **espantapájaros** *m inv* scarecrow; **espantar 1** *v/t* (*asustar*) frighten, scare; (*ahuyentar*) frighten away; F (*horrorizar*) horrify; **espanto** *m* (*susto*) fright; *L.Am.* (*fantasma*) ghost; ***nos llenó de ~*** *desagrado* we were horrified; ***¡qué ~!*** how awful!; ***de ~*** terrible; **espantoso** horrific; *para enfatizar* terrible, dreadful; ***hace un calor ~*** it's incredibly hot
España Spain; **español 1** *adj* Spanish **2** *m*, **-a** *f* Spaniard; ***los ~es*** the Spanish **3** *m idioma* Spanish; **españolismo** *m* (*afición*) love of Spain;

cualidad Spanishness
esparadrapo *m* Band-Aid®, *Br* (sticking) plaster
esparcir *papeles* scatter; *rumor* spread; **esparcirse** *de papeles* be scattered; *de rumor* spread
espárrago *m* asparagus
esparto *m* BOT esparto grass
espasmo *m* spasm
especia *f* spice
especial special; (*difícil*) fussy; ***en ~*** especially; **especialidad** *f* specialty, *Br* speciality; **especialista** *m/f* specialist; *en cine* stuntman; *mujer* stuntwoman; **especializarse** specialize (***en*** in); **especialmente** specially
especie *f* BIO species *sg*; (*tipo*) kind, sort
especificar specify; **específico** specific
espectacular spectacular; **espectáculo** *m* TEA show; (*escena*) sight; ***dar el ~*** *fig* make a spectacle of o.s.; **espectador** *m*, **~a** *f en cine etc* member of the audience; DEP spectator; (*observador*) on-looker
espectro *m* FÍS spectrum; (*fantasma*) ghost
especular speculate
espejismo *m* mirage; **espejo** *m* mirror; ***~ retrovisor*** rear-view mirror
espeluznante horrific, horrifying
espera *f* wait; ***sala de ~*** waiting room; ***en ~ de*** pending; ***estar a la ~ de*** be waiting for
esperanza *f* hope; ***~ de vida*** life expectancy
esperar 1 *v/t* (*aguardar*) wait for; *con esperanza* hope; (*suponer, confiar en*) expect **2** *v/i* (*aguardar*) wait
esperma *f* sperm
espeso thick; *vegetación, niebla* thick, dense; **espesor** *m* thickness
espía *m/f* spy; **espiar 1** *v/t* spy on **2** *v/i* spy
espiga *f* BOT ear, spike
espina *f de planta* thorn; *de pez* bone; ***~ dorsal*** spine, backbone
espinacas *fpl* spinach
espinilla *f de la pierna* shin; *en la piel* pimple, spot
espino *m* BOT hawthorn; **espinoso** *tb fig* thorny
espionaje *m* spying, espionage
espiral *f/adj* spiral (*atr*)
espirar exhale
espíritu *m* spirit; **espiritual** spiritual
espléndido splendid, magnificent; (*generoso*) generous; **esplendor** *m* splendor, *Br* splendour
espliego *m* lavender
esponja *f* sponge; **esponjoso** spongy; *toalla* soft, fluffy
espontáneo spontaneous
esposa *f* wife; **esposas** *fpl* (*manillas*) handcuffs *pl*; **esposo** *m* husband
esprint *m* sprint
espuma *f* foam; *de jabón* lath-

er; *de cerveza* froth; **~ de afeitar** shaving foam; **~ moldeadora** styling mousse; **espumoso** frothy, foamy; *caldo* sparkling
esquela *f aviso* death notice, obituary
esqueleto *m* skeleton; *Méx, C.Am., Pe, Bol fig* blank form
esquema *m* (*croquis*) sketch, diagram; (*sinopsis*) outline, summary
esquí *m* ski; *deporte* skiing; **~ de fondo** cross-country skiing; **~ náutico** o **acuático** waterskiing; **esquiador** *m*, **~a** *f* skier; **esquiar** ski
esquina *f* corner
esquirol *m/f* strikebreaker, scab F
esquivar avoid, dodge F
esquizofrenia *f* schizophrenia; **esquizofrénico** schizophrenic
esta ☞ **este**[2]
estabilidad *f* stability; **estable** stable
establecer establish; *negocio* set up; **establecimiento** *m* establishment
establo *m* stable
estaca *f* stake
estación *f* station; *del año* season; **~ espacial** *o* **orbital** space station; **~ de invierno** *o* **invernal** winter resort; **~ de servicio** service station; **~ de trabajo** INFOR work station; **estacionamiento** *m* AUTO *acción* parking; *L.Am. parking* parking lot, *Br* car park; **estacionar** AUTO park
estadio *m* DEP stadium
estadística *f cifra* statistic; *ciencia* statistics *sg*
estado *m* state; MED condition; **~ civil** marital status; **en buen ~** in good condition; **el Estado** the State; **~ del bienestar** welfare state; **los Estados Unidos** (**de América**) the United States (of America)
estadounidense **1** *adj* American, US *atr* **2** *m/f* American
estafa *f* swindle, cheat; **estafador** *m*, **~a** *f* con artist F, fraudster; **estafar** cheat (**a** out of)
estallar explode; *de guerra* break out; *de escándalo* break; **estalló en llanto** she burst into tears; **estallido** *m* explosion; *de guerra* outbreak
estampa *f de libro* illustration; (*aspecto*) appearance; REL prayer card; **estampado** *tejido* patterned; **estampar** *sello* put; *tejido* print; *pasaporte* stamp
estampilla *f L.Am.* stamp
estancar *río* dam up; *fig* bring to a standstill; **estancarse** stagnate; *fig* come to a standstill
estancia *f* stay; *Rpl* (*hacienda*) farm, ranch
estanco **1** *adj* watertight **2** *m shop selling cigarettes etc*

estándar *m* standard; **estandarizar** standardize
estandarte *m* standard, banner
estanque *m* pond
estante *m* shelf; **estantería** *f* shelves *pl*; *para libros* bookcase
estaño *m* tin
estar be; ***¿está Javier?*** is Javier in?; ***estamos a 3 de enero*** it's January 3rd; ***ahora estoy con Vd.*** I'll be with you in just a moment; **~ *a bien / mal con alguien*** be on good / bad terms with s.o.; **~ *de*** *ocupación* work as, be; **~ *en algo*** be working on sth; **~ *para hacer algo*** be about to do sth; ***no ~ para algo*** not be in a mood for sth; ***está por hacer*** it hasn't been done yet; ***¡ya estoy!*** I'm ready!; ***¡ya está!*** that's it!; **estarse** stay; **~ *quieto*** keep still
estatal state *atr*
estatua *f* statue; **estatura** *f* height; **estatuto** *m* statute; **~*s*** articles of association
este[1] *m* east
este[2], **esta, estos, estas** this; *pl* these
éste, ésta, éstos, éstas this (one); *pl* these (ones)
estela *f* MAR wake; AVIA, *fig* trail
estepa *f* steppe
estera *f* mat
estéreo stereo
estéril MED sterile; *trabajo, esfuerzo etc* futile; **esterilizar** *tb persona* sterilize
esterlina: ***libra* ~** pound sterling
esteticista *m/f* beautician; **estético** esthetic, *Br* aesthetic
estiércol *m* dung; (*abono*) manure
estigma *m tb fig* stigma
estilo *m* style; ***algo por el* ~** something like that; ***son todos por el* ~** they're all the same
estilográfica *f* fountain pen
estima *f* esteem, respect; **estimación** *f* (*cálculo*) estimate; (*estima*) esteem, respect; **estimar** respect, hold in high regard; ***estimo conveniente que*** I consider it advisable to
estimulante 1 *adj* stimulating **2** *m* stimulant; **estimular** stimulate; (*animar*) encourage; **estímulo** *m* stimulus; (*incentivo*) incentive
estío *m literario* summertime
estipulación *f* stipulation
estirar stretch; (*alisar*) smooth out; **estirón** *m* (*tirón*) tug; ***dar un* ~** F *de niño* shoot up
estirpe *f* stock
estival summer *atr*
esto this; **~ *es*** that is to say; ***por* ~** this is why; ***a todo* ~** (*mientras tanto*) meanwhile; (*a propósito*) incidentally
estofado stewed
estómago *m* stomach
Estonia Estonia; **estonio 1**

adj Estonian **2** *m*, **-a** *f* Estonian **3** *m idioma* Estonian
estorbar 1 *v/t* (*dificultar*) hinder **2** *v/i* get in the way; **estorbo** *m* hindrance
estornino *m* ZO starling
estornudar sneeze
estragón *m* BOT tarragon
estragos *mpl* devastation; ***causar ~ entre*** wreak havoc among
estrambótico F eccentric; *ropa* outlandish
estrangular strangle
estratagema *f* stratagem; **estrategia** *f* strategy; **estratégico** strategic
estrato *m fig* stratum
estrechar 1 *v/t ropa* take in; *mano* shake; ***~ entre los brazos*** hug, embrace; **estrecho 1** *adj* narrow; (*apretado*) tight; *amistad* close; ***~ de miras*** narrow-minded **2** *m* strait, straits *pl*
estrella *f tb de cine etc* star; ***~ fugaz*** falling star; ***~ de mar*** ZO starfish; ***~ polar*** Pole star; **estrellarse** crash (***contra*** into)
estremecer shock, shake; **estremecerse** shake, tremble; *de frío* shiver; *de horror* shudder; **estremecimiento** *m* shaking, trembling; *de frío* shiver; *de horror* shudder
estreñimiento *m* constipation
estrépito *m* noise, racket; **estrepitoso** noisy
estrés *m* stress; **estresado** stressed out; **estresar** stress; **estresante** stressful
estría *f en piel* stretch mark
estribo *m* stirrup; ***perder los ~s*** *fig* fly off the handle F
estribor *m* MAR starboard
estricto strict
estridente shrill, strident
estrofa *f* stanza, verse
estropeado (*averiado*) broken; **estropear** *aparato* break; *plan* ruin, spoil
estructura *f* structure
estruendo *m* racket, din
estrujar F crumple up; *trapo* wring out; *persona* squeeze
estuche *m* case, box
estuco *m* stucco work
estudiante *m/f* student; **estudiar** study; **estudio** *m disciplina* study; *apartamento* studio, *Br* studio flat; *de cine, música* studio; **estudioso** studious
estufa *f* heater
estupefaciente *m* narcotic (drug); **estupefacto** stupefied, speechless
estupendo fantastic, wonderful
estupidez *f cualidad* stupidity; *acción* stupid thing; **estúpido 1** *adj* stupid **2** *m*, **-a** *f* idiot
esturión *m* ZO sturgeon
etapa *f* stage
eternidad *f* eternity; **eterno** eternal; ***la película se me hizo -a*** the movie seemed to go on for ever
etiqueta *f* label; (*protocolo*)

etiquette
eucalipto *m* BOT eucalyptus
Europa Europe; **europeo 1** *adj* European **2** *m*, **-a** *f* European
eusquera *m/adj* Basque
evacuación *f* evacuation; **evacuar** evacuate
evadir avoid; *impuestos* evade; **evadirse** *tb fig* escape
evaluación *f* evaluation, assessment; (*prueba*) test; **evaluar** assess, evaluate
evangélico evangelical; **evangelio** *m* gospel
evaporación *f* evaporation; **evaporarse** evaporate; *fig* F vanish into thin air
evasión *f tb fig* escape; ***~ de capitales*** flight of capital; ***~ fiscal*** tax evasion; **evasiva** *f* evasive reply; **evasivo** evasive
evento *m* event; **eventual** possible; *trabajo* casual, temporary; ***en el caso ~ de*** in the event of; **eventualidad** *f* eventuality
evidencia *f* evidence, proof; ***poner en ~*** demonstrate; ***poner a alguien en ~*** show s.o. up; **evidente** evident, clear
evitable avoidable; **evitar** avoid; (*impedir*) prevent; *molestias* save; ***no puedo ~lo*** I can't help it
evocar evoke
evolución *f* BIO evolution; (*desarrollo*) development; **evolucionar** BIO evolve; (*desarrollar*) develop
exactitud *f* accuracy; **exacto** accurate, exact; ***¡~!*** exactly!, precisely!
exageración *f* exaggeration; **exagerar** exaggerate
exaltado excited, worked up; **exaltarse** get excited, get worked up (***por*** about)
examen *m* test, exam; MED examination; (*análisis*) study; ***~ de conducir*** driving test; **examinar** examine; **examinarse** take an exam
excavación *f* excavation; **excavadora** *f* digger; **excavar** excavate; *túnel* dig
excedente 1 *adj* surplus; *empleado* on extended leave of absence **2** *m* surplus; **exceder** exceed; **excederse** go too far, get carried away
excelencia *f* excellence; ***Su Excelencia la...*** Her Excellency the ...; ***por ~*** par excellence; **excelente** excellent
excéntrico 1 *adj* eccentric **2** *m*, **-a** *f* eccentric
excepción *f* exception; ***a ~ de*** except for; **excepcional** exceptional; **excepto** except; **exceptuar** except; ***exceptuando*** with the exception of, except for
excesivo excessive; **exceso** *m* excess; ***~ de equipaje*** excess baggage; ***~ de velocidad*** speeding; ***en ~*** in excess, too much
excitación *f* excitement, agi-

tation; **excitante 1** *adj* exciting; ***una bebida ~*** a stimulant **2** *m* stimulant; **excitar** excite; *sentimientos, sexualmente* arouse; **excitarse** get excited; *sexualmente* become aroused
exclamación *f* exclamation; **exclamar** exclaim
excluir leave out (***de*** of), exclude (***de*** from); *posibilidad* rule out; **exclusión** *f* exclusion; ***con ~ de*** with the exception of; **exclusiva** *f privilegio* exclusive rights *pl* (***de*** to); *reportaje* exclusive; **exclusivo** exclusive
excomulgar REL excommunicate
excremento *m* excrement
excursión *f* trip, excursion
excusa *f* excuse; ***~s*** apologies
excusar excuse
exento exempt (***de*** from); ***~ de impuestos*** tax-exempt, tax-free
exhausto exhausted
exhibición *f* display, demonstration; *de película* screening, showing; **exhibir** show, display; *película* screen, show; *cuadro* exhibit
exhortar exhort (***a*** to)
exigencia *f* demand; **exigente** demanding; **exigir** demand; (*requerir*) call for, demand
exiliar exile; **exiliarse** go into exile; **exilio** *m* exile; ***en el ~*** in exile
existencia *f* existence; (*vida*) life; ***~s*** COM supplies, stocks; **existir** exist; ***existen muchos problemas*** there are a lot of problems
éxito *m* success; ***~ de taquilla*** box office hit; ***tener ~*** be successful, be a success; **exitoso** successful
exótico exotic
expansión *f* expansion; (*recreo*) recreation; **expansivo** expansive
expatriarse leave one's country
expectación *f* sense of anticipation; **expectante** expectant; **expectativa** *f* (*esperanza*) expectation; ***estar a la ~ de algo*** be waiting for sth; ***~s*** (*perspectivas*) prospects
expedición *f* expedition
expediente *m* file, dossier; (*investigación*) investigation, inquiry; ***~ académico*** student record; ***~ disciplinario*** disciplinary proceedings *pl*
expedir *documento* issue; *mercancías* send, dispatch
experiencia *f* experience
experimentar 1 *v/t* try out, experiment with **2** *v/i* experiment (***con*** on); **experimento** *m* experiment
experto 1 *adj* expert; ***~ en hacer algo*** expert at doing sth **2** *m* expert (***en*** on)
expiar expiate, atone for
expirar expire
explicable explainable, explicable; **explicación** *f* ex-

planation; **explicar** explain; **explicarse** (*comprender*) understand; (*hacerse comprender*) express o.s.; **explicativo** explanatory

exploración *f* exploration; **explorador** *m*, **~a** *f* explorer; MIL scout; **explorar** explore

explosión *f* explosion; **~ *demográfica*** population explosion; ***hacer* ~** go off, explode; **explosionar** explode; **explosivo** *m/adj* explosive

explotación *f de mina, tierra* exploitation, working; *de negocio* running, operation; *de trabajador* exploitation; **explotar 1** *v/t tierra, mina* work, exploit; *situación* take advantage of, exploit; *trabajador* exploit **2** *v/i* go off, explode; *fig* explode

exponer *teoría* set out, put forward; (*revelar*) expose; *pintura* exhibit, show; (*arriesgar*) risk; **exponerse: *~ a algo*** (*arriesgarse*) lay o.s. open to sth

exportación *f* export; **exportar** export; **exportador** *m*, **~a** *f* exporter

exposición *f* exhibition; **expositor** *m*, **~a** *f* exhibitor

expresar express; **expresión** *f* expression; **expresivo** expressive

expreso 1 *adj* express *atr*; ***tren* ~** express (train) **2** *m tren* express (train); *café* espresso

exprimidor *m* lemon squeezer; *eléctrico* juicer; **exprimir** squeeze; (*explotar*) exploit

expropiar expropriate

expulsar expel, throw out F; DEP expel from the game, *Br* send off; **expulsión** *f* expulsion; DEP sending off

exquisito *comida* delicious; (*bello*) exquisite; (*refinado*) refined

éxtasis *m tb droga* ecstasy

extender *brazos* stretch out; (*untar*) spread; *tela, papel* spread out; (*ampliar*) extend; **extenderse** *de campos* stretch; *de influencia* extend; (*difundirse*) spread; (*durar*) last; *explayarse* go into detail; **extensible** extending; **extensión** *f tb* TELEC extension; *superficie* expanse, area; **extenso** extensive, vast; *informe* lengthy, long

exterior 1 *adj aspecto* external, outward; *capa* outer; *apartamento* overlooking the street; POL foreign; ***la parte* ~** the outside **2** *m* (*fachada*) exterior, outside; *aspecto* exterior, outward appearance; ***viajar al* ~** (*al extranjero*) travel abroad

exterminar exterminate, wipe out

externo 1 *adj aspecto* external, outward; *influencia* external, outside; *capa* outer; *deuda* foreign **2** *m*, **-a** *f* EDU *student who attends a boarding school but returns home each evening*, *Br* day boy / girl

extinción *f*: ***en peligro de ~*** in danger of extinction; **extinguidor** *m L.Am.*: **~ (*de incendios*)** (fire) extinguisher; **extinguir** BIO, ZO wipe out; *fuego* extinguish, put out; **extinguirse** BIO, ZO become extinct, die out; *de fuego* go out; *de plazo* expire; **extintor** *m* fire extinguisher

extirpar MED remove; *vicio* eradicate, stamp out

extorsión *f* extortion

extra 1 *adj excelente* top quality; *adicional* extra; ***horas ~*** overtime; ***paga ~*** extra month's pay **2** *m/f de cine* extra **3** *m gasto* additional expense

extracción *f* extraction; **extracto** *m* extract; (*resumen*) summary; GASTR, QUÍM extract; ***~ de cuenta*** bank statement; **extractor** *m* extractor; ***~ de humos*** extractor fan

extradición *f* extradition; **extraditar** extradite

extraer extract, pull out; *conclusión* draw

extranjero 1 *adj* foreign **2** *m*, **-a** *f* foreigner; ***en el ~*** abroad

extrañar *L.Am.* miss; **extrañarse** be surprised (***de*** at); **extrañeza** *f* strangeness; (*sorpresa*) surprise; **extraño 1** *adj* strange, odd **2** *m*, **-a** *f* stranger

extraordinario extraordinary

extraterrestre extraterrestial, alien

extraviar lose, mislay; **extraviarse** get lost, lose one's way

extremar maximize

extremaunción *f* REL extreme unction

extremidad *f* end; ***~es*** extremities; **extremista 1** *adj* extreme **2** *m/f* POL extremist; **extremo 1** *adj* extreme **2** *m* extreme; *parte primera o última* end; *punto* point; ***llegar al ~ de*** reach the point of **3** *m/f*: ***~ derecho / izquierdo*** DEP right / left wing; ***en ~*** in the extreme

exuberante exuberant; *vegetación* lush

eyacular ejaculate

F

fabada *f* GASTR *Asturian stew with pork sausage, bacon and beans*

fábrica *f* plant, factory; **fabricación** *f* manufacturing; **fabricante** *m* manufacturer, maker; **fabricar** manufacture

fabuloso fabulous

faceta *f fig* facet

facha 1 *f* look; (*cara*) face **2** *m/f desp* fascist; **fachada** *f tb fig* façade

facial facial

fácil easy; ***es ~ que*** it's likely that; **facilidad** *f* ease; ***tener ~ para algo*** have a gift for sth; ***~es de pago*** credit facilities, credit terms; **facilitar** facilitate, make easier; (*hacer factible*) make possible; *medios, dinero etc* provide
factible feasible
factor *m* factor
factoría *f esp L.Am.* plant, factory
factura *f* COM invoice; *de luz, gas etc* bill; **facturación** *f* COM invoicing; *volumen de negocio* turnover; AVIA check-in; **facturar** COM invoice, bill; *volumen de negocio* turn over; AVIA check in
facultad *f* faculty; (*autoridad*) authority
faena *f* task, job; ***hacer una ~ a alguien*** play a dirty trick on s.o.
fagot *m* MÚS bassoon
faisán *m* ZO pheasant
faja *f prenda interior* girdle
falda *f* skirt; *de montaña* side; **falda-pantalón** *f* divided skirt, culottes *pl*
falla *f* fault; *de fabricación* flaw; **fallar 1** *v/i* fail; (*no acertar*) miss; *de sistema etc* go wrong; JUR find (***en favor de*** for; ***en contra de*** against); ***~ a alguien*** let s.o. down **2** *v/t* JUR pronounce judg(e)ment in; *pregunta* get wrong; ***~ el tiro*** miss
fallecer pass away; **fallecimiento** *m* demise
fallo *m* mistake; TÉC fault; JUR judg(e)ment; ***~ cardiaco*** heart failure
falsedad *f* falseness; (*mentira*) lie; **falsificación** *f de moneda* counterfeiting; *de documentos, firma* forgery; **falsificar** *moneda* counterfeit; *documento, firma* forge, falsify; **falso** false; *joyas* fake; *documento, firma* forged; ***jurar en ~*** commit perjury
falta *f* (*escasez*) lack, want; (*error*) mistake; (*ausencia*) absence; *en tenis* fault; *en fútbol* foul; (*tiro libre*) free kick; ***hacerle ~ a alguien*** foul s.o.; ***~ de*** lack of, shortage of; ***sin ~*** without fail; ***buena ~ le hace*** it's about time; ***echar en ~ a alguien*** miss s.o.; ***hacer ~*** be necessary
faltar be missing; ***falta una hora*** there's an hour to go; ***sólo falta hacer la salsa*** there's only the sauce to do; ***~ a*** be absent from; ***~ a alguien*** be disrespectful to s.o.; ***~ a su palabra*** not keep one's word; **falto: *~ de*** lacking in, devoid of; ***~ de recursos*** short of resources
fama *f* fame; (*reputación*) reputation; ***tener mala ~*** have a bad reputation
familia *f* family; ***sentirse como en ~*** feel at home; **familiar 1** *adj* family *atr*; (*conocido*), *lenguaje* familiar **2** *m/f* relation, relative

famoso 1 *adj* famous **2** *m*, **-a** *f* celebrity
fanático 1 *adj* fanatical **2** *m*, **-a** *f* fanatic; **fanatismo** *m* fanaticism
fanfarrón 1 *adj* boastful **2** *m*, **-ona** *f* boaster; **fanfarronear** boast, brag
fango *m tb fig* mud
fantasía *f* fantasy; (*imaginación*) imagination; ***joyas de ~*** costume jewelry *o Br* jewellery; **fantasma** *m* ghost; **fantástico** fantastic
fardo *m* bundle
faringe *f* ANAT pharynx; **faringitis** *f* MED pharyngitis
farmacéutico 1 *adj* pharmaceutical **2** *m*, **-a** *f* pharmacist, *Br tb* chemist; **farmacia** *f* pharmacy, *Br tb* chemist's; *estudios* pharmacy; ***~ de guardia*** 24-hour pharmacist, *Br* emergency chemist; **fármaco** *m* medicine
faro *m* MAR lighthouse; AUTO headlight, headlamp; ***~ antiniebla*** fog light; **farol** *m* lantern; (*farola*) streetlight, streetlamp; *en juegos de cartas* bluff
farsa *f tb fig* farce; **farsante** *m/f* fraud, fake
fascinación *f* fascination; **fascinar** fascinate
fascismo *m* fascism; **fascista** *m/f & adj* fascist
fase *f* phase
fastidiar annoy; F (*estropear*) spoil; **fastidio** *m* annoyance; ***¡qué ~!*** what a nuisance!; **fastidioso** annoying
fatal 1 *adj* fatal; (*muy malo*) dreadful, awful **2** *adv* very badly; **fatalidad** *f* misfortune
fatiga *f* tiredness, fatigue; **fatigado** tired; **fatigar** tire; **fatigoso** tiring
favor *m* favor, *Br* favour; ***a ~ de*** in favor of; ***por ~*** please; ***hacer un ~*** do a favor; **favorable** favorable, *Br* favourable; **favorecer** favor, *Br* favour ; *de ropa, color* suit; **favoritismo** *m* favoritism, *Br* favouritism; **favorito 1** *adj* favorite, *Br* favourite **2** *m*, **-a** *f* favorite
fax *m* fax; ***enviar un ~ a alguien*** send s.o. a fax, fax s.o.
faz *f* face
fe *f* faith (***en*** in)
fealdad *f* ugliness
febrero *m* February
febril feverish
fecha *f* date; ***~ límite de consumo*** best before date; ***~ de nacimiento*** date of birth; **fechar** date
fecundar fertilize; **fecundidad** *f* fertility; **fecundo** fertile
federación *f* federation; **federal** federal
felicidad *f* happiness; ***¡~es!*** congratulations!; **felicitación** *f* letter of congratulations; ***¡felicitaciones!*** congratulations!; **felicitar** congratulate (***por*** on); **feliz** happy; ***¡~ Navidad!*** Merry Christmas!

felpa *f* toweling, *Br* towelling
femenino 1 *adj* feminine; *moda, equipo* women's **2** GRAM feminine; **femin(e)idad** *f* femininity; **feminismo** *m* feminism; **feminista** *m/f & adj* feminist
fenomenal 1 *adj* F fantastic F, phenomenal F **2** *adv*: ***lo pasé ~*** F I had a fantastic time F; **fenómeno 1** *m* phenomenon; *persona* genius **2** *adj* F fantastic F, great F
feo 1 *adj* ugly; *fig* nasty **2** *m*: ***hacer un ~ a alguien*** F snub s.o.
féretro *m* casket, coffin
feria *f* COM fair; *L.Am.* (*mercado*) market; *Méx* (*calderilla*) small change; ***~ de muestras*** trade fair; **feriado 1** *adj L.Am.*: ***día ~*** public holiday **2** *m L.Am.* public holiday; **ferial 1** *adj*: ***recinto ~*** fairground **2** *m* fair
fermentación *f* fermentation; **fermentar** ferment
ferocidad *f* ferocity; **feroz** fierce; (*cruel*) cruel
férreo *tb fig* iron *atr*; *del ferrocarril* rail *atr*; **ferretería** *f* hardware store; **ferrocarril** *m* railroad, *Br* railway; **ferroviario** rail *atr*
ferry *m* ferry
fértil fertile; **fertilidad** *f* fertility; **fertilizante** *m* fertilizer; **fertilizar** fertilize
ferviente *fig* fervent
festival *m* festival; ***~ cinematográfico*** film festival; **festivo** festive
fétido fetid
feto *m* fetus
fiable trustworthy; *datos, máquina etc* reliable; **fiado**: ***al ~*** F on credit; **fiador 1** *m* TÉC safety catch **2** *m*, **~a** *f* JUR guarantor
fiambre *m* cold cut, *Br* cold meat; P (*cadáver*) stiff P
fianza *f* deposit; JUR bail; ***bajo ~*** on bail
fiar give credit; **fiarse**: ***~ de alguien*** trust s.o.; ***no me fío*** I don't trust him / them *etc*
fibra *f* fiber, *Br* fibre; ***~ óptica*** optical fiber; ***~ de vidrio*** fiberglass
ficha *f* file card, index card; *en juegos de mesa* counter; *en un casino* chip; *en damas* checker, *Br* draught; *en ajedrez* man, piece; TELEC token; **fichar 1** *v/t* DEP sign; JUR open a file on **2** *v/i* DEP sign (***por*** for); **fichero** *m* file cabinet, *Br* filing cabinet; INFOR file
fidelidad *f* fidelity
fideo *m* noodle
fiebre *f* fever; (*temperatura*) temperature; ***~ del heno*** hay fever
fiel 1 *adj* faithful; (*leal*) loyal **2** *mpl*: ***los ~es*** REL the faithful *pl*
fieltro *m* felt
fiera *f* wild animal
fierro *m L.Am.* iron
fiesta *f* festival; (*reunión social*) party; (*día festivo*) pub-

lic holiday; ***estar de ~*** be in a party mood
figura *f* figure; (*estatuilla*) figurine; (*forma*) shape; *naipes* face card, *Br* picture card; **figurado** figurative; **figurante** *m*, **-a** *f en película* extra; TEA walk-on; **figurar** appear (***en*** in); **figurarse** imagine
fijación *f* fixing; (*obsesión*) fixation; **fijador** *m* FOT, PINT fixative, fixer; *para el pelo* hairspray; **fijar** fix; *cartel* stick; *fecha*, *objetivo* set; *residencia* establish; *atención* focus; **fijarse** (*establecerse*) settle; (*prestar atención*) pay attention (***en*** to); ***~ en algo*** (*darse cuenta*) notice sth; **fijo** fixed; *trabajo* permanent; *fecha* definite
fila *f* line, *Br* queue; *de asientos* row; ***en ~ india*** in single file; ***~s*** MIL ranks
filete *m* GASTR fillet
Filipinas *fpl* Philippines; **filipino 1** *adj* Philippine, Filipino **2** *m*, **-a** *f* Filipino **3** *m idioma* Philipino, Filipino
film(e) *m* movie, film; **filmación** *f* filming, shooting; **filmar** film, shoot
filólogo *m*, **-a** *f* philologist
filosofía *f* philosophy; **filosófico** philosophical; **filósofo** *m*, **-a** *f* philosopher
filtrar filter; *información* leak; **filtrarse** filter (***por*** through); *de agua*, *información* leak; **filtro** *m* filter
fin *m* end; (*objetivo*) aim, purpose; ***~ de semana*** weekend; ***a ~es de mayo*** at the end of May; ***al ~ y al cabo*** at the end of the day; ***en ~*** anyway
final *f*/*adj* final; **finalidad** *f* purpose, aim; **finalista 1** *adj*: ***las dos selecciones ~s*** the two teams that reached the final **2** *m*/*f* finalist; **finalización** *f* completion; **finalizado** complete; **finalizar** end, finish; **finalmente** eventually
financiación *f* funding; **financiar** fund, finance; **financista** *m*/*f L.Am.* financier; **finanzas** *fpl* finances
finca *f* (*bien inmueble*) property; *L.Am.* (*granja*) farm
finés 1 *adj* Finnish **2** *m*, **-esa** Finn **3** *m idioma* Finnish
fineza *f cualidad* fineness; *dicho* compliment
fingir pretend, feign *fml*
finlandés 1 *adj* Finnish **2** *m*, **-esa** *f* Finn **3** *m idioma* Finnish; **Finlandia** Finland
fino *calidad* fine; *libro*, *tela* thin; (*esbelto*) slim; *modales*, *gusto* refined; *sentido de humor* subtle; **finura** *f de calidad* fineness; *de tela* thinness; (*esbeltez*) slimness; *de modales*, *gusto* refinement; *de sentido de humor* subtlety
firma *f* signature; *acto* signing; COM firm; **firmar** sign
firme firm; (*estable*) steady; ***en ~*** COM firm; **firmeza** *f* firmness

fiscal 1 *adj* tax *atr*, fiscal **2** *m/f* district attorney, *Br* public prosecutor
física *f* physics; **físico 1** *adj* physical **2** *m*, **-a** *f* physicist **3** *m de una persona* physique
fisioterapia *f* physical therapy, *Br* physiotherapy
fisura *f* crack; MED fracture
flác flabby
flaco thin; ***punto ~*** weak point
flamante (*nuevo*) brand-new
flamenco 1 *adj* MÚS flamenco **2** *m* MÚS flamenco; ZO flamingo
flaqueza *f fig* weakness
flash *m* FOT flash
flato *m* MED stitch
flauta *f* flute; *Méx* GASTR fried taco; ***~ dulce*** recorder; ***~ travesera*** (transverse) flute; **flautista** *m/f* flautist
flecha *f* arrow
flequillo *m del pelo* bangs *pl*, *Br* fringe
fletar charter; (*embarcar*) load
flexible flexible
flirtear flirt (***con*** with)
flojo loose; *café, argumento* weak; COM *actividad* slack; *redacción* poor; *L.Am.* (*perezoso*) lazy
flor *f* flower; **florecer** BOT flower. bloom; *de negocio, civilización* flourish; **florero** *m* vase; **florista** *m/f* florist; **floristería** *f* florist
flota *f* fleet; **flotador** *m* float; **flotar** float
fluctuación *f* fluctuation; **fluctuar** fluctuate
fluido 1 *adj* fluid; *tráfico* free-flowing; *lenguaje* fluent **2** *m* fluid; **fluir** flow; **flujo** *m* flow
fluorescente 1 *adj* fluorescent **2** *m* strip light
fluvial river *atr*
foca *f* ZO seal
foco *m* focus; TEA, TV spotlight; *de infección* center, *Br* centre; *de incendio* seat; *L.Am.* (*bombilla*) lightbulb; *de auto* headlight; *de calle* streetlight
fogón *m de cocina* stove; TÉC burner; *L.Am. fuego* bonfire
follaje *m* foliage
follar V fuck V, screw V
folleto *m* pamphlet
follón *m* argument; (*lío*) mess
fomentar foster; COM promote; *rebelión* foment, incite; **fomento** *m* COM promotion
fonda *f* cheap restaurant; (*pensión*) boarding house
fondo *m* bottom; *de sala, cuarto* back; *de pasillo* end; (*profundidad*) depth; PINT, FOT background; *de un museo* collection; COM fund; ***~ de inversión*** investment fund; ***~ de pensiones*** pension fund; ***Fondo Monetario Internacional*** International Monetary Fund; ***~s*** money, funds; ***tiene buen ~*** he's got a good heart; ***en el ~*** deep down

fontanería *f* plumbing; **fontanero** *m* plumber
footing *m* DEP jogging; ***hacer ~*** go jogging, jog
forastero 1 *adj* foreign **2** *m*, **-a** *f* outsider, stranger
forestal forest *atr*
forjar *metal* forge
forma *f* form; (*apariencia*) shape; (*manera*) way; ***de todas ~s*** in any case, anyway; ***estar en ~*** be fit; **formación** *f* formation; (*entrenamiento*) training; ***~ profesional*** vocational training; **formal** formal; *niño* well-behaved; (*responsable*) responsible; **formalidad** *f* formality; **formar** form; (*educar*) educate
formatear format; **formato** *m* format
formidable huge; (*estupendo*) tremendous
fórmula *f* formula; **formular** *teoría* formulate; *queja* make, lodge; **formulario** *m* form
forraje *m* fodder
fortalecer *tb fig* strengthen; **fortaleza** *f* strength of character; MIL fortress; **fortificación** *f* fortification; **fortificar** MIL fortify
fortuito chance *atr*, accidental
fortuna *f* fortune; (*suerte*) luck; ***por ~*** fortunately, luckily
forzado forced; **forzar** force; (*violar*) rape; **forzoso** *aterrizaje* forced
fosa *f* pit; (*tumba*) grave; ***~s nasales*** nostrils
fósforo *m* QUÍM phosphorus; *L.Am.* (*cerilla*) match
foso *m* ditch; TEA, MÚS pit; *de castillo* moat
foto *f* photo; **fotocopia** *f* photocopy; **fotocopiadora** *f* photocopier; **fotocopiar** photocopy; **fotogénico** photogenic; **fotografía** *f* photography; **fotografiar** photograph; **fotógrafo** *m*, **-a** *f* photographer
fracasado 1 *adj* unsuccessful **2** *m*, **-a** *f* loser; **fracasar** fail; **fracaso** *m* failure
fracción *f* fraction; POL faction
fractura *f* MED fracture; **fracturar** MED fracture
frágil fragile
fragmento *m* fragment; *de novela, poema* excerpt, extract
fragua *f* forge
fraile *m* friar, monk
frambuesa *f* raspberry
francés 1 *adj* French **2** *m* Frenchman; *idioma* French; **francesa** *f* Frenchwoman; **Francia** France
franco (*sincero*) frank; (*evidente*) distinct, marked; COM free
franela *f* flannel
franja *f* fringe; *de tierra* strip
franquear *carta* pay the postage on; *camino, obstáculo* clear; **franqueo** *m* postage; **franqueza** *f* frankness
frasco *m* bottle

frase *f* phrase; (*oración*) sentence; *~ **hecha*** set phrase
fraternal brotherly
fraude *m* fraud; **fraudulento** fraudulent
frecuencia *f* frequency; ***con ~*** frequently; **frecuentar** frequent; **frecuente** frequent; (*común*) common
fregadero *m* sink; **fregar** *platos* wash; *el suelo* mop; *L.Am.* F bug F; **fregona** *f* mop; *L.Am.* F pain in the neck F
freidora *f* deep fryer; **freír** fry; F (*matar*) waste P
frenar 1 *v/i* AUTO brake **2** *v/t fig* slow down; *impulsos* check; **freno** *m* brake; ***poner ~ a algo*** *fig* curb sth, check sth; ***~ de mano*** parking brake, *Br* handbrake
frente 1 *f* forehead **2** *m* MIL, METEO front; ***de ~*** *colisión* head-on; ***de ~ al grupo*** *L.Am.* facing the group; ***hacer ~ a*** face up to **3** *prp*: ***~ a*** opposite
fresa *f* strawberry
fresco 1 *adj* cool; *pescado etc* fresh; *persona* F fresh F, *Br* cheeky F **2** *m*, **-a** *f*: ***¡eres un ~!*** F you've got nerve! F **3** *m* fresh air; *C.Am. bebida* fruit drink; **frescura** *f* freshness; (*frío*) coolness; *fig* nerve
fresno *m* BOT ash tree
fresón *m* strawberry
frialdad *f tb fig* coldness
fricción *f* TÉC, *fig* friction
frigorífico 1 *adj* refrigerated **2** *m* icebox, *Br* fridge
fríjol *m*, **frijol** *m L.Am.* bean
frío 1 *adj tb fig* cold **2** *m* cold; ***tener ~*** be cold
fritar *L.Am.* fry; **frito 1** *part* ☞ ***freír*** **2** *adj* fried **3** *mpl*: ***~s*** fried food
frívolo frivolous
frontal frontal; *ataque etc* head-on; (*delantero*) front *atr*
frontera *f* border; **fronterizo** border *atr*
frotar rub
fructuoso *fig* fruitful
fruncir *material* gather; ***~ el ceño*** frown
frustración *f* frustration; **frustrar** frustrate; *plan* thwart; **frustrarse** fail
fruta *f* fruit; **frutal 1** *adj* fruit *atr* **2** *m* fruit tree; **frutería** *f* fruit store, *Br* greengrocer's; **frutilla** *f S.Am.* strawberry; **fruto** *m tb fig* fruit; *nuez, almendra etc* nut; ***~s secos*** nuts
fuego *m* fire; ***¿tienes ~?*** do you have a light?; ***~s artificiales*** fireworks; ***pegar*** *o* ***prender ~ a*** set fire to
fuel(-oil) *m* fuel oil
fuelle *m* bellows *pl*
fuente *f* fountain; *recipiente* dish; *fig* source
fuera 1 *vb* ☞ ***ir, ser*** **2** *adv* outside; (*en otro lugar*) away; (*en otro país*) abroad; ***por ~*** on the outside; ***¡~!*** get out! **3** *prp*: ***~ de*** outside; ***¡sal ~ de aquí!*** get out of here!; ***~***

del país abroad

fuerte 1 *adj* strong; *dolor* intense; *lluvia* heavy; *aumento* sharp; *ruido* loud; *fig* P incredible F **2** *adv* hard **3** *m* MIL fort; **fuerza** *f* strength; (*violencia*) force; ELEC power; **~ *aérea*** air force; **~ *de voluntad*** willpower; **~*s armadas*** armed forces; **~*s de seguridad*** security forces; ***a ~ de*** by (dint of)

fuga *f* escape; *de gas, agua* leak; ***darse a la ~*** flee; **fugarse** run away; *de la cárcel* escape; **fugaz** *fig* fleeting; **fugitivo 1** *adj* runaway *atr* **2** *m*, **-a** *f* fugitive

fulana *f* so-and-so; F (*prostituta*) hooker P; **fulano** *m* so-and-so

fulminante sudden

fumador *m*, **~a** *f* smoker; **fumar** smoke

función *f* purpose, function; *en el trabajo* duty; TEA performance; ***en ~ de*** according to; **funcional** functional; **funcionamiento** *m* working; **funcionar** work; ***no funciona*** out of order; **funcionario** *m*, **-a** *f* government employee, civil servant

funda *f* cover; *de gafas* case; *de almohada* pillowcase

fundación *f* foundation; **fundador** *m*, **~a** *f* founder

fundamental fundamental; **fundamentalismo** *m* fundamentalism; **fundamentalista** *m/f* fundamentalist; **fundamentalmente** fundamentally; **fundamento** *m* foundation; **~*s*** (*nociones*) fundamentals; **fundar** *fig* base (***en*** on); **fundarse** be based (***en*** on)

fundición *f* smelting; (*fábrica*) foundry; **fundir** *hielo* melt; *metal* smelt; COM merge; **fundirse** melt; *de bombilla* fuse; *de plomos* blow; COM merge; *L.Am. de empresa* go under

fúnebre funeral *atr*, *fig*: *ambiente* gloomy; **funeral** *m* funeral; **funeraria** *f* funeral parlor, *Br* undertaker's

funesto disastrous

funicular *m* funicular; (*teleférico*) cable car

furcia *f* P whore P

furgón *m* van; FERR boxcar, *Br* goods van; **~ *de equipajes*** baggage car, *Br* luggage van; **furgoneta** *f* van

furia *f* fury; **furioso** furious; **furor** *m*: ***hacer ~*** *fig* be all the rage F

furtivo furtive

fusible *m* ELEC fuse

fusil *m* rifle; **fusilamiento** *m* execution (*by firing squad*); **fusilar** shoot; *fig* F (*plagiar*) lift F

fusión *f* FÍS fusion; COM merger; **fusionar** COM merge; **fusionarse** merge

fútbol *m* soccer, *Br* football; **~ *americano*** football, *Br* American football; **~ *sala***

five-a-side soccer; **futbolín** *m* Foosball®, table football; **futbolista** *m/f* soccer player, *Br* footballer, *Br* football player

futuro *m/adj* future (*atr*)

G

gabardina *f prenda* raincoat; *material* gabardine

gabinete *m* (*despacho*) office; *en una casa* study; POL cabinet; *L.Am. de médico* office, *Br* surgery

gafas *fpl* glasses; ***~ de sol*** sunglasses

gaita *f* MÚS bagpipes *pl*

gala *f* gala; ***traje de ~*** formal dress

galante gallant

galardón *m* award; **galardonar:** ***fue galardonado con...*** he was awarded ...

galería *f* gallery; ***~ de arte*** art gallery

galgo *m* greyhound

gallego 1 *adj* Galician; *Rpl* F Spanish **2** *m*, **-a** *f* Galician; *Rpl* F Spaniard **3** *m idioma* Galician

galleta *f* cookie, *Br* biscuit

gallina 1 *f* hen **2** *m* F chicken; **gallinero** *m* henhouse

gallo *m* rooster, *Br* cock

galopar gallop; **galope** *m* gallop

gama *f* range

gamba *f* shrimp, *Br* prawn

gamberro *m*, **-a** *f* troublemaker

gamo *m* fallow deer

gamuza *f* chamois

gana *f*: ***de mala ~*** unwillingly, grudgingly; ***no me da la ~*** I don't want to; ***... me da ~s de*** ... makes me want to; ***tener ~s de*** (***hacer***) ***algo*** feel like (doing) sth

ganadería *f* stockbreeding; **ganadero** *m*, **-a** *f* stockbreeder; **ganado** *m* cattle *pl*

ganador *m* winner; **ganancia** *f* profit; **ganar 1** *v/t* win; *mediante el trabajo* earn **2** *v/i mediante el trabajo* earn; (*vencer*) win; (*mejorar*) improve; **ganarse** earn; *a alguien* win over; ***~ la vida*** earn a living

ganchillo *m* crochet; **gancho** *m* hook; *L.Am., Arg fig* F sex-appeal; ***hacer ~*** *L.Am.* (*ayudar*) lend a hand; ***tener ~*** F *de un grupo, una campaña* be popular; *de una persona* have that certain something

gandul *m* lazybones *sg*

ganga *f* bargain

ganso *m* goose; *macho* gander

garaje *m* garage

garantía *f* guarantee; **garantizar** guarantee

garapiñado candied

garbanzo *m* BOT chickpea

garbo *m al moverse* grace
garganta *f* ANAT throat; GEOG gorge; **gargantilla** *f* choker
gárgaras *fpl*: ***hacer ~*** gargle
garra *f* claw; *de ave* talon; ***caer en las ~s de alguien*** *fig* fall into s.o.'s clutches; ***tener ~*** F be compelling
garrafa *f* carafe
garrapata *f* ZO tick
garza *f* ZO heron
gas *m* gas; ***~es*** MED gas, wind; ***con ~*** carbonated, *Br* fizzy; ***sin ~*** still
gasa *f* gauze
gaseosa *f* lemonade; **gasoducto** *m* gas pipeline; **gasoil, gasóleo** *m* oil; *para motores* diesel; **gasolina** *f* gas, *Br* petrol; **gasolinera** *f* gas station, *Br* petrol station
gastar *dinero* spend; *energía, electricidad etc* use; (*llevar*) wear; (*desperdiciar*) waste; (*desgastar*) wear out; ***¿qué número gastas?*** what size do you take?; **gastarse** *dinero* spend; *de gasolina, agua* run out of; *de pila* run down; *de ropa, zapatos* wear out;
gasto *m* expense
gastronomía *f* gastronomy; **gastrónomo** *m*, **-a** *f* gastronome
gata *f* (female) cat; *Méx* servant, maid; ***a ~s*** F on all fours; **gatear** crawl
gatillo *m* trigger
gato *m* cat; AUTO jack; ***cuatro ~s*** a handful of people
gavilán *m* sparrowhawk
gaviota *f* (sea)gull
gay *m/adj* gay
gazpacho *m* gazpacho (*cold soup made with tomatoes, peppers, garlic etc*)
gel *m* gel
gelatina *f* gelatin(e); GASTR Jell-O®, *Br* jelly
gemelo 1 *adj* twin *atr* **2** *mpl*: ***~s*** twins; *de camisa* cuff links; (*prismáticos*) binoculars
Géminis *m/f inv* ASTR Gemini
gemir moan, groan
generación *f* generation
generador *m* ELEC generator
general 1 *adj* general; ***en ~*** in general; ***por lo ~*** generally **2** *m* general; **generalidad** *f* (*mayoría*) majority; (*vaguedad*) general nature; **generalizar 1** *v/t* make more widespread **2** *v/i* generalize; **generalmente** generally
generar generate
género *m* (*tipo*) type; *de literatura* genre; GRAM gender; COM goods *pl*, merchandise
generosidad *f* generosity; **generoso** generous
genética *f* genetics; **genéticamente** genetically; ***~ modificado*** genetically modified; **genético** genetic; **genetista** *m/f* geneticist
genial brilliant; F (*estupendo*) fantastic F, great F; **genio** *m* genius; (*carácter*) temper; ***tener mal ~*** be bad-tempered
genitales *mpl* genitals

gente *f* people *pl*; *L.Am.* (*persona*) person
gentil kind, courteous; REL Gentile; **gentileza** *f* kindness; ***por ~ de*** by courtesy of
gentío *m* crowd
geografía *f* geography; **geografico** geographical
geología *f* geology; **geologico** geological; **geólogo** *m*, **-a** *f* geologist
geometría *f* geometry; **geometrico** geometrical
geranio *m* geranium
gerencia *f* management; *oficina* manager's office; **gerente** *m/f* manager
geriatría *f* geriatrics
germano 1 *adj* Germanic **2** *m*, **-a** *f* German
germen *m* germ; **germinar** *tb fig* germinate
gesticular gesticulate
gestión *f* management; ***gestiones*** (*trámites*) formalities, procedure; **gestionar** *trámites* take care of; *negocio* manage
gesto *m* gesture; (*expresión*) expression
gestoría *f Esp agency offering clients help with official documents*
giba *f* hump, hunch
gigante *m/adj* giant (*atr*); **gigantesco** gigantic
gilipollas *m/f inv* P jerk P
gilipollez *f Esp* V bullshit V
gimnasia *f* gymnastics; ***hacer ~*** do exercises; **gimnasio** *m* gymnasium, gym
ginebra *f* gin
ginecólogo *m*, **-a** *f* gynecologist, *Br* gynaecologist
gira *f* tour; **girar 1** *v/i* turn; *alrededor de algo* revolve; *fig* (*tratar*) revolve (***en torno a*** around) **2** *v/t* COM transfer; **girasol** *m* BOT sunflower; **giratorio** revolving; **giro** *m* turn; GRAM idiom; ***~ postal*** COM money order
gitano 1 *adj* gypsy *atr* **2** *m*, **-a** *f* gypsy
glacial icy; **glaciar** *m* glacier
glándula *f* ANAT gland
glaucoma *m* MED glaucoma
glicerina *f* glycerin(e)
global global; *visión, resultado* overall; *cantidad* total; **globalización** f globalization;
globo *m aerostático, de niño* balloon; *terrestre* globe; ***~ terráqueo*** globe
gloria *f* glory; (*delicia*) delight; ***estar en la ~*** F be in seventh heaven; **glorificar** glorify; **glorioso** glorious
glosa *f* gloss; **glosar** gloss; **glosario** *m* glossary
glotón 1 *adj* greedy **2** *m*, **-ona** *f* glutton
glucosa *f* glucose
glúteo *m* gluteus
gobernador *m* governor; **gobernar** rule, govern; **gobierno** *m* government
goce *m* pleasure, enjoyment
gol *m* DEP goal
golf *m* DEP golf
golfillo *m* (street) urchin
golfista *m/f* golfer

golfo 1 *m* GEOG gulf **2** *m*, **-a** *f* good-for-nothing; *niño* little devil; **Golfo de California** Gulf of California; **Golfo de México** Gulf of Mexico
golondrina *f* ZO swallow
golosina *f* candy, *Br* sweet; **goloso** sweet-toothed
golpe *m* knock, blow; ***~ de Estado*** coup d'état; ***de ~*** suddenly; ***no da ~*** F she doesn't do a thing; **golpear** hit
goma *f* (*caucho*) rubber; (*pegamento*) glue; (*banda elástica*) rubber band; F (*preservativo*) condom, rubber P; *C.Am.* F (*resaca*) hangover; ***~ (de borrar)*** eraser; ***~ espuma*** foam rubber
gonorrea *f* gonorrhea, *Br* gonorrhoea
gordo 1 *adj* fat **2** *m*, **-a** *f* fat person **3** *m premio* jackpot; **gordura** *f* fat
gorila *m* gorilla
gorra *f* cap; ***de ~*** F for free F
gorrino *m fig* pig
gorrión *m* sparrow
gorro *m* cap; ***estar hasta el ~ de algo*** F be fed up to the back teeth with sth F
gorrón *m*, **-ona** *f* F scrounger
gota *f* drop; ***ni ~*** F not a drop; *de pan* not a scrap; **gotear** drip; *filtrarse* leak; **gotera** *f* leak; (*mancha*) stain
gótico *m*/*adj* Gothic
gozar enjoy o.s.; ***~ de*** (*disfrutar de*) enjoy; (*poseer*) have, enjoy; **gozo** *m* (*alegría*) joy; (*placer*) pleasure; **gozoso** happy
grabación *f* recording; **grabado** *m* engraving; **grabadora** *f* tape recorder; **grabar** *video etc* record; PINT, *fig* engrave
gracia *f*: ***tener ~*** (*ser divertido*) be funny; (*tener encanto*) be graceful; ***me hace ~*** I think it's funny; ***dar las ~s a alguien*** thank s.o.; ***~s*** thank you; **gracioso** funny
gradas *fpl* DEP stands, grandstand; **graderío** *m* stands
grado *m* degree; ***de buen ~*** with good grace, readily
graduación *f* TÉC *etc* adjustment; *de alcohol* alcohol content; EDU graduation; MIL rank; **gradual** gradual; **gradualmente** gradually; **graduar** TÉC *etc* adjust; ***~ las gafas*** *o* ***la vista*** have one's eyes tested; **graduarse** graduate, get one's degree
gráfico 1 *adj* graphic **2** *m* MAT graph; INFOR graphic; **grafista** *m*/*f* graphic designer
gragea *f* tablet, pill
gramática *f* grammar; **gramático** grammatical
gramo *m* gram
Gran Bretaña Great Britain
gran *short form of* **grande** *before a noun*
granada *f* BOT pomegranate; ***~ de mano*** MIL hand grenade
grande 1 *adj* big; ***a lo ~*** in

style **2** *m/f L.Am.* (*adulto*) grown-up, adult; (*mayor*) eldest; ***pasarlo en ~*** F have a great time; **grandeza** *f* greatness; **grandioso** magnificent
grandilocuente grandiloquent
granel *m*: ***vender a ~*** COM sell in bulk
granizado *m type of soft drink made with crushed ice*; **granizar** hail; **granizo** *m* hail
granja *f* farm
grano *m* grain; *de café* bean; *en la piel* pimple, spot
granuja *m* rascal
grapa *f* staple; **grapadora** *f* stapler
grasa *f* BIO, GASTR fat; *lubricante, suciedad* grease; ***sin ~s*** fat-free; **grasiento** greasy; **graso** greasy; *carne* fatty; ***de bajo contenido ~*** low-fat
gratificación *f* gratification; **gratificar** reward; **gratificante** gratifying
gratinar cook au gratin
gratis free; **gratitud** *f* gratitude; **gratuito** free
grato pleasant
grava *f* gravel
gravamen *m* tax; **gravar** tax
grave serious; *tono* grave, solemn; *nota* low; *voz* deep; ***estar ~*** be seriously ill; **gravedad** *f* seriousness, gravity; FÍS gravity
gravilla *f* grave
gravitación *f* gravitation
Grecia Greece
gremio *m* (*oficio manual*) trade; (*profesión*) profession
gres *m* (*arcilla*) earthenware; *para artesano* potter's clay
gresca *f* (*pelea*) fight; (*escándalo*) uproar
griego **1** *adj* Greek **2** *m*, **-a** *f* Greek **3** *m idioma* Greek
grieta *f* crack
grifo **1** *adj Méx* F high **2** *m* faucet, *Br* tap; *Pe* (*gasolinera*) gas station, *Br* petrol station
grillo *m* ZO cricket
gripe *f* flu, influenza
gris gray, *Br* grey
gritar shout, yell; **griterío** *m* shouting; **grito** *m* cry, shout; ***a ~ pelado*** at the top of one's voice; ***pedir algo a ~s*** F be crying out for sth
grosella *f* redcurrant
grosería *f* rudeness; **grosero** **1** *adj* rude **2** *m*, **-a** *f* rude person
grúa *f* crane; AUTO wrecker, *Br* breakdown truck
grueso thick; *persona* stout
grulla *f* ZO crane
gruñir (*quejarse*) grumble; *de perro* growl; *de cerdo* grunt
grupo *m* group
gruta *f* cave; *artificial* grotto
guacho **1** *adj S.Am.* (*sin casa*) homeless; (*huérfano*) orphaned **2** *m*, **-a** *f S.Am. sin casa* homeless person; (*huérfano*) orphan
guadaña *f* scythe
guagua *f W.I., Ven, Canaries*

bus; *Pe, Bol, Chi* (*niño*) baby
guante *m* glove; **guantera** *f* AUTO glove compartment
guapo *hombre* handsome, good-looking; *mujer* beautiful; *S.Am.* (*valiente*) bold, gutsy F
guarda *m/f* keeper; **guardabarros** *m inv* AUTO fender, *Br* mudguard; **guardabosques** *m/f inv* forest ranger; **guardacoches** *m/f inv* parking lot attendant, *Br* car park attendant; **guardacostas** *m inv* coastguard vessel; **guardaespaldas** *m/f inv* bodyguard; **guarda jurado** security guard; **guardameta** *m/f* DEP goalkeeper
guardar keep; *poner en un lugar* put (away); *recuerdo* have; *apariencias* keep up; INFOR save; **~ *silencio*** keep silent; **guardarse** keep; **~ *de*** refrain from
guardarropa *m* checkroom, *Br* cloakroom; (*ropa, armario*) wardrobe
guardería *f* nursery
guardia 1 *f* guard; ***de*~** on duty **2** *m/f* MIL guard; (*policía*) police officer; **~ *civil*** *Esp* civil guard; **~ *de seguridad*** security guard; **~ *de tráfico*** traffic warden
guardián 1 *adj*: ***perro*~** guard dog **2** *m*, **-ana** *f* guard; *fig* guardian
guarida *f* ZO den; *de personas* hideout
guarnecer adorn (***de*** with); GASTR garnish (***con*** with); **guarnición** *f* GASTR accompaniment; MIL garrison
guarro 1 *adj* F (*sucio*) filthy **2** *m tb fig* F pig
guasa *f L.Am.* joke; ***de*~** as a joke
Guatemala Guatemala; **guatemalteco 1** *adj* Guatemalan **2** *m*, **-a** *f* Guatemalan
guateque *m* party
guay *Esp* F cool F, neat F
gubernamental governmental, government *atr*
guerra *f* war; **~ *civil*** civil war; **~ *mundial*** world war; ***dar*~ *a alguien*** F give s.o. trouble; **guerrero 1** *adj* warlike **2** *m* warrior; **guerrilla** *f* guerillas *pl*; **guerrillero** *m* guerilla
guía 1 *m/f* guide; **~ *turístico*** tour guide **2** *f libro* guide (book); **~ *telefónica*** *o* ***de teléfonos*** phone book; **guiar** guide
guijarro *m* pebble
guinda 1 *adj L.Am.* purple **2** *f fresca* morello cherry; *en dulce* glacé cherry
guindilla *f* GASTR chil(l)i
guiñar: ***le guiñó un ojo*** she winked at him
guión *m de película* script; GRAM *corto* hyphen; *largo* dash
guirnalda *f* garland
guisante *m* pea; **guisar** GASTR stew, casserole; **guiso** *m* GASTR stew, casserole
guitarra *f* guitar; **guitarrista**

m/f guitarist, guitar player
gusano *m* worm
gustar: *me gusta viajar* I like to travel, I like traveling; ***¿te gusta...?*** do you like ...?; ***no me gusta*** I don't like it; **gusto** *m* taste; (*placer*) pleasure; ***a ~*** at ease; ***con mucho ~*** with pleasure; ***de buen ~*** in good taste, tasteful; ***de mal ~*** in bad taste; ***mucho*** *o* ***tanto ~*** how do you do; **gustoso: *hacer algo ~*** do sth gladly
Guyana Francesa French Guyana; **Guyana** Guyana; **guyanés 1** *adj* Guyanese **2** *m*, **-esa** *f* Guyanese

H

haba *f* broad bean
Habana: *La ~* Havana; **habanero 1** *adj* of / from Havana, Havana *atr* **2** *m*, **-a** *f* citizen of Havana; **habano 1** *adj* of / from Havana, Havana *atr* **2** *m*, **-a** *f* citizen of Havana **3** *m* Havana (cigar)
haber 1 *v/aux* have; ***hemos llegado*** we've arrived; ***he de levantarme pronto*** I have to *o* I've got to get up early; ***has de ver*** *Méx* you ought to see it **2** *v/impers*: ***hay*** there is *sg*, there are *pl*; ***hubo un incendio*** there was a fire; ***¿qué hay?***, *Méx* ***¿qué hubo?*** how's it going?; ***hay que hacerlo*** it has to be done; ***no hay de qué*** not at all **3** *m* asset; *pago* fee; *de cuenta bancaria* credit
habichuela *f* kidney bean
hábil skilled; (*capaz*) capable; (*astuto*) clever, smart; **habilidad** *f* skill; (*capacidad*) ability; (*astucia*) cleverness; **habilitar** *lugar* fit out; *persona* authorize
habitable habitable; **habitación** *f* room; (*dormitorio*) bedroom; ***~ doble / individual*** double / single room; **habitante** *m/f* inhabitant; **habitar** live (***en*** in)
hábito *m tb* REL habit; (*práctica*) knack; **habitual 1** *adj* usual, regular **2** *m/f* regular; **habituar: *~ a alguien a algo*** get s.o. used to sth; **habituarse: *~ a algo*** get used to sth
habla *f* speech; ***¡al ~!*** TELEC speaking; ***quedarse sin ~*** *fig* be speechless; **hablada** *f L.Am.* piece of gossip; ***~s*** gossip; **hablador** talkative; *Méx* boastful; **habladurías** *fpl* gossip; **hablante** *m/f* speaker; **hablar** speak; (*conversar*) talk; ***~ con alguien*** talk to s.o., talk with s.o.; ***~ de*** *de libro etc* be about; ***¡ni ~!*** no way!; **hablarse** speak to one another
hacendado 1 *adj* land-own-

ing **2** *m*, **-a** *f* land-owner

hacer 1 *v/t* (*realizar*) do; (*elaborar, crear*) make; **~ una pregunta** ask a question; **¡qué le vamos a ~!** that's life; **le hicieron ir** they made him go **2** *v/i*: **haces bien / mal en ir** you are doing the right / wrong thing by going; **me hace mal** it's making me ill; **esto hará de mesa** *de objeto* this will do as a table; **~ como que o como si** act as if; **no le hace** *L.Am.* it doesn't matter; **se me hace qué** *L.Am.* it seems to me that **3** *v/impers*: **hace calor / frío** it's hot / cold; **hace tres días** three days ago; **desde hace un año** for a year; **hacerse** *traje* make; *casa* build o.s.; (*cocinarse*) cook; (*convertirse, volverse*) get, become; **~ viejo** get old; **se hace tarde** it's getting late; **~ el sordo** pretend to be deaf; **~ a algo** get used to sth; **~ con algo** get hold of sth

hacha *f* ax, *Br* axe

hachís *m* hashish

hacia toward; **~ adelante** forward; **~ abajo** down; **~ arriba** up; **~ atrás** back(ward); **~ las cuatro** about four (o'clock)

hacienda *f L.Am.* (*granja*) ranch, estate

Hacienda *f ministerio* Treasury Department, *Br* Treasury; *oficina* Internal Revenue Service, *Br* Inland Revenue

hacinar stack

hada *f* fairy

halagar flatter; **halago** *m* flattery

halagüeño encouraging

halcón *m* falcon

hall *m* hall

hallar find; (*descubrir*) discover; *muerte, destino* meet; **hallarse** be; (*sentirse*) feel; **hallazgo** *m* find; (*descubrimiento*) discovery

halógeno halogen

halterofilia *f* DEP weight-lifting

hamaca *f* hammock; (*tumbona*) deck chair; *L.Am.* (*mecedora*) rocking chair

hambre *f* hunger; **tener ~** be hungry **morirse de ~** *fig* be starving; **hambriento** *tb fig* hungry (**de** for)

hamburguesa *f* hamburger

hampa *f* underworld

harapiento ragged; **harapo** *m* rag

harina *f* flour

hartar 1 *v/t*: **~ a alguien con algo** tire s.o. with sth; **~ a alguien de algo** give s.o. too much of sth; **harto 1** *adj* fed up F; (*lleno*) full (up) **2** *adv* very much; *delante del adjetivo* extremely; **me gusta ~** *L.Am.* I like it a lot

hasta 1 *prp* until, till; **llegó ~ Bilbao** he went as far as Bilbao; **~ ahora** so far; **~ aquí** up to here; **¿~ cuándo?** how long?; **~ que** until; **¡~**

luego!, ***¡~ la vista!*** see you (later) **2** *adv* even
hastío *m* boredom
hato *m L.Am.* bundle
hay ☞ ***haber***
haya *f* BOT beech
haz *m* bundle; *de luz* beam
hazaña *f* achievement
hebilla *f* buckle
hebra *f de hilo* thread
hechizar *fig* bewitch; **hechizo** *m* spell, charm
hecho 1 *part* ☞ ***hacer***, ***~ a mano*** hand-made; ***¡bien ~!*** well done!; ***muy ~*** *carne* well-done **2** *adj* finished; ***un hombre ~ y derecho*** a fully grown man **3** *m* fact; ***de ~*** in fact; **hechura** *f de ropa* making
hectárea *f* hectare (*approx. 2.5 acres*)
hedor *m* stink, stench
helada *f* frost; **heladería** *f* ice cream parlor *o Br* parlour; **helado 1** *adj* frozen; *fig* icy; ***quedarse ~*** be stunned **2** *m* ice cream; **helarse** *tb fig* freeze
helecho *m* BOT fern
hélice *f* propeller
helicóptero *m* helicopter
helipuerto *m* heliport
hematoma *m* bruise
hembra *f* female
hemisferio *m* hemisphere
hemorragia *f* MED hemorrhage, *Br* haemorrhage, bleeding; **hemorroides** *fpl* MED hemorrhoids, *Br* haemorrhoids, piles
hender, **henderse** crack; **hendidura** *f* crack
heno *m* hay
hepático liver *atr*, hepatic; **hepatitis** *f* MED hepatitis
heredar inherit (***de*** from); **heredera** *f* heiress; **heredero** *m* heir; **hereditario** hereditary
hereje *m* heretic; **herejía** *f* heresy
herencia *f* inheritance
herida *f* wound; (*lesión*) injury; *mujer* wounded woman; *mujer lesionada* injured woman; **herir** wound; (*lesionar*) injure
hermana *f* sister; **hermanastra** *f* stepsister; **hermanastro** *m* stepbrother; **hermandad** *f de hombres* brotherhood, fraternity; *de mujeres* sisterhood; **hermano** *m* brother
hermoso beautiful; **hermosura** *f* beauty
hernia *f* MED hernia
héroe *m* hero; **heroico** heroic; **heroína** *f mujer* heroine; *droga* heroin
herradura *f* horseshoe
herramienta *f* tool
herrumbre *f* rust
hervidero *m fig* hotbed; **hervir 1** *v/i* boil; *fig* seethe (***de*** with) **2** *v/t* boil
hidrato *m*: ***~ de carbono*** carbohydrate
hidráulico hydraulic
hidroavión *m* seaplane; **hidrocarburo** *m* hydrocarbon;

hidroeléctrico hydroelectric; **hidrógeno** *m* hydrogen
hiedra *f* BOT ivy
hielo *m* ice
hiena *f* ZO hyena
hierba *f* grass; ***mala ~*** weed; **hierbabuena** *f* BOT mint
hierro *m* iron
hígado *m* liver
higiene *f* hygiene; **higiénico** hygienic
higo *m* BOT fig; **higuera** *f* BOT fig tree
hija *f* daughter; **hijastra** *f* stepdaughter; **hijastro** *m* stepson; **hijo** *m* son; ***~s*** children *pl*; ***~ de puta*** P son of a bitch V, bastard P; ***~ único*** only child
hilar 1 *v/t* spin **2** *v/i*: ***~ delgado o fino*** *fig* split hairs; **hilo** *m* thread; ***~ dental*** dental floss; ***sin ~s*** TELEC cordless; ***perder el ~*** *fig* lose the thread
himno *m* hymn; ***~ nacional*** national anthem
hincapié *m*: ***hacer ~*** put special emphasis (***en*** on)
hincha *m* F fan, supporter; **hinchado** swollen; **hinchar** inflate, blow up; *Rpl* P annoy; **hincharse** MED swell; *fig* stuff o.s (***de*** with); (*mostrarse orgulloso*) swell with pride; **hinchazón** *f* swelling
hinojo *m* BOT fennel
hipermercado *m* supermarket, *Br tb* supermarket; **hipertensión** *f* MED high blood pressure, hypertension; **hipertexto** *m* hypertext
hípica *f* equestrian sports *pl*
hipo *m* hiccups *pl*; ***quitar el ~*** F take one's breath away
hipócrita 1 *adj* hypocritical **2** *m/f* hypocrite
hipódromo *m* racetrack
hipopótamo *m* hippopotamus
hipoteca *f* COM mortgage; **hipotecar** COM mortgage; *fig* compromise
hipótesis *f* hypothesis; **hipotético** hypothetical
hirviente boiling
hispánico Hispanic; **hispanidad** *f*: ***la ~*** the Spanish-speaking world; **hispano 1** *adj* (*español*) Spanish; (*hispanohablante*) Spanish-speaking; *en EE.UU.* Hispanic **2** *m*, **-a** *f* (*español*) Spaniard; (*hispanohablante*) Spanish speaker; *en EE.UU.* Hispanic
histérico hysterical
historia *f* history; (*cuento*) story; ***una ~ de drogas*** F some drugs business; ***déjate de ~s*** F stop making excuses; **histórico** historical; (*importante*) historic
hito *m tb fig* milestone
hockey *m* field hockey, *Br* hockey; ***~ sobre hielo*** hockey, *Br* ice hockey
hogar *m fig* home
hoguera *f* bonfire
hoja *f* BOT leaf; *de papel* sheet; *de libro* page; *de cuchillo* blade; ***~ de afeitar*** razor blade; ***~ de cálculo*** INFOR

spreadsheet; **hojalata** *f* tin; **hojear** leaf through
hola hello, hi F
Holanda Holland; **holandés** **1** *adj* Dutch **2** *m* Dutchman; ***los holandeses*** the Dutch **3** *m idioma* Dutch; **holandesa** *f* Dutchwoman
holgado loose, comfortable; ***estar ~ de tiempo*** have time to spare
holgazán *m* idler
hollín *m* soot
hombre *m* man; ***~ de negocios*** businessman; ***~ rana*** frogman; ***¡claro, ~!*** you bet!, sure thing!; ***¡~, qué alegría!*** that's great!
hombrera *f* shoulder pad; MIL epaulette; **hombro** *m* shoulder; ***~ con ~*** shoulder to shoulder
homenaje *m* homage; **homenajear** pay homage to
homeópata *m/f* homeopath
homicidio *m* homicide
homogéneo homogenous
homosexual *m/f & adj* homosexual
honda *f de cuero* sling(shot); *Rpl* (*tirachinas*) slingshot, *Br* catapult
hondo deep; **hondura** *f* depth
Honduras Honduras; **hondureño** **1** *adj* Honduran **2** *m*, **-a** *f* Honduran
honesto honorable, *Br* honourable, decent
hongo *m* fungus
honor *m* honor, *Br* honour; ***en ~ a*** in honor of; ***hacer ~ a*** live up to; ***palabra de ~*** word of honor; **honorable** honorable, *Br* honourable; **honorario** honorary; **honorarios** *mpl* fees; **honra** *f* honor, *Br* honour; **honradez** *f* honesty; **honrado** honest; **honrar** honor, *Br* honour; **honrarse: *~ de hacer algo*** be honored *o Br* honoured to do sth; **honroso** honorable, *Br* honourable
hora *f* hour; ***~s extraordinarias*** overtime; ***~ local*** local time; ***~ punta*** rush hour; ***a la ~ de...*** *fig* when it comes to …; ***¡ya era ~!*** about time too!; ***tengo ~ con el dentista*** I have an appointment with the dentist; ***¿qué ~ es?*** what time is it?; **horario** *m* schedule, *Br* timetable; ***~ comercial*** business hours *pl*; ***~ flexible*** flextime, *Br* flexitime; ***~ de trabajo*** (working) hours *pl*
horca *f* gallows *pl*
horchata *f drink made from tiger nuts*
horizontal horizontal; **horizonte** *m* horizon
horma *f* form, mold, *Br* mould; *de zapatos* last
hormiga *f* ant
hormigón *m* concrete; ***~ armado*** reinforced concrete
hormiguero *m* ant hill
hormona *f* hormone
hornillo *m de fogón* burner; *de gas* gas ring; *transportable* camping stove

horno *m* oven; ***alto ~*** blast furnace
horóscopo *m* horoscope
horquilla *f para pelo* hairpin
horrendo horrendous
horrible horrible, dreadful; **horror** *m* horror (***a*** of); ***tener ~ a*** be terrified of; ***me gusta ~es*** F I like it a lot; ***¡qué ~!*** how awful!; **horroroso** terrible; (*feo*) hideous
hortaliza *f* vegetable
horticultura *f* horticulture
hospedaje *m* accommodations *pl*, *Br* accommodation; ***dar ~ a alguien*** put s.o. up; **hospedar** put up; **hospedarse** stay (***en*** at); **hospital** *m* hospital; **hospitalario** hospitable; MED hospital *atr*; **hospitalidad** *f* hospitality
hostal *m* hostel; **hostelería** *f* hotel industry; *como curso* hotel management
hostia *f* REL host
hostil hostile; **hostilidad** *f* hostility
hotel *m* hotel
hoy today; ***de ~ en adelante*** from now on; ***~ por ~*** at the present time; ***~ en día*** nowadays
hoyo *m* hole; (*depresión*) hollow; **hoyuelo** *m* dimple
hucha *f* money box
hueco 1 *adj* hollow; (*vacío*) empty; *fig*: *persona* shallow **2** *m* gap; (*agujero*) hole; *de ascensor* shaft
huelga *f* strike; ***~ de celo*** work-to-rule; ***~ de hambre*** hunger strike; ***declararse en ~, ir a la ~*** go on strike; **huelguista** *m/f* striker
huella *f* mark; *de animal* track; ***~s dactilares*** finger prints
huérfano 1 *adj* orphan *atr* **2** *m*, **-a** *f* orphan
huerta *f* truck farm, *Br* market garden; **huerto** *m* kitchen garden
hueso *m* bone; *de fruta* pit, stone; *persona* tough guy; *Méx* F cushy number F; *Méx* F (*influencia*) influence, pull F; ***~ duro de roer*** *fig* F hard nut to crack F
huésped *m/f* guest
huevera *f para servir* eggcup; *para almacenar* egg box; **huevo** *m* egg; P (*testículo*) ball P; ***~ duro*** hard-boiled egg; ***~ escalfado*** poached egg; ***~ frito*** fried egg; ***~ pasado por agua*** soft-boiled egg; ***~s revueltos*** scrambled eggs; ***un ~ de*** P a load of F
huida *f* flight, escape; **huir** flee, escape (***de*** from); ***~ de algo*** avoid sth
hule *m* oilcloth; *L.Am.* (*caucho*) rubber
hulla *f* coal
humanidad *f* humanity; **humano** human
humareda *f* cloud of smoke; **humear** *con humo* smoke; *con vapor* steam
humedad *f* humidity; *de una*

casa damp(ness); **humedecer** dampen; **húmedo** humid; *toalla* damp
humildad *f* humility; **humilde** humble; (*sin orgullo*) modest; *clase social* lowly; **humillación** *f* humiliation; **humillante** humiliating; **humillar** humiliate
humo *m* smoke; (*vapor*) steam
humor *m* humor, *Br* humour; ***estar de buen / mal ~*** be in a good / bad mood; ***sentido del ~*** sense of humor; **humorista** *m/f* humorist; (*cómico*) comedian
hundimiento *m* sinking; **hundir** sink; *fig*: *empresa* ruin; *persona* devastate; **hundirse** sink; *fig*: *de empresa* collapse; *de persona* go to pieces
húngaro 1 *adj* Hungarian **2** *m*, **-a** *f* Hungarian **3** *m idioma* Hungarian; **Hungría** Hungary
huracán *m* hurricane
hurtadillas *fpl*: ***a ~*** furtively
hurtar steal; **hurto** *m* theft
husmear F nose around F

I

ibérico Iberian; **ibero, íbero** *m*, **-a** *f* Iberian; **iberoamericano** Latin American
ibicenco Ibizan
iceberg *m* iceberg
ida *f* outward journey; (***billete de***) ***~ y vuelta*** round trip (ticket), *Br* return (ticket)
idea *f* idea; ***no tener ni ~*** not have a clue; **ideal** *m/adj* ideal; **idealismo** *m* idealism; **idealista 1** *adj* idealistic **2** *m/f* idealist; **idear** think up
idéntico identical; **identidad** *f* identity; **identifición** *f* identification; INFOR user name; ***~ genética*** genetic fingerprint; **identificar** identify; **identificarse** identify o.s.
ideología *f* ideology
idilio *m* idyll; (*relación amorosa*) romance
idioma *m* language
idiota 1 *adj* idiotic **2** *m/f* idiot; **idiotez** *f* stupid thing to say / do
ídolo *m tb fig* idol
idóneo suitable
iglesia *f* church
ignorancia *f* ignorance; **ignorante** ignorant; **ignorar** not know, not be aware of
igual 1 *adj* (*idéntico*) same (***a***, ***que*** as); (*proporcionado*) equal (***a*** to); (*constante*) constant; ***al ~ que*** like, the same as; ***me da ~*** I don't mind **2** *m/f* equal; ***no tener ~*** have no equal; **igualar 1** *v/t precio*, *marca* equal, match; (*nivelar*) level off; ***~ algo*** MAT make sth equal (***con***, ***a*** to) **2** *v/i* DEP tie the game, *Br*

equalize; **igualdad** *f* equality; ~ ***de oportunidades*** equal opportunities; **igualmente** equally
ilegal illegal; **ilegalidad** *f* illegality
ilegible illegible
ilegítimo unlawful; *hijo* illegitimate
ileso unhurt
ilícito illicit
ilimitado unlimited
iluminación *f* illumination; **iluminar** *edificio, calle etc* light, illuminate; *fig* light up
ilusión *f* illusion; (*deseo, esperanza*) hope; **iluso 1** *adj* gullible **2** *m*, **-a** *f* dreamer; **ilusorio** illusory
ilustración *f* illustration; **ilustrado** illustrated; (*culto*) learned; **ilustrar** illustrate; (*aclarar*) explain; **ilustre** illustrious
imagen *f tb fig* image; ***ser la viva ~ de*** be the spitting image of; **imaginable** imaginable; **imaginación** *f* imagination; **imaginar, imaginarse** imagine; **imaginativo** imaginative
imán *m* magnet
imbécil 1 *adj* stupid **2** *m/f* idiot, imbecile
imitación *f* imitation; **imitar** imitate
impaciencia *f* impatience; **impacientarse** lose (one's) patience; **impaciente** impatient
impacto *m tb fig* impact; ~ ***de bala*** bullet wound
impar *número* odd
imparable unstoppable
imparcial impartial
impartir impart; *clase, bendición* give
impávido fearless
impecable impeccable
impedir prevent; (*estorbar*) impede
impenetrable impenetrable
impensado unexpected
imperar rule; *fig* prevail
imperceptible imperceptible
imperdible *m* safety pin
imperdonable unpardonable, unforgivable
imperfecto *m/adj* imperfect
imperial imperial; **imperio** *m* empire; **imperioso** *necesidad* pressing; *persona* imperious
impermeable 1 *adj* waterproof **2** *m* raincoat
impertérrito unperturbed, unmoved
impertinente 1 *adj* impertinent **2** *m/f*: ***¡eres un ~!*** you've got nerve!
ímpetu *m* impetus; **impetuoso** impetuous
implacable implacable
implantar *programa* implement; *democracia* establish; *pena de muerte* bring in; MED implant; **implantarse** be introduced
implicar mean, imply; (*involucrar*) involve; *en un delito* implicate (***en*** in)
implorar beg for

imponente impressive; F terrific; **imponer 1** *v/t* impose; *miedo, respeto* inspire **2** *v/i* be imposing *o* impressive; **imponerse** (*hacerse respetar*) assert o.s.; DEP win; (*prevalecer*) prevail; (*ser necesario*) be imperative; ***~ una tarea*** set o.s. a task
impopular unpopular
importación *f* import
importancia *f* importance; ***darse ~*** give o.s. airs; ***tener ~*** be important; **importante** important; **importar** matter; ***no importa*** it doesn't matter; ***eso a ti no te importa*** that's none of your business; ***¿qué importa?*** what does it matter?; ***¿le importa...?*** do you mind ...?; **importe** *m* amount; (*coste*) cost
importuno inopportune
imposibilidad *f* impossibility; **imposible** impossible
imposición *f* imposition; (*exigencia*) demand; COM deposit
impotencia *f* impotence, helplessness; MED impotence; **impotente** helpless, impotent; MED impotent
impracticable impracticable
impregnar saturate (***de*** with); TÉC impregnate (***de*** with)
imprenta *f taller* print shop; *arte, técnica* printing; *máquina* printing press
imprescindible essential; *persona* indispensable
impresión *f* impression; *acto* printing; (*tirada*) print run; ***la sangre le da ~*** he can't stand the sight of blood; **impresionante** impressive; **impresionismo** *m* impressionism; **impresionar: *~le a alguien*** impress s.o.; (*conmover*) move s.o.; (*alterar*) shock s.o.; **impreso** *m* form; ***~s*** printed matter; **impresora** *f* INFOR printer; ***~ de chorro de tinta*** inkjet (printer); ***~ de inyección de tinta*** inkjet (printer); ***~ láser*** laser (printer)
imprevisto 1 *adj* unforeseen, unexpected **2** *m* unexpected event
imprimir *tb* INFOR print; *fig* transmit
improbable unlikely, improbable
improductivo unproductive
improvisar improvise
imprudente reckless, rash
impuesto *m* tax; ***~ sobre el valor añadido*** *sales tax*, *Br* value-added tax; ***~ sobre la renta*** income tax
impugnar challenge
impulsar TÉC propel; COM boost
impulsivo impulsive; **impulso** *m* impulse; (*empuje*) impetus; COM boost; *fig* urge, impulse; ***tomar ~*** take a run up
impunidad *f* impunity
imputar attribute
inacabable endless; **inacabado** unfinished

inaccesible inaccessible
inaceptable unacceptable
inadmisible inadmissible
inadvertido: ***pasar ~*** go unnoticed
inagotable inexhaustible
inaguantable unbearable
inalámbrico **1** *adj* TELEC cordless **2** *m* TELEC cordless (telephone)
inarrugable crease-resistant
inaudito unprecedented
inauguración *f* official opening, inauguration; **inaugurar** (officially) open, inaugurate
incansable tireless
incapacidad *f* disability; (*falta de capacidad*) inability; (*ineptitud*) incompetence; **incapaz** incapable (***de*** of)
incautarse: ***~ de*** seize
incauto unwary
incendiar set fire to; **incendio** *m* fire
incentivo *m* incentive
incertidumbre *f* uncertainty
incidente *m* incident
incienso *m* incense
incierto *m* uncertain
incineración *f de cadáver* cremation
incisivo cutting; *fig* incisive; ***diente ~*** incisor
incitar incite
inclinación *f* inclination; *de un terreno* slope; *muestra de respeto* bow; *fig* tendency; **inclinar** tilt; ***~ la cabeza*** nod (one's head); ***me inclina a creer que...*** it makes me think that ...; **inclinarse** bend (down); *de un terreno* slope; *desde la vertical* lean; *en señal de respeto* bow; ***~ a*** *fig* tend to, be inclined to
incluir include; **inclusive** inclusive; **incluso** even
incoherente incoherent
incoloro colorless, *Br* colourless
incomodar inconvenience; (*enfadar*) annoy; **incomodarse** feel uncomfortable; (*enfadarse*) get annoyed (***por*** about); **incómodo** uncomfortable; (*fastidioso*) inconvenient
incomparable incomparable
incompatible incompatible
incompetente incompetent
incompleto incomplete
incomprensible incomprehensible
incomunicado isolated, cut off; JUR in solitary confinement
inconfundible unmistakable
inconsciente MED unconscious; (*ignorante*) unaware; (*irreflexivo*) thoughtless
inconstante fickle
incontestable indisputable
inconveniente **1** *adj* (*inoportuno*) inconvenient; (*impropio*) inappropriate **2** *m* (*desventaja*) drawback; (*estorbo*) problem; ***no tengo ~*** I don't mind
incorporar incorporate; **incorporarse** sit up; ***~ a*** MIL join

incorrecto incorrect, wrong; *comportamiento* impolite; **incorregible** incorrigible
incrédulo incredulous; **increíble** incredible
incremento *m* growth
incubadora *f* incubator; **incubar** incubate
inculpar JUR accuse
inculto ignorant, uneducated
incurable incurable
indecente indecent; *película* obscene
indeciso undecided; *por naturaleza* indecisive
indefinido (*impreciso*) vague; (*ilimitado*) indefinite
indemnización *f* compensation; **indemnizar** compensate (***por*** for)
independencia *f* independence; **independiente** independent; **independientemente** independently
indescriptible indescribable
indeterminado indeterminate; (*indefinido*) indefinite
India: (***la***) ~ India; **indio 1** *adj* Indian **2** *m*, **-a** *f* Indian
indicación *f* indication; (*señal*) sign; ***indicaciones*** *para llegar* directions; (*instrucciones*) instructions; **indicador** *m* indicator; **indicar** show, indicate; (*señalar*) point out; (*sugerir*) suggest; **índice** *m* index; ***dedo*** ~ index finger; **indicio** *m* indication, sign; (*vestigio*) trace
indiferencia *f* indifference; **indiferente** indifferent; (*irrelevante*) immaterial
indígena 1 *adj* indigenous, native **2** *m/f* native
indigente destitute
indigestión *f* indigestion; **indigesto** indigestible
indignar: ~ ***a alguien*** make s.o. indignant; **indignarse** become indignant
indirecta *f* insinuation; (*sugerencia*) hint; **indirecto** indirect
indiscreción *f* indiscretion; (*declaración*) indiscreet remark; **indiscreto** indiscreet
indiscutible indisputable
indisoluble insoluble; *matrimonio* indissoluble
indispensable indispensable
indispuesto indisposed, unwell
indistinto vague; *sonido* faint
individual individual; *cama, habitación* single; **individuo** *m* individual
indivisible indivisible
índole *f* nature
indolencia *f* laziness, indolence; **indolente** lazy, indolent
indomable *animal* untameable; *persona* indomitable
indudable undoubted
indulgencia *f* indulgence
indultar pardon; **indulto** *m* pardon
indumentaria *f* clothing
industria *f* industry; **industrial 1** *adj* industrial **2** *m/f* industrialist
inédito unpublished; *fig* un-

precedented
ineficacia *f* inefficiency; *de un procedimiento* ineffectiveness; **ineficaz** inefficient; *procedimiento* ineffective
ineficiencia *f* inefficiency; **ineficiente** inefficient
inepto 1 *adj* inept, incompetent **2** *m*, **-a** *f* incompetent fool
inequívoco unequivocal
inesperado unexpected
inestable unstable; *tiempo* unsettled
inestimable invaluable
inevitable inevitable
inexperto inexperienced
inexplicable inexplicable
infalible infallible
infame loathsome; (*terrible*) dreadful
infamia *f* (*deshonra*) disgrace; *acción* dreadful thing to do; *dicho* slander, slur
infancia *f* infancy; **infanta** *f* infanta, princess
infantería *f* MIL infantry
infantil children's *atr*; *naturaleza* childlike; *desp* infantile, childish
infarto *m* MED heart attack
infatigable tireless, indefatigable
infección *f* MED infection; **infeccioso** infectious; **infectar** infect
infeliz 1 *adj* unhappy, miserable **2** *m/f* poor devil
inferior 1 *adj* inferior (***a*** to); *en el espacio* lower (***a*** than) **2** *m/f* inferior; **inferioridad** *f* inferiority
infertilidad *f* infertility
infestar infest; (*invadir*) overrun
infiel 1 *adj* unfaithful **2** *m/f* unbeliever
infierno *m* hell
ínfimo *cantidad* very small; *calidad* very poor
infinidad *f*: ***~ de*** countless; **infinito 1** *adj* infinite **2** *m* infinity
inflación *f* inflation
inflamable flammable; **inflamación** *f* MED inflammation; **inflamarse** MED become inflamed
inflar inflate; **inflarse** swell (up); *fig* F get conceited
inflexible *fig* inflexible
influencia *f* influence; ***tener ~s*** have contacts; **influir: *~ en alguien / algo*** influence s.o. / sth, have an influence on s.o. / sth; **influjo** *m* influence; **influyente** influential
infografía *f* computer graphics *pl*
información *f* information; (*noticias*) news *sg*; **informal** informal; *persona* unreliable; **informar** inform (***de***, ***sobre*** about); **informática** *f* information technology, IT; **informático 1** *adj* computer *atr* **2** *m*, **-a** *f* IT specialist
informe 1 *adj* shapeless **2** *m* report; ***~s*** (*referencias*) references

infracción *f* offense, *Br* offence
infraestructura *f* infrastructure
infrarrojo infrared
infrecuente infrequent
infructuoso fruitless
ingeniero *m*, **-a** *f* engineer; **ingenio** *m* ingenuity; (*aparato*) device; **~ azucarero** *L.Am.* sugar refinery; **ingenioso** ingenious
Inglaterra England
ingle *f* groin
inglés 1 *adj* English **2** *m* Englishman; *idioma* English; **inglesa** *f* Englishwoman
ingratitud *f* ingratitude; **ingrato** ungrateful; *tarea* thankless
ingravidez *f* weightlessness
ingrediente *m* ingredient
ingresar 1 *v/i*: **~ en** *en universidad* go to; *en asociación* join; *en hospital* be admitted to **2** *v/t cheque* pay in; **ingreso** *m* entry; *en una asociación* joining; *en hospital* admission; COM deposit; **~s** income
inhabitado uninhabited
inhalar inhale
inhibición *f* inhibition; JUR disqualification
inhumano inhuman
inicial *f/adj* initial; **iniciar** initiate; *curso* start, begin; **iniciativa** *f* initiative; **inicio** *m* start, beginning
inigualable incomparable; *precio* unbeatable
injerencia *f* interference
injuria *f* insult; **injuriar** insult
injusticia *f* injustice; **injusto** unjust
inmediaciones *fpl* immediate area (**de** of), vicinity (**de** of); **inmediatamente** immediately; **inmediato** immediate; **de ~** immediately
inmejorable unbeatable
inmenso immense
inmigración *f* immigration; **inmigrante** *m/f* immigrant; **inmigrar** immigrate
inminente imminent
inmoral immoral
inmortal immortal
inmóvil *persona* motionless; *vehículo* stationary
inmueble *m* building
inmune immune; **inmunidad** *f* MED, POL immunity; **inmunizar** immunize; **inmunológico: sistema ~** MED immune system
innato innate, inborn
innecesario unnecessary
innovación *f* innovation
innumerable innumerable, countless
inocencia *f* innocence; **inocente** innocent
inodoro *m* toilet
inofensivo inoffensive, harmless
inolvidable unforgettable
inoportuno inopportune; (*molesto*) inconvenient
inoxidable: acero ~ stainless steel
inquietar worry; **inquietarse**

worry; **inquietud** *f* worry, anxiety; *intelectual* interest; **inquieto** worried
inquilino *m* tenant
inquisitivo inquisitive
insalubre unhealthy
insano unhealthy
insatisfacción *f* dissatisfaction; **insatisfactorio** unsatisfactory; **insatisfecho** dissatisfied
inscribir 1 *v/t* (*grabar*) inscribe; *en lista* register, enter; *en curso* enroll, *Br* enrol, register; **inscripción** *f* inscription; *en lista* registration, entry; *en curso* enrollment, *Br* enrolment, registration
insecticida *m* insecticide; **insecto** *m* insect
inseguridad *f de una persona* insecurity; *de estructura* unsteadiness; (*peligro*) dangerousness; **inseguro** insecure; *estructura* unsteady; (*peligroso*) dangerous, unsafe
insensato foolish
insensible insensitive (***a*** to)
insertar insert
inservible useless
insignificante insignificant
insinuar insinuate
insípido insipid
insistir insist; **~ *en hacer algo*** insist on doing sth; **~ *en algo*** stress sth
insolación *f* MED sunstroke
insolencia *f* insolence; **insolente** insolent
insólito unusual
insoluble insoluble
insolvencia *f* insolvency
insomnio *m* insomnia
insonorizar soundproof; **insonoro** soundless
insoportable unbearable, intolerable
inspección *f* inspection; **inspeccionar** inspect; **inspector** *m*, **~a** *f* inspector
inspiración *f* inspiration; MED inhalation; **inspirar** inspire; MED inhale
instalación *f acto* installation; ***instalaciones deportivas*** sports facilities; **instalar** install, *Br* instal; (*colocar*) put; *un negocio* set up; **instalarse** *en un sitio* install *o Br* instal o.s.
instancia *f* JUR petition; (*petición por escrito*) application; ***a ~s de*** at the request of
instantánea *f* FOT snapshot; **instantáneo** immediate, instantaneous; **instante** *m* moment, instant; ***al ~*** right away, immediately
instinto *m* instinct
institución *f* institution; **instituir** institute; **instituto** *m* institute; *Esp* high school, *Br* secondary school; ***~ de belleza*** beauty salon; **institutriz** *f* governess
instrucción *f* education; (*formación*) training; MIL drill; INFOR instruction; JUR hearing; ***instrucciones de uso*** instructions, directions (for use); **instruido** educated; **instruir** educate; (*formar*)

train; JUR *pleito* hear; **instructivo** educational
instrumento *m* instrument; (*herramienta*), *fig* tool; **~ musical** musical instrument
insuficiencia *f* lack; MED failure; **insuficiente 1** *adj* insufficient, inadequate **2** *m* EDU *nota* fail
insultar insult; **insulto** *m* insult
insuperable insurmountable
intachable faultless
intacto intact; (*sin tocar*) untouched
integrar integrate; *equipo* make up; **íntegro** whole, entire; ***un hombre ~*** *fig* a man of integrity
intelectual *m/f & adj* intellectual
inteligencia *f* intelligence; **inteligente** intelligent
intemperie *f*: ***a la ~*** in the open air
intempestivo untimely
intemporal timeless
intención *f* intention; ***doble*** *o* ***segunda ~*** ulterior motive; **intencional** intentional
intensidad *f* intensity; (*fuerza*) strength; **intensificar** intensify; **intensificarse** intensify; **intensivo** intensive; **intenso** intense; (*fuerte*) strong
intentar try, attempt; **intento** *m* attempt, try; *Méx* (*intención*) aim; **intentona** *f*: **~ (*golpista*)** POL putsch, coup
interacción *f* interaction; **interactivo** interactive
intercalar insert
intercambio *m* exchange, swap
interceder intercede (***por*** for)
interceptar *tb* DEP intercept
interés *m tb* COM interest; *desp* self-interest; ***sin ~*** interest-free; **interesado 1** *adj* interested **2** *m*, **-a** *f* interested party; **interesante** interesting; **interesar** interest; **interesarse: ~ *por*** take an interest in
interface *m*, **interfaz** *f* INFOR interface
interferencia *f* interference; **interferir 1** *v/t* interfere with **2** *v/i* interfere (***en*** in)
interino substitute *atr*; (*provisional*) provisional, acting *atr*
interior 1 *adj* interior; *bolsillo* inside *atr*; COM, POL domestic **2** *m* interior; DEP inside-forward; ***en su ~*** *fig* inwardly
interlocutor *m*, **~a** *f* speaker; ***mi ~*** the person I was talking to
intermediario *m* COM intermediary, middle-man; **intermedio 1** *adj nivel* intermediate; *tamaño, calidad* medium **2** *m* intermission
intermitente 1 *adj* intermittent **2** *m* AUTO turn signal, *Br* indicator
internacional *m/f & adj* international
internado *m* boarding school
internauta *m/f* INFOR Inter-

net user, Net surfer
internet *m* Internet; ***en ~*** on the Internet
interno 1 *adj* internal; POL domestic, internal **2** *m*, **-a** *f* EDU boarder; (*preso*) inmate; MED intern, *Br* houseman
interpretar interpret; TEA play; **intérprete** *m/f* interpreter
interrogación *f* interrogation; ***signo de ~*** question mark; **interrogar** question; **interrogatorio** *m* questioning, interrogation
interrumpir 1 *v/t* interrupt; *servicio* suspend; *vacaciones* cut short **2** *v/i* interrupt; **interrupción** *f* interruption; *de servicio* suspension; *de vacaciones* cutting short; ***sin ~*** non-stop; **interruptor** *m* ELEC switch
intervalo *m tb* MÚS interval; (*espacio*) gap
intervención *f* intervention; *en debate* participation; *en película* appearance; MED operation; **intervenir 1** *v/i* intervene; *en debate* take part, participate; *en película* appear **2** *v/t* TELEC tap; *contrabando* seize; MED operate on
intestinal intestinal; **intestino** *m* intestine
intimidad *f* intimacy; (*lo privado*) privacy; ***en la ~*** in private
intimidar intimidate
íntimo intimate; (*privado*) private; *amigos* close
intolerable intolerable; **intolerante** intolerant
intoxicación *f* poisoning; **intoxicar** poison
intranquilo uneasy; (*nervioso*) restless
intransferible non-transferable
intransigente intransigent
intransitable impassable
intratable: *es ~* he is impossible (to deal with)
intravenoso MED intravenous
intrépido intrepid
intriga *f* intrigue; *de novela* plot; **intrigar 1** *v/t* (*interesar*) intrigue **2** *v/i* plot, scheme
introducción *f* introduction; *acción de meter* insertion; INFOR input; **introducir** introduce; (*meter*) insert; INFOR input
intuición *f* intuition; **intuir** sense
inundación *f* flood; **inundar** flood
inusitado unusual
inútil 1 *adj* useless; MIL unfit **2** *m/f*: ***es un ~*** he's useless
invadir invade; *de un sentimiento* overcome
invalidar invalidate; **invalidez** *f* disability; **inválido 1** *adj persona* disabled; *documento* invalid **2** *m*, **-a** *f* disabled person
invariable invariable
invasión *f* MIL invasion
invencible invincible; *miedo*

insurmountable
invención *f* invention; **inventar** invent; **inventario** *m* inventory; **invento** *m* invention; **inventor** *m* inventor
invernadero *m* greenhouse; **invernal** winter *atr*
inverosímil unlikely
inversión *f* reversal; COM investment; **inverso** opposite; *orden* reverse; ***a la -a*** the other way around; **inversor** *m*, **~a** *f* investor; **invertir** reverse; COM invest (***en*** in)
investigación *f* investigation; EDU, TÉC research; ***~ y desarrollo*** research and development; **investigador** *m*, **~a** *f* researcher; **investigar** investigate; EDU, TÉC research
invidente *m/f* blind person
invierno *m* winter
invisible invisible
invitación *f* invitation; **invitado** *m*, **-a** *f* guest; **invitar** invite (***a*** to); (*convidar*) treat (***a*** to)
involuntario involuntary
inyección *f* injection; **inyectar** inject
ir 1 *v/i* go (***a*** to); ***~ en avión*** fly; ***¡ya voy!*** I'm coming!; ***~ a por algo*** go and fetch sth; ***~ bien / mal*** go well / badly; ***iba de amarillo*** she was wearing yellow; ***van dos a dos*** DEP the score is two all; ***¿de qué va la película?*** what's the movie about?; ***¡qué va!*** you must be joking! F; ***¡vamos!*** come on!; ***¡vaya!*** well! **2** *v/aux*: ***va a llover*** it's going to rain; ***ya voy comprendiendo*** I'm beginning to understand; ***~ para viejo*** be getting old; **irse** go (away), leave; ***¡vete!*** go away!; ***¡vámonos!*** let's go
ira *f* anger
Irak Iraq, Irak
Irán Iran; **iraní** *m/f & adj* Iranian
iraquí *m/f & adj* Iraqi, Iraki
iris *m inv* ANAT iris; ***arco ~*** rainbow
Irlanda Ireland; **irlandés 1** *adj* Irish **2** *m* Irishman; **irlandesa** *f* Irishwoman
ironía *f* irony; **irónico** ironic
irradiación *f* irradiation
irregular irregular; *superficie* uneven; **irregularidad** *f* irregularity; *de superficie* unevenness
irrelevante irrelevant
irreprochable irreproachable
irresistible irresistible
irresponsable irresponsible
irrevocable irrevocable
irrigar MED, AGR irrigate
irritación *f* irritation; **irritar** *tb* MED irritate; **irritarse** get irritated
irrompible unbreakable
irrumpir burst in
isla *f* island
Israel Israel; **israelí** *m/f & adj* Israeli
Italia Italy; **italiano 1** *adj* Italian **2** *m*, **-a** *f* Italian; **3** *m idioma* Italian

itinerario *m* itinerary

IVA *m* (= ***impuesto sobre el valor añanido*** *o L.Am.* ***agregado***) sales tax, *Br* VAT (= value added tax)

izar hoist

izquierda *f tb* POL left; **izquierdista** POL **1** *adj* left-wing **2** *m/f* left-winger; **izquierdo** left

J

jabalí *m* ZO wild boar

jabalina *f* javelin

jabón *m* soap; **~ *de afeitar*** shaving soap; **jabonera** *f* soap dish

jacinto *m* hyacinth

jactarse boast (***de*** about)

jadear pant

jaguar *m* ZO jaguar

jalea *f* jelly

jaleo *m* (*ruido*) racket, uproar; (*lío*) mess

Jamaica Jamaica; **jamaicano 1** *adj* Jamaican **2** *m*, **-a** *f* Jamaican

jamás never; ***¿viste ~ algo así?*** did you ever see anything like it?; ***nunca ~*** never ever; ***por siempre ~*** for ever and ever

jamón *m* ham; **~ *de York*** cooked ham; **~ *serrano*** cured ham

Japón Japan; **japonés 1** *adj* Japanese **2** *m*, **-esa** *f* Japanese **3** *m idioma* Japanese

jaque *m* check; **~ *mate*** checkmate; ***dar ~ a*** checkmate

jaqueca *f* MED migraine

jarabe *m* syrup; *Méx type of folk dance*

jardín *m* garden; **~ *de infancia*** kindergarten; **jardinera** *f* jardiniere; **jardinería** *f* gardening; **jardinero** *m*, **-a** *f* gardener

jarra *f* pitcher, *Br* jug; ***en ~s*** with hands on hips; **jarro** *m* pitcher, *Br* jug

jaula *f* cage

jazmín *m* BOT jasmine

jefatura *f* headquarters *pl*; (*dirección*) leadership; **~ *de policía*** police headquarters; **jefe** *m*, **-a** *f de departamento, organización* head; (*superior*) boss; POL leader; *de tribu* chief; **~ *de cocina*** (head) chef; **~ *de estado*** head of state

jengibre *m* BOT ginger

jeque *m* sheik

jerez *m* sherry

jerga *f* jargon; (*argot*) slang

jersey *m* sweater

jibia *f* ZO cuttlefish

jilguero *m* ZO goldfinch

jinete *m* rider; *en carrera* jockey

jirafa *f* ZO giraffe

jocoso humorous, joking

joder V (*follar*) screw V, fuck V; (*estropear*) screw up V, fuck up V; *L.Am.* F (*fasti-*

diar) annoy

jornada *f* (working) day; *distancia* day's journey; **~ *laboral*** work day; **~ *partida*** split shift; **jornal** *m* day's wage; **jornalero** *m*, **-a** *f* day laborer, *Br* day laborer

joroba *f* hump; *fig* pain F; **jorobado** hump-backed; *fig* F in a bad way F; **jorobar** F (*molestar*) bug F; *planes* ruin

joven 1 *adj* young **2** *m/f* young man; *mujer* young woman; ***los jóvenes*** young people

joya *f* jewel; *persona* gem; **~*s*** jewelry, *Br* jewellery; **joyería** *f* jewelry store, *Br* jeweller's; **joyero 1** *m*, **-a** *f* jeweler, *Br* jeweller **2** *m* jewelry *o Br* jewellery box

juanete *m* MED bunion

jubilación *f* retirement; **~ *anticipada*** early retirement; **jubilado 1** *adj* retired **2** *m*, **-a** *f* retiree, *Br* pensioner; **jubilarse** retire; **júbilo** *m* jubilation

judía *f* BOT bean; **~ *verde*** green bean, runner bean

judicial judicial

judío 1 *adj* Jewish **2** *m*, **-a** *f* Jew

juego *m* game; *acción* play; *por dinero* gambling; (*conjunto de objetos*) set; **~ *de azar*** game of chance; **~ *de café*** coffee set; **~ *de manos*** conjuring trick; **~ *de mesa*** board game; **~ *de sociedad*** game; ***Juegos Olímpicos*** Olympic Games; ***estar en ~*** *fig* be at stake; ***fuera de ~*** DEP offside; ***hacer ~ con*** go with, match

juerga *f* F partying F

jueves *m inv* Thursday

juez *m/f* judge; **~ *de línea*** *en fútbol* assistant referee; *en fútbol americano* line judge

jugada *f* play, *Br* move; *en ajedrez* move; ***hacerle una mala ~ a alguien*** play a dirty trick on s.o.; **jugador** *m*, **~a** *f* player; **jugar 1** *v/t* play **2** *v/i* play; *con dinero* gamble; **~ *al baloncesto*** play basketball; **jugarse** risk; **jugarreta** *f* F dirty trick F

jugo *m* juice; **jugoso** *tb fig* juicy

juguete *m* toy; **juguetería** *f* toy store, *Br* toy shop

juicio *m* judg(e)ment; JUR trial; (*sensatez*) sense; (*cordura*) sanity; ***a mi ~*** in my opinion; ***estar en su ~*** be in one's right mind; ***perder el ~*** lose one's mind

julio *m* July

junco *m* BOT reed

jungla *f* jungle

junio *m* June

junta *f* POL (regional) government; *militar* junta; COM board; (*sesión*) meeting; TÉC joint; **~ *directiva*** board of directors; **juntar** put together; *gente* gather together; *bienes* collect; **juntarse** (*reunirse*) meet, assemble; *de pareja*: *empezar a salir* start going out; *empezar a vi-*

vir juntos move in together; *de caminos, ríos* meet, join; **~ con alguien** *socialmente* mix with s.o.; **junto 1** *adj* together **2** *prp*: **~ a** next to, near; **~ con** together with

juntura *f* TÉC joint

jurado *m* JUR jury; **juramento** *m* oath; ***bajo ~*** under oath; **jurar** swear; **jurídico** legal; **jurisdicción** *f* jurisdiction; **jurista** *m/f* jurist

justicia *f* justice; ***la ~*** (*la ley*) the law; **justificante** *m de pago* receipt; *de ausencia, propiedad* certificate; **justificar** *tb* TIP justify; **justo** just, fair; (*exacto*) right, exact; ***lo ~*** just enough; ***¡~!*** right!, exactly!

juvenil youthful; **juventud** *f* youth

K

kárate *m* karate; **karateca** *m/f* karate expert

kilo *m* kilo; *fig* F million; **kilobyte** *m* kilobyte; **kilogramo** *m* kilogram, *Br* kilogramme; **kilómetro** *m* kilometer, *Br* kilometre; **kilovatio** *m* kilowatt

kiosco *m* kiosk

kiwi *m* BOT kiwi (fruit)

L

la 1 *art* the; ***~ que está embarazada*** the one who is pregnant; ***~ más grande*** the biggest (one); ***dame ~ roja*** give me the red one **2** *pron complemento directo sg* her; *a usted* you; *algo* it

laberinto *m* labyrinth, maze

labia *f*: ***tener mucha ~*** have the gift of the gab; **labio** *m* lip

labor *f* work; (*tarea*) task, job; ***hacer ~es*** do needlework; ***no estar por la ~*** F not be enthusiastic about the idea; **laborable**: ***día ~*** workday; **laboral** labor *atr*, *Br* labour *atr*; **laboratorio** *m* laboratory, lab F; **labrador** *m* farm worker; **labrar** *tierra* work; *piedra* carve

laca *f* lacquer; ***~ de uñas*** nail varnish *o* polish

lactante *madre* nursing; *bebé* being breastfed

ladera *f* slope

lado *m* side; (*lugar*) place; ***al ~*** nearby; ***al ~ de*** beside, next to; ***de ~*** sideways; ***ir por otro ~*** go another way; ***por un ~... por otro ~*** on the one hand … on the other hand

ladrar bark

ladrillo *m* brick

ladrón *m* thief
lagartija *f* ZO small lizard; **lagarto** *m* ZO lizard
lago *m* lake
lágrima *f* tear
laguna *f* lagoon; *fig* gap
laico lay *atr*
lamentable deplorable; **lamentablemente** regretfully; **lamentar** regret, be sorry about; *muerte* mourn; **lamentarse** complain (***de*** about); **lamento** *m* whimper; *por dolor* groan
lamer lick
lámina *f* sheet
lámpara *f* lamp; ***~ de pie*** floor lamp
lana *f* wool; *Méx* P dough F
lance *m* incident, episode; ***de ~*** secondhand
lancha *f* launch; ***~ fueraborda*** outboard
langosta *f insecto* locust; *crustáceo* spiny lobster; **langostino** *m* king prawn
lánguido languid
lanzamiento *m* MIL, COM launch; ***~ de disco / de martillo*** discus / hammer (throw); ***~ de peso*** shot put; **lanzar** throw; *cohete, producto* launch; *bomba* drop; **lanzarse** throw o.s. (***en*** into); (*precipitarse*) pounce (***sobre*** on)
lápiz *m* pencil; ***~ de ojos*** eyeliner; ***~ labial*** *o* ***de labios*** lipstick
largarse F clear off F; **largo 1** *adj* long; *persona* tall; ***a la -a*** in the long run; ***a lo ~ del día*** throughout the day; ***a lo ~ de la calle*** along the street; ***¡~!*** F scram! F; ***pasar de ~*** go (straight) past **2** *m* length; **largometraje** *m* feature film
laringe *f* larynx
las 1 *art fpl* the **2** *pron complemento directo pl* them; *a ustedes* you; ***llévate ~ que quieras*** take the ones *o* those you want; ***~ de...*** those of ...; ***~ de Juan*** Juan's
lascivo lewd
láser *m* laser; ***rayo ~*** laser beam
lástima *f* pity, shame; **lastimarse** hurt o.s.
lastre *m* ballast; *fig* burden
lata *f* can, *Br tb* tin; *fig* F drag F; ***dar la ~*** F be a drag F
lateral 1 *adj* side *atr* **2** *m* DEP: ***~ derecho / izquierdo*** right / left back
latido *m* beat
latifundio *m* large estate
látigo *m* whip
latín *m* Latin; **latino** Latin; **Latinoamérica** Latin America; **latinoamericano 1** *adj* Latin American **2** *m*, **-a** *f* Latin American
latir beat
latitud *f* latitude
latón *m* brass
laurel *m* BOT laurel; ***dormirse en los ~es*** *fig* rest on one's laurels
lavable washable; **lavabo** *m* washbowl; **lavado** *m* washing; ***~ de cerebro*** *fig* brain-

washing; **lavadora** *f* washing machine; **lavandería** *f* laundry; **lavaplatos** *m inv* dishwasher; *L.Am.* (*fregadero*) sink; **lavar 1** *v/t* wash; ***~ los platos*** wash the dishes; ***~ la ropa*** do the laundry; ***~ en seco*** dry-clean **2** *v/i* (*lavar los platos*) do the dishes; *de detergente* clean; **lavarse** wash up, *Br* have a wash; ***~ los dientes*** brush one's teeth; ***~ las manos*** wash one's hands; **lavativa** *f* MED enema; **lavavajillas** *m inv líquido* dishwashing liquid, *Br* washing-up liquid; *electrodoméstico* dishwasher

laxante *m/adj* MED laxative

lazo *m* knot; *de adorno* bow; *para atrapar animales* lasso

le *complemento indirecto* (to) him; (*a ella*) (to) her; (*a usted*) (to) you; (*a algo*) (to) it; *complemento directo* him; (*a usted*) you

leal loyal; **lealtad** *f* loyalty

lección *f* lesson

leche *f* milk; **lechería** *f* dairy; **lechero 1** *adj* dairy *atr* **2** *m* milkman

lecho *m tb de río* bed

lechón *m* suckling pig

lechuga *f* lettuce

lechuza *f* ZO barn-owl; *Cuba, Méx* P hooker F

lector *m*, **~a** *f* reader; **lectura** *f* reading

leer read

legación *f* legation

legal legal; *fig* F *persona* great F; **legalidad** *f* legality; **legalizar** legalize

legar leave

legendario legendary

legislación *f* legislation; **legislar** legislate; **legislativo** legislative

legitimar justify; *documento* authenticate; **legítimo** legitimate; (*verdadero*) authentic

lego lay *atr*; *fig* ignorant

legua *f*: ***se ve a la ~*** *fig* F you can see it a mile off F; *hecho* it's blindingly obvious F

legumbre *f* BOT pulse

lejanía *f* distance; ***en la ~*** in the distance; **lejano** distant

lejía *f* bleach

lejos 1 *adv* far (away); ***Navidad queda ~*** Christmas is a long way off; ***a lo ~*** in the distance; ***ir demasiado ~*** *fig* go too far; ***llegar ~*** *fig* go far **2** *prp*: ***~ de*** far from

lema *m* slogan

lencería *f* lingerie

lengua *f* tongue; ***~ materna*** mother tongue; ***irse de la ~*** let the cat out of the bag; **lenguado** *m* ZO sole; **lenguaje** *m* language

lente *f* lens; ***~s de contacto*** contact lenses; **lentes** *mpl L.Am.* glasses

lenteja *f* BOT lentil

lentejuela *f* sequin

lentillas *fpl* contact lenses

lentitud *f* slowness; **lento** slow; ***a fuego ~*** on a low heat

leña *f* (fire)wood; ***echar ~ al fuego*** *fig* add fuel to the fire;

leñador *m* woodcutter
Leo *m/f inv* ASTR Leo
león *m* lion; *L.Am.* puma; **~ *marino*** sealion
leopardo *m* leopard
leotardo *m de gimnasta* leotard; **~*s*** tights, *Br* heavy tights
lerdo (*torpe*) slow(-witted)
les *pl complemento indirecto* (to) them; (*a ustedes*) (to) you; *complemento directo* them; (*a ustedes*) you
lesbiana *f* lesbian
lesión *f* injury; **lesionar** injure
letal lethal
letón 1 *adj* Latvian **2** *m*, **-ona** *f* Latvian **3** *m idioma* Latvian; **Letonia** *f* Latvia
letra *f* letter; *de canción* lyrics *pl*; **~ *de cambio*** COM bill of exchange; **~ *de imprenta*** block capital; **~ *mayúscula*** capital letter; ***al pie de la ~*** word for word; **letrado 1** *adj* learned **2** *m*, **-a** *f* lawyer
letrero *m* sign
levadura *f* yeast
levantamiento *m* raising; (*rebelión*) rising; *de embargo* lifting; **levantar** raise; *bulto* lift (up); *del suelo* pick up; *edificio, estatua* put up; *embargo* lift; **~ *sospechas*** arouse suspicion; ***¡levanta los ánimos!*** cheer up!; **levantarse** get up; (*ponerse de pie*) stand up; *de un edificio, una montaña* rise; *en rebelión* rise up; **levante** *m* east
leve slight; *sonrisa* faint
léxico *m* lexicon
ley *f* law; ***con todas las de la ~*** fairly and squarely
leyenda *f* legend
liar tie (up); *en papel* wrap (up); *cigarillo* roll; *persona* confuse
libanés 1 *adj* Lebanese **2** *m*, **-esa** *f* Lebanese; **Líbano** Lebanon
liberación *f* release; *de un país* liberation; **liberal** liberal; **liberar** (set) free, release; *país* liberate; *energía* release; **libertad** *f* freedom, liberty; **~ *bajo fianza*** JUR bail; **~ *condicional*** JUR probation
libertinaje *m* licentiousness
Libia Libya; **libio 1** *adj* Libyan **2** *m*, **-a** *f* Libyan
libra *f* pound; **~ *esterlina*** pound (sterling)
Libra *m/f inv* ASTR Libra
librar 1 *v/t* free (**de** from); *cheque* draw; *batalla* fight **2** *v/i*: ***libro los lunes*** I have Mondays off; **libre** free; **librecambio** *m* free trade
librería *f* bookstore; **librero** *m* bookseller; *L.Am. mueble* bookcase; **libreta** *f* notebook; **~ *de ahorros*** bankbook, passbook; **libro** *m* book; **~ *de bolsillo*** paperback (book); **~ *de cocina*** cookbook; **~ *de familia*** *booklet recording family births, marriages and deaths*

licencia *f* permit, license, *Br* licence; (*permiso*) permission; MIL leave; ***~ de manejar o conducir*** *L.Am.* driver's license, *Br* driving licence; ***tomarse demasiadas ~s*** take liberties; **licenciado** *m*, **-a** *f* graduate; **licenciar** MIL discharge; **licenciarse** graduate; MIL be discharged; **licenciatura** *f* EDU degree

licitar *L.Am. en subasta* bid for

licor *m* liquor, *Br* spirits *pl*

licuadora *f* blender

líder 1 *m/f* leader **2** *adj* leading

lidia *f* bullfighting

liebre *f* hare

lienzo *m* canvas

liga *f* POL, DEP league; *de medias* garter; **ligamento** *m* ANAT ligament; **ligar 1** *v/t* bind; (*atar*) tie **2** *v/i*: ***~ con*** F pick up F

ligero 1 *adj* light; (*rápido*) rapid; *movimiento* agile; (*leve*) slight; ***~ de ropa*** scantily clad; ***a la -a*** (*sin pensar*) lightly **2** *adv* quickly

ligue *m* F: ***estar de ~*** be on the pick-up F

liguero *m* garter belt, *Br* suspender belt

lija *f*: ***papel de ~*** sandpaper

lila *f* BOT lilac

lima *f* file; BOT lime; ***~ de uñas*** nail file; **limar** file; *fig* polish

limitar 1 *v/t* limit **2** *v/i*: ***~ con*** border on; **limitarse** limit o.s. (***a*** to); **límite 1** *m* limit; (*línea de separación*) boundary; ***~ de velocidad*** speed limit **2** *adj*: ***situación ~*** life-threatening situation

limón *m* lemon; **limonada** *f* lemonade; **limonero** *m* lemon tree

limosna *f*: ***una ~, por favor*** can you spare some change?

limpiabotas *m/f inv* bootblack; **limpiaparabrisas** *m inv* AUTO windshield wiper, *Br* windscreen wiper; **limpiar** clean; *con un trapo* wipe; *fig* clean up; ***~ a alguien*** F clean s.o. out F; **limpieza** *f estado* cleanliness; *acto* cleaning; ***~ general*** spring cleaning; ***~ en seco*** dry-cleaning; **limpio** clean; (*ordenado*) neat, tidy; *político* honest; ***quedarse ~*** *S.Am.* F be broke F; ***sacar algo en ~*** *fig* make sense of sth

linaje *m* lineage

linaza *f* BOT linseed

lince *m* ZO lynx

lindante adjacent (***con*** to), bordering (***con*** on); **lindar**: ***~ con algo*** adjoin sth; *fig* border on sth

lindo 1 *adj* lovely; ***de lo ~*** a lot, a great deal **2** *adv L.Am. jugar, bailar* beautifully

línea *f* line; ***en ~*** on line; ***~ aérea*** airline; ***mantener la ~*** watch one's figure; ***de pri-***

mera ~ *fig* first-rate; ***tecnología de primera ~*** cutting edge technology; ***entre ~s*** *fig* between the lines

lingüístico linguistic

lino *m* linen; BOT flax

linterna *f* flashlight, *Br* torch

lío *m* bundle; F (*desorden*) mess; F (*jaleo*) fuss; ***~ amoroso*** F affair; ***hacerse un ~*** get into a muddle

liposucción *f* liposuction

liquidación *f* COM *de deuda* settlement; *de negocio* liquidation; ***~ total*** clearance sale; **liquidar** *cuenta*, *deuda* settle; COM *negocio* wind up, liquidate; *existencias* sell off; F (*matar*) liquidate F, bump off F; **líquido 1** *adj* liquid; COM net **2** *m* liquid

lira *f* lira

lírica *f* lyric poetry

lisiado 1 *adj* crippled **2** *m* cripple

liso smooth; *terreno* flat; *pelo* straight; (*sin adornos*) plain; ***-a y llanamente*** plainly and simply

lisonja *f* flattery; **lisonjear** flatter

lista *f* list; ***~ de boda*** wedding list; ***~ de correos*** general delivery, *Br* poste restante; ***~ de espera*** waiting list; **listado** *m* INFOR printout; **listín** *m*: ***~ (telefónico)*** phone book

listo (*inteligente*) clever; (*preparado*) ready

listón *m de madera* strip; DEP bar

litera *f* bunk; *de tren* couchette

literario literary; **literatura** *f* literature

litoral 1 *adj* coastal **2** *m* coast

litro *m* liter, *Br* litre

Lituania Lithuania; **lituano 1** *adj* Lithuanian **2** *m*, **-a** *f* Lithuanian **3** *m idioma* Lithuanian

liviano light; (*de poca importancia*) trivial

llaga *f* ulcer

llama *f* flame; ZO llama

llamada *f* call; *en una puerta* knock; *en timbre* ring; ***~ a cobro revertido*** collect call; ***~ de auxilio*** distress call; **llamamiento** *m* call; ***hacer un ~ a algo*** call for sth; **llamar** call; TELEC call, *Br tb* ring; ***~ a la puerta*** knock at the door; *con timbre* ring the bell; ***el fútbol no me llama nada*** football doesn't appeal to me in the slightest; **llamarse** be called; ***¿cómo te llamas?*** what's your name?

llamativo eyecatching; *color* loud

llanito *m*, **-a** *f* F Gibraltarian

llano 1 *adj terreno* level; *trato* natural; *persona* unassuming **2** *m* flat ground

llanta *f* wheel rim; *C.Am.*, *Méx* (*neumático*) tire, *Br* tyre

llanto *m* sobbing

llanura *f* plain

llave *f* key; *para tuerca* wrench, *Br tb* spanner; ~

de contacto AUTO ignition key; **~ *inglesa*** TÉC monkey wrench; **~ *en mano*** available for immediate occupancy; ***bajo* ~** under lock and key; ***cerrar con* ~** lock; **llavero** *m* key ring

llegada *f* arrival; **llegar** arrive; (*alcanzar*) reach; ***la comida no llegó para todos*** there wasn't enough food for everyone; ***me llega hasta las rodillas*** it comes down to my knees; **~ *a saber*** find out; **~ *a ser*** get to be; **~ *a viejo*** live to a ripe old age

llenar 1 *v/t* fill; *impreso* fill out *o* in **2** *v/i* be filling; **lleno** full (***de*** of); *pared* covered (***de*** with); ***de* ~** fully

llevar 1 *v/t* take; *ropa*, *gafas* wear; *ritmo* keep up; **~ *las de perder*** be likely to lose; ***me lleva dos años*** he's two years older than me; ***llevo ocho días aquí*** I've been here a week **2** *v/i* lead (***a*** to); **llevarse** take; *susto*, *sorpresa* get; **~ *bien* / *mal*** get on well / badly; ***se lleva el color rojo*** red is fashionable

llorar cry, weep

llover rain; ***llueve*** it is raining

llovizna *f* drizzle; **lloviznar** drizzle

lluvia *f* rain; *Rpl* (*ducha*) shower; **lluvioso** rainy

lo 1 *art* the; ***no sabes* ~ *difícil que es*** you don't know how difficult it is **2** *pron*: *a él* him; *a usted* you; *algo* it; **~ *sé*** I know **3** *pron rel*: **~ *que*** what; **~ *cual*** which

lobo *m* wolf; **~ *marino*** seal; **~ *de mar*** *fig* sea dog

local 1 *adj* local **2** *m* premises *pl*; **localidad** *f* town; TEA seat; **localizar** locate; *incendio* contain

loción *f* lotion

loco 1 *adj* mad, crazy; ***a lo* ~** F (*sin pensar*) hastily **2** *m* madman

locomoción *f* locomotion; ***medio de* ~** means of transport; **locomotora** *f* locomotive

locuaz talkative, loquacious *fml*

locura *f* madness

locutor *m*, **~a** *f* RAD, TV presenter

lodo *m* mud

lógica *f* logic; **lógico** logical

logrado excellent; **lograr** achieve; (*obtener*) obtain; **~ *hacer algo*** manage to do sth; **logro** *m* achievement

lombarda *f* BOT red cabbage

lomo *m* back; GASTR loin

lona *f* canvas

loncha *f* slice

Londres London

longaniza *f type of dried sausage*

longitud *f* longitude; (*largo*) length

lonja *f de pescado* fish market; (*loncha*) slice

loro *m* parrot

los 1 *art mpl* the **2** *pron complemento directo pl* them; *a*

ustedes you; ***llévate ~ que quieras*** take the ones *o* those you want; ***~ de...*** those of ...; ***~ de Juan*** Juan's
losa *f* flagstone
lote *m en reparto* share, part; *L.Am.* (*solar*) lot; **lotería** *f* lottery; **lotero** *m*, **-a** *f* lottery ticket seller
loza *f* china
lubina *f* ZO sea bass
lubri(fi)cante 1 *adj* lubricating **2** *m* lubricant; **lubri(fi)car** lubricate
lucha *f* fight, struggle; DEP wrestling; ***~ libre*** DEP all-in wrestling; **luchar** fight (***por*** for)
lúcido lucid, clear
luciérnaga *f* ZO glowworm
lucio *m* ZO pike
lucir 1 *v/i* shine; *L.Am.* (*verse bien*) look good **2** *v/t ropa, joya* wear; **lucirse** *tb irónico* excel o.s.
lucrativo lucrative; **lucro** *m* profit; ***sin ánimo de ~*** not-for-profit
luego 1 *adv* (*después*) later; *en orden, espacio* then; *L.Am.* (*en seguida*) right now; ***~ ~*** *Méx* straight away **2** *conj* therefore; ***~ que*** *L.Am.* after
lugar *m* place; ***~ común*** cliché; ***en ~ de*** instead of; ***en primer ~*** in the first place, first(ly); ***fuera de ~*** out of place; ***yo en tu ~*** if I were you, (if I were) in your place; ***dar ~ a*** give rise to; ***tener ~*** take place
lujo *m* luxury; **lujoso** luxurious
lumbago *m* MED lumbago; **lumbar** lumbar
lumbre *f* fire; **luminoso** luminous; *lámpara, habitación* bright
luna *f* moon; *de tienda* window; *de vehículo* windshield, *Br* windscreen; ***~ de miel*** honeymoon; ***~ llena*** / ***nueva*** full / new moon; ***media ~*** *L.Am.* GASTR croissant; **lunar 1** *adj* lunar **2** *m en la piel* mole; ***de ~es*** spotted, polka-dot
lunes *m inv* Monday
luneta *f*: ***~ térmica*** AUTO heated windshield, *Br* heated windscreen
lupa *f* magnifying glass; ***mirar algo con ~*** *fig* go through sth with a fine-tooth comb
lúpulo *m* BOT hop
luso 1 *adj* Portuguese **2** *m*, **-a** *f* Portuguese
lustrar polish; **lustre** *m* shine; *fig* luster, *Br* lustre
luto *m* mourning; ***estar de ~ por alguien*** be in mourning for s.o.
Luxemburgo *m* Luxemb(o)urg; **luxemburgués 1** *adj* of / from Luxemb(o)urg, Luxemb(o)urg *atr* **2** *m*, **-guesa** *f* Luxemb(o)urger
luz *f* light; ***~ trasera*** AUTO rear light; ***luces de carretera*** *o* ***largas*** AUTO full *o* main beam headlights; ***luces de cruce*** *o* ***cortas*** AUTO dipped

headlights; **~ verde** *tb fig* green light; **arrojar ~ sobre algo** *fig* shed light on s.th.; **dar a ~** give birth to; **salir a la ~** *fig* come to light; **a todas luces** evidently

M

macabro 1 *adj* macabre **2** *m*, **-a** *f* ghoul
macarrones *mpl* macaroni *sg*
macedonia *f*: **~ de frutas** fruit salad
maceta *f* flowerpot
machacar crush; *fig* thrash
machete *m* machete
machismo *m* male chauvinism; **machista 1** *adj* sexist **2** *m* sexist, male chauvinist
macho 1 *adj* male; (*varonil*) tough; *desp* macho **2** *m* male; *apelativo* F man F, *L.Am.* (*plátano*) banana
macizo 1 *adj* solid **2** *m* GEOG massif; ***Macizo de Brasil*** Brazilian Highlands; **~ de flores** flower bed
madeja *f* hank
madera *f* wood; **tener ~ de** have the makings of; **madero** *m* P cop P
madrastra *f* step-mother
madre 1 *f* mother; **~ soltera** single mother **2** *adj Méx, C.Am.* F great F; **madreselva** *f* BOT honeysuckle
madrileño 1 *adj* of / from Madrid, Madrid *atr* **2** *m*, **-a** *f* native of Madrid
madrina *f* godmother
madrugada *f* early morning; (*amanecer*) dawn; **de ~** in the small hours; **madrugador** *m*, **~a** *f* early riser; **madrugar** *L.Am.* (*quedar despierto*) stay up till the small hours; (*levantarse temprano*) get up early
madurar 1 *v/t fig*: *idea* think through **2** *v/i de persona* mature; *de fruta* ripen; **madurez** *f mental* maturity; *edad* middle age; *de fruta* ripeness; **maduro** *mentalmente* mature; *de edad* middle-aged; *fruta* ripe
maestría *f* mastery; *Méx* EDU master's (degree); **maestro 1** *adj* master *atr* **2** *m*, **-a** *f* EDU teacher; MÚS maestro
magia *f tb fig* magic; **mágico** magic
magistrado *m* judge; **magistral** masterly
magnético magnetic
magnetofón *m* tape recorder; **magnetoscopio** *m* VCR, video (cassette recorder)
magnífico magnificent
magnitud *f* magnitude
mago *m tb fig* magician; ***los Reyes Magos*** the Three Wise Men
magro *carne* lean
magulladura *f* bruise

mahometano 1 *adj* Muslim **2** *m*, **-a** *f* Muslim
maíz *m* corn
majadero F **1** *adj* idiotic, stupid **2** *m*, **-a** *f* idiot
majestad *f* majesty; **majestuoso** majestic
majo F nice; (*bonito*) pretty
mal 1 *adj* ☞ ***malo* 2** *adv* badly; ***~ que bien*** one way or the other; ***¡menos ~!*** thank goodness!; ***ponerse a ~ con alguien*** fall out with s.o.; ***tomarse algo a ~*** take sth badly **3** *m* MED illness; ***el ~ menor*** the lesser of two evils
malaria *f* MED malaria
malcriado spoilt
maldad *f* evil
maldecir curse; **maldición** *f* curse; **maldito** F damn F; ***¡-a sea!*** (god)damn it!
maleante *m/f* & *adj* criminal
malecón *m* breakwater
maleducado rude, bad-mannered
malentendido *m* misunderstanding
malestar *m* MED discomfort; *social* unrest
maleta *f* bag, suitcase; *L.Am.* AUTO trunk, *Br* boot; ***hacer la ~*** pack one's bags; **maletero** *m* trunk, *Br* boot; **maletín** *m* briefcase
maleza *f* undergrowth
malformación *f* malformation
malgastar waste
malhechor *m*, **~a** *f* criminal
malhumorado bad-tempered
malicia *f* (*mala intención*) malice; (*astucia*) cunning; ***no tener ~*** F be very naive; **malicioso** (*malintencionado*) malicious; (*astuto*) cunning, sly
maligno harmful; MED malignant
malintencionado malicious
malla *f* mesh; *Rpl* (*bañador*) swimsuit
Mallorca *f* Majorca; **mallorquín 1** *adj* Majorcan **2** *m*, **-quina** *f* Majorcan
malo 1 *adj* bad; *calidad* poor; (*enfermo*) sick, ill; ***por las buenas*** *o* ***por las -as*** like it or not; ***por las -as*** by force; ***ponerse ~*** fall ill **2** *m* bad guy, baddy F
malogrado *muerto* dead before one's time; **malograrse** fail; *de plan* come to nothing; *fallecer* die before one's time; *S.Am.* (*descomponerse*) break down; (*funcionar mal*) go wrong
maloliente stinking
malparado: ***salir ~ de algo*** come out badly from sth
malta *f* malt
maltratar mistreat
maltrecho weakened; *cosa* damaged
malvado evil
malversación *f*: ***~ de fondos*** embezzlement
Malvinas: ***las ~*** the Falklands, the Falkland Islands

mama *f* breast
mamá *f* mom, *Br* mum
mamar suck; ***dar de ~*** (breast)feed
mamífero *m* mammal
mampara *f* screen
manada *f* herd; *de lobos* pack
manantial *m* spring
manar flow
mancha *f* (dirty) mark; *de grasa, sangre etc* stain; **manchar** get dirty; *de grasa, sangre etc* stain
Mancha: *Canal de la ~* English Channel; ***la ~*** La Mancha
manco *de mano* one-handed; *de brazo* one-armed
mandamás *m inv* F big shot F
mandar 1 *v/t* order; (*enviar*) send; ***~ hacer algo*** have sth done **2** *v/i* be in charge; ***¿mande?*** *Méx* can I help you?; *Méx* TELEC hallo?; (*¿cómo?*) what did you say?
mandarina *f* mandarin (orange)
mandato *m* order; POL mandate
mandíbula *f* ANAT jaw
mandil *m* leather apron
mando *m* command; ***~ a distancia*** TV remote control; ***tablero de -s*** AUTO dashboard; **mandón** F bossy F
manecilla *f* hand
manejar 1 *v/t* handle; *máquina* operate; *L.Am.* AUTO drive **2** *v/i L.Am.* AUTO drive; **manejo** *m* handling; *de una máquina* operation
manera *f* way; ***~s*** manners; ***lo hace a su ~*** he does it his way; ***de ~ que*** so (that); ***de ninguna ~*** certainly not; ***no hay ~ de*** it is impossible to; ***de todas ~s*** anyway
manga *f* sleeve; ***~ de riego*** hosepipe; ***en ~s de camisa*** in one's shirtsleeves; ***traer algo en la ~*** F have sth up one's sleeve
mangar P pinch F
mango *m* BOT mango; *CSur* F (*dinero*) dough F; ***estoy sin un ~*** *CSur* F I'm broke F, I don't have a bean F
manguera *f* hose(pipe)
manguito *m* TÉC sleeve; ***~s*** *para nadar* armbands
maní *m S.Am.* peanut
manía *f* (*costumbre*) habit; (*antipatía*) dislike; (*obsesión*) obsession; ***tiene sus -s*** she has her little ways
manicomio *m* lunatic asylum
manicura *f* manicure
manifestación *f de gente* demonstration; (*muestra*) show; (*declaración*) statement; **manifestante** *m/f* demonstrator; **manifestar** (*demostrar*) show; (*declarar*) declare, state; **manifestarse** demonstrate; **manifiesto 1** *adj* clear, manifest **2** *m* manifesto
manillar *m* handlebars *pl*
maniobra *f* maneuver, *Br* manoeuvre; **maniobrar** maneuver, *Br* manoeuvre
manipulación *f* manipula-

tion; (*manejo*) handling; **manipular** manipulate; (*manejar*) handle
maniquí 1 *m* dummy **2** *m/f* model
manivela *f* handle
manjar *m* delicacy
mano 1 *f* hand; **~ *de obra*** manpower; **~ *de pintura*** coat of paint; ***a ~ izquierda*** on the lefthand side; ***de segunda ~*** second-hand; ***echar una ~ a alguien*** give s.o. a hand; ***estar a ~s*** *L.Am.* F be even; ***traerse algo entre ~s*** be plotting sth; ***~s libres*** hands-free **2** *m Méx* F buddy F; **manojo** *m* handful; **~ *de llaves*** bunch of keys; **~ *de nervios*** *fig* bundle of nerves
manopla *f* mitten
manosear handle; *persona* F grope F
mansión *f* mansion
manso docile; *persona* mild
manta *f* blanket
manteca *f* fat; *Rpl* butter; **~ *de cacao*** cocoa butter; **~ *de cerdo*** lard; **mantecado** *m type of cupcake, traditionally eaten at Christmas*
mantel *m* tablecloth; **~ *individual*** table mat; **mantelería** *f* table linen
mantener (*sujetar*) hold; *techo etc* hold up; (*preservar*) keep; *conversación, relación* have; *económicamente* support; (*afirmar*) maintain; **mantenerse** (*sujetarse*) be held; *económicamente* support o.s.; *en forma* keep; **mantenimiento** *m* maintenance; *económico* support; ***gimnasia de ~*** gymnasium
mantequilla *f* butter
mantilla *f de bebé* shawl
manto *m* GEOL layer, stratum; (*capa*) cloak; ***un ~ de nieve*** a blanket of snow
mantón *m* shawl
manual *m/adj* manual; **manualidades** *fpl* handicrafts
manuscrito 1 *adj* handwritten **2** *m* manuscript
manutención *f* maintenance
manzana *f* apple; *de casas* block; **manzanilla** *f* camomile tea; **manzano** *m* apple tree
maña *f* skill
mañana 1 *f* morning; ***por la ~*** in the morning; ***~ por la ~*** tomorrow morning; ***de la ~ a la noche*** from morning until night; ***de la noche a la ~*** *fig* overnight **2** *adv* tomorrow; ***pasado ~*** the day after tomorrow
mapa *m* map; **~ *de carreteras*** road map
maqueta *f* model
maquillaje *m* make-up; **maquillar** make up; **maquillarse** put on one's make-up
máquina *f* machine; FERR locomotive; *C.Am., W.I.* AUTO car; **~ *de afeitar*** (electric) shaver; **~ *de coser*** sewing machine; **~ *de fotos*** camera; **~ *recreativa*** arcade game; **~**

de respiración asistida life support machine; ***a toda ~*** at top speed; **maquinaciones** *fpl* scheming; **maquinador 1** *adj* scheming **2** *m*, **~a** *f* schemer; **maquinal** *fig* mechanical; **maquinar** plot; **maquinaria** *f* machinery; ; **maquinilla** *f*: **~ *de afeitar*** razor; **~ *eléctrica*** electric razor; **maquinista** *m/f* FERR engineer, *Br* train driver
mar *m* (*also f*) sea; ***llover a ~es*** *fig* F pour, bucket down F; ***alta ~*** high seas *pl*; ***Mar Bermejo*** Gulf of California; ***mar Caribe*** Caribbean Sea
maraña *f de hilos* tangle; (*lío*) jumble
maravilla *f* marvel, wonder; BOT marigold; ***a las mil ~s*** marvelously, *Br* marvellously; **maravillarse** be amazed (***de*** at); **maravilloso** marvelous, *Br* marvelous
marca *f* mark; COM brand; **~ *registrada*** registered trademark; ***de ~*** brand-name *atr*; **marcador** *m* DEP (*resultado*) score; (*tablero*) scoreboard; **marcapasos** *m inv* MED pacemaker; **marcar** mark; *número de teléfono* dial; *gol* score; *res* brand; *de termómetro, contador etc* read, register
marcha *f* (*salida*) departure; (*velocidad*) speed; (*avance*) progress; MIL march; AUTO gear; **~ *atrás*** AUTO reverse (gear); ***a ~s forzadas*** *fig* flat out; ***a toda ~*** at top speed; ***ponerse en ~*** get going; **marchante** *m L.Am.* regular customer; **marchar** (*progresar*) go; (*funcionar*) work; (*caminar*) walk; MIL march; **marcharse** leave, go
marchitarse wilt; **marchito** *flor* withered; *juventud* faded
marco *m de cuadro, puerta* frame; *fig* framework
marea *f* tide; **~ *alta*** high tide; **~ *baja*** low tide; **~ *negra*** oil slick; **marearse** feel nauseous, *Br* feel sick; **marejada** *f* heavy sea; **mareo** *m* seasickness
marfil *m* ivory
margarina *f* margarine
margarita *f* BOT daisy
margen *m tb fig* margin; ***al ~ de eso*** apart from that; **marginal** marginal
maricón *m* P fag P, *Br* poof P; **mariconera** *f* man's handbag
marido *m* husband
marina *f* navy; **~ *mercante*** merchant navy
marinero 1 *adj* sea *atr* **2** *m* sailor; **marino 1** *adj brisa* sea *atr*; *planta, animal* marine; ***azul ~*** navy blue **2** *m* sailor
marioneta *f tb fig* puppet
mariposa *f* butterfly
mariquita *f* ladybug, *Br* ladybird
marisco *m* seafood
marítimo maritime
marmita *f* pot, pan

mármol *m* marble
marqués *m* marquis; **marquesa** *f* marchioness
marquesina *f* marquee, *Br* canopy
marrano 1 *adj* filthy **2** *m* hog, *Br* pig; F *persona* pig F
marrón *m/adj* brown
marroquí *m/f* & *adj* Moroccan; **Marruecos** Morocco
marta *f* ZO marten
martes *m inv* Tuesday
martillar hammer; **martillo** *m* hammer; **~ *neumático*** pneumatic drill
mártir *m/f* martyr; **martirio** *m tb fig* martyrdom; **martirizar** *tb fig* martyr
marzo *m* March
más 1 *adj* more **2** *adv* more; *superlativo* most; MAT plus; ***~ grande*** bigger; ***~ importante*** more important; ***el ~ grande*** the biggest; ***el ~ importante*** the most important; ***trabajar ~*** work harder; ***~ bien*** rather; ***¿qué ~?*** what else?; ***no ~*** *L.Am.* ☞ ***nomás***; ***por ~ que*** however much; ***sin ~*** without more ado
mas *conj* but
masa *f* mass; GASTR dough
masacre *f* massacre
masaje *m* massage; **masajista** *m/f* masseur; *mujer* masseuse
mascar 1 *v/t* chew **2** *v/i L.Am.* chew tobacco
máscara *f* mask; **mascarilla** *f* mask; *cosmética* face pack
mascota *f* mascot; *animal doméstico* pet
masculino masculine
masivo massive
masón *m* mason
masoquismo *m* masochism; **masoquista 1** *adj* masochistic **2** *m/f* masochist
máster *m* master's (degree)
masticar chew
mástil *m* mast; *de tienda* pole
mata *f* bush
matadero *m* slaughterhouse; **matanza** *f* slaughter; **matar** kill; *ganado* slaughter; **matarse** kill o.s.; *morir* be killed
matasellos *m inv* postmark
mate 1 *adj* matt **2** *m en ajedrez* mate; *L.Am.* (*infusión*) maté
matemáticas *fpl* mathematics, math, *Br* maths; **matemático 1** *adj* mathematical **2** *m*, **-a** *f* mathematician
materia *f* matter; (*material*) material; (*tema*) subject; ***~ prima*** raw material; ***en ~ de*** as regards; **material** *m/adj* material
maternal maternal; **maternidad** *f* maternity; ***casa de ~*** maternity hospital; **materno:** ***por parte -a*** on one's mother's side, maternal
matinal morning *atr*
matiz *m de ironía* touch; *de color* shade; **matizar** *comentarios* qualify
matón *m* bully; (*criminal*) thug
matorral *m* thicket
matrícula *f* AUTO license plate, *Br* numberplate; EDU

registration; **matricular** register

matrimonial marriage *atr*, marital; **matrimonio** *m* marriage; *boda* wedding

matriz *f* matrix; ANAT womb

matutino morning *atr*

maxilar 1 *adj* maxillary **2** *m* jaw(bone)

máxima *f* maxim; **máximo** maximum

mayo *m* May

mayonesa *f* mayonnaise

mayor ◇ *comparativo*: *en tamaño* larger, bigger; *en edad* older; *en importancia* greater; ***ser ~ de edad*** be an adult; JUR be of legal age; ***al por ~*** COM wholesale ◇ *superlativo*: ***el ~*** *en edad* the oldest, the eldest; *en tamaño* the largest, the biggest; *en importancia* the greatest; ***los ~es*** adults; ***la ~ parte*** the majority; **mayoría** *f* majority; ***alcanzar la ~ de edad*** come of age; ***la ~ de*** the majority of, most (of); **mayorista** *m/f* wholesaler

mayúscula *f* capital (letter), upper case letter

maza *f* mace

mazapán *m* marzipan

mazorca *f* cob

me *complemento directo* me; *complemento indirecto* (to) me; *reflexivo* myself

mear F pee F

mecánica *f* mechanics; **mecánico 1** *adj* mechanical **2** *m*, **-a** *f* mechanic; **mecanismo** *m* mechanism; **mecanizar** mechanize

mecanografía *f* typing; **mecanógrafo** *m*, **-a** *f* typist

mecedora *f* rocking chair

mecenas *m inv* patron, sponsor

mecer, mercerse rock

mecha *f* wick; *de explosivo* fuse; *del pelo* highlight; *Méx* F fear; **mechero** *m* cigarette lighter; **mechón** *m de pelo* lock

medalla *f* medal; **medallista** *m/f* medalist, *Br* medallist

media *f* stocking; ***~s*** pantyhose *pl*, *Br* tights *pl*

mediación *f* mediation; **mediado:** ***a ~s de junio*** in mid-June; **mediador** *m*, **~a** *f* mediator; **mediana** *f* AUTO median strip, *Br* central reservation; **mediano** medium, average; **medianoche** *f* midnight; **mediante** by means of; **mediar** mediate

mediático media *atr*

medicamento *m* medicine, drug; **medicina** *f* medicine; **medicinal** medicinal; **médico 1** *adj* medical **2** *m/f* doctor; ***~ de cabecera*** *o* ***de familia*** family doctor; ***~ de urgencia*** emergency doctor

medida *f* measure; *acto* measurement; (*grado*) extent; ***hecho a ~*** made to measure; ***a ~ que*** as

medieval medieval

medio 1 *adj* half; *tamaño* medium; (*de promedio*) average; ***las tres y -a*** half past three, three-thirty **2** *m* environment; (*centro*) middle; (*manera*) means; ***~ ambiente*** environment; ***por ~ de*** by means of; ***en ~ de*** in the middle of; ***~s*** *dinero* means; ***~s de comunicación*** *o* ***de información*** (mass) media **3** *adv* half; ***hacer algo a -as*** half do sth; ***ir a -as*** go halves; ***día por ~*** *L.Am.* every other day

medioambiental environmental

mediocre mediocre

mediodía *m* midday

medir 1 *v/t* measure **2** *v/i*: ***mide 2 metros de ancho / alto*** it's 2 meters wide / high

meditación *f* meditation; **meditar 1** *v/t* ponder **2** *v/i* meditate

médula *f* marrow; ***~ espinal*** spinal cord

medusa *f* ZO jellyfish

mejicano 1 *adj* Mexican **2** *m*, **-a** *f* Mexican; **Méjico** *país* Mexico; *Méx DF* Mexico City

mejilla *f* cheek

mejillón *m* ZO mussel

mejor better; ***el ~*** the best; ***lo ~*** the best thing; ***lo ~ posible*** as well as possible; ***a lo ~*** perhaps; **mejora** *f* improvement

mejorana *f* BOT marjoram

mejorar improve; ***¡que te mejores!*** get well soon!; **mejoría** *f* improvement

melena *f* long hair; *de león* mane

mellizo 1 *adj* twin *atr* **2** *m*, **-a** *f* twin

melocotón *m* peach

melón *m* melon

meloso F sickly sweet

membrana *f* membrane

membrete *m* heading, letterhead; ***papel con ~*** letterhead, headed paper

membrillo *m* quince; ***dulce de ~*** quince jelly

memorable memorable

memoria *f tb* INFOR memory; (*informe*) report; ***de ~*** by heart; ***~s*** (*biografía*) memoirs; **memorizar** memorize

mención *f*: ***hacer ~ de*** mention; **mencionar** mention

mendigar beg for; **mendigo** *m* beggar

menear shake; *las caderas* sway; ***~ la cola*** wag its tail

menester *m* (*trabajo*) job; ***~es*** F tools, gear; ***ser ~*** (*necessario*) be necessary

menguante decreasing; *luna* waning; **menguar** decrease; *de la luna* wane

meningitis *f* MED meningitis

menopausia *f* menopause

menor less; *en tamaño* smaller; *en edad* younger; ***ser ~ de edad*** be a minor; ***al por ~*** COM retail; ***el ~*** *en tamaño* the smallest; *en edad* the youngest

Menorca *f* Minorca; **menorquín 1** *adj* Minorcan **2** *m*, **-quina** *f* Minorcan

menos 1 *adj en cantidad* less; *en número* fewer **2** *adv comparativo en cantidad* less; *superlativo en cantidad* least; MAT minus; ***es ~ guapa que Ana*** she is not as pretty as Ana; ***a ~ que*** unless; ***al ~, por lo ~*** at least; ***echar de ~*** miss; ***ni mucho ~*** far from it; ***son las dos ~ diez*** it's ten of two, it's ten to two
menospreciar underestimate; (*desdeñar*) look down on; **menosprecio** *m* contempt
mensaje *m* message; ***~ de texto*** text (message); **mensajero** *m* courrier
menstruación *f* menstruation
mensual monthly; **mensualidad** *f* monthly payment
menta *f* BOT mint
mental mental; **mentalidad** *f* mentality; **mente** *f* mind
mentar mention
mentir lie; **mentira** *f* lie; **mentiroso 1** *adj*: ***ser muy ~*** tell a lot of lies **2** *m*, **-a** *f* liar
menú *m tb* INFOR menu; ***~ de ayuda*** help menu
menudeo *m L.Am.* retail trade; **menudo 1** *adj* small; ***¡-a suerte!*** *fig* F lucky devil!; ***a ~*** often **2** *m L.Am.* small change; ***~s*** GASTR giblets
meñique *m/adj*: (***dedo***) ~ little finger
meollo *m fig* heart
mercadería *f L.Am.* merchandise; **mercado** *m* market; ***Mercado Común*** Common Market; ***~ negro*** black market; **mercancía** *f* merchandise; **mercantil** commercial
mercenario *m/adj* mercenary
mercería *f* notions *pl*, *Br* haberdashery
mercurio *m* mercury
merecer deserve; ***no ~ la pena*** it's not worth it
merendar have an afternoon snack
merengue *m* GASTR meringue
meridiano *m/f* meridian; **meridional 1** *adj* southern **2** *m* southerner
merienda *f* afternoon snack
mérito *m* merit
merluza *f* ZO hake
merma *f* reduction, decrease; **mermar 1** *v/t* reduce **2** *v/i* diminish
mermelada *f* jam
mero 1 *adj* mere; ***el ~ jefe*** *Méx* F the big boss **2** *m* ZO grouper
mes *m* month
mesa *f* table; ***poner / quitar la ~*** set / clear the table; **meseta** *f* plateau; **mesilla, mesita** *f*: ~ (***de noche***) night stand, *Br* bedside table
mesón *m traditional rustic-style restaurant*
mestizo *m* person of mixed race
mesura *f*: ***con ~*** in moderation; **mesurado** moderate
meta *f en fútbol* goal; *en carre-*

ra finish line; *fig* (*objetivo*) goal, objective
metabolismo *m* metabolism
metal *m* metal; **metálico 1** *adj* metallic **2** *m*: ***en ~*** (in) cash
meteorología *f* meteorology; **meteorológico** weather *atr*, meteorological
meter put; (*involucrar*) involve; **meterse**: ***~ en algo*** get into sth; (*involucrarse*) get involved in sth; ***~ con alguien*** pick on s.o.; ***¿dónde se ha metido?*** where has he got to?
meticuloso meticulous
metódico methodical; **método** *m* method
metro *m medida* meter, *Br* metre; *para medir* rule; *transporte* subway, *Br* underground
metrópolis *f inv* metropolis; **metropolitano** metropolitan
mexicano 1 *adj* Mexican **2** *m*, **-a** Mexican; **México** *país* Mexico; *Méx DF* Mexico City
mezcla *f sustancia* mixture; *de tabaco, café etc* blend; *acto* mixing; *de tabaco, café etc* blending; **mezclar** mix; *tabaco, café etc* blend; ***~ a alguien en algo*** get s.o. mixed up in sth; **mezclarse** mix; ***~ en algo*** get mixed up in sth
mezquino mean
mezquita *f* mosque
mí me; *reflexivo* myself
mi, mis my
microbio *m* microbe; **microbús** *m* minibus; **microchip** *m* (micro)chip; **microfilm(e)** *m* microfilm; **micrófono** *m* microphone; ***~ oculto*** bug; **microondas** *m inv* microwave; **microprocesador** *m* microprocessor; **microscopio** *m* microscope
miedo *m* fear (***a*** of); ***dar ~*** be frightening; ***me da ~ la oscuridad*** I'm frightened of the dark; ***tener ~ de que*** be afraid that; ***de ~*** F awesome F; **miedoso** timid; ***¡no seas tan ~!*** don't be scared!
miel *f* honey
miembro *m* member; ANAT limb
mientras 1 *conj* while; ***~ que*** whereas **2** *adv*: ***~ tanto*** in the meantime
miércoles *m inv* Wednesday
mierda *f* P shit P, crap P; ***una ~ de película*** a crap movie P
miga *f de pan* crumb; ***hacer buenas / malas ~s*** *fig* F get on well / badly
migración *f* migration
milagro *m* miracle; **milagroso** miraculous
milicia *f* militia
milímetro *m* millimeter, *Br* millimetre
militar 1 *adj* military **2** *m* soldier; ***los ~es*** the military **3** *v/i* POL: ***~ en*** be a member of
milla *f* mile
millar *m* thousand
millón *m* million; ***mil millo-***

nes billion; **millonario** *m* millionaire
mimar spoil, pamper
mimbre *m* BOT willow; ***muebles de ~*** wicker furniture
mímica *f* mime
mina *f* MIN mine; *Rpl* F broad F, *Br* bird F; **minar** mine; *fig* undermine
mineral *m/adj* mineral; **minería** *f* mining; **minero 1** *adj* mining **2** *m* miner
minifalda *f* miniskirt
minimizar minimize; **mínimo** *m/adj* minimum
ministerio *m* POL department; ***~ de Asuntos Exteriores***, *L.Am.* ***~ de Relaciones Exteriores*** State Department, *Br* Foreign Office; ***~ de Hacienda*** Treasury Department, *Br* Treasury; ***~ del Interior*** Department of the Interior, *Br* Home Office; **ministro** *m*, **-a** *f* minister; ***~ del Interior*** Secretary of the Interior, *Br* Home Secretary; ***primer ~*** Prime Minister
minoría *f* minority
minorista COM **1** *adj* retail *atr* **2** *m/f* retailer
minuciosidad *f* attention to detail; **minucioso** meticulous, thorough
minúscula *f* small letter, lower case letter; **minúsculo** tiny, minute
minusválido 1 *adj* disabled **2** *m*, **-a** *f* disabled person; ***los ~s*** the disabled
minuta *f* GASTR menu; (*cuenta de los honorarios*) bill
minuto *m* minute
mío, mía mine; ***el ~ / la -a*** mine
miope short-sighted; **miopía** *f* short-sightedness
mirada *f* look; ***echar una ~*** take a look (***a*** at); **mirador** *m* viewpoint; **mirar 1** *v/t* look at; (*observar*) watch; *L.Am.* (*ver*) see **2** *v/i* look; ***~ por la ventana*** look out of the window
mirlo *m* ZO blackbird
misa *f* REL mass
misal *m* missal
miserable wretched; **miseria** *f* poverty; *fig* misery; **misericordia** *f* mercy; **mísero** wretched; *sueldo* miserable
misil *m* missile
misión *f* mission; **misionero** *m*, **-a** *f* missionary
mismo 1 *adj* same; ***yo ~*** I myself; ***me da lo ~*** it's all the same to me **2** *adv*: ***aquí ~*** right here; ***ahora ~*** right now
misterio *m* mystery; **misterioso** mysterious
mística *f* mysticism; **místico** mystic(al)
mitad *f* half; ***a ~ del camino*** halfway; ***a ~ de la película*** halfway through the movie; ***a ~ de precio*** half-price
mitigar mitigate; *ansiedad, dolor etc* ease
mitin *m* POL meeting
mito *m* myth; **mitología** *f* mythology

mixto mixed; *comisión* joint
mobiliario *m* furniture
mocedad *f* youth
mochila *f* backpack; **mochilero** *m*, **-a** *f* backpacker
moción *f* POL motion
moco *m*: ***tener ~s*** have a runny nose; **mocoso** *m*, **-a** *f* F snotty-nosed kid F
moda *f* fashion; ***de ~*** in fashion; ***estar pasado de ~*** be out of fashion
modales *mpl* manners
modalidad *f* form; DEP discipline; ***~ de pago*** method of payment
modelar model; **modelo 1** *m* model **2** *m/f persona* model
moderación *f* moderation; **moderador** *m*, **~a** *f* TV presenter; **moderar** moderate; *impulsos* control; *velocidad, gastos* reduce; *debate* chair
modernización *f* modernization; **modernizar** modernize; **moderno** modern
modestia *f* modesty; **modesto** modest
módico *precio* reasonable
modificar modify
modismo *m* idiom
modista *m/f* dressmaker; *diseñador* fashion designer
modo *m* way; ***a ~ de*** as; ***de ~ que*** so that; ***de ningún ~*** not at all; ***en cierto ~*** in a way; ***de todos ~s*** anyway
mofa *f* mockery; **mofarse: *~ de*** make fun of
moho *m* mold, *Br* mould; **mohoso** moldy, *Br* mouldy
mojado (*húmedo*) damp, moist; (*empapado*) wet; **mojar** (*humedecer*) dampen, moisten; (*empapar*) wet; *galleta* dunk, dip
mojón *m tb fig* milestone
molar P **1** *v/t*: ***me mola ese tío*** I like the guy a lot **2** *v/i* be cool F
molde *m* mold; *Br* mould; *para bizcocho* (cake) tin; ***romper ~s*** *fig* break the mold; **moldeado** *m* molding; *Br* moulding; **moldear** mold; *Br* mould; **moldura** *f* ARQUI molding; *Br* moulding
molécula *f* molecule
moler grind; *fruta* mash; ***carne molida*** ground meat, *Br* mince
molestar bother, annoy; (*doler*) trouble; ***no ~*** do not disturb; **molestarse** get upset; (*ofenderse*) take offense *o* *Br* offence; (*enojarse*) get annoyed; ***~ en hacer algo*** take the trouble to do sth; **molestia** *f* nuisance; ***~s*** MED discomfort; **molesto** annoying; (*incómodo*) inconvenient
molinillo *m*: ***~ de café*** coffee grinder *o* mill; **molino** *m* mill; ***~ de viento*** windmill
molleja *f de ave* gizzard; ***~s*** GASTR sweetbreads
molusco *m* ZO mollusk, *Br* mollusc
momentáneo momentary; **momento** *m* moment; ***al ~*** at once; ***por el ~, de ~*** for the moment

momia *f* mummy
monarca *m* monarch; **monarquía** *f* monarchy
monasterio *m* monastery
mondadientes *m inv* toothpick
mondar peel; *árbol* prune
moneda *f* coin; (*divisa*) currency; **monedero** *m* change purse, *Br* purse; **monetario** monetary
monitor[1] *m* TV, INFOR monitor
monitor[2] *m*, **~a** *f* (*profesor*) instructor
monja *f* nun; **monje** *m* monk
mono 1 *m* ZO monkey; *prenda* coveralls *pl*, *Br* boilersuit **2** *adj* pretty, cute; **monopatín** *m* skateboard; **monopolio** *m* monopoly; **monótono** monotonous
monovolumen *m* AUTO minivan, *Br* people carrier, MPV
monstruo *m* monster; (*fenómeno*) phenomenon; **monstruosidad** *f* monstrosity; **monstruoso** monstrous
montacargas *m inv* hoist
montador *m*, **~a** *f* TÉC fitter; *de película* editor; **montaje** *m* TÉC assembly; *de película* editing; TEA staging; *fig* F con F
montaña *f* mountain; **~ *rusa*** rollercoaster; **montañoso** mountainous
montar 1 *v/t* TÉC assemble; *tienda* put up; *negocio* set up; *película* edit; *caballo* mount; **~ *la guardia*** mount guard **2** *v/i*: **~ *en bicicleta*** ride a bicycle; **~ *a caballo*** ride a horse
monte *m* mountain; (*bosque*) woodland
montón *m* pile, heap; ***montones de*** F piles of F
montura *f de gafas* frame
monumental monumental; **monumento** *m* monument
monzón *m* monsoon
moño *m* bun
moqueta *f* (wall-to-wall) carpet
mora *f de zarza* blackberry; *de morera* mulberry
morado purple
moral 1 *adj* moral **2** *f* (*moralidad*) morals *pl*; (*ánimo*) morale; **moralidad** *f* morality
morboso perverted
morcilla *f* blood sausage, *Br* black pudding
mordaz biting; **morder** bite; **mordisco** *m* bite
moreno *pelo, piel* dark; (*bronceado*) tanned
morfina *f* morphine
morir die (***de*** of); **morirse** die; **~ *por*** *fig* be dying for
morisco Moorish
moro 1 *adj* North African **2** *m*, **-a** *f* North African
moroso COM **1** *adj* slow to pay **2** *m*, **-a** *f* slow payer
mortal 1 *adj* mortal; *accidente, herida* fatal; *dosis* lethal **2** *m/f* mortal; **mortalidad** *f* mortality
mortero *m tb* MIL mortar

mortífero lethal
mosaico *m* mosaic
mosca *f* fly; ***por si las ~s*** F just to be on the safe side
Moscú Moscow
mosquearse F get hot under the collar F; (*sentir recelo*) smell a rat F
mosquitero *m* mosquito net; **mosquito** *m* mosquito
mostaza *f* mustard
mosto *m* grape juice
mostrador *m* counter; *en bar* bar; ***~ de facturación*** check-in desk; **mostrar** show
mote *m* nickname; *S.Am.* boiled corn *o Br* maize
motín *m* mutiny; *en una cárcel* riot
motivar motivate; **motivo** *m* motive, reason; MÚS, PINT motif; ***con ~ de*** because of
moto *f* motorcycle, motorbike; ***~ acuática*** *o* ***de agua*** jet ski; **motocicleta** *f* motorcycle; **motociclista** *m/f* motorcyclist
motor *m* engine; *eléctrico* motor; **motora** *f* motorboat; **motorismo** *m* motorcycling; **motorista** *m/f* motorcyclist
motriz motor
mover move; (*agitar*) shake; (*impulsar, incitar*) drive; **movible** movable; *fig precio, opinión* fickle
móvil 1 *adj* mobile **2** *m* TELEC cell(phone), *Br* mobile (phone); **movilidad** *f* mobility; **movilizar** mobilize; **movimiento** *m* movement; COM, *fig* activity
moza *f* girl; *camarera* waitress;
mozo 1 *adj*: ***en mis años ~s*** in my youth **2** *m* boy; *camarero* waiter
muchacha *f* girl; **muchacho** *m* boy
muchedumbre *f* crowd
mucho 1 *adj cantidad* a lot of, lots of; *esp neg* much; ***no tengo ~ dinero*** I don't have much money; ***~s*** a lot of, lots of, many; *esp neg* many; ***no tengo ~s amigos*** I don't have many friends; ***tengo ~ frío*** I am very cold; ***es ~ coche para mí*** it's too big a car for me **2** *adv* a lot; *esp neg* much; ***no me gustó ~*** I didn't like it very much; ***¿dura / tarda ~?*** does it last / take long?; ***como ~*** at the most; ***ni ~ menos*** far from it; ***por ~ que*** however much **3** *pron* a lot, much; ***~s*** a lot of people, many people
mucosa *f* ANAT mucous membrane; **mucosidad** *f* mucus
muda *f de ropa* change of clothes; **mudanza** *f de casa* move; **mudar** change; ZO shed; **mudarse:** ***~ de casa*** move house; ***~ de ropa*** change (one's clothes)
mudo mute; *letra* silent
mueble *m* piece of furniture; ***~s*** furniture
mueca *f de dolor* grimace; ***hacer ~s*** make faces
muela *f* tooth; ANAT molar; ~

del juicio wisdom tooth
muelle *m* TÉC spring; MAR wharf
muerte *f* death; **muerto 1** *part* ☞ ***morir* 2** *adj* dead **3** *m*, **-a** *f* dead person; ***los*~*s*** the dead
muesca *f* notch, groove
muestra *f* sample; (*señal*) sign; (*exposición*) show
mugre *f* filth; **mugriento** filthy
mujer *f* woman; (*esposa*) wife; **mujeriego** *m* womanizer
mula *f* ZO mule; *Méx* (*basura*) trash, *Br* rubbish
mulato *m* mulatto
muleta *f* crutch; TAUR cape
mulo *m* ZO mule
multa *f* fine; **multar** fine
multicine *m* multiplex; **multicolor** multicolored, *Br* multicoloured; **multicultural** multicultural; **multinacional** *f* multinational
múltiple multiple; **multiplicación** *f* multiplication; **multiplicar, multiplicarse** multiply; **múltiplo** *m* MAT multiple; **multisalas** *m inv* multiplex; **multitarea** *f* multitasking
multitud *f* crowd; ~ ***de*** thousands of; **multitudinario** mass *atr*
multiuso multipurpose
mundial 1 *adj* world *atr* **2** *m*: ***el*** ~ ***de fútbol*** the World Cup; **mundo** *m* world; ***todo el*** ~ everybody, everyone
munición *f* ammunition
municipal municipal; **municipio** *m* municipality
muñeca *f* doll; ANAT wrist; **muñeco** *m* doll; *fig* puppet; ~ ***de nieve*** snowman
mural 1 *adj* wall *atr* **2** *m* mural; **muralla** *f de ciudad* wall
murciélago *m* ZO bat
murmurar murmur; *criticar* gossip
muro *m* wall
muscular muscular; **músculo** *m* muscle; **musculoso** muscular; **musculatura** *f* muscles *pl*
museo *m* museum; *de pintura* art gallery
musgo *m* BOT moss
música *f* music; ~ ***de fondo*** background music; **musical** *m/adj* musical; **músico** *m*, **-a** *f* musician
muslo *m* thigh
mutación *f* BIO mutation; TEA scene change
mutilado *m*, **-a** *f* disabled person; **mutilar** mutilate
mutuo mutual
muy very; (*demasiado*) too; ~ ***valorado*** highly valued

N

nabo *m* **1** *adj Arg* F dumb F **2** *m* turnip
nácar *m* mother-of-pearl
nacer be born; *de un huevo* hatch; *de una planta* sprout; *de un río, del sol* rise; (*surgir*) arise (***de*** from); **nacido** born; ***mal ~*** wicked; **nacimiento** *m* birth; *de Navidad* crèche, nativity scene
nación *f* nation; **nacional** national; **nacionalidad** *f* nationality; **nacionalizar** COM nationalize; *persona* naturalize
nada 1 *pron* nothing; ***no hay ~*** there isn't anything, there's nothing; ***~ más*** nothing else; ***~ menos que*** no less than; ***¡de ~!*** you're welcome, not at all; ***no es ~*** it's nothing **2** *adv* not at all; ***no ha llovido ~*** it hasn't rained at all **3** *f* nothingness
nadador *m*, **~a** *f* swimmer; **nadar** swim
nadie nobody, no-one; ***no había ~*** there was nobody there, there wasn't anyone there
nado: ***atravesar a ~*** swim across
naipe *m* (playing) card
nalga *f* buttock
naranja 1 *f* orange; ***media ~*** F (*pareja*) other half **2** *adj* orange; **naranjo** *m* orange tree
narciso *m* BOT daffodil
narcótico *m*/*adj* narcotic; **narcotráfico** *m* drug trafficking
nariz *f* nose; ***¡narices!*** F nonsense!
narración *f* narration; **narrar: *~ algo*** tell the story of sth
nasal nasal
nata *f* cream; ***~ montada*** whipped cream
natación *f* swimming
natal native; **natalidad** *f* birthrate
natillas *fpl* custard
nativo *m*, **-a** *f* native
natural 1 *adj* natural; ***ser ~ de*** come froml **2** *m*: ***fruta al ~*** fruit in its own juice; **naturaleza** *f* nature; **naturalidad** *f* naturalness; **naturalizar** naturalize; **naturalizarse** become naturalized; **naturalmente** naturally; **naturista 1** *adj* nudist, naturist; *medicina* natural **2** *m*/*f* nudist, naturist
naufragar be shipwrecked; *fig* fail; **naufragio** *m* shipwreck; **náufrago 1** *adj* shipwrecked **2** *m*, **-a** *f* shipwrecked person
náuseas *fpl* nausea
náutico nautical
navaja *f* knife
naval naval; **nave** *f* ship; *de iglesia* nave; ***~ espacial***

spaceship, spacecraft; **navegable** navigable; **navegación** *f* navigation; ~ ***a vela*** sailing; **navegar 1** *v/i* sail; *por el aire, espacio* fly; ~ ***por la red*** *o* ***por Internet*** INFOR surf the Net **2** *v/t* sail
navegador *m* INFOR browser; **navegante** *m/f* navigator
Navidad *f* Christmas
naviero *m* shipowner; **navío** *m* ship
neblina *f* mist; **nebuloso** *fig* hazy, nebulous
necesario necessary; **neceser** *m* toilet kit, *Br* toilet bag; **necesidad** *f* need; (*cosa esencial*) necessity; ***de primera*** ~ essential; ***en caso de*** ~ if necessary; ***hacer sus -es*** F relieve o.s.; **necesitado** needy; **necesitar** need
necio brainless
necrología *f*, **necrológica** *f* obituary
neerlandés 1 *adj* Dutch **2** *m* Dutchman; *idioma* Dutch; **neerlandesa** *f* Dutchwoman
negación *f* negation; *de acusación* denial; **negar** *acusación* deny; (*no conceder*) refuse; **negarse** refuse (***a*** to); **negativa** *f* refusal; *de acusación* denial; **negativo** *m/adj* negative
negligencia *f* JUR negligence; **negligente** negligent
negociación *f* negotiation; ***negociaciones*** talks; **negociante** *m/f* businessman; *mujer* businesswoman; *desp* money-grubber; **negociar** negotiate; **negocio** *m* business; (*trato*) deal
negra *f* black woman; MÚS quarter note, *Br* crotchet; *L.Am.* (*querida*) honey, dear; **negrita** *f* bold; **negro 1** *adj* black; ***estar*** ~ F be furious **2** *m* black man; *L.Am.* (*querido*) honey, dear
nena *f* F little girl, kid F; **nene** *m* F little boy, kid F
neocelandés ☞ ***neozelandés***
neoyorquino 1 *adj* New York *atr* **2** *m*, **-a** New Yorker
neozelandés 1 *adj* New Zealand *atr* **2** *m*, **-esa** *f* New Zealander
nervio *m* ANAT nerve; **nerviosismo** *m* nervousness; **nervioso** nervous; ***ponerse*** ~ get nervous; (*agitado*) get agitated; ***poner a alguien*** ~ get on s.o.'s nerves
neto COM net
neumático 1 *adj* pneumatic **2** *m* AUTO tire, *Br* tyre
neumonía *f* MED pneumonia
neuralgia *f* neuralgia
neurólogo *m*, **-a** *f* neurologist
neurosis *f inv* neurosis; **neurótico** neurotic
neutral neutral; **neutralidad** *f* neutrality; **neutro** neutral
nevada *f* snowfall; **nevar** snow; **nevera** *f* refrigerator, fridge; ~ ***portátil*** cooler
ni neither; ~... ~ neither ...

nor; ~ ***siquiera*** not even
Nicaragua Nicaragua; **nicaragüense** *m/f & adj* Nicaraguan
nicho *m* niche
nido *m* nest
niebla *f* fog
nieta *f* granddaughter; **nieto** *m* grandson; ~***s*** grandchildren
nieve *f* snow; *Méx* water ice, sorbet
ninfa *f* nymph
ningún ☞ ***ninguno***
ninguno no; ***no hay -a razón*** there's no reason why, there isn't any reason why
niña *f* girl; *forma de cortesía* young lady; **niñera** *f* nanny; **niñez** *f* childhood; **niño** **1** *adj* young; *desp* childish **2** *m* boy; *forma de cortesía* young man; ~***s*** children *pl*; ~ ***de pecho*** infant
nipón **1** *adj* Japanese **2** *m*, **-ona** *f* Japanese
níquel *m* nickel
níspero *m* BOT loquat
nitidez *f* clarity; FOT sharpness; **nítido** clear; *imagen* sharp
nitrógeno *m* nitrogen
nivel *m* level; (*altura*) height; ~ ***del mar*** sea level; ~ ***de vida*** standard of living; **nivelar** level
no no; *para negar verbo* not; ***no entiendo*** I don't understand, I do not understand; ~ ***te vayas*** don't go; ~ ***bien*** as soon as; ~ ***del todo*** not entirely; ***ya*** ~ not any more; ~ ***más*** *L.Am.* ☞ ***nomás***; ***así*** ~ ***más*** *L.Am.* just like that; ***te gusta, ¿~?*** you like it, don't you?; ***te ha llamado, ¿~?*** he called you, didn't he?
noble *m/f & adj* noble; **nobleza** *f* nobility
noche *f* night; ***de ~, por la ~*** at night; ***¡buenas ~s!*** *saludo* good evening; *despedida* good night; **Nochebuena** *f* Christmas Eve; **Nochevieja** *f* New Year's Eve
noción *f* notion; **nociones** *mpl* basic knowledge
nocivo harmful
nocturno night *atr*, ZO nocturnal; ***clase -a*** evening class
nogal *m* BOT walnut
nomás *L.Am.* just; ***llévaselo*** ~ just take it away; ~ ***lo vio*** as soon as she saw him
nombrado famous, renowned; **nombramiento** *m* appointment; **nombrar** mention; *para un cargo* appoint; **nombre** *m* name; GRAM noun; ~ ***de familia*** family name, surname; ~ ***de pila*** first name name; ~ ***de soltera*** maiden name
nómina *f* pay slip; **nominal** nominal; **nominar** nominate
nor(d)este *m* northeast
noria *f de agua* waterwheel; *en feria* ferris wheel
norirlandés **1** *adj* of / from Northern Ireland, Northern

Ireland *atr* **2** *m*, **~esa** *f* man / woman from Northern Ireland
norma *f* standard; (*regla*) rule, regulation; **normal** normal; **normalizar** standardize
noroeste *m* northwest
norte *m* north
Norteamérica North America; **norteamericano 1** *adj* North American **2** *m*, **-a** *f* North American
Noruega Norway; **noruego 1** *adj* Norwegian **2** *m*, **-a** *f* Norwegian **3** *m idioma* Norwegian
nos *complemento directo* us; *complemento indirecto* (to) us; *reflexivo* ourselves
nosotros, nosotras we; *complemento* us; ***ven con ~*** come with us; ***somos ~*** it's us
nostalgia *f* nostalgia; *por la patria* homesickness
nota *f tb* MÚS note; EDU grade, mark; ***~ a pie de página*** footnote; ***tomar ~ de algo*** make a note of sth; **notable** remarkable, notable; **notar** notice; (*sentir*) feel; ***hacer ~ algo a alguien*** point sth out to s.o.; ***se nota que*** you can tell that; ***hacerse ~*** draw attention to o.s.
notario *m*, **-a** *f* notary
noticia *f* piece of news; *en noticiario* news story; ***~s*** news *sg*
notificación *f* notification; **notificar** notify
notorio famous, well-known
novato *m*, **-a** *f* beginner
novedad *f* novelty; *cosa* new thing; (*noticia*) piece of news; *acontecimiento* new development; ***llegar sin ~*** arrive safely; **novela** *f* novel; ***~ negra*** crime novel; ***~ rosa*** romantic novel; **novelista** *m/f* novelist
noveno ninth; **noventa** ninety
novia *f* girlfriend; *el día de la boda* bride
noviembre *m* November
novillada *f bullfight featuring novice bulls*; **novillo** *m* young bull; *vaca* heifer
novio *m* boyfriend; *el día de la boda* bridegroom; ***los ~s*** the bride and groom; (*recién casados*) the newly-weds
nube *f* cloud; ***estar en las ~s*** *fig* be miles away; **nublado 1** *adj* cloudy **2** *m* storm cloud; **nublarse** cloud over; **nuboso** cloudy; **nubosidad** *f* clouds *pl*
nuca *f* nape of the neck
nuclear nuclear; **núcleo** *m* nucleus; *de problema* heart
nudillo *m* knuckle
nudismo *m* nudism; **nudista** *m/f* nudist; ***playa ~*** nudist beach
nudo *m* knot
nuera *f* daughter-in-law
nuestro 1 *adj* our **2** *pron* ours
Nueva York New York
Nueva Zelanda New Zealand

nueve nine
nuevo new; (*otro*) another; ***de ~*** again
nuez *f* BOT walnut; ANAT Adam's apple
nulo null and void; F *persona* hopeless; (*inexistente*) non-existent
numeración *f* numbering; (*números*) numbers *pl*; **numerar** number; **numérico** numerical; ***teclado ~*** numeric keypad, number pad; **número** *m* number; *de publicación* issue; *de zapato* size; ***~ secreto*** PIN (number); ***en ~s rojos*** *fig* in the red; ***montar un ~*** F make a scene; **numeroso** numerous
nunca never; ***~ jamás*** *o* ***más*** never again; ***más que ~*** more than ever
nupcial wedding *atr*
nutria *f* ZO otter
nutrición *f* nutrition; **nutrir** nourish; *fig*: *esperanzas* cherish; **nutritivo** nutritious, nourishing
ñame *m* BOT yam
ñandú *m* ZO rhea
ñoñería *f* feebleness F; **ñoño** **1** *adj* feeble F, wimpish F **2** *m*, -a *f* drip F, wimp F
ñu *m* ZO gnu

O

o or; ***~... ~*** either ... or
oasis *m inv* oasis
obcecado (*terco*) obstinate; (*obsesionado*) obsessed
obedecer obey; *de una máquina* respond; ***~ a*** *fig* be due to; **obediencia** *f* obedience; **obediente** obedient
obertura *f* MÚS overture
obesidad *f* obesity; **obeso** obese
obispo *m* bishop
objeción *f* objection; **objetar** **1** *v/t* object; ***tener algo que ~*** have any objection **2** *v/i* become a conscientious objector
objetivo **1** *adj* objective **2** *m* objective; MIL target; FOT lens
objeto *m* object; ***con ~ de*** with the aim of
objetor *m*, ***~a*** *f* objector
oblea *f* wafer
oblícuo oblique, slanted
obligación *f* obligation, duty; COM bond; **obligar**: ***~ a alguien*** oblige *o* force s.o. (***a*** to); *de una ley* apply to s.o.; **obligarse**: ***~ a hacer algo*** force o.s. to do sth; **obligatorio** obligatory
oboe *m* MÚS oboe
obra *f* work; ***~s*** *de construcción* building work; *en la vía pública* road works; ***~ de arte*** work of art; ***~ maestra*** masterpiece; ***~ de teatro*** play; **obrar** act; **obrero** **1** *adj* working **2** *m*, -a *f* worker

obsceno obscene
obsequiar: *~ **a alguien con algo*** present s.o. with sth; **obsequio** *m* gift
observación *f* observation; JUR observance; **observar** observe; **observatorio** *m* observatory
obsesión *f* obsession; **obsesionar** obsess; **obsesionarse** become obsessed (***con*** with); **obsesivo** obsessive
obstaculizar hinder; **obstáculo** *m* obstacle
obstante: ***no ~*** nevertheless
obstetricia *f* obstetrics
obstinación *f* obstinacy; **obstinado** obstinate; **obstinarse** insist (***en*** on)
obstrucción *f* obstruction, blockage; **obstruir** obstruct, block
obtener get, obtain *fml*
obturador *m* shutter
obvio obvious
oca *f* goose
ocasión *f* occasion; (*oportunidad*) chance, opportunity; ***con ~ de*** on the occasion of; ***de ~*** COM cut-price, bargain *atr*; *de segunda mano* second-hand; **ocasionar** cause
ocaso *m del sol* setting; *de un imperio* decline
occidental 1 *adj* western **2** *m/f* Westerner; **occidente** *m* west
océano *m* ocean
ochenta eighty; **ocho** eight
ocio *m* leisure time; *desp* idleness; **ocioso** idle
octava *f* MÚS octave; **octavilla** *f* leaflet; **octavo 1** *adj* eighth **2** *m* eighth; DEP ***~s de final*** last 16
octubre *m* October
ocular eye *atr*; **oculista** *m/f* ophthalmologist
ocultar hide, conceal; **oculto** hidden; (*sobrenatural*) occult
ocupación *f tb* MIL occupation; (*actividad*) activity; **ocupado** busy; *asiento* taken; **ocupante** *m/f* occupant; **ocupar** *espacio* take up, occupy; (*habitar*) live in, occupy; *obreros* employ; *periodo de tiempo* spend, occupy; MIL occupy; **ocuparse:** ***~ de*** deal with; (*cuidar de*) look after
ocurrencia *f* occurrence; (*chiste*) quip, witty remark; **ocurrente** witty; **ocurrir** happen, occur; ***se me ocurrió*** it occurred to me, it struck me
odiar hate; **odio** *m* hatred, hate; **odioso** odious, hateful
odontología *f* dentistry; **odontólogo** *m* odontologist
oeste *m* west
ofender offend; **ofenderse** take offense *o Br* offence (***por*** at); **ofensa** *f* insult; **ofensiva** *f* offensive
oferta *f* offer; ***~ pública de adquisición*** takeover bid
oficial 1 *adj* official **2** *m/f* MIL officer; **oficina** *f* office; ***~ de correos*** post office; ***~ de***

empleo employment office; ***~ de turismo*** tourist office; **oficio** *m trabajo* trade; **oficioso** unofficial; **oficialista** *L.Am.* pro-government; **oficinista** *m/f* office worker
ofimática *f* INFOR office automation
ofrecer offer; **ofrecimiento** *m* offer
oftalmólogo *m*, **-a** *f* ophthalmologist
oída *f*: ***conocer algo de ~s*** have heard of sth; **oído** *m* hearing; ***hacer ~s sordos*** turn a deaf ear; ***ser todo ~s*** *fig* be all ears; **oír** *tb* JUR hear; *(escuchar)* listen to; ***¡oye!*** listen!
ojal *m* buttonhole
ojalá: ***¡~!*** let's hope so; ***¡~ venga!*** I hope he comes
ojeada *f* glance; **ojeras** *fpl* bags under the eyes; **ojete** **1** *m* eyelet **2** *m/f Méx* V bastard P, son of a bitch V ; **ojo** *m* ANAT eye; ***¡~!*** F watch out!; ***~ de la cerradura*** keyhole; ***a ~*** roughly; ***andar con ~*** F keep one's eyes open F; ***no pegar ~*** F not sleep a wink F
ola *f* wave; ***~ de calor*** heat wave; ***~ de frío*** cold spell; **oleada** *f fig* wave, flood; **oleaje** *m* swell
olé olé
oleada *f fig* wave, flood; **oleaje** *m* swell
óleo *m* oil; **oleoducto** *m* (oil) pipeline; **oleoso** oily
oler smell (***a*** of); **olfatear** sniff; **olfato** *m* sense of smell; *fig* nose
olimpíada, olimpiada *f* Olympics *pl*
oliva *f* BOT olive; **olivo** *m* olive tree
olla *f* pot; ***~ exprés*** *o* ***a presión*** pressure cooker
olmo *m* BOT elm
olor *m* smell; *agradable tb* scent; ***~ corporal*** BO; **oloroso** scented
olvidar forget; **olvidarse:** ***~ de algo*** forget sth; **olvido** *m* oblivion
ombligo *m* ANAT navel
omisión *f* omission; **omitir** omit, leave out
omnipotente omnipotent; **omnisciente** omniscient
omóplato, omoplato *m* ANAT shoulder blade
once eleven
onda *f* wave; ***estar en la ~*** F be with it F; **ondear** *de bandera* wave; **ondulación** *f* undulation; **ondular** **1** *v/i* undulate **2** *v/t pelo* wave
oneroso onerous
onoro sonorous
onza *f* ounce
OPA *f* (= ***oferta pública de adquisición***) takeover bid
opaco opaque
ópera *f* MÚS opera; ***~ prima*** first work
operación *f* operation; **operador** *m*, **~a** *f* TELEC, INFOR operator; ***~ turístico*** tour operator; **operar** **1** *v/t* MED

operate on; *cambio* bring about **2** *v/i* operate; COM do business (***con*** with); **operarse** MED have an operation (***de*** on); *de un cambio* occur; **operario** *m*, **-a** *f* operator, operative
opereta *f* MÚS operetta
opinar 1 *v/t* think (***de*** about) **2** *v/i* express an opinion; **opinión** *f* opinion
opio *m* opium
oponente *m/f* opponent; **oponer** *resistencia* put up (***a*** to); *razón, argumento* put forward (***a*** against); **oponerse** be opposed (***a*** to); (*manifestar oposición*) object (***a*** to)
oporto *m* port
oportunidad *f* opportunity; **oportunista 1** *adj* opportunistic **2** *m/f* opportunist; **oportuno** timely; *momento* opportune; *respuesta, medida* suitable
oposición *f* POL opposition; ***oposiciones*** official entrance exams
opresión *f* oppression; **oprimir** oppress; *botón* press; *de zapatos* be too tight for
optar (*elegir*) opt (***por*** for); ***~ a*** be in the running for
óptica *f* optician, *Br* optician's; FÍS optics; *fig* point of view; **óptico 1** *adj* optical **2** *m*, **-a** *f* optician
optimismo *m* optimism; **optimista 1** *adj* optimistic **2** *m/f* optimist
óptimo ideal
opuesto 1 *part* ☞ ***oponer*** **2** *adj* opposite
opulencia *f* opulence; **opulento** opulent
oración *f* REL prayer; GRAM sentence
oráculo *m* oracle
orador *m*, **~a** *f* orator; **oral** oral; ***prueba de inglés ~*** English oral (exam)
orden 1 *m* order; ***~ del día*** agenda; ***poner en ~*** tidy up **2** *f* (*mandamiento*) order; ***¡a la ~!*** yes, sir; ***por ~ de*** by order of; **ordenado** tidy; **ordenador** *m* INFOR computer; ***~ de escritorio*** desktop (computer); ***~ personal*** personal computer; ***~ portátil*** laptop; ***asistido por ~*** computer aided; **ordenanza 1** *f* bylaw **2** *m* office junior, gofer F; MIL orderly; **ordenar** *habitación* tidy up; *alfabéticamente* arrange; (*mandar*) order
ordeñar milk
ordinario ordinary; *desp* vulgar; ***de ~*** ordinarily
oreja *f* ear; **orejeras** *fpl* earmuffs
orfanato *m* orphanage
orfebre *m/f* goldsmith / silversmith
orgánico organic
organillo *m* barrel organ
organismo *m* organism; POL agency, organization
organista *m/f* organist
organización *f* organization;

Organización de las Naciones Unidas United Nations; **organizador 1** *adj* organizing **2** *m*, **~a** *f* organizer; **organizar** organize
órgano *m* MÚS, ANAT, *fig* organ
orgasmo *m* orgasm
orgía *f* orgy
orgullo *m* pride; **orgulloso** proud (***de*** of)
orientación *f* orientation; (*ayuda*) guidance; ***sentido de la ~*** sense of direction
oriental 1 *adj* oriental, eastern **2** *m/f* Oriental
orientar (*aconsejar*) advise; ***~ algo hacia algo*** turn sth toward sth; **orientarse** get one's bearings; *de una planta* turn (***hacía*** toward)
oriente *m* east; ***Oriente*** Orient; ***Oriente Medio*** Middle East; ***Extremo*** *o* ***Lejano Oriente*** Far East
orificio *m* hole; *en cuerpo* orifice
origen *m* origin; ***dar ~ a*** give rise to; **original** *m/adj* original; **originalidad** *f* originality; **originar** give rise to; **originario** original; (*nativo*) native (***de*** of)
orilla *f* shore; *de un río* bank
orín *m* rust
orina *f* urine; **orinal** *m* urinal; **orinar** urinate
ornamentar adorn; **ornamento** *m* ornament; ***~s*** REL vestments
oro *m* gold; ***~s*** (*en naipes*) *suit in Spanish deck of cards*
orquesta *f* orchestra
orquídea *f* BOT orchid
ortiga *f* BOT nettle
ortodoncia *f* MED orthodontics
ortodoxo orthodox
ortografía *f* spelling
ortopédico 1 *adj* orthopedic, *Br* orthopaedic **2** *m*, **-a** *f* orthopedist, *Br* orthopaedist
oruga *f* ZO caterpillar; TÉC (caterpillar) track
orujo *m liquor made from the remains of grapes*
orzuelo *m* MED stye
os *complemento directo* you; *complemento indirecto* (to) you; *reflexivo* yourselves
osado daring; **osar** dare
oscilar oscillate; *de precios* fluctuate
oscurecer 1 *v/t* darken; *logro, triunfo* overshadow **2** *v/i* get dark; **oscuridad** *f* darkness; **oscuro** dark; *fig* obscure; ***a -as*** in the dark
óseo bone *atr*
oso *m* bear; ***~ hormiguero*** anteater; ***~ panda*** panda; ***~ polar*** polar bear
ostensible obvious
ostentar flaunt; *cargo* hold
ostra *f* oyster; ***¡~s!*** F hell! F
OTAN *f* (= ***Organización del Tratado del Atlántico Norte***) NATO (= North Atlantic Treaty Organization)
otoñal fall *atr*, *Br* autumnal; **otoño** *m* fall, *Br* autumn
otorgar award; *favor* grant

otorrino F, **otorrinolaringólogo** *m* MED ear, nose and throat specialist
otro 1 *adj* (*diferente*) another; *con el, la* other; **~s** other; **~s dos libros** another two books **2** *pron* (*adicional*) another (one); (*persona distinta*) someone *o* somebody else; (*cosa distinta*) another one, a different one; **~s** others **3** *siguiente*: **¡hasta -a!** see you soon **4** *pron recíproco*: **amar el uno al ~** love one another
ovación *f* ovation
oval, ovalado oval
ovario *m* ANAT ovary
oveja *f* sheep
ovillo *m* ball
ovino *m* sheep; **~s** sheep *pl*
óvulo *m* egg
oxidarse rust, go rusty; **óxido** *m* QUÍM oxide; (*herrumbre*) rust; **oxígeno** *m* oxygen
oyente *m/f* listener
ozono *m* ozone; **capa de ~** ozone layer

P

pabellón *m* pavilion; *edificio* block; MÚS bell; MAR flag
pacer graze
paciencia *f* patience; **paciente** *m/f & adj* patient
pacífico 1 *adj* peaceful; *persona* peaceable **2** *m*: **el Pacífico** the Pacific; **pacifista** *m/f & adj* pacifist
pacotilla *f*: **de ~** third-rate, lousy F
pactar 1 *v/t* agree; **~ un acuerdo** reach (an) agreement **2** *v/i* reach (an) agreement; **pacto** *m* agreement, pact
padecer suffer; **~ de** have trouble with
padrastro *m* step-father; **padre** *m* father; REL Father; **~s** parents; **¡qué ~!** *Méx* F brilliant!; **padrenuestro** *m* Lord's Prayer; **padrino** *m* *en bautizo* godfather; (*en boda*) *man who gives away the bride*
paga *f* pay; *de niño* allowance, *Br* pocket money
pagano pagan
pagar pay; *compra, gastos, crimen* pay for; *favor* repay; **¡me las pagarás!** you'll pay for this!; **pagaré** *m* IOU
página *f* page; **~ web** web page; **~s amarillas** yellow pages
pago *m* payment; *Rpl* (*quinta*) piece of land
país *m* country; **los Países Bajos** the Netherlands; **paisaje** *m* landscape; **paisajista** *m/f* landscape artist; *jardinero* landscape gardener
paisano *m*: **de ~** MIL in civilian clothes; *policía* in plain clothes
paja *f* straw; **pajar** *m* hayloft

pajarita *f corbata* bow tie; **pájaro** *m* bird; *fig* nasty piece of work F; **~ carpintero** woodpecker
pala *f* spade; *raqueta* paddle; *para servir* slice; *para recoger* dustpan
palabra *f tb fig* word; **bajo ~** on parole; **tomar la ~** speak; **palabrota** *f* swearword
palacio *m* palace; **~ de deportes** sports center *o Br* centre; **~ de justicia** law courts
paladar *m* palate
palanca *f* lever; **~ de cambios** AUTO gearshift, *Br* gear lever
palangana *f* washbowl, *Br* washing-up bowl
palco *m* TEA box
paleta *f* PINT palette; TÉC trowel; **paletilla** *f* GASTR shoulder
paliar alleviate; *dolor* relieve
palidecer *de persona* turn pale; **palidez** *f* paleness; **pálido** pale
palillo *m para dientes* toothpick; *para comer* chopstick
paliza 1 *f* beating; (*derrota*) thrashing F; (*pesadez*) drag F **2** *m/f* F drag F
palma *f* palm; **dar ~s** clap (one's hands); **palmada** *f* pat; (*manotazo*) slap
palmera *f* BOT palm tree; (*dulce*) *heart-shaped pastry*
palmo *m* hand's breadth; **~ a ~** inch by inch
palo *m de madera etc* stick; MAR mast; *de portería* post, upright; **~ de golf** golf club; **~ mayor** MAR mainmast; **a medio ~** *L.Am.* F half-drunk; **a ~ seco** *whisky* straight up, *Br* neat; **ser un ~** *L.Am.* F be fantastic
paloma *f* pigeon; *blanca* dove
palomita *f Méx* checkmark, *Br* tick; **~s de maíz** popcorn
palpable *fig* palpable; **palpar** feel
palpitación *f* palpitation; **palpitar** *del corazón* pound; *Rpl fig* have a hunch F
paludismo *m* MED malaria
pampa *f* pampa, prairie; **a la ~** *Rpl* in the open
pan *m* bread; **un ~** a loaf; **~ integral** wholewheat *o Br* wholemeal bread; **~ de molde** sliced bread; **~ de barra** French bread; **~ rallado** breadcrumbs *pl*; **~ tostado** toast
pana *f* corduroy
panacea *f* panacea
panadería *f* bakery; **panadero** *m*, **-a** *f* baker
panal *m* honeycomb
Panamá Panama; **el Canal de ~** the Panama Canal; **Ciudad de ~** Panama city; **panameño 1** *adj* Panamanian **2** *m*, **-a** *f* Panamanian
pancarta *f* placard
páncreas *m inv* ANAT pancreas
pandereta *f*, **pandero** *m* tambourine
pandilla *f* group; *de delincuentes* gang

panecillo *m* (bread) roll
pánico *m* panic
pantaleta *f C.Am.*, *Méx* panties *pl*
pantalla *f* TV, INFOR screen; *de lámpara* shade
pantalón *m*, **pantalones** *mpl* pants *pl*, *Br* trousers *pl*
pantano *m* reservoir
pantanoso swampy
pantera *f* ZO panther
pantorrilla *f* ANAT calf
panty *m* pantyhose *pl*, *Br* tights *pl*
panza *f de persona* belly
pañal *m* diaper, *Br* nappy
paño *m* cloth; ***~ de cocina*** dishtowel; **pañuelo** *m* handkerchief
papa 1 *m* Pope **2** *f L.Am.* potato
papá *m* F pop F, dad F; ***~s*** *L.Am.* parents; ***Papá Noel*** Santa Claus
papada *f* double chin
papagayo *m* ZO parrot
papaya *f* BOT papaya
papel *m* paper; *trozo* piece of paper; TEA, *fig* role; ***~ de aluminio*** aluminum foil, *Br* aluminium foil; ***~ de envolver*** wrapping paper; ***~ de regalo*** giftwrap; ***~ higiénico*** toilet paper; **papelera** *f* waste basket, *Br* wastepaper basket; **papelería** *f* stationery store, stationer's shop
paperas *fpl* MED mumps
papilla *f para bebés* baby food; *para enfermos* purée
paquete *m* package, parcel; *de cigarrillos* packet
Paquistán Pakistan; **paquistaní** *m/f & adj* Pakistani
par 1 *f* par; ***a la ~ que*** as well as **2** *m* pair; ***abierto de ~ en ~*** wide open
para for; *dirección* toward; ***ir ~*** head for; ***diez ~ las ocho*** *L.Am.* ten of eight, ten to eight; ***lo hace ~ ayudarte*** he does it (in order) to help you; ***~ que*** so that; ***¿~ qué te marchas?*** what are you leaving for?; ***lo heredó todo ~ morir a los 30*** he inherited it all, only to die at 30
parabólica *f* satellite dish
parabrisas *m inv* AUTO windshield, *Br* windscreen; **paracaídas** *m inv* parachute; **paracaidista** *m/f* parachutist; MIL paratrooper, para; **parachoques** *m inv* AUTO bumper
parada *f* stop; ***~ de autobús*** bus stop; ***~ de taxis*** taxi stand, *Br* taxi rank
paradero *m* whereabouts *sg*; *L.Am.* ☞ ***parada***
parado 1 *adj* unemployed; *L.Am.* (*de pie*) standing (up); ***salir bien / mal ~*** come off well / badly **2** *m*, **-a** *f* unemployed person
paradójico paradoxical
parador *m Esp* parador (*state-run luxury hotel*)
paraguas *m inv* umbrella
Paraguay Paraguay; **paraguayo 1** *adj* Paraguayan **2** *m* , **-a** *f* Paraguayan

paraíso *m* paradise; ~ ***fiscal*** tax haven
paraje *m* place, spot
paralela *f* MAT parallel; DEP ~***s*** parallel bars; **paralelo** *m/adj* parallel
parálisis *f tb fig* paralysis; **paralítico 1** *adj* paralytic **2** *m*, **-a** *f* person who is paralyzed; **paralizar** MED paralyze; *actividad* bring to a halt; **paralizarse** *por miedo* be paralyzed (***por*** by); *fig actividad* be brought to a halt
paranoia *f* paranoia; **paranoico 1** *adj* paranoid **2** *m*, **-a** *f* person suffering from paranoia
parapente *m* hang glider; *actividad* hang gliding
parapeto *m* parapet
parapléjico 1 *adj* MED paraplegic **2** *m*, **-a** *f* paraplegic
parar 1 *v/t* stop; *L.Am.* (*poner de pie*) stand up **2** *v/i* stop; *en alojamiento* stay; ~ ***de llover*** stop raining; **pararse** stop; *L.Am.* (*ponerse de pie*) stand up
pararrayos *m inv* lightning rod, *Br* lightning conductor
parásito *m* parasite
parasol *m* parasol; *en la playa* (beach) umbrella
parcela *f* lot, *Br* plot
parche *m* patch
parcial (*partidario*) bias(s)ed
parco moderate, frugal; ***es*** ~ ***en palabras*** he's a man of few words
pardo 1 *adj color* dun; *L.Am. desp* half-breed *desp*, *Br tb* half-caste *desp* **2** *m color* dun; *L.Am. desp* half-breed *desp*
parecer 1 *m* opinion, view; ***al*** ~ apparently **2** *v/i* seem, look; ***¿qué te parece?*** what do you think?; **parecerse** resemble each other; ~ ***a alguien*** resemble s.o.; **parecido 1** *adj* similar **2** *m* similarity
pared *f* wall
pareja *f* pair; *en una relación* couple; *de una persona* partner; *de un objeto* other one
parentela *f* relatives *pl*, family; **parentesco** *m* relationship
paréntesis *m inv* parenthesis; *fig* break; ***entre*** ~ *fig* by the way
paridad *f* COM parity
pariente *m/f* relative
parir 1 *v/i* give birth **2** *v/t* give birth to
parking *m* parking lot, *Br* car park
parlamento *m* parliament
paro *m* unemployment; ***estar en*** ~ be unemployed; ~ ***cardíaco*** cardiac arrest
parodia *f* parody; **parodiar** parody
parpadear blink; **párpado** *m* eyelid
parque *m* park; *para bebé* playpen; ~ ***de atracciones*** amusement park; ~ ***de bomberos*** fire station; ~ ***natural*** nature reserve; ~ ***temático***

theme park
parqué *m* parquet
parquímetro *m* parking meter
párrafo *m* paragraph
parrilla *f* broiler, *Br* grill; ***a la ~*** broiled, *Br* grilled; **parrillada** *f L.Am.* barbecue
párroco *m* parish priest; **parroquia** *f* REL parish; COM clientele, customers *pl*; **parroquiano** *m*, **-a** *f* parishioner
parte 1 *m* report; ***dar ~ a alguien*** inform s.o. **2** *f trozo* part; JUR party; ***alguna ~*** somewhere; ***ninguna ~*** nowhere; ***otra ~*** somewhere else; ***de ~ de*** on behalf of; ***en ~*** partly; ***en*** *o* ***por todas ~s*** everywhere; ***por otra ~*** moreover; ***estar de ~ de alguien*** be on s.o.'s side; ***tomar ~ en*** take part in
parterre *m* flowerbed
participación *f* participation; **participante** *m/f* participant; **participar 1** *v/t una noticia* announce **2** *v/i* take part (***en*** in), participate (***en*** in)
particular 1 *adj clase, propiedad* private; *asunto* personal; (*específico*) particular; (*especial*) peculiar; ***en ~*** in particular **2** *m* (*persona*) individual; ***~es*** particulars; **particularidad** *f* peculiarity
partida *f en juego* game; (*remesa*) consignment; *documento* certificate; ***~ de nacimiento*** birth certificate;
partidario 1 *adj*: ***ser ~ de*** be in favor *o Br* favour of **2** *m*, **-a** *f* supporter; **partido** *m* POL party; DEP game; ***sacar ~ de*** take advantage of; ***tomar ~*** take sides
partir 1 *v/t* (*dividir, repartir*) split; (*romper*) break open, split open; (*cortar*) cut **2** *v/i* (*irse*) leave; ***a ~ de hoy*** (starting) from today; ***a ~ de ahora*** from now on; ***~ de*** *fig* start from
parto *m* birth; *fig* creation
party line *f* chatline
parvulario *m* kindergarten
pasa *f* raisin
pasada *f con trapo* wipe; *de pintura* coat; ***de ~*** in passing; ***¡qué ~!*** F that's incredible! F; **pasado 1** *adj tiempo* last; ***el lunes ~*** last Monday **2** *m* past
pasador *m para el pelo* barrette, *Br* (hair) slide; (*pestillo*) bolt; GASTR strainer
pasaje *m* (*billete*) ticket; MÚS, *de texto* passage; **pasajero 1** *adj* temporary; *relación* brief **2** *m*, **-a** *f* passenger
pasamano(s) *m* handrail
pasaporte *m* passport
pasar 1 *v/t* pass; *tiempo* spend; *un lugar* go past; *frontera* cross; *problemas, dificultades* experience; AUTO (*adelantar*) pass, *Br* overtake; *una película* show; ***para ~ el tiempo*** to pass the time; ***~lo bien*** have a good time **2** *v/i* (*suceder*) happen; *en juegos* pass;

paso de coger el teléfono F I can't be bothered to pick up the phone; ***pasé a visitarla*** I dropped by to see her; ~ ***de moda*** go out of fashion; ~ ***por*** go by; ***pasa por aquí*** come this way; ***dejar*** ~ *oportunidad* miss; ***hacerse*** ~ ***por*** pass o.s. off as; ***pasaré por tu casa*** I'll drop by your house; ***¡pasa!*** come in; ***¿qué pasa?*** what's happening?, what's going on?; ***¿qué te pasa?*** what's the matter?; **pasarse** *tb fig* go too far; *del tiempo* pass, go by; (*usar el tiempo*) spend; *de molestia, dolor* go away; ~ ***al enemigo*** go over to the enemy; ***se le pasó llamar*** he forgot to call

pasarela *f de modelos* runway, *Br* catwalk

Pascua *f* Easter; ***¡felices ~s!*** Merry Christmas!

pase *m tb* DEP, TAUR pass; *en el cine* showing; ~ ***de modelos*** fashion show

pasearse walk; **paseo** *m* walk; ~ ***marítimo*** seafront; ***dar un*** ~ go for a walk

pasillo *m* corridor; *en avión, cine* aisle

pasión *f* passion

pasivo passive

pasmar amaze; **pasmarse** be amazed; ~ ***de frío*** freeze

paso *m* step; (*manera de andar*) walk; (*ritmo*) pace, rate; *de agua* flow; *de tráfico* movement; (*cruce*) crossing; *de tiempo* passing; (*huella*) footprint; ~ ***a nivel*** grade crossing, *Br* level crossing; ~ ***de peatones*** crosswalk, *Br* pedestrian crossing; ***de*** ~ on the way; ***estar de*** ~ be passing through

pasota F *actitud* couldn't-care-less

pasta *f sustancia* paste; GASTR pasta; P (*dinero*) dough P; ~ ***de dientes*** toothpaste

pastel *m* GASTR cake; *pintura, color* pastel; **pastelería** *f* cake shop

pastilla *f* tablet; *de jabón* bar; ***a toda*** ~ F at top speed F

pasto *m* (*hierba*) grass; ***a todo*** ~ F for all one is worth F;

pastor *m* shepherd; REL pastor; ~ ***alemán*** German shepherd

pata *f* leg; ***a cuatro ~s*** on all fours; ***meter la*** ~ F put one's foot in it F; **patada** *f* kick; ***dar una*** ~ kick; **patalear** stamp one's feet

Patagonia Patagonia; **patagónico** Patagonian

patata *f* potato; ***~s fritas*** *de sartén* French fries, *Br* chips; *de bolsa* chips, *Br* crisps

paté *m* paté

patear *L.Am. de animal* kick

patente 1 *adj* clear, obvious **2** *f* patent; *L.Am.* AUTO license plate, *Br* numberplate

paternal paternal, fatherly; **paternidad** *f* paternity, fatherhood; **paterno** paternal

patético pitiful

patíbulo *m* scaffold
patilla *f de gafas* arm; **~s** *barba* sideburns
patín *m* skate; **~ (*de ruedas*) *en línea*** rollerblade®, inline skate; **patinador** *m*, **~a** *f* skater; **patinaje** *m* skating; ***~ artístico*** figure skating; ***~ sobre hielo*** ice-skating; ***~ sobre ruedas*** roller-skating; **patinar** skate; **patinete** *m* scooter
patio *m* courtyard, patio; ***~ de butacas*** TEA orchestra, *Br* stalls *pl*
pato *m* ZO duck
patológico pathological
patraña *f* tall story
patria *f* homeland; **patrimonio** *m* heritage; **patriota** *m/f* patriot; **patriótico** patriotic
patrocinador *m*, **~a** *f* sponsor; **patrocinar** sponsor
patrón *m* (*jefe*) boss; REL patron saint; *para costura* pattern; (*modelo*) standard; MAR skipper; **patrona** *f* (*jefa*) boss; REL patron saint
patrulla *f* patrol; **patrullar** patrol
paulatino gradual
pausa *f* pause; *en una actividad* break; MÚS rest; ***~ publicitaria*** commercial break; **pausado** slow, deliberate
pava *f animal* (hen) turkey; F (*colilla*) cigarette butt
pavimento *m* pavement, *Br* road surface
pavo 1 *adj L.Am.* F stupid **2** *m* ZO turkey; ***~ real*** peacock
payaso *m* clown
paz *f* peace; ***dejar en ~*** leave alone
peaje *m* toll
peatón *m* pedestrian
peca *f* freckle
pecado *m* sin; **pecador** *m*, **~a** *f* sinner; **pecar** sin; ***~ de ingenuo / generoso*** be very naive / generous
pecho *m* (*caja torácica*) chest; (*mama*) breast; ***tomar algo a ~*** take sth to heart; **pechuga** *f* GASTR breast; *L.Am. fig* F (*caradura*) nerve F
pecoso freckled
peculiar peculiar, odd; (*característico*) typical
pedagógico educational
pedal *m* pedal
pedante 1 *adj* pedantic; (*presuntuoso*) pretentious **2** *m/f* pedant; (*presuntuoso*) pretentious individual; **pedantería** *f* pedantry; (*presunción*) pretentiousness
pedazo *m* piece, bit; ***hacer ~s*** F smash to bits F
pediatra *m/f* pediatrician, *Br* paediatrician
pedicura *f* pedicure
pedido *m* order; **pedir 1** *v/t* ask for; (*necesitar*) need; *en restaurante* order; ***me pidió que no fuera*** he asked me not to go **2** *v/i mendigar* beg; *en restaurante* order
pedo 1 *adj* drunk **2** *m* F fart F
pegadizo catchy; **pegajoso**

sticky; *fig*: *persona* clingy; **pegamento** *m* glue; **pegar 1** *v/t* (*golpear*) hit; (*adherir*) stick, glue; *bofetada*, *susto*, *resfriado* give **2** *v/i* (*golpear*) hit; (*adherir*) stick; *del sol* beat down; (*armonizar*) go (together); **pegarse** *resfriado* catch; *acento* pick up; *susto* give o.s.; **~ *un golpo / un tiro*** hit / shoot o.s.; **pegatina** *f* sticker

peinado *m* hairstyle; **peinar 1** *v/t tb fig* comb; **~ *a alguien*** comb s.o.'s hair; **peine** *m* comb; **peineta** *f* ornamental comb

p. ej. (= ***por ejemplo***) eg (= for example)

pelaje *m* ZO coat; *fig* (*aspecto*) look; **pelar** *manzana*, *patata etc* peel

peldaño *m* step

pelea *f* fight; **pelear, pelearse** fight

peletería *f* furrier

película *f* movie, film; FOT film; **~ *del Oeste*** Western; ***de* ~** F awesome F

peligro *m* danger; ***correr* ~** be in danger; ***poner en* ~** endanger, put at risk; **peligroso** dangerous

pelirrojo red-haired, red-headed

pellejo *m de animal* skin, hide

pellizcar pinch

pelo *m de persona*, *de perro* hair; *de animal* fur; ***a* ~** F (*sin preparación*) unprepared; ***montar a* ~** ride bareback; ***tomar el* ~ *a alguien*** F pull s.o.'s leg F

pelota 1 *f* ball; **~*s*** F nuts F, balls F; ***en* ~*s*** P stark naked **2** *m/f* F creep F

peluca *f* wig

peluche *m* soft toy; ***oso de* ~** teddy bear

peludo *persona* hairy; *animal* furry

peluquería *f* hairdressing salon, *Br* hairdresser's; **peluquero** *m*, **-a** *f* hairdresser; **peluquín** *m* hairpiece

pelusa *f* fluff

pelvis *f inv* ANAT pelvis

pena *f* (*tristeza*) sadness, sorrow; (*congoja*) grief; (*lástima*) pity; JUR sentence; **~ *capital*** death penalty, capital punishment; **~ *de muerte*** death penalty; ***no vale*** *o* ***no merece la* ~** it's not worth it; ***¡qué* ~!** what a shame *o* pity!; ***a duras* ~*s*** with great difficulty; ***me da* ~** *L.Am.* I'm ashamed; **penal** penal; ***derecho* ~** criminal law; **penalizar** penalize

pender hang (***sobre*** over); **pendiente 1** *adj* unfinished; *cuenta* unpaid **2** *m* earring **3** *f* slope

péndulo *m* pendulum

pene *m* ANAT penis

penetración *f* penetration; **penetrante** *mirada* penetrating; *sonido* piercing; *frío* bitter; *herida* deep; *análisis* incisive; **penetrar** penetrate; (*entrar*) enter; *de un líquido*

seep in
penicilina *f* penicillin
península *f* peninsula
penitencia *f* penitence
penoso distressing; *trabajo* laborious
pensamiento *m* thought; BOT pansy; **pensar 1** *v/t* think about; (*opinar*) think; ***¡ni ~lo!*** don't even think about it **2** *v/i* think (***en*** about); **pensativo** thoughtful
pensión *f* rooming house, *Br* guesthouse; *dinero* pension; ***~ alimenticia*** child support, *Br* maintenance; ***~ completa*** American plan, *Br* full board; **pensionista** *m/f* pensioner
Pentecostés *m* Pentecost
penúltimo penultimate
penuria *f* shortage (***de*** of); (*pobreza*) poverty
peña *f* crag, cliff; (*roca*) rock; F *de amigos* group; **peñón** *m*: ***el Peñon de Gibraltar*** the Rock of Gibraltar
peón *m en ajedrez* pawn; *trabajador* laborer, *Br* labourer
peor worse; ***de mal en ~*** from bad to worse
pepinillo *m* gherkin; **pepino** *m* cucumber
pepita *f* pip
pequeñez *f* smallness; **pequeño 1** *adj* small, little; ***de ~*** when I was small *o* little **2** *m*, **-a** *f* little one
pera *f* pear; **peral** *m* pear tree
perca *f pez* perch
percance *m* mishap
percatarse notice; ***~ de algo*** notice sth
percebe *m* ZO barnacle
percepción *f* perception; COM *acto* receipt; **perceptible** perceptible
percha *f* coat hanger; *gancho* coat hook
percibir perceive; COM *sueldo* receive
percusión *f* MÚS percussion
perdedor *m*, **~a** *f* loser; **perder 1** *v/t* lose; *tren, avión etc* miss; *el tiempo* waste **2** *v/i* lose; ***echar a ~*** ruin; ***echarse a ~*** *de alimento* go bad; **perderse** get lost; **pérdida** *f* loss
perdigón *m* pellet
perdiz *f* ZO partridge
perdón *m* pardon; REL forgiveness; ***pedir ~*** say sorry, apologize; ***¡~!*** sorry; ***¿~?*** pardon me?; **perdonar** forgive; JUR pardon; ***~ algo a alguien*** forgive s.o. sth; ***¡perdone!*** sorry; ***perdone, ¿tiene hora?*** excuse me, do you have the time?
perdurable enduring; **perdurar** endure
perecedero perishable; **perecer** perish
peregrinación *f* pilgrimage; **peregrinar** go on a pilgrimage; **peregrino** *m*, **-a** *f* pilgrim
perejil *m* BOT parsley
perezoso 1 *adj* lazy **2** *m* ZO sloth
perfección *f* perfection; ***a la ~***

perfectly, to perfection; **perfeccionar** perfect; **perfecto** perfect
pérfido treacherous
perfil *m* profile; ***de ~*** in profile, from the side
perfilar *dibujo* outline; *proyecto* put the finishing touches to; **perfilarse** emerge
perforar pierce; *calle* dig up
perfumar perfume; **perfume** *m* perfume; **perfumería** *f* perfume shop
pergamino *m* parchment
pericia *f* expertise
periferia *f* periphery; *de ciudad* outskirts *pl*
perímetro *m* perimeter
periódico 1 *adj* periodic **2** *m* newspaper; **periodismo** *m* journalism; **periodista** *m/f* journalist; **período, periodo** *m* period
peripecia *f* adventure
periquito *m* ZO budgerigar
perito 1 *adj* expert **2** *m*, **-a** *f* expert; COM *en seguros* loss adjuster
perjudicar harm, damage; **perjudicial** harmful, damaging; **perjuicio** *m* harm, damage; ***sin ~ de*** without affecting
perjurio *m* perjury
perla *f* pearl
permanecer remain, stay; **permanencia** *f* stay; **permanente 1** *adj* permanent **2** *f* perm
permeable permeable
permisible permissible; **permiso** *m* permission; *documento* permit; ***~ de conducir*** driver's license, *Br* driving licence; ***~ de residencia*** residence permit; ***con ~*** excuse me; ***estar de ~*** be on leave; **permitir** permit, allow
permuta *f* exchange
pernicioso harmful
pernoctar spend the night
pero 1 *conj* but **2** *m* flaw, defect; ***no hay ~s que valgan*** no excuses
perogrullada *f* platitude
perpendicular perpendicular
perpetrar *crimen* perpetrate, commit
perpetuar perpetuate; **perpetuo** *fig* perpetual
perplejo puzzled, perplexed
perra *f* dog; **perro** *m* dog; ***~ callejero*** stray; ***~ guardián*** guard dog; ***~ lazarillo*** seeing eye dog®, *Br* guide dog; ***~ pastor*** sheepdog; ***hace un tiempo de ~s*** F the weather is lousy F
persecución *f* pursuit; (*acoso*) persecution; **perseguidor** *m*, **~a** *f* persecutor; **perseguir** pursue; *delincuente* look for; (*molestar*) pester; (*acosar*) persecute
perseverancia *f* perseverance; **perseverante** persistent; **perseverar** persevere (***en*** with)
persiana *f* blind
persignarse cross o.s.

persistencia *f* persistence; **persistente** persistent; **persistir** persist

persona *f* person; ***quince ~s*** fifteen people; **personaje** *m* TEA character; *famoso* celebrity; **personal 1** *adj* personal **2** *m* personnel, staff; **personalidad** *f* personality; **personarse** arrive, turn up; **personificar** personify, embody

perspectiva *f* perspective; *fig* point of view; **~s** outlook, prospects

perspicacia *f* shrewdness, perspicacity; **perspicaz** shrewd, perspicacious

persuadir persuade; **persuasión** *f* persuasion; **persuasivo** persuasive

pertenecer belong (***a*** to); **perteneciente: ~ *a*** belonging to

pértiga *f* pole; ***salto con ~*** DEP pole vault

pertinaz persistent; (*terco*) obstinate

pertinente relevant, pertinent

pertrechar equip, supply (***de*** with); **pertrecharse** equip o.s.; **pertrechos** *mpl* MIL equipment

perturbación *f* disturbance; **perturbado** *m* , **-a** *f*: **~ (*mental*)** mentally disturbed person; **perturbador** disturbing; **perturbar** disturb; *reunión* disrupt

Perú Peru; **peruano 1** *adj* Peruvian **2** *m* , **-a** *f* Peruvian

perversidad *f* wickedness, evil; **perversión** *f* perversion; **perverso** perverted; **pervertir** pervert

pesa *f para balanza* weight; DEP shot; *C.Am* butcher's shop

pesadez *f fig* drag F

pesadilla *f* nightmare

pesado 1 *adj objeto* heavy; *libro, clase etc* tedious, boring; *trabajo* tough **2** *m*, **-a** *f* bore; ***¡qué ~ es!*** F he's a real pain F

pesadumbre *f* grief, sorrow

pésame *m* condolences *pl*

pesar 1 *v/t* weigh **2** *v/i* be heavy; (*influir*) carry weight; *fig* weigh heavily (***sobre*** on) **3** *m* sorrow; ***a ~ de*** in spite of, despite

pesca *f actividad* fishing; (*peces*) fish *pl*; **pescadería** *f* fish shop; **pescadero** *m*, **-a** *f* fish dealer, *Br* fishmonger; **pescado** *m* GASTR fish; **pescador** *m* fisherman; **pescar 1** *v/t un pez, resfriado etc* catch; (*intentar tomar*) fish for; *trabajo, marido etc* land F **2** *v/i* fish

pescuezo *m* neck

pese: ~ *a* despite

pesebre *m* (*comedero*) manger; (*belén*) crèche

pesimismo *m* pessimism; **pesimista 1** *adj* pessimistic **2** *m/f* pessimist

pésimo awful, terrible

peso *m* weight; *moneda* peso;

de ~ *fig* weighty
pesquisa *f* investigation
pestaña *f* eyelash; **pestañear** flutter one's eyelashes; ***sin ~*** *fig* without batting an eyelid
peste *f* MED plague; F *olor* stink F; ***echar ~s*** F curse and swear
pestillo *m* (*picaporte*) door handle; (*cerradura*) bolt
petardo 1 *m* firecracker **2** *m*, **-a** *f* F nerd F
petición *f* request
petrificar petrify (*tb fig*); **petrificarse** become petrified
petróleo *m* oil, petroleum; **petrolero 1** *adj* oil *atr* **2** *m* MAR oil tanker
petulancia *f* smugness; **petulante** smug
pez *m* ZO fish; ***~ espada*** swordfish; ***~ gordo*** F big shot F
pezón *m* nipple
piadoso pious
pianista *m/f* pianist; **piano** *m* piano; ***~ de cola*** grand piano
pica *f* TAUR goad; *palo de la baraja* spade
picadero *m* *escuela* riding school; **picadura** *f de reptil, mosquito* bite; *de avispa* sting; *tabaco* cut tobacco
picadillo *m* GASTR *de lomo: marinated ground meat*
picado 1 *adj diente* decayed; *mar* rough, choppy; *carne* ground, *Br* minced; *verdura* minced, *Br* finely chopped; *fig* offended **2** *m L.Am.* dive; ***caer en ~*** *de precios* nosedive
picador *m* TAUR picador; MIN face worker
picante 1 *adj* hot, spicy; *chiste* risqué **2** *m* hot spice
picar 1 *v/t de mosquito, serpiente* bite; *de avispa* sting; *de ave* peck; *carne* grind, *Br* mince; *verdura* mince, *Br* finely chop; TAUR jab with a lance; (*molestar*) annoy **2** *v/i tb fig* take the bait; *L.Am. de la comida* be hot; (*producir picor*) itch; *del sol* burn
picardía *f* (*astucia*) craftiness, slyness; (*travesura*) mischievousness; *Méx* (*taco, palabrota*) swearing, swearwords *pl*
pícaro *persona* crafty, sly; *comentario* mischievous
picarse (*agujerearse*) rust; (*cariarse*) decay; F (*molestarse*) get mad F
pichón *m L.Am. pollo* chick; F (*novato*) rookie F
pico *m* ZO beak; F (*boca*) mouth; *de montaña* peak; *herramienta* pickax, *Br* pickaxe; ***a las tres y ~*** some time after three o'clock
picor *m* itch
picotear peck
pie *m* foot; *de estatua, lámpara* base; ***a ~*** on foot; ***de ~*** standing; ***no tiene ni ~s ni cabeza*** I can't make head nor tail of it
piedad *f* pity; (*clemencia*)

mercy
piedra *f tb* MED stone
piel *f de persona, fruta* skin; *de animal* hide, skin; (*cuero*) leather; ***abrigo de ~es*** fur coat
pienso *m* animal feed
pierna *f* leg; ***dormir a ~ suelta*** sleep like a log
pieza *f de un conjunto*, MÚS piece; *de aparato* part; TEA play; (*habitación*) room; ***~ de recambio*** spare (part)
pijama *m* pajamas *pl*, *Br* pyjamas *pl*
pila *f* ELEC battery; (*montón*) pile; (*fregadero*) sink
pilar *m tb fig* pillar
píldora *f* pill
pileta *f Rpl* sink; (*alberca*) swimming pool
pillar (*tomar*) seize; (*atrapar*) catch; (*atropellar*) hit; *chiste* get
pillo 1 *adj* mischievous **2** *m*, **-a** *f* rascal
pilotar AVIA fly, pilot; AUTO drive; MAR steer; **piloto** *m* AVIA, MAR pilot; AUTO driver; ELEC pilot light; ***~ automático*** autopilot
pimentón *m* paprika; **pimienta** *f* pepper; **pimiento** *m* pepper; ***me importa un ~*** F I couldn't care less F
pincel *m* paintbrush
pinchadiscos *m/f* F disc jockey, DJ
pinchar 1 *v/t* prick; AUTO puncture; TELEC tap; F (*molestar*) bug F; ***~le a alguien*** MED give s.o. a shot **2** *v/i* prick; AUTO get a flat (tire), *Br* get a puncture; **pinchazo** *m herida* prick; *dolor* sharp pain; AUTO flat (tire), *Br* puncture; F (*fracaso*) flop F
pincho *m* GASTR bar snack
pingüino *m* ZO penguin
pino *m* BOT pine; ***hacer el ~*** do a handstand
pinta *f* pint; *aspecto* looks *pl*; ***tener buena ~*** *fig* look inviting
pintada *f* graffiti; **~s** graffiti *pl o sg*
pintar paint; ***no ~ nada*** *fig* F not count; **pintarse** put on one's make-up
pintor *m*, **~a** *f* painter; **~ (*de brocha gorda*)** (house) painter; **pintoresco** picturesque; **pintura** *f sustancia* paint; *obra* painting
pinza *f* clothes pin, *Br* clothes peg; ZO claw; ***~s*** tweezers; *L.Am.* (*alicates*) pliers
piña *f del pino* pine cone; *fruta* pineapple; **piñón** *m* BOT pine nut; TÉC pinion
pío pious
piojo *m* ZO louse; ***~s*** lice *pl*
pionero 1 *adj* pioneering **2** *m*, **-a** *f tb fig* pioneer
pipa *f* pipe; ***~s*** *semillas* sunflower seeds; ***pasarlo ~*** F have a great time
pipí *m* F pee F; ***hacer ~*** F pee F
pique *m* resentment; (*rivalidad*) rivalry; ***irse a ~*** *fig* go under

piqueta *f herramienta* pickax, *Br* pickaxe; *en cámping* tent peg
piquete *m* POL picket
piragüismo *m* canoeing
pirámide *f* pyramid
pirata *m/f* pirate; **~ *informático*** hacker; **piratería** *f* piracy
pirenaico Pyrenean; **Pirineos** *mpl* Pyrenees
piropo *m* compliment
pirotécnico fireworks *atr*
pisada *f* footstep; *huella* footprint; **pisar** step on; *uvas* tread; *fig* (*maltratar*) walk all over; *idea* steal; ***~ a alguien*** step on s.o.'s foot
piscina *f* swimming pool
Piscis *m/f inv* ASTR Pisces
piso *m* apartment, *Br* flat; (*planta*) floor
pisotear trample
pista *f* track, trail; (*indicio*) clue; *de atletismo* track; ***~ de aterrizaje*** AVIA runway; ***~ de baile*** dance floor; ***~ de tenis / squash*** tennis / squash court
pistacho *m* BOT pistachio
pistola *f* pistol; **pistolero** *m* gunman
pistón *m* piston
pita *f* BOT agave, pita
pitar 1 *v/i* whistle; *con bocina* hoot; *L.Am.* (*fumar*) smoke; ***salir pitando*** F dash off F **2** *v/t* (*abuchear*) whistle at; *penalti, falta etc* call, *Br* blow for; *silbato* blow
pitillera *f* cigarette case; **pitillo** *m* cigarette; *hecho a mano* roll-up
pito *m* whistle; (*bocina*) horn
piyama *m L.Am.* pajamas *pl*, *Br* pyjamas *pl*
pizarra *f* blackboard; *piedra* slate
placa *f* (*lámina*) sheet; (*plancha*) plate; (*letrero*) plaque; *Méx* AUTO license plate, *Br* number plate; ***~ madre*** INFOR motherboard; ***~ (dental)*** plaque; ***~ de matrícula*** AUTO license plate, *Br* number plate
placer 1 *v/i* please **2** *m* pleasure
plaga *f* AGR pest; MED plague; *fig* scourge; (*abundancia*) glut; **plagado** infested; (*lleno*) full; ***~ de gente*** swarming with people
plan *m* plan
plancha *f para planchar* iron; *en cocina* broiler, *Br* grill; *de metal* sheet; F (*metedura de pata*) goof F; ***a la ~*** GASTR broiled, *Br* grilled; **planchado 1** *adj* F **shattered** F **2** *m* ironing; **planchar** iron; *Méx* F (*dar plantón*) stand up F; *L.Am.* (*lisonjear*) flatter
planeador *m* glider; **planear 1** *v/t* plan **2** *v/i* AVIA glide
planeta *m* planet
planicie *f* plain
planificar plan
plano 1 *adj* flat **2** *m* ARQUI plan; *de ciudad* map; *en cine* shot; MAT plane; *fig* level
planta *f* BOT plant; (*piso*) floor; ***~ del pie*** sole of the

foot; **plantación** *f* plantation; **plantar 1** *v/t árbol etc* plant; *tienda de campaña* put up; **~ *a alguien*** F stand s.o. up F
plantear *problema* pose, create; *cuestión* raise
plantilla *f para zapato* insole; (*personal*) staff; DEP squad; *para cortar*, INFOR template
plantón *m*: ***dar un ~ a alguien*** F stand s.o. up F
plástico *m* plastic
plata *f* silver; *L.Am.* F (*dinero*) cash, dough F
plataforma *f tb* POL platform; **~ *petrolífera*** oil rig
plátano *m* banana
platea *f* TEA orchestra, *Br* stalls *pl*
plateado *Méx* wealthy
platicar 1 *v/t L.Am.* tell **2** *v/i Méx* chat, talk
platillo *m*: **~ *volante*** flying saucer; ***~s*** MÚS cymbals
platina *f de microscopio* slide; *de estéreo* tape deck
platino *m* platinum
plató *m de película* set; TV studio
plato *m* plate; GASTR dish; **~ *combinado*** mixed platter; **~ *hondo*** soup dish; **~ *preparado*** ready meal; **~ *principal*** main course; **~ *sopero*** soup dish
playa *f* beach; **~ *de estacionamiento*** *L.Am.* parking lot, *Br* car park; **playeras** *fpl* canvas shoes
plaza *f* square; (*vacante*) job opening; *en vehículo* seat; *de trabajo* position; **~ *de toros*** bull ring
plazo *f* period; (*pago*) installment, *Br* instalment; ***a corto / largo ~*** in the short / long term; ***a ~s*** in installments
plegable collapsible, folding; **plegar** fold (up); **plegarse** *fig* submit (***a*** to)
pleito *m* JUR lawsuit; *fig* dispute; ***poner un ~ a alguien*** sue s.o.
pleno 1 *adj* full; ***en ~ día*** in broad daylight **2** *m* plenary session
pliego 1 *vb* ☞ ***plegar*** **2** *m* (*hoja de papel*) sheet (of paper); (*carta*) sealed letter *o* document; **pliegue** *m* fold, crease
plomero *m Méx* plumber; **plomo** *m* lead; ELEC fuse; *fig* F drag F; ***sin ~*** AUTO unleaded
pluma *f* feather; *para escribir* fountain pen
plural *m/adj* plural
población *f gente* population; (*ciudad*) city, town; (*pueblo*) village; *Chi* shanty town; **poblado 1** *adj* populated; *barba* bushy; **~ *de*** *fig* full of **2** *m* (*pueblo*) settlement; **poblador** *m*, **~a** *f Chi* shanty town dweller; **poblar** populate
pobre 1 *adj* poor **2** *m/f* poor person; ***los ~s*** the poor; **pobreza** *f* poverty
pocilga *f* pigpen, *Br* pigsty
poco 1 *adj sg* little, not much;

pl few, not many; ***un ~ de*** a little; ***unos ~s*** a few **2** *adv* little; ***trabaja ~*** he doesn't work much; ***estuvo ~ por aquí*** he wasn't around much; ***~ a ~*** little by little; ***dentro de ~*** soon, shortly; ***hace ~*** a short time ago, not long ago; ***por ~*** nearly **3** *m*: ***un ~*** a little, a bit

podar AGR prune

poder 1 *v/aux capacidad* can, be able to; *permiso* can, be allowed to; *posibilidad* may, might; ***no pude hablar con ella*** I wasn't able to talk to her; ***¿puedo ir contigo?*** can *o* may I come with you?; ***¡podías habérselo dicho!*** you could have *o* you might have told him **2** *v/i*: ***~ con*** (*sobreponerse a*) manage, cope with; ***me puede*** he can beat me; ***no puedo más*** I can't take any more, I've had enough; ***puede ser*** perhaps, maybe; ***puede que*** perhaps, maybe; ***¿se puede?*** may I come in? **3** *m tb* POL power; ***en ~ de alguien*** in s.o.'s hands; **poderoso** powerful

podio *m* podium

podólogo *m*, **-a** *f* MED podiatrist, *Br* chiropodist

podrido *tb fig* rotten

poema *m* poem; **poesía** *f género* poetry; (*poema*) poem; **poeta** *m/f* poet; **poético** poetic; **poetisa** *f* poet

polaco 1 *adj* Polish **2** *m*, **-a** *f* Pole **3** *m idioma* Polish

polea *f* TÉC pulley

policía 1 *f* police **2** *m/f* police officer, policeman; *mujer* police officer, policewoman; **policíaco, policiaco** detective *atr*

polideportivo *m* sports center, *Br* sports centre

polifacético versatile, multifaceted

poligamia *f* polygamy

polilla *f* ZO moth

polio *f* MED polio

política *f* politics; **político 1** *adj* political **2** *m*, **-a** *f* politician

póliza *f* policy; ***~ de seguros*** insurance policy

polizón *m/f* stowaway

pollo *m* ZO, GASTR chicken

polo *m* GEOG, ELEC pole; *prenda* polo shirt; DEP polo; ***Polo Norte*** North Pole; ***Polo Sur*** South Pole

Polonia Poland

polución *f* pollution; **polucionar** pollute

polvo *m* dust; *en química, medicina etc* powder; ***~s de talco*** talcum powder; ***echar un ~*** V have a screw V; **pólvora** *f* gunpowder; **polvoriento** dusty

pomada *f* cream

pomelo *m* BOT grapefruit

pompa *f* pomp; ***~ de jabón*** bubble; ***~s fúnebres*** *ceremonia* funeral ceremony; *establecimiento* funeral home

ponedero *m* nest(ing) box

ponencia *f* presentation; EDU paper
ponente *m/f* speaker
poner put; (*añadir*) put in; RAD, TV turn on, switch on; *la mesa* set; *ropa* put on; (*escribir*) put down; *en libro etc* say; *negocio* set up; *huevos* lay; **~ a alguien furioso** make s.o. angry; **~le una multa a alguien** fine s.o.; **pongamos que** let's suppose *o* assume that; **ponerse** *ropa* put on; **ponte en el banco** go and sit on the bench; **se puso ahí** she stood over there; **dile que se ponga** TELEC tell her to come to the phone; **~ palido** turn pale; **~ furioso** get angry; **~ enfermo** become *o* fall ill; **~ a** start to
popa *f* MAR stern
popular popular; (*del pueblo*) folk *atr*, *barrio* lower-class;
popularizar popularize
por ◇ *motivo* for, because of; **lo hizo ~ amor** she did it out of love ◇ *medio* by; **~ avión** by air ◇ *tiempo*: **~ un segundo** *L.Am.* for a second; **~ la mañana** in the morning ◇ movimiento: **~ la calle** down the street; **~ un tunel** through a tunnel; **~ aquí** this way ◇ *posición aproximada* around, about; **está ~ aquí** it's around here (somewhere) ◇ *cambio*: **~ cincuenta pesos** for fifty pesos ◇ otros usos: **~ hora** an *o* per hour; **dos ~ dos** two times two; **¿~ qué?** why?
porcelana *f* porcelain, china
porcentaje *m* percentage
porche *f* porch
porción *f* portion
pormenor *m* detail
pornografía *f* pornography
poro *m* pore; **poroso** porous
porque because; **~ sí** just because
porqué *m* reason
porquería *f* filth; F *cosa de poca calidad* piece of trash F
porra *f* baton; (*palo*) club
porro *m* F joint F
porrón *m container from which wine is poured straight into the mouth*
portaaviones *m inv* aircraft carrier
portada *f* TIP front page; *de revista* cover; ARQUI front
portador *m*, **~a** *f* COM bearer; MED carrier
portal *m* foyer; (*entrada*) doorway
portaminas *m inv* automatic pencil, *Br* propelling pencil
portarse behave
portátil portable
portavoz *m/f* spokesman; *mujer* spokeswoman
porte *m* (*aspecto*) appearance; (*gasto de correo*) postage
porteño *Arg* **1** *adj* of Buenos Aires **2** *m*, **-a** *f* native of Buenos Aires
portería *f* reception; *casa* superintendent's apartment, *Br* caretaker's flat; DEP goal;

portero *m* doorman; *de edificio* superintendent, *Br* caretaker; DEP goalkeeper; **~ automático** intercom, *Br* entryphone
pórtico *m* portico
portorriqueño 1 *adj* Puerto Rican **2** *m*, **-a** *f* Puerto Rican
Portugal Portugal; **portugués 1** *m/adj* Portuguese **2** *m*, **-esa** *f persona* Portuguese **3** *m idioma* Portuguese
porvenir *m* future
pos(t)venta after-sales *atr*
posada *f C.Am., Méx* Christmas party; (*fonda*) inn
posar *mano* lay, place (**sobre** on); **~ la mirada en** gaze at; **posarse** *de ave, insecto*, AVIA land
pose *f* pose
poseer possess; (*ser dueño de*) own, possess; **posesión** *f* possession; **tomar ~ (de un cargo)** POL take up office
posguerra *f* postwar period
posibilidad *f* possibility; **posibilitar** make possible; **posible** possible; **en lo ~** as far as possible; **hacer todo lo ~** do everything possible; **es ~ que...** perhaps ...
posición *f tb* MIL, *fig* position; *social* standing, status
positivo positive
postal 1 *adj* mail *atr*, postal **2** *f* postcard; **poste** *m* post
postergar postpone
posterior later, subsequent; (*trasero*) rear *atr*, back *atr*; **posterioridad** *f*: **con ~** later, subsequently; **con ~ a** later than, subsequent to
postizo 1 *adj* false **2** *m* hairpiece
postre *m* dessert; **a la ~** in the end
postura *f tb fig* position
potable drinkable; *fig* F passable; **agua ~** drinking water
potaje *m* GASTR stew
potasio *m* potassium
pote *m* (*olla*) pot; GASTR stew
potencia *f* power; **en ~** potential; **potente** powerful
potro *m* ZO colt
pozo *m* well; MIN shaft; *Rpl en calle* pothole; **un ~ sin fondo** *fig* a bottomless pit
práctica *f* practice; **practicable** *tarea* feasible, practicable; *camino* passable; **practicar** practice, *Br* practise; *deporte* play; **~ la equitación** ride; **práctico** practical
pradera *f* prairie, grassland; **prado** *m* meadow
pragmático pragmatic; **pragmatismo** *m* pragmatism
precario precarious
precaución *f* precaution
precedente 1 *adj* previous **2** *m* precedent; **preceder** precede
precintar *paquete* seal; *lugar* seal off; **precinto** *m* seal
precio *m* price; **precioso** (*de valor*) precious; (*hermoso*) beautiful
precipicio *m* precipice
precipitación *f* (*prisa*) hurry, haste; **precipitaciones** rain;

precipitado hasty, sudden; **precipitar** (*lanzar*) throw, hurl; (*acelerar*) hasten; **precipitarse** rush; *fig* be hasty
precisar (*aclarar*) specify; (*necesitar*) need; **precisión** *f* precision; **preciso** precise, accurate; ***ser* ~** be necessary
precoz early; *niño* precocious
precursor *m*, **~a** *f* precursor, forerunner
predecesor *m*, **~a** *f* predecessor
predecir predict
predicar preach
predicción *f* prediction
predilecto favorite, *Br* favourite
predispuesto predisposed (***a*** to)
predominar predominate; **predominio** *m* predominance
prefacio *m* preface, foreword
preferencia *f* preference; **preferente** preferential; **preferido** **1** *part* ☞ ***preferir*** **2** *adj* favorite, *Br* favourite; **preferir** prefer
prefijo *m* prefix; TELEC area code, *Br* dialling code
pregunta *f* question; **preguntar** ask; ***~ por algo*** ask about sth; ***~ por alguien*** *paradero* ask for s.o.; *salud etc* ask about s.o.
prejuicio *m* prejudice
prematuro **1** *adj* premature **2** *m*, **-a** *f* premature baby
premiar award a prize to; **premio** *m* prize
prenda *f* item of clothing, garment; *garantía* security; *en juegos* forfeit
prendedor *m* broach, *Br* brooch
prender **1** *v/t a fugitivo* capture; *sujetar* pin up; *L.Am. fuego* light; *L.Am. luz* turn on; ***~ fuego a*** set fire to **2** *v/i de planta* take; (*empezar a arder*) catch; *de moda* catch on
prensa *f* press; ***~ amarilla*** gutter press; **prensar** press
preocupación *f* worry, concern; **preocupado** worried, concerned (***por*** about); **preocupante** worrying; **preocupar** worry, concern; **preocuparse** worry (***por*** about); ***~ de*** (*encargarse*) look after, take care of
preparación *f* preparation; (*educación*) education; *para trabajo* training; **preparado** ready, prepared; **preparar** prepare, get ready; **preparativos** *mpl* preparations
preponderar predominate
preposición *f* GRAM preposition
presa *f* (*dique*) dam; (*embalse*) reservoir; (*víctima*) prey; *L.Am. para comer* bite to eat
prescribir JUR prescribe; **prescripción** *f* JUR *de contrato* expiry, expiration
presencia *f* presence; ***buena ~*** smart appearance; **presenciar** witness; (*estar presente a*) attend, be present at

presentación *f* presentation; COM launch; *entre personas* introduction; **presentador** *m*, **~a** *f* TV presenter; **presentar** present; *a alguien* introduce; *producto* launch; *solicitud* submit; **presentarse** *en sitio* show up; (*darse a conocer*) introduce o.s.; *a examen* take; *de problema, dificultad* arise; *a elecciones* run
presente 1 *adj* present; ***tener algo ~*** bear sth in mind; ***¡~!*** here! **2** *m tiempo* present **3** *m/fpl*: ***los ~s*** those present
presentir foresee; ***presiento que...*** I have a feeling that ...
preservar protect; **preservativo** *m* condom
presidencia *f* presidency; *de compañía* presidency, *Br* chairmanship; *de comité* chairmanship; **presidente** *m*, **-a** *f* president; *de gobierno* premier, prime minister; *de compañía* president, *Br* chairman, *Br mujer* chairwoman; *de comité* chair
presidio *m* prison
presidir be president of; *reunión* chair
presión *f* pressure; ***~ sanguínea*** blood pressure; **presionar** *botón* press; *fig* put pressure on, pressure
preso 1 *part* ☞ ***prender*** **2** *m*, **-a** *f* prisoner
prestación *f* provision; ***~ social sustitutoria*** MIL community service in lieu of military service; **préstamo** *m* loan; ***~ bancario*** bank loan; **prestar** *dinero* lend; *ayuda* give; *L.Am.* borrow; ***~ atención*** pay attention
prestidigitador *m*, **~a** *f* conjurer
prestigio *m* prestige; **prestigioso** prestigious
presumido conceited; (*coqueto*) vain; **presumir 1** *v/t* presume **2** *v/i* show off; ***~ de algo*** boast about sth; ***presume de listo*** he thinks he's very clever; **presunto** alleged, suspected; **presuntuoso** conceited
presuponer assume; **presupuesto 1** *part* ☞ ***presuponer*** **2** *m* POL budget
pretencioso pretentious
pretender: ***pretendía convencerlos*** he was trying to persuade them; **pretendiente** *m de mujer* suitor; **pretensión** *f L.Am.* (*arrogancia*) vanity; ***sin pretensiones*** unpretentious
pretexto *m* pretext
prevención *f* prevention; **prevenir** prevent; (*avisar*) warn (***contra*** against); **preventivo** preventive, preventative
prever foresee
previo previous; ***sin ~ aviso*** without (prior) warning
previsión *f* (*predicción*) forecast; (*preparación*) foresight
prima *f de seguro* premium;

(*pago extra*) bonus
primavera *f* spring; BOT primrose
primer first; **primero 1** *adj* first; ***~s auxilios*** first aid **2** *m*, **-a** *f* first (one) **3** *adv* first
primitivo primitive; (*original*) original
primo *m*, **-a** *f* cousin
primordial fundamental
princesa *f* princess
principal main, principal; ***lo ~*** the main *o* most important thing
príncipe *m* prince
principiante 1 *adj* inexperienced **2** *m/f* beginner; **principio** *m* principle; *en tiempo* beginning; ***a ~s de abril*** at the beginning of April
prioridad *f* priority; **prioritario** priority *atr*
prisa *f* hurry, rush; ***darse ~*** hurry (up); ***tener ~*** be in a hurry *o* rush
prisión *f* prison, jail; **prisionero 1** *adj* captive **2** *m*, **-a** *f* prisoner
prismáticos *mpl* binoculars
privado 1 *part* ☞ ***privar*** **2** *adj* private; **privar: *~ a alguien de algo*** deprive s.o. of sth; **privarse** deprive o.s.; **privatizar** privatize
privilegiado privileged; (*excelente*) exceptional; **privilegiar** privilege; (*dar importancia a*) favor, *Br* favour; **privilegio** *m* privilege
proa *f* MAR bow
probabilidad *f* probability;
probable probable, likely
probar 1 *v/t teoría* test, try out; (*comer un poco de*) taste, try; (*comer por primera vez*) try **2** *v/i* try; ***~ a hacer*** try doing; **probeta** *f* test tube
problema *m* problem; **problemático** problematic
procedencia *f* origin; **procedente: *~ de*** from; **proceder 1** *v/i* come (***de*** from); (*actuar*) proceed; (*ser conveniente*) be fitting; ***~ a*** proceed to; ***~ contra alguien*** initiate proceedings against s.o. **2** *m* conduct; **procedimiento** *m* procedure, method; JUR proceedings *pl*
procesamiento *m*: ***~ de textos*** word processing; **procesar** INFOR process; JUR prosecute; **procesión** *f* procession; **proceso** *m* process; JUR trial; ***~ de datos / textos*** data / word processing
proclamación *f* proclamation; **proclamar** proclaim
procurador *m*, **~a** *f* JUR attorney, lawyer; **procurar** try
prodigio *m* wonder, miracle; *persona* prodigy
producción *f* production; **producir** produce; (*causar*) cause; **productividad** *f* productivity; **productivo** productive; *empresa* profitable; **producto** *m* product; **productor** *m*, **~a** *f* producer
profanar defile, desecrate
profesión *f* profession; **profesional** *m/f* & *adj* profes-

sional; **profesor** *m*, **~a** *f* teacher; *de universidad* professor, *Br* lecturer

profeta *m* prophet

profundidad *f* depth; **profundo** deep; *pensamiento*, *persona* profound

programa *m* program, *Br* programme; INFOR program; EDU syllabus; **~ *de estudios*** syllabus, curriculum; **programador** *m*, **~a** *f* programmer; **programar** *aparato* program, *Br* programme; INFOR program; (*planear*) schedule

progresar progress, make progress; **progresivo** progressive; **progreso** *m* progress

prohibición *f* ban (***de*** on); **prohibido** forbidden; **~ *fumar*** no smoking; **prohibir** forbid, ban

prolijo long-winded; (*minucioso*) detailed

prólogo *m* preface

prolongar extend, prolong

promedio *m* average

promesa *f* promise; **prometedor** bright, promising; **prometer** promise; **prometida** *f* fiancée; **prometido 1** *part* ☞ ***prometer*** **2** *adj* engaged **3** *m* fiancé

prominente prominent

promoción *f* promotion; EDU year; **promocionar** promote; **promotor** *m*, **~a** *f* promoter; **~ *inmobiliario*** developer; **promover** promote; (*causar*) provoke, cause

promulgar *ley* promulgate

pronombre *m* GRAM pronoun

pronóstico *m* prognosis; **~ *del tiempo*** weather forecast

pronto 1 *adj* prompt **2** *adv* (*dentro de poco*) soon; (*temprano*) early; ***de ~*** suddenly; ***tan ~ como*** as soon as

pronunciación *f* pronunciation; **pronunciar** pronounce; (*decir*) say; **~ *un discurso*** give a speech

propagación *f* spread; **propaganda** *f* advertising; POL propaganda; **propagar** spread

propenso prone (***a*** to)

propicio favorable, *Br* favourable

propiedad *f* property; **propietario** *m*, **-a** *f* owner, proprietor

propina *f* tip

propio own; (*característico*) characteristic (***de*** of), typical (***de*** of); (*adecuado*) suitable (***para*** for); ***la -a directora*** the director herself

proponer propose, suggest; **proponerse: ~ *hacer algo*** decide to do sth

proporción *f* proportion; **proporcional** proportional; **proporcionar** provide, supply; *satisfacción* give

proposición *f* proposal, suggestion

propósito *m* (*intención*) intention; (*objetivo*) purpose;

a ~ on purpose; (*por cierto*) by the way
propuesta *f* proposal
propulsión *f* TÉC propulsion
prórroga *f* DEP overtime, *Br tb* extra time; **prorrogar** *plazo* extend
prosa *f* prose
proseguir carry on, continue
prospecto *m* directions for use *pl*; *de propaganda* leaflet
prosperar prosper, thrive; **prosperidad** *f* prosperity; **próspero** prosperous, thriving
prostitución *f* prostitution; **prostituta** *f* prostitute
protagonista *m/f personaje* main character; *actor, actriz* star; *de una hazaña* hero; *mujer* heroine
protección *f* protection; **proteger** protect (**de** from)
proteína *f* protein
protesta *f* protest; **protestante** *m/f* Protestant; **protestar** **1** *v/t* protest **2** *v/i* (*quejarse*) complain (**por**, **de** about); (*expresar oposición*) protest (**contra**, **por** about, against)
protocolo *m* protocol
provecho *m* benefit; **¡buen ~!** enjoy (your meal); **sacar ~ de** benefit from; **provechoso** beneficial
proveedor *m*, **~a** *f* supplier; **~ de (acceso a) Internet** Internet Service Provider, ISP; **proveer** supply; **~ a alguien de algo** supply s.o. with sth
proverbio *m* proverb
providencia *f* providence
provincia *f* province; **provincial** provincial
provisión *f* provision; **provisional** provisional; **provisorio** *S.Am.* provisional
provocar cause; *al enfado* provoke; *sexualmente* lead on; **¿te provoca un café?** *S.Am.* how about a coffee?; **provocativo** provocative
proxeneta *m* pimp
proximidad *f* proximity; **próximo** (*siguiente*) next; (*cercano*) near, close
proyección *f* MAT, PSI projection; *de película* showing; **proyectar** project; (*planear*) plan; *película* show; *sombra* cast; **proyectil** *m* missile; **proyecto** *m* plan; *trabajo* project; **~ de ley** bill; **tenir en ~ hacer algo** plan to do sth; **proyector** *m* projector
prudencia *f* caution, prudence; **prudente** careful, cautious
prueba *f tb* TIP proof; JUR piece of evidence; DEP event; EDU test; **a ~ de bala** bulletproof; **poner algo a ~** put sth to the test
psicología *f* psychology; **psicológico** psychological; **psicólogo** *m*, **-a** *f* psychologist; **psicópata** *m/f* psychopath
psiquiatra *m/f* psychiatrist; **psiquiatría** *f* psychiatry; **psiquiátrico** psychiatric; **psíquico** psychic

púa *f* ZO spine, quill; MÚS plectrum, pick
publicación *f* publication; **publicar** publish; **publicarse** come out, be published; **publicidad** *f* (*divulgación*) publicity; COM advertising; (*anuncios*) advertisements *pl*; **publicitario 1** *adj* advertising *atr* **2** *m*, **-a** *f* advertising executive; **público 1** *adj* public; *escuela* public, *Br* state **2** *m* public; TEA audience; DEP spectators *pl*, crowd
puchero *m* GASTR (cooking) pot; ***hacer ~s*** *fig* pout
pudín *m* pudding
pudor *m* modesty
pudrirse rot; ***~ de envidia*** be green with envy
pueblo *m* village; *más grande* town
puente *m* bridge; ***hacer ~*** *have a day off between a weekend and a public holiday*
puerco 1 *adj* dirty; *fig* filthy F **2** *m* ZO pig; ***~ espín*** porcupine
pueril childish, puerile
puerro *m* BOT leek
puerta *f* door; *en valla* gate; DEP goal; ***~ de embarque*** gate
puerto *m* MAR port; GEOG pass
Puerto Rico Puerto Rico
pues well; *fml* (*porque*) as, since; ***~ bien*** well; ***¡~ sí!*** of course!
puesta *f*: ***~ a punto*** tune-up; ***~ de sol*** sunset
puesto 1 *part* ☞ **poner 2** *m lugar* place; *en mercado* stand, stall; MIL post; ***~*** (***de trabajo***) job **3** *conj*: ***~ que*** since, given that
pulcro immaculate
pulga *f* ZO flea
pulgada *f* inch; **pulgar** *m* thumb
pulgón *m* ZO aphid, *Br* greenfly
pulido 1 *adj* polished **2** *m acción* polishing; *efecto* polish;
pulir polish
pulmón *m* lung; **pulmonar** pulmonary, lung *atr*; **pulmonía** *f* MED pneumonia
pulpa *f* pulp
púlpito *m* pulpit
pulpo *m* ZO octopus
pulsación *f* beat; *de tecla* keystroke; **pulsar** *botón, tecla* press
pulso *m* pulse; *fig* steady hand; ***tomar el ~ a alguien*** take s.o.'s pulse
pulverizador *m* spray; **pulverizar** spray; (*convertir en polvo*) pulverize, crush
puma *m* ZO puma, mountain lion
punible punishable
punta *f* tip; (*extremo*) end; *de lápiz*, GEOG point; *L.Am.* (*grupo*) group; ***sacar ~ a*** sharpen; **puntada** *f* stitch; **puntapié** *m* kick; **puntilla** *f*: ***de ~s*** on tippy-toe, *Br* on tiptoe

punto *m* point; *señal* dot; *signo de puntuación* period, *Br* full stop; *en costura, sutura* stitch; ***dos ~s*** colon; ***~ muerto*** AUTO neutral; ***~ de vista*** point of view; ***~ y coma*** semicolon; ***a ~*** (*listo*) ready; (*a tiempo*) in time; ***de ~*** knitted; ***en ~*** on the dot; ***estar a ~ de*** be about to; ***hacer ~*** knit

puntuación *f* punctuation; DEP score; EDU grade, *Br* mark; **puntual** punctual; **puntualidad** *f* punctuality; **puntualizar** (*señalar*) point out; (*aclarar*) clarify

puñal *m* dagger

puñetazo *m* punch

puño *m* fist; *de camisa* cuff; *de bastón, paraguas* handle

pupila *f* pupil

pupitre *m* desk

puré *m* purée; *sopa* cream; ***~ de patatas*** *o L.Am.* ***papas*** mashed potatoes

pureza *f* purity

purgante *m/adj* laxative, purgative; **purgar** MED, POL purge; **purgarse** take a laxative; **purgatorio** *m* REL purgatory

purificar purify; **puro 1** *adj* pure; *Méx* (*único*) sole, only; ***la -a verdad*** the honest truth **2** *m* cigar

púrpura *f* purple

pus *m* pus

pústula *f* MED pustule

puta *f* P whore P; **putada** *f* P dirty trick

Q

que 1 *pron rel sujeto*: *persona* who, that; *cosa* which, that; *complemento*: *persona* that, whom *fml*; *cosa* that, which; ***el coche ~ ves*** the car you can see, the car that *o* which you can see **2** *conj* that; ***lo mismo ~ tú*** the same as you; ***más grande ~*** bigger than; ***¡~ entre!*** tell him to come in; ***¡~ descanses!*** sleep well; ***¡~ sí!*** I said yes; ***¡~ no!*** I said no; ***es ~...*** the thing is …; ***yo ~ tú*** if I were you

qué 1 *adj & pron interr* what; ***¿~ día es?*** what day is it? **2** *adj & pron int*: ***¡~ moto!*** what a motorbike!; ***¡~ de flores!*** what a lot of flowers! **3** *adv*: ***¡~ alto es!*** he's so tall!; ***¡~ bien!*** great!

quebradizo brittle; **quebrado 1** *adj* broken **2** *m* MAT fraction; **quebrar 1** *v/t* break **2** *v/i* COM go bankrupt *o* bust F

quedar (*permanecer*) stay; *en un estado* be; (*sobrar*) be left; ***te queda bien / mal*** *de estilo* it suits you / doesn't suit you; *de talla* it fits you / doesn't fit you; ***~ cerca*** be nearby; ***~ con alguien*** F arrange to meet (with) s.o.; **~ en algo** agree to sth; **quedarse** stay; **~ ciego** go blind; **~ con algo** keep sth; **me quedé sin comer** I ended up not eating

quehaceres *mpl* tasks

queja *f* complaint; **quejarse** complain (**a** to; **de** about)

quema *f* burning; **quemadura** *f* burn; **quemar 1** *v/t* burn; *con agua* scald; F *recursos* use up; F *dinero* blow F **2** *v/i* be very hot

querella *f* JUR lawsuit

querer (*desear*) want; (*amar*) love; **~ decir** mean; **sin ~** unintentionally; **quisiera...** I would like ...; **querido 1** *part* ☞ **querer 2** *adj* dear **3** *m*, **-a** *f* darling

queso *m* cheese

quicio *m*: **sacar de ~ a alguien** F drive s.o. crazy F

quiebra *f* COM bankruptcy

quien *rel sujeto* who, that; *objeto* who, whom *fml*, that

quién who; **¿de ~ es este libro?** whose is this book?, who does this book belong to?

quieto still; **quietud** *f* peacefulness

quilate *m* carat

quilla *f* keel

química *f* chemistry; **químico 1** *adj* chemical **2** *m*, **-a** *f* chemist

quince fifteen; **quincena** *f* two weeks, *Br* fortnight

quiniela *f lottery where the winners are decided by soccer results*, *Br* football pools

quinientos five hundred

quinina *f* quinine

quinta *f* MIL draft, *Br* call-up; **es de mi ~** he's my age

quinto 1 *adj* fifth **2** *m* MIL conscript

quiosco *m* kiosk; **~ de prensa** newsstand, *Br* newsagent's

quirófano *m* operating room, *Br* operating theatre

quirúrgico surgical

quitaesmalte *m* nail varnish remover; **quitamanchas** *m inv* stain remover; **quitanieves** *m* snowplow, *Br* snowplough

quitar 1 *v/t ropa* take off, remove; *obstáculos* remove; **~ algo a alguien** take sth (away) from s.o.; **~ la mesa** clear the table **2** *v/i*: **¡quita!** get out of the way!; **quitarse** *ropa, gafas* take off; (*apartarse*) get out of the way; **~ algo / a alguien de encima** get rid of sth / s.o.

quitasol *m* sunshade

quizá(s) perhaps, maybe

R

rabanito *m* BOT wild radish; **rábano** *m* BOT radish

rabia *f* MED rabies *sg*; ***dar ~ a alguien*** make s.o. mad; ***tener ~ a alguien*** have it in for s.o.; **rabiar:** ***~ de dolor*** be in agony; ***~ por*** be dying for

rabioso MED rabid; *fig* furious

rabo *m* tail

racha *f* spell

racial racial

racimo *m* bunch

ración *f* share; (*porción*) serving, portion; **racional** rational; **racionalizar** rationalize; **racionar** ration

racismo *m* racism; **racista** *m/f & adj* racist

radar *m* radar

radiación *f* radiation; **radiactividad** *f* radioactivity; **radiactivo** radioactive; **radiador** *m* radiator; **radiante** radiant; **radiar** radiate

radical *m/f & adj* radical

radio 1 *m* MAT radius; QUÍM radium; *L.Am.* radio; ***~ de acción*** range **2** *f* radio; ***~ despertador*** clock radio; **radioaficionado** *m* radio ham; **radiocasete** *m* radio cassette player; **radiografía** *f* X-ray; **radiología** *f* radiology; **radiopatrulla** *f* radio patrol car; **radiotaxi** *m* radio taxi; **radioterapia** *f* radiotherapy; **radioyente** *m/f* listener

ráfaga *f* gust; *de balas* burst

rafia *f* raffia

raído threadbare

rail, raíl *m* rail

raíz *f* root; ***~ cuadrada*** MAT square root; ***a ~ de*** as a result of

raja *f* (*rodaja*) slice; (*corte*) cut; (*grieta*) crack; **rajar 1** *v/t fruta* cut, slice; *cerámica* crack; *neumático* slash **2** *v/i* F gossip; **rajarse** *fig* F back out

rallador *m* grater; **rallar** GASTR grate

rama *f* branch; POL wing; ***andarse por las ~s*** beat about the bush

ramera *f* whore, prostitute

ramificarse branch out

ramo *m* COM sector; ***~ de flores*** bunch of flowers

rampa *f* ramp; ***~ de lanzamiento*** launch pad

rana *f* ZO frog

rancho *m Méx* small farm; *L.Am.* (*barrio de chabolas*) shanty town

rancio rancid; *fig* ancient

ranura *f* slot

rapaz 1 *adj* predatory **2** *m*, **-a** *f* F kid F

rape *m pescado* anglerfish; ***al ~ pelo*** cropped

rapidez *f* speed, rapidity;

rápido 1 *adj* quick, fast **2** *m* rapids *pl*
rapiña *f* pillage
raptar kidnap; **rapto** *m* kidnap
raqueta *f* racket
rareza *f* scarcity, rarity; **raro** rare
ras *m*: ***a ~ de tierra*** at ground level
rascacielos *m inv* skyscraper; **rascar** scratch; *superficie* scrape, scratch
rasgar tear (up); **rasgo** *m* feature; ***a grandes ~s*** broadly speaking
rasguñar scratch; **rasguño** *m* MED scratch
raso 1 *adj* flat, level; ***soldado ~*** private **2** *m material* satin; ***al ~*** in the open air
raspado *m Méx* water ice; **raspar 1** *v/t* scrape; *con lija* sand **2** *v/i* be rough
rastrear 1 *v/t persona* track; *bosque, zona* comb **2** *v/i* rake; **rastrillo** *m* rake; **rastro** *m* flea market; (*huella*) trace; **rastrojo** *m* stubble
rata *f* ZO rat
ratero *m*, **-a** *f* petty thief
raticida *m* rat poison
ratificar POL ratify
rato *m* time; ***~s libres*** spare time; ***al poco ~*** after a short time *o* while; ***todo el ~*** all the time
ratón *m* ZO, INFOR mouse; **ratonera** *f* mouse trap
raya *f* GRAM dash; ZO ray; *de pelo* part, *Br* parting; ***a*** *o* ***de ~s*** striped; ***pasarse de la ~*** overstep the mark, go too far; **rayado** *disco, superficie* scratched
rayar 1 *v/t* scratch; (*tachar*) cross out **2** *v/i* border (***en*** on)
rayo *m* FÍS ray; METEO (bolt of) lightning; ***~ láser*** laser beam; ***~ X*** X-ray
raza *f* race; *de animal* breed
razón *f* reason; ***a ~ de*** *precio* at; ***dar la ~ a alguien*** admit that s.o. is right; ***entrar en ~*** see sense; ***perder la ~*** lose one's mind; ***tener ~*** be right; **razonable** *precio* reasonable
reacción *f* reaction (***a*** to); ***avión a ~*** jet (aircraft); **reaccionar** react (***a*** to); **reaccionario 1** *adj* reactionary **2** *m*, **-a** *f* reactionary
reacio reluctant (***a*** to)
reactor *m* reactor; (*motor*) jet engine
real (*regio*) royal; (*verdadero*) real; **realidad** *f* reality; ***en ~*** in fact, in reality; **realista 1** *adj* realistic **2** *m/f* realist; **realizador** *m*, **~a** *f de película* director; RAD, TV producer; **realizar** *tarea* carry out; RAD, TV produce; COM realize
realzar highlight
reanimar revive
reanudar resume
rebaja *f* reduction; ***~s de verano*** summer sale; **rebajar** reduce
rebanada *f* slice
rebaño *m* flock

rebasar *Méx* AUTO pass, *Br* overtake
rebatir *razones* rebut, refute
rebeca *f* cardigan
rebelarse rebel; **rebelde 1** *adj* rebel *atr* **2** *m/f* rebel; **rebelión** *f* rebellion
rebosar overflow
rebotar 1 *v/t* bounce; (*disgustar*) annoy **2** *v/i* bounce; **rebote** *m* bounce; ***de ~*** on the rebound
rebozar GASTR coat
rebuscado over-elaborate
recado *m* errand; *Rpl* (*arnés*) harness; ***dejar un ~*** leave a message
recaer *fig*: *de responsabilidad* fall (***en*** to); MED have a relapse; JUR reoffend; **recaída** *f* MED relapse
recalentar *comida* warm *o* heat up
recargar *batería* recharge; *recipiente* refill; ***~ un 5%*** charge 5% extra; **recargo** *m* surcharge
recauchutado *m* retread
recaudación *f acción* collection; *cantidad* takings *pl*; **recaudador** *m*, **~a** *f* collector; **recaudar** *impuestos, dinero* collect
recelar suspect; ***~ de alguien*** not trust s.o.; **recelo** *m* mistrust; **receloso** suspicious
recepción *f* reception; **recepcionista** *m/f* receptionist; **receptor** *m* receiver
receta *f* GASTR recipe; ***~ médica*** prescription; **recetar** MED prescribe
rechazar reject; MIL repel; **rechazo** *m* rejection
rechinar creak, squeak
recibir receive; **recibo** *m* (sales) receipt
reciclable recyclable; **reciclado, reciclaje** *m* recycling; **reciclar** recycle
recién newly; *L.Am.* (*hace poco*) just; ***~ casados*** newly-weds; ***~ nacido*** newborn; ***~ pintado*** wet paint; ***~ llegamos*** we've only just arrived; **reciente** recent
recinto *m* premises *pl*; *área* grounds *pl*
recipiente *m* container
recíproco reciprocal
recital *m* recital; **recitar** recite
reclamación *f* complaint; POL claim, demand; **reclamar 1** *v/t* claim, demand **2** *v/i* complain
reclamo *m* lure
reclinar rest; **reclinarse** lean, recline (***contra*** against)
recluta *m/f* recruit; **reclutar** recruit
recobrar recover
recodo *m* bend
recogedor *m* dustpan; **recoger** pick up, collect; *habitación* tidy up; AGR harvest; (*mostrar*) show; **recogida** *f* collection; ***~ de basuras*** garbage collection, *Br* refuse collection; ***~ de equipajes*** baggage reclaim
recolección *f* harvest; **recolectar** harvest

recomendable recommendable; **recomendación** *f* recommendation; **recomendar** recommend
recompensa *f* reward; **recompensar** reward
reconciliación *f* reconciliation; **reconciliar** reconcile; **reconciliarse** make up (***con*** with), be reconciled (***con*** with)
reconocer recognize; *errores* admit, acknowledge; *area* reconnoiter, *Br* reconnoitre; MED examine; **reconocido** grateful; **reconocimiento** *m* recognition; *de error* acknowledg(e)ment; MED examination, check-up; MIL reconnaissance
reconquista *f* reconquest
reconstruir *fig* reconstruct
récord 1 *adj* record(-breaking) **2** *m* record
recordar remember, recall; ***~ algo a alguien*** remind s.o. of sth
recorrer *distancia* cover; *a pie* walk; *territorio, país* travel around; *camino* go along, travel along; **recorrido** *m* route; DEP round
recortar cut out; *fig* cut; **recorte** *m fig* cutback; ***~ de periódico*** cutting, clipping; ***~ salarial*** salary cut
recrear recreate; **recrearse** amuse o.s.; **recreativo** recreational; ***juegos ~s*** amusements; **recreo** *m* recreation; EDU recess, *Br* break
recriminar reproach
recrudecer worsen; **recrudecerse** intensify
rectángulo *m* rectangle
rectificar correct, rectify; *camino* straighten
recto straight; (*honesto*) honest
recuerdo *m* memory; ***da ~s a Luís*** give my regards to Luís
recuperación *f tb fig* recovery; **recuperar** *tiempo* make up; *algo perdido* recover; **recuperarse** recover (***de*** from)
recurrir 1 *v/t* JUR appeal against **2** *v/i*: ***~ a*** resort to, turn to; **recurso** *m* JUR appeal; *material* resource; ***~s humanos*** human resources
red *f* net; INFOR, *fig* network; ***caer en las ~es de*** *fig* fall into the clutches of
redacción *f* writing; *de editorial* editorial department; EDU essay; **redactar** write, compose; **redactor** *m*, **~a** *f* editor
redada *f* raid
redecilla *f* hairnet
redención *f* redemption; **redimir** redeem
rédito *m* return, yield
redoblar redouble; **redoblarse** double; **redoble** *m* MÚS (drum)roll
redonda *f*: ***a la ~*** around; **redondear** *para más* round up; *para menos* round down; (*rematar*) round off; **redondo** round; *negocio* excellent; ***ca-***

er ~ flop down
reducción *f* reduction; MED setting; **reducir** reduce (***a*** to); MIL overcome
reeducar reeducate
reelección *f* reelection; **reelegir** re-elect
reembolsar refund; **reembolso** *m* refund; ***contra ~*** collect on delivery, *Br* cash on delivery, COD
reemplazar replace; **reemplazo** *m* replacement; DEP substitute; MIL recruit
reexpedir forward
referencia *f* reference; ***~s*** COM references; **referente:** ***~ a*** referring to; **referir** tell, relate; **referirse** refer (***a*** to)
refinación *f* refining; **refinado 1** *adj tb fig* refined **2** *m* refining; **refinamiento** *m* refining; **refinar** refine; **refinería** *f* refinery
reflejar *tb fig* reflect; **reflejo** *m* reflex; *imagen* reflection; **reflexión** *f fig* reflection, thought; **reflexionar** reflect on, ponder; **reflexivo** GRAM reflexive
reflujo *m* ebb
reforestación *f* reforestation; **reforestar** reforest
reforma *f* reform; ***~s*** (*obras*) refurbishment; (*reparaciones*) repairs; **reformar** reform; *edificio* refurbish; (*reparar*) repair
reforzar reinforce; *vigilancia* increase, step up
refractario TÉC heat-resistant, fireproof; *fig* ***ser ~ a algo*** be against sth
refrán *m* saying
refregar scrub
refrescar 1 *v/t tb fig* refresh; *conocimientos* brush up **2** *v/i* cool down; **refresco** *m* soda, *Br* soft drink
refrigeración *f de alimentos* refrigeration; *aire acondicionado* air-conditioning; *de motor* cooling; **refrigerador** *m* refrigerator; **refrigerar** refrigerate; **refrigerio** *m* snack
refuerzo *m* reinforcement; ***~s*** MIL reinforcements
refugiado *m*, **-a** *f* refugee; **refugiarse** take refuge; **refugio** *m* refuge
refundir rework
refutar refute
regadera *f* watering can; *Méx* (*ducha*) shower; **regadío** *m*: ***tierra de ~*** irrigated land
regalar: ***~ algo a alguien*** give sth to s.o., give s.o. sth
regaliz *m* BOT licorice, *Br* liquorice
regalo *m* gift, present
regañar 1 *v/t* tell off **2** *v/i* quarrel
regar water; AGR irrigate
regata *f* regatta
regatear DEP get past, dodge; ***no ~ esfuerzos*** spare no effort; **regateo** *m* haggling
regazo *m* lap
regenerar regenerate
régimen *m* POL regime; MED diet; ***estar a ~*** be on a diet
regio regal, majestic; *S.Am.* F

(*estupendo*) great F
región *f* region; **regional** regional
regir 1 *v/t* rule, govern **2** *v/i* apply, be in force
registrar register; *casa* search; **registro** *m* register; *de casa* search; **~ civil** register of births, marriages and deaths
regla *f* (*norma*) rule; *para medir* ruler; MED period; ***por ~ general*** as a rule
reglamentar regulate; **reglamentario** regulation *atr*; **reglamento** *m* regulation
regocijo *m* delight
regresar 1 *v/i* return **2** *v/t Méx* return, give back; **regreso** *m* return
regulable adjustable; **regulación** *f* regulation; *de temperatura* control; **regular 1** *adj* regular; (*común*) ordinary; (*no muy bien*) so-so **2** *v/t* TÉC regulate; *temperatura* control; **regularidad** *f* regularity
rehabilitación *f* rehabilitation; ARQUI restoration; **rehabilitar** ARQUI restore
rehén *m* hostage
rehuir shy away from
rehusar refuse, decline
reimpresión *f* reprinting
reina *f* queen; **reinado** *m* reign; **reinar** *tb fig* reign
reincidente 1 *adj* repeat **2** *m/f* repeat offender; **reincidir** reoffend
reino *m tb fig* kingdom; ***el Reino Unido*** the United Kingdom
reintegrar, reintegrarse return (***a*** to); **reintegro** *m* (*en lotería*) *prize in the form of a refund of the stake money*
reír, reírse laugh (***de*** at)
reiterar repeat, reiterate
reivindicar claim; ***~ un atentado*** claim responsibility for an attack
reja *f* AGR plowshare, *Br* ploughshare; (*barrote*) bar, railing; ***meter entre ~s*** *fig* F put behind bars; **rejilla** *f* FERR luggage rack
rejoneador *m bullfighter on horseback*
rejuvenecer rejuvenate
relación *f* relationship; ***relaciones públicas*** public relations, PR *sg*; **relacionar** relate (***con*** to), connect (***con*** with); **relacionarse** be connected (***con*** to), be related (***con*** to); (*mezclarse*) mix
relajación *f* relaxation; **relajar, relajarse** relax
relámpago *m* flash of lightning; ***viaje ~*** flying visit
relampaguear: ***relampagueó y tronó mucho*** there was a lot of thunder and lightning
relativo relative; ***~ a*** regarding, about
relato *m* short story
relax *m* relaxation
relegar relegate
relevar MIL relieve; ***~ a alguien de algo*** relieve s.o.

of sth; **relevo** *m* MIL change; (*sustituto*) relief, replacement; ***carrera de ~s*** relay (race); ***tomar el ~ de alguien*** take over from s.o., relieve s.o.

relieve *m* relief; ***poner de ~*** highlight

religión *f* religion; **religiosa** *f* nun; **religiosidad** *f* religiousness; **religioso 1** *adj* religious **2** *m* monk

relinchar neigh

rellano *m* landing

rellenar fill; GASTR *pollo* stuff; *formulario* fill out, fill in; **relleno 1** *adj* GASTR stuffed; *pastel* filled **2** *m* stuffing; *en pastel* filling

reloj *m* clock; *de pulsera* watch, wristwatch; ***~ de sol*** sundial; **relojería** *f* watchmaker's; **relojero** *m*, **-a** *f* watchmaker

relucir sparkle, glitter

remachar *mesa, silla* rivet; *orden* repeat

remanente *m* remainder, surplus

remar row

rematar 1 *v/t* finish off; *L.Am.* COM auction **2** *v/i en fútbol* shoot; **remate** *m L.Am.* COM auction, sale; *en fútbol* shot; ***ser tonto de ~*** be a complete idiot

remediar remedy; ***no puedo ~lo*** I can't do anything about it; **remedio** *m* remedy; ***sin ~*** hopeless; ***no hay más ~ que...*** there's no alternative but to ...

remendar *con parche* patch; (*zurcir*) darn

remero *m* rower, oarsman

remesa *f* (*envío*) shipment, consignment; *L.Am. dinero* remittance

remiendo *m* (*parche*) patch; (*zurcido*) darn

remilgado fussy, finicky; **remilgo** *m*; ***tener / hacer ~s*** be fussy

remisión *f* remission; *en texto* reference; **remitente** *m/f* sender; **remitir 1** *v/t* send, ship; *en texto* refer (***a*** to) **2** *v/i* MED go into remission; *de crisis* ease (off)

remo *m pala* oar; *deporte* rowing

remodelar redesign, remodel

remojar soak; *L.Am.* F *acontecimiento* celebrate

remolacha *f* beet, *Br* beetroot; ***~ azucarera*** sugar beet

remolcador *m* tug; **remolcar** AUTO, MAR tow

remolino *m de aire* eddy; *de agua* whirlpool

remolque *m* AUTO trailer

remordimiento *m* remorse

remoto remote

remover (*agitar*) stir; *L.Am.* (*destituir*) dismiss; *C.Am., Méx* (*quitar*) remove

remplazar ☞ ***reemplazar***

remuneración *f* remuneration; **remunerar** pay

Renacimiento *m* Renaissance

renacuajo *m* ZO tadpole; F

persona shrimp F
renal ANAT renal, kidney *atr*
rencor *m* resentment; ***guardar ~ a alguien*** bear s.o. a grudge; **rencoroso** resentful
rendición *f* surrender
rendido exhausted
rendija *f* crack; (*hueco*) gap
rendimiento *m* performance; FIN yield; (*producción*) output; **rendir 1** *v/t honores* pay; *beneficio* produce, yield **2** *v/i* perform; **rendirse** surrender
renegado 1 *adj* renegade *atr* **2** *m* renegade; **renegar:** ***~ de alguien*** disown s.o.; ***~ de algo*** renounce sth
renglón *m* line; ***a ~ seguido*** immediately after
reno *m* ZO reindeer
renombrado famous, renowned; **renombre** *m*: ***de ~*** famous, renowned
renovación *f* renewal; **renovar** renew
renta *f* income; *de casa* rent; **rentable** profitable; **rentar** (*arrendar*) rent out; (*alquiler*) rent
renuncia *f* resignation; **renunciar:** ***~ a*** *tabaco, alcohol etc* give up; *puesto* resign; *demanda* drop
reñir 1 *v/t* tell off **2** *v/i* quarrel, fight F
reo *m*, **-a** *f* accused
reorganizar reorganize
reparación *f* repair; *fig* reparation; **reparar 1** *v/t* repair **2** *v/i*: ***~ en algo*** notice sth; **reparo** *m*: ***poner ~s a*** find problems with; **repartir** (*dividir*) share out, divide up; *productos* deliver; **reparto** *m* (*división*) share-out, distribution; TEA cast; ***~ a domicilio*** home delivery
repasar *trabajo* go over again; EDU review, *Br* revise
repaso *m de lección* review, *Br* revision; *de últimas novedades* review; TÉC *de motor* service; ***dar un ~ a alguien*** tell s.o. off
repatriación *f* repatriation; **repatriarse** go home
repelente 1 *adj fig* repellent, repulsive; F *niño* horrible **2** *m* repellent; **repeler** repel
repente: ***de ~*** suddenly; **repentino** sudden
repercusión *f fig* repercussion; **repercutir** have repercussions (***en*** on)
repertorio *m* TEA, MÚS repertoire
repetición *f* repetition; **repetir** repeat
repicar 1 *v/t campanas* ring; *castañuelas* click **2** *v/i* ring out; **repique** *m de campanas* ringing; *de castañuelas* clicking
repisa *f* shelf
repleto full (***de*** of)
réplica *f* replica
replicar reply
repoblación *f* repopulation, restocking
repollo *m* BOT cabbage
reponer *existencias* replace;

TEA *obra* revive; **~ *fuerzas*** get one's strength back; **reponerse** recover (**de** from)

reportaje *m* story, report; **reportero** *m*, **-a** *f* reporter; **~ *gráfico*** press photographer

reposacabezas *m inv* AUTO headrest; **reposado** calm; **reposar** rest; *de vino* settle

reposición *f* TEA revival; TV repeat

reposo *m* rest

repostar refuel

repostería *f* pastries *pl*

reprender scold, tell off

represa *f* dam; (*embalse*) reservoir

represalia *f* reprisal

representación *f* representation; TEA performance; ***en ~ de*** on behalf of; **representante** *m/f* representative; **representar** represent; *obra* put on, perform; *papel* play; **~ *menos años*** look younger

represión *f* repression

reprimenda *f* reprimand

reprimir *tb* PSI repress

reprobable reprehensible; **reprobación** *f* condemnation; **reprobar** condemn; *L.Am.* EDU fail

reprochar reproach; **reproche** *m* reproach

reproducción *f* BIO reproduction; **reproducir** reproduce; **reproducirse** BIO reproduce, breed; **reproductor 1** *adj* breeding **2** *m* breeding animal

reptar creep

reptil *m* ZO reptile

república *f* republic; ***República Dominicana*** Dominican Republic; **republicano 1** *adj* republican **2** *m*, **-a** *f* republican

repudiar *fml* repudiate; *herencia* renounce

repuesto 1 *part* ☞ ***reponer*** **2** *m* spare part; ***de ~*** spare

repugnancia *f* disgust, repugnance; **repugnante** disgusting, repugnant; **repugnar** disgust, repel

repulsión *f* repulsion; **repulsivo** repulsive

reputación *f* reputation; **reputado** reputable

requemar burn

requerimiento *m* request, requirement; **requerir** require; JUR summons

requesón *m* cottage cheese

requisar *Arg*, *Chi* MIL requisition; **requisito** *m* requirement

res *f L.Am.* bull; ***carne f de ~*** beef; ***~es*** cattle *pl*

resaca *f* MAR undertow; *de beber* hangover

resaltar 1 *v/t* highlight, stress **2** *v/i* ARQUI jut out; *fig* stand out

resbaladizo slippery; *fig* tricky; **resbalar** slide; *fig* slip (up)

rescatar rescue, save; **rescate** *m de peligro* rescue; *en secuestro* ransom

rescindir cancel; *contrato* ter-

minate
resentido resentful; **resentimiento** *m* resentment; **resentirse** get upset; *de rendimiento, calidad* suffer
reseña *f de libro etc* review
reserva 1 *f* reservation; ***~ natural*** nature reserve; ***sin ~s*** without reservation; **2** *m/f* DEP reserve; **reservado 1** *adj* reserved **2** *m* private room; **reservar** (*guardar*) set aside, put by; *billete* reserve
resfriado 1 *adj*: ***estar ~*** have a cold **2** *m* cold; **resfriarse** catch (a) cold
resguardar protect (***de*** from); **resguardo** *m* COM counterfoil
residencia *f* residence; ***~ de ancianos*** *o* ***para la tercera edad*** retirement home; **residir** reside; ***~ en*** *fig* lie in; **residuo** *m* residue; ***~s*** waste
resignación *f actitud* resignation; **resignarse** resign o.s. (***a*** to)
resina *f* resin
resistencia *f* resistance; ELEC, TÉC resistor; **resistente** (*fuerte*) strong, tough; ***~ al calor*** heat-resistant; ***~ al fuego*** fireproof; **resistir 1** *v/i* resist; (*aguantar*) hold out **2** *v/t tentación* resist; *frío, dolor etc* stand, bear; **resistirse** be reluctant (***a*** to)
resolución *f actitud* determination; *de problema* solution (***de*** to); JUR ruling; **resolver** *problema* solve; **resolverse** decide (***a*** to; ***por*** on)
resonancia *f* TÉC resonance; ***tener ~*** have an impact; **resonar** echo
resorte *m* spring
respaldar back, support; **respaldo** *m de silla* back; *fig* backing, support
respectivo respective; **respecto** *m*: ***al ~*** on the matter; ***con ~ a*** regarding
respetable respectable; **respetar** respect; **respeto** *m* respect; **respetuoso** respectful
respiración *f* breathing; ***estar con ~ asistida*** MED be on a respirator; **respirar** breathe; **respiro** *m fig* breather, break
resplandecer shine, gleam; **resplandor** *m* shine, gleam
responder 1 *v/t* answer **2** *v/i*: ***~ a*** answer, reply to; MED respond to; *descripción* fit, match; (*ser debido a*) be due to
responsabilidad *f* responsibility; **responsable 1** *adj* responsible (***de*** for) **2** *m/f* person responsible (***de*** for)
respuesta *f* (*contestación*) reply, answer; *fig* response
restablecer re-establish; **restablecerse** recover; **restablecimiento** *m* re-establishment; *de enfermo* recovery
restante 1 *adj* remaining **2** *m/fpl*: ***los / las ~s*** the rest *pl*, the remainder *pl*; **restar**

1 *v/t* subtract; **~ *importancia a*** play down the importance of **2** *v/i* remain, be left
restaurante *m* restaurant
restaurar restore
restitución *f* restitution; *de confianza, calma* restoration; *en cargo* reinstatement; **restituir** restore; *en cargo* reinstate
resto *m* rest, remainder; ***los ~s mortales*** the (mortal) remains
restricción *f* restriction; **restringir** restrict, limit
resuelto 1 *part* ☞ ***resolver*** **2** *adj* decisive, resolute
resultado *m* result; ***sin ~*** without success; **resultar** turn out; **~ *caro*** turn out to be expensive
resumen *m* summary; ***en ~*** in short; **resumir** summarize
resurrección *f* REL resurrection
retablo *m* altarpiece
retaguardia *f* MIL rearguard
retal *m* remnant
retama *f* BOT broom
retar challenge; *Rpl* (*regañar*) scold, tell off
retardar delay; **retardarse** be late
retención *f* MED retention; *de persona* detention; **~ *fiscal*** tax deduction; **retener** *dinero etc* withhold, deduct; *persona* detain
retina *f* ANAT retina
retirada *f* MIL retreat,. withdrawal; **retirar** take away, remove; *acusación, dinero* withdraw; **retirarse** MIL withdraw; **retiro** *m lugar* retreat
reto *m* challenge; *Rpl* (*regañina*) scolding
retocar FOT retouch, touch up; (*acabar*) put the finishing touches to
retorcer twist; **retorcerse** writhe
retorno *m* return
retractar retract, withdraw
retransmisión *f* RAD, TV transmission, broadcast; **retransmitir** transmit, broadcast
retrasado 1 *part* ☞ ***retrasar*** **2** *adj tren, entrega* late; *con trabajo, pagos* behind; ***está ~ en clase*** he's lagging behind in class; **~ *mental*** mentally handicapped; **retrasar 1** *v/t* hold up; *reloj* put back; *reunión* postpone, put back **2** *v/i de reloj* lose time; *en los estudios* be behind; **retrasarse** (*atrasarse*) be late; *de reloj* lose time; *con trabajo, pagos* get behind; **retraso** *m* delay; ***ir con ~*** be late
retratar FOT take a picture of; *fig* depict; **retrato** *m* picture; ***~-robot*** composite photo, E-Fit®
retrete *m* bathroom
retrovisor *m* AUTO rear-view mirror; **~ *exterior*** wing mirror
retumbar boom
reuma, reúma *m* MED rheu-

matism
reunificación *f* POL reunification; **reunificar** reunify, reunite
reunión *f* meeting; *de amigos* get-together; **reunir** *personas* bring together; *requisitos* meet; *datos* gather (together); **reunirse** meet up, get together; COM meet
revalorizar revalue
revancha *f* revenge
revelado *m* development; **revelar** FOT develop
reventa *f* resale
reventar 1 *v/i* burst; ***lleno a ~*** full to bursting **2** *v/t puerta etc* break down; **reventón** *m* AUTO blowout
reverencia *f* reverence; *saludo*: *de hombre* bow; *de mujer* curtsy
reversible *ropa* reversible; **reverso** *m* reverse, back
revés *m* setback; *tenis* backhand; ***al*** *o* ***del ~*** back to front; *con el interior fuera* inside out
revestimiento *m* TÉC covering, coating; **revestir** TÉC cover (***de*** with); ***~ gravedad*** be serious
revisar check, inspect; **revisión** *f* check, inspection; AUTO service; ***~ técnica*** roadworthiness test, *Br* MOT (test); ***~ médica*** check-up; **revisor** *m*, **~a** *f* FERR (ticket) inspector
revista *f* magazine; ***pasar ~ a*** MIL inspect, review; *fig* review; **revistero** *m* magazine rack
revocar *pared* render; JUR revoke
revolución *f* revolution; **revolucionar** revolutionize
revolver 1 *v/t* GASTR stir; *estómago* turn; (*desordenar*) mess up **2** *v/i* rummage (***en*** in)
revólver *m* revolver
revuelo *m* stir
revuelta *f* uprising
rey *m* king
rezar 1 *v/t oración* say **2** *v/i* pray; *de texto* say
ribera *f* shore, bank
ribete *m* trimming, edging; ***~s*** *fig* elements
rico 1 *adj* rich; *comida* delicious; F *niño* cute, sweet **2** *m* rich man; ***nuevo ~*** nouveau riche
ridículo 1 *adj* ridiculous **2** *m* ridicule; ***hacer el ~, quedar en ~*** make a fool of o.s.
riego 1 *vb* ☞ ***regar*** **2** *m* AGR irrigation; ***~ sanguíneo*** blood flow
riel *m* FERR rail; ***~ para cortinas*** curtain rail
rienda *f* rein; ***dar ~ suelta a*** give free rein to
riesgo *m* risk; ***correr el ~*** run the risk (***de*** of); **riesgoso** *L.Am.* risky
rifa *f* raffle
rifle *m* rifle
rigidez *f* rigidity; *de carácter* inflexibility; *fig* strictness; **rígido** rigid; *carácter* inflexi-

ble; *fig* strict; **rigor** *m* rigor, *Br* rigour; **riguroso** rigorous, harsh
rima *f* rhyme; **rimar** rhyme
rímel *m* mascara
rincón *m* corner; **rinconera** *f* corner unit
rinoceronte *m* ZO rhinoceros, rhino
riña *f* quarrel, fight
riñón *m* ANAT kidney
riñonera *f* fanny pack, *Br* bum bag
río 1 *m* river; **~ abajo / arriba** down / up river **2** *vb* ☞ **reír**
riqueza *f* wealth
risa *f* laugh; **~s** laughter; **dar ~** be funny; **morirse de ~** kill o.s. laughing; **tomar algo a ~** treat sth as a joke
risueño cheerful
ritmo *m* rhythm; *de desarrollo* rate, pace
rito *m* rite; **ritual** *m/adj* ritual
rival *m/f* rival; **rivalizar: ~ con** rival
rizado curly; **rizar** curl; **rizo** *m* curl
robar *persona, banco* rob; *objeto* steal; *naipe* take
roble *m* BOT oak
robo *m* robbery; *en casa* burglary
robot *m* robot; **~ de cocina** food processor
robusto robust, sturdy
roca *f* rock
rociar spray; **rocío** *m* dew
rodaballo *m* ZO turbot
rodaja *f* slice
rodaje *m de película* shooting, filming; **rodar 1** *v/i* roll; *de coche* go, travel (**a** at); *sin rumbo fijo* wander **2** *v/t película* shoot
rodear surround; **rodeo** *m* detour; *con caballos y vaqueros etc* rodeo; **andarse con ~s** beat about the bush; **hablar sin ~s** not beat about the bush
rodilla *f* knee; **de ~s** kneeling, on one's knees; **hincarse** *o* **ponerse de ~s** kneel (down)
roedor *m* rodent; **roer** gnaw; *fig* eat into
rogar ask for; (*implorar*) beg for, plead for; **hacerse de ~** play hard to get
rojo 1 *adj* red; **al ~ vivo** red hot **2** *m color* red **3** *m*, **-a** *f* POL red, commie F
rollo *m* FOT roll; *fig* F drag F; **buen / mal ~** F good / bad atmosphere
románico *m/adj* Romanesque; **romano 1** *adj* Roman **2** *m*, **-a** *f* Roman; **romántico 1** *adj* romantic **2** *m*, **-a** *f* romantic
romería *f* procession
romper 1 *v/t* break; (*hacer añicos*) smash; *tela, papel* tear **2** *v/i* break; **~ a** start to; **~ con alguien** break up with s.o.
ron *m* rum
roncar snore
ronco hoarse; **quedarse ~** go hoarse
ronda *f* round
ronquera *f* hoarseness
ropa *f* clothes *pl*; **~ de cama**

bedclothes *pl*; ~ ***interior*** underwear; ~ ***íntima*** *L.Am.* underwear; **ropero** *m* closet, *Br* wardrobe

rosa 1 *adj* pink **2** *f* BOT rose; **rosado 1** *adj* pink; *vino* rosé **2** *m* rosé; **rosario** *m* REL rosary; *fig* string

rosbif *m* GASTR roast beef

rosca *f* TÉC thread; GASTR F *pastry similar to a donut*

rostro *m* face

rotación *f* rotation

roto 1 *part* ☞ ***romper* 2** *adj pierna etc* broken; (*hecho añicos*) smashed; *tela, papel* torn **3** *m*, **-a** *f Chi* one of the urban poor

rotonda *f* traffic circle, *Br* roundabout

rotulador *m* fiber-tip, *Br* fibre-tip, felt-tip; **rotular** label; **rótulo** *m* sign

rotura *f* breakage; ***una ~ de cadera*** MED a broken hip

rozar 1 *v/t* rub; (*tocar ligeramente*) brush; *fig* touch on **2** *v/i* rub

rubeola, rubéola *f* MED German measles *sg*

rubí *m* ruby

rubio blond; ***tabaco ~*** Virginia tobacco

rudo rough

rueda *f* wheel; ~ ***dentada*** cogwheel; ~ ***de prensa*** press conference; ~ ***de recambio*** spare wheel

ruedo *m* TAUR bullring

ruego 1 *vb* ☞ ***rogar* 2** *m* request

rufián *m* rogue

ruido *m* noise; ***mucho ~ y pocas nueces*** all talk and no action; **ruidoso** noisy

ruina *f* ruin; ***llevar a alguien a la ~*** *fig* bankrupt s.o.

ruiseñor *m* ZO nightingale

ruleta *f* roulette

rulo *m* roller

Rumania Romania; **rumano 1** *adj* Romanian **2** *m*, **-a** *f* Romanian **3** *m idioma* Romanian

rumbo *m* course; ***tomar ~ a*** head for; ***perder el ~*** *fig* lose one's way

rumor *m* rumor, *Br* rumour

ruptura *f de relaciones* breaking off; *de pareja* break-up

rural 1 *adj* rural **2** *m Rpl* station wagon, *Br* estate car; ***~es*** *Méx* (rural) police

Rusia Russia; **ruso 1** *adj* Russian **2** *m*, **-a** *f* Russian **3** *m idioma* Russian

rústico rustic

ruta *f* route

rutina *f* routine; **rutinario** routine *atr*

S

S.A. (= ***sociedad anónima***) inc. (= incorporated), *Br* plc (= public limited company)
sábado *m* Saturday
sabana *f* savanna(h)
sábana *f* sheet; **~ *ajustable*** fitted sheet
saber 1 *v/t* know (***de*** about); **~ *hacer algo*** know how to do sth, be able to do sth; ***hacer ~ algo a alguien*** let s.o. know sth; ***¡qué sé yo!*** who knows?; ***que yo sepa*** as far as I know **2** *v/i* taste (***a*** of); ***me sabe mal*** *fig* it upsets me **3** *m* knowledge, learning; **sabido** well-known
sabio 1 *adj* wise; (*sensato*) sensible **2** *m*, **-a** *f* wise person; (*experto*) expert
sable *m* saber, *Br* sabre
sabor *m* flavor, *Br* flavour, taste; **saborear** savor, *Br* savour; *fig* relish
sabotaje *m* sabotage; **sabotear** sabotage
sabroso tasty; *fig* juicy; *L.Am.* (*agradable*) nice
sacacorchos *m inv* corkscrew; **sacapuntas** *m inv* pencil sharpener
sacar *v/t* take out; *mancha* take out, remove; *información* get; *disco*, *libro* bring out; *lengua* stick out; *fotocopias* make; **~ *a alguien a bailar*** ask s.o. to dance; **~ *algo en claro*** (*entender*) make sense of sth; **~ *de paseo*** take for a walk
sacarina *f* saccharin(e)
sacerdote *m* priest
saco *m* sack; *L.Am.* jacket; **~ *de dormir*** sleeping bag
sacramento *m* sacrament
sacrificar sacrifice; (*matar*) slaughter; **sacrificio** *m* sacrifice; **sacrilegio** *m* sacrilege; **sacristán** *m* sexton; **sacristía** *f* vestry
sacudida *f* shake, jolt; ELEC shock; **sacudir** *tb fig* shake; F *niño* beat
sagaz shrewd, sharp
Sagitario *m/f inv* ASTR Sagittarius
sagrado sacred, holy
sal 1 *f* salt; **~ *común*** cooking salt **2** *vb* ☞ ***salir***
sala *f* room, hall; *de cine* screen; JUR court room; **~ *de chat*** chat room; **~ *de embarque*** AVIA departure lounge; **~ *de espera*** waiting room; **~ *de estar*** living room; **~ *de fiestas*** night club; **~ *de sesiones*** *o* ***de juntas*** boardroom
salado salted; (*con demasiada sal*) salty; (*no dulce*) savory, *Br* savoury; *fig* funny, witty; *C.Am.*, *Chi*, *Rpl* F pric(e)y F

salar 1 *v/t* add salt to, salt; *para conservar* salt **2** *m Arg* salt mine
salario *m* salary
salchicha *f* sausage; **salchichón** *m type of spiced sausage*
saldar *disputa* settle; *deuda* settle, pay; *géneros* sell off; **saldo** *m* COM balance; (*resultado*) result; *~ acreedor* credit balance; *~ deudor* debit balance; *de ~* reduced, on sale
salero *m* salt cellar; *fig* wit
salida *f* exit, way out; TRANSP departure; *de carrera* start; *~ de emergencia* emergency exit
saliente projecting, protruding; *presidente* outgoing
salir leave, go out; (*aparecer*) appear, come out; INFOR log out *o* off; *~ de* (*ir fuera de*) leave, go out of; (*venir fuera de*) leave, come out of; *~ a alguien* take after s.o.; *~ a 1000 dólares* cost 1000 dollars; *~ bien / mal* turn out well / badly; *no me salió el trabajo* I didn't get the job; *~ con alguien* date s.o.; *~ perdiendo* end up losing; **salirse** *de líquido* overflow; (*dejar*) leave; *~ con la suya* get what one wants
saliva *f* saliva; *tragar ~* hold one's tongue
salmo *m* psalm
salmón *m* ZO salmon
salón *m* living room; *~ de actos* auditorium, hall; *~ de baile* dance hall; *~ de belleza* beauty salon
salpicar splash, spatter (*con* with); *fig* sprinkle, pepper
salsa *f* GASTR sauce; *baile* salsa; *en su ~ fig* in one's element; **salsera** *f* sauce boat
saltar 1 *v/i* jump, leap; *~ a la vista fig* be obvious; *~ sobre* pounce on; *~ a la comba* jump rope, *Br* skip **2** *v/t valla* jump
salto *m* leap, jump; *~ de agua* waterfall; *~ de altura* high jump; *~ de longitud* broad jump, *Br* long jump; *~ mortal* somersault
salubridad *f L.Am.* health; *Salubridad L.Am.* Department of Health
salud *f* health; *¡(a tu) ~!* cheers!; **saludable** healthy; **saludar** say hello to, greet; MIL salute; **saludo** *m* greeting; MIL salute; *~s en carta* best wishes
salvación *f* REL salvation; **salvador** *m* REL savior, *Br* saviour
salvadoreño 1 *adj* Salvador(e)an **2** *m*, **-a** *f* Salvador(e)an
salvaje 1 *adj* wild; (*bruto*) brutal **2** *m/f* savage
salvamento *m* rescue; *buque de ~* lifeboat; **salvar** save; *obstáculo* get over; **salvapantallas** *m inv* INFOR screensaver; **salvavidas** *m inv* life belt

salvia *f* BOT sage
salvo 1 *adj*: ***estar a ~*** be safe (and sound); ***ponerse a ~*** reach safety **2** *adv & prp* except, save
San Saint
sanar 1 *v/t* cure **2** *v/i de persona* get well, recover; *de herida* heal; **sanatorio** *m* sanitarium, clinic
sanción *f* JUR penalty, sanction; **sancionar** penalize; (*multar*) fine
sandalia *f* sandal
sandía *f* watermelon
saneamiento *m* cleaning up; COM restructuring; **sanear** clean up; COM restructure
sangrar bleed; **sangre** *f* blood; ***~ fría*** *fig* coolness; ***a ~ fría*** *fig* in cold blood; **sangría** *f* GASTR sangria; **sangriento** bloody
sanidad *f* health; **sano** healthy; ***~ y salvo*** safe and well; ***cortar por lo ~*** take drastic measures
santiguarse cross o.s., make the sign of the cross
santo 1 *adj* holy **2** *m* saint; ***~ y seña*** F password; ***¿a ~ de qué?*** F what on earth for? F; **santuario** *m fig* sanctuary
sapo *m* ZO toad
saque *m en tenis* serve; ***~ de banda*** *en fútbol* throw-in; ***~ de esquina*** corner (kick); ***tener buen ~*** F have a big appetite; **saquear** sack, ransack
sarampión *m* MED measles
sarcasmo *m* sarcasm; **sarcástico** sarcastic
sardina *f* sardine; ***como ~s en lata*** like sardines
sargento *m* sergeant
sarna *f* MED scabies *sg*
sarro *m* tartar
sartén *f* frying pan
sastre *m* tailor; **sastrería** *f* tailoring; (*taller*) tailor's shop
satélite *m* satellite; ***ciudad ~*** satellite town
sátira *f* satire; **satírico 1** *adj* satirical **2** *m*, **-a** *f* satirist
satisfacción *f* satisfaction; **satisfacer** satisfy; *requisito, exigencia tb* meet; *deuda* settle, pay off; **satisfactorio** satisfactory; **satisfecho 1** *part* ☞ ***satisfacer*** **2** *adj* satisfied; (*lleno*) full; ***darse por ~*** be satisfied (***con*** with)
sauce *m* BOT willow; ***~ llorón*** weeping willow
saúco *m* BOT elder
saudí *m/f & adj* Saudi; **saudita** *m/f* Saudi
sauna *f* sauna
sazonar GASTR season
scooter *m* motor scooter
se ◇ *complemento indirecto*: *a él* (to) him; *a ella* (to) her; *a usted, ustedes* (to) you; *a ellos* (to) them; ***~ lo daré*** I will give it to him / her / you / them ◇ *reflexivo*: *con él* himself; *con ella* herself; *cosa* itself; *con usted* yourself; *con ustedes* yourselves; *con ellos* themselves; ***~ vistió***

he got dressed, he dressed himself; ***se lavó las manos*** she washed her hands; **~ *abrazaron*** they hugged each other ◇ *oración impersonal*: **~ *cree*** it is thought; **~ *habla español*** Spanish spoken
sebo *m* grease, fat
secador *m*: **~ (*de pelo*)** hair dryer; **secadora** *f* dryer; **secar, secarse** dry
sección *f* section
seco dry; *fig*: *persona* curt, brusque; ***parar en* ~** stop dead
secretaria *f* secretary; **~ *de dirección*** executive secretary; **secretaría** *f* secretary's office; *de organización* secretariat; **secretario** *m tb* POL secretary; **secreto 1** *adj* secret **2** *m* secret; ***un* ~ *a voces*** an open secret
secta *f* sect
sector *m* sector
secuela *f* MED after-effect
secuestrar *barco, avión* hijack; *persona* abduct, kidnap; **secuestro** *m de barco, avión* hijacking; *de persona* abduction, kidnapping; **~ *aéreo*** hijacking
secular secular, lay
secundario secondary
sed *f tb fig* thirst; ***tener* ~** be thirsty
seda *f* silk
sedante *m* sedative
sede *f de organización* headquarters; *de acontecimiento* site; **~ *social*** head office
sediento thirsty; ***estar* ~ *de*** *fig* thirst for
seducción *f* seduction; (*atracción*) attraction; **seducir** seduce; (*atraer*) attract; (*cautivar*) captivate, charm; **seductor 1** *adj* seductive; (*atractivo*) attractive; *oferta* tempting **2** *m* seducer; **seductora** *f* seductress
segadora *f* reaper, harvester; **segar** reap, harvest
seguida *f*: ***en* ~** at once, immediately; **seguido 1** *adj* consecutive, successive; ***ir todo* ~** go straight on **2** *adv L.Am.* often, frequently; **seguir 1** *v/t* follow **2** *v/i* continue, carry on; ***sigue enfadado conmigo*** he's still angry with me
según 1 *prp* according to **2** *adv* it depends
segundo *m/adj* second
seguridad *f* safety; *contra crimen* security; (*certeza*) certainty; ***Seguridad Social*** *Esp* Welfare, *Br* Social Security; **seguro 1** *adj* safe; (*estable*) steady; (*cierto*) sure; ***es* ~** (*cierto*) it's a certainty; **~ *de sí mismo*** self-confident, sure of o.s. **2** *adv* for sure **3** *m* COM insurance; *de puerta, coche* lock; *L.Am.* (*imperdible*) safety pin; ***poner el* ~** lock the door; ***ir sobre* ~** be on the safe side
seis six
seísmo *m* earthquake

selección *f* selection; **~ *nacional*** DEP national team; **seleccionar** choose, select; **selecto** select

sellar seal; **sello** *m* stamp; *fig* hallmark; **~ *discográfico*** (record) label

selva *f* (*bosque*) forest; (*jungla*) jungle; **~ *tropical*** tropical rain forest

semáforo *m* traffic light

semana *f* week; ***Semana Santa*** Holy Week, Easter; **semanal** weekly; **semanario** *m* weekly

sembradora *f* seed drill; *mujer* sower; **sembrar** sow; *fig*: *pánico etc* spread

semejante 1 *adj* similar; ***jamás he oído ~ tontería*** I've never heard such nonsense **2** *m* fellow human being, fellow creature

semen *m* BIO semen

semestre *m* six-month period; EDU semester

semicírculo *m* semicircle; **semicorchea** *f* MÚS sixteenth note, *Br* semiquaver; **semifinal** *f* DEP semifinal

semilla *f* seed

seminario *m* seminary

sémola *f* semolina

senado *m* senate; **senador** *m*, **~a** *f* senator

sencillez *f* simplicity; **sencillo 1** *adj* simple **2** *m L.Am.* small change

senda *f* path, track; **sendero** *m* path, track

senil senile

seno *m tb fig* bosom; **~*s*** breasts

sensación *f* feeling, sensation; ***causar ~*** *fig* cause a sensation; **sensacional** sensational

sensato sensible

sensibilidad *f* feeling; (*emotividad*) sensitivity; **sensible** sensitive; (*apreciable*) appreciable, noticeable; **sensual** sensual; **sensualidad** *f* sensuality

sentado sitting, seated; ***dar por ~*** *fig* take for granted, assume; **sentar 1** *v/t fig* establish, create **2** *v/i*: **~ *bien a alguien*** *de comida* agree with s.o.; ***le sienta bien esa chaqueta*** that jacket suits her; **sentarse** sit down

sentencia *f* JUR sentence

sentido *m* sense; (*significado*) meaning; **~ *común*** common sense; **~ *del humor*** sense of humor *o Br* humour; ***perder / recobrar el ~*** lose / regain consciousness

sentimental emotional; ***ser ~*** be sentimental; **sentimiento** *m* feeling; ***lo acompaño en el ~*** my condolences

sentir 1 *m* feeling, opinion **2** *v/t* feel; (*percibir*) sense; ***lo siento*** I'm sorry

seña *f* gesture, sign; **~*s*** address; ***hacer ~s*** wave

señal *f* signal; *fig* sign, trace; COM deposit; ***en ~ de*** as a token of; **señalar** indicate, point out

señor 1 *m* gentleman, man; *trato* sir; *escrito* Mr; ***el ~ López*** Mr López; ***los ~es López*** Mr and Mrs López; **señora** *f* lady, woman; *trato* ma'am, *Br* madam; *escrito* Mrs, Ms; ***la ~ López*** Mrs Lopez; ***mi ~*** my wife; ***~s y señores*** ladies and gentlemen; **señorita** *f* young lady, young woman; *tratamiento* miss; *escrito* Miss; ***la ~ López*** Ms López, Miss López
Señor *m* Lord
separación *f* separation; ***~ de bienes*** JUR division of property; **separado** separated; ***por ~*** separately; **separar** separate; **separarse** separate, split up F; **separatismo** *m* separatism; **separatista** *m/f & adj* separatist
sepia *f* ZO cuttlefish
septiembre *m* September
séptimo seventh
sepulcro *m* tomb; **sepultar** bury; **sepultura** *f* burial; (*tumba*) tomb; ***dar ~ a alguien*** bury s.o.
sequía *f* drought
séquito *m* retinue, entourage
ser 1 *v/i* be; ***es de Juan*** it's Juan's, it belongs to Juan; ***a no ~ que*** unless; ***¡eso es!*** exactly!, that's right!; ***es de esperar*** it's to be hoped; ***¿cuánto es?*** how much is it?; ***¿qué es de ti?*** how's life?, how're things?; ***o sea*** in other words **2** *m* being
Serbia Serbia; **serbio 1** *adj* Serb(ian) **2** *m*, **-a** *f* Serb **3** *m idioma* Serbian
serenidad *f* calmness, serenity; **sereno 1** *m*: ***dormir al ~*** sleep outdoors **2** *adj* calm, serene
serial *m* TV, RAD series *sg*
serie *f* series *sg*; ***fuera de ~*** out of this world
seriedad *f* seriousness; **serio** serious; (*responsable*) reliable; ***en ~*** seriously
sermón *m* sermon
seropositivo MED HIV positive
serpentina *f* streamer; **serpiente** *f* ZO snake; ***~ de cascabel*** rattlesnake
serrar saw; **serrín** *m* sawdust; **serrucho** *m* handsaw
servicio *m* service; ***~s*** restroom, *Br* toilets; ***~ militar*** military service; ***~ de atención al cliente*** customer service; ***estar de ~*** be on duty; **servidor** *m* INFOR server; **servidumbre** *f* (*criados*) servants *pl*; (*condición*) servitude; **servil** servile; **servilleta** *f* napkin, serviette; **servir 1** *v/t* serve **2** *v/i* be of use; ***¿para qué sirve esto?*** what is this (used) for?; ***no ~ de nada*** be no use at all; **servirse** help o.s.; *comida* help oneself to
sésamo *m* sesame
sesenta sixty
sesión *f* session; *en cine, teatro* show, performance
seso *m* ANAT brain; *fig* brains

pl, sense
seta *f* BOT mushroom; *venenosa* toadstool
setenta seventy
seto *m* hedge
seudónimo *m* pseudonym
severo severe
sexismo *m* sexism; **sexista** *m/f & adj* sexist; **sexo** *m* sex
sexto sixth
sexual sexual; **sexualidad** *f* sexuality
sí 1 *adv* yes **2** *pron tercera persona*: *singular masculino* himself; *femenino* herself; *cosa*, *animal* itself; *pl* themselves; *usted* yourself; *ustedes* yourselves; ***por ~ solo*** by himself / itself, on his / its own
si if; ***~ no*** if not; ***como ~*** as if; ***por ~*** in case; ***me pregunto si vendrá*** I wonder whether he'll come
SIDA *m* (= ***síndrome de inmunidad deficiente adquirida***) Aids (= acquired immune deficiency syndrome)
sidra *f* cider
siembra *f* sowing
siempre always; ***~ que*** providing that, as long as; ***lo de ~*** the same old story; ***para ~*** for ever
sien *f* ANAT temple
sierra *f* saw; GEOG mountain range
siesta *f* siesta, nap; ***dormir la ~*** have a siesta *o* nap
siete seven
sífilis *f* MED syphilis
sifón *m* TÉC siphon
sigla *f* abbreviation, acronym
siglo *m* century; ***hace ~s*** *o* ***un ~ que no le veo*** *fig* I haven't seen him in a long long time
significado *m* meaning; **significar** mean, signify; **significativo** meaningful, significant
signo *m* sign; ***~ de admiración*** exclamation mark; ***~ de interrogación*** question mark; ***~ de puntuación*** punctuation mark
siguiente 1 *adj* next, following **2** *pron* next (one)
sílaba *f* syllable
silbar whistle; **silbato** *m* whistle; **silbido** *m* whistle
silenciador *m* AUTO muffler, *Br* silencer; **silenciar** silence; **silencio** *m* silence; **silencioso** silent
silla *f* chair; ***~ de montar*** saddle; ***~ de ruedas*** wheelchair; **sillón** *m* armchair, easy chair
silueta *f* silhouette
silvestre wild
simbólico symbolic; **simbolismo** *m* symbolism; **simbolizar** symbolize; **símbolo** *m* symbol
simétrico symmetrical
similar similar
simpatía *f* warmth, friendliness; **simpático** nice, lik(e)able
simple 1 *adj* simple; (*mero*)

ordinary **2** *m* simpleton; **simplicidad** *f* simplicity; **simplificar** simplify; **simplista** simplistic
simulación *f* simulation; **simulacro** *m* (*cosa falsa*) pretense, *Br* pretence, sham; (*simulación*) simulation; **~ *de incendio*** fire drill; **simulador** *m* simulator; **simular** simulate
simultáneo simultaneous
sin without; **~ *que*** without; **~ *preguntar*** without asking
sinceridad *f* sincerity; **sincero** sincere
sindical union *atr*; **sindicato** *m* (labor *o Br* trade) union
sinfonía *f* MÚS symphony
singular 1 *adj* singular; *fig* outstanding, extraordinary **2** *m* GRAM singular
siniestro 1 *adj* sinister **2** *m* accident; (*catástrofe*) disaster
sino 1 *m* fate **2** *conj* but; (*salvo*) except
síntesis *f inv* synthesis; (*resumen*) summary; **sintético** synthetic
síntoma *m* symptom
sinvergüenza *m/f* swine; ***¡qué ~!*** (*descarado*) what a nerve!
siquiera: *ni* ~ not even; **~ *bebe algo*** *L.Am.* at least have a drink
sirena *f* siren
sirvienta *f* maid; **sirviente** *m* servant
sistema *m* system; **~ *operativo*** operating system; **sistemático** systematic
sitiar surround, lay siege to; **sitio** *m* place; (*espacio*) room; ***hacer* ~** make room; ***en ningún* ~** nowhere; **~ *web*** web site; **situación** *f* situation; **situado** situated; ***estar* ~** be situated; ***bien* ~** *fig* in a good position; **situar** place, put; **situarse** be
slalom *m* slalom
sobaco *m* armpit
soberbio proud, arrogant; *fig* superb
sobornar bribe; **soborno** *m* bribe
sobra *f* surplus, excess; ***hay de* ~** there's more than enough; **~*s*** leftovers; **sobrar: *sobra comida*** there's food left over; **sobrado 1** *adj* ***estar** o **andar* ~ *de algo*** have plenty of sth; ***no andar muy* ~ *de algo*** not have much sth **2** *adv* easily; ***te conozco* ~** I know you well enough; **sobrante** remaining, left over
sobre 1 *m* envelope **2** *prp* on; **~ *esto*** about this; **~ *las tres*** about three o'clock; **~ *todo*** above all, especially
sobrecargar overload
sobreestimar overestimate
sobremanera exceedingly
sobremesa *f*: ***de* ~** afternoon *atr*
sobrenombre *m* nickname
sobresaliente outstanding, excellent
sobrevivir survive

sobrina *f* niece; **sobrino** *m* nephew
sobrio sober; *comida, decoración* simple; (*moderado*) restrained
socarrón sarcastic, snide F
social social; **socialismo** *m* socialism; **socialista** *m/f & adj* socialist
sociedad *f* society; **~ *anónima*** public corporation, *Br* public limited company; **~ *de consumo*** consumer society
socio *m*, **-a** *f de club etc* member; COM partner
sociología *f* sociology
socorrer help, assist; **socorro** *m* help, assistance; ***¡~!*** help!
soda *f* soda (water)
sodio *m* sodium
soez *f* crude, coarse
sofá *m* sofa; **sofá-cama** *m* sofa bed
sofisticación *f* sophistication; **sofisticado** sophisticated
sofocar suffocate; *incendio* put out
soga *f* rope
soja *f* soy, *Br* soya
sol *m* sun; ***hace ~*** it's sunny; ***tomar el ~*** sunbathe
solamente only
solar *m* vacant lot
solario, solárium *m* solarium
soldado *m/f* soldier
soldar weld, solder
soleado sunny
soledad *f* solitude, loneliness
solemne solemn; **solemnidad** *f* solemnity; ***de ~*** extremely
soler: *~ hacer algo* usually do sth; ***suele venir temprano*** he usually comes early; ***solía visitarme*** he used to visit me
solicitante *m/f* applicant; **solicitar** request; *empleo, beca* apply for; **solícito** attentive; **solicitud** *f* application, request
solidario supportive, understanding
solidez *f* solidity; *fig* strength; **sólido** solid; *fig* sound
solista *m/f* soloist
solitaria *f* ZO tapeworm; **solitario 1** *adj* solitary; *lugar* lonely **2** *m* solitaire, *Br* patience; ***actuó en ~*** he acted alone
sollozar sob; **sollozo** *m* sob
sólo only, just
solo single; ***estar ~*** be alone; ***sentirse ~*** feel lonely; ***un ~ día*** a single day; ***a solas*** alone, by o.s.; ***por sí ~*** by o.s.
solomillo *m* GASTR sirloin
soltar let go of; (*librar*) release, let go; *olor* give off
soltera *f* single *o* unmarried woman; **soltero 1** *adj* single, not married **2** *m* bachelor, unmarried man; **solterona** *f desp* old maid
soltura *f* fluency, ease
soluble soluble; **solución** *f* solution; **solucionar** solve
solvente solvent
sombra *f* shadow; ***a la ~ de un árbol*** in the shade of a tree;

a la ~ de *fig* under the protection of; ***~ de ojos*** eye shadow
sombrero *m* hat
sombrilla *f* sunshade, beach umbrella
sombrío *fig* somber, *Br* sombre
someter subject; ***~ algo a votación*** put sth to the vote
somier *m* bed base
somnífero *m* sleeping pill
somnolencia *f* sleepiness; **somnoliento** sleepy
son 1 *m* sound; ***al ~ de*** to the sound of **2** *vb* ☞ ***ser***
sonar ring out; ***~ a*** sound like; ***me suena esa voz*** I know that voice
sonda *f* MED catheter; ***~ espacial*** space probe; **sondear** *fig* survey, poll; **sondeo** *m*: ***~ (de opinión)*** survey, (opinion) poll
sonido *m* sound
sonreír smile; **sonrisa** *f* smile
sonrojar: ***~ a alguien*** make s.o. blush; **sonrojarse** blush; **sonrojo** *m* blush
soñar dream (***con*** about)
soñoliento sleepy
sopa *f* soup; **sopera** *f* soup tureen
soplar 1 *v/i del viento* blow **2** *v/t vela* blow out; *polvo* blow away; ***~ algo a la policía*** tip the police off about sth; **soplo** *m*: ***en un ~*** F in an instant; **soplón** *m* F informer
soportable bearable; **soportar** *fig* put up with, bear; ***no puedo ~ a José*** I can't stand José; **soporte** *m* support, stand; ***~ lógico*** INFOR software; ***~ físico*** INFOR hardware
soprano MÚS *m/f* soprano
sorber sip
sorbete *m* sorbet; *C.Am.* ice cream
sorbo *m* sip
sordera *f* deafness
sordo 1 *adj* deaf **2** *m*, **-a** *f* deaf person; ***hacerse el ~*** turn a deaf ear; **sordomudo 1** *adj* deaf and dumb **2** *m*, **-a** *f* deaf-mute
soroche *m Pe, Bol* altitude sickness
sorprendente surprising; **sorprender** surprise; **sorpresa** *f* surprise; ***de*** *o* ***por ~*** by surprise
sortear draw lots for; *obstáculo* get around; **sorteo** *m* (*lotería*) lottery, (prize) draw
sortija *f* ring
sosiego *m* calm, quiet
soso 1 *adj* tasteless, insipid; *fig* dull **2** *m*, **-a** *f* stick-in-the-mud F
sospecha *f* suspicion; **sospechar 1** *v/t* suspect **2** *v/i* be suspicious; ***~ de alguien*** suspect someone; **sospechoso 1** *adj* suspicious **2** *m*, **-a** *f* suspect
sostén *m* brassiere, bra; *fig* pillar, mainstay; **sostener** *familia* support; *opinión* hold
sota *f naipes* jack

sótano *m* basement
su, sus *de él* his; *de ella* her; *de cosa* its; *de usted, ustedes* your; *de ellos* their; *de uno* one's
suave soft, smooth; *sabor, licor* mild; **suavizante** *m de pelo, ropa* conditioner; **suavizar** *tb fig* soften
subasta *f* auction; ***sacar a ~*** put up for auction; **subastar** auction (off)
subcontratar subcontract, outsource
súbdito *m* subject
subestimar underestimate
subida *f* rise; **subido: *~ de tono*** *fig* risqué, racy; **subir 1** *v/t cuesta, escalera* go up, climb; *objeto* raise, lift; *intereses, precio* raise **2** *v/i para indicar acercamiento* come up; *para indicar alejamiento* go up; *de precio* rise, go up; *a un tren, autobús* get on; *a un coche* get in
súbito: *de ~* suddenly, all of a sudden
subjetivo subjective
subjuntivo *m* GRAM subjunctive
sublevar 1 *v/t* incite to revolt; *fig* infuriate, get angry
sublime sublime, lofty
submarinismo *m* scuba diving; **submarino 1** *adj* underwater **2** *m* submarine
subnormal subnormal
subordinado 1 *adj* subordinate **2** *m*, **-a** *f* subordinate
subrayar *tb fig* underline
subsidio *m* welfare, *Br* benefit; ***~ de paro*** *o* ***desempleo*** unemployment compensation *o Br* benefit
subsistencia *f* subsistence, survival; *de pobreza, tradición* persistence; **subsistir** live, survive; *de pobreza, tradición* live on, persist
subsuelo *m* subsoil; *Rpl en edificio* basement
subterráneo 1 *adj* underground **2** *m L.Am.* subway, *Br* underground
subtítulo *m* subtitle
suburbio *m* slum area
subvención *f* subsidy
suceder happen, occur; ***~ a*** follow; ***¿qué sucede?*** what's going on?; **sucesión** *f* succession; **sucesivo** successive; ***en lo ~*** from now on; **suceso** *m* event; **sucesor** *m*, **~a** *f* successor
suciedad *f* dirt; **sucio** *tb fig* dirty
sucumbir succumb, give in
sucursal *f* COM branch
sudadera *f* sweatshirt; **sudar** sweat
Sudáfrica South Africa; **sudafricano 1** *adj* South African **2** *m*, **-a** *f* South African; **Sudamérica** South America; **sudamericano 1** *adj* South American **2** *m*, **-a** *f* South American; **sudeste** *m* southeast; **sudoeste** *m* southwest
sudor *m* sweat; **sudoroso** sweaty

Suecia Sweden; **sueco 1** *adj* Swedish **2** *m*, **-a** *f* Swede **3** *m idioma* Swedish

suegra *f* mother-in-law; **suegro** *m* father-in-law

suela *f de zapato* sole

sueldo *m* salary

suelo *m en casa* floor; *en el exterior* earth, ground; AGR soil; ***estar por los ~s*** F be at rock bottom F

suelto 1 *adj* loose, free; ***un pendiente ~*** a single earring; ***andar ~*** be at large **2** *m* loose change

sueño *m (estado de dormir)* sleep; *(fantasía, imagen mental)* dream; ***tener ~*** be sleepy

suero *m* MED saline solution; *sanguíneo* blood serum

suerte *f* luck; ***por ~*** luckily; ***echar a ~s*** toss for, draw lots for; ***probar ~*** try one's luck

suéter *m* sweater

suficiente 1 *adj* enough, sufficient **2** *m* EDU pass

sufrir 1 *v/t fig* suffer, put up with **2** *v/i* suffer (***de*** from)

sugerencia *f* suggestion; **sugerir** suggest

suicida 1 *adj* suicidal **2** *m/f* suicide victim; **suicidarse** commit suicide; **suicidio** *m* suicide

Suiza Switzerland; **suizo 1** *adj* Swiss **2** *m*, **-a** *f* Swiss **3** *m* GASTR *sugar topped bun*

sujetador *m* brassiere, bra; **sujetar** hold (down), keep in place; *(sostener)* hold; **sujeto 1** *adj* secure **2** *m* individual; GRAM subject

suma *f* sum; ***en ~*** in short; **sumamente** extremely; **sumar 1** *v/t* add; ***5 y 6 suman 11*** 5 and 6 make 11 **2** *v/i* add up; **sumario** *m* summary; JUR indictment; **sumarse: *~ a*** join

sumergir submerge

sumidero *m* drain

suministrar supply, provide; **suministro** *m* supply

sumisión *f* submission; **sumiso** submissive

sumo supreme; ***con ~ cuidado*** with the utmost care; ***a lo ~*** at the most

suntuoso sumptuous

superar *persona* beat; *límite* go beyond, exceed; *obstáculo* overcome, surmount

superávit *m* surplus

superficial superficial, shallow; **superficie** *f* surface

superfluo superfluous

superior 1 *adj* upper; *en jerarquía* superior; ***ser ~ a*** be superior to **2** *m* superior; **superioridad** *f* superiority

supermercado *m* supermarket

supersónico supersonic

superstición *f* superstition; **supersticioso** superstitious

suplementario supplementary; **suplemento** *m* supplement

suplente *m/f* substitute, stand-in

suplicar *cosa* plead for, beg for; *persona* beg

suplicio *m fig* torment, ordeal
suponer suppose, assume; **suposición** *f* supposition
supositorio *m* MED suppository
supremacía *f* supremacy; **supremo** supreme
supresión *f* suppression; *de impuesto*, *ley* abolition; *de restricción* lifting; *de servicio* withdrawal; **suprimir** suppress; *ley*, *impuesto* abolish; *restricción* lift; *servicio* withdraw; *puesto de trabajo* cut
supuesto 1 *part* ☞ ***suponer*** **2** *adj* supposed, alleged; ***por ~*** of course **3** *m* assumption
supurar weep, ooze
sur *m* south
surafricano ☞ ***sudafricano***
suramericano ☞ ***sudamericano***
surcar sail
surco *m* AGR furrow
surf(ing) *m* surfing; **surfista** *m/f* surfer
surgimiento *m* emergence; **surgir** *fig* emerge; *de problema* come up; *de agua* spout
surtido 1 *adj* assorted; ***bien ~*** COM well stocked **2** *m* assortment, range; **surtidor** *m*: ***~ de gasolina*** *o* ***de nafta*** gas pump, *Br* petrol pump; **surtir 1** *v/t* supply; ***~ efecto*** have the desired effect **2** *v/i* spout
susceptible touchy; ***ser ~ de mejora*** leave room for improvement
suscitar arouse; *polémica* generate; *escándalo* provoke
suscribir subscribe to; **suscripción** *f* subscription; **suscriptor** *m*, **~a** *f* subscriber
suspender 1 *v/t empleado*, *alumno* suspend; *objeto* hang; *reunión* adjourn; *examen* fail **2** *v/i* EDU fail; **suspensión** *f* suspension; **suspenso 1** *adj* ***alumnos ~s*** students who have failed; ***en ~*** suspended **2** *m* fail
suspicacia *f* suspicion; **suspicaz** suspicious
suspirar sigh; ***~ por algo*** yearn for sth, long for sth; **suspiro** *m* sigh
sustancia *f* substance; **sustancial** substantial; **sustantivo** *m* GRAM noun
sustituir: ***~ X por Y*** replace X with Y, substitute Y for X; **sustituto** *m* substitute
susto *m* fright, scare; ***dar*** *o* ***pegar un ~ a alguien*** give s.o. a fright
sustraer subtract, take away; (*robar*) steal
susurrar whisper; **susurro** *m* whisper
sutil *fig* subtle; **sutileza** *f fig* subtlety
sutura *f* MED suture
suyo, suya *de él* his; *de ella* hers; *de usted*, *ustedes* yours; *de ellos* theirs; ***los ~s*** his / her etc folks, his / her etc family; ***salirse con la -a*** get one's own way

T

tabaco *m* tobacco
tábano *m* ZO horsefly
taberna *f* bar
tabique *m* partition
tabla *f de madera* board, plank; PINT panel; (*cuadro*) table; ***~ de planchar*** ironing board; ***~ de surf*** surfboard; ***acabar*** *o* ***quedar en ~s*** end in a tie
tablado *m en un acto* platform; *de escenario* stage
tablero *m* board, plank; *de juego* board; ***~ de mandos*** *o* ***de instrumentos*** AUTO dashboard; **tableta** *f*: ***~ de chocolate*** chocolate bar
taburete *m* stool
tacaño 1 *adj* F miserly **2** *m*, **-a** *f* F miser F
tachar cross out
tácito tacit
taco *m* F (*palabrota*) swear word; *L.Am.* heel; GASTR taco (*filled tortilla*)
tacón *m de zapato* heel; ***zapatos de ~*** high-heeled shoes
táctica *f* tactics *pl*
tacto *m* (sense of) touch; *fig* tact, discretion
tafetán *m* taffeta
tajada *f* GASTR slice; ***agarrar una ~*** F get drunk; **tajante** categorical
tal 1 *adj* such; ***no dije ~ cosa*** I said no such thing; ***un ~ Lucas*** someone called Lucas **2** *adv*: ***~ como*** such as; ***dejó la habitación ~ cual la encontró*** she left the room just as she found it; ***~ para cual*** two of a kind; ***~ vez*** maybe, perhaps; ***¿qué ~?*** how's it going?; ***¿que ~ la película?*** what was the movie like?; ***con ~ de que*** + *subj* as long as
taladradora *f* drill; **taladrar** drill; **taladro** *m* drill
talar *árbol* fell, cut down
talento *m* talent
talla *f* size; (*estatura*) height; *C.Am.* F (*mentira*) lie; ***dar la ~*** *fig* make the grade; **tallar** carve; *piedra preciosa* cut
tallarín *m* noodle
talle *m* waist
taller *m* workshop; ***~ mecánico*** AUTO repair shop; ***~ de reparaciones*** repair shop
tallo *m* BOT stalk, stem
talón *m* ANAT heel; COM stub; ***pisar los talones a alguien*** be hot on s.o.'s heels; **talonario** *m*: ***~ de cheques*** check book, *Br* cheque book
tamaño 1 *adj*: ***~ problema*** such a great problem **2** *m* size
tambalearse stagger, lurch; *de coche* sway
también also, too, as well; ***yo ~*** me too
tambor *m* drum; *persona*

drummer
tamiz *m* sieve
tampoco neither; ***él ~ va*** he's not going either
tampón *m* tampon; *de tinta* ink-pad
tan so; ***~... como...*** as … as …; ***~ sólo*** merely
tanda *f* series *sg*, batch; (*turno*) shift; *L.Am.* (commercial) break; ***~ de penaltis*** DEP penalty shootout
tanque *m tb* MIL tank
tanto 1 *pron* so much; *igual cantidad* as much; ***un ~*** a little; ***~s*** so many *pl*; *igual número* as many; ***tienes ~*** you have so much; ***a las -as de la noche*** in the small hours **2** *adv* so much; *igual cantidad* as much; *periodo* as long; ***~ mejor*** so much the better; ***no es para ~*** it's not such a big deal; ***estar al ~*** be informed (***de*** about); ***por lo ~*** therefore, so **3** *m* point; ***~ por ciento*** percentage
tapa *f* lid; ***~ dura*** hardback
tapacubos *m inv* AUTO hubcap
tapadera *f* lid; *fig* front; **tapar** cover; *recipiente* put the lid on
tapete *m* tablecloth; ***poner algo sobre el ~*** bring sth up for discussion
tapia *f* wall; ***más sordo que una ~*** as deaf as a post
tapicero *m*, **-a** *f* upholsterer; **tapiz** *m* tapestry; **tapizar** upholster
tapón *m* top, cap; *de baño* plug; *de tráfico* traffic jam; **taponar** block; *herida* swab
taquigrafía *f* shorthand; **taquigrafiar** take down in shorthand; **taquígrafo** *m*, **-a** *f* stenographer, shorthand writer
taquilla *f* ticket office; TEA box-office; *C.Am.* (*bar*) small bar
taquímetro *m* tachometer
tara *f* defect; COM tare
tarántula *f* ZO tarantula
tardanza *f* delay; **tardar** take a long time; ***tardamos dos horas*** we were two hours overdue *o* late; ***¡no tardes!*** don't be late; ***a más ~*** at the latest; ***¿cuánto se tarda …?*** how long does it take to …?; **tarde 1** *adv* late; ***~ o temprano*** sooner or later **2** *f hasta las 5 ó 6* afternoon; *desde las 5 ó 6* evening; ***¡buenas ~s!*** good afternoon / evening; ***por la ~*** in the afternoon / evening; ***de ~ en ~*** from time to time; **tardío** late
tardo slow
tarea *f* task, job; ***~s domésticas*** housework
tarifa *f* rate; *de tren* fare; ***~ plana*** flat rate
tarima *f* platform; ***suelo de ~*** wooden floor
tarjeta *f* card; ***~ amarilla*** DEP yellow card; ***~ de crédito*** credit card; ***~ de débito*** debit card; ***~ de embarque*** AVIA

boarding card; ~ ***de sonido*** INFOR sound card; ~ ***de visita*** (business) card; ~ ***gráfica*** INFOR graphics card; ~ ***inteligente*** smart card; ~ ***postal*** postcard; ~ ***roja*** DEP red card; ~ ***telefónica*** phonecard

tarro *m* jar; P (*cabeza*) head

tarta *f* cake; *plana* tart; ~ ***helada*** ice-cream cake

tartamudear stutter, stammer

tarugo *m* F blockhead F

tasa *f* rate; (*impuesto*) tax; ~ ***de desempleo*** *o* ***paro*** unemployment rate; **tasar** fix a price for; (*valorar*) assess

tasca *f* F bar

tatuaje *m* tattoo

taurino bullfighting *atr*; **Tauro** *m/f inv* ASTR Taurus; **tauromaquia** *f* bullfighting

taxi *m* cab, taxi; **taxista** *m/f* cab *o* taxi driver

taza *f* cup; *del wáter* bowl

te *directo* you; *indirecto* (to) you; *reflexivo* yourself

té *m* tea

tea *f* torch

teatral *fig* theatrical; **teatro** *m tb fig* theater, *Br* theatre

tebeo *m* children's comic

techo *m* ceiling; (*tejado*) roof; ~ ***solar*** AUTO sun-roof; ***los sin*** ~ the homeless; ***tocar*** ~ *fig* peak

tecla *f* key; **teclado** *m* MÚS, INFOR keyboard; **teclear** key; **teclista** *m/f* INFOR keyboarder; MÚS keyboard player

técnica *f* technique; **técnico** **1** *adj* technical **2** *m/f* technician; *de televisor, lavadora etc* repairman; **tecnología** *f* technology; ***alta*** ~ hi-tech; ~ ***punta*** state-of-the-art technology, leading-edge technology

tedio *m* tedium

teja *f* roof tile; ***a toca*** ~ in hard cash; **tejado** *m* roof

tejano **1** *adj* Texan, of / from Texas **2** *m*, **-a** *f* Texan; **Tejas** Texas; **tejanos** *mpl* jeans

tejer **1** *v/t* weave; (*hacer punto*) knit; F *intriga* devise **2** *v/i L.Am.* F plot, scheme; **tejido** *m* fabric; ANAT tissue

tejón *m* ZO badger

tela *f* fabric, material; ~ ***de araña*** spiderweb; ***poner en*** ~ ***de juicio*** call into question; ***hay*** ~ ***para rato*** F there's a lot to be done

telar *m* loom; **telaraña** *f* spiderweb

teleadicto, *m* **-a** *f* F couch potato F, teleaddict F

telecomedia *f* sitcom

telecomunicaciones *fpl* telecommunications

telediario *m* TV (television) news *sg*

teledirigido remote-controlled

teleférico *m* cable car

telefonear call, phone; **telefónico** (tele)phone *atr*; **teléfono** *m* (tele)phone; ~ ***inalámbrico*** cordless (phone); ~ ***móvil*** cell (phone), *Br* mobile (phone)

telefonema *m L.Am.* (phone) message

telenovela *f* soap (opera)

telescopio *m* telescope

telesilla *f* chair lift

telespectador *m*, **~a** *f* (television) viewer

telesquí *m* drag lift

teletexto *m* teletext

teletrabajo *m* teleworking; **teletrabajador** *m*, **~a** *f* teleworker

televidente *m/f* (television) viewer; **televisión** *f* television; ~ ***por cable*** cable (television); ~ ***de pago*** pay-per-view television; ~ ***vía satélite*** satellite television; **televisivo** television *atr*; **televisor** *m* TV, television (set)

telón *m* TEA curtain; ***el ~ de acero*** POL the Iron Curtain; ~ ***de fondo*** *fig* backdrop, background

tema *m* subject, topic; MÚS, *de novela* theme

temblar tremble, shake; *de frío* shiver; **temblor** *m* trembling, shaking; *de frío* shivering; *L.Am.* (*terremoto*) earthquake; ~ ***de tierra*** earth tremor; **tembloroso** trembling, shaking; *de frío* shivering

temer be afraid of; **temerse** be afraid; ~ ***lo peor*** fear the worst

temerario rash, reckless; **temeridad** *f* rashness, recklessness

temeroso fearful, frightened; **temible** terrifying; **temor** *m* fear

temperamento *m* temperament; **temperante** *Méx* teetotal

temperatura *f* temperature

tempestad *f* storm; **tempestuoso** *tb fig* stormy

templado warm; *clima* temperate; *fig* moderate; **templar** *ira, nervios* calm

templo *m* temple

temporada *f* season; ***una ~*** a time, some time; **temporal 1** *adj* temporary **2** *m* storm;

temprano early

tenacidad *f* tenacity; **tenaz** determined, tenacious; **tenaza** *f* pincer, claw; **~s** pincers; *para las uñas* pliers

tendedero *m* clotheshorse

tendencia *f* tendency; (*corriente*) trend; **tendencioso** tendentious

tender 1 *v/t ropa* hang out; *cable* lay; ***le tendió la mano*** he held out his hand to her **2** *v/i*: ~ ***a*** tend to

tendón *m* ANAT tendon

tenebroso dark, gloomy

tenedor *m* fork

tener have; ~ ***10 años*** be 10 (years old); ~ ***un metro de ancho / largo*** be one meter wide / long; ~ ***por*** consider to be; ***tengo que madrugar*** I must get up early, I have to *o* I've got to get up early; **tenerse** stand up; *fig* stand

firm; ***se tiene por atractivo*** he thinks he's attractive
tenia *f* ZO tapeworm
teniente *m/f* MIL lieutenant
tenis *m* tennis; **~ *de mesa*** table tennis; **tenista** *m/f* tennis player
tenor *m* MÚS tenor; ***a ~ de*** along the lines of
tensión *f* tension; ELEC voltage; MED blood pressure; **tenso** tense; *cuerda* taut
tentación *f* temptation; **tentador** tempting; **tentar** tempt, entice
tentativa *f* attempt
tenue faint
teñir dye; *fig* tinge
teología *f* theology
teoría *f* theory; ***en ~*** in theory; **teórico 1** *adj* theoretical **2** *m*, **-a** *f* theorist
terapeuta *m/f* therapist; **terapéutico** therapeutic; **terapia** *f* therapy
tercer third; ***Tercer Mundo*** Third World; **tercero** *m/adj* third; **tercio** *m* third
terciopelo *m* velvet
terco stubborn
termal thermal
termas *fpl* hot springs
terminación *f* GRAM ending; **terminal 1** *m* INFOR terminal **2** *f* AVIA terminal; **~ *de autobuses*** bus terminal; **terminar 1** *v/t* end, finish **2** *v/i* end, finish; (*parar*) stop; **término** *m* end, conclusion; (*palabra*) term; **~ *municipal*** municipal area; ***por ~ medio*** on average; ***poner ~ a algo*** put an end to sth
termo *m* thermos® (flask)
termómetro *m* thermometer; **termostato** *m* thermostat
ternera *f* calf; GASTR veal; **ternero** *m* calf
terno *m CSur* suit
ternura *f* tenderness
terraplén *m* embankment; **terrateniente** *m/f* landowner
terraza *f* terrace; (*balcón*) balcony; (*café*) sidewalk *o Br* pavement café
terremoto *m* earthquake
terreno *m* land; *fig* field; ***un ~*** a plot *o* piece of land; **~ *de juego*** DEP field
terrestre *animal* land *atr*; *transporte* surface *atr*; ***la atmósfera ~*** the earth's atmosphere
terrible terrible, awful
territorio *m* territory
terrón *m* lump; **~ *de azúcar*** sugar lump
terror *m* terror; **terrorismo** *m* terrorism; **terrorista 1** *adj* terrorist *atr* **2** *m/f* terrorist; **~ *suicida*** suicide bomber
terso smooth
tertulia *f* TV debate, round table discussion
tesis *f inv* thesis
tesorería *f oficio* post of treasurer; *oficina* treasury; (*activo disponsible*) liquid assets *pl*
testaferro *m* front man
testamento *m* JUR will
testarudo stubborn

testículo *m* ANAT testicle
testificar 1 *v/t* (*probar, mostrar*) be proof of; **~ *que*** JUR testify that, give evidence that **2** *v/i* testify, give evidence; **testigo 1** *m/f* JUR witness; **~ *de cargo*** witness for the prosecution; **~ *ocular*** *o* ***presencial*** eye witness **2** *m* DEP baton
testimoniar testify; **testimonio** *m* testimony, evidence
teta *f* F boob F; ZO teat, nipple
tétanos *m* MED tetanus
tetera *f* teapot
tétrico gloomy
textil 1 *adj* textile *atr* **2** *mpl*: **~*es*** textiles
texto *m* text; **textual** textual
textura *f* texture
tez *f* complexion
ti you; *reflexivo* yourself
tía *f* aunt; F (*chica*) girl, chick F
tibia *f* ANAT tibia
tibio *tb fig* lukewarm
tiburón *m* ZO, *fig* F shark
ticket *m* (sales) receipt
tiempo *m* time; (*clima*) weather; GRAM tense; **~ *real*** INFOR real time; ***a*** **~** in time; ***a un*** **~**, ***al mismo*** **~** at the same time; ***antes de*** **~** *llegar* ahead of time, early; *celebrar* too soon; ***con*** **~** in good time, early; ***hace buen / mal*** **~** the weather's fine / bad
tienda *f* store, shop; **~ *de campaña*** tent; ***ir de*** **~*s*** go shopping
tierno soft; *carne* tender; *pan* fresh
tierra *f* land; *materia* soil, earth; (*patria*) native land; ***la Tierra*** the earth; **~ *firme*** dry land, terra firma; ***echar por*** **~** ruin, wreck
tieso stiff, rigid
tiesto *m* flowerpot
tifus *m* MED typhus
tigre *m* ZO tiger; *L.Am.* puma; *L.Am.* (*leopardo*) jaguar
tijeras *fpl* scissors
tila *f* lime blossom tea
tildar: **~ *a alguien de*** *fig* brand s.o. as
tilde *f* accent; *en ñ* tilde
tilo *m* BOT lime (tree)
timador *m*, **~*a*** *f* cheat; **timar** cheat
timbal *m* MÚS kettle drum
timbre *m de puerta* bell; *Méx* (postage) stamp
timidez *f* shyness, timidity; **tímido** shy, timid
timo *m* confidence trick, swindle
timón *m* MAR, AVIA rudder; **timonel** MAR **1** *m* helmsman **2** *f* helmswoman
tímpano *m* ANAT eardrum
tina *f* large jar; *L.Am.* (*bañera*) (bath)tub
tinerfeño of / from Tenerife
tinieblas *fpl* darkness
tinta *f* ink; ***de buena*** **~** *fig* on good authority; ***medias*** **~*s*** *fig* half measures; **tinte** *m* dye; *fig* veneer, gloss
tinto: ***vino*** **~** red wine
tintorería *f* dry cleaner

tío *m* uncle; F (*tipo*) guy F; F *apelativo* pal F
tiovivo *m* carousel, merry-go--round
típico typical (***de*** of); **tipo** *m* type, kind; F *persona* guy F; COM rate; ***~ de cambio*** exchange rate; ***~ de interés*** interest rate; ***tener buen ~*** be well built; *de mujer* have a good figure
tipografía *f* typography
tíquet, tiquete *m L.Am.* receipt
tira *f* strip; ***la ~ de*** F loads of F; ***~ y afloja*** *fig* give and take
tirada *f* TIP print run; ***de una ~*** in one go; **tirado** P (*barato*) dirt-cheap F; ***estar ~*** F (*fácil*) be a piece of cake F
tirador *m* shot, marksman; *de puerta* handle; **tiradores** *mpl Arg* suspenders, *Br* braces
tiranía *f* tyranny; **tiránico** tyrannical; **tiranizar** tyrannize; **tirano 1** *adj* tyrannical **2** *m*, **-a** *f* tyrant
tirante 1 *adj* taut; *fig* tense **2** *m* strap; ***~s*** suspenders, *Br* braces; **tirantez** *f fig* tension
tirar 1 *v/t* throw; *edificio, persona* knock down; (*volcar*) knock over; *basura, dinero* throw away; TIP print; F *en examen* fail **2** *v/i* pull, attract; (*disparar*) shoot; ***~ a*** tend toward; ***~ de algo*** pull sth; ***ir tirando*** F get by, manage; **tirarse** throw o.s.; F *tiempo* spend
tirita *f* MED Band-Aid®, *Br* plaster
tiritar shiver
tiro *m* shot; ***~ al blanco*** target practice; ***al ~*** *CSur* F right away; ***de ~s largos*** F dressed up; ***ni a ~s*** F for love nor money
tiroides *m* ANAT thyroid (gland)
tirón *m* tug, jerk; ***de un ~*** at a stretch, without a break
tiroteo *m* shooting
tisana *f* herbal tea
títere *m tb fig* puppet; ***no dejar ~ con cabeza*** F spare no-one
titiritero *m*, **-a** *f* acrobat
titubear waver, hesitate
titular *m de periódico* headline; **título** *m* title; *universitario* degree; JUR title; COM bond; ***tener muchos ~s*** be highly qualified; ***a ~ de*** as; ***~s de crédito*** credits
tiza *f* chalk
toalla *f* towel; **toallero** *m* towel rail
tobillo *m* ankle
tobogán *m* slide
tocadiscos *m inv* record player
tocado: *estar ~* *fig* F be crazy
tocador *m* dressing-table
tocante: *en lo ~ a...* with regard to ...
tocar 1 *v/t* touch; MÚS play **2** *v/i L.Am. a la puerta* knock (on the door); *L.Am.* (*sonar la campanita*) ring the doorbell; ***te toca jugar*** it's your turn

tocino *m* bacon
tocólogo *m*, **-a** *f* obstetrician
todavía still, yet; ***~ no ha llegado*** he still hasn't come, he hasn't come yet; ***~ no*** not yet
todo 1 *adj* all; ***~s los domingos*** every Sunday; ***-a la clase*** the whole *o* the entire class **2** *adv* all; ***estaba ~ sucio*** it was all dirty; ***con ~*** all the same; ***del ~*** entirely, absolutely **3** *pron* all, everything; *pl* everybody, everyone; ***ir a por -as*** go all out
todoterreno *m* AUTO off-road *o* all-terrain vehicle
toldo *m* awning; *L.Am.* Indian hut
tolerable tolerable; **tolerancia** *f* tolerance; **tolerante** tolerant; **tolerar** tolerate
toma *f* FOT shot, take; ***~ de conciencia*** realization; ***~ de corriente*** outlet, *Br* socket; ***~ de posesión*** POL taking office; **tomar 1** *v/t* take; *bebida, comida* have; ***~ la con alguien*** F have it in for s.o. F; ***~ el sol*** sunbathe; ***¡toma!*** here (you are); ***toma y daca*** give and take **2** *v/i L.Am.* (*beber*) drink; ***~ por la derecha*** turn right, take a right
tomate *m* tomato
tomavistas *m inv* movie camera
tomillo *m* BOT thyme
tomo *m* volume, tome
tonel *m* barrel, cask; **tonelada** *f peso* ton; **tonelaje** *m* tonnage
tónica *f* tonic; **tónico** *m* MED tonic; **tono** *m* MÚS, MED, PINT tone
tontería *f fig* stupid *o* dumb F thing; ***~s*** nonsense; **tonto 1** *adj* silly, foolish **2** *m*, **-a** *f* fool, idiot; ***hacer el ~*** play the fool; ***hacerse el ~*** act dumb F
toparse: ***~ con alguien*** bump into s.o., run into s.o.
tope *m* limit; *pieza* stop; *Méx en la calle* speed bump; ***pasarlo a ~*** F have a great time
tópico *m* cliché, platitude
topo *m* ZO mole
topográfico topographic(al)
toque *m*: ***~ de queda*** MIL, *fig* curfew; ***dar los últimos ~s*** put the finishing touches (***a*** to)
torbellino *m* whirlwind
torcer 1 *v/t* twist; (*doblar*) bend; (*girar*) turn **2** *v/i* turn; ***~ a la derecha*** turn right; **torcerse** twist, bend; *fig* go wrong; ***~ un pie*** sprain one's ankle; **torcido** twisted, bent
tordo *m pájaro* thrush; *caballo* dapple-gray, *Br* dapple-grey
torear 1 *v/i* fight bulls **2** *v/t* fight; *fig* dodge, sidestep; **toreo** *m* bullfighting; **torero** *m* bullfighter
tormenta *f* storm; **tormento** *m* torture
torneo *m* competition, tournament
tornillo *m* screw; *con tuerca* bolt; ***le falta un ~*** F he's got a screw loose F

torniquete *m* turnstile; MED tourniquet
torno *m de alfarería* wheel; ***en ~ a*** around, about
toro *m* bull; ***ir a los ~s*** go to a bullfight
torpe clumsy; (*tonto*) dense, dim
torpedo *m* MIL torpedo
torpeza *f* clumsiness; (*necedad*) stupidity
torre *f* tower; ***~ de control*** AVIA control tower
torrencial torrential; **torrente** *m fig* avalanche, flood
tórrido torrid
torsión *f* twisting; TÉC torsion, torque
torta *f* cake; *plana* tart; F (*bofetada*) slap
tortilla *f* omelet, *Br* omelette; *L.Am.* tortilla
tórtola *f* ZO turtledove
tortuga *f* ZO tortoise; *marina* turtle; ***a paso de ~*** *fig* at a snail's pace
tortuoso *fig* tortuous
tortura *f tb fig* torture; **torturar** torture
tos *f* cough
tosco *fig* rough, coarse
toser cough
tostada *f* piece of toast; **tostador** *m* toaster; **tostar** toast; *café* roast; *al sol* tan
total 1 *adj* total; ***en ~*** in total **2** *m* total; **totalidad** *f* totality
tóxico toxic; **toxicómano** *m*, **-a** *f* drug addict
tozudo obstinate
traba *f* obstacle; ***poner ~s*** raise objections; ***sin ~s*** without a hitch
trabajador 1 *adj* hard-working **2** *m*, **~a** *f* worker; ***~ eventual*** casual worker; **trabajar 1** *v/i* work **2** *v/t* work; *tema*, *músculos* work on; **trabajo** *m* work; ***~ en equipo*** team work; ***~ a tiempo parcial*** part-time work; **trabajoso** hard, laborious
trabar *amistad* strike up
tracción *f* TÉC traction; ***~ delantera / trasera*** front / rear-wheel drive
tractor *m* tractor
tradición *f* tradition; **tradicional** traditional
traducción *f* translation; **traducir** translate; **traductor** *m*, **~a** *f* translator
traer bring; *de periódico* carry; ***~ consigo*** involve, entail
traficante *m* dealer; **traficar** deal (***en*** in); **tráfico** *m* traffic; ***~ de drogas*** drug trafficking; *en pequeña escala* drug dealing
tragaluz *m* skylight; **tragaperras** *f inv* slot machine
tragar swallow; ***no lo trago*** I can't stand him
tragedia *f* tragedy; **trágico** tragic
trago *m* mouthful; F *bebida* drink; ***de un ~*** in one gulp; ***pasar un mal ~*** *fig* have a hard time
traición *f* treachery, betrayal; **traicionar** betray; **traidor 1** *adj* treacherous **2** *m*, **~a** *f*

traitor
traje 1 *m* suit; **~ *de baño*** swimsuit **2** *vb* ☞ ***traer***
trajín *m* hustle and bustle
trama *f* (*tema*) plot; **tramar** *complot* hatch
tramitación *f* processing; **tramitar** *documento*: *de persona* apply for; *de banco etc* process; **trámite** *m* formality
trampa *f* trap; (*truco*) scam F, trick; ***hacer ~s*** cheat
trampolín *m* diving board
tramposo *m*, **-a** *f* cheat, crook
trance *m* (*momento difícil*) tough time; ***en ~*** *de médium* in a trance
tranquilidad *f* calm, quietness; **tranquilizar**: ***~ a alguien*** calm s.o. down; **tranquilo** calm, quiet; ***¡~!*** don't worry; ***déjame ~*** leave me alone; ***quedarse tan ~*** not bat an eyelid
transacción *f* COM deal, transaction
transatlántico 1 *adj* transatlantic **2** *m* liner
transbordador *m* ferry; ***~ espacial*** space shuttle; **transbordo** *m*: ***hacer ~*** TRANSP transfer, change
transcripción *f* transcription
transcurrir *de tiempo* pass, go by; **transcurso** *m* course; *de tiempo* passing
transeúnte *m/f* passer-by
transferencia *f* COM transfer; **transferible** transferable; **transferir** transfer
transformación *f* transformation; **transformador** *m* ELEC transformer; **transformar** transform
transfusión *f*: ***~ de sangre*** blood transfusion
transgénico genetically modified, GM
transgredir infringe; **transgresión** *f* infringement, transgression
transición *f* transition
transigente accommodating; **transigir** compromise, make concessions
transistor *m* transistor
transitable passable; **transitar** *de persona* walk; *de vehículo* travel (***por*** along)
transitivo GRAM transitive
tránsito *m* COM transit; *L.Am.* (*circulación*) traffic
transmisión *f* transmission; ***~ de datos*** data transmission; ***enfermedad de ~ sexual*** sexually transmitted disease; **transmitir** spread; RAD, TV broadcast, transmit
transparencia *f para proyectar* transparency, slide; **transparente** transparent
transpirar perspire
transportar transport; **transporte** *m* transport; **transportista** *m/f* haulage contractor
transversal transverse, cross *atr*
tranvía *m* streetcar, *Br* tram
trapecio *m* trapeze
trapo *m viejo* rag; *para limpiar* cloth; ***~s*** F clothes

tráquea *f* ANAT windpipe, trachea
tras *en el espacio* behind; *en el tiempo* after
trascendental, trascendente momentous; *en filosofía* transcendental
trasero 1 *adj* rear *atr*, back *atr* **2** *m* F butt F
trasfondo *m* background; *fig* undercurrent
trasladar move; *trabajador* transfer; **trasladarse** move (***a*** to); ***se traslada*** *Méx*: *en negocio* under new management; **traslado** *m* move; *de trabajador* transfer; ***~ al aeropuerto*** airport transfer
traslucirse be visible; *fig* be evident, show
trasnochador *m* night owl; **trasnochar** (*acostarse tarde*) go to bed late, stay up late; (*no dormir*) stay up all night; *L.Am.* (*pernoctar*) stay the night
traspapelar mislay
traspasar (*atravesar*) go through; COM transfer; **traspaso** *m* COM transfer
trasplantar AGR, MED transplant; **trasplante** *m* AGR, MED transplant
trastero *m* lumber room; **trasto** *m desp* piece of junk; *persona* good-for-nothing
trastornar upset; (*molestar*) inconvenience; **trastorno** *m* inconvenience; MED disorder
trata *f* trade
tratado *m esp* POL treaty
tratamiento *m* treatment; ***~ de datos / textos*** data / word processing; **tratar 1** *v/t* treat; (*manejar*) handle; (*dirigirse a*) address (***de*** as); *gente* come into contact with; *tema* deal with **2** *v/i*: ***~ con alguien*** deal with s.o.; ***~ de*** (*intentar*) try to; **tratarse: *¿de qué se trata?*** what's it about?; **trato** *m* treatment; COM deal; ***malos ~s*** abuse,; ***tener ~ con alguien*** have dealings with s.o.; ***¡~ hecho!*** it's a deal; **tratante** *m/f* dealer, trader
trauma *m* trauma; **traumatismo** *m* MED trauma, injury; **traumático** traumatic
través *m*: ***a ~ de*** through; **travesaño** *m en fútbol* crossbar; **travesía** *f* crossing
travesti *m* transvestite
travesura *f* bit of mischief, prank; **travieso** *niño* mischievous
trayecto *m* journey; ***10 dólares por ~*** 10 dollars each way; **trayectoria** *f fig* course, path
trazado *m acción* drawing; (*diseño*) plan, design; *de camino* route; **trazar** (*dibujar*) draw; *ruta* plot, trace; (*describir*) outline, describe; **trazo** *m* line
trébol *m* BOT clover
trece thirteen
trecho *m* stretch, distance
tregua *f* truce, cease-fire; ***sin***

~ relentlessly
treinta thirty
tremendo awful, dreadful; *éxito*, *alegría* tremendous
tren *m* FERR train; ***~ de lavado*** car wash; ***vivir a todo ~*** F live in style; ***estar como un ~*** F be absolutely gorgeous
trenza *f* braid, *Br* plait; **trenzar** plait; *pelo* braid, *Br* plait
trepar climb (***a*** up), scale (***a*** sth)
trepidar vibrate, shake
tres three
tresillo *m* living-room suite, *Br* three-piece suite
triangular triangular; **triángulo** *m* triangle
tribu *f* tribe
tribuna *f* grandstand
tribunal *m* court
tributario 1 *adj* COM tax *atr* **2** *m* tributary; **tributo** *m* tribute; (*impuesto*) tax
triciclo *m* tricycle
tricolor tricolor, *Br* tricolour
trigo *m* wheat
trilladora *f* thresher; **trillar** AGR thresh
trimestral quarterly; **trimestre** *m* quarter; *escolar* semester, *Br* term
trinchar GASTR carve
trinchera *f* MIL trench
trineo *m* sled, sleigh
trinidad *f* REL trinity
tripa *f* F belly F, gut F
triple *m* triple; ***el ~ que el año pasado*** three times as much as last year
trípode *m* tripod
tripulación *f* AVIA, MAR crew; **tripular** crew, man
triste sad; **tristeza** *f* sadness
triturar grind
triunfador 1 *adj* winning **2** *m*, ***~a*** *f* winner, victor; **triunfar** triumph, win; **triunfo** *m* triumph, victory; *en naipes* trump
trivial trivial; **trivialidad** *f* triviality
trofeo *m* trophy
trombón *m* MÚS trombone
trompa 1 *adj* F wasted F **2** *f* MÚS horn; ZO trunk
trompeta *f* MÚS trumpet; **trompetista** *m/f* MÚS trumpeter
trompo *m* spinning top
tronar thunder
tronco *m* trunk; *cortado* log; ***dormir como un ~*** sleep like a log
trono *m* throne
tropa *f* MIL ordinary soldier; ***~s*** troops
tropezar trip, stumble
tropical tropical; **trópico** *m* tropic
tropiezo *m* *fig* setback
trote *m* trot
trozo *m* piece
trucha *f* ZO trout
truco *m* trick; ***coger el ~ a algo*** F get the hang of sth F
trueno *m* thunder
trueque *m* barter
trufa *f* BOT truffle
tu, tus your
tú you

tuberculosis *f* MED tuberculosis, TB
tubería *f* pipe; **tubo** *m* tube; **~ *de escape*** AUTO exhaust (pipe); ***por un ~*** F an enormous amount
tuerca *f* TÉC nut
tuétano *m*: ***hasta los ~s*** *fig* through and through
tulipán *m* BOT tulip
tumba *f* tomb, grave
tumbar knock down; **tumbona** *f* (sun) lounger
tumor *m* MED tumor, *Br* tumour
tumulto *m* uproar; **tumultuoso** uproarious
tuna *f Méx fruta* prickly pear
tunecino 1 *adj* Tunisian **2** *m*, **-a** *f* Tunisian
túnel *m* tunnel; **~ *de lavado*** car wash
Túnez *país* Tunisia; *ciudad* Tunis
turbar (*emocionar*) upset; *paz* disturb; (*avergonzar*) embarrass
turbina *f* turbine
turbio cloudy, murky; *fig* shady, murky
turbulencia *f* turbulence; **turbulento** turbulent
turco 1 *adj* Turkish **2** *m*, **-a** *f* Turk **3** *m idioma* Turkish
turismo *m* tourism; *automóvil* sedan, *Br* saloon (car); **turista** *m/f* tourist
turnarse take it in turns; **turno** *m* turn; **~ *de noche*** night shift; ***por ~s*** in turns
turquesa *f* turquoise; ***azul ~*** turquoise
Turquía Turkey
turrón *m* nougat
tutear address as 'tu'
tutela *f autoridad* guardianship; *cargo* tutorship
tutor *m*, **~a** *f* EDU tutor
tuyo, tuya yours; ***los tuyos*** your folks, your family

U

u (*instead of* **o** *before words starting with o*) or
ubicación *f L.Am.* location; (*localización*) finding; **ubicado** located, situated; **ubicar** *L.Am.* place, put; (*localizar*) locate
ubre *f* udder
Ud. ☞ ***usted***
Uds. ☞ ***ustedes***
úlcera *f* MED ulcer
ulterior subsequent
últimamente lately; **ultimar** finalize; *L.Am.* (*rematar*) finish off; **último** last; (*más reciente*) latest; *piso* top *atr*; ***-as noticias*** latest news *sg*; ***por ~*** finally
ultraje *m* outrage; (*insulto*) insult
ultramar *m*: ***de ~*** overseas, foreign
ultrasonido *m* ultrasound
ulular *de viento* howl; *de búho*

hoot
umbral *m fig* threshold
un, una a; *antes de vocal y h muda* an; **~os coches / pájaros** some cars / birds; **~os cuantos** a few, some; **-as mil pesetas** about a thousand pesetas
unánime unanimous
ungüento *m* ointment
únicamente only; **único** only; (*sin par*) unique; **hijo ~** only child; **lo ~ que...** the only thing that ...
unidad *f* MIL, MAT unit; (*cohesión*) unity; **~ de cuidados intensivos, ~ de vigilancia intensiva** MED intensive care unit; **~ de disco** INFOR disk drive; **unido** united; *familia* close-knit; **unificar** unify
uniformar *fig* standardize; **uniforme 1** *adj* uniform; *superficie* even **2** *m* uniform
unión *f* union; **Unión Europea** European Union
unir join; *personas* unite; *características* combine (**con** with); *ciudades* link; **unirse** join together; **~ a** join
universal universal
universidad *f* university; **~ a distancia** *university correspondence school*, *Br* Open University; **universitario 1** *adj* university *atr* **2** *m*, **-a** *f* (*estudiante*) university student
universo *m* universe
uno 1 *pron* one; **es la -a** it's one o'clock; **me lo dijo ~** someone *o* somebody told me; **~ a ~, ~ por ~, de ~ en ~** one by one **2** *m* one; **el ~ de enero** January first, the first of January
untar spread
uña *f* ANAT nail; ZO claw; **ser ~ y carne** *personas* be extremely close
uranio *m* uranium
urbanismo *m* city planning, *Br* town planning; **urbanización** *f* (urban) development; (*colonia*) housing development, *Br* housing estate; **urbanizar** *terreno* develop; **urbano** urban; (*cortés*) courteous; **guardia ~** local police officer
urgencia *f* urgency; (*prisa*) haste; MED emergency; **~s** emergency room, *Br* casualty; **urgente** urgent
urinario *m* urinal
urna *f* urn; **~ electoral** ballot box
urólogo *m* MED urologist
urraca *f* ZO magpie
Uruguay Uruguay; **uruguayo 1** *adj* Uruguayan **2** *m*, **-a** *f* Uruguayan
usanza *f* usage, custom; **usado** (*gastado*) worn; (*de segunda mano*) second hand; **usar 1** *v/t* use; *ropa*, *gafas* wear **2** *v/i*: **listo para ~** ready to use; **uso** *m* use; (*costumbre*) custom; **en buen ~** still in use
usted you; **~es** you; **de ~ / ~es** your; **es de ~ / ~es**

it's yours
usual common, usual
usuario *m*, **-a** *f* user; **~ *final*** end user
usura *f* usury
utensilio *m* tool; *de cocina* utensil; **~s** equipment; **~s *de pesca*** fishing tackle
útero *m* ANAT uterus
útil 1 *adj* useful **2** *m* tool; **~es *de pesca*** fishing tackle; **utilidad** *f* usefulness; **utilitario 1** *adj* functional, utilitarian **2** *m* AUTO compact; **utilizar** use
utopía *f* utopia; **utópico** utopian
uva *f* BOT grape; ***estar de mala* ~** F be in a foul mood; ***tener mala* ~** F be a nasty piece of work F
úvula *f* ANAT uvula

V

vaca *f* cow; GASTR beef; **~ *marina*** manatee, sea cow
vacaciones *fpl* vacation, *Br* holiday; ***de* ~** on vacation, *Br* on holiday
vacante 1 *adj* vacant, empty **2** *f* job opening, position, *Br tb* vacancy; ***cubrir una* ~** fill a position; **vaciar** empty
vacío 1 *adj* empty **2** *m* FÍS vacuum; *fig espacio* void; **~ *de poder*** power vacuum; **~ *legal*** loophole; ***dejar un* ~** *fig* leave a gap; ***envasado al* ~** vacuum-packed; ***hacer el* ~ *a alguien*** *fig* ostracize s.o.
vacuna *f* vaccine; **vacunación** *f* vaccination; **vacunar** vaccinate
vacuno bovine; ***ganado* ~** cattle *pl*
vado *m* ford; *en la calle* entrance ramp
vagabundo 1 *adj perro* stray **2** *m*, **-a** *f* hobo, *Br* tramp; **vagar** wander
vagina *f* ANAT vagina
vago (*holgazán*) lazy; (*indefinido*) vague; ***hacer el* ~** laze around
vagón *m de carga* wagon; *de pasajeros* car, *Br* coach; **~ *restaurante*** dining car, *Br tb* restaurant car
vaho *m* (*aliento*) breath; (*vapor*) steam
vaina *f* BOT pod; *S.Am.* F (*molestia*) drag F
vainilla *f* vanilla
vaivén *m* to-and-fro; ***vaivenes*** *fig* ups and downs
vajilla *f* dishes *pl*; *juego* dinner service, set of dishes
vale *m* voucher, coupon; **~ *de regalo*** gift certificate, *Br* gift token; **valer 1** *v/t* be worth; (*costar*) cost **2** *v/i de billete, carné* be valid; (*estar permitido*) be allowed; (*tener valor*) be worth; (*servir*) be of use; ***no* ~ *para algo*** be no

good at sth; ***vale más caro*** it's more expensive; ***más vale...*** it's better to ...; ***más te vale...*** you'd better ...; ***¡vale!*** okay, sure; **valerse** manage (by o.s.); ~ ***de*** make use of
validez *f* validity; **válido** valid
valiente brave; *irónico* fine
valija *f* (*maleta*) bag, suitcase, *Br tb* case
valioso valuable
valla *f* fence; DEP, *fig* hurdle; ~ ***publicitaria*** billboard, *Br* hoarding; ***carrera de ~s*** DEP hurdles; **vallar** fence in
valle *m* valley
valor *m* value; (*valentía*) courage; ~ ***añadido***, *L.Am.* ~ ***agregado*** added value; ***objetos de ~*** valuables; ***~es*** COM securities; **valorar** value (***en*** at)
vals *m* waltz
válvula *f* ANAT, ELEC valve; ~ ***de escape*** *fig* safety valve
vampiresa *f* vamp, femme fatale; **vampiro** *m fig* vampire
vanagloriarse boast (***de*** about), brag (***de*** about)
vandálico destructive; **vandalismo** *m* vandalism; **vándalo** *m*, **-a** *f* vandal
vanguardia *f* MIL vanguard; ***de ~*** *fig* avant-garde
vanidad *f* vanity; **vanidoso** conceited, vain; **vano** futile, vain; ***en ~*** in vain
vapor *m* vapor, *Br* vapour *de agua* steam; ***cocinar al ~*** steam; **vaporizador** *m* spray, vaporizer **vaporizar** vaporize
vaquero 1 *adj tela* denim; ***pantalones ~s*** jeans **2** *m* cowboy, cowhand; ~**(*s*)** *pantalones* jeans
vara *f* stick; TÉC rod; (*bastón de mando*) staff
variable variable; *tiempo* changeable; **variación** *f* variation; **variado** varied; **variante** *f* variant; **variar** vary; ***para ~*** for a change
varicela *f* MED chickenpox
variedad *f* variety; ***~es*** vaudeville, *Br* variety
vario varied; **variopinto** varied, diverse; **varios** several, various
varón *m* man, male; **varonil** manly, virile
vasija *f* container, vessel; **vaso** *m* glass; ANAT vessel
vástago *m* BOT shoot; TÉC rod
vasto vast
vatio *m* ELEC watt
Vd. ☞ ***usted***
Vds. ☞ ***ustedes***
vecinal neighborhood *atr*, *Br* neighbourhood *atr*; **vecindad** *f Méx* poor area; **vecindario** *m* neighborhood, *Br* neighbourhood; **vecino 1** *adj* neighboring, *Br* neighbouring **2** *m*, **-a** *f* neighbor, *Br* neighbour
veda *f en caza* closed season; **vedar** ban, prohibit
vega *f* plain

vegetación *f* vegetation; **vegetal 1** *adj* vegetable, plant *atr* **2** *m* vegetable; **vegetar** *fig* vegetate; **vegetariano 1** *adj* vegetarian **2** *m*, **-a** *f* vegetarian
vehemencia *f* vehemence; **vehemente** vehement
vehículo *m tb fig* vehicle; MED carrier
veinte *m/adj* twenty
vejación *f* humiliation
vejez *f* old age
vejiga *f* ANAT bladder
vela *f para alumbrar* candle; DEP sailing; *de barco* sail; ***a toda ~*** F flat out F; ***pasar la noche en ~*** stay up all night; **velada** *f* evening; **velar: *~ por algo*** look after sth; **velero** *m* MAR sailing ship
veleta 1 *f* weathervane **2** *m/f fig* weathercock
vello *m* (body) hair
velo *m* veil
velocidad *f* speed; (*marcha*) gear; **velocímetro** *m* speedometer; **velocista** *m/f* DEP sprinter
velódromo *m* velodrome
veloz fast, speedy
vena *f* ANAT vein; ***estar en ~*** F be on form
venado *m* ZO deer
vencedor 1 *adj* winning **2** *m*, **~a** *f* winner; **vencer 1** *v/t* defeat; *fig* (*superar*) overcome **2** *v/i* win; COM *de plazo etc* expire; **vencimiento** *m* expiration, *Br* expiry; *de bono* maturity
venda *f* bandage; **vendaje** *m* MED dressing; **vendar** MED bandage, dress; ***~ los ojos a alguien*** blindfold s.o.
vendedor *m*, **~a** *f* seller; **vender** sell; *fig* (*traicionar*) betray; ***se vende*** for sale
vendimia *f* grape harvest
veneno *m* poison; **venenoso** poisonous
venerar venerate, worship
venezolano 1 *adj* Venezuelan **2** *m*, **-a** *f* Venezuelan; **Venezuela** Venezuela
venganza *f* vengeance, revenge; **vengarse** take revenge (***de*** on; ***por*** for); **vengativo** vengeful
venidero future
venir come; ***~ bien*** be convenient; ***~ mal*** be inconvenient; ***viene a ser lo mismo*** it comes down to the same thing; ***el año que viene*** next year; ***¡venga!*** come on; ***¿a qué viene eso?*** why do you say that?
venta *f* sale; ***~ por correo*** *o* ***por catálogo*** mail order; ***~ al detalle*** *o* ***al por menor*** retail; ***en ~*** for sale
ventaja *f* advantage; DEP *en carrera, partido* lead; **ventajoso** advantageous
ventana *f* window; ***~ de la nariz*** nostril; **ventanilla** *f* AVIA, AUTO, FERR window; MAR porthole
ventilación *f* ventilation; **ventilador** *m* fan; **ventilar**

air; *fig*: *problema* talk over

ventoso windy

ver 1 *v/t* see; *televisión* watch; JUR *pleito* hear; *L.Am.* (*mirar*) look at; ***está por ~*** it remains to be seen; ***no puede verla*** *fig* he can't stand the sight of her; ***no tiene nada que ~ con*** it doesn't have anything to do with; ***¡a ~!*** let's see; ***¡hay que ~!*** would you believe it!; ***ya veremos*** we'll see **2** *v/i L.Am.* (*mirar*) look

veraneante *m/f* vacationer, *Br* holidaymaker; **veranear** spend the summer vacation *o Br* holidays; **veraneo** *m* summer vacation *o Br* holidays; ***ir de ~*** go on one's summer vacation *o Br* holidays; **verano** *m* summer

veras *f*: ***de ~*** really, truly

verbal GRAM verbal

verbena *f* (*fiesta*) party

verbo *m* GRAM verb

verdad *f* truth; ***a decir ~*** to tell the truth; ***de ~*** real, proper; ***no te gusta, ¿~?*** you don't like it, do you?; ***vas a venir, ¿~?*** you're coming, aren't you?; ***es ~*** it's true, it's the truth; **verdadero** true; (*cierto*) real

verde 1 *adj* green; *fruta* unripe; F *chiste* blue; ***viejo ~*** dirty old man; ***poner ~ a alguien*** F criticize s.o. **2** *m* green; ***los ~s*** POL the Greens

verdugo *m* executioner

verdura *f*: **~(s)** (*hortalizas*) greens *pl*, (green) vegetables *pl*

vereda *f S.Am.* sidewalk, *Br* pavement

veredicto *m* JUR, *fig* verdict

vergonzoso disgraceful, shameful; (*tímido*) shy; **vergüenza** *f* shame; (*escándalo*) disgrace; ***me da ~*** I'm embarrassed

verídico true

verificación *f* verification; **verificar** verify

verja *f* railing; (*puerta*) iron gate

vermú, vermut *m* vermouth

verruga *f* wart

versado well-versed (***en*** in)

versátil fickle; *artista* versatile

versión *f* version; ***en ~ original*** *película* original language version

verso *m* verse

vértebra *f* ANAT vertebra

vertedero *m* dump, tip; **verter** dump; (*derramar*) spill; *fig*: *opinión* voice

vertical vertical

vertiente *f L.Am.* (*cuesta*) slope; (*lado*) side

vertiginoso dizzy; (*rápido*) frantic; **vértigo** *m* MED vertigo; ***darle a alguien ~*** make s.o. dizzy

vesícula *f* blister; ***~ biliar*** ANAT gall-bladder

vestíbulo *m de casa* hall; *de edifico público* lobby

vestido *m* dress; *L.Am. de hombre* suit

vestigio *m* vestige, trace
vestir 1 *v/t* dress; (*llevar puesto*) wear **2** *v/i* dress; ***~ de negro*** wear black, dress in black; **vestirse** get dressed; (*disfrazarse*) dress up; ***~ de algo*** wear sth
veterano 1 *adj* veteran; (*experimentado*) experienced **2** *m*, **-a** *f* veteran
veterinario 1 *adj* veterinary **2** *m*, **-a** *f* veterinarian, vet
vez *f* time; ***a la ~*** at the same time; ***a su ~*** for his / her part; ***de ~ en cuando*** from time to time; ***en ~ de*** instead of; ***érase una ~*** once upon a time, there was; ***otra ~*** again; ***tal ~*** perhaps, maybe; ***una ~*** once; ***a veces*** sometimes; ***muchas veces*** (*con frecuencia*) often; ***hacer las veces de*** *de objeto* serve as; *de persona* act as
vía 1 *f* FERR track; ***~ estrecha*** FERR narrow gauge; ***darle ~ libre a alguien*** give s.o. a free hand; ***por ~ aérea*** by air; ***en ~s de*** *fig* in the process of **2** *prp* via
viable viable, feasible
viaducto *m* viaduct
viajante *m/f* sales rep; **viajar** travel; **viaje** *m* trip, journey; ***sus ~s por...*** his travels in ...; ***~ organizado*** package tour; ***~ de ida*** outward journey; ***~ de ida y vuelta*** round trip; ***~ de novios*** honeymoon; ***~ de vuelta*** return journey; **viajero** *m*, **-a** *f* traveler, *Br* traveller
viario road *atr*, ***educación -a*** instruction in road safety
víbora *f tb fig* viper
vibración *f* vibration; **vibrar** vibrate
vicepresidente *m*, **-a** *f* POL vice-president; COM vice-president, *Br* deputy chairman
viceversa: *y ~* and vice versa
vicio *m* vice; ***pasarlo de ~*** F have a great time F; **vicioso** vicious; (*corrompido*) depraved
víctima *f* victim
victoria *f* victory; ***cantar ~*** claim victory; **victorioso** victorious
vid *f* vine
vida *f* life; ***de por ~*** for life; ***en mi ~*** never (in my life); ***ganarse la ~*** earn a living; ***~ mía*** my love
vidente *m/f* seer, clairvoyant
vídeo *m* video; **videocámara** *f* video camera; **videocas(s)et(t)e** *m* video cassette; **videoteca** *f* video library; **videoteléfono** *m* videophone
vidriera *f L.Am.* store *o Br* shop window; **vidriero** *m*, **-a** *f* glazier; **vidrio** *m L.Am.* glass; (*ventana*) window
viejo 1 *adj* old **2** *m* old man; ***mis ~s*** F my folks F
viento *m* wind; ***hacer ~*** be windy; ***proclamar a los cuatro ~s*** *fig* shout from the rooftops

vientre *m* belly
viernes *m inv* Friday; ***Viernes Santo*** Good Friday
viga *f* beam, girder
vigente *legislación* in force
vigilancia *f* watchfulness, vigilance; **vigilante 1** *adj* watchful, vigilant **2** *m L.Am.* policeman; ~ ***nocturno*** night watchman; ~ ***jurado*** security guard; **vigilar 1** *v/i* keep watch **2** *v/t* watch; *a un preso* guard
vigor *m* vigor, *Br* vigour; ***en*** ~ in force; **vigoroso** vigorous
vil vile, despicable
villa *f* town
villancico *m* Christmas carol
vilo: ***en*** ~ in the air; *fig* in suspense
vinagre *m* vinegar; **vinagrera** *f* vinegar bottle; *S.Am.* (*indigestión*) indigestion; ~***s*** cruet
vínculo *m* link; *fig* (*relación*) tie, bond
vino 1 *m* wine; ~ ***blanco*** white wine; ~ ***de mesa*** table wine; ~ ***tinto*** red wine **2** *vb* ☞ ***venir***
viña *f* vineyard; **viñedo** *m* vineyard
viola *f* MÚS viola
violación *f* rape; *de derechos* violation; **violar** rape
violencia *f* violence; **violento** violent; (*embarazoso*) embarrassing; *persona* embarrassed
violeta 1 *f* BOT violet **2** *m/adj* violet
violín *m* violin; **violinista** *m/f* violinist; **violonc(h)elo** *m* cello
viraje *m* MAR tack; AVIA bank; AUTO swerve; *fig* change of direction; **virar** MAR, AVIA turn
virgen 1 *adj* virgin; *cinta* blank; ***lana*** ~ pure new wool **2** *f* virgin
Virgo *m/f inv* ASTR Virgo
viril virile, manly; **virilidad** *f* virility, manliness; *edad* manhood
virtud *f* virtue; ***en*** ~ ***de*** by virtue of; **virtuoso 1** *adj* virtuous **2** *m*, **-a** *f* virtuoso
viruela *f* MED smallpox
virulento MED, *fig* virulent
virus *m inv* MED virus; ~ ***informático*** computer virus
visa *f L.Am.* visa; **visado** *m* visa
vísceras *fpl* guts, entrails
visera *f de gorra* peak; *de casco* visor
visibilidad *f* visibility; **visible** visible; *fig* obvious
visillo *m* sheer, *Br* net curtain
visión *f* vision, sight; *fig* vision; (*opinión*) view; ***tener*** ~ ***de futuro*** be forward looking
visita *f* visit; ~ ***a domicilio*** house call; ~ ***guiada*** guided tour; **visitante 1** *adj* visiting; DEP away **2** *m/f* visitor; **visitar** visit
visón *m* ZO mink
visor *m* FOT viewfinder; *en arma de fuego* sight
víspera *f* eve; ***en*** ~***s de*** on the eve of

vista *f* (eye)sight; JUR hearing; **~ *cansada*** MED tired eyes; ***a la ~*** COM at sight; ***a primera ~*** at first sight; ***con ~s a*** with a view to; ***en ~ de*** in view of; ***hasta la ~*** bye!, see you!; ***tener ~ para algo*** *fig* have a good eye for sth; ***volver la ~ atrás*** *tb fig* look back; **vistazo** *m* look; ***echar un ~ a*** take a (quick) look at

visto 1 *part* ☞ **ver 2** *adj*: ***está bien ~*** it's the done thing; ***está mal ~*** it's not the done thing; ***está ~ que*** it's obvious that; ***por lo ~*** apparently **3** *m* check(mark), *Br* tick; ***dar el ~ bueno*** give one's approval; **vistoso** eye-catching

vital vital; *persona* lively; **vitalidad** *f* vitality, liveliness

vitamina *f* vitamin

viticultor *m*, **~a** *f* wine grower; **viticultura** *f* wine-growing

vitrina *f* display cabinet; *L.Am.* shop window

viuda *f* widow; **viudo 1** *adj* widowed **2** *m* widower; ***quedarse ~*** be widowed

vivaz bright, sharp

vivencia *f* experience

víveres *mpl* provisions

vivienda *f* housing; (*casa*) house

vivir 1 *v/t* live through, experience **2** *v/i* live; ***~ de algo*** live on sth; **vivo** alive; *color* bright; *ritmo* lively; *fig* F sharp, smart

Vizcaya Biscay; ***Golfo de ~*** Bay of Biscay

vocablo *m* word; **vocabulario** *m* vocabulary

vocación *f* vocation

vocal 1 *m/f* member **2** *f* vowel

vocero *m*, **-a** *f esp L.Am.* spokesperson

volante 1 *adj* flying **2** *m* AUTO steering wheel; *de vestido* flounce; MED referral (slip); **volar 1** *v/i* fly; *fig* vanish **2** *v/t* fly; *edificio* blow up

volcán *m* volcano; **volcánico** volcanic

volcar 1 *v/t* knock over; (*vaciar*) empty; *barco, coche* overturn **2** *v/i de coche, barco* overturn

voleibol *m* volleyball

voltaje *m* ELEC voltage; **voltio** *m* ELEC volt

volumen *m* volume; **voluminoso** bulky; *vientre* ample; *historial* lengthy

voluntad *f* will; ***buena / mala ~*** good / ill will; **voluntario 1** *adj* volunteer **2** *m*, **-a** *f* volunteer

voluptuoso voluptuous

volver 1 *v/t página, mirada etc* turn (***a*** to; ***hacia*** toward); ***~ loco*** drive crazy **2** *v/i* return; ***~ a hacer algo*** do sth again; **volverse** turn around; ***~ loco*** go crazy

vomitar 1 *v/t* throw up; *lava* hurl, throw out **2** *v/i* throw up, be sick; ***tengo ganas de ~*** I feel nauseous, *Br* I feel sick; **vómito** *m* vomit

voraz voracious; *incendio*

fierce
vos *sg Rpl, C.Am., Ven* you
vosotros, vosotras *pl* you
votar vote; **voto** *m* vote; ***~ en blanco*** spoiled ballot paper
voz *f* voice; *fig* rumor, *Br* rumour; ***a media ~*** in a hushed voice; ***a ~ en grito*** at the top of one's voice; ***en ~ alta*** aloud; ***en ~ baja*** in a low voice; ***correr la ~*** spread the word; ***no tener ~ ni voto*** *fig* not have a say; ***~ en off*** voice-over
vuelo 1 *vb* ☞ ***volar* 2** *m* flight; ***~ chárter*** charter flight; ***~ nacional*** domestic flight; ***al ~*** *coger, cazar* in mid-air; ***una falda con ~*** a full skirt
vuelta *f* return; *en carrera* lap; ***~ de carnero*** *L.Am.* half-somersault; ***~ al mundo*** round-the-world trip; ***a la ~*** on the way back; ***a la ~ de la esquina*** *fig* just around the corner; ***dar la ~*** *llave etc* turn; ***dar media ~*** turn around; ***dar una ~*** go for a walk
vuestro 1 *adj* your **2** *pron* yours
vulcanizar vulcanize
vulgar vulgar, common; *abundante* common
vulnerable vulnerable; **vulnerar** violate; *fig* damage

W

walkman® *m* personal stereo, walkman®
wáter *m* bathroom, toilet
windsurf(ing) *m* windsurfing; **windsurfista** *m/f* windsurfer

X

xenofobia *f* xenophobia; **xenófobo 1** *adj* xenophobic **2** *m*, **-a** *f* xenophobe
xilófono *m* MÚS xylophone

y and
ya already; (*ahora mismo*) now; ***¡~!*** *incredulidad* oh, yeah!, sure!; *comprensión* I know; *asenso* OK, sure; *al terminar* finished!, done!; ***~ no vive aquí*** he doesn't live here any more, he no longer lives here; ***~ que*** since, as; ***~ lo sé*** I know; ***~... ~...*** either … or …

yacer lie; **yacimiento** *m* MIN deposit
yanqui *m/f* Yankee
yate *m* yacht
yaya *f* grandma; **yayo** *m* grandpa
yegua *f* ZO mare
yema *f* yolk; **~ *del dedo*** fingertip
yerba *f L.Am.* grass; **~ *mate*** maté
yerno *m* son-in-law
yeso *m* plaster
yo I; ***soy* ~** it's me; **~ *que tú*** if I were you
yodo *m* iodine
yogur *m* yog(h)urt
yugo *m* yoke
yunque *m* anvil
yunta *f* yoke, team
yute *m* jute
yuyo *m L.Am.* weed

Z

zafiro *m* sapphire
zambullida *f* dive; **zambullirse** dive (***en*** into); *fig* throw o.s. (***en*** into)
zamparse F wolf down F
zanahoria *f* carrot
zanco *m* stilt
zancudo *m L.Am.* mosquito
zángano *m* ZO drone; *fig* F lazybones *sg*
zanja *f* ditch; **zanjar** *fig problemas* settle; *dificultades* overcome
zapatería *f* shoe store, shoe shop; **zapatero** *m*, **-a** *f* shoemaker; **~ *remendón*** shoe mender; **zapatilla** *f* slipper; *de deporte* sneaker, *Br* trainer; **zapato** *m* shoe
Zaragoza Saragossa
zarpa *f* paw
zarpar MAR set sail (***para*** for)
zarza *f* BOT bramble; **zarzamora** *f* BOT blackberry
zarzuela *f type of operetta*
zigzag *m* zigzag
zinc *m* zinc
zócalo *m* baseboard, *Br* skirting board
zodíaco, zodiaco *m* zodiac
zona *f* area, zone
zonzo *L.Am.* F stupid
zoo *m* zoo; **zoología** *f* zoology; **zoológico 1** *adj* zoological **2** *m* zoo
zorra *f* ZO vixen; P whore P; **zorro 1** *adj* sly, crafty **2** *m* ZO fox; *fig* old fox
zorzal *m* ZO thrush
zozobrar MAR overturn; *fig* go under
zueco *m* clog
zumbar 1 *v/i* buzz **2** *v/t golpe, bofetada* give
zumo *m* juice
zurcir *calcetines* darn; *chaqueta, pantalones* patch
zurdo 1 *adj* left-handed **2** *m, f* left-hander
zurra *f* TÉC tanning; *fig* F hiding F; **zurrar** TÉC tan; **~ *a alguien*** F tan s.o.'s hide F

A

a [ə] un(a)
abandon [ə'bændən] abandonar
abbreviate [ə'bri:vieit] abreviar; **abbreviation** abreviatura *f*
abduct [əb'dʌkt] raptar
ability [ə'bɪlətɪ] capacidad *f*, habilidad *f*
able ['eɪbl] (*skillful*) capaz, hábil; ***be ~ to*** poder
abnormal [æb'nɔ:rml] anormal
aboard [ə'bɔ:rd] **1** *prep* a bordo de **2** *adv* a bordo
abolish [ə'bɑ:lɪʃ] abolir; **abolition** abolición *f*
abort [ə'bɔ:rt] cancelar; **abortion** aborto *m* (*provocado*); ***have an ~*** abortar; **abortive** fallido
about [ə'baʊt] **1** *prep* (*concerning*) acerca de, sobre; ***what's it ~?*** *of book* ¿de qué trata? **2** *adv* (*roughly*) más o menos; ***be ~ to*** (*be going to*) estar a punto de
above [ə'bʌv] **1** *prep* por encima de; ***~ all*** sobre todo **2** *adv*: ***on the floor ~*** en el piso de arriba
abrasive [ə'breɪsɪv] *personality* abrasivo
abreast [ə'brest] de frente, en fondo; ***keep ~ of*** mantenerse al tanto de
abridge [ə'brɪdʒ] abreviar
abroad [ə'brɒ:d] *live* en el extranjero; *go* al extranjero
abrupt [ə'brʌpt] brusco
abscess ['æbsɪs] absceso *m*
absence ['æbsəns] *of person* ausencia *f*; (*lack*) falta *f*; **absent** ausente; **absentee** ausente *m/f*; **absenteeism** absentismo *m*; **absent-minded** despistado, distraído
absolute ['æbsəlu:t] *power* absoluto; *idiot* completo; *mess* total; **absolution** REL absolución *f*; **absolve** absolver
absorb [əb'sɔ:rb] absorber; **absorbent** absorbente; **absorbent cotton** algodón *m* hidrófilo; **absorbing** absorbente
abstain [əb'steɪn] *in vote* abstenerse; **abstention** *in vote* abstención *f*
abstract ['æbstrækt] abstracto
absurd [əb'sɜ:rd] absurdo; **absurdity** lo absurdo
abundance [ə'bʌndəns] abundancia *f*; **abundant** abundante
abuse[1] [ə'bju:s] *n* (*insults*) insultos *mpl*; ***(child) ~*** malos tratos *mpl* a menores; *sexual* agresión *f* sexual a menores
abuse[2] [ə'bju:z] *v/t* abusar de; *verbally* insultar
abysmal [ə'bɪʒml] F (*very*

bad) desastroso F
academic [ækəˈdemɪk] **1** *n* académico(-a) *m*(*f*), profesor(a) *m*(*f*) **2** *adj* académico; **academy** academia *f*
accelerate [əkˈseləreɪt] acelerar; **acceleration** aceleración *f*; **accelerator** acelerador *m*
accent [ˈæksənt] acento *m*; (*emphasis*) énfasis *m*; **accentuate** acentuar
accept [əkˈsept] aceptar; **acceptable** aceptable; **acceptance** aceptación *f*
access [ˈækses] **1** *n* acceso *m* **2** *v/t also* COMPUT acceder a; **accessible** accesible
accessory [əkˈsesərɪ] *for wearing* accesorio *m*; LAW cómplice *m/f*
accident [ˈæksɪdənt] accidente *m*; ***by ~*** por casualidad; **accidental** accidental; **accidentally** sin querer
acclimate, acclimatize [əˈklaɪmət, əˈklaɪmətaɪz] aclimatarse
accommodate [əˈkɑːmədeɪt] alojar; *needs* hacer frente a; **accommodations** alojamiento *m*
accompaniment [əˈkʌmpənɪmənt] MUS acompañamiento *m*; **accompany** *also* MUS acompañar
accomplice [əˈkʌmplɪs] cómplice *m/f*
accomplished [əˈkʌmplɪʃt] consumado; **accomplishment** *of task* realización *f*; (*talent*) habilidad *f*; (*achievement*) logro *m*
accord [əˈkɔːrd] acuerdo *m*; ***of one's own ~*** de motu propio
accordance [əˈkɔːrdəns]: ***in ~ with*** de acuerdo con
according [əˈkɔːrdɪŋ]: ***~ to*** según; **accordingly** (*consequently*) por consiguiente; (*appropriately*) como corresponde
account [əˈkaʊnt] *financial* cuenta *f*; (*report*) relato *m*, descripción *f*; ***give an ~ of*** relatar, describir; ***on no ~*** de ninguna manera; ***on ~ of*** a causa de; ***take sth into ~*** tener algo en cuenta; **accountable** responsable (***to*** ante); **accountant** contable *m/f*, *L.Am.* contador(a) *m*(*f*); **accounts** contabilidad *f*
accumulate [əˈkjuːmjʊleɪt] **1** *v/t* acumular **2** *v/i* acumularse; **accumulation** acumulación *f*
accuracy [ˈækjʊrəsɪ] precisión *f*; **accurate** preciso; **accurately** con precisión
accusation [ækjuːˈzeɪʃn] acusación *f*; **accuse:** ***~ s.o. of sth*** acusar a alguien de algo; **accused** LAW acusado(-a) *m*(*f*); **accusing** acusador
accustom [əˈkʌstəm]: ***get ~ed to*** acostumbrarse a
ace [eɪs] *in cards* as *m*; (*in tennis: shot*) ace *m*

ache [eɪk] **1** *n* dolor *m* **2** *v/i* doler

achieve [ə'ʧiːv] conseguir, lograr; **achievement** logro *m*

acid ['æsɪd] ácido *m*

acknowledge [ək'nɑːlɪdʒ] reconocer; ***~ receipt of*** acusar recibo de; **acknowledg(e)ment** reconocimento *m*

acoustics [ə'kuːstɪks] acústica *f*

acquaint [ə'kweɪnt] *fml*: ***be ~ed with*** conocer; **acquaintance** *person* conocido(-a) *m(f)*

acquire [ə'kwaɪr] adquirir; **acquisition** adquisición *f*

acquit [ə'kwɪt] LAW absolver; **acquittal** LAW absolución *f*

acre ['eɪkər] acre *m* (*4.047m²*)

across [ə'krɑːs] **1** *prep* al otro lado de; ***sail ~ the Atlantic*** cruzar el Atlántico navegando **2** *adv* de un lado a otro; ***10 m ~*** 10 *m* de ancho

act [ækt] **1** *v/i* THEA actuar **2** *n* (*deed*), *of play* acto *m*; *in vaudeville* número *m*; (*law*) ley *f*

action ['ækʃn] acción *f*; ***take ~*** actuar

active ['æktɪv] activo; *party member* en activo; **activist** POL activista *m/f*; **activity** actividad *f*

actor ['æktər] actor *m*

actress ['æktrɪs] actriz *f*

actual ['ækʧʊəl] verdadero, real; **actually** en realidad

acute [ə'kjuːt] *pain* agudo; *sense* muy fino

AD [eɪ'diː] (= ***anno Domini***) D.C. (= después de Cristo)

ad [æd] ☞ ***advertisement***

adamant ['ædəmənt] firme

adapt [ə'dæpt] **1** *v/t* adaptar **2** *v/i of person* adaptarse; **adaptability** adaptabilidad *f*; **adaptable** adaptable; **adaptation** *of play etc* adaptación *f*; **adapter** *electrical* adaptador *m*

add [æd] **1** *v/t* añadir; MATH sumar **2** *v/i of person* sumar

◆ **add on** sumar

◆ **add up 1** *v/t* sumar **2** *v/i fig* cuadrar

addict ['ædɪkt] adicto(-a) *m(f)*; ***drug ~*** drogadicto(-a) *m(f)*; **addicted** adicto; **addiction** adicción *f*; **addictive** adictivo

addition [ə'dɪʃn] MATH suma *f*; *to list, company etc* incorporación *f*; ***in ~*** además (***to*** de); **additional** adicional; **additive** aditivo *m*; **add-on** extra *m*, accesorio *m*

address [ə'dres] **1** *n* dirección *f* **2** *v/t letter* dirigir; *audience* dirigirse a; **addressee** destinatario(-a) *m(f)*

adequate ['ædɪkwət] suficiente; (*satisfactory*) aceptable; **adequately** suficientemente; (*satisfactorily*) aceptablemente

◆ **adhere to** *surface* adherirse a; *rules* cumplir

adhesive [əd'hiːsɪv] adhesivo *m*

adjacent [ə'dʒeɪsnt] adyacen-

te
adjective ['ædʒɪktɪv] adjetivo *m*
adjoining [ə'dʒɔɪnɪŋ] contiguo
adjourn [ə'dʒɜːrn] *of meeting* aplazar; **adjournment** aplazamiento *m*
adjust [ə'dʒʌst] ajustar, regular; **adjustable** ajustable, regulable; **adjustment** ajuste *m*; *psychological* adaptación *f*
ad lib [æd'lɪb] **1** *adj* improvisado **2** *v/i* improvisar
administer [əd'mɪnɪstər] administrar; **administration** administración *f*; **administrative** administrativo; **administrator** administrador(a) *m(f)*
admirable ['ædmərəbl] admirable; **admiration** admiración *f*; **admire** admirar; **admirer** admirador(a) *m(f)*; **admiring** de admiración; **admiringly** con admiración
admissible [əd'mɪsəbl] admisible; **admission** (*confession*) confesión *f*; **~ *free*** entrada gratis; **admit** *to place* dejar entrar; *to organization* admitir; *to hospital* ingresar; (*confess*) confesar; (*accept*) admitir; **admittance** admisión *f*; ***no* ~** prohibido el paso
adolescence [ædə'lesns] adolescencia *f*; **adolescent** **1** *n* adolescente *m/f* **2** *adj* de adolescente
adopt [ə'dɑːpt] adoptar; **adoption** adopción *f*
adorable [ə'dɔːrəbl] encantador; **adoration** adoración *f*; **adore** adorar
adrenalin [ə'drenəlɪn] adrenalina *f*
adult ['ædʌlt] **1** *n* adulto(-a) *m(f)* **2** *adj* adulto; **adultery** adulterio *m*
advance [əd'væns] **1** *n money* adelanto *m*; *in science*, MIL avance *m*; ***in* ~** con antelación; *get money* por adelantado **2** *v/i* MIL avanzar; (*make progress*) avanzar, progresar **3** *v/t theory* presentar; *money* adelantar; *knowledge*, *cause* hacer avanzar; **advanced** avanzado
advantage [əd'væntɪdʒ] ventaja *f*; ***take* ~ *of*** aprovecharse de; **advantageous** ventajoso
adventure [əd'ventʃər] aventura *f*; **adventurous** aventurero; *investment* arriesgado
adverb ['ædvɜːrb] adverbio *m*
adversary ['ædvərserɪ] adversario(-a) *m(f)*
adverse ['ædvɜːrs] adverso
advertise ['ædvərtaɪz] **1** *v/t* anunciar **2** *v/i* anunciarse, poner un anuncio; **advertisement** anuncio *m*; **advertiser** anunciante *m/f*; **advertising** publicidad *f*
advice [əd'vaɪs] consejo *m*; ***some* ~** un consejo; **advisable** aconsejable; **advise** aconsejar; *government* ase-

sorar
advocate ['ædvəkeɪt] abogar por
aerial ['erɪəl] *Br* antena *f*; **aerial photograph** fotografía *f* aérea
aerobics [e'roubɪks] aerobic *m*
aerodynamic [eroudaɪ'næmɪk] aerodinámico
aeroplane ['erouplein] *Br* avión *m*
aerosol ['erəsɑːl] aerosol *m*
aesthetic *Br* ☞ ***esthetic***
affair [ə'fer] (*matter*) asunto *m*; (*love* ~) aventura *f*, lío *m*
affection [ə'fekʃn] afecto *m*; **affectionate** afectuoso; **affectionately** con afecto
affirmative [ə'fɜːrmətɪv] afirmativo
affluence ['æfluəns] prosperidad *f*; **affluent** próspero
afford [ə'fɔːrd] permitirse
afloat [ə'flout] *boat* a flote
afraid [ə'freɪd]: ***be ~*** tener miedo (***of*** de); ***I'm ~*** *expressing regret* me temo
afresh [ə'freʃ] de nuevo
Africa ['æfrɪkə] África; **African 1** *adj* africano **2** *n* africano(-a) *m(f)*; **African-American 1** *adj* afroamericano **2** *n* afroamericano(-a) *m(f)*
after ['æftər] **1** *prep* después de; ***it's ten ~ two*** son las dos y diez **2** *adv* (*afterward*) después; ***the day ~*** el día siguiente
afternoon [æftər'nuːn] tarde *f*; ***good ~*** buenas tardes
'after sales service servicio *m* posventa; **aftershave** after shave *m*; **afterward** después
again [ə'geɪn] otra vez; ***I never saw him ~*** no lo volví a ver
against [ə'genst] contra
age [eɪdʒ] **1** *n* edad *f*; (*era*) era *f*; ***she's 5 years of ~*** tiene 5 años **2** *v/i* envejecer; **aged: *~ 16*** con 16 años de edad; **age group** grupo *m* de edades; **age limit** límite *m* de edad
agency ['eɪdʒənsɪ] agencia *f*
agenda [ə'dʒendə] orden *m* del día
agent ['eɪdʒənt] agente *m/f*
aggravate ['ægrəveɪt] agravar; (*annoy*) molestar
aggression [ə'greʃn] agresividad *f*; **aggressive** agresivo; **aggressively** agresivamente
aghast [ə'gæst] horrorizado
agile ['ædʒəl] ágil; **agility** agilidad *f*
agitated ['ædʒɪteɪtɪd] agitado; **agitation** agitación *f*; **agitator** agitador(a) *m(f)*
agnostic [æg'nɑːstɪk] agnóstico(-a) *m(f)*
ago [ə'gou]: ***two days ~*** hace dos días; ***long ~*** hace mucho tiempo
agonize ['ægənaɪz] atormentarse (***over*** por); **agonizing** *pain* atroz; *wait* angustioso; **agony** agonía *f*
agree [ə'griː] **1** *v/i* estar de acuerdo; *of figures* coincidir;

(*reach agreement*) ponerse de acuerdo **2** *v/t price* acordar; **agreeable** (*pleasant*) agradable; **agreement** acuerdo *m*
agricultural [ægrɪ'kʌltʃərəl] agrícola; **agriculture** agricultura *f*
ahead [ə'hed] delante; *movement* adelante; *in race* por delante; ***be ~ of*** estar por delante de; ***plan ~*** planear con antelación
aid [eɪd] **1** *n* ayuda *f* **2** *v/t* ayudar
aide [eɪd] asistente *m/f*
Aids [eɪdz] sida *m*
ailing ['eɪlɪŋ] *economy* débil
ailment ['eɪlmənt] achaque *m*
aim [eɪm] **1** *n* (*objective*) objetivo *m* **2** *v/i in shooting* apuntar; ***~ to do sth*** tener como intención hacer algo **3** *v/t*: ***be ~ed at*** *of remark* estar dirigido a; *of gun* estar apuntando a; **aimless** sin objetivos
air [er] **1** *n* aire *m*; ***by ~*** *travel* en avión; *send mail* por correo aéreo; ***in the open ~*** al aire libre **2** *v/t room, views* airear; **airbag** airbag *m*; **air-conditioned** con aire acondicionado, climatizado; **air-conditioning** aire *m* acondicionado; **aircraft** avión *m*; **aircraft carrier** portaaviones *m inv*; **air force** fuerza *f* aérea; **air hostess** azafata *f*, *L.Am.* aeromoza *f*; **airline** línea *f* aérea; **airliner** avión *m* de pasajeros; **airmail**: ***by ~*** por correo aéreo; **airplane** avión *m*; **airport** aeropuerto *m*; **air terminal** terminal *f* aérea; **air-traffic controller** controlador(a) *m(f)* del tráfico aéreo
aisle [aɪl] pasillo *m*
ajar [ə'dʒɑːr]: ***be ~*** estar entreabierto
alarm [ə'lɑːrm] **1** *n* alarma *f* **2** *v/t* alarmar; **alarming** alarmante; **alarmingly** de forma alarmante
album ['ælbəm] álbum *m*
alcohol ['ælkəhɑːl] alcohol *m*; **alcoholic 1** *n* alcohólico(-a) *m(f)* **2** *adj* alcohólico
alert [ə'lɜːrt] **1** *n signal* alerta *f* **2** *v/t* alertar **3** *adj* alerta
alibi ['ælɪbaɪ] coartada *f*
alien ['eɪlɪən] **1** *n* extranjero(-a) *m(f)*; *from space* extraterrestre *m/f* **2** *adj* extraño; **alienate** alienar
align [ə'laɪn] alinear
alike [ə'laɪk] **1** *adj*: ***be ~*** parecerse **2** *adv* igual; ***old and young ~*** viejos y jóvenes sin distinción
alimony ['ælɪmənɪ] pensión *f* alimenticia
alive [ə'laɪv]: ***be ~*** estar vivo
all [ɒːl] **1** *adj* todo(s) **2** *pron* todo; ***~ of us / them*** todos nosotros / ellos; ***for ~ I know*** por lo que sé **3** *adv*: ***~ at once*** (*suddenly*) de repente; (*at the same time*) a la vez; ***~ but*** (*except*) todos menos; (*nearly*) casi; ***~ the better*** mucho mejor; ***they're not at ~ alike*** no

se parecen en nada; ***not at ~!*** ¡en absoluto!; ***two ~*** SP empate a dos

allegation [ælɪ'geɪʃn] acusación *f*; **allege** alegar; **alleged** presunto; **allegedly** presuntamente

allegiance [ə'liːdʒəns] lealtad *f*

allergic [ə'lɜːrdʒɪk] alérgico

alleviate [ə'liːvɪeɪt] aliviar

alley ['ælɪ] callejón *m*

alliance [ə'laɪəns] alianza *f*

allocate ['æləkeɪt] asignar; **allocation** asignación *f*

allot [ə'lɑːt] asignar

allow [ə'laʊ] (*permit*) permitir; (*calculate for*) calcular

◆ **allow for** tener en cuenta

allowance [ə'laʊəns] (*money*) asignación *f*; (*pocket money*) paga *f*

alloy ['ælɔɪ] aleación *f*

all-'purpose multiuso; **all-round** completo

◆ **allude to** [ə'luːd] aludir a

alluring [ə'luːrɪŋ] atractivo

all-wheel 'drive con tracción a las cuatro ruedas

ally ['ælaɪ] aliado(-a) *m(f)*

almond ['ɑːmənd] almendra *f*

almost ['ɒːlmoʊst] casi

alone [ə'loʊn] solo

along [ə'lɒːŋ] **1** *prep* (*situated beside*) a lo largo de; ***walk ~ this path*** sigue por esta calle **2** *adv*: ***would you like to come ~?*** ¿te gustaría venir con nosotros?; ***~ with*** junto con; ***all ~*** (*all the time*) todo el tiempo

alongside [əlɒːŋ'saɪd] (*in cooperation with*) junto a; (*parallel to*) al lado de

aloof [ə'luːf] distante

aloud [ə'laʊd] en voz alta

alphabet ['ælfəbet] alfabeto *m*; **alphabetical** alfabético

already [ɒːl'redɪ] ya

alright [ɒːlraɪt] (*not hurt, in working order*) bien; ***that's ~*** (*don't mention it*) de nada; (*I don't mind*) no importa

altar ['ɒːltər] altar *m*

alter ['ɒːltər] alterar; **alteration** alteración *f*

alternate 1 ['ɒːltərneɪt] *v/i* alternar **2** ['ɒːltərnət] *adj* alterno

alternative [ɒːlt'ɜːrnətɪv] **1** *n* alternativa *f* **2** *adj* alternativo; **alternatively** si no

although [ɒːl'ðoʊ] aunque, si bien

altitude ['æltɪtuːd] altitud *f*; *of mountain* altura *f*

altogether [ɒːltə'geðər] (*completely*) completamente; (*in all*) en total

altruism ['æltruːɪzm] altruismo *m*; **altruistic** altruista

aluminium [æljʊ'mɪnɪəm] *Br*, **aluminum** [ə'luːmənəm] aluminio *m*

always ['ɒːlweɪz] siempre

a.m. ['eɪem] (= ***ante meridiem***) a.m.; ***at 11 ~*** a las 11 de la mañana

amass [ə'mæs] acumular

amateur ['æmətʃʊr] *unskilled* aficionado(-a) *m(f)*; SP amateur *m/f*; **amateurish** *pej* chapucero

amaze [ə'meɪz] asombrar; **amazed** asombrado; **amazement** asombro *m*; **amazing** asombroso; F (*very good*) alucinante F; **amazingly** increíblemente

Amazon ['æməzən] *n*: ***the ~*** el Amazonas

ambassador [æm'bæsədər] embajador(a) *m*(*f*)

amber ['æmbər] ámbar

ambience ['æmbɪəns] ambiente *m*

ambiguity [æmbɪ'gju:ətɪ] ambigüedad *f*; **ambiguous** ambiguo

ambition [æm'bɪʃn] *also pej* ambición *f*; **ambitious** ambicioso

ambivalent [æm'bɪvələnt] ambivalente

amble ['æmbl] deambular

ambulance ['æmbjʊləns] ambulancia *f*

ambush ['æmbʊʃ] **1** *n* emboscada *f* **2** *v/t* tender una emboscada a

amend [ə'mend] enmendar; **amendment** enmienda *f*; **amends: *make ~ for*** compensar

amenities [ə'mi:nətɪz] servicios *mpl*

America [ə'merɪkə] *continent* América; *USA* Estados *mpl* Unidos; **American 1** *adj North American* estadounidense **2** *n North American* estadounidense *m/f*

amicable ['æmɪkəbl] amistoso; **amicably** amistosamente

ammunition [æmjʊ'nɪʃn] munición *f*

amnesia [æm'ni:zɪə] amnesia *f*

amnesty ['æmnəstɪ] amnistía *f*

among(st) [ə'mʌŋ(st)] entre

amoral [eɪ'mɔ:rəl] amoral

amount [ə'maʊnt] cantidad *f*

◆ **amount to** ascender a

amphibian [æm'fɪbɪən] anfibio *m*

ample ['æmpl] abundante

amplifier ['æmplɪfaɪr] amplificador *m*; **amplify** amplificar

amputate ['æmpjʊteɪt] amputar; **amputation** amputación *f*

amuse [ə'mju:z] (*make laugh*) divertir; (*entertain*) entretener; **amusement** (*merriment*) diversión *f*; (*entertainment*) entretenimiento *m*; **amusement park** parque *m* de atracciones; **amusing** divertido

an [æn] ☞ ***a***

anaemia *Br* ☞ ***anemia***

anaesthetic *Br* ☞ ***anesthetic***

analog ['ænəlɑ:g] analógico; **analogy** analogía *f*

analysis [ə'næləsɪs] análisis *m inv*; PSYCH psicoanálisis *m inv*; **analyst** analista *m/f*; PSYCH psicoanalista *m/f*; **analytical** analítico; **analyze** analizar; PSYCH psicoanalizar

anarchy ['ænərkɪ] anarquía *f*

ancestor ['ænsestər] antepasado(-a) *m(f)*
anchor ['æŋkər] **1** *n* NAUT ancla *f*; TV presentador(a) *m(f)* **2** *v/i* NAUT anclar
ancient ['eɪnʃənt] antiguo
and [ænd] y
Andean ['ændɪən] andino; **Andes:** ***the ~*** los Andes
anemia [ə'niːmɪə] anemia *f*; **anemic** anémico
anesthetic [ænəs'θetɪk] anestesia *f*
angel ['eɪndʒl] ángel *m*
anger ['æŋgər] **1** *n* enfado *m* **2** *v/t* enfadar
angle ['æŋgl] ángulo *m*
angry ['æŋgrɪ] enfadado
animal ['ænɪml] animal *m*
animated ['ænɪmeɪtɪd] animado; **animated cartoon** dibujos *mpl* animados; **animation** animación *f*
animosity [ænɪ'mɑːsətɪ] animosidad *f*
ankle ['æŋkl] tobillo *m*
annex ['æneks] **1** *n building* edificio *m* anexo **2** *v/t state* anexionar
annihilate [ə'naɪəleɪt] aniquilar; **annihilation** aniquilación *f*
anniversary [ænɪ'vɜːrsərɪ] aniversario *m*
announce [ə'nauns] anunciar; **announcement** anuncio *m*; **announcer** TV, RAD presentador(a) *m(f)*
annoy [ə'nɔɪ] irritar; **annoyance** (*anger*) irritación *f*; (*nuisance*) molestia *f*; **annoying** irritante
annual ['ænuəl] anual
annul [ə'nʌl] anular; **annulment** anulación *f*
anonymous [ə'nɑːnɪməs] anónimo
anorexia [ænə'reksɪə] anorexia *f*
another [ə'nʌðər] **1** *adj* otro **2** *pron* otro(-a) *m(f)*; ***they helped one ~*** se ayudaron (el uno al otro)
answer ['ænsər] **1** *n* respuesta *f*, contestación *f*; *to problem* solución *f* **2** *v/t* responder, contestar; **answerphone** contestador *m*
ant [ænt] hormiga *f*
antagonism [æn'tægənɪzm] antagonismo *m*; **antagonistic** hostil; **antagonize** antagonizar, enfadar
Antarctic [ænt'ɑːrktɪk]: ***the ~*** el Antártico
antenatal [æntɪ'neɪtl] prenatal
antenna [æn'tenə] antena *f*
antibiotic [æntɪbaɪ'ɑːtɪk] antibiótico *m*
anticipate [æn'tɪsɪpeɪt] esperar, prever; **anticipation** expectativa *f*, previsión *f*
antics ['æntɪks] payasadas *fpl*
antidote ['æntɪdout] antídoto *m*
antifreeze ['æntɪfriːz] anticongelante *m*
antipathy [æn'tɪpəθɪ] antipatía *f*
antiquated ['æntɪkweɪtɪd] anticuado

antique [æn'tiːk] antigüedad *f*
antiseptic [æntɪ'septɪk] **1** *adj* antiséptico **2** *n* antiséptico *m*
antisocial [æntɪ'soʊʃl] antisocial, poco sociable
antivirus program [æntɪ'vaɪrəs] COMPUT antivirus *m inv*
anxiety [æŋ'zaɪətɪ] ansiedad *f*; **anxious** preocupado; (*eager*) ansioso
any ['enɪ] **1** *adj*: ***are there ~ glasses?*** ¿hay vasos?; ***there isn't ~ bread*** no hay pan; ***have you ~ idea at all?*** ¿tienes alguna idea?; *no matter which* cualquier(a) **2** *pron* alguno(-a); ***there isn't ~ left*** no queda
anybody ['enɪbɒːdɪ] alguien; *no matter who* cualquiera; ***there wasn't ~ there*** no había nadie allí
anyhow ['enɪhaʊ] en todo caso, de todos modos
anyone ['enɪwʌn] ☞ ***anybody***
anything ['enɪθɪŋ] algo; *with negatives* nada; ***I didn't hear ~*** no oí nada; ***~ but*** todo menos
anyway ['enɪweɪ] ☞ ***anyhow***
anywhere ['enɪwer] en alguna parte; ***I can't find it ~*** no lo encuentro por ninguna parte
apart [ə'pɑːrt] aparte; ***~ from*** aparte de
apartment [ə'pɑːrtmənt] apartamento *m*, *Span* piso *m*; **apartment block** bloque *m* de apartamentos *or Span* pisos
ape [eɪp] simio *m*
aperitif [ə'perɪtiːf] aperitivo *m*
apologize [ə'pɑːlədʒaɪz] disculparse; **apology** disculpa *f*
appalling [ə'pɒːlɪŋ] horroroso
apparatus [æpə'reɪtəs] aparatos *mpl*
apparent [ə'pærənt] aparente, evidente; **apparently** al parecer, por lo visto
appeal [ə'piːl] (*charm*) atractivo *m*; *for funds etc* llamamiento *m*; LAW apelación *f*
◆ **appeal for** solicitar
◆ **appeal to** (*be attractive to*) atraer a
appealing [ə'piːlɪŋ] *idea, offer* atractivo
appear [ə'pɪr] aparecer; *in court* comparecer; (*seem*) parecer; **appearance** aparición *f*; *in court* comparecencia *f*; (*look*) apariencia *f*, aspecto *m*
appendicitis [əpendɪ'saɪtɪs] apendicitis *m*
appendix [ə'pendɪks] MED, *of book* apéndice *m*
appetite ['æpɪtaɪt] *also fig* apetito *m*; **appetizer** aperitivo *m*; **appetizing** apetitoso
applaud [ə'plɒːd] aplaudir; **applause** aplauso *m*
apple ['æpl] manzana *f*
appliance [ə'plaɪəns] aparato *m*; *household* electrodoméstico *m*

applicable [ə'plɪkəbl] aplicable; **applicant** solicitante *m/f*; **application** *for job etc* solicitud *f*; **apply 1** *v/t rules, ointment* aplicar **2** *v/i of rule, law* aplicarse

◆ **apply for** *job, passport* solicitar; *university* solicitar el ingreso en

◆ **apply to** (*contact*) dirigirse a; (*affect*) aplicarse a

appoint [ə'pɔɪnt] *to position* nombrar; **appointment** *to position* nombramiento *m*; *meeting* cita *f*

appraisal [ə'preɪz(ə)l] evaluación *f*

appreciable [ə'priːʃəbl] apreciable; **appreciate 1** *v/t* (*value*) apreciar; (*be grateful for*) agradecer; (*acknowledge*) ser consciente de **2** *v/i* FIN revalorizarse; **appreciative** agradecido

apprehensive [æprɪ'hensɪv] aprensivo, temeroso

approach [ə'prouʧ] **1** *n* aproximación *f*; (*proposal*) propuesta *f*; *to problem* enfoque *m* **2** *v/t* (*get near to*) aproximarse a; (*contact*) ponerse en contacto con; *problem* enfocar; **approachable** accesible

appropriate [ə'prouprɪət] apropiado, adecuado

approval [ə'pruːvl] aprobación *f*; **approve 1** *v/i*: ***my parents don't*** ~ a mis padres no les parece bien **2** *v/t* aprobar

approximate [ə'prɑːksɪmət] aproximado; **approximately** aproximadamente

apricot ['æprɪkɑːt] albaricoque *m*, *L.Am.* damasco *m*

April ['eɪprəl] abril *m*

apt [æpt] *remark* oportuno; **aptitude** aptitud *f*

aquarium [ə'kwerɪəm] acuario *m*

Arab ['ærəb] **1** *adj* árabe **2** *n* árabe *m/f*; **Arabic 1** *adj* árabe **2** *n* árabe *m*

arbitrary ['ɑːrbɪtrerɪ] arbitrario

arbitrate ['ɑːrbɪtreɪt] arbitrar; **arbitration** arbitraje *m*

arch [ɑːrʧ] arco *m*

archaeology *Br* ☞ ***archeology***

archaic [ɑːr'keɪɪk] arcaico

archeological [ɑːrkɪə'lɑːdʒɪkl] arqueológico; **archeologist** arqueólogo(-a) *m(f)*; **archeology** arqueología *f*

architect ['ɑːrkɪtekt] arquitecto(-a) *m(f)*; **architectural** arquitectónico; **architecture** arquitectura *f*

archives ['ɑːrkaɪvz] archivos *mpl*

Arctic ['ɑːrktɪk]: ***the*** ~ el Ártico

ardent ['ɑːrdənt] ardiente

arduous ['ɑːrdjuəs] arduo

area ['erɪə] área *f*; *f*; **area code** TELEC prefijo *m*

arena [ə'riːnə] SP estadio *m*

Argentina [ɑːrdʒən'tiːnə] Argentina; **Argentinian 1** *adj* argentino **2** *n* argentino(-a)

m(f)
arguably ['ɑːrgjʊəblɪ] posiblemente; **argue** discutir; (*reason*) argumentar; **argument** discusión *f*; (*reasoning*) argumento *m*
arid ['ærɪd] *land* árido
arise [ə'raɪz] *of situation* surgir
arithmetic [ə'rɪθmətɪk] aritmética *f*
arm[1] [ɑːrm] *n* brazo *m*
arm[2] [ɑːrm] *v/t* armar
armaments ['ɑːrməmənts] armamento *m*
armchair ['ɑːrmtʃer] sillón *m*
armed [ɑːrmd] armado; **armed forces** fuerzas *fpl* armadas; **armed robbery** atraco *m* a mano armada
'armpit sobaco *m*
arms [ɑːrmz] (*weapons*) armas *fpl*
army ['ɑːrmɪ] ejército *m*
around [ə'raʊnd] **1** *prep* (*enclosing*) alrededor de; ***it's ~ the corner*** está a la vuelta de la esquina **2** *adv* (*in the area*) por ahí; (*encircling*) alrededor; (*roughly*) alrededor de; (*with expressions of time*) en torno a
arouse [ə'raʊz] despertar; *sexually* excitar
arrange [ə'reɪndʒ] (*put in order*) ordenar; *flowers, music* arreglar; *meeting etc* organizar; *time and place* acordar; ***I've ~d to meet her*** he quedado con ella; **arrangement** (*plan*) plan *m*, preparativo *m*; (*agreement*) acuerdo *m*; (*layout*) disposición *f*; *of flowers, music* arreglo *m*
arrears [ə'rɪərz] atrasos *mpl*
arrest [ə'rest] **1** *n* detención *f*, arresto *m* **2** *v/t* detener, arrestar
arrival [ə'raɪvl] llegada *f*; **arrive** llegar
◆ **arrive at** llegar a
arrogance ['ærəgəns] arrogancia *f*; **arrogant** arrogante
arrow ['æroʊ] flecha *f*
arson ['ɑːrsn] incendio *m* provocado
art [ɑːrt] arte *m*
artery ['ɑːrtərɪ] arteria *f*
art gallery museo *m*; *private* galería *f* de arte
arthritis [ɑːr'θraɪtɪs] artritis *f*
artichoke ['ɑːrtɪtʃoʊk] alcachofa *f*, *L.Am.* alcaucil *m*
article ['ɑːrtɪkl] artículo *m*
articulate [ɑːr'tɪkjʊlət] *person* elocuente
artificial [ɑːrtɪ'fɪʃl] artificial
artillery [ɑːr'tɪlərɪ] artillería *f*
artist ['ɑːrtɪst] artista *m/f*; **artistic** artístico
'arts degree licenciatura *f* en letras
as [æz] **1** *conj* (*while, when*) cuando; (*because, like*) como; ***~ if*** como si; ***~ usual*** como de costumbre **2** *adv* como; ***~ high ~ ...*** tan alto como…; ***~ much ~ that?*** ¿tanto? **3** *prep* como; ***work ~ a teacher*** trabajar como profesor; ***~ for*** por lo que respecta a; ***~ from*** or ***of*** a partir de

ash [æʃ] ceniza *f*
ashamed [ə'ʃeɪmd] avergonzado, *L.Am.* apenado
'ash can cubo *m* de la basura
ashore [ə'ʃɔːr] en tierra; ***go ~*** desembarcar
ashtray ['æʃtreɪ] cenicero *m*
Asia ['eɪʃə] Asia; **Asian 1** *adj* asiático **2** *n* asiático(-a) *m(f)*; **Asian American** norteamericano(-a) *m(f)* de origen asiático
aside [ə'saɪd] a un lado
ask [æsk] *person* preguntar; *question* hacer; *(invite)* invitar; *favor* pedir; ***~ s.o. for sth*** pedir algo a alguien
◆ **ask after** *person* preguntar por
◆ **ask for** pedir
◆ **ask out** invitar a salir
asleep [ə'sliːp] dormido; ***fall ~*** dormirse
asparagus [ə'spærəgəs] espárragos *mpl*
aspect ['æspekt] aspecto *m*
aspiration [æspə'reɪʃn] aspiración *f*
aspirin ['æsprɪn] aspirina *f*
ass[1] [æs] *(idiot)* burro(-a) *m(f)*
ass[2] [æs] P *(butt)* culo P
assassin [ə'sæsɪn] asesino(-a) *m(f)*; **assassinate** asesinar; **assassination** asesinato *m*
assault [ə'sɒːlt] **1** *n* agresión *f*; *(attack)* ataque *m* **2** *v/t* atacar, agredir
assemble [ə'sembl] **1** *v/t parts* montar **2** *v/i of people* reunirse; **assembly** *of parts* montaje *m*; POL asamblea *f*; **assembly line** cadena *f* de montaje
assent [ə'sent] asentir
assertive [ə'sɜːrtɪv] *person* seguro y firme
assess [ə'ses] *situation* evaluar; *value* valorar; **assessment** evaluación *f*
asset ['æset] FIN activo *m*; *fig* ventaja *f*
assign [ə'saɪn] asignar; **assignment** *(task)* trabajo *m*
assimilate [ə'sɪmɪleɪt] asimilar; *in group* integrar
assist [ə'sɪst] ayudar; **assistance** ayuda *f*, asistencia *f*; **assistant** ayudante *m/f*; **assistant manager** subdirector(a) *m(f)*
associate [ə'soʊʃɪeɪt] **1** *v/t* asociar **2** *v/i*: ***~ with*** relacionarse con **3** *n* colega *m/f*; **association** asociación *f*
assortment [ə'sɔːrtmənt] *of food* surtido *m*; *of people* diversidad *f*
assume [ə'suːm] *(suppose)* suponer; **assumption** suposición *f*
assurance [ə'ʃʊrəns] garantía *f*; *(confidence)* seguridad *f*; **assure** *(reassure)* asegurar
asthma ['æsmə] asma *f*
astonish [ə'stɑːnɪʃ] asombrar; **astonishing** asombroso; **astonishment** asombro *m*
astound [ə'staʊnd] pasmar
astride [ə'straɪd] a horcajadas

sobre
astrology [ə'strɑːlədʒɪ] astrología *f*
astronaut ['æstrənɒːt] astronauta *m/f*
astronomer [ə'strɑːnəmər] astrónomo(-a) *m(f)*; **astronomical** *price etc* astronómico; **astronomy** astronomía *f*
astute [ə'stuːt] astuto, sagaz
asylum [ə'saɪləm] asilo *m*; *mental* manicomio *m*
at [æt] *with places* en; **~ *Joe's*** *house* en casa de Joe; **~ *the door*** a la puerta; **~ *10 dollars*** a 10 dólares; **~ *the age of 18*** a los 18 años; **~ *5 o'clock*** a las 5; ***be good ~ sth*** ser bueno haciendo algo
atheist ['eɪθɪɪst] ateo(-a) *m(f)*
athlete ['æθliːt] atleta *m/f*; **athletic** atlético; **athletics** atletismo *m*
Atlantic [ət'læntɪk]: ***the ~*** el Atlántico
atlas ['ætləs] atlas *m inv*
ATM [eɪtiː'em] (= ***automatic teller machine***) cajero *m* automático
atmosphere ['ætməsfɪr] atmósfera *f*; (*ambience*) ambiente *m*
atom ['ætəm] átomo *m*; **atomic** atómico
atone [ə'toʊn]: **~ *for*** expiar
atrocious [ə'troʊʃəs] atroz; **atrocity** atrocidad *f*
at-'seat TV *televisor en el respaldo del asiento*
attach [ə'tætʃ] sujetar, fijar; *importance* atribuir; **attachment** *to e-mail* archivo *m* adjunto
attack [ə'tæk] **1** *n* ataque *m* **2** *v/t* atacar
attempt [ə'tempt] **1** *n* intento *m* **2** *v/t* intentar
attend [ə'tend] acudir a
◆ **attend to** ocuparse de
attendance [ə'tendəns] asistencia *f*; **attendant** *in museum etc* vigilante *m/f*
attention [ə'tenʃn] atención *f*; ***pay ~*** prestar atención; **attentive** atento
attic ['ætɪk] ático *m*
attitude ['ætɪtuːd] actitud *f*
attorney [ə'tɜːrnɪ] abogado(-a) *m(f)*
attract [ə'trækt] atraer; **attraction** atracción *f*; **attractive** atractivo
auction ['ɒːkʃn] subasta *f*, *L.Am.* remate *m*
audacity [ɒː'dæsətɪ] audacia *f*
audible ['ɒːdəbl] audible
audience ['ɒːdɪəns] público *m*; TV audiencia *f*
audio ['ɒːdɪoʊ] de audio; **audiovisual** audiovisual
audit ['ɒːdɪt] **1** *n* auditoría *f* **2** *v/t* auditar; *course* asistir de oyente a
audition [ɒː'dɪʃn] **1** *n* audición *f* **2** *v/i* hacer una prueba
auditor ['ɒːdɪtər] FIN auditor(a) *m(f)*
auditorium [ɒːdɪ'tɔːrɪəm] *of theater etc* auditorio *m*
August ['ɒːgəst] agosto *m*
aunt [ænt] tía *f*
au pair [oʊ'per] au pair *m/f*

aura ['ɒːrə] aura *f*
auspicious [ɒː'spɪʃəs] propicio
austere [ɒː'stiːr] austero; **austerity** austeridad *f*
Australia [ɒː'streɪlɪə] Australia; **Australian 1** *adj* australiano **2** *n* australiano(-a) *m(f)*
Austria ['ɒːstrɪə] Austria; **Austrian 1** *adj* austriaco **2** *n* austriaco(-a) *m(f)*
authentic [ɒː'θentɪk] auténtico; **authenticity** autenticidad *f*
author ['ɒːθər] escritor(a) *m(f)*; *of text* autor(a) *m(f)*
authoritarian [əθɑːrɪ'terɪən] autoritario; **authoritative** autorizado; **authority** autoridad *f*; *(permission)* autorización *f*; **authorization** autorización *f*; **authorize** autorizar
autistic [ɒː'tɪstɪk] autista
autobiography [ɒːtəbaɪ'ɑːgrəfɪ] autobiografía *f*
autocratic [ɒːtə'krætɪk] autocrático
autograph ['ɒːtəgræf] autógrafo *m*
automate ['ɒːtəmeɪt] automatizar; **automatic 1** *adj* automático **2** *n car* (coche *m*) automático *m*; **automatically** automáticamente; **automation** automatización
automobile ['ɒːtəmoubiːl] automóvil *m*, coche *m*, *L.Am.* carro *m*, *Rpl* auto *m*; **automobile industry** industria *f* automovilística
autonomous [ɒː'tɑːnəməs] autónomo
autopilot ['ɒːtoupaɪlət] piloto *m* automático
autopsy ['ɒːtɑːpsɪ] autopsia *f*
autumn ['ɒːtəm] *Br* otoño *m*
auxiliary [ɒːg'zɪljərɪ] auxiliar
available [ə'veɪləbl] disponible
avalanche ['ævəlænʃ] avalancha *f*, alud *m*
avenue ['ævənuː] avenida *f*; *fig* camino *m*
average ['ævərɪdʒ] **1** *adj* medio; *(mediocre)* regular **2** *n* promedio *m*, media *f*; ***on ~*** como promedio, de media
◆ **average out at** salir a
averse [ə'vɜːrs]: ***not be ~ to*** no ser reacio a; **aversion** aversión *f*
avid ['ævɪd] ávido
avocado [ɑːvə'kɑːdou] aguacate *m*, *S.Am.* palta *f*
avoid [ə'vɔɪd] evitar
await [ə'weɪt] aguardar, esperar
awake [ə'weɪk] despierto
award [ə'wɔːrd] **1** *n* *(prize)* premio *m* **2** *v/t prize, damages* conceder; **awards ceremony** ceremonia *f* de entrega de premios
aware [ə'wer]: ***be ~ of sth*** ser consciente de algo; ***become ~ of sth*** darse cuenta de algo; **awareness** conciencia *f*
away [ə'weɪ]: ***look ~*** mirar ha-

cia otra parte; ***it's 5 miles ~*** está a 5 millas; ***take sth ~ from s.o.*** quitar algo a alguien; ***be ~*** estar fuera; **away game** SP partido *m* fuera de casa

awesome ['ɒːsəm] F alucinante F; **awful** horrible

awkward ['ɒːkwərd] (*clumsy*) torpe; (*difficult*) difícil; (*embarrassing*) embarazoso; ***feel ~*** sentirse incómodo

ax, *Br* **axe** [æks] **1** *n* hacha *f* **2** *v/t project* suprimir; *budget*, *job* recortar

axle ['æksl] eje *m*

B

baby ['beɪbɪ] bebé *m*; **baby-sit** hacer de *Span* canguro *or L.Am.* babysitter

bachelor ['bætʃələr] soltero *m*

back [bæk] **1** *n of person*, *clothes* espalda *f*; *of car*, *bus*, *house* parte *f* trasera; *of paper*, *book* dorso *m*; *of drawer* fondo *m*; *of chair* respaldo *m*; SP defensa *m/f*; ***in ~*** *in store* en la trastienda; ***in the ~*** ***(of the car)*** atrás (del coche); ***~ to front*** del revés **2** *adj* trasero **3** *adv* atrás; ***give sth ~ to s.o.*** devolver algo a alguien; ***she'll be ~ tomorrow*** volverá mañana **4** *v/t* (*support*) apoyar; *horse* apostar por

◆ **back down** echarse atrás

◆ **back out** *of commitment* echarse atrás

◆ **back up 1** *v/t* (*support*) respaldar; *file* hacer una copia de seguridad de **2** *v/i in car* dar marcha atrás

'backache dolor *m* de espalda; **backbone** columna *f* vertebral; **backdate: *~d to ...*** con efecto retroactivo a partir del...; **backdoor** puerta *f* trasera; **backer: *the ~s of the movie*** las personas que financiaron la película; **background** fondo *m*; *of person* origen *m*; *of situation* contexto *m*; **backhand** *in tennis* revés *m*; **backing** (*support*) apoyo *m*; MUS acompañamiento *m*; **backing group** grupo *m* de acompañamiento; **backlash** reacción *f* violenta; **backlog** acumulación *f*; **backpack** mochila *f*; **backpacker** mochilero(-a) *m(f)*; **back seat** asiento *m* trasero; **back streets** callejuelas *fpl*; *poorer part* zonas *fpl* deprimidas; **backstroke** SP espalda *f*; **backtrack** volver atrás; **backup** (*support*) apoyo *m*; *for police* refuerzos *mpl*; COMPUT copia *f* de seguridad; **backyard** jardín *m* trasero

bacon ['beɪkn] tocino *m*, *Span* bacon *m*

bacteria [bæk'tɪrɪə] bacterias *fpl*
bad [bæd] malo; *before singular masculine noun* mal; *headache etc* fuerte; *mistake, accident* grave; ***that's really too ~*** (*shame*) es una verdadera pena
badge [bædʒ] insignia *f*; *of policeman* placa *f*
bad 'language palabrotas *fpl*; **badly** *injured* gravemente; *damaged* seriamente; *work* mal; ***he ~ needs ...*** necesita urgentemente…
badminton ['bædmɪntən] bádminton *m*
bad-tempered [bæd'tempərd] malhumorado
baffle ['bæfl] confundir
bag [bæg] bolsa *f*; *for school* cartera *f*; (*purse*) bolso *m*, *S.Am.* cartera *f*
baggage ['bægɪdʒ] equipaje *m*; **baggage check** consigna *f*
baggy ['bægɪ] ancho
bail [beɪl] LAW libertad *f* bajo fianza; (*money*) fianza *f*; ***on ~*** bajo fianza
bait [beɪt] cebo *m*
bake [beɪk] hornear; **baked potato** *Span* patata *f or L.Am.* papa *f* asada (*con piel*); **baker** panadero(-a) *m(f)*; **bakery** panadería *f*
balance ['bæləns] **1** *n* equilibrio *m*; (*remainder*) resto *m*; *of bank account* saldo *m* **2** *v/t* poner en equilibrio **3** *v/i* mantenerse en equilibrio; *of accounts* cuadrar; **balanced** (*fair*) objetivo; *diet, personality* equilibrado; **balance sheet** balance *m*
balcony ['bælkənɪ] balcón *m*; *in theater* anfiteatro *m*
bald [bɒːld] calvo; **balding** medio calvo
ball [bɒːl] pelota *f*; *football size* balón *m*, pelota *f*; *billiard-ball size* bola *f*
ballad ['bæləd] balada *f*
ballet [bæ'leɪ] ballet *m*; **ballet dancer** bailarín(-ina) *m(f)*
'ball game (*baseball*) partido *m* de béisbol
ballistic missile [bə'lɪstɪk] misil *m* balístico
balloon [bə'luːn] globo *m*
ballot ['bælət] **1** *n* voto *m* **2** *v/t members* consultar por votación; **ballot box** urna *f*; **ballot paper** papeleta *f*
'ballpark (*baseball*) campo *m* de béisbol; **ballpark figure** F cifra *f* aproximada; **ballpoint (pen)** bolígrafo *m*, *Mex* pluma *f*, *Rpl* birome *m*
balls [bɒːlz] V huevos *mpl* V
bamboo [bæm'buː] bambú *m*
ban [bæn] **1** *n* prohibición *f* **2** *v/t* prohibir
banal [bə'næl] banal
banana [bə'nænə] plátano *m*, *Rpl* banana *f*
band [bænd] banda *f*; *pop* grupo *m*
bandage ['bændɪdʒ] **1** *n* vendaje *m* **2** *v/t* vendar
'Band-Aid® *Span* tirita *f*,

L.Am. curita *f*
bandit ['bændɪt] bandido *m*
bandy ['bændɪ] *legs* arqueado
bang [bæŋ] **1** *n noise* estruendo *m*; (*blow*) golpe *m* **2** *v/t door* cerrar de un portazo; (*hit*) golpear
bangle ['bæŋgl] brazalete *m*
bangs [bæŋz] flequillo *m*
banisters ['bænɪstərz] barandilla *f*
banjo ['bændʒou] banjo *m*
bank¹ [bæŋk] *of river* orilla *f*
bank² [bæŋk] FIN banco *m*
◆ **bank on** contar con
'**bank account** cuenta *f* (bancaria); **banker** banquero *m*; **banker's card** tarjeta *f* bancaria; **banking** banca *f*; **bank loan** préstamo *m* bancario; **bank manager** director(a) *m(f)* de banco; **bank rate** tipo *m* de interés bancario; **bankroll** financiar; **bankrupt** en bancarrota *or* quiebra; ***go*** ~ quebrar; **bankruptcy** quiebra *f*, bancarrota *f*
banner ['bænər] pancarta *f*
banquet ['bæŋkwɪt] banquete *m*
baptism ['bæptɪzm] bautismo *m*; **baptize** bautizar
bar¹ [bɑːr] *n of iron* barra *f*; *of chocolate* tableta *f*; *for drinks* bar *m*; (*counter*) barra *f*
bar² [bɑːr] *v/t from premises* prohibir la entrada a
barbaric [bɑːr'bærɪk] brutal
barbecue ['bɑːrbɪkjuː] **1** *n* barbacoa *f* **2** *v/t* cocinar en la barbacoa
barbed wire [bɑːrbd] alambre *f* de espino
barber ['bɑːrbər] barbero *m*
'**bar code** código *m* de barras
bare [ber] desnudo; *room* vacío; *floor* descubierto; **barefoot** descalzo; **bare-headed** sin sombrero; **barely** apenas
bargain ['bɑːrgɪn] **1** *n* (*deal*) trato *m*; (*good buy*) ganga *f* **2** *v/i* regatear
barge [bɑːrdʒ] NAUT barcaza *f*
◆ **barge into** *person* tropezarse con; *room* irrumpir en
baritone ['bærɪtoun] barítono *m*
bark¹ [bɑːrk] **1** *n of dog* ladrido *m* **2** *v/i* ladrar
bark² [bɑːrk] *n of tree* corteza *f*
barn [bɑːrn] granero *m*
barometer [bə'rɑːmɪtər] *also fig* barómetro *m*
barracks ['bærəks] MIL cuartel *m*
barrel ['bærəl] tonel *m*, barril *m*
barren ['bærən] *land* yermo
barrette [bə'ret] pasador *m*
barricade [bærɪ'keɪd] barricada *f*
barrier ['bærɪər] barrera *f*
'**bar tender** camarero(-a) *m(f)*, *L.Am.* mesero(-a) *m(f)*, *Rpl* mozo(-a) *m(f)*
barter ['bɑːrtər] **1** *n* trueque *m* **2** *v/t* trocar (***for*** por)
base [beɪs] **1** *n* base *f* **2** *v/t* basar (***on*** en); **baseball** béisbol *m*; *ball* pelota *f* de béisbol;

baseball cap gorra *f* de béisbol; **baseboard** rodapié *m*; **basement** *of house* sótano *m*
basic ['beɪsɪk] (*rudimentary*) básico; *room* sencillo; *skills* elemental; (*fundamental*) fundamental; **basically** básicamente
basin ['beɪsn] *for washing* barreño *m*; *in bathroom* lavabo *m*
basis ['beɪsɪs] base *f*
bask [bæsk] tomar el sol
basket ['bæskɪt] cesta *f*; *in basketball* canasta *f*; **basketball** *game* baloncesto *m*, *L.Am.* básquetbol *m*; *ball* balón *m or* pelota *f* de baloncesto
Basque [bæsk] **1** *adj* vasco **2** *n person* vasco(-a) *m(f)*; *language* vasco *m*
bass [beɪs] bajo *m*; *instrument* contrabajo *m*
bastard ['bæstərd] P cabrón (-ona) *m(f)* P
bat[1] [bæt] **1** *n baseball* bate *m*; *table tennis* pala *f* **2** *v/i in baseball* batear
bat[2] [bæt] (*animal*) murciélago *m*
batch [bætʃ] *of students* tanda *f*; *of bread* hornada *f*; *of products* lote *m*
bath [bæθ] baño *m*
bathe [beɪð] bañarse
'bathrobe albornoz *m*; **bathroom** cuarto *m* de baño; (*toilet*) servicio *m*, *L.Am.* baño *m*; **bath towel** toalla *f* de baño; **bathtub** bañera *f*
batter ['bætər] asa *f*; *in baseball* bateador(a) *m(f)*; **battered** maltratado
battery ['bætərɪ] pila *f*; *in computer, car* batería *f*
battle ['bætl] **1** *n* batalla *f* **2** *v/i against illness etc* luchar; **battleship** acorazado *m*
bawl [bɒːl] (*shout*) gritar, vociferar; (*weep*) berrear
bay [beɪ] (*inlet*) bahía *f*
BC [biː'siː] (= ***before Christ***) A.C. (= antes de Cristo)
be [biː] ◇ *permanent characteristics, profession, nationality* ser; *position, temporary condition* estar; ***there is, there are*** hay; ◇ ***has the mailman been?*** ¿ha venido el cartero?; ***I've never been to Japan*** no he estado en Japón; ◇ *tags*: ***that's right, isn't it?*** eso es, ¿no?; ***she's Chinese, isn't she?*** es china, ¿verdad? ◇ *passive*: ***he was arrested*** fue detenido, lo detuvieron
beach [biːtʃ] playa *f*; **beachwear** ropa *f* playera
beads [biːdz] cuentas *fpl*
beak [biːk] pico *m*
beam [biːm] **1** *n in ceiling etc* viga *f* **2** *v/i* (*smile*) sonreír de oreja a oreja
bean [biːn] judía *f*, alubia *f*, *L.Am.* frijol *m*, *S.Am.* poroto *m*
bear[1] [ber] *n animal* oso(-a) *m(f)*
bear[2] [ber] *v/t weight* resistir;

costs correr con; (*tolerate*) soportar; **bearable** soportable
beard [bɪrd] barba *f*
beat [biːt] **1** *n of heart* latido *m*; *of music* ritmo *m* **2** *v/i of heart* latir; *of rain* golpear **3** *v/t in competition* derrotar, ganar a; (*hit*) pegar a; (*pound*) golpear
◆ **beat up** dar una paliza a
beaten ['biːtən]: ***off the ~ track*** retirado; **beating** *physical* paliza *f*; **beat-up** F destartalado F
beautiful ['bjuːtɪfl] bonito, precioso, *L.Am.* lindo; *smell, taste, meal* delicioso, *L.Am.* rico; *vacation* estupendo; **beautifully** *cooked, done* perfectamente; **beauty** belleza *f*
beaver ['biːvər] castor *m*
because [bɪ'kɑːz] porque; ***~ of*** debido a, a causa de
become [bɪ'kʌm] hacerse, volverse; ***it became clear that ...*** quedó claro que...; ***what's ~ of her?*** ¿qué fue de ella?; **becoming** favorecedor
bed [bed] cama *f*; *of flowers* macizo; *of sea* fondo *m*; *of river* cauce *m*; ***go to ~*** ir a la cama; **bedding** ropa *f* de cama; **bedridden: *be ~*** estar postrado en cama; **bedroom** dormitorio *m*, *L.Am.* cuarto *m*; **bedtime** hora *f* de irse a la cama
bee [biː] abeja *f*
beech [biːʧ] haya *f*
beef [biːf] carne *f* de vaca; **beefburger** hamburguesa *f*
beep [biːp] **1** *n* pitido *m* **2** *v/i* pitar
beer [bɪr] cerveza *f*
beet [biːt] remolacha *f*
beetle ['biːtl] escarabajo *m*
before [bɪ'fɔːr] **1** *prep* antes de **2** *adv* antes; ***I've seen this movie ~*** ya he visto esta película; ***the week ~*** la semana anterior **3** *conj* antes de que; **beforehand** de antemano
befriend [bɪ'frend] hacerse amigo de
beg [beg] **1** *v/i* mendigar, pedir **2** *v/t*: ***~ s.o. to do sth*** suplicar a alguien que haga algo; **beggar** mendigo(-a) *m(f)*
begin [bɪ'gɪn] empezar, comenzar (***to do*** a hacer); **beginner** principiante *m/f*; **beginning** principio *m*, comienzo *m*; (*origin*) origen *m*
behalf [bɪ'hɑːf]: ***on ~ of*** en nombre de
behave [bɪ'heɪv] comportarse, portarse; ***~ (yourself)!*** ¡pórtate bien!; **behavior,** *Br* **behaviour** comportamiento *m*, conducta *f*
behind [bɪ'haɪnd] **1** *prep* detrás de; ***be ~ ...*** (*responsible*) estar detrás de...; (*support*) respaldar... **2** *adv* (*at the back*) detrás; ***leave sth ~*** dejarse algo
beige [beɪʒ] beige, *Span* beis
being ['biːɪŋ] ser *m*
belated [bɪ'leɪtɪd] tardío

belch [beltʃ] **1** *n* eructo *m* **2** *v/i* eructar
Belgian ['beldʒən] **1** *adj* belga **2** *n* belga *m/f*; **Belgium** Bélgica
belief [bɪ'li:f] creencia *f*; **believe** creer
◆ **believe in** creer en
believer [bɪ'li:vər] REL creyente *m/f*; *fig* partidario(-a) *m(f)* (**in** de)
Belize [be'li:z] Belice
bell [bel] timbre *m*; *of church* campana *f*; **bellhop** botones *m inv*
belligerent [bɪ'lɪdʒərənt] beligerante
bellow ['belou] bramar
belly ['belɪ] estómago *m*; *fat* barriga *f*; *of animal* panza *f*
◆ **belong to** pertenecer a
belongings [bɪ'lɒ:ŋɪŋz] pertenencias *fpl*
beloved [bɪ'lʌvɪd] querido
below [bɪ'lou] **1** *prep* debajo de; *in amount, level* por debajo de **2** *adv* abajo; *in text* más abajo; ***10 degrees ~*** 10 grados bajo cero
belt [belt] cinturón *m*
benchmark ['bentʃmɑ:rk] punto *m* de referencia
bend [bend] **1** *n* curva *f* **2** *v/t* doblar **3** *v/i* torcer, girar; *of person* flexionarse
◆ **bend down** agacharse
beneath [bɪ'ni:θ] **1** *prep* debajo de **2** *adv* abajo
benefactor ['benɪfæktər] benefactor(a) *m(f)*
beneficial [benɪ'fɪʃl] beneficioso
benefit ['benɪfɪt] **1** *n* beneficio *m* **2** *v/t* beneficiar **3** *v/i* beneficiarse
benevolent [bɪ'nevələnt] benevolente
benign [bɪ'naɪn] agradable; MED benigno
bequeath [bɪ'kwi:ð] *also fig* legar; **bequest** legado *m*
beret [bə'reɪ] boina *f*
berry ['berɪ] baya *f*
berth [bɜ:rθ] *on ship* litera *f*; *on train* camarote *m*; *for ship* amarradero *m*
beside [bɪ'saɪd] al lado de; ***be ~ o.s.*** estar fuera de sí; ***that's ~ the point*** eso no tiene nada que ver
besides [bɪ'saɪdz] **1** *adv* además **2** *prep* (*apart from*) además de
best [best] **1** *adj & adv* mejor; ***which did you like ~?*** ¿cuál te gustó más? **2** *n*: ***do one's ~*** hacer todo lo posible; ***the ~*** el / la mejor; ***all the ~!*** ¡que te vaya bien!; **best before date** fecha *f* de caducidad; **best man** *at wedding* padrino *m*
bet [bet] **1** *n* apuesta *f* **2** *v/t & v/i* apostar; ***you ~!*** ¡ya lo creo!
betray [bɪ'treɪ] traicionar; *husband, wife* engañar; **betrayal** traición *f*; *of husband, wife* engaño *m*
better ['betər] **1** *adj & adv* mejor; ***get ~*** mejorar; ***I'd really ~ not*** mejor no; ***I like her ~***

me gusta más ella; **better-off** (*wealthier*) más rico
between [bɪ'twiːn] entre
beware [bɪ'wer]: **~ *of*** tener cuidado con
bewilder [bɪ'wɪldər] desconcertar; **bewilderment** desconcierto *m*
beyond [bɪ'jɑːnd] más allá de
bias ['baɪəs] *against* prejuicio *m*; *in favor* favoritismo *m*; **bias(s)ed** parcial
Bible ['baɪbl] Biblia *f*; **biblical** bíblico
bicentennial [baɪsen'tenɪəl] bicentenario *m*
bicker ['bɪkər] reñir, discutir
bicycle ['baɪsɪkl] bicicleta *f*
bid [bɪd] **1** *n at auction* puja *f*; (*attempt*) intento *m* **2** *v/i at auction* pujar; **bidder** postor(a) *m*(*f*)
biennial [baɪ'enɪəl] bienal
big [bɪg] **1** *adj* grande; *before singular nouns* gran; ***my ~ brother* / *sister*** mi hermano / hermana mayor **2** *adv*: ***talk ~*** alardear
bigamist ['bɪgəmɪst] bígamo(-a) *m*(*f*)
'bighead F creído(-a) *m*(*f*) F
bigot ['bɪgət] fanático(-a) *m*(*f*), intolerante *m*/*f*
bike [baɪk] F bici *f* F; *motorbike* moto *f* F; **biker** motero(-a) *m*(*f*)
bikini [bɪ'kiːnɪ] biquini *m*
bilingual [baɪ'lɪŋgwəl] bilingüe
bill [bɪl] *for gas, electricity* factura *f*; (*money*) billete *m*; POL proyecto *m* de ley; (*poster*) cartel *m*; *Br in restaurant etc* cuenta *f*; **billboard** valla *f* publicitaria; **billfold** cartera *f*, billetera *f*
billion ['bɪljən] mil millones *mpl*, millardo *m*
bin [bɪn] cubo *m*
bind [baɪnd] (*connect*) unir; (*tie*) atar; LAW obligar; **binding** *agreement* vinculante
binoculars [bɪ'nɑːkjʊlərz] prismáticos *mpl*
biodegradable [baɪoʊdɪ'greɪdəbl] biodegradable
biographer [baɪ'ɑːgrəfər] biógrafo(-a) *m*(*f*); **biography** biografía *f*
biological [baɪoʊ'lɑːdʒɪkl] biológico; **biology** biología *f*
bird [bɜːrd] ave *f*, pájaro *m*
biro® ['baɪroʊ] *Br* bolígrafo *m*, *Mex* pluma *f*, *Rpl* birome *m*
birth [bɜːrθ] nacimiento *m*; (*labor*) parto *m*; ***give ~ to*** *child* dar a luz; *of animal* parir; ***date of ~*** fecha *f* de nacimiento; **birth certificate** partida *f* de nacimiento; **birth control** control *m* de natalidad; **birthday** cumpleaños *m inv*; ***happy ~!*** ¡feliz cumpleaños!
biscuit ['bɪskɪt] bollo *m*, panecillo *m*; *Br* galleta *f*
bisexual ['baɪsekʃʊəl] **1** *adj* bisexual **2** *n* bisexual *m*/*f*
bishop ['bɪʃəp] obispo *m*
bit [bɪt] (*piece*) trozo *m*; (*part*) parte *f*; *of puzzle* pieza *f*; COMPUT bit *m*; ***a ~ of*** (*a little*)

un poco de

bitch [bɪtʃ] **1** *n dog* perra *f*; F *woman* zorra *f* F **2** *v/i* F (*complain*) quejarse

bite [baɪt] **1** *n of dog* mordisco *m*; *of mosquito, snake* picadura *f*; *of food* bocado *m* **2** *v/t & v/i of dog* morder; *of mosquito, flea, snake* picar

bitter ['bɪtər] amargo; *person* resentido

black [blæk] **1** *adj* negro; *coffee* solo; *tea* sin leche **2** *n* (*color*) negro *m*; (*person*) negro(-a) *m*(*f*)

◆ **black out** (*faint*) perder el conocimiento

'**blackboard** pizarra *f*, encerado *m*; **black coffee** café *m* solo; **black economy** economía *f* sumergida; **black eye** ojo *m* morado; **blacklist** lista *f* negra; **blackmail 1** *n* chantaje *m* **2** *v/t* chantajear; **black market** mercado *m* negro; **blackness** oscuridad *f*; **blackout** ELEC apagón *m*; MED desmayo *m*

bladder ['blædər] vejiga *f*

blade [bleɪd] hoja *f*; *of propeller* pala *f*; *of grass* brizna *f*

blame [bleɪm] **1** *n* culpa *f* **2** *v/t* culpar

bland [blænd] *smile* insulso; *food* insípido

blank [blæŋk] **1** *adj* (*not written on*) en blanco; *tape* virgen; *look* inexpresivo **2** *n* (*empty space*) espacio *m* en blanco; **blank check,** *Br* **blank cheque** cheque *m* en blanco

blanket ['blæŋkɪt] manta *f*, *L.Am.* frazada *f*

blast [blæst] **1** *n* (*explosion*) explosión *f*; (*gust*) ráfaga *f* **2** *v/t tunnel* abrir (con explosivos); *rock* volar; **~!** F ¡mecachis! F; **blast-off** despegue *m*

blatant ['bleɪtənt] descarado

blaze [bleɪz] **1** *n* (*fire*) incendio *m* **2** *v/i of fire* arder

blazer ['bleɪzər] americana *f*

bleach [bliːtʃ] **1** *n for clothes* lejía *f*; *for hair* decolorante *m* **2** *v/t hair* aclarar, desteñir

bleak [bliːk] *countryside* inhóspito; *weather* desapacible; *future* desolador

bleary-eyed ['blɪrɪaɪd] con ojos de sueño

bleat [bliːt] *of sheep* balar

bleed [bliːd] sangrar; **bleeding** hemorragia *f*

bleep [bliːp] **1** *n* pitido *m* **2** *v/i* pitar

blemish ['blemɪʃ] imperfección *f*

blend [blend] **1** *n of coffee etc* mezcla *f*; *fig* combinación *f* **2** *v/t* mezclar; **blender** *machine* licuadora *f*

bless [bles] bendecir; **~ *you!*** *in response to sneeze* ¡Jesús!; **blessing** bendición *f*

blind [blaɪnd] **1** *adj* ciego; *corner* sin visibilidad **2** *v/t of sun* cegar; **blind alley** callejón *m* sin salida; **blind date** cita *f* a ciegas; **blindfold 1** *n* venda *f* **2** *v/t* vendar los ojos a; **blind-**

ing *light* cegador; *headache* terrible; **blindly** a ciegas; *fig* ciegamente; **blind spot** *in road* punto *m* sin visibilidad; *in driving mirror* ángulo *m* muerto

blink [blɪŋk] parpadear

blizzard ['blɪzərd] ventisca *f*

bloc [blɑːk] POL bloque *m*

block [blɑːk] **1** *n* bloque *m*; *buildings* manzana *f*, *L.Am.* cuadra *f*; (*blockage*) bloqueo *m* **2** *v/t* bloquear; *sink* atascar; **blockage** obstrucción *f*; **blockbuster** gran éxito *m*; **block letters** letras *fpl* mayúsculas

blond [blɑːnd] rubio; **blonde** *woman* rubia *f*

blood [blʌd] sangre *f*; **blood donor** donante *m/f* de sangre; **blood group** grupo *m* sanguíneo; **blood poisoning** septicemia *f*; **blood pressure** tensión *f* (arterial); **blood sample** muestra *f* de sangre; **bloodshed** derramamiento *m* de sangre; **bloodshot** enrojecido; **bloodstained** ensangrentado; **blood test** análisis *m inv* de sangre; **bloodthirsty** sanguinario; *movie* macabro

bloom [bluːm] *also fig* florecer

blossom ['blɑːsəm] **1** *n* flores *fpl* **2** *v/i also fig* florecer

blot [blɑːt] mancha *f*

◆ **blot out** borrar; *sun*, *view* ocultar

blouse [blaʊz] blusa *f*

blow[1] [bloʊ] *n* golpe *m*

blow[2] [bloʊ] **1** *v/t smoke* exhalar; *whistle* tocar **2** *v/i of wind*, *person* soplar; *of whistle* sonar; *of fuse* fundirse; *of tire* reventarse

◆ **blow out 1** *v/t candle* apagar **2** *v/i of candle* apagarse

◆ **blow over 1** *v/t* derribar **2** *v/i* derrumbarse; *of storm* amainar; *of argument* calmarse

◆ **blow up 1** *v/t with explosives* volar; *balloon* hinchar; *photograph* ampliar **2** *v/i* explotar

'blow-dry secar (*con secador*); **blowout** *of tire* reventón *m*

blue [bluː] azul; F *movie* porno *inv* F; **blueberry** arándano *m*; **blue chip** puntero, de primera fila; **blues** MUS blues *m inv*; ***have the*** ~ estar deprimido

bluff [blʌf] **1** *n* (*deception*) farol *m* **2** *v/i* ir de farol

blunder ['blʌndər] error *m* de bulto

blunt [blʌnt] *pencil* sin punta; *knife* desafilado; *person* franco; **bluntly** francamente

blur [blɜːr] **1** *n* imagen *f* desenfocada **2** *v/t* desdibujar

◆ **blurt out** [blɜːrt] soltar

blush [blʌʃ] **1** *n* rubor *m* **2** *v/i* ruborizarse; **blusher** *cosmetic* colorete *m*

blustery ['blʌstərɪ] tempestuoso

BO [biː'oʊ] (= ***body odor***) olor *m* corporal

board [bɔːrd] **1** *n* tablón *m*, tabla *f*; *for game* tablero *m*; *for notices* tablón *m*; ~ **(of directors)** consejo *m* de administración; **on ~** a bordo **2** *v/t airplane etc* embarcar; *train* subir a **3** *v/i of passengers* embarcar

◆ **board up** cubrir con tablas

boarder ['bɔːrdər] *in house* huésped *m/f*; **board game** juego *m* de mesa; **boarding card** tarjeta *f* de embarque; **boarding school** internado *m*; **board meeting** reunión *f* del consejo de administración; **board room** sala *f* de reuniones *or* juntas

boast [boʊst] **1** *n* presunción *f* **2** *v/i* presumir (**about** de)

boat [boʊt] barco *m*; *small, for leisure* barca *f*

bodily ['bɑːdɪlɪ] **1** *adj* corporal; *needs* físico; *function* fisiológico **2** *adv eject* en volandas; **body** cuerpo *m*; *dead* cadáver *m*; **bodyguard** guardaespaldas *m/f inv*; **bodywork** MOT carrocería *f*

bogus ['boʊgəs] falso

boil[1] [bɔɪl] *n* (*swelling*) forúnculo

boil[2] [bɔɪl] **1** *v/t* hervir; *egg, vegetables* cocer **2** *v/i* hervir

◆ **boil down to** reducirse a

boiler ['bɔɪlər] caldera *f*

boisterous ['bɔɪstərəs] escandaloso

bold [boʊld] **1** *adj* valiente, audaz; *text* en negrita **2** *n print* negrita *f*

Bolivia [bə'lɪvɪə] Bolivia; **Bolivian 1** *adj* boliviano **2** *n* boliviano(-a) *m(f)*

bolster ['boʊlstər] *confidence* reforzar

bolt [boʊlt] **1** *n on door* cerrojo *m*; *with nut* perno *m* **2** *adv*: **~ upright** erguido **3** *v/t* (*fix with bolts*) atornillar; *close* cerrar con cerrojo **4** *v/i* (*run off*) fugarse

bomb [bɑːm] **1** *n* bomba *f* **2** *v/t* MIL bombardear; *of terrorist* poner una bomba en; **bombard** *also fig* bombardear; **bomb attack** atentado *m* con bomba; **bomber** bombardero *m*; *terrorist* terrorista *m/f* (*que pone bombas*); **bomb scare** amenaza *f* de bomba; **bombshell** *fig*: *news* bomba *f*

bond [bɑːnd] **1** *n* (*tie*) unión *f*; FIN bono *m* **2** *v/i of glue* adherirse

bone [boʊn] hueso *m*; *of fish* espina *f*

bonnet ['bɑːnɪt] *Br of car* capó *m*

bonus ['boʊnəs] *money* plus *m*, bonificación *f*; (*extra*) ventaja *f* adicional

boob [buːb] P (*breast*) teta *f* P

booboo ['buːbuː] F metedura *f* de pata

book [bʊk] **1** *n* libro *m* **2** *v/t* reservar; *of policeman* multar; **bookcase** estantería *f*, librería *f*; **booked up** lleno, completo; *person* ocupado; **bookie** F corredor(a) *m(f)* de apuestas; **booking** reserva *f*; **bookkeeper** tenedor(a) *m(f)* de libros; **bookkeeping** contabilidad *f*; **booklet** folleto *m*; **bookmaker** corredor(a) *m(f)* de apuestas; **books** (*accounts*) contabilidad *f*; **bookseller** librero(-a) *m(f)*; **bookstore** librería *f*

boom[1] [buːm] **1** *n* boom *m* **2** *v/i of business* experimentar un boom

boom[2] [buːm] *n noise* estruendo *m*

boost [buːst] **1** *n* impulso *m* **2** *v/t* estimular; *morale* levantar

boot [buːt] bota *f*; *Br of car* maletero *m*, *C.Am.*, *Mex* cajuela *f*, *Rpl* baúl *m*

◆ **boot up** COMPUT arrancar

booth [buːð] *at market* cabina *f*; *at exhibition* puesto *m*, stand *m*

booze [buːz] F bebida *f*, *Span* priva *f* F

border ['bɔːrdər] **1** *n* frontera *f*; (*edge*) borde *m* **2** *v/t country* limitar con

◆ **border on** limitar con; (*be almost*) rayar en

bore[1] [bɔːr] *v/t hole* taladrar

bore[2] [bɔːr] **1** *n person* pesado(-a) *m(f)* **2** *v/t* aburrir

bored [bɔːrd] aburrido; **boredom** aburrimiento *m*; **boring** aburrido

born [bɔːrn]: ***be ~*** nacer

borrow ['bɑːrou] tomar prestado

bosom ['buzm] pecho *m*

boss [bɑːs] jefe(-a) *m(f)*

◆ **boss around** dar órdenes a

bossy ['bɑːsɪ] mandón

botanical [bə'tænɪkl] botánico

botch [bɑːtʃ] arruinar

both [bouθ] **1** *adj & pron* ambos, los dos; ***~ of them*** ambos, los dos **2** *adv*: ***~ my mother and I*** tanto mi madre como yo

bother ['bɑːðər] **1** *n* molestias *fpl* **2** *v/t* (*disturb*) molestar; (*worry*) preocupar

bottle ['bɑːtl] botella *f*, *for baby* biberón *m*

◆ **bottle up** *feelings* reprimir

'bottle bank contenedor *m* de vidrio; **bottled water** agua *f* embotellada; **bottleneck** embotellamiento *m*; *in production* cuello *m* de botella; **bottle-opener** abrebotellas *m inv*

bottom ['bɑːtəm] **1** *adj* inferior, de abajo **2** *n of case*, *garden* fondo *m*; *of hill*, *page* pie *m*; *of pile* parte *f* inferior; (*underside*) parte *f* de abajo; *of street* final *m*; (*buttocks*) trasero *m*

◆ **bottom out** tocar fondo

bottom 'line *financial* saldo *m* final; (*real issue*) realidad *f*

boulder ['bouldər] roca *f* redondeada

bounce [bauns] **1** *v/t ball* botar **2** *v/i of ball* (re)botar; *of rain* rebotar; *of check* ser rechazado; **bouncer** portero

m, gorila *m*
bound[1] [baʊnd] *adj*: ***he's ~ to ...*** (*sure to*) seguro que…
bound[2] [baʊnd] *adj*: ***be ~ for*** *of ship* llevar destino a
bound[3] [baʊnd] *n* (*jump*) salto *m*
boundary ['baʊndərɪ] límite *m*; *of countries* frontera *f*
bouquet [bʊ'keɪ] ramo *m*
bourbon ['bɜːrbən] bourbon *m*
bout [baʊt] MED ataque *m*; *in boxing* combate *m*
bow[1] [baʊ] **1** *n as greeting* reverencia *f* **2** *v/i* saludar con la cabeza **3** *v/t head* inclinar
bow[2] [boʊ] *n* (*knot*) lazo *m*; MUS, *for archery* arco *m*
bow[3] [baʊ] *n of ship* proa *f*
bowels ['baʊəlz] entrañas *fpl*
bowl[1] [boʊl] *n for rice etc* cuenco *m*; *for soup* plato *m* sopero; *for salad* ensaladera *f*; *for washing* barreño *m*
bowl[2] [boʊl] **1** *n* (*ball*) bola *f* **2** *v/i in bowling* lanzar la bola
bowling ['boʊlɪŋ] bolos *mpl*; **bowling alley** bolera *f*
bow tie [boʊ] pajarita *f*
box[1] [bɑːks] *n* caja *f*; *on form* casilla *f*
box[2] [bɑːks] *v/i* boxear
boxer ['bɑːksər] boxeador(a) *m*(*f*); **boxing** boxeo *m*; **boxing glove** guante *m* de boxeo; **boxing match** combate *m* de boxeo
'box number *at post office* apartado *m* de correos; **box office** taquilla *f*, *L.Am.* boletería *f*
boy [bɔɪ] niño *m*, chico *m*
boycott ['bɔɪkɑːt] **1** *n* boicot *m* **2** *v/t* boicotear
'boyfriend novio *m*
bra [brɑː] sujetador *m*
bracelet ['breɪslɪt] pulsera *f*
bracket ['brækɪt] *for shelf* escuadra *f*
brag [bræg] fanfarronear
braid [breɪd] *in hair* trenza *f*; *trimming* trenzado *m*
braille [breɪl] braille *m*
brain [breɪn] cerebro *m*; **brainless** F estúpido; **brains** (*intelligence*) inteligencia *f*; **brain surgeon** neurocirujano(-a) *m*(*f*); **brain tumor,** *Br* **brain tumour** tumor *m* cerebral; **brainwash** lavar el cerebro a
brake [breɪk] **1** *n* freno *m* **2** *v/i* frenar
branch [bræntʃ] *of tree* rama *f*; *of company* sucursal *f*
brand [brænd] **1** *n* marca *f* **2** *v/t*: ***be ~ed a liar*** ser tildado de mentiroso; **brand image** imagen *f* de marca
brandish ['brændɪʃ] blandir
brand 'leader marca *f* líder del mercado; **brand name** nombre *m* comercial; **brand-new** nuevo, flamante
brandy ['brændɪ] brandy *m*
brassière [brə'zɪr] sujetador *m*, sostén *m*
brat [bræt] *pej* niñato(-a) *m*(*f*)
brave [breɪv] valiente, valeroso; **bravery** valentía *f*, valor

m

brawl [brɒːl] **1** *n* pelea *f* **2** *v/i* pelearse

Brazil [brə'zɪl] Brasil; **Brazilian 1** *adj* brasileño **2** *n* brasileño(-a) *m(f)*

breach [briːʧ] (*violation*) infracción *f m*; *in party* ruptura *f*; **breach of contract** incumplimiento *m* de contrato

bread [bred] pan *m*

breadth [bredθ] ancho *m*; *of knowledge* amplitud *f*

'**breadwinner:** ***be the ~*** ser el que gana el pan

break [breɪk] **1** *n* fractura *f*, rotura *f*; (*rest*) descanso *m* **2** *v/t also promise* romper; *rules*, *law* violar; *news* dar; *record* batir **3** *v/i* romperse; *of news* saltar; *of storm* estallar

◆ **break down 1** *v/i of vehicle* averiarse, estropearse; *of machine* estropearse; *of talks* romperse; *in tears* romper a llorar; *mentally* venirse abajo **2** *v/t door* derribar; *figures* desglosar

◆ **break even** cubrir gastos

◆ **break in** (*interrupt*) interrumpir; *of burglar* entrar

◆ **break up 1** *v/t into parts* descomponer; *fight* poner fin a **2** *v/i of ice* romperse; *of couple*, *band* separarse; *of meeting* terminar

breakable ['breɪkəbl] rompible, frágil; **breakage** rotura *f*; **breakdown** *of vehicle*, *machine* avería *f*; *of talks* ruptura *f*; (*nervous*) crisis *f inv* nerviosa; *of figures* desglose *m*

breakfast ['brekfəst] desayuno *m*; ***have ~*** desayunar

'**break-in** entrada *f* (*mediante la fuerza*); *robbery* robo *m*; **breakthrough** *in negotiations* paso *m* adelante; *of technology* avance *m*; **breakup** *of partnership* ruptura *f*, separación *f*

breast [brest] pecho *m*; **breastfeed** amamantar; **breaststroke** braza *f*

breath [breθ] respiración *f*; ***be out of ~*** estar sin respiración

breathe [briːð] respirar

◆ **breathe in** aspirar, inspirar

◆ **breathe out** espirar

breathing ['briːðɪŋ] respiración *f*

breathtaking ['breθteɪkɪŋ] impresionante

breed [briːd] **1** *n* raza *f* **2** *v/t* criar; *plants* cultivar; *fig* causar **3** *v/i of animals* reproducirse; **breeding** *of animals* cría *f*; *of person* educación *f*

breeze [briːz] brisa *f*; **breezy** ventoso

brew [bruː] **1** *v/t beer* elaborar **2** *v/i of storm* avecinarse; *of trouble* fraguarse; **brewery** fábrica *f* de cerveza

bribe [braɪb] **1** *n* soborno *m*, *Mex* mordida *f*, *S.Am.* coima *f* **2** *v/t* sobornar; **bribery** soborno *m*, *Mex* mordida *f*, *S.Am.* coima *f*

brick [brɪk] ladrillo *m*

bride [braɪd] novia *f* (*en boda*); **bridegroom** novio *m* (*en*

boda); **bridesmaid** dama *f* de honor
bridge [brɪdʒ] **1** *n also* NAUT puente *m* **2** *v/t gap* superar
bridle [braɪdl] brida *f*
brief[1] [bri:f] *adj* breve, corto
brief[2] [bri:f] **1** *n* (*mission*) misión *f* **2** *v/t*: **~ *s.o. on sth*** informar a alguien de algo
'briefcase maletín *m*; **briefing** reunión *f* informativa; **briefly** brevemente; (*in few words*) en pocas palabras; (*to sum up*) en resumen; **briefs** *for women* bragas *fpl*; *for men* calzoncillos *mpl*
bright [braɪt] *color* vivo; *smile* radiante; (*sunny*) luminoso; (*intelligent*) inteligente; **brightly** *shine* intensamente; *smile* alegremente
brilliance ['brɪljəns] *of person* genialidad *f*; *of color* resplandor *m*; **brilliant** *sunshine etc* resplandeciente; (*very good*) genial; (*very intelligent*) brillante
brim [brɪm] *of container* borde *m*; *of hat* ala *f*
bring [brɪŋ] traer
◆ **bring back** (*return*) devolver; (*re-introduce*) reinstaurar; *memories* traer
◆ **bring down** *government* derrocar; *airplane* derribar; *price* reducir
◆ **bring on** *illness* provocar
◆ **bring out** *product* sacar
◆ **bring up** *child* criar; *subject* mencionar; (*vomit*) vomitar
brink [brɪŋk] borde *m*
brisk [brɪsk] *person* enérgico; *walk* rápido; *trade* animado
bristles ['brɪslz] *on chin* pelos *mpl*; *of brush* cerdas *fpl*
Britain ['brɪtn] Gran Bretaña; **British 1** *adj* británico **2** *npl*: ***the ~*** los británicos
brittle ['brɪtl] frágil
broach [broʊtʃ] broche *m*
broad [brɒ:d] **1** *adj* ancho; *smile* amplio; (*general*) general **2** *n* F (*woman*) tía *f* F; ***in ~ daylight*** a plena luz del día; **broadcast 1** *n* emisión *f* **2** *v/t* emitir; **broadcaster** presentador(a) *m(f)*; **broadjump** salto *m* de longitud; **broadly** en general; **broadminded** tolerante, abierto
broccoli ['brɑ:kəlɪ] brécol *m*, brócoli *m*
brochure ['broʊʃər] folleto *m*
broil [brɔɪl] asar a la parrilla; **broiler** *on stove* parrilla *f*; *chicken* pollo *m* (para asar)
broke [broʊk] F: ***be ~*** estar sin blanca F; *long-term* estar arruinado; **broken** *adj* roto; *home* deshecho; **broker** corredor(a) *m(f)*
bronchitis [brɑ:ŋ'kaɪtɪs] bronquitis *f*
bronze [brɑ:nz] bronce *m*
brooch [broʊtʃ] *Br* broche *m*
brothel ['brɑ:θl] burdel *m*
brother ['brʌðər] hermano *m*; **brother-in-law** cuñado *m*; **brotherly** fraternal
brow [braʊ] (*forehead*) frente *f*; *of hill* cima *f*
brown [braʊn] **1** *n* marrón *m*,

L.Am. color *m* café **2** *adj* marrón; *eyes, hair* castaño; (*tanned*) moreno; **brownie** (*cake*) pastel *m* de chocolate y nueces; **brown paper bag** bolsa *f* de cartón

browse [braʊz] *in store* echar una ojeada; COMPUT navegar; **browser** COMPUT navegador *m*

bruise [bru:z] magulladura *f*, cardenal *f*; *on fruit* maca *f*

brunette [bru:'net] morena *f*

brush [brʌʃ] **1** *n* cepillo *m*; *conflict* roce *m* **2** *v/t* cepillar; (*touch lightly*) rozar

◆ **brush aside** hacer caso omiso a

◆ **brush up** repasar

brusque [brʊsk] brusco

brutal ['bru:tl] brutal; **brutality** brutalidad *f*; **brutally** brutalmente; **brute** bestia *m/f*

bubble ['bʌbl] burbuja *f*

buck[1] [bʌk] *n* F (*dollar*) dólar *m*

buck[2] [bʌk] *v/i of horse* corcovear

bucket ['bʌkɪt] cubo *m*

buckle[1] ['bʌkl] **1** *n* hebilla *f* **2** *v/t belt* abrochar

buckle[2] ['bʌkl] *v/i of metal* combarse

bud [bʌd] BOT capullo *m*

buddy ['bʌdɪ] F amigo(-a) *m(f)*

budge [bʌdʒ] **1** *v/t* mover **2** *v/i* moverse

budget ['bʌdʒɪt] presupuesto *m*

buff [bʌf] aficionado(-a) *m(f)*

buffalo ['bʌfəloʊ] búfalo *m*

buffer ['bʌfər] RAIL tope *m*; COMPUT búfer *m*; *fig* barrera *f*

buffet ['bʊfeɪ] *meal* bufé *m*

bug [bʌg] **1** *n insect* bicho *m*; *virus* virus *m inv*; (*for spying*) micrófono *m* oculto; COMPUT error *m* **2** *v/t room* colocar un micrófono en; F (*annoy*) fastidiar F

buggy ['bʌgɪ] *for baby* silla *f* de paseo

build [bɪld] **1** *n of person* constitución *f* **2** *v/t* construir

◆ **build up** **1** *v/t strength* aumentar; *relationship* fortalecer **2** *v/i of dirt* acumularse; *of pressure etc* aumentar

builder ['bɪldər] albañil *m/f*; *company* constructora *f*; **building** edificio *m*; *activity* construcción *f*; **building site** obra *f*; **building society** *Br* caja *f* de ahorros; **building trade** industria *f* de la construcción; **build-up** accumulación *f*; ***after all the ~*** *publicity* después de tantas expectativas; **built-in** *cupboard* empotrado; *flash* incorporado

bulb [bʌlb] BOT bulbo *m*; (*light ~*) bombilla *f*, *L.Am.* foco *m*

bulge [bʌldʒ] **1** *n* bulto *m* **2** *v/i of wall* abombarse

bulky ['bʌlkɪ] voluminoso

bull [bʊl] *animal* toro *m*; **bulldozer** bulldozer *m*

bullet ['bʊlɪt] bala *f*
bulletin ['bʊlɪtɪn] boletín *m*; **bulletin board** tablón *m* de anuncios
'**bullet-proof** antibalas *inv*
'**bull fight** corrida *f* de toros; **bull fighter** torero(-a) *m*(*f*); **bull fighting** tauromaquia *f*, los toros; **bull ring** plaza *f* de toros; **bull's-eye** diana *f*, blanco *m*; **bullshit** *n* V *Span* gilipollez *f* V, *L.Am.* pendejada *f* V
bully ['bʊlɪ] **1** *n* matón(-ona) *m*(*f*); *child* abusón(-ona) *m*(*f*) **2** *v/t* intimidar; **bullying** intimidación *f*
bum [bʌm] F **1** *n* (*tramp*) vagabundo(-a) *m*(*f*); (*worthless person*) inútil *m/f* **2** *v/t cigarette etc* gorronear
bump [bʌmp] **1** *n* (*swelling*) chichón *m*; *on road* bache *m* **2** *v/t* golpear; **bumper** MOT parachoques *m inv*; **bumpy** con baches; *flight* movido
bunch [bʌntʃ] *of people* grupo *m*; *of keys* manojo *m*; *of flowers* ramo *m*; *of grapes* racimo *m*; ***thanks a ~ iron*** no sabes lo que te lo agradezco
bungle ['bʌŋgl] echar a perder
bunk [bʌŋk] litera *f*
buoy [bɔɪ] NAUT boya *f*; **buoyant** optimista; *economy* boyante
burden ['bɜːrdn] **1** *n also fig* carga *f* **2** *v/t*: ***~ s.o. with sth*** *fig* cargar a alguien con algo
bureau ['bjʊroʊ] (*chest of drawers*) cómoda *f*; (*office*) departamento *m*, oficina *f*; **bureaucrat** burócrata *m/f*; **bureaucratic** burocrático
burger ['bɜːrgər] hamburguesa *f*
burglar ['bɜːrglər] ladrón (-ona) *m*(*f*); **burglar alarm** alarma *f* antirrobo; **burglarize** robar; **burglary** robo *m*
burial ['berɪəl] entierro *m*
burn [bɜːrn] **1** *n* quemadura *f* **2** *v/t* quemar **3** *v/i* quemarse
◆ **burn down** **1** *v/t* incendiar **2** *v/i* incendiarse
burp [bɜːrp] **1** *n* eructo *m* **2** *v/i* eructar
burst [bɜːrst] **1** *n in pipe* rotura *f* **2** *adj tire* reventado **3** *v/t & v/i* reventar; ***~ into tears*** echarse a llorar; ***~ out laughing*** echarse a reír
bus [bʌs] *local* autobús *m*, *Mex* camión *m*, *Arg* colectivo *m*, *C.Am.* guagua *f*; *long distance* autobús *m*, *Span* autocar *m*
bush [bʊʃ] *plant* arbusto *m*; **bushy** *beard* espeso
business ['bɪznɪs] negocios *mpl*; (*company*) empresa *f*; (*sector*) sector *m*; (*affair, matter*) asunto *m*; *as subject of study* empresariales *fpl*; ***on ~*** de negocios; ***mind your own ~!*** ¡no te metas en lo que no te importa!; **business card** tarjeta *f* de visita; **business class** clase *f* eje-

cutiva; **businesslike** eficiente; **businessman** hombre *m* de negocios; **business meeting** reunión *f* de negocios; **business school** escuela *f* de negocios; **business studies** empresariales *mpl*; **business trip** viaje *m* de negocios; **businesswoman** mujer *f* de negocios, ejecutiva *f*

bust[1] [bʌst] *n of woman* busto *m*

bust[2] [bʌst] *adj* F (*broken*) escacharrado F

'bus station estación *f* de autobuses; **bus stop** parada *f* de autobús

'bust-up F corte *m* F; **busty** pechugona

busy ['bɪzɪ] *also* TELEC ocupado; *full of people* abarrotado; *restaurant etc: making money* ajetreado; **busybody** metomentodo *m/f*

but [bʌt] **1** *conj* pero **2** *prep*: ***all ~ him*** todos excepto él; ***the last ~ one*** el penúltimo; ***~ for you*** si no hubiera sido por ti

butcher ['bʊtʃər] carnicero(-a) *m(f)*

butt [bʌt] **1** *n of cigarette* colilla *f*; F (*buttocks*) trasero *m* F **2** *v/t of bull* embestir

butter ['bʌtər] mantequilla *f*; **butterfly** mariposa *f*

buttocks ['bʌtəks] nalgas *fpl*

button ['bʌtn] botón *m*; (*badge*) chapa *f*

buy [baɪ] comprar

◆ **buy out** COM comprar la parte de

buyer ['baɪr] comprador(a) *m(f)*

buzz [bʌz] **1** *n* zumbido *m* **2** *v/i of insect* zumbar; **buzzer** timbre *m*

by [baɪ] *to show agent* por; (*near, next to*) al lado de, junto a; (*no later than*) no más tarde de; *mode of transport* en; ***~ day*** de día; ***~ bus*** en autobús; ***~ my watch*** en mi reloj; ***a play ~ ...*** una obra de...; ***~ o.s.*** *without company* solo

bye(-bye) [baɪ] adiós

'bypass circunvalación *f*; MED bypass *m*; **by-product** subproducto *m*; **bystander** transeúnte *m/f*

C

cab [kæb] taxi *m*; *of truck* cabina *f*; **cab driver** taxista *m/f*

cabin ['kæbɪn] *of plane* cabina *f*; *of ship* camarote *m*; **cabin attendant** auxiliar *m/f* de vuelo; **cabin crew** personal *m* de a bordo

cabinet ['kæbɪnɪt] armario *m*; POL gabinete *m*

cable ['keɪbl] cable *m*; **cable car** teleférico *m*; **cable television** televisión *f* por cable

'cab stand parada *f* de taxis
cactus ['kæktəs] cactus *m inv*
cadaver [kə'dævər] cadáver *m*
caddie ['kædɪ] *in golf* caddie *m/f*
Caesarean *Br* ☞ ***Cesarean***
café ['kæfeɪ] café *m*; **cafeteria** cafetería *f*, cantina *f*
caffeine ['kæfi:n] cafeína *f*
cage [keɪdʒ] jaula *f*; **cagey** cauteloso
cake [keɪk] tarta *f*; *small* pastel *m*
calculate ['kælkjʊleɪt] calcular; **calculating** calculador; **calculation** cálculo *m*; **calculator** calculadora *f*
calendar ['kælɪndər] calendario *m*
calf[1] [kæf] *of cow* ternero(-a) *m(f)*
calf[2] [kæf] *of leg* pantorrilla *f*
caliber, *Br* **calibre** ['kælɪbər] *of gun* calibre *m*
call [kɒ:l] **1** *n* llamada *f*; (*demand*) llamamiento *m* **2** *v/t also* TELEC llamar; *meeting* convocar; ***be ~ ed ...*** llamarse… **3** *v/i also* TELEC llamar; (*visit*) pasarse
◆ **call back 1** *v/t* (*phone again*) volver a llamar; (*return call*) devolver la llamada; (*summon*) hacer volver **2** *v/i on phone* volver a llamar; (*make another visit*) volver a pasar
◆ **call for** (*collect*) pasar a recoger; (*demand*) pedir, exigir; (*require*) requerir
◆ **call off** cancelar
caller ['kɒ:lər] *on phone* persona *f* que llama; (*visitor*) visitante *m/f*
callous ['kæləs] cruel
calm [kɑ:m] **1** *adj* tranquilo; *weather* apacible **2** *n* calma *f*
◆ **calm down 1** *v/t* calmar **2** *v/i* calmarse
calmly ['kɑ:mlɪ] con calma, tranquilamente
calorie ['kælərɪ] caloría *f*
camcorder ['kæmkɔ:rdər] videocámara *f*
camera ['kæmərə] cámara *f*; **cameraman** cámara *m*, camarógrafo *m*
camouflage ['kæməflɑ:ʒ] **1** *n* camuflaje *m* **2** *v/t* camuflar
camp [kæmp] **1** *n* campamento *m* **2** *v/i* acampar
campaign [kæm'peɪn] **1** *n* campaña *f* **2** *v/i* hacer campaña (***for*** a favor de)
camper ['kæmpər] campista *m/f*; *vehicle* autocaravana *f*; **camping** campada *f*; *on campsite* camping *m*; **campsite** camping *m*
campus ['kæmpəs] campus *m*
can[1] [kæn] *v/aux* poder; ***~ you swim?*** ¿sabes nadar?; ***~ you hear me?*** ¿me oyes?; ***~ I have a beer?*** ¿me pones una cerveza?
can[2] [kæn] *n for drinks etc* lata *f*
Canada ['kænədə] Canadá; **Canadian 1** *adj* canadiense **2** *n* canadiense *m/f*
canal [kə'næl] *waterway* canal

m

Canary Islands, Canaries [kə'neriz]: ***the ~*** las Islas Canarias

cancel ['kænsl] cancelar; **cancellation** cancelación *f*

cancer ['kænsər] cáncer *m*

candid ['kændɪd] sincero

candidacy ['kændɪdəsɪ] candidatura *f*; **candidate** candidato(-a) *m(f)*

candle ['kændl] vela *f*

candor, *Br* **candour** ['kændər] sinceridad *f*

candy ['kændɪ] (*sweet*) caramelo *m*; (*sweets*) dulces *mpl*

cane [keɪn] caña *f*

canister ['kænɪstər] bote *m*

canned [kænd] enlatado, en lata; (*recorded*) grabado

cannot ['kænɑːt] ☞ ***can not***

canny ['kænɪ] (*astute*) astuto

canoe [kə'nuː] canoa *f*, piragua *f*

'can opener abrelatas *m inv*

can't [kænt] = ***can not***

canteen [kæn'tiːn] *in plant* cantina *f*, cafetería *f*

canvas ['kænvəs] *for painting* lienzo *m*; *material* lona *f*

canyon ['kænjən] cañón *m*

cap [kæp] *hat* gorro *m*; *with peak* gorra *f*

capability [keɪpə'bɪlətɪ] capacidad *f*; **capable** capaz

capacity capacidad *f*; *of engine* cilindrada *f*

capital ['kæpɪtl] *city* capital *f*; *letter* mayúscula *f*; *money* capital *m*; **capitalism** capitalismo *m*; **capitalist 1** *adj* capitalista **2** *n* capitalista *m/f*; **capital punishment** pena *f* capital

capsize [kæp'saɪz] volcar

capsule ['kæpsʊl] cápsula *f*

captain ['kæptɪn] capitán (-ana) *m(f)*; *of aircraft* comandante *m/f*

caption ['kæpʃn] pie *m* de foto

captivate ['kæptɪveɪt] cautivar; **captive 1** *adj* prisionero **2** *n* prisionero(-a) *m(f)*; **captivity** cautividad *f*; **capture 1** *n of city* toma *f*, *of criminal, animal* captura *f* **2** *v/t person, animal* capturar; *city, building* tomar; *market share* ganar

car [kɑːr] coche *m*, *L.Am.* carro *m*, *Rpl* auto *m*; *of train* vagón *m*; ***by ~*** en coche

carbon monoxide [kɑːrbənmən'ɑːksaɪd] monóxido *m* de carbono

carbureter, carburetor [kɑːrbʊ'retər] carburador *m*

carcass ['kɑːrkəs] cadáver *m*

card [kɑːrd] tarjeta *f*; (*post~*) (tarjeta *f*) postal *f*; (*playing ~*) carta *f*, naipe *m*; **cardboard** cartón *m*

cardiac ['kɑːrdɪæk] cardíaco

cardinal ['kɑːrdɪnl] REL cardenal *m*

care [ker] **1** *n* cuidado *m*; *medical* asistencia *f* médica; (*worry*) preocupación *f*; ***care of*** ☞ ***c/o***; ***take ~*** (*be cautious*) tener cuidado; ***take ~ of*** cuidar; (*deal with*) ocuparse de **2**

v/i preocuparse; ***I don't ~!*** ¡me da igual!

◆ **care about** preocuparse por

◆ **care for** (*look after*) cuidar

career [kə'rɪr] carrera *f*

careful ['kerfl] cuidadoso; ***be ~*** tener cuidado; **carefully** con cuidado; *worded etc* cuidadosamente; **careless** descuidado; **carelessly** descuidadamente

caress [kə'res] acariciar

'car ferry ferry *m*, transbordador *m*

cargo ['kɑːrgoʊ] cargamento *m*

Caribbean [kə'ɪbiən]: ***the ~*** el Caribe

caricature ['kærɪkətʃər] caricatura *f*

carnival ['kɑːrnɪvl] feria *f*

carpenter ['kɑːrpɪntər] carpintero(-a) *m(f)*

carpet ['kɑːrpɪt] alfombra *f*

'car phone teléfono *m* de coche; **carpool** *compartir el vehículo para ir al trabajo*; **car rental** alquiler *m* de automóviles

carrier ['kærɪər] *company* transportista *m*; *airline* línea *f* aérea; *of disease* portador(a) *m(f)*

carrot ['kærət] zanahoria *f*

carry ['kærɪ] **1** *v/t* llevar; *disease* ser portador de; *of ship, bus etc* transportar **2** *v/i of sound* oírse

◆ **carry on 1** *v/i* continuar **2** *v/t business* efectuar

◆ **carry out** *survey etc* llevar a cabo

cart [kɑːrt] carro *m*; *for shopping* carrito *m*

carton ['kɑːrtn] caja *f* de cartón; *for milk, cigarettes* cartón *m*

cartoon [kɑːr'tuːn] tira *f* cómica; *on TV* dibujos *mpl* animados

carve [kɑːrv] *meat* trinchar; *wood* tallar

case¹ [keɪs] *container* funda *f*; *of wine etc* caja *f*; *Br* (*suitcase*) maleta *f*

case² [keɪs] *instance, criminal,* MED caso *m*; LAW causa *f*; ***in ~ ...*** por si...; ***in any ~*** en cualquier caso

cash [kæʃ] **1** *n* efectivo *m* **2** *v/t check* hacer efectivo; **cash desk** caja *f*; **cash flow** flujo *m* de caja, cash-flow *m*; **cashier** *in store etc* cajero(-a) *m(f)*; **cashpoint** *Br* cajero *m* automático; **cash register** caja *f* registradora

casino [kə'siːnoʊ] casino *m*

casket ['kæskɪt] (*coffin*) ataúd *m*

casserole ['kæsəroʊl] *meal* guiso *m*; *container* cacerola *f*

cassette [kə'set] cinta *f*, casete *f*; **cassette player, cassette recorder** casete *m*

cast [kæst] **1** *n of play* reparto *m*; (*mold*) molde *m* **2** *v/t doubt* proyectar; *metal* fundir

Castilian [kæs'tɪlɪən] castellano

cast 'iron hierro *m* fundido
castle ['kæsl] castillo *m*
casual ['kæʒʊəl] (*chance*) casual; (*offhand*) despreocupado; (*not formal*) informal; **casually** *dressed* de manera informal; *say* a la ligera; **casualty** víctima *f*
cat [kæt] gato *m*
Catalan ['kætəlæn] catalán
catalog, *Br* **catalogue** ['kætəlɑːg] catálogo *m*
catalyst ['kætəlɪst] catalizador *m*
catastrophe [kə'tæstrəfɪ] catástrofe *f*; **catastrophic** catastrófico
catch [kæʧ] **1** *n* parada *f* (*sin que la pelota toque el suelo*); *of fish* captura *f*, (*lock*) cierre *m*; (*problem*) pega *f* **2** *v/t ball* agarrar, *Span* coger; *animal* atrapar; *escapee* capturar; (*get on*: *bus*, *train*) tomar, *Span* coger; (*not miss*: *bus*, *train*) alcanzar, *Span* coger; *fish* pescar; *illness* agarrar, *Span* coger; **catching** *also fig* contagioso; **catchy** pegadizo
categoric [kætə'gɑːrɪk] categórico; **category** categoría *f*
caterer ['keɪtərər] hostelero(-a) *m*(*f*)
cathedral [kə'θiːdrl] catedral *f*
Catholic ['kæθəlɪk] **1** *adj* católico **2** *n* católico(-a) *m*(*f*); **Catholicism** catolicismo *m*
cattle ['kætl] ganado *m*
cause [kɒːz] **1** *n* causa *f*; (*grounds*) motivo *m* **2** *v/t* causar, provocar
caution ['kɒːʃn] **1** *n* precaución *f* **2** *v/t* (*warn*) prevenir; **cautious** cauto, prudente; **cautiously** cautelosamente
cave [keɪv] cueva *f*
cavity ['kævətɪ] caries *f inv*
CD [siː'diː] (= ***compact disc***) CD *m* (= disco *m* compacto); **CD player** (reproductor *m* de) CD *m*; **CD-ROM** CD-ROM *m*
cease [siːs] **1** *v/i* cesar **2** *v/t* suspender; **cease-fire** alto *m* el fuego
ceiling ['siːlɪŋ] techo *m*; (*limit*) tope *m*
celebrate ['selɪbreɪt] **1** *v/i*: ***let's ~ with a bottle of champagne*** celebrémoslo con una botella de champán **2** *v/t* celebrar; **celebrated** célebre; **celebration** celebración *f*; **celebrity** celebridad *f*
cell [sel] *in prison*, *spreadsheet* celda *f*; BIO célula *f*
cellar ['selər] sótano *m*; *for wine* bodega *f*
cello ['ʧeloʊ] violonchelo *m*
cell phone, cellular phone ['seljələr] (teléfono *m*) móvil *m*, *L.Am.* (teléfono *m*) celular *m*
cement [sɪ'ment] cemento *m*
cemetery ['seməterɪ] cementerio *m*
censor ['sensər] censor(a) *m*(*f*)
census ['sensəs] censo *m*
cent [sent] céntimo *m*

centenary [sen'tiːnərɪ] centenario *m*
center ['sentər] **1** *n* centro *m* **2** *v/t* centrar
centigrade ['sentɪgreɪd] centígrado
centimeter, *Br* **centimetre** ['sentɪmiːter] centímetro *m*
central ['sentrəl] central; *location, apartment* céntrico; **Central America** Centroamérica, América Central; **Central American 1** *adj* centroamericano, de (la) América *f* Central **2** n centroamericano(-a) *m*(*f*); **central heating** calefacción *f* central; **centralize** centralizar; **central locking** MOT cierre *m* centralizado
centre *Br* ☞ ***center***
century ['sentʃərɪ] siglo *m*
CEO [siːiː'oʊ] (= ***Chief Executive Officer***) consejero(-a) *m*(*f*) delegado
ceramic [sɪ'ræmɪk] de cerámica
cereal ['sɪrɪəl] cereal *m*; *for breakfast* cereales *mpl*
ceremonial [serɪ'moʊnɪəl] **1** *adj* ceremonial **2** *n* ceremonial *m*; **ceremony** ceremonia *f*
certain ['sɜːrtn] (*sure*) seguro; (*particular*) cierto; **certainly** (*definitely*) claramente; (*of course*) por supuesto; **certainty** (*confidence*) certeza *f*; (*inevitability*) seguridad *f*
certificate [sər'tɪfɪkət] (*qualification*) título *m*; (*official paper*) certificado *m*
certified public accountant ['sɜːrtɪfaɪd] censor(a) *m*(*f*) jurado de cuentas; **certify** certificar
Cesarean [sɪ'zerɪən] cesárea *f*
CFO [siːef'oʊ] (= ***Chief Financial Officer***) director(-a) *m*(*f*) financiero(a)
chain [tʃeɪn] **1** *n also of hotels etc* cadena *f* **2** *v/t* encadenar
chair [tʃer] **1** *n* silla *f*; (*arm~*) sillón *m*; *at university* cátedra *f* **2** *v/t meeting* presidir; **chair lift** telesilla *f*; **chairman** presidente *m*; **chairmanship** presidencia *f*; **chairperson** presidente(-a) *m*(*f*)
chalk [tʃɒːk] tiza *f*; *in soil* creta *f*
challenge ['tʃælɪndʒ] **1** *n* (*difficulty*) desafío *m*; *in competition* ataque *m* **2** *v/t* desafiar; (*call into question*) cuestionar; **challenger** aspirante *m/f*; **challenging** *job* estimulante
Chamber of 'Commerce Cámara *f* de Comercio
champagne [ʃæm'peɪn] champán *m*
champion ['tʃæmpɪən] **1** *n* SP campeón(-ona) *m*(*f*) **2** *v/t cause* abanderar; **championship** campeonato *m*
chance [tʃæns] posibilidad *f*; (*opportunity*) oportunidad *f*; (*luck*) casualidad *f*; ***by ~*** por casualidad; ***take a ~*** correr el riesgo
change [tʃeɪndʒ] **1** *n* cambio

m; (*small coins*) suelto *m*; *from purchase* cambio *m*, *L.Am.* vuelto *m*; ***for a ~*** para variar **2** *v/t* cambiar **3** *v/i* cambiar; (*put on different clothes*) cambiarse; (*take different train / bus*) hacer transbordo; **changeover** transición *f* (***to*** a); **changing room** SP vestuario *m*; *in shop* probador *m*

channel ['ʧænl] canal *m*

chant [ʧænt] **1** *n* REL canto *m*; *of fans* cántico *m*; *of demonstrators* consigna *f* **2** *v/i* gritar **3** *v/t* corear

chaos ['keɪɑːs] caos *m*; **chaotic** caótico

chapel ['ʧæpl] capilla *f*

chapter ['ʧæptər] capítulo *m*

character ['kærɪktər] carácter *m*; *person, in book* personaje *m*; **characteristic 1** *n* característica *f* **2** *adj* característico; **characterize** (*be typical of*) caracterizar; (*describe*) describir

charge [ʧɑːrdʒ] **1** *n* (*fee*) tarifa *f*; LAW acusación *f*; ***free of ~*** gratis; ***be in ~*** estar a cargo **2** *v/t sum of money* cobrar; (*put on account*) pagar con tarjeta; LAW acusar (***with*** de); *battery* cargar **3** *v/i* (*attack*) cargar; **charge account** cuenta *f* de crédito; **charge card** tarjeta *f* de compra

charitable ['ʧærɪtəbl] de caridad; *person* caritativo; **charity** caridad *f*; *organization* entidad *f* benéfica

charm [ʧɑːrm] **1** *n* encanto *m*; *on bracelet etc* colgante *m* **2** *v/t* (*delight*) encantar; **charming** encantador

charred [ʧɑːrd] carbonizado

chart [ʧɑːrt] gráfico *m*; (*map*) carta *f* de navegación

charter flight ['ʧɑːrtər] vuelo *m* chárter

chase [ʧeɪs] **1** *n* persecución *f* **2** *v/t* perseguir

◆ **chase away** ahuyentar

chassis ['ʃæsɪ] *of car* chasis *m inv*

chat [ʧæt] **1** *n* charla *f* **2** *v/i* charlar; **chatline** party line *f*; **chat room** sala *f* de chat

chatter ['ʧætər] **1** *n* cháchara *f* **2** *v/i talk* parlotear; *of teeth* castañetear

chauffeur ['ʃoʊfər] chófer *m*, *L.Am.* chofer *m*

chauvinist ['ʃoʊvɪnɪst] (*male ~*) machista *m*

cheap [ʧiːp] barato; (*nasty*) chabacano; (*mean*) tacaño

cheat [ʧiːt] **1** *n* (*person*) tramposo(-a) *m(f)* **2** *v/t* engañar **3** *v/i in exam* copiar; *in cards etc* hacer trampa

check[1] [ʧek] **1** *adj shirt* a cuadros **2** *n* cuadro *m*

check[2] [ʧek] *n* FIN cheque *m*; *in restaurant etc* cuenta *f*

check[3] [ʧek] **1** *n to verify sth* comprobación *f* **2** *v/t* (*verify*) comprobar; *machinery* inspeccionar; *with a ~mark* poner un tic en; *coat* dejar en el guardarropa **3** *v/i* comprobar

◆ **check in** *at airport* facturar; *at hotel* registrarse
◆ **check out 1** *v/i of hotel* dejar el hotel **2** *v/t* (*look into*) investigar; *club etc* probar
◆ **check up on** investigar
'checkbook talonario *m* de cheques, *L.Am.* chequera *f*; **checked** *material* a cuadros
checkered ['ʧekərd] *shirt* a cuadros; *career* accidentado
'check-in (counter) mostrador *m* de facturación; **checking account** cuenta *f* corriente; **checklist** lista *f* de verificación; **check mark** tic *m*; **check-out** caja *f*; **checkpoint** control *m*; **checkroom** *for coats* guardarropa *m*; *for baggage* consigna *f*; **checkup** revisión *f* (médica)
cheek [ʧi:k] ANAT mejilla *f*
cheer [ʧɪr] **1** *n* ovación *f* **2** *v/t* ovacionar **3** *v/i* lanzar vítores
◆ **cheer up 1** *v/i* animarse **2** *v/t* animar
cheerful ['ʧɪrfəl] alegre; **cheering** vítores *mpl*; **cheerleader** animadora *f*
cheese [ʧi:z] queso *m*
chef [ʃef] chef *m*, jefe *m* de cocina
chemical ['kemɪkl] **1** *adj* químico **2** *n* producto *m* químico; **chemist** *in laboratory* químico(-a) *m(f)*; *Br dispensing* farmaceútico(-a) *m(f)*; **chemistry** química *f*
chemotherapy [ki:mou'θerəpɪ] quimioterapia *f*
cheque [ʧek] *Br* ☞ ***check²***
chess [ʧes] ajedrez *m*
chest [ʧest] pecho *m*; *box* cofre *m*
chew [ʧu:] mascar, masticar; *of dog*, *rats* mordisquear; **chewing gum** chicle *m*
chick [ʧɪk] pollito *m*; *young bird* polluelo *m*; F *girl* nena *f* F
chicken ['ʧɪkɪn] **1** *n* gallina *f*; *food* pollo *m*
chief [ʧi:f] **1** *n* jefe(-a) *m(f)* **2** *adj* principal; **chiefly** principalmente
child [ʧaɪld] niño(-a) *m(f)*; **childhood** infancia *f*; **childish** *pej* infantil; **childlike** infantil
children ['ʧɪldrən] *pl* ☞ ***child***
Chile ['ʧɪlɪ] Chile; **Chilean 1** *adj* chileno **2** *n* chileno(-a) *m(f)*
chil(l)i (pepper) ['ʧɪlɪ] chile *m*, *Span* guindilla *f*
◆ **chill out** P relajarse; (*calm down*) tranquilizarse
chilly ['ʧɪlɪ] *also fig* fresco
chimney ['ʧɪmnɪ] chimenea *f*
chin [ʧɪn] barbilla *f*
China ['ʧaɪnə] China
china ['ʧaɪnə] porcelana *f*
Chinese [ʧaɪ'ni:z] **1** *adj* chino **2** *n* (*language*) chino *m*; (*person*) chino(-a) *m(f)*
chip [ʧɪp] **1** *n damage* mella *f*; *in gambling* ficha *f*; **~s** patatas *fpl* fritas **2** *v/t* (*damage*) mellar; **chipmunk** ardilla *f* listada
chisel ['ʧɪzl] *for stone* cincel

m; *for wood* formón *m*
chlorine ['klɔːriːn] cloro *m*
chocolate ['tʃɑːkələt] chocolate *m*
choice [tʃɔɪs] **1** *n* elección *f*; (*selection*) selección *f*; ***I had no ~*** no tuve alternativa **2** *adj* (*top quality*) selecto
choir [kwaɪr] coro *m*
choke [tʃoʊk] **1** *v/i* ahogarse **2** *v/t* estrangular
cholesterol [kə'lestəroʊl] colesterol *m*
choose [tʃuːz] elegir, escoger; **choosey** F exigente
chop [tʃɑːp] **1** *n meat* chuleta *f* **2** *v/t wood* cortar; *meat* trocear; *vegetables* picar
◆ **chop down** *tree* talar
chore [tʃɔːr] tarea *f*
choreography [kɔːrɪ'ɑːgrəfɪ] coreografía *f*
chorus ['kɔːrəs] *singers* coro *m*; *of song* estribillo *m*
Christ [kraɪst] Cristo
christen ['krɪsn] bautizar
Christian ['krɪstʃən] **1** *n* cristiano(-a) *m*(*f*) **2** *adj* cristiano; **Christianity** cristianismo *m*
Christmas ['krɪsməs] Navidad(es) *f*(*pl*); ***Merry ~!*** ¡Feliz Navidad!; **Christmas card** crismas *m inv*; **Christmas Day** día *m* de Navidad; **Christmas Eve** Nochebuena *f*; **Christmas present** regalo *m* de Navidad; **Christmas tree** árbol *m* de Navidad
chronic ['krɑːnɪk] crónico
chubby ['tʃʌbɪ] rechoncho
chuck [tʃʌk] F tirar
chuckle ['tʃʌkl] **1** *n* risita *f* **2** *v/i* reírse por lo bajo
chunk [tʃʌŋk] trozo *m*
church [tʃɜːrtʃ] iglesia *f*; **church service** oficio *m* religioso; **churchyard** cementerio *m* (al lado de iglesia)
chute [ʃuːt] rampa *f*; *for garbage* colector *m* de basura
cigar [sɪ'gɑːr] puro *m*
cigarette [sɪgə'ret] cigarrillo *m*; **cigarette lighter** encendedor *m*
cinema ['sɪnɪmə] *Br* cine *m*
circle ['sɜːrkl] **1** *n* círculo *m* **2** *v/i of plane* volar en círculo
circuit ['sɜːrkɪt] circuito *m*; (*lap*) vuelta *f*; **circuit board** COMPUT placa *f or* tarjeta *f* de circuitos
circular ['sɜːrkjʊlər] **1** *n* circular *f* **2** *adj* circular; **circulate** **1** *v/i* circular **2** *v/t memo* hacer circular; **circulation** circulación *f*; *of newspaper* tirada *f*
circumstances ['sɜːrkəmstənsɪs] circunstancias *fpl*; *financial* situación *f* económica
circus ['sɜːrkəs] circo *m*
cistern ['sɪstɜːrn] cisterna *f*
citizen ['sɪtɪzn] ciudadano(-a) *m*(*f*); **citizenship** ciudadanía *f*
city ['sɪtɪ] ciudad *f*; **city center**, *Br* **city centre** centro *m* de la ciudad; **city hall** ayuntamiento *m*

civic ['sɪvɪk] cívico

civil ['sɪvl] civil; (*polite*) cortés; **civil ceremony** ceremonia *f* civil; **civil engineer** ingeniero(-a) *m*(*f*) civil; **civilian** civil *m*/*f*; **civilization** civilización *f*; **civilize** civilizar; **civil rights** derechos *mpl* civiles; **civil servant** funcionario(-a) *m*(*f*); **civil service** administración *f* pública; **civil war** guerra *f* civil

claim [kleɪm] **1** *n* (*request*) reclamación *f* (***for*** de); (*assertion*) afirmación *f* **2** *v/t* (*ask for as a right*) reclamar; (*assert*) afirmar; *lost property* reclamar; **claimant** reclamante *m*/*f*

clam [klæm] almeja *f*

clammy ['klæmɪ] húmedo

clamp [klæmp] *fastener* abrazadera *f*

◆ **clamp down** actuar contundentemente (***on*** contra)

clandestine [klæn'destɪn] clandestino

clap [klæp] (*applaud*) aplaudir

clarification [klærɪfɪ'keɪʃn] aclaración *f*; **clarify** aclarar; **clarity** claridad *f*

clash [klæʃ] **1** *n* choque *m* **2** *v/i* chocar; *of colors* desentonar; *of events* coincidir

clasp [klæsp] **1** *n* broche *m* **2** *v/t in hand* estrechar

class [klæs] **1** *n* clase *f* **2** *v/t* clasificar (***as*** como)

classic ['klæsɪk] **1** *adj* clásico **2** *n* clásico *m*; **classical** clásico; **classification** clasificación *f*; **classified information** reservado; **classified ad** anuncio *m* por palabras; **classify** clasificar; **classroom** clase *f*, aula *f*; **classy** F con clase

clause [klɒ:z] cláusula *f*

claustrophobia [klɒ:strə'foubɪə] claustrofobia *f*

claw [klɒ:] garra *f*; *of lobster* pinza *f*

clay [kleɪ] arcilla *f*

clean [kli:n] **1** *adj* limpio **2** *adv* F (*completely*) completamente **3** *v/t* limpiar

cleaner ['kli:nər] *person* limpiador(a) *m*(*f*); (***dry***) ~ tintorería *f*

cleanse [klenz] *skin* limpiar; **cleanser** *for skin* loción *f* limpiadora

clear [klɪr] **1** *adj* claro; *sky* despejado; *water* transparente; *conscience* limpio **2** *v/t roads etc* despejar; (*acquit*) absolver; (*authorize*) autorizar **3** *v/i of mist* despejarse

◆ **clear out 1** *v/t closet* ordenar, limpiar **2** *v/i* marcharse

◆ **clear up 1** *v/i* ordenar; *of weather* despejarse; *of illness* desaparecer **2** *v/t* (*tidy*) ordenar; *problem* aclarar

clearance ['klɪrəns] *space* espacio *m*; (*authorization*) autorización *f*; **clearance sale** liquidación *f*; **clearing** claro *m*; **clearly** claramente

cleavage ['kli:vɪdʒ] escote *m*

clench [klentʃ] apretar

clergy ['klɜːrdʒɪ] clero *m*; **clergyman** clérigo *m*
clerk [klɜːrk] oficinista *m/f*; *in store* dependiente(-a) *m/f*
clever ['klevər] listo; *idea, gadget* ingenioso
click [klɪk] **1** *n* COMPUT clic *m* **2** *v/i* hacer clic
◆ **click on** COMPUT hacer clic en
client ['klaɪənt] cliente *m/f*; **clientele** clientela *f*
climate ['klaɪmət] *also fig* clima *m*
climax ['klaɪmæks] clímax *m*
climb [klaɪm] **1** *n up mountain* ascensión *f* **2** *v/t & v/i* subir; **climber** *person* escalador(a) *m(f)*, *L.Am.* andinista *m/f*
clinch [klɪntʃ] *deal* cerrar
cling [klɪŋ] *of clothes* pegarse al cuerpo
◆ **cling to** aferrarse a
clingy ['klɪŋɪ] *person* pegajoso
clinic ['klɪnɪk] clínica *f*; **clinical** clínico
clip[1] [klɪp] **1** *n fastener* clip *m* **2** *v/t*: **~ sth to sth** sujetar algo a algo
clip[2] [klɪp] **1** *n extract* fragmento *m* **2** *v/t hair, grass* cortar; **clipping** *from press* recorte *m*
clock [klɑːk] reloj *m*; **clock radio** radio *m* despertador; **clockwise** en el sentido de las agujas del reloj
clone [kloʊn] **1** *n* clon *m* **2** *v/t* clonar; **cloning** clonación *f*
close[1] [kloʊs] *adv* cerca; **~ to the school** cerca del colegio; *adj family* cercano; *friend* íntimo; **be ~ to s.o.** *emotionally* estar muy unido a alguien
close[2] [kloʊz] *v/t* cerrar
closed-circuit 'television circuito *m* cerrado de televisión; **close-knit** muy unido; **closely** *watch* atentamente; *cooperate* de cerca
closet ['klɑːzɪt] armario *m*
close-up ['kloʊsʌp] primer plano *m*
closing date ['kloʊzɪŋ] fecha *f* límite
closure ['kloʊʒər] cierre *m*
clot [klɑːt] **1** *n of blood* coágulo *m* **2** *v/i* coagularse
cloth [klɑːθ] tela *f*, tejido *m*; *for cleaning* trapo *m*
clothes [kloʊðz] ropa *f*; **clothing** ropa *f*
cloud [klaʊd] nube *f*; **cloudless** despejado; **cloudy** nublado
clout [klaʊt] *fig* influencia *f*
clove of garlic [kloʊv] diente *m* de ajo
clown [klaʊn] *also fig* payaso *m*
club [klʌb] palo *m*; *organization* club *m*
clue [kluː] pista *f*
clumsiness ['klʌmzɪnɪs] torpeza *f*; **clumsy** torpe
cluster ['klʌstər] grupo *m*
clutch [klʌtʃ] **1** *n* MOT embrague *m* **2** *v/t* agarrar
◆ **clutch at** agarrarse a
Co. (= ***Company***) Cía. (= Compañía *f*)

c/o (= ***care of***) en el domicilio de

coach [koʊʧ] **1** *n* (*trainer*) entrenador(a) *m*(*f*); *Br* (*bus*) autobús *m* **2** *v/t footballer* entrenar; *singer* preparar; **coaching** entrenamiento *m*

coagulate [koʊ'ægjʊleɪt] *of blood* coagularse

coal [koʊl] carbón *m*

coalition [koʊə'lɪʃn] coalición *f*

coalmine mina *f* de carbón

coarse [kɔːrs] áspero; *hair*, (*vulgar*) basto; **coarsely** (*vulgarly*) de manera grosera

coast [koʊst] costa *f*; **coastal** costero; **coastguard** servicio *m* de guardacostas; *person* guardacostas *m*/*f inv*; **coastline** litoral *m*, costa *f*

coat [koʊt] **1** *n* chaqueta *f*, *L.Am.* saco *m*; (*over*~) abrigo *m*; *of animal* pelaje *m*; *of paint* capa *f* **2** *v/t* (*cover*) cubrir (***with*** de); **coathanger** percha *f*; **coating** capa *f*

coax [koʊks] persuadir

cocaine [kə'keɪn] cocaína *f*

cock [kɑːk] *chicken* gallo *m*; *any male bird* macho *m*; **cockpit** *of plane* cabina *f*; **cockroach** cucaracha *f*; **cocktail** cóctel *m*

cocoa ['koʊkoʊ] cacao *m*

coconut ['koʊkənʌt] coco *m*; **coconut palm** cocotero *m*

code [koʊd] código *m*; ***in*** ~ cifrado

coeducational [koʊedʊ'keɪʃnl] mixto

coerce [koʊ'ɜːrs] coaccionar

coexist [koʊɪg'zɪst] coexistir; **coexistence** coexistencia *f*

coffee ['kɑːfɪ] café *m*; **coffee maker** cafetera *f* (para preparar); **coffee pot** cafetera *f* (para servir); **coffee shop** café *m*

cohabit [koʊ'hæbɪt] cohabitar

coherent [koʊ'hɪrənt] coherente

coil [kɔɪl] **1** *n of rope* rollo *m*; *of snake* anillo *m* **2** *v/t*: ~ (***up***) enrollar

coin [kɔɪn] moneda *f*

coincide [koʊɪn'saɪd] coincidir; **coincidence** coincidencia *f*

Coke® [koʊk] Coca-Cola® *f*

cold [koʊld] **1** *adj* frío; ***I'm*** ~ tengo frío; ***it's*** ~ *of weather* hace frío **2** *n* frío *m*; MED resfriado *m*; **cold-blooded** de sangre fría; *murder* a sangre fría; **coldly** fríamente, con frialdad; **coldness** frialdad *f*; **cold sore** calentura *f*

collaborate [kə'læbəreɪt] colaborar (***on*** en); **collaboration** colaboración *f*; **collaborator** colaborador(a) *m*(*f*); *with enemy* colaboracionista *m*/*f*

collapse [kə'læps] desplomarse; **collapsible** plegable

collar ['kɑːlər] cuello *m*; *for dog* collar *m*

colleague ['kɑːliːg] colega *m*/*f*

collect [kə'lekt] **1** *v/t* recoger;

as hobby coleccionar **2** *v/i* (*gather together*) reunirse; **collect call** llamada *f* a cobro revertido; **collection** colección *f*; *in church* colecta *f*; **collective** colectivo; **collector** coleccionista *m/f*

college ['kɑːlɪdʒ] universidad *f*

collide [kə'laɪd] chocar, colisionar; **collision** choque *m*, colisión *f*

Colombia [kə'lʌmbɪə] Colombia; **Colombian 1** *adj* colombiano **2** *n* colombiano(-a) *m(f)*

colon ['koʊlən] *punctuation* dos puntos *mpl*

colonel ['kɜːrnl] coronel *m*

colonial [kə'loʊnɪəl] colonial; **colonize** colonizar; **colony** colonia *f*

color ['kʌlər] color *m f*; **color-blind** daltónico; **colored** *person* de color; **colorful** lleno de colores; *account* colorido

colossal [kə'lɑːsl] colosal

colour *Br* ☞ ***color***

colt [koʊlt] potro *m*

Columbus [kə'lʌmbəs] Colón

column ['kɑːləm] columna *f*; **columnist** columnista *m/f*

coma ['koʊmə] coma *m*

comb [koʊm] **1** *n* peine *m* **2** *v/t hair, area* peinar; ~ ***one's hair*** peinarse

combat ['kɑːmbæt] **1** *n* combate *m* **2** *v/t* combatir

combination [kɑːmbɪ'neɪʃn] combinación *f*; **combine 1** *v/t* combinar; *ingredients* mezclar **2** *v/i* combinarse

come [kʌm] venir

◆ **come across** (*find*) encontrar

◆ **come along** (*come too*) venir; (*turn up*) aparecer; (*progress*) marchar

◆ **come back** volver

◆ **come down 1** *v/i* bajar; *of rain, snow* caer **2** *v/t*: ***come down the stairs*** bajar las escaleras

◆ **come for** (*attack*) atacar; (*collect*: *thing*) venir a por; (*collect*: *person*) venir a buscar a

◆ **come forward** presentarse

◆ **come from** (*travel*) venir de; (*originate*) ser de

◆ **come in** entrar; *of train* llegar; *of tide* subir

◆ **come in for** *criticism* recibir

◆ **come off** *of handle etc* soltarse; *of paint etc* quitarse

◆ **come out** salir; *of book* publicarse; *of stain* irse

◆ **come to 1** *v/t place* llegar a; *of hair, water* llegar hasta **2** *v/i* (*regain consciousness*) volver en sí

◆ **come up** subir; *of sun* salir

'comeback regreso *m*

comedian [kə'miːdɪən] humorista *m/f*; *pej* payaso(-a) *m(f)*; **comedy** comedia *f*

comfort ['kʌmfərt] **1** *n* comodidad *f*, confort *m*; (*consolation*) consuelo *m* **2** *v/t* consolar; **comfortable** cómodo

comic ['kɑːmɪk] **1** *n to read* cómic *m*; (*comedian*) cómico(-a) *m*(*f*) **2** *adj* cómico; **comical** cómico; **comic book** cómic *m*; **comics** tiras *fpl* cómicas; **comic strip** tira *f* cómica

comma ['kɑːmə] coma *f*

command [kə'mænd] **1** *n* orden *f* **2** *v/t* ordenar, mandar

commandeer [kɑːmən'dɪr] requisar

commander [kə'mændər] comandante *m/f*; **commander-in-chief** comandante *m/f* en jefe

commemorate [kə'meməreɪt] conmemorar

commence [kə'mens] comenzar

commendable [kə'mendəbl] encomiable; **commendation** *for bravery* mención *f*

comment ['kɑːment] **1** *n* comentario *m* **2** *v/i* hacer comentarios (***on*** sobre); **commentary** comentarios *mpl*; **commentator** comentarista *m/f*

commerce ['kɑːmɜːrs] comercio *m*; **commercial 1** *adj* comercial **2** *n* (*ad*) anuncio *m* (publicitario); **commercial break** pausa *f* publicitaria; **commercialize** comercializar

commission [kə'mɪʃn] (*payment*, *committee*) comisión *f*; (*job*) encargo *m*

commit [kə'mɪt] *crime* cometer; *money* comprometer; **commitment** compromiso *m* (***to*** con); **committee** comité *m*

commodity [kə'mɑːdətɪ] *raw material* producto *m* básico; *product* bien *m* de consumo

common ['kɑːmən] común; ***have sth in ~*** tener algo en común; **commonly** comúnmente; **common sense** sentido *m* común

commotion [kə'moʊʃn] alboroto *m*

communal [kə'mjuːnl] comunal

communicate [kə'mjuːnɪkeɪt] **1** *v/i* comunicarse **2** *v/t* comunicar; **communication** comunicación *f*; **communicative** comunicativo

Communion [kə'mjuːnjən] REL comunión *f*

Communism ['kɑːmjʊnɪzəm] comunismo *m*; **Communist 1** *adj* comunista **2** *n* comunista *m/f*

community [kə'mjuːnətɪ] comunidad *f*

commute [kə'mjuːt] **1** *v/i* viajar al trabajo **2** *v/t* LAW conmutar

compact 1 [kəm'pækt] *adj* compacto **2** ['kɑːmpækt] *n* MOT utilitario *m*; **companion** [kəm'pænjən] compañero(-a) *m*(*f*)

company ['kʌmpənɪ] compañía *f*; COM *also* empresa *f*

comparable ['kɑːmpərəbl] comparable; **comparative**

adj relativo; *study* comparado; **compare** comparar; **comparison** comparación *f*
compartment [kəm'pɑːrtmənt] compartimento *m*
compass ['kʌmpəs] brújula *f*; *for geometry* compás *m*
compassion [kəm'pæʃn] compasión *f*; **compassionate** compasivo
compatibility [kəmpætə'bɪlɪtɪ] compatibilidad *f*; **compatible** compatible
compel [kəm'pel] obligar
compensate ['kɑːmpənseɪt] **1** *v/t* compensar **2** *v/i*: **~ *for*** compensar; **compensation** (*money*) indemnización *f*; (*reward, comfort*) compensación *f*
compete [kəm'piːt] competir (***for*** por)
competence ['kɑːmpɪtəns] competencia *f*; **competent** competente
competition [kɑːmpə'tɪʃn] (*contest*) concurso *m*; SP competición *f*; (*competitors*) competencia *f*; **competitive** competitivo; **competitiveness** COM competitividad *f*; *of person* espíritu *m* competitivo; **competitor** *in contest* concursante *m/f*; SP competidor(a) *m(f)*, contrincante *m/f*; COM competidor(a) *m(f)*
complacent [kəm'pleɪsənt] complaciente
complain [kəm'pleɪn] quejarse; **complaint** queja *f*; MED dolencia *f*
complementary [kɑːmplɪ'mentərɪ] complementario
complete [kəm'pliːt] **1** *adj* (*total*) absoluto, total; (*full*) completo; (*finished*) finalizado **2** *v/t task, building etc* finalizar; *course* completar; *form* rellenar; **completely** completamente; **completion** finalización *f*
complex ['kɑːmpleks] **1** *adj* complejo **2** *n also* PSYCH complejo *m*; **complexion** *facial* tez *f*; **complexity** complejidad *f*
compliance [kəm'plaɪəns] cumplimiento *m* (***with*** de)
complicate ['kɑːmplɪkeɪt] complicar; **complicated** complicado; **complication** complicación *f*
complimentary [kɑːmplɪ'mentərɪ] elogioso; (*free*) de regalo, gratis
comply [kəm'plaɪ] cumplir; **~ *with*** cumplir
component [kəm'pounənt] pieza *f*, componente *m*
compose [kəm'pouz] *also* MUS componer; **composed** (*calm*) sereno; **composer** MUS compositor(a) *m(f)*; **composition** *also* MUS composición *f*; **composure** compostura *f*
compound ['kɑːmpaund] *chemical* compuesto *m*
comprehend [kɑːmprɪ'hend] comprender; **comprehen-**

sion comprensión *f*; **comprehensive** detallado
compress [kəm'pres] comprimir; *information* condensar
comprise [kəm'praɪz] comprender; ***be ~d of*** constar de
compromise ['kɑːmprəmaɪz] **1** *n* solución *f* negociada **2** *v/i* transigir, efectuar concesiones **3** *v/t principles* traicionar; (*jeopardize*) poner en peligro
compulsion [kəm'pʌlʃn] PSYCH compulsión *f*; **compulsive** *behavior* compulsivo; *reading* absorbente; **compulsory** obligatorio
computer [kəm'pjuːtər] *Span* ordenador *m*, *L.Am.* computadora *f*; **computer game** juego *m* de *Span* ordenador *or L.Am.* computadora; **computerize** informatizar, *L.Am.* computarizar; **computer science** informática *f*, *L.Am.* computación *f*; **computing** informática *f*, *L.Am.* computación *f*
comrade ['kɑːmreɪd] compañero(-a) *m*(*f*); POL camarada *m/f*; **comradeship** camaradería *f*
conceal [kən'siːl] ocultar; **concealment** ocultación *f*
conceit [kən'siːt] engreimiento; **conceited** engreido
conceivable [kən'siːvəbl] concebible; **conceive** *of woman* concebir
concentrate ['kɑːnsəntreɪt] **1** *v/i* concentrarse **2** *v/t energies* concentrar; **concentration** concentración *f*
concept ['kɑːnsept] concepto *m*; **conception** *of child* concepción *f*
concern [kən'sɜːrn] **1** *n* (*anxiety*, *care*) preocupación *f*; (*business*) asunto *m*; (*company*) empresa *f* **2** *v/t* (*involve*) concernir; (*worry*) preocupar; **concerned** preocupado (***about*** por); (*involved*) en cuestión; **concerning** en relación con
concert ['kɑːnsərt] concierto *m*; **concerted** concertado
concession [kən'seʃn] concesión *f*
concise [kən'saɪs] conciso
conclude [kən'kluːd] concluir (***from*** de); **conclusion** conclusión *f*; **conclusive** concluyente
concrete ['kɑːŋkriːt] **1** *adj* concreto **2** *n* hormigón *m*, *L.Am.* concreto *m*
concussion [kən'kʌʃn] conmoción *f* cerebral
condemn [kən'dem] condenar; **condemnation** condena *f*
condescend [kɑːndɪ'send]: ***he ~ed to speak to me*** se dignó a hablarme; **condescending** condescendiente
condition [kən'dɪʃn] **1** *n* (*state*) condiciones *fpl*; *of health* estado *m*; *illness* enfermedad *f*; (*requirement*, *term*) condición *f* **2** *v/t* PSYCH con-

dicionar; **conditioning** PSYCH condicionamiento *m*
condo ['kɑːndoʊ] F apartamento *m*, *Span* piso *m*; *building* bloque de apartamentos
condolences [kən'doʊlənsɪz] condolencias *fpl*
condom ['kɑːndəm] condón *m*, preservativo *m*
condominium [kɑːndə'mɪnɪəm] ☞ ***condo***
condone [kən'doʊn] justificar
conduct 1 ['kɑːndʌkt] *n* conducta *f* **2** [kən'dʌkt] *v/t* (*carry out*) realizar, hacer; ELEC conducir; MUS dirigir; **conducted tour** visita *f* guiada; **conductor** MUS director(a) *m(f)* de orquesta; *on train* revisor(-a) *m(f)*
cone [koʊn] cono *m*; *for ice cream* cucurucho *m*; *of pine tree* piña *f*
conference ['kɑːnfərəns] congreso *m*; *discussion* conferencia *f*; **conference room** sala *f* de conferencias
confess [kən'fes] **1** *v/t* confesar **2** *v/i* confesar; REL confesarse; **confession** confesión *f*
confide [kən'faɪd] **1** *v/t* confiar **2** *v/i*: **~ *in s.o.*** confiarse a alguien; **confidence** confianza *f*; **confident** (*self-assured*) seguro de sí mismo; (*convinced*) seguro; **confidential** confidencial; **confidently** con seguridad
confine [kən'faɪn] (*imprison*) confinar, recluir; (*restrict*) limitar; **confined** *space* limitado
confirm [kən'fɜːrm] confirmar; **confirmation** confirmación *f*
confiscate ['kɑːnfɪskeɪt] confiscar
conflict 1 ['kɑːnflɪkt] *n* conflicto *m* **2** [kən'flɪkt] *v/i* chocar
confront [kən'frʌnt] hacer frente a; **confrontation** confrontación *f*
confuse [kən'fjuːz] confundir; **confused** *person* confundido; *situation* confuso; **confusing** confuso; **confusion** confusión *f*
congestion [kən'dʒestʃn] congestión *f*
congratulate [kən'grætʃʊleɪt] felicitar; **congratulations** felicitaciones *fpl*
congregate ['kɑːŋgrɪgeɪt] congregarse; **congregation** REL congregación *f*
Congress ['kɑːŋgres] Congreso *m*; **Congressional** del Congreso; **Congressman** congresista *m*; **Congresswoman** congresista *f*
conjecture [kən'dʒektʃər] conjetura *f*
con man ['kɑːnmæn] F timador *m* F
connect [kə'nekt] conectar; (*link*) relacionar, vincular; *to power supply* enchufar; **connected: *be well-~*** estar bien relacionado; ***be ~ with*** estar relacionado con; **con-**

nection conexión *f*; (*personal contact*) contacto *m*

connoisseur [kɑːnə'sɜːr] entendido(-a) *m(f)*

conquer ['kɑːŋkər] conquistar; *fear etc* vencer; **conqueror** conquistador(a) *m(f)*; **conquest** conquista *f*

conscience ['kɑːnʃəns] conciencia *f*; **conscientious** concienzudo; **conscientiousness** aplicación *f*

conscious ['kɑːnʃəs] consciente; **consciously** conscientemente; **consciousness** conciencia *f*

consecutive [kən'sekjutɪv] consecutivo

consensus [kən'sensəs] consenso *m*

consent [kən'sent] **1** *n* consentimiento *m* **2** *v/i* consentir (***to*** en)

consequence ['kɑːnsɪkwəns] consecuencia *f*; **consequently** por consiguiente

conservation [kɑːnsər'veɪʃn] conservación *f*; **conservationist** ecologista *m/f*; **conservative** conservador; *estimate* prudente; **conserve** **1** *n* (*jam*) compota *f* **2** *v/t* conservar

consider [kən'sɪdər] considerar; (*show regard for*) mostrar consideración por; **considerable** considerable; **considerably** considerablemente; **considerate** considerado; **considerately** con consideración; **consideration** consideración *f*; (*factor*) factor *m*; ***take sth into ~*** tomar algo en consideración

◆ **consist of** [kən'sɪst] consistir en

consistency [kən'sɪstənsɪ] (*texture*) consistencia *f*; (*unchangingness*) coherencia *f*; *of player* regularidad *f*; **consistent** *person* coherente; *improvement* constante

consolidate [kən'sɑːlɪdeɪt] consolidar

conspicuous [kən'spɪkjuəs] llamativo

conspiracy [kən'spɪrəsɪ] conspiración *f*; **conspirator** conspirador(a) *m(f)*; **conspire** conspirar

constant ['kɑːnstənt] constante; **constantly** constantemente

constipated ['kɑːnstɪpeɪtɪd] estreñido; **constipation** estreñimiento *m*

constitute ['kɑːnstɪtuːt] constituir; **constitution** constitución *f*; **constitutional** POL constitucional

constraint [kən'streɪnt] restricción *f*, limite *m*

construct [kən'strʌkt] construir; **construction** construcción *f*; **constructive** constructivo

consul ['kɑːnsl] cónsul *m/f*; **consulate** consulado *m*

consult [kən'sʌlt] consultar; **consultancy** *company* consultoría *f*; (*advice*) asesoramiento *m*; **consultant** asesor(a) *m(f)*, consultor(a) *m(f)*; **consultation** consulta *f*

consume [kən'suːm] consumir; **consumer** consumidor(a) *m(f)*; **consumption** consumo *m*

contact ['kɑːntækt] **1** *n* contacto **2** *v/t* contactar con; **contact lens** lentes *fpl* de contacto, *Span* lentillas *fpl*

contagious [kən'teɪdʒəs] contagioso

contain [kən'teɪn] contener; **container** recipiente *m*; COM contenedor *m*

contaminate [kən'tæmɪneɪt] contaminar; **contamination** contaminación *f*

contemporary [kən'tempərerɪ] **1** *adj* contemporáneo **2** *n* contemporáneo(-a) *m(f)*

contempt [kən'tempt] desprecio *m*; **contemptible** despreciable; **contemptuous** despectivo

contender [kən'tendər] contendiente *m/f*; *against champion* aspirante *m/f*

content[1] ['kɑːntent] *n* contenido *m*

content[2] [kən'tent] **1** *adj* satisfecho **2** *v/t*: ~ ***o.s. with*** contentarse con; **contented** satisfecho; **contentment** satisfacción *f*

contents ['kɑːntents] contenido *m*

contest[1] ['kɑːntest] *n* (*competition*) concurso *m*; (*struggle*) lucha *f*

contest[2] [kən'test] *v/t leadership* presentarse como candidato a; *decision, will* impugnar

contestant [kən'testənt] concursante *m/f*; *in sport* competidor(a) *m(f)*

context ['kɑːntekst] contexto *m*

continent ['kɑːntɪnənt] continente *m*; **continental** continental

continual [kən'tɪnjʊəl] continuo; **continually** continuamente; **continuation** continuación *f*; **continue** continuar; **continuous** continuo; **continuously** continuamente

contort [kən'tɔːrt] *face* contraer; *body* contorsionar

contraception [kɑːntrə'sepʃn] anticoncepción *f*; **contraceptive** anticonceptivo *m*

contract[1] ['kɑːntrækt] *n* contrato *m*

contract[2] [kən'trækt] **1** *v/i* (*shrink*) contraerse **2** *v/t illness* contraer

contractor [kən'træktər] contratista *m/f*; **contractual** [kən'træktʊəl] contractual

contradict [kɑːntrə'dɪkt] *statement* desmentir; *person* contradecir; **contradiction** contradicción *f*; **contradictory** contradictorio

contrary[1] ['kɑːntrərɪ] **1** *adj* contrario; ~ ***to*** al contrario de **2** *n*: ***on the*** ~ al contrario

contrary[2] [kən'treri] *adj* (*perverse*) difícil
contrast ['kɑːntræst] **1** *n* contraste *m* **2** *v/t & v/i* contrastar; **contrasting** opuesto
contravene [kɑːntrə'viːn] contravenir
contribute [kən'tribjuːt] **1** *v/i* contribuir (***to*** a) **2** *v/t money, suggestion* contribuir con, aportar; **contribution** contribución *f*; *to political party, church* donación *f*; **contributor** *of money* donante *m/f*; *to magazine* colaborador(a) *m(f)*
control [kən'troul] **1** *n* control *m*; ***be in ~ of*** controlar **2** *v/t* controlar
controversial [kɑːntrə'vɜːrʃl] polémico, controvertido; **controversy** polémica *f*, controversia *f*
convenience [kən'viːniəns] conveniencia *f*; **convenience store** tienda *f* de barrio; **convenient** conveniente; *time* oportuno
convent ['kɑːnvənt] convento *m*
convention [kən'venʃn] convención *f*; (*meeting*) congreso *m*; **conventional** convencional
conversation [kɑːnvər'seiʃn] conversación *f*; **conversational** coloquial
conversion [kən'vɜːrʃn] conversión *f*; **convert 1** *n* converso(-a) *m(f)* (***to*** a) **2** *v/t* convertir; **convertible** *car* descapotable *m*
convey [kən'vei] (*transmit*) transmitir; (*carry*) transportar; **conveyor belt** cinta *f* transportadora
convict 1 ['kɑːnvikt] *n* convicto(-a) *m(f)* **2** [kən'vikt] *v/t* LAW: ***~ s.o. of sth*** declarar a alguien culpable de algo; **conviction** LAW condena *f*; (*belief*) convicción *f*
convince [kən'vins] convencer
convoy ['kɑːnvɔi] convoy *m*
cook [kuk] **1** *n* cocinero(-a) *m(f)* **2** *v/t & v/i* cocinar; **cookbook** libro *m* de cocina; **cookery** cocina *f*; **cookie** galleta *f*; **cooking** cocina *f*
cool [kuːl] **1** *n*: ***keep one's ~*** F mantener la calma **2** *adj* fresco; *drink* frío; (*calm*) tranquilo; (*unfriendly*) frío; P (*great*) *Span* guay P, *L.Am.* chévere P, *Mex* padre P, *Rpl* copante P **3** *v/i* enfriarse; *of tempers* calmarse **4** *v/t*: ***~ it*** F cálmate
◆ **cool down 1** *v/i* enfriarse; *of weather* refrescar; *of tempers* calmarse **2** *v/t food* enfriar; *fig* calmar
cooperate [kou'ɑːpəreit] cooperar; **cooperation** cooperación *f*; **cooperative** (*helpful*) cooperativo
coordinate [kou'ɔːrdineit] coordinar; **coordination** coordinación *f*
cop [kɑːp] F poli *m/f* F
cope [koup] arreglárselas; ***~ with*** poder con

copier ['kɑːpɪər] *machine* fotocopiadora *f*
copper ['kɑːpər] cobre *m*
copy ['kɑːpɪ] **1** *n* copia *f*; *of book* ejemplar *m* **2** *v/t* copiar
cord [kɔːrd] (*string*) cuerda *f*, cordel *m*; (*cable*) cable *m*
cordon ['kɔːrdn] cordón *m*
cords [kɔːrdz] *pants* pantalones *mpl* de pana
core [kɔːr] **1** *n of fruit* corazón *m*; *of party* núcleo *m* **2** *adj issue* central
cork [kɔːrk] corcho *m*; **corkscrew** sacacorchos *m inv*
corn [kɔːrn] *grain* maíz *m*
corner ['kɔːrnər] **1** *n of page, street* esquina *f*; *of room* rincón *m*; *on road* curva *f*; *in soccer* córner *m*, saque *m* de esquina **2** *v/t person* arrinconar; **~ *a market*** monopolizar un mercado **3** *v/i of driver, car* girar
coronary ['kɑːrənerɪ] **1** *adj* coronario **2** *n* infarto *m* de miocardio
coroner ['kɑːrənər] *oficial encargado de investigar muertes sospechosas*
corporal ['kɔːrpərəl] cabo *m/f*; **corporal punishment** castigo *m* corporal
corporate ['kɔːrpərət] COM corporativo, de empresa; **corporation** (*business*) sociedad *f* anónima
corpse [kɔːrps] cadáver *m*
corral [kə'ræl] corral *m*
correct [kə'rekt] **1** *adj* correcto; *time* exacto **2** *v/t* corregir;
correction corrección *f*;
correctly correctamente
correspond [kɑːrɪ'spɑːnd] (*match*) corresponderse; **correspondence** correspondencia *f*; **correspondent** (*reporter*) corresponsal *m/f*
corridor ['kɔːrɪdər] pasillo *m*
corroborate [kə'rɑːbəreɪt] corroborar
corrosion [kə'roʊʒn] corrosión *f*
corrupt [kə'rʌpt] **1** *adj* corrupto; COMPUT corrompido **2** *v/t* corromper; (*bribe*) sobornar; **corruption** corrupción *f*
cosmetic [kɑːz'metɪk] cosmético; *fig* superficial; **cosmetics** cosméticos *mpl*; **cosmetic surgery** cirugía *f* estética
cosmopolitan [kɑːzmə'pɑːlɪtən] cosmopolitano
cost [kɑːst] **1** *n also fig* costo *m*, *Span* coste *m* **2** *v/t* costar; *project* estimar el costo de; ***how much does it ~?*** ¿cuánto cuesta?
Costa Rica [kɑːstə'riːkə] Costa Rica; **Costa Rican** **1** *adj* costarricense **2** *n* costarricense *m/f*
'cost-effective rentable; **cost of living** costo *m or Span* coste *m* de la vida
costume ['kɑːstuːm] *for actor* traje *m*
cosy *Br* ☞ ***cozy***
cot [kɑːt] (*camp-bed*) catre *m*

cottage ['kɑːtɪdʒ] casa *f* de campo, casita *f*

cotton ['kɑːtn] **1** *n* algodón *m* **2** *adj* de algodón; **cotton candy** algodón *m* dulce; **cotton wool** *Br* algodón *m* (hidrófilo)

couch [kaʊʧ] sofá *m*; **couch potato** F teleadicto(-a) *m*(*f*) F

cough [kɑːf] **1** *n* tos *f* **2** *v/i* toser; *to get attention* carraspear; **cough medicine** jarabe *m* para la tos

could [kʊd]: **~ *I have my key?*** ¿me podría dar la llave?; **~ *you help me?*** ¿me podrías ayudar?; ***you ~ be right*** puede que tengas razón; ***you ~ have warned me!*** ¡me podías haber avisado!

council ['kaʊnsl] consejo *m*; **councilor** concejal(a) *m*(*f*)

counsel ['kaʊnsl] **1** *n* (*advice*) consejo *m*; (*lawyer*) abogado(-a) *m*(*f*) **2** *v/t* (*advise*) aconsejar; *person* ofrecer apoyo psicológico a; **counseling,** *Br* **counselling** apoyo *m* psicológico; **counsellor** *Br*, **counselor** *of student* orientador(a) *m*(*f*); LAW abogado(-a) *m*(*f*)

count [kaʊnt] **1** *n* cuenta *f*; (*action of* ~*ing*) recuento *m* **2** *v/t* & *v/i* contar

◆ **count on** contar con

countdown cuenta *f* atrás

counter ['kaʊntər] *in shop* mostrador *m*; *in café* barra *f*; *in game* ficha *f*

'**counteract** contrarrestar; **counter-attack 1** *n* contraataque *m* **2** *v/i* contraatacar; **counterclockwise** en sentido contrario al de las agujas del reloj; **counterespionage** contraespionaje *m*; **counterfeit 1** *v/t* falsificar **2** *adj* falso; **counterpart** (*person*) homólogo(-a) *m*(*f*); **counterproductive** contraproducente

countless ['kaʊntlɪs] incontables

country ['kʌntrɪ] país *m*; *as opposed to town* campo *m*

county ['kaʊntɪ] condado *m*

coup [kuː] POL golpe *m* (de Estado); *fig* golpe *m* de efecto

couple ['kʌpl] pareja *f*; ***a ~ of*** un par de

courage ['kʌrɪdʒ] valor *m*, coraje *m*; **courageous** valiente

courier ['kʊrɪr] mensajero(-a) *m*(*f*); *with tourist party* guía *m/f*

course [kɔːrs] (*lessons*) curso *m*; *of meal* plato *m*; *of ship, plane* rumbo *m*; *for horse race* circuito *m*; *for golf* campo *m*; *for marathon* recorrido *m*; ***of ~*** por supuesto

court [kɔːrt] LAW tribunal *m*; (*courthouse*) palacio *m* de justicia; SP pista *f*, cancha *f*; **court case** proceso *m*, causa *f*

courtesy ['kɜːrtəsɪ] cortesía *f*

'**courthouse** palacio *m* de

justicia; **courtroom** sala *f* de juicios; **courtyard** patio *m*
cousin ['kʌzn] primo(-a) *m(f)*
cover ['kʌvər] **1** *n protective* funda *f*; *of book, magazine* portada *f*; (*shelter*) protección *f*; (*insurance*) cobertura *f* **2** *v/t* cubrir
◆ **cover up 1** *v/t* cubrir; *scandal* encubrir **2** *v/i* disimular
coverage ['kʌvərɪdʒ] *by media* cobertura *f* informativa
covert ['koʊvɜːrt] encubierto
'cover-up encubrimiento *m*
cow [kaʊ] vaca *f*
coward ['kaʊərd] cobarde *m/f*; **cowardice** cobardía *f*
'cowboy vaquero *m*
co-worker ['koʊwɜːrkər] compañero(a) *m(f)* de trabajo
cozy ['koʊzɪ] *room* acogedor; *job* cómodo
crab [kræb] cangrejo *m*
crack [kræk] **1** *n* grieta *f*; *in cup* raja *f*; (*joke*) chiste *m* (malo) **2** *v/t cup* rajar; *nut* cascar; *code* descifrar; F (*solve*) resolver **3** *v/i* rajarse; **crack (cocaine)** crack *m*; **cracked** *cup* rajado; **cracker** *to eat* galleta *f* salada
cradle ['kreɪdl] cuna *f*
craft[1] [kræft] NAUT embarcación *f*
craft[2] [kræft] (*skill*) arte *m*; (*trade*) oficio *m*; **craftsman** artesano *m*; **crafty** astuto
crag [kræg] *rock* peñasco *m*
cram [kræm] embutir
cramps [kræmps] calambre *m*; ***stomach* ~** retorcijón *m*
crane [kreɪn] **1** *n machine* grúa *f* **2** *v/t*: **~ *one's neck*** estirar el cuello
crank [kræŋk] *person* maniático(-a) *m(f)*; **cranky** (*badtempered*) gruñón
crap [kræp] P mierda *f* P; (*nonsense*) *Span* gilipolleces *fpl* P, *L.Am.* pendejadas *fpl* P, *Rpl* boludeces *fpl* P
crash [kræʃ] **1** *n noise* estruendo *m*; *accident* accidente *m*; COM quiebra *f*, crac *m*; COMPUT bloqueo *m* **2** *v/i of car, airplane* estrellarse (***into*** con); *of market* hundirse; COMPUT bloquearse **3** *v/t car* estrellar; **crash course** curso *m* intensivo; **crash diet** dieta *f* drástica; **crash helmet** casco *m* protector; **crash-land** realizar un aterrizaje forzoso
crate [kreɪt] caja *f*
crater ['kreɪtər] cráter *m*
crave [kreɪv] ansiar; **craving** ansia *f m*
crawl [krɒːl] **1** *n in swimming* crol *m* **2** *v/i on floor* arrastrarse; *of baby* andar a gatas; (*move slowly*) avanzar lentamente
crayon ['kreɪɑːn] lápiz *m* de color
craze [kreɪz] locura *f* (***for*** de); **crazy** loco
creak [kriːk] *of hinge* chirriar; *of floor, shoes* crujir; **creaky** que chirría; *floor, shoes* que

cruje
cream [kriːm] **1** *n for skin* crema *f*; *for coffee, cake* nata *f* **2** *adj* crema
crease [kriːs] **1** *n* arruga *f*; *deliberate* raya *f* **2** *v/t* arrugar
create [kriː'eɪt] crear; **creation** creación *f*; **creative** creativo; **creator** creador(a) *m(f)* *f*
creature ['kriːʧər] criatura
credibility [kredə'bɪlətɪ] credibilidad *f*; **credible** creíble
credit ['kredɪt] crédito *m*; **creditable** estimable; **credit card** tarjeta *f* de crédito; **credit limit** límite *m* de crédito; **creditor** acreedor(a) *m(f)*; **creditworthy** solvente
creep [kriːp] **1** *n pej* asqueroso(-a) *m(f)* **2** *v/i* moverse sigilosamente; **creepy** F espeluznante F
cremate [krɪ'meɪt] incinerar; **cremation** incineración *f*
crest [krest] *of hill* cima *f*; *of bird* cresta *f*
crevice ['krevɪs] grieta *f*
crew [kruː] tripulación *f*; **crew cut** rapado *m*
crib [krɪb] *for baby* cuna *f*
crime [kraɪm] delito *m*; *serious, also fig* crimen *m*; **criminal 1** *n* delincuente *m/f*, criminal *m/f* **2** *adj* criminal; (LAW: *not civil*) penal; (*shameful*) vergonzoso; *act* delictivo
crimson ['krɪmzn] carmesí
cripple ['krɪpl] **1** *n* inválido(-a) *m(f)* **2** *v/t person* dejar inválido; *fig* paralizar
crisis ['kraɪsɪs] crisis *f inv*
crisp [krɪsp] *weather* fresco; *lettuce* crujiente; *dollar bill* flamante; **crisps** *Br* patatas *fpl* fritas, *L.Am* papas *fpl* fritas
criterion [kraɪ'tɪrɪən] criterio *m*
critic ['krɪtɪk] crítico(-a) *m(f)*; **critical** crítico; *moment* decisivo; **criticism** crítica *f*; **criticize** criticar
crocodile ['krɑːkədaɪl] cocodrilo *m*
crony ['kroʊnɪ] F amiguete *m/f* F
crook [krʊk] ladrón (-ona) *m(f)*; *dishonest trader* granuja *m/f*; **crooked** torcido; (*dishonest*) deshonesto
crop [krɑːp] **1** *n also fig* cosecha *f*; *plant grown* cultivo *m* **2** *v/t hair* cortar; *photo* recortar
◆ **crop up** salir
cross [krɑːs] **1** *adj* (*angry*) enfadado **2** *n* cruz *f* **3** *v/t* (*go across*) cruzar; **~ *o.s.*** REL santiguarse **4** *v/i* (*go across*) cruzar; *of lines* cruzarse
◆ **cross off** tachar
'**crosscheck 1** *n* comprobación *f* **2** *v/t* comprobar; **cross-examine** interrogar; **cross-eyed** bizco; **crossing** NAUT travesía *f*; **crossroads** *also fig* encrucijada *f*; **crosswalk** paso *m* de peatones; **crossword (puzzle)** crucigrama *m*
crotch [krɑːʧ] entrepierna *f*

crouch [kraʊʧ] agacharse
crowd [kraʊd] multitud *f*, muchedumbre *f*; *at sports event* público *m*; **crowded** abarrotado (***with*** de)
crown [kraʊn] corona *f*
crucial ['kruːʃl] crucial
crucifix ['kruːsɪfɪks] crucifijo *m*; **crucifixion** crucifixión *f*; **crucify** *also fig* crucificar
crude [kruːd] **1** *adj* (*vulgar*) grosero; (*unsophisticated*) primitivo **2** *n*: ~ (***oil***) crudo *m*
cruel ['kruːəl] cruel (***to*** con); **cruelty** crueldad *f*
cruise [kruːz] **1** *n* crucero *m* **2** *v/i of people* hacer un crucero; *of car* ir a velocidad de crucero; *of plane* volar
crumb [krʌm] miga *f*
crumble ['krʌmbl] *of bread* desmigajarse; *of stonework* desmenuzarse; *fig*: *of opposition* desmoronarse
crumple ['krʌmpl] (*crease*) arrugar
crush [krʌʃ] **1** *n* (*crowd*) muchedumbre *f* **2** *v/t* aplastar; (*crease*) arrugar
crust [krʌst] *on bread* corteza *f*
crutch [krʌʧ] *walking aid* muleta *f*
cry [kraɪ] **1** *n* (*call*) grito *m* **2** *v/i* (*weep*) llorar
◆ **cry out** gritar
cryptic ['krɪptɪk] críptico
crystal ['krɪstl] cristal *m*
cu [siː'juː] *in texting* A2 (*adiós*)
Cuba ['kjuːbə] Cuba; **Cuban** **1** *adj* cubano **2** *n* cubano(-a) *m*(*f*)
cube [kjuːb] cubo *m*; **cubic** cúbico
cubicle ['kjuːbɪkl] (*changing room*) cubículo *m*
cuddle ['kʌdl] abrazar
cue [kjuː] *for actor etc* pie *m*; *for pool* taco *m*
cuff [kʌf] *of shirt* puño *m*; *of pants* vuelta *f*; (*blow*) cachete *m*
culminate ['kʌlmɪneɪt] culminar (***in*** en); **culmination** culminación *f*
culprit ['kʌlprɪt] culpable *m/f*
cult [kʌlt] (*sect*) secta *f*
cultivate ['kʌltɪveɪt] *also fig* cultivar; **cultivated** *person* culto; **cultivation** *of land* cultivo *m*
cultural ['kʌlʧərəl] cultural; **culture** cultura *f*; **cultured** culto
cumulative ['kjuːmjʊlətɪv] acumulativo
cunning ['kʌnɪŋ] **1** *n* astucia *f* **2** *adj* astuto
cup [kʌp] taza *f*; *trophy* copa *f*
cupboard ['kʌbərd] armario *m*
curb [kɜːrb] **1** *n of street* bordillo *m*; *on powers etc* freno *m* **2** *v/t* frenar
cure [kjʊr] **1** *n* MED cura *f* **2** *v/t* MED, *meat* curar
curiosity [kjʊrɪ'ɑːsətɪ] curiosidad *f*; **curious** curioso
curl [kɜːrl] **1** *n in hair* rizo *m*;

of smoke voluta **2** *v/t hair* rizar; (*wind*) enroscar **3** *v/i of hair* rizarse; *of paper* ondularse

◆ **curl up** acurrucarse

curly ['kɜːrlɪ] *hair* rizado; *tail* enroscado

currency ['kʌrənsɪ] *money* moneda *f*; ***foreign ~*** divisas *fpl*; **current 1** *n in sea*, ELEC corriente *f* **2** *adj* actual; **current affairs** la actualidad

curse [kɜːrs] **1** *n* (*spell*) maldición *f*; (*swearword*) palabrota *f* **2** *v/t* maldecir **3** *v/i* (*swear*) decir palabrotas

cursor ['kɜːrsər] COMPUT cursor *m*

cursory ['kɜːrsərɪ] superficial

curt [kɜːrt] brusco, seco

curtain ['kɜːrtn] cortina *f*; THEA telón *m*

curve [kɜːrv] **1** *n* curva *f* **2** *v/i* curvarse

cushion ['kʊʃn] **1** *n* cojín *m* **2** *v/t blow*, *fall* amortiguar

custody ['kʌstədɪ] *of children* custodia *f*; ***in ~*** LAW detenido

custom ['kʌstəm] costumbre *f*; COM clientela *f*; **customer** cliente(-a) *m*(*f*); **customer service** atención *f* al cliente

customs ['kʌstəmz] aduana *f*; **customs officer** funcionario(-a) *m*(*f*) de aduanas

cut [kʌt] **1** *n* corte *m*; (*reduction*) recorte (***in*** de) **2** *v/t* cortar; (*reduce*) recortar; *hours* acortar; ***get one's hair ~*** cortarse el pelo

◆ **cut down 1** *v/t tree* talar, cortar **2** *v/i in expenses* gastar menos; *in smoking* fumar menos

◆ **cut off** cortar; (*isolate*) aislar

◆ **cut up** trocear

cutback recorte *m*

cute [kjuːt] guapo, lindo; (*clever*) listo

cut-off date fecha *f* límite; **cut-price** rebajado; *store* de productos rebajados; **cut-throat** *competition* despiadado; **cutting 1** *n from newspaper* recorte *m* **2** *adj remark* hiriente

cyber ... ['saɪbər] ciber...

cycle ['saɪkl] **1** *n* bicicleta *f*; *of events* ciclo *m* **2** *v/i* ir en bicicleta; **cycling** ciclismo *m*; **cyclist** ciclista *m/f*

cylinder ['sɪlɪndər] cilindro *m*; **cylindrical** cilíndrico

cynic ['sɪnɪk] escéptico(-a) *m*(*f*); **cynical** escéptico; **cynicism** escepticismo *m*

Czech [ʧek] **1** *adj* checo; ***the ~ Republic*** la República Checa **2** *n person* checo(-a) *m*(*f*); *language* checho *m*

D

DA [diː'eɪ] (= ***district attorney***) fiscal *m/f* (del distrito)

◆ **dabble in** ['dæbl] ser aficionado a

dad [dæd] *talking to him* papá *m*; *talking about him* padre *m*

daily ['deɪlɪ] **1** *n* (*paper*) diario *m* **2** *adj* diario

'dairy products productos *mpl* lácteos

dam [dæm] **1** *n for water* presa *f* **2** *v/t river* embalsar

damage ['dæmɪdʒ] **1** *n* daños *mpl*; *to reputation etc* daño *m* **2** *v/t also fig* dañar; **damages** LAW daños *mpl* y perjuicios; **damaging** perjudicial

damn [dæm] F **1** *int* ¡mecachis! F **2** *adj* maldito F **3** *adv* muy; **damning** *evidence* condenatorio; *report* crítico

damp [dæmp] húmedo

dance [dæns] **1** *n* baile *m* **2** *v/i* bailar; **dancer** bailarín (-ina) *m(f)*; **dancing** baile *m*

Dane [deɪn] danés(-esa) *m(f)*

danger ['deɪndʒər] peligro *m*; **dangerous** peligroso

dangle ['dæŋgl] **1** *v/t* balancear **2** *v/i* colgar

Danish ['deɪnɪʃ] **1** *adj* danés **2** *n language* danés *m*; **Danish (pastry)** pastel *m* de hojaldre (*dulce*)

dare [der] atreverse; ~ ***to do sth*** atreverse a hacer algo; ~ ***s.o. to do sth*** desafiar a alguien para que haga algo; **daring** atrevido

dark [dɑːrk] **1** *n* oscuridad *f* **2** *adj* oscuro; **dark glasses** gafas *fpl* oscuras, *L.Am.* lentes *fpl* oscuras; **darkness** oscuridad *f*

darling ['dɑːrlɪŋ] cielo *m*

dart [dɑːrt] **1** *n for throwing* dardo *m* **2** *v/i* lanzarse

dash [dæʃ] **1** *n punctuation* raya *f*; (*small amount*) chorrito *m* **2** *v/i* correr **3** *v/t hopes* frustrar; **dashboard** salpicadero *m*

data ['deɪtə] datos *mpl*; **database** base *f* de datos

date[1] [deɪt] *fruit* dátil *m*

date[2] [deɪt] fecha *f*; (*meeting*) cita *f*; (*person*) pareja *f*; ***out of*** ~ *clothes* pasado de moda; *passport* caducado; ***up to*** ~ al día; **dated** anticuado

daughter ['dɒːtər] hija *f*; **daughter-in-law** nuera *f*

dawn [dɒːn] amanecer *m*, alba *f*; *fig* albores *mpl*

day [deɪ] día *m*; ***the*** ~ ***after*** el día siguiente; ***the*** ~ ***after tomorrow*** pasado mañana; ***the*** ~ ***before*** el día anterior; ***the*** ~ ***before yesterday*** anteayer; ***in those*** ~***s*** en aquellos tiempos; ***the other*** ~ (*recently*) el otro día; **daybreak** amanecer *m*, alba *f*; **daydream** **1** *n* fantasía *f* **2** *v/i* soñar despierto; **daylight** luz *f* del día; **day spa** centro *m* de salud

dazed [deɪzd] aturdido

dazzle ['dæzl] *also fig* deslumbrar

dead [ded] **1** *adj* muerto; *battery* agotado; *light bulb* fundido; *place* muerto F **2** *adv* F (*very*) tela de F; **~ *beat*, ~ *tired*** hecho polvo **3** *npl*: ***the ~*** los muertos; **dead end** *street* callejón *m* sin salida; **dead heat** empate *m*; **deadline** fecha *f* tope; *for newspaper* hora *f* de cierre; ***meet a ~*** cumplir un plazo; **deadlock** *in talks* punto *m* muerto; **deadly** mortal

deaf [def] sordo; **deafening** ensordecedor; **deafness** sordera *f*

deal [di:l] **1** *n* acuerdo *m*; ***a great ~ of*** mucho(s) **2** *v/t cards* repartir

◆ **deal in** COM comerciar con

◆ **deal with** tratar; *situation* hacer frente a; *customer*, *applications* encargarse de; (*do business with*) hacer negocios con

dealer ['di:lər] comerciante *m/f*; (*drug ~*) traficante *m/f*; **dealing** (*drug ~*) tráfico *m*; **dealings** (*business*) tratos *mpl*

dear [dɪr] querido; (*expensive*) caro; ***Dear Sir*** Muy Sr. Mío

death [deθ] muerte *f*; **death toll** saldo *m* de víctimas mortales

debatable [dɪ'beɪtəbl] discutible; **debate 1** *n* debate *m* **2** *v/t & v/i* debatir

debit ['debɪt] **1** *n* cargo *m* **2** *v/t account* cargar en; *amount* cargar; **debit card** tarjeta *f* de débito

debris [də'bri:] *nsg of building* escombros *mpl*; *of airplane* restos *mpl*

debt [det] deuda *f*; ***be in ~*** estar endeudado; **debtor** deudor(-a) *m(f)*

debug [di:'bʌg] COMPUT depurar

decade ['dekeɪd] década *f*

decadent ['dekədənt] decadente

decaffeinated [dɪ'kæfɪneɪtɪd] descafeinado

decay [dɪ'keɪ] **1** *n of plant* putrefacción *f*; *of civilization* declive *m*; *in teeth* caries *f inv* **2** *v/i of plant* pudrirse; *of civilization* decaer; *of teeth* cariarse

deceased [dɪ'si:st]: ***the ~*** el difunto / la difunta

deceit [dɪ'si:t] engaño *m*, mentira *f*; **deceitful** mentiroso; **deceive** engañar

December [dɪ'sembər] diciembre *m*

decency ['di:sənsɪ] decencia *f*; **decent** decente

deception [dɪ'sepʃn] engaño *m*; **deceptive** engañoso

decide [dɪ'saɪd] decidir; **decided** (*definite*) tajante

decimal ['desɪml] decimal *m*

decipher [dɪ'saɪfər] descifrar

decision [dɪ'sɪʒn] decisión *f*; **decisive** decidido; (*crucial*) decisivo
deck [dek] *of ship* cubierta *f*; *of cards* baraja *f*
declaration [deklə'reɪʃn] declaración *f*; **declare** declarar
decline [dɪ'klaɪn] **1** *n* descenso *m*; *in standards* caída *f*; *in health* empeoramiento *m* **2** *v/t invitation* declinar **3** *v/i* (*refuse*) rehusar; (*decrease*) declinar; *of health* empeorar
decode [di:'koʊd] descodificar
décor ['deɪkɔ:r] decoración *f*
decorate ['dekəreɪt] *with paint* pintar; *with paper* empapelar; (*adorn*) decorar; *soldier* condecorar; **decoration** *paint* pintado *m*; *paper* empapelado *m*; (*ornament*) decoración *f*; **decorator** (*interior* ~) decorador(a) *m*(*f*)
decoy ['di:kɔɪ] señuelo *m*
decrease 1 ['di:kri:s] *n* disminución *f* (***in*** de) **2** [dɪ'kri:s] *v/t & v/i* disminuir
dedicate ['dedɪkeɪt] *book* dedicar; **dedicated** dedicado; **dedication** dedicación *f*; *in book* dedicatoria *f*
deduce [dɪ'du:s] deducir
deduct [dɪ'dʌkt] descontar; **deduction** deducción *f*
deed [di:d] (*act*) acción *f*, obra *f*; LAW escritura *f*
deep [di:p] profundo; *color* intenso; **deepen 1** *v/t* profundizar **2** *v/i* hacerse más profundo; *of mystery* agudizarse; **deep freeze** congelador *m*
deer [dɪr] ciervo *m*
deface [dɪ'feɪs] desfigurar
defamation [defə'meɪʃn] difamación *f*; **defamatory** difamatorio
defeat [dɪ'fi:t] **1** *n* derrota *f* **2** *v/t* derrotar
defect ['di:fekt] defecto *m*; **defective** defectuoso
de'fence *Br* ☞ ***defense***
defend [dɪ'fend] defender; **defendant** acusado(-a) *m*(*f*); *in civil case* demandado(-a) *m*(*f*); **defense** defensa *f*; **defenseless** indefenso; **Defense Secretary** POL ministro(-a) *m*(*f*) de Defensa; *in USA* secretario *m* de Defensa; **defensive 1** *n* : ***go on the*** ~ ponerse a la defensiva **2** *adj* defensivo
defer [dɪ'fɜ:r] (*postpone*) aplazar, diferir
defiance [dɪ'faɪəns] desafío *m*; **defiant** desafiante
deficiency [dɪ'fɪʃənsɪ] deficiencia *f*
deficit ['defɪsɪt] déficit *m*
define [dɪ'faɪn] definir
definite ['defɪnɪt] definitivo; *improvement* claro; (*certain*) seguro; **definitely** con certeza, sin lugar a dudas
definition [defɪ'nɪʃn] definición *f*
deformity [dɪ'fɔ:rmɪtɪ] deformidad *f*
defrost [di:'frɒ:st] descongelar

defuse [diː'fjuːz] *bomb* desactivar; *situation* calmar
defy [dɪ'faɪ] desafiar
degrading [dɪ'greɪdɪŋ] degradante
degree [dɪ'griː] grado *m*; *from university* título *m*
dehydrated [diːhaɪ'dreɪtɪd] deshidratado
deign [deɪn]: ~ **to** dignarse a
dejected [dɪ'dʒektɪd] abatido, desanimado
delay [dɪ'leɪ] **1** *n* retraso *m* **2** *v/t* retrasar; ***be ~ed*** llevar retraso **3** *v/i* retrasarse
delegate ['delɪgeɪt] **1** *n* delegado(-a) *m(f)* **2** *v/t task* delegar; *person* delegar en; **delegation** delegación *f*
delete [dɪ'liːt] borrar; (*cross out*) tachar; **deletion** borrado *m*
deliberate **1** [dɪ'lɪbərət] *adj* deliberado **2** [dɪ'lɪbəreɪt] *v/i* deliberar; **deliberately** deliberadamente
delicate ['delɪkət] delicado; *health* frágil
delicatessen [delɪkə'tesn] *tienda de productos alimenticios de calidad*
delicious [dɪ'lɪʃəs] delicioso
delight [dɪ'laɪt] placer *m*; **delighted** encantado; **delightful** encantador
deliver [dɪ'lɪvər] entregar, repartir; *message* dar; *baby* dar a luz; *speech* pronunciar; **delivery** entrega *f*, reparto *m*; *of baby* parto *m*; **delivery date** fecha *f* de entrega
de luxe [də'luːks] de lujo
demand [dɪ'mænd] **1** *n* exigencia *f*; *by union* reivindicación *f*; COM demanda *f*; ***in ~*** solicitado **2** *v/t* exigir; (*require*) requirir; **demanding** *job* que exige mucho; *person* exigente
demo ['demoʊ] (*protest*) manifestación *f*; *of video etc* maqueta *f*
democracy [dɪ'mɑːkrəsɪ] democracia *f*; **democrat** demócrata *m/f*; **democratic** democrático
demolish [dɪ'mɑːlɪʃ] demoler; *argument* destruir; **demolition** demolición *f*; *of argument* destrucción *f*
demonstrate ['demənstreɪt] **1** *v/t* demostrar **2** *v/i politically* manifestarse; **demonstration** demostración *f*; (*protest*) manifestación *f*; **demonstrator** (*protester*) manifestante *m/f*
demoralized [dɪ'mɔːrəlaɪzd] desmoralizado; **demoralizing** desmoralizador
demote [diː'moʊt] degradar
den [den] (*study*) estudio *m*
denial [dɪ'naɪəl] *of accusation* negación *f*; *of request* denegación *f*
denim ['denɪm] tela *f* vaquera
Denmark ['denmɑːrk] Dinamarca
denomination [dɪnɑːmɪ'neɪʃn] *of money* valor *m*; *religious* confesión *f*
dense [dens] denso; *foliage*

espeso; *crowd* compacto; **density** *of population* densidad *f*
dent [dent] **1** *n* abolladura *f* **2** *v/t* abollar
dental ['dentl] dental
dented ['dentɪd] abollado
dentist ['dentɪst] dentista *m/f*; **dentures** dentadura *f* postiza
Denver boot ['denvər] cepo *m*
deny [dɪ'naɪ] *charge* negar; *right, request* denegar
deodorant [diː'oudərənt] desodorante *m*
department [dɪ'pɑːrtmənt] departamento *m*; *of government* ministerio *m*; **Department of State** Ministerio *m* de Asuntos Exteriores; **department store** grandes almacenes *mpl*
departure [dɪ'pɑːrtʃər] salida *f*; *from job* marcha *f*; (*deviation*) desviación *f*; **departure lounge** sala *f* de embarque; **departure time** hora *f* de salida
depend [dɪ'pend] depender; ***that ~s*** depende; **dependence** dependencia *f*
depict [dɪ'pɪkt] describir
deplorable [dɪ'plɔːrəbl] deplorable; **deplore** deplorar
deploy [dɪ'plɔɪ] (*use*) utilizar; (*position*) desplegar
deport [dɪ'pɔːrt] deportar; **deportation** deportación *f*
deposit [dɪ'pɑːzɪt] **1** *n* depósito *m*; *of coal* yacimiento *m* **2** *v/t money* depositar, *Span* ingresar; (*put down*) depositar; **deposition** LAW declaración *f*
depot ['diːpou] *for storage* depósito *m*
depreciation [dɪpriːʃɪ'eɪʃn] FIN depreciación *f*
depress [dɪ'pres] *person* deprimir; **depressed** deprimido; **depressing** deprimente; **depression** depresión *f*; *meteorological* borrasca *f*
deprivation [deprɪ'veɪʃn] privación *f*; **deprive** privar; **deprived** desfavorecido
depth [depθ] profundidad *f*; *of color* intensidad *f*; ***in ~*** en profundidad
deputy ['depjutɪ] segundo(-a) *m(f)*
derail [dɪ'reɪl]: ***be ~ed*** descarrilar
derelict ['derəlɪkt] en ruinas
deride [dɪ'raɪd] ridiculizar, mofarse de; **derision** burla *f*, mofa *f*; **derisory** irrisorio
derivative [dɪ'rɪvətɪv] poco original; **derive** obtener; ***be ~d from*** *of word* derivar(se) de
dermatologist [dɜːrmə'tɑːlədʒɪst] dermatólogo(-a) *m(f)*
derogatory [dɪ'rɑːgətɔːrɪ] despectivo
descendant [dɪ'sendənt] descendiente *m/f*; **descent** descenso *m*; (*ancestry*) ascendencia *f*
describe [dɪ'skraɪb] descri-

bir; **description** descripción *f*

desegregate [diː'segrəgeɪt] acabar con la segregación racial en

desert[1] ['dezərt] *n* desierto *m*

desert[2] [dɪ'zɜːrt] **1** *v/t* abandonar **2** *v/i of soldier* desertar; **deserted** desierto; **deserter** MIL desertor(a) *m(f)*; **desertion** abandono *m*; MIL deserción *f*

deserve [dɪ'zɜːrv] merecer

design [dɪ'zaɪn] **1** *n* diseño *m*; (*pattern*) motivo *m* **2** *v/t* diseñar

designate ['dezɪgneɪt] *person* designar; *area* declarar

designer [dɪ'zaɪnər] diseñador(a) *m(f)*; **designer clothes** ropa *f* de diseño

desirable [dɪ'zaɪrəbl] deseable; *house* apetecible; **desire** deseo *m*

desk [desk] *in classroom* pupitre *m*; *in office* mesa *f*; *in hotel* recepción *f*; **desk clerk** recepcionista *m/f*; **desktop publishing** autoedición *f*

desolate ['desələt] *place* desolado

despair [dɪ'sper] **1** *n* desesperación *f*; ***in ~*** desesperado **2** *v/i* desesperarse; **desperate** desesperado; ***be ~ for sth*** necesitar algo desesperadamente; **desperation** desesperación *f*

despicable [dɪs'pɪkəbl] despreciable; **despise** despreciar

despite [dɪ'spaɪt] a pesar de

dessert [dɪ'zɜːrt] postre *m*

destination [destɪ'neɪʃn] destino *m*

destroy [dɪ'strɔɪ] destruir; **destroyer** NAUT destructor *m*; **destruction** destrucción *f*; **destructive** destructivo; *child* revoltoso

detach [dɪ'tætʃ] separar, soltar; **detached** (*objective*) distanciado; **detachment** (*objectivity*) distancia *f*

detail ['diːteɪl] detalle *m*; **detailed** detallado

detain [dɪ'teɪn] (*hold back*) entretener; *as prisoner* detener; **detainee** detenido(-a) *m(f)*

detect [dɪ'tekt] percibir; *of device* detectar; **detection** *of criminal* descubrimiento *m*; *of smoke etc* detección *f*; **detective** detective *m/f*; **detector** detector *m*

détente ['deɪtɑːnt] POL distensión *f*

deter [dɪ'tɜːr] disuadir

detergent [dɪ'tɜːrdʒənt] detergente *m*

deteriorate [dɪ'tɪrɪəreɪt] deteriorarse; *of weather* empeorar

determination [dɪtɜːrmɪ'neɪʃn] determinación *f*; **determine** (*establish*) determinar; **determined** resuelto, decidido

detest [dɪ'test] detestar; **detestable** detestable

detour ['diːtʊr] rodeo *m*; (*di-*

version) desvío *m*
devaluation [diːvælju'eɪʃn] devaluación *f*; **devalue** devaluar
devastate ['devəsteɪt] devastar; *fig*: *person* asolar
develop [dɪ'veləp] **1** *v/t film* revelar; *site* urbanizar; *business* desarrollar; (*improve on*) perfeccionar; *illness* contraer **2** *v/i* (*grow*) desarrollarse; **developing country** país *m* en vías de desarrollo; **development** *of film* revelado *m*; *of site* urbanización *f*; *of business*, *country* desarrollo *m*; (*event*) acontecimiento *m*; (*improving*) perfeccionamiento *m*
device [dɪ'vaɪs] *tool* aparato *m*, dispositivo *m*
devil ['devl] *also fig* diablo *m*
devise [dɪ'vaɪz] idear
devote [dɪ'voʊt] dedicar (***to*** a); **devoted** *son etc* afectuoso; **devotion** devoción *f*
devour [dɪ'vaʊər] devorar
devout [dɪ'vaʊt] devoto
diabetes [daɪə'biːtiːz] *nsg* diabetes *f*; **diabetic** diabético(-a) *m*(*f*)
diagnose ['daɪəgnoʊz] diagnosticar; **diagnosis** diagnóstico *m*
diagonal [daɪ'ægənl] diagonal; **diagonally** diagonalmente, en diagonal
diagram ['daɪəgræm] diagrama *m*
dial ['daɪl] **1** *n of clock* esfera *f*; *of instrument* cuadrante *m* **2** *v/t* & *v/i* TELEC marcar
dialog, *Br* **dialogue** ['daɪəlɑːg] diálogo *m*
'**dial tone** tono *m* de marcar
diameter [daɪ'æmɪtər] diámetro *m*
diamond ['daɪmənd] diamante *m*; *shape* rombo *m*
diaper ['daɪpər] pañal *m*
diaphragm ['daɪəfræm] diafragma *m*
diarrhea, *Br* **diarrhoea** [daɪə'riːə] diarrea *f*
diary ['daɪrɪ] diario *m*; *for appointments* agenda *f*
dice [daɪs] dado *m*; *pl* dados *mpl*
dictate [dɪk'teɪt] dictar; **dictator** POL dictador(a) *m*(*f*); **dictatorship** dictadura *f*
dictionary ['dɪkʃənerɪ] diccionario *m*
die [daɪ] morir
◆ **die down** *of storm* amainar; *of excitement* calmarse
◆ **die out** desaparecer
diet ['daɪət] **1** *n* dieta *f* **2** *v/i* hacer dieta
differ ['dɪfər] ser distinto; (*disagree*) discrepar; **difference** diferencia *f*; **different** diferente, distinto (***from*** de); **differently** de manera diferente
difficult ['dɪfɪkəlt] difícil; **difficulty** dificultad *f*
dig [dɪg] cavar
digest [daɪ'dʒest] *also fig* digerir; **digestion** digestión *f*
digit ['dɪdʒɪt] dígito *m*; **digital** digital; **digital camera**

cámara *f* digital; **digital photo** foto *f* digital
dignified ['dɪgnɪfaɪd] digno; **dignity** dignidad *f*
dilapidated [dɪ'læpɪdeɪtɪd] destartalado
dilemma [dɪ'lemə] dilema *m*
dilute [daɪ'lu:t] diluir
dim [dɪm] **1** *adj room* oscuro; *light* tenue; *outline* borroso; (*stupid*) tonto **2** *v/i of lights* atenuarse
dime [daɪm] *moneda de diez centavos*
dimension [daɪ'menʃn] dimensión *f*
diminish [dɪ'mɪnɪʃ] disminuir
din [dɪn] estruendo *m*
dine [daɪn] *fml* cenar
dinghy ['dɪŋgɪ] *small yacht* bote *m* de vela; *rubber boat* lancha *f* neumática
dining car ['daɪnɪŋ] RAIL coche *m* comedor; **dining room** comedor *m*
dinner ['dɪnər] cena *f*; *at midday* comida *f*; (*formal*) cena *f* de gala; **dinner party** cena *f*
dip [dɪp] **1** *n for food* salsa *f*; (*slope*) inclinación *f*; (*depression*) hondonada *f* **2** *v/i of road* bajar
diploma [dɪ'ploʊmə] diploma *m*
diplomacy [dɪ'ploʊməsɪ] diplomacia *f*; **diplomat** diplomático(-a) *m(f)*; **diplomatic** diplomático
direct [daɪ'rekt] **1** *adj* directo **2** *v/t* dirigir; **direction** dirección *f*; **~s** *to a place* indicaciones *fpl*; (*instructions*) instrucciones *fpl*; *for medicine* posología *f*; *to a place* indicazioni *fpl*; *for use* istruzioni *fpl*; **directly** (*straight*) directamente; (*soon*) pronto; (*immediately*) ahora mismo; **director** director(a) *m(f)*; **directory** directorio *m*; TELEC guía *f* telefónica
dirt [dɜ:rt] suciedad *f*; **dirty 1** *adj* sucio; (*pornographic*) pornográfico **2** *v/t* ensuciar
disability [dɪsə'bɪlətɪ] discapacidad *f*; **disabled** discapacitado
disadvantage [dɪsəd'væntɪdʒ] desventaja *f*; **disadvantaged** desfavorecido
disagree [dɪsə'gri:] no estar de acuerdo; **disagreeable** desagradable; **disagreement** desacuerdo *m*; (*argument*) discusión *f*
disappear [dɪsə'pɪr] desaparecer; **disappearance** desaparición *f*
disappoint [dɪsə'pɔɪnt] desilusionar, decepcionar; **disappointing** decepcionante; **disappointment** desilusión *f*, decepción *f*
disapproval [dɪsə'pru:vl] desaprobación *f*; **disapprove** desaprobar, estar en contra; **disapproving** desaprobatorio
disarm [dɪs'ɑ:rm] desarmar; **disarmament** desarme *m*
disaster [dɪ'zæstər] desastre *m*; **disastrous** desastroso

disband [dɪs'bænd] **1** *v/t* disolver **2** *v/i* disolverse
disbelief [dɪsbə'liːf] incredulidad *f*
disc [dɪsk] (CD) compact *m* (disc)
discard [dɪ'skɑːrd] desechar; *boyfriend* deshacerse de
disciplinary [dɪsɪ'plɪnərɪ] disciplinario; **discipline** disciplina *f*
'disc jockey disc jockey *m/f*, *Span* pinchadiscos *m/f inv*
disclaim [dɪs'kleɪm] negar
disclose [dɪs'klous] revelar
disco ['dɪskou] discoteca *f*
discomfort [dɪs'kʌmfərt] (*pain*) molestia *f*; (*embarrassment*) incomodidad *f*
disconcert [dɪskən'sɜːrt] desconcertar
disconnect [dɪskə'nekt] desconectar
discontent [dɪskən'tent] descontento *m*
discontinue [dɪskən'tɪnjuː] *product* dejar de producir; *bus service* suspender
discotheque ['dɪskətek] discoteca *f*
discount ['dɪskaunt] descuento *m*
discourage [dɪs'kʌrɪdʒ] (*dissuade*) disuadir (***from*** de); (*dishearten*) desanimar
discover [dɪ'skʌvər] descubrir; **discovery** descubrimiento *m*
discredit [dɪs'kredɪt] desacreditar
discreet [dɪ'skriːt] discreto
discrepancy [dɪ'skrepənsɪ] discrepancia *f*
discretion [dɪ'skreʃn] discreción *f*
discriminate [dɪ'skrɪmɪneɪt] discriminar (***against*** contra); **discriminating** entendido; **discrimination** *sexual etc* discriminación *f*
discuss [dɪ'skʌs] discutir; *of article* analizar; **discussion** discusión *f*
disease [dɪ'ziːz] enfermedad *f*
disembark [dɪsəm'bɑːrk] desembarcar
disentangle [dɪsən'tæŋgl] desenredar
disfigure [dɪs'fɪgər] desfigurar
disgrace [dɪs'greɪs] **1** *n* vergüenza *f* **2** *v/t* deshonrar; **disgraceful** vergonzoso
disguise [dɪs'gaɪz] **1** *n* disfraz *m* **2** *v/t voice etc* cambiar; *fear, anxiety* disfrazar
disgust [dɪs'gʌst] **1** *n* asco *m*, repugnancia *f* **2** *v/t* dar asco a, repugnar; **disgusting** asqueroso, repugnante
dish [dɪʃ] plato *m*
disheartening [dɪs'hɑːrtnɪŋ] descorazonador
dishonest [dɪs'ɑːnɪst] deshonesto; **dishonesty** deshonestidad *f*
dishonor [dɪs'ɑːnər] deshonra *f*; **dishonorable** deshonroso; **dishonour** *etc Br* ☞ ***dishonor etc***
disillusion [dɪsɪ'luːʒn] desilu-

sionar; **disillusionment** desilusión *f*

disinfect [dɪsɪn'fekt] desinfectar; **disinfectant** desinfectante *m*

disinherit [dɪsɪn'herɪt] desheredar

disintegrate [dɪs'ɪntəgreɪt] desintegrarse; *of marriage* deshacerse

disjointed [dɪs'dʒɔɪntɪd] deshilvanado

disk [dɪsk] *also* COMPUT disco *m*; **disk drive** COMPUT unidad *f* de disco; **diskette** disquete *m*

dislike [dɪs'laɪk] **1** *n* antipatía *f* **2** *v/t*: ***I ~ him*** no me gusta

dislocate ['dɪsləkeɪt] dislocar

disloyal [dɪs'lɔɪəl] desleal

dismal ['dɪzməl] *weather* horroroso; *prospect* negro; *person* (*sad*) triste; *person* (*negative*) negativo; *failure* estrepitoso

dismantle [dɪs'mæntl] desmantelar

dismay [dɪs'meɪ] (*alarm*) consternación *f*; (*disappointment*) desánimo *m*

dismiss [dɪs'mɪs] *worker* despedir; *suggestion* rechazar; *idea* descartar; **dismissal** *of worker* despido *m*

disobedience [dɪsə'bi:dɪəns] desobediencia *f*; **disobedient** desobediente; **disobey** desobedecer

disorganized [dɪs'ɔ:rgənaɪzd] desorganizado

disoriented [dɪs'ɔ:rɪəntɪd] desorientado

disparaging [dɪ'spærɪdʒɪŋ] despreciativo

disparity [dɪ'spærətɪ] disparidad *f*

dispassionate [dɪ'spæʃənət] desapasionado

dispatch [dɪ'spætʃ] (*send*) enviar

disperse [dɪ'spɜ:rs] *of crowd* dispersarse; *of mist* disiparse

display [dɪ'spleɪ] **1** *n* muestra *f*; *in store window* objetos *mpl* expuestos; COMPUT pantalla *f* **2** *v/t emotion* mostrar; *for sale* exponer; COMPUT visualizar

displease [dɪs'pli:z] desagradar; **displeasure** desagrado *m*

disposable [dɪ'spoʊzəbl] desechable; **disposal** eliminación *f*; ***put sth at s.o.'s ~*** poner algo a disposición de alguien

◆ **dispose of** [dɪ'spoʊz] (*get rid of*) deshacerse de

disprove [dɪs'pru:v] refutar

dispute [dɪ'spju:t] **1** *n* disputa *f*; *industrial* conflicto *m* laboral **2** *v/t* discutir; (*fight over*) disputarse

disqualification [dɪskwɑ:lɪfɪ'keɪʃn] descalificación *f*; **disqualify** descalificar

disregard [dɪsrə'gɑ:rd] **1** *n* indiferencia *f* **2** *v/t* no tener en cuenta

disreputable [dɪs'repjʊtəbl] poco respetable

disrespect [dɪsrə'spekt] falta

f de respeto; **disrespectful** irrespetuoso
disrupt [dɪs'rʌpt] *train service* alterar; *meeting, class* interrumpir; **disruption** *of train service* alteración *f*; *of meeting, class* interrupción *f*
dissatisfaction [dɪssætɪs'fækʃn] insatisfacción *f*; **dissatisfied** insatisfecho
dissident ['dɪsɪdənt] disidente *m/f*
dissolve [dɪ'zɑːlv] **1** *v/t* disolver **2** *v/i* disolverse
distance ['dɪstəns] distancia *f*; ***in the ~*** en la lejanía; **distant** distante
distaste [dɪs'teɪst] desagrado *m*; **distasteful** desagradable
distinct [dɪ'stɪŋkt] *(clear)* claro; *(different)* distinto; **distinctive** característico; **distinctly** claramente, con claridad; *(decidedly)* verdaderamente
distinguish [dɪ'stɪŋgwɪʃ] distinguir (***between*** entre); **distinguished** distinguido
distort [dɪ'stɔːrt] distorsionar
distract [dɪ'strækt] distraer; **distraught** [dɪ'strɒːt] angustiado, consternado
distress [dɪ'stres] **1** *n* sufrimiento *m* **2** *v/t (upset)* angustiar; **distressing** angustiante
distribute [dɪ'strɪbjuːt] distribuir; **distribution** distribución *f*; **distributor** COM distribuidor(a) *m(f)*
district ['dɪstrɪkt] zona *f*; *(neighborhood)* barrio *m*; **district attorney** fiscal *m/f* del distrito
distrust [dɪs'trʌst] desconfianza *f*
disturb [dɪ'stɜːrb] *(interrupt)* molestar; *(upset)* preocupar; **disturbance** *(interruption)* molestia *f*; **~s** *(civil unrest)* disturbios *mpl*; **disturbed** preocupado; *mentally* perturbado; **disturbing** inquietante
disused [dɪs'juːzd] abandonado
ditch [dɪʧ] **1** *n* zanja *f* **2** *v/t* F *plan* abandonar
dive [daɪv] **1** *n* salto *m* de cabeza; *underwater* inmersión *f*; *of plane* descenso *m* en picado; F *bar etc* antro *m* F **2** *v/i* tirarse de cabeza; *underwater* bucear; *of plane* descender en picado; **diver** *underwater* buceador(a) *m(f)*
diverge [daɪ'vɜːrdʒ] bifurcarse
diversification [daɪvɜːrsɪfɪ'keɪʃn] COM diversificación *f*; **diversify** COM diversificarse
diversion [daɪ'vɜːrʃn] *for traffic* desvío *m*; *to distract attention* distracción *f*; **divert** desviar
divide [dɪ'vaɪd] dividir
dividend ['dɪvɪdend] FIN dividendo *m*
diving ['daɪvɪŋ] *from board* salto *m* de trampolín; *(scuba ~)* buceo *m*; **diving board**

trampolín *m*
division [dɪ'vɪʒn] división *f*
divorce [dɪ'vɔːrs] **1** *n* divorcio *m* **2** *v/t* divorciarse de **3** *v/i* divorciarse; **divorced** divorciado; **divorcee** divorciado(-a) *m(f)*
divulge [daɪ'vʌldʒ] divulgar
DIY [diːaɪ'waɪ] (= ***do it yourself***) bricolaje *m*
dizziness ['dɪzɪnɪs] mareo *m*; **dizzy** mareado
DJ ['diːdʒeɪ] (= ***disc jockey***) disc jockey *m/f*, *Span* pinchadiscos *m/f inv*
DNA [diːen'eɪ] (= ***deoxyribonucleic acid***) AND *m* (= ácido *m* desoxirribonucleico)
do [duː] **1** *v/t* hacer; *100 mph etc* ir a; ***~ one's hair*** arreglarse el pelo **2** *v/i*: ***that'll ~ nicely*** eso bastará; ***that will ~!*** ¡ya vale!; ***~ well*** *of business* ir bien; ***he's ~ing well*** le van bien las cosas; ***well done!*** (*congratulations!*) ¡bien hecho!; ***how ~ you ~?*** encantado de conocerle
◆ **do away with** abolir
◆ **do up** (*renovate*) renovar; *coat* abrocharse; *laces* atarse
◆ **do with:** ***I could do with ...*** no me vendría mal...
◆ **do without** pasar sin
docile ['doʊsəl] dócil
dock[1] [dɑːk] **1** *n* NAUT muelle *m* **2** *v/i of ship* atracar; *of spaceship* acoplarse
dock[2] [dɑːk] *n* LAW banquillo *m* (de los acusados)
doctor ['dɑːktər] médico *m*; *form of address* doctor *m*; **doctorate** doctorado *m*
doctrine ['dɑːktrɪn] doctrina *f*
document ['dɑːkjʊmənt] documento *m*; **documentary** documental *m*; **documentation** documentación *f*
dodge [dɑːdʒ] *blow, person* esquivar; *question* eludir
dog [dɒːg] **1** *n* perro(-a) *m(f)* **2** *v/t of bad luck* perseguir
dogma ['dɒːgmə] dogma *m*; **dogmatic** dogmático
'**dog tag** MIL chapa *f* de identificación; **dog-tired** F hecho polvo F
do-it-yourself [duːɪtjər'self] bricolaje *m*
doldrums ['doʊldrəmz]: ***be in the ~*** *of economy* estar en un bache; *of person* estar deprimido
doll [dɑːl] *toy* muñeca *f*; F *woman* muñeca *f* F
dollar ['dɑːlər] dólar *m*
dolphin ['dɑːlfɪn] delfín *m*
dome [doʊm] cúpula *f*
domestic [də'mestɪk] **1** *adj chores* doméstico; *news, policy* nacional **2** *n* empleado(-a) *m(f)* del hogar; **domestic flight** vuelo *m* nacional
dominant ['dɑːmɪnənt] dominante; **dominate** dominar; **domination** dominación *f*; **domineering** dominante
donate [doʊ'neɪt] donar; **donation** donación *f*
donkey ['dɑːŋkɪ] burro *m*

donor ['dounər] donante *m/f*
donut ['dounʌt] dónut *m*
doom [du:m] (*fate*) destino *m*; (*ruin*) fatalidad *f*; **doomed** *project* condenado al fracaso
door [dɔ:r] puerta *f*; **doorbell** timbre *m*; **doorman** portero *m*; **doorway** puerta *f*
dope [doup] (*drugs*) droga *f*; F (*idiot*) lelo(-a) *m(f)*
dormant ['dɔ:rmənt] *volcano* inactivo
dormitory ['dɔ:rmɪtɔ:rɪ] (*hall of residence*) residencia *f* de estudiantes; *Br* dormitorio *m* (colectivo)
dose [dous] dosis *f inv*
dot [dɑ:t] punto *m*
double ['dʌbl] **1** *n person* doble *m/f* **2** *adj* doble **3** *v/t* doblar **4** *v/i* doblarse; **double bed** cama *f* de matrimonio; **doublecheck** volver a comprobar; **double click** COMPUT hacer doble clic (**on** en); **doublecross** engañar; **double park** aparcar en doble fila; **double room** habitación *f* doble; **doubles** *in tennis* dobles *mpl*
doubt [daut] **1** *n* duda *f*; (*uncertainty*) dudas *fpl*; ***no ~*** (*probably*) sin duda **2** *v/t* dudar; **doubtful** *look* dubitativo; ***be ~*** *of person* tener dudas; **doubtless** sin duda
dough [dou] masa *f*
dove [dʌv] *also fig* paloma *f*
down [daun] **1** *adv* (*downward*) (hacia) abajo; ***~ there*** allá abajo; ***$200 ~*** (*as deposit*) una entrada de 200 dólares; ***~ south*** hacia el sur; ***be ~*** *of price* haber bajado; *of numbers* haber descendido; (*not working*) no funcionar; F (*depressed*) estar deprimido **2** *prep*: ***run ~ the stairs*** bajar las escaleras corriendo; ***walk ~ the street*** andar por la calle; **down-and-out** vagabundo(-a) *m(f)*; **download** COMPUT **1** *v/t* descargar, bajar **2** *n* descarga *f*; **downmarket** *Br* barato; **down payment** entrada *f*; **downplay** quitar importancia a; **downpour** chaparrón *m*; **downscale** barato; **downside** (*disadvantage*) desventaja *f*; **downsize** *car* reducir el tamaño de; *company* reajustar la plantilla de; **downstairs** en el piso de abajo; ***I ran ~*** bajé corriendo; **downtown** **1** *n* centro *m* **2** *adj* del centro **3** *adv live* en el centro; *go* al centro
doze [douz] echar una cabezada
dozen ['dʌzn] docena *f*
draft [dræft] **1** *n of air* corriente *f*; *of document* borrador *m*; MIL reclutamiento *m*; ***~ beer*** cerveza *f* de barril **2** *v/t document* redactar un borrador de; MIL reclutar; **draft dodger** prófugo(-a) *m(f)*; **draftsman** delineante *m/f*
drag [dræg] **1** *v/t* (*pull*) arrastrar; (*search*) dragar **2** *v/i of movie* ser pesado

drain [dreɪn] **1** *n pipe* sumidero *m*; *under street* alcantarilla *f* **2** *v/t water, vegetables* escurrir; *land* drenar; *tank, oil* vaciar; *person* agotar; **drainage** (*drains*) desagües *mpl*; *of water from soil* drenaje *m*; **drainpipe** tubo *m* de desagüe

drama ['drɑːmə] drama *m*; (*excitement*) dramatismo *m*; **dramatic** dramático; *scenery* espectacular; **dramatist** dramaturgo(-a) *m(f)*; **dramatize** *also fig* dramatizar

drapes [dreɪps] cortinas *fpl*

drastic ['dræstɪk] drástico

draught [dræft] *Br* ☞ ***draft***

draw [drɒː] **1** *n in game* empate *m*; *in lottery* sorteo *m*; (*attraction*) atracción *f* **2** *v/t picture* dibujar; *curtain* correr; *in lottery* sortear; *knife* sacar; (*attract*) atraer; (*lead*) llevar; *from bank account* sacar **3** *v/i* dibujar; *in game* empatar

◆ **draw back 1** *v/i* (*recoil*) echarse atrás **2** *v/t* (*pull back*) retirar

◆ **draw out** sacar

◆ **draw up 1** *v/t document* redactar; *chair* acercar **2** *v/i of vehicle* parar

drawback desventaja *f*

drawer [drɒːr] *of desk* cajón *m*

drawing ['drɒːɪŋ] dibujo *m*

drawl [drɒːl] acento *m* arrastrado

dread [dred] tener pavor a; **dreadful** horrible

dream [driːm] **1** *n* sueño *m* **2** *v/i* soñar

◆ **dream up** inventar

dreary ['drɪrɪ] triste

dress [dres] **1** *n for woman* vestido *m*; (*clothing*) traje *m* **2** *v/t person* vestir; *wound* vendar; ***get ~ed*** vestirse **3** *v/i* vestirse

◆ **dress up** vestirse elegante; (*wear a disguise*) disfrazarse (***as*** de)

'dress circle piso *m* principal; **dresser** (*dressing table*) tocador *m*; *in kitchen* aparador *m*; **dressing** *for salad* aliño *m*, *Span* arreglo *m*; *for wound* vendaje *m*; **dress rehearsal** ensayo *m* general

dribble ['drɪbl] *of baby* babear; *of water* gotear; SP driblar

dried [draɪd] *fruit etc* seco; **drier** ['draɪr] ☞ ***dryer***

drift [drɪft] *of snow* amontonarse; *of ship* ir a la deriva; (*go off course*) desviarse del rumbo; *of person* vagar; **drifter** vagabundo(-a) *m(f)*

drill [drɪl] **1** *n tool* taladro *m*; *exercise* simulacro *m*; MIL instrucción *f* **2** *v/t hole* taladrar **3** *v/i for oil* hacer perforaciones; MIL entrenarse

drily ['draɪlɪ] *say* secamente

drink [drɪŋk] **1** *n* bebida *f* **2** *v/t* beber **3** *v/i* beber, *L.Am.* tomar; **drinkable** potable; **drinker** bebedor(a) *m(f)*; **drinking water** agua *f* potable

drip [drɪp] **1** *n* gota *f*; MED gotero *m* **2** *v/i* gotear

drive [draɪv] **1** *n outing* paseo *m* (en coche); (*energy*) energía *f*; COMPUT unidad *f*; (*campaign*) campaña *f* **2** *v/t vehicle* conducir, *L.Am.* manejar; (*own*) tener; (*take in car*) llevar (en coche); TECH impulsar **3** *v/i* conducir, *L.Am.* manejar

'drive-in *movie theater* autocine *m*

drivel ['drɪvl] tonterías *fpl*

driver ['draɪvər] conductor(a) *m(f)*; COMPUT controlador *m*; **driver's license** carné *m* de conducir; **drivethru** *restaurante / banco etc en el que se atiende al cliente sin que salga del coche*; **driveway** camino *m* de entrada

drizzle ['drɪzl] **1** *n* llovizna *f* **2** *v/i* lloviznar

drop [drɑːp] **1** *n* gota *f*; *in price, temperature* caída *f* **2** *v/t object* dejar caer; *person from car* dejar; *person from team* excluir; (*stop seeing*) abandonar; *charges etc* retirar; (*give up*) dejar **3** *v/i* caer; *of wind* amainar

◆ **drop in** pasar a visitar

◆ **drop off 1** *v/t person* dejar; (*deliver*) llevar **2** *v/i* (*fall asleep*) dormirse; (*decline*) disminuir

◆ **drop out** (*withdraw*) retirarse; ***drop out of school*** abandonar el colegio

drought [draʊt] sequía *f*

drown [draʊn] ahogarse

drug [drʌg] **1** *n* droga *f* **2** *v/t* drogar; **drug addict** drogadicto(-a) *m(f)*; **drug dealer** traficante *m/f* (de drogas); **druggist** farmacéutico(-a) *m(f)*; **drugstore** *tienda en la que se venden medicinas, cosméticos, periódicos y que a veces tiene un bar*; **drug trafficking** tráfico *m* de drogas

drum [drʌm] MUS tambor *m*; *container* barril *m*; **~*s*** *in band* batería *f*; **drumstick** MUS baqueta *f*

drunk [drʌŋk] **1** *n* borracho(-a) *m(f)* **2** *adj* borracho; ***get* ~** emborracharse; **drunk driving** conducción *f* bajo los efectos del alcohol

dry [draɪ] **1** *adj* seco **2** *v/t & v/i* secar; **dryclean** limpiar en seco; **dry cleaner** tintorería *f*; **dryer** *machine* secadora *f*

dual ['duːəl] doble

dub [dʌb] *movie* doblar

dubious ['duːbɪəs] dudoso; (*having doubts*) inseguro

duck [dʌk] **1** *n* pato *m*, pata *f* **2** *v/i* agacharse

dud [dʌd] F (*false bill*) billete *m* falso

due [duː] debido; ***payment is now* ~** el pago se debe hacer efectivo ahora

dull [dʌl] *weather* gris; *sound, pain* sordo; (*boring*) aburrido, soso

duly ['duːlɪ] (*as expected*) tal y como se esperaba; (*properly*) debidamente

dumb [dʌm] (*mute*) mudo; F (*stupid*) estúpido
dump [dʌmp] **1** *n for garbage* vertedero *m*; (*unpleasant place*) lugar *m* de mala muerte **2** *v/t* (*deposit*) dejar; (*dispose of*) deshacerse de; *waste* verter
dune [du:n] duna *f*
duplex (apartment) ['du:pleks] dúplex *m*
duplicate ['du:plɪkət] duplicado *m*
durable ['dʊrəbl] duradero
during ['dʊrɪŋ] durante
dusk [dʌsk] crepúsculo *m*
dust [dʌst] **1** *n* polvo *m* **2** *v/t* quitar el polvo a; **duster** trapo *m* del polvo; **dustpan** recogedor *m*; **dusty** polvoriento
Dutch [dʌtʃ] holandés; **Dutchman** holandés *m*; **Dutchwoman** holandesa *f*
duty ['du:tɪ] deber *m*; (*task*) tarea *f*; *on goods* impuesto *m*; ***be on ~*** estar de servicio; **duty-free** libre de impuestos
DVD [di:vi:'di:] (= ***digital versatile disk***) DVD *m*; **DVD-ROM** DVD-ROM *m*
dwarf [dwɔ:rf] **1** *n* enano *m* **2** *v/t* empequeñecer
dwindle ['dwɪndl] menguar
dye [daɪ] **1** *n* tinte *m* **2** *v/t* teñir
dying ['daɪɪŋ] moribundo; *tradition etc* en vías de desaparición
dynamic [daɪ'næmɪk] dinámico; **dynamism** dinamismo *m*
dynasty ['daɪnəstɪ] dinastía *f*
dyslexic [dɪs'leksɪk] **1** *adj* disléxico **2** *n* disléxico(-a) *m(f)*

E

each [i:tʃ] **1** *adj* cada **2** *adv*: ***he gave us one ~*** nos dio uno a cada uno; ***they're $1.50 ~*** valen 1.50 dólares cada uno **3** *pron* cada uno; ***~ other*** el uno al otro; ***we love ~ other*** nos queremos
eager ['i:gər] ansioso; **eagerly** ansiosamente; **eagerness** entusiasmo *m*
eagle ['i:gl] águila *f*; **eagle-eyed** con vista de lince
ear¹ [ɪr] oreja *f*
ear² [ɪr] *of corn* espiga *f*
earache dolor *m* de oídos
early ['ɜ:rlɪ] **1** *adj* (*not late*) temprano; (*ahead of time*) anticipado; (*farther back in time*) primero; (*in the near future*) pronto; *music* antiguo **2** *adv* (*not late*) pronto, temprano; (*ahead of time*) antes de tiempo; **early bird** madrugador(a) *m(f)*
earmark ['ɪrmɑ:rk] destinar
earn [ɜ:rn] *salary* ganar; *interest* devengar; *holiday, drink etc* ganarse
earnest ['ɜ:rnɪst] serio
earnings ['ɜ:rnɪŋz] ganancias

fpl

'earphones auriculares *mpl*; **earring** pendiente *m*

earth [ɜːrθ] tierra *f*; **earthenware** loza *f*; **earthly** terrenal; ***it's no ~ use*** F no sirve para nada; **earthquake** terremoto *m*; **earth-shattering** extraordinario

ease [iːz] **1** *n* facilidad *f*; ***feel at ~*** sentirse cómodo **2** *v/t* (*relieve*) aliviar

easel ['iːzl] caballete *m*

easily ['iːzəlɪ] fácilmente; (*by far*) con diferencia

east [iːst] **1** *n* este *m* **2** *adj* oriental, este; *wind* del este **3** *adv travel* hacia el este

Easter ['iːstər] Pascua *f*; *period* Semana *f* Santa; **Easter Day** Domingo *m* de Resurrección; **Easter egg** huevo *m* de pascua

easterly ['iːstərlɪ] del este

Easter 'Monday Lunes *m* Santo

eastern ['iːstərn] del este; (*oriental*) oriental; **easterner** *habitante de la costa este estadounidense*

Easter 'Sunday Domingo *m* de Resurrección

eastward ['iːstwərd] hacia el este

easy ['iːzɪ] fácil; (*relaxed*) tranquilo; **easy chair** sillón *m*; **easy-going** tratable

eat [iːt] comer

◆ **eat out** comer fuera

eatable ['iːtəbl] comestible

eavesdrop ['iːvzdrɑːp] escuchar a escondidas (***on s.o.*** alguien)

ebb [eb] *of tide* bajar

e-book ['iːbʊk] libro *m* electrónico; **e-business** comercio *m* electrónico

eccentric [ɪk'sentrɪk] **1** *adj* excéntrico **2** *n* excéntrico(-a) *m*(*f*); **eccentricity** excentricidad *f*

echo ['ekoʊ] **1** *n* eco *m* **2** *v/i* resonar **3** *v/t words* repetir; *views* mostrar acuerdo con

eclipse [ɪ'klɪps] **1** *n* eclipse *m* **2** *v/t fig* eclipsar

ecological [iːkə'lɑːdʒɪkl] ecológico; **ecologically** ecológicamente; **ecologically friendly** ecológico; **ecologist** ecologista *m/f*; **ecology** ecología *f*

economic [iːkə'nɑːmɪk] económico; **economical** (*cheap*) económico; (*thrifty*) cuidadoso; **economics** economía *f*; *financial aspects* aspecto *m* económico; **economist** economista *m/f*; **economize** economizar

◆ **economize on** economizar, ahorrar

economy [ɪ'kɑːnəmɪ] economía *f*; (*saving*) ahorro *m*; **economy class** clase *f* turista

ecosystem ['iːkoʊsɪstm] ecosistema *m*; **ecotourism** ecoturismo *m*

ecstasy ['ekstəsɪ] éxtasis *m*; **ecstatic** extasiado

Ecuador ['ekwədɔːr] Ecua-

dor; **Ecuadorean 1** *adj* ecuatoriano **2** n ecuatoriano(-a) *m(f)*
eczema ['eksmə] eczema *f*
edge [edʒ] **1** *n of knife* filo *m*; *of table, road, cliff* borde *m*; ***on ~*** tenso **2** *v/i* (*move slowly*) acercarse despacio; **edgewise: *I couldn't get a word in ~*** no me dejó decir una palabra; **edgy** tenso
edible ['edɪbl] comestible
edit ['edɪt] *text* corregir; *book* editar; *newspaper* dirigir; *TV program* montar; **edition** edición *f*; **editor** *of text, book* editor(a) *m(f)*; *of newspaper* director(a) *m(f)*; *of TV program* montador(a) *m(f)*; **editorial 1** *adj* editorial **2** *n in newspaper* editorial *m*
educate ['edʒəkeɪt] *child* educar; *consumers* concienciar; **educated** culto; **education** educación *f*; **educational** educativo; (*informative*) instructivo
eerie ['ɪrɪ] escalofriante
effect [ɪ'fekt] efecto *m*; **effective** efectivo; (*striking*) impresionante
effeminate [ɪ'femɪnət] afeminado
efficiency [ɪ'fɪʃənsɪ] *of person* eficiencia *f*; *of machine* rendimiento *m*; *of system* eficacia *f*; *in motel* cuarto *m* con cocina; **efficient** *person* eficiente; *machine* de buen rendimiento; *method* eficaz; **efficiently** eficientemente
effort ['efərt] esfuerzo *m*; **effortless** fácil
e.g. [iː'dʒiː] p. ej.
egg [eg] huevo *m*; **eggcup** huevera *f*; **egghead** F cerebrito(-a) *m(f)* F; **eggplant** berenjena *f*
ego ['iːgoʊ] PSYCH ego *m*; (*self-esteem*) amor *m* propio; **egocentric** egocéntrico; **egoism** egoismo *m*; **egoist** egoísta *m/f*
eiderdown ['aɪdərdaʊn] *quilt* edredón *m*
eight [eɪt] ocho; **eighteen** dieciocho; **eighteenth** decimoctavo; **eighth** octavo; **eightieth** octogésimo; **eighty** ochenta
either ['aɪðər] **1** *adj & pron* cualquiera de los dos; *with negative constructions* ninguno de los dos; (*both*) cada, ambos **2** *adv* tampoco; ***I won't go ~*** yo tampoco iré **3** *conj*: ***~ ... or*** *choice* o... o; *with negative constructions* ni... ni
eject [ɪ'dʒekt] **1** *v/t* expulsar **2** *v/i from plane* eyectarse
◆ **eke out** [iːk] (*make last*) hacer durar; ***~ a living*** ganarse la vida a duras penas
el [el] ferrocarril *m* elevado
elaborate 1 [ɪ'læbərət] *adj* elaborado **2** [ɪ'læbəreɪt] *v/t* elaborar **3** [ɪ'læbəreɪt] *v/i* dar detalles
elapse [ɪ'læps] pasar
elastic [ɪ'læstɪk] **1** *adj* elástico **2** *n* elástico *m*; **elasticated**

elástico
elated [ɪ'leɪtɪd] eufórico; **elation** euforia *f*
elbow ['elboʊ] codo *m*
elder ['eldər] **1** *adj* mayor **2** *n* mayor *m/f*; **elderly 1** *adj* mayor **2** *npl*: ***the ~*** las personas mayores; **eldest 1** *adj* mayor **2** *n* mayor *m/f*
elect [ɪ'lekt] elegir; **elected** elegido; **election** elección *f*; **election campaign** campaña *f* electoral; **election day** día *m* de las elecciones; **electorate** electorado *m*
electric [ɪ'lektrɪk] eléctrico; *fig atmosphere* electrizado; **electrical** eléctrico; **electric chair** silla *f* eléctrica; **electrician** electricista *m/f*; **electricity** electricidad *f*; **electrify** electrificar; *fig* electrizar
electrocute [ɪ'lektrəkju:t] electrocutar
electron [ɪ'lektrɑ:n] electrón *m*; **electronic** electrónico; **electronics** electrónica *f*
elegance ['elɪgəns] elegancia *f*; **elegant** elegante
element ['elɪmənt] elemento *m*; **elementary** (*rudimentary*) elemental; **elementary school** escuela *f* primaria
elephant ['elɪfənt] elefante *m*
elevate ['elɪveɪt] elevar; **elevated railroad** ferrocarril *m* elevado; **elevation** (*altitude*) altura *f*; **elevator** ascensor *m*
eleven [ɪ'levn] once; **eleventh** undécimo
eligible ['elɪdʒəbl] que reúne los requisitos; ***be ~ to do sth*** tener derecho a hacer algo
eliminate [ɪ'lɪmɪneɪt] eliminar; *poverty* acabar con; (*rule out*) descartar; **elimination** eliminación *f*
elite [eɪ'li:t] **1** *n* élite *f* **2** *adj* de élite
eloquence ['eləkwəns] elocuencia *f*; **eloquent** elocuente
El Salvador [el'sælvədɔ:r] El Salvador
else [els]: ***anything ~?*** ¿algo más?; ***nothing ~*** nada más; ***no one ~*** nadie más; ***everyone ~ is going*** todos (los demás) van; ***someone ~*** otra persona; ***something ~*** algo más; ***let's go somewhere ~*** vamos a otro sitio; ***or ~*** si no; **elsewhere** en otro sitio
elude [ɪ'lu:d] (*escape from*) escapar de; (*avoid*) evitar; **elusive** evasivo
emaciated [ɪ'meɪsɪeɪtɪd] demacrado
e-mail ['i:meɪl] **1** *n* correo *m* electrónico **2** *v/t person* mandar un correo electrónico a; **e-mail address** dirección *f* electrónica
emancipation [ɪmænsɪ'peɪʃn] emancipación *f*
embalm [ɪm'bɑ:m] embalsamar
embankment [ɪm'bæŋkmənt] *of river* dique *m*; RAIL terraplén *m*

embargo [em'bɑːrgoʊ] embargo *m*
embark [ɪm'bɑːrk] embarcar
embarrass [ɪm'bærəs] avergonzar; **embarrassed** avergonzado; **embarrassing** embarazoso; **embarrassment** embarazo *m*
embassy ['embəsɪ] embajada *f*
embezzle [ɪm'bezl] malversar; **embezzlement** malversación *f*
emblem ['embləm] emblema *m*
embodiment [ɪm'bɑːdɪmənt] personificación *f*; **embody** personificar
embrace [ɪm'breɪs] **1** *n* abrazo *m* **2** *v/t* (*hug*) abrazar; (*take in*) abarcar **3** *v/i of two people* abrazarse
embroider [ɪm'brɔɪdər] bordar; *fig* adornar
embryo ['embrɪoʊ] embrión *m*; **embryonic** *fig* embrionario
emerald ['emərəld] esmeralda *f*
emerge [ɪ'mɜːrdʒ] emerger, salir; *of truth* aflorar
emergency [ɪ'mɜːrdʒənsɪ] emergencia *f*; **emergency exit** salida *f* de emergencia; **emergency landing** aterrizaje *m* forzoso; **emergency services** servicios *mpl* de urgencia
emigrate ['emɪgreɪt] emigrar; **emigration** emigración *f*
Eminence ['emɪnəns] REL: ***His ~*** Su Eminencia; **eminent** eminente
emission [ɪ'mɪʃn] *of gases* emisión *f*; **emit** emitir; *heat, odor* desprender
emotion [ɪ'moʊʃn] emoción *f*; **emotional** *problems* sentimental; (*full of emotion*) emotivo
emphasis ['emfəsɪs] *in word* acento *m*; *fig* énfasis *m*; **emphasize** *syllable* acentuar; *fig* hacer hincapié en; **emphatic** enfático
empire ['empaɪr] imperio *m*
employ [ɪm'plɔɪ] emplear; **employee** empleado(-a) *m*(*f*); **employer** empresario(-a) *m*(*f*); **employment** empleo *m*; (*work*) trabajo *m*
emptiness ['emptɪnɪs] vacío *m*; **empty** **1** *adj* vacío **2** *v/t drawer, pockets* vaciar; *glass, bottle* acabar **3** *v/i of room, street* vaciarse
emulate ['emjʊleɪt] emular
enable [ɪ'neɪbl] permitir
enchanting [ɪn'ʧæntɪŋ] encantador
encircle [ɪn'sɜːrkl] rodear
enclose [ɪn'kloʊz] *in letter* adjuntar; *area* rodear; **enclosure** *with letter* documento *m* adjunto
encore ['ɑːŋkɔːr] bis *m*
encounter [ɪn'kaʊntər] **1** *n* encuentro *m* **2** *v/t person* encontrarse con; *problem, resistance* tropezar con
encourage [ɪn'kʌrɪdʒ] ani-

mar; *violence* fomentar; **encouragement** ánimo *m*; **encouraging** alentador
encyclopedia [ɪsaɪklə'piːdɪə] enciclopedia *f*
end [end] **1** *n of journey, month* final *m*; (*extremity*) extremo *m*; (*conclusion, purpose*) fin *m*; ***in the ~*** al final **2** *v/t & v/i* terminar
◆ **end up** acabar
endanger [ɪn'deɪndʒər] poner en peligro; **endangered species** especie *f* en peligro de extinción
endeavor, *Br* **endeavour** [ɪn'devər] **1** *n* esfuerzo *m* **2** *v/t* procurar
endemic [ɪn'demɪk] endémico
ending ['endɪŋ] final *m*; GRAM terminación *f*; **endless** interminable
endorse [ɪn'dɔːrs] apoyar; *product* representar; **endorsement** apoyo *m*; *of product* representación *f*
end 'product producto *m* final
endurance [ɪn'dʊrəns] resistencia *f*; **endure 1** *v/t* resistir **2** *v/i* (*last*) durar; **enduring** duradero
enemy ['enəmɪ] enemigo(-a) *m*(*f*)
energetic [enər'dʒetɪk] enérgico; **energy** energía *f*; **energy supply** suministro *m* de energía
enforce [ɪn'fɔːrs] hacer cumplir
engage [ɪn'geɪdʒ] **1** *v/t* (*hire*) contratar **2** *v/i* TECH engranar; **engaged** *to be married* prometido; *Br* TELEC ocupado; ***get ~*** prometerse; **engagement** compromiso *m*; MIL combate *m*; **engagement ring** anillo *m* de compromiso
engine ['endʒɪn] motor *m*; **engineer** ingeniero(-a) *m*(*f*); NAUT, RAIL maquinista *m/f*; **engineering** ingeniería *f*
England ['ɪŋglənd] Inglaterra; **English 1** *adj* inglés (-esa) **2** *n language* inglés *m*; ***the ~*** los ingleses; **Englishman** inglés *m*; **Englishwoman** inglesa *f*
engrave [ɪn'greɪv] grabar; **engraving** grabado *m*
engrossed [ɪn'groʊst] absorto (***in*** en)
engulf [ɪn'gʌlf] devorar
enhance [ɪn'hæns] realzar
enigma [ɪ'nɪgmə] enigma *m*
enjoy [ɪn'dʒɔɪ] disfrutar; ***~ o.s.*** divertirse; ***~ (your meal)!*** ¡que aproveche!; **enjoyable** agradable; **enjoyment** diversión *f*
enlarge [ɪn'lɑːrdʒ] ampliar; **enlargement** ampliación *f*
enlighten [ɪn'laɪtn] educar
enlist [ɪn'lɪst] MIL alistarse
enmity ['enmətɪ] enemistad *f*
enormous [ɪ'nɔːrməs] enorme; *satisfaction, patience* inmenso
enough [ɪ'nʌf] **1** *adj & pron*

suficiente, bastante; ***will $50 be ~?*** ¿llegará con 50 dólares?; ***that's ~!*** ¡ya basta! **2** *adv* suficientemente, bastante; ***big ~*** suficientemente *or* bastante grande

enquire [ɪn'kwaɪr] ☞ ***inquire***

enroll, *Br* **enrol** [ɪn'roʊl] matricularse

en suite ['ɑːnswiːt]: ***~ bathroom*** baño *m* privado

ensure [ɪn'ʃʊər] asegurar

entail [ɪn'teɪl] conllevar

entangle [ɪn'tæŋgl] *in rope* enredar

enter ['entər] **1** *v/t room, house* entrar en; *competition* participar en; COMPUT introducir **2** *v/i* entrar; THEA entrar en escena; *in competition* inscribirse **3** *n* COMPUT intro *m*

enterprise ['entərpraɪz] (*initiative*) iniciativa *f*; (*venture*) empresa *f*; **enterprising** con iniciativa

entertain [entər'teɪn] (*amuse*) entretener; (*consider*) considerar; **entertainer** artista *m/f*; **entertaining** entretenido; **entertainment** entretenimiento *m*

enthusiasm [ɪn'θuːzɪæzm] entusiasmo *m*; **enthusiast** entusiasta *m/f*; **enthusiastic** entusiasta; **enthusiastically** con entusiasmo

entire [ɪn'taɪr] entero; **entirely** completamente

entitle [ɪn'taɪtld]: ***~ s.o. to sth*** dar derecho a alguien a algo; ***be ~d to*** tener derecho a

entrance ['entrəns] entrada *f*

entranced [ɪn'trænst] encantado

'entrance exam(ination) examen *m* de acceso

entrant ['entrənt] participante *m/f*

entrepreneur [ɑːntrəprə'nɜːr] empresario(-a) *m(f)*; **entrepreneurial** empresarial

entrust [ɪn'trʌst] confiar

entry ['entrɪ] entrada *f*; *for competition* inscripción *f*; **entryphone** portero *m* automático

envelop [ɪn'veləp] cubrir

envelope ['envəloʊp] sobre *m*

enviable ['envɪəbl] envidiable; **envious** envidioso

environment [ɪn'vaɪrənmənt] (*nature*) medio *m* ambiente; (*surroundings*) entorno *m*, ambiente *m*; **environmental** medioambiental; **environmentalist** ecologista *m/f*; **environmentally friendly** ecológico; **environs** alrededores *mpl*

envisage [ɪn'vɪzɪdʒ] imaginar

envoy ['envɔɪ] enviado(-a) *m(f)*

envy ['envɪ] **1** *n* envidia *f* **2** *v/t* envidiar

epic ['epɪk] **1** *n* epopeya *f* **2** *adj journey* épico

epicenter, *Br* **epicentre** ['epɪsentər] epicentro *m*

epidemic [epɪ'demɪk] epidemia *f*

episode ['epɪsoʊd] episodio *m*

epitaph ['epɪtæf] epitafio *m*
equal ['iːkwl] **1** *adj* igual **2** *n* igual *m/f* **3** *v/t with numbers* equivaler; (*be as good as*) igualar; ***be ~ to*** *a task* estar capacitado para; **equality** igualdad *f*; **equalize 1** *v/t* igualar **2** *v/i Br* SP empatar; **equalizer** *Br* SP gol *m* del empate; **equally** igualmente; *share, divide* en partes iguales; **equal rights** igualdad *f* de derechos
equation [ɪ'kweɪʒn] MATH ecuación *f*
equator [ɪ'kweɪtər] ecuador *m*
equip [ɪ'kwɪp] equipar; **equipment** equipo *m*
equity ['ekwətɪ] FIN acciones *fpl* ordinarias
equivalent [ɪ'kwɪvələnt] **1** *adj* equivalente **2** *n* equivalente *m*
era ['ɪrə] era *f*
eradicate [ɪ'rædɪkeɪt] erradicar
erase [ɪ'reɪz] borrar
erect [ɪ'rekt] **1** *adj* erguido **2** *v/t* levantar, erigir; **erection** construcción *f*; *of penis* erección *f*
ergonomic [ɜːrgoʊ'nɑːmɪk] ergonómico
erode [ɪ'roʊd] *also fig* erosionar; **erosion** erosión *f*
errand ['erənd] recado *m*
erratic [ɪ'rætɪk] irregular; *course* errático
error ['erər] error *m*
erupt [ɪ'rʌpt] *of volcano* entrar en erupción; *of violence* brotar; *of person* explotar; **eruption** *of volcano* erupción *f*; *of violence* brote *m*
escalate ['eskəleɪt] intensificarse; **escalation** intensificación *f*; **escalator** escalera *f* mecánica
escape [ɪ'skeɪp] **1** *n* fuga *f* **2** *v/i of prisoner, animal, gas* escaparse
escort 1 ['eskɔːrt] *n* acompañante *m/f*; (*guard*) escolta *m/f* **2** [ɪ'skɔːrt] *v/t* escoltar; *socially* acompañar
especially [ɪ'speʃlɪ] especialmente
espionage ['espɪənɑːʒ] espionaje *m*
espresso (coffee) [es'presoʊ] café *m* exprés
essay ['eseɪ] *creative* redacción *f*; *factual* trabajo *m*
essential [ɪ'senʃl] esencial
establish [ɪ'stæblɪʃ] *company* fundar; (*create, determine*) establecer; **establishment** *firm, shop etc* establecimiento *m*
estate [ɪ'steɪt] *land* finca *f*; *of dead person* patrimonio *m*
esthetic [ɪs'θetɪk] estético
estimate ['estɪmət] **1** *n* estimación *f*; *for job* presupuesto *m* **2** *v/t* estimar
estuary ['estʃəwerɪ] estuario *m*
etc [et'setrə] etc
eternal [ɪ'tɜːrnl] eterno; **eternity** eternidad *f*
ethical ['eθɪkl] ético; **ethics**

ética *f*
ethnic ['eθnɪk] étnico
EU [iː'juː] (= ***European Union***) UE *f* (= Unión *f* Europea)
euphemism ['juːfəmɪzm] eufemismo *m*
euro ['jʊroʊ] euro *m*
Europe ['jʊrəp] Europa; **European 1** *adj* europeo **2** *n* europeo(-a) *m(f)*
euthanasia [jʊθə'neɪzɪə] eutanasia *f*
evacuate [ɪ'vækjʊeɪt] evacuar
evade [ɪ'veɪd] evadir
evaluate [ɪ'væljʊeɪt] evaluar; **evaluation** evaluación *f*
evaporate [ɪ'væpəreɪt] evaporarse; *of confidence* desvanecerse; **evaporation** evaporación *f*
evasion [ɪ'veɪʒn] evasión *f*; **evasive** evasivo
eve [iːv] víspera *f*
even ['iːvn] **1** *adj* (*regular*) regular; (*level*) llano; *number* par; *distribution* igualado; ***I'll get ~ with him*** me las pagará **2** *adv* incluso; ***~ bigger*** incluso *or* aún mayor; ***not ~*** ni siquiera; ***~ so*** aun así; ***~ if*** aunque **3** *v/t*: ***~ the score*** igualar el marcador
evening ['iːvnɪŋ] tarde *f*; *after dark* noche *f*; ***in the ~*** por la tarde / noche; ***yesterday ~*** anoche *f*; ***good ~*** buenas noches; **evening class** clase *f* nocturna; **evening dress** *for woman* traje *f* de noche; *for man* traje *f* de etiqueta
evenly ['iːvnlɪ] (*regularly*) regularmente
event [ɪ'vent] acontecimiento *m*; SP prueba *f*; **eventful** agitado, lleno de incidentes
eventually [ɪ'ventʃʊəlɪ] finalmente
ever ['evər]: ***have you ~ been to Colombia?*** ¿has estado alguna vez en Colombia?; ***for ~*** siempre; ***~ since*** desde entonces; ***~ since I've known him*** desde que lo conozco; **everlasting** *love* eterno
every ['evrɪ] cada; ***I see him ~ day*** le veo todos los días; **everybody** ☞ ***everyone***; **everyday** cotidiano; **everyone** todo el mundo; **everything** todo; **everywhere** en *or* por todos sitios; (*wherever*) dondequiera que
evict [ɪ'vɪkt] desahuciar
evidence ['evɪdəns] prueba(s) *f(pl)*; ***give ~*** prestar declaración; **evident** evidente; **evidently** (*clearly*) evidentemente; (*apparently*) aparentemente, al parecer
evil ['iːvl] **1** *adj* malo **2** *n* mal *m*
evolution [iːvə'luːʃn] evolución *f*; **evolve** evolucionar
ex [eks] F (*former wife, husband*) ex *m/f* F
exact [ɪg'zækt] exacto; **exacting** exigente; *task* duro; **exactly** exactamente
exaggerate [ɪg'zædʒəreɪt] exagerar; **exaggeration** exa-

geración *f*
exam [ɪg'zæm] examen *m*; **examination** examen *m*; *of patient* reconocimiento *m*; **examine** examinar; *patient* reconocer
example [ɪg'zæmpl] ejemplo *m*; ***for ~*** por ejemplo
excavate ['ekskəveɪt] excavar; **excavation** excavación *f*
exceed [ɪk'si:d] (*be more than*) exceder; (*go beyond*) sobrepasar; **exceedingly** sumamente
excel [ɪk'sel] **1** *v/i* sobresalir (***at*** en) **2** *v/t*: **~ *o.s.*** superarse a sí mismo; **excellence** excelencia *f*; **excellent** excelente
except [ɪk'sept] excepto; **~ *for*** a excepción de; **exception** excepción *f*; **exceptional** excepcional
excerpt ['eksɜ:rpt] extracto *m*
excess [ɪk'ses] **1** *n* exceso *m* **2** *adj* excedente; **excessive** excesivo
exchange [ɪks'ʧeɪndʒ] **1** *n* intercambio *m* **2** *v/t* cambiar; **exchange rate** FIN tipo *m* de cambio
excite [ɪk'saɪt] (*make enthusiastic*) entusiasmar; **excited** emocionado, excitado; ***get ~*** (***about***) emocionarse *or* excitarse (con); **excitement** emoción *f*, excitación *f*; **exciting** emocionante, excitante
exclaim [ɪk'skleɪm] exclamar; **exclamation** exclamación *f*; **exclamation point** signo *m* de admiración
exclude [ɪk'sklu:d] excluir; *possibility* descartar; **excluding** excluyendo; **exclusive** exclusivo
excuse 1 [ɪk'skju:s] *n* excusa *f* **2** [ɪk'skju:z] *v/t* (*forgive*) excusar, perdonar; (*allow to leave*) disculpar; **~ *me*** perdone
ex-di'rectory *Br*: ***be ~*** no aparecer en la guía telefónica
execute ['eksɪkju:t] *criminal, plan* ejecutar; **execution** *of criminal, plan* ejecución *f*; **executive** ejecutivo(-a) *m(f)*
exempt [ɪg'zempt] exento
exercise ['eksərsaɪz] **1** *n* ejercicio *m* **2** *v/t muscle* ejercitar; *dog* pasear; *caution* proceder con **3** *v/i* hacer ejercicio
exhale [eks'heɪl] exhalar
exhaust [ɪg'zɒ:st] **1** *n fumes* gases *mpl* de la combustión; *pipe* tubo *m* de escape **2** *v/t* (*tire*) cansar; (*use up*) agotar; **exhausted** (*tired*) agotado; **exhausting** agotador; **exhaustion** agotamiento *m*; **exhaustive** exhaustivo
exhibit [ɪg'zɪbɪt] **1** *n* objeto *m* expuesto **2** *v/t of gallery* exhibir; *of artist* exponer; (*give evidence of*) mostrar; **exhibition** exposición *f*; *of bad behavior, skill* exhibición *f*
exhilarating [ɪg'zɪləreɪtɪŋ] estimulante
exile ['eksaɪl] **1** *n* exilio *m*; *person* exiliado(-a) *m(f)* **2** *v/t*

exiliar
exist [ɪg'zɪst] existir; **~ on** subsistir a base de; **existence** existencia *f*; ***be in ~*** existir; **existing** existente
exit ['eksɪt] **1** *n* salida *f* **2** *v/i* COMPUT salir
exonerate [ɪg'zɑːnəreɪt] exonerar de
exotic [ɪg'zɑːtɪk] exótico
expand [ɪk'spænd] **1** *v/t* expandir **2** *v/i* expandirse; *of metal* dilatarse; **expanse** extensión *f*; **expansion** expansión *f*; *of metal* dilatación *f*
expect [ɪk'spekt] **1** *v/t* esperar; (*suppose*) suponer, imaginar(se); (*demand*) exigir **2** *v/i*: ***be ~ing*** (*be pregnant*) estar en estado; ***I ~ so*** creo que sí; **expectant mother** futura madre *f*; **expectation** expectativa *f*
expedition [ekspɪ'dɪʃn] expedición *f*
expel [ɪk'spel] expulsar
expendable [ɪk'spendəbl] prescindible
expenditure [ɪk'spendɪʧər] gasto *m*
expense [ɪk'spens] gasto *m*; **expenses** gastos *mpl*; **expensive** caro
experience [ɪk'spɪrɪəns] **1** *n* experiencia *f* **2** *v/t* experimentar; **experienced** experimentado
experiment [ɪk'sperɪmənt] **1** *n* experimento *m* **2** *v/i* experimentar; **experimental** experimental
expert ['ekspɜːrt] **1** *adj* experto **2** *n* experto(-a) *m*(*f*); **expertise** destreza *f*
expiration date [ɪkspɪ'reɪʃn] fecha *f* de caducidad; **expire** caducar; **expiry** *of contract* vencimiento *m*; *of passport* caducidad *f*; **expiry date** *Br* fecha *f* de caducidad
explain [ɪk'spleɪn] explicar; **explanation** explicación *f*; **explanatory** explicativo
explicit [ɪk'splɪsɪt] explícito
explode [ɪk'sploʊd] **1** *v/i of bomb* explotar **2** *v/t bomb* hacer explotar
exploit[1] ['eksplɔɪt] *n* hazaña *f*
exploit[2] [ɪk'splɔɪt] *v/t person, resources* explotar
exploitation [eksplɔɪ'teɪʃn] explotación *f*
exploration [eksplə'reɪʃn] exploración *f*; **explore** *country etc* explorar; *possibility* estudiar; **explorer** explorador(a) *m*(*f*)
explosion [ɪk'sploʊʒn] explosión *f*; **explosive** explosivo *m*
export ['ekspɔːrt] **1** *n* exportación *f*; *item* producto *m* de exportación; ***~s*** exportaciones *fpl* **2** *v/t also* COMPUT exportar; **exporter** exportador(a) *m*(*f*)
expose [ɪk'spoʊz] (*uncover*) exponer; *scandal* sacar a la luz; **exposure** exposición *f*; PHOT foto(grafía) *f*
express [ɪk'spres] **1** *adj* (*fast*) rápido; (*explicit*) expreso **2** *n*

train expreso *m* **3** *v/t* expresar; **expression** *voiced* muestra *f*; *phrase*, *on face* expresión *f*; **expressive** expresivo; **expressly** *state* expresamente; *forbid* terminantemente; **expressway** autopista *f*

expulsion [ɪk'spʌlʃn] expulsión *f*

extend [ɪk'stend] **1** *v/t house* ampliar; *runway*, *path* alargar; *contract* prorrogar **2** *v/i of garden etc* llegar; **extension** *to house* ampliación *f*; *of contract* prórroga *f*; TELEC extensión *f*; **extensive** *damage* cuantioso; *knowledge* considerable; *search* extenso, amplio; **extent** alcance *m*; ***to a certain ~*** hasta cierto punto

exterior [ɪk'stɪrɪər] **1** *adj* exterior **2** *n* exterior *m*

exterminate [ɪk'stɜːrmɪneɪt] exterminar

external [ɪk'stɜːrnl] exterior, externo

extinct [ɪk'stɪŋkt] *species* extinguido; **extinction** *of species* extinción *f*; **extinguish** extinguir, apagar; *cigarette* apagar; **extinguisher** extintor *m*

extortion [ɪk'stɔːrʃn] extorsión *f*

extra ['ekstrə] **1** *n* extra *m* **2** *adj* extra; ***be ~*** (*cost more*) pagarse aparte **3** *adv* super

extra 'time *Br* SP prórroga *f*

extract[1] ['ekstrækt] *n* extracto *m*

extract[2] [ɪk'strækt] *v/t* sacar; *oil*, *tooth* extraer; *information* sonsacar; **extraction** *of oil*, *tooth* extracción *f*

extradite ['ekstrədaɪt] extraditar; **extradition** extradición *f*

extramarital [ekstrə'mærɪtl] extramarital

extraordinary [ɪk'strɔːrdɪnerɪ] extraordinario

extravagance [ɪk'strævəgəns] *with money* despilfarro *m*; *of claim etc* extravagancia *f*; **extravagant** *with money* despilfarrador; *claim* extravagante

extreme [ɪk'striːm] **1** *n* extremo *m* **2** *adj* extremo; *views* extremista; **extremely** extremadamente; **extremist** extremista *m/f*

extrovert ['ekstrəvɜːrt] **1** *adj* extrovertido **2** *n* extrovertido(-a) *m*(*f*)

exuberant [ɪg'zuːbərənt] exuberante

eye [aɪ] **1** *n* ojo *m* **2** *v/t* mirar; **eye-catching** llamativo; **eyeglasses** gafas *fpl*, *L.Am.* anteojos *mpl*, *L.Am.* lentes *mpl*; **eyeliner** lápiz *m* de ojos; **eyeshadow** sombra *f* de ojos; **eyesight** vista *f*; **eyewitness** testigo *m/f* ocular

F

fabric ['fæbrɪk] tejido *m*
fabulous ['fæbjʊləs] fabuloso, estupendo
façade [fə'sɑːd] fachada *f*
face [feɪs] **1** *n* cara *f* **2** *v/t* (*be opposite*) estar enfrente de; (*confront*) enfrentarse a
◆ **face up to** hacer frente a
'facecloth toallita *f*; **facelift** lifting *m*
facial ['feɪʃl] limpieza *f* de cutis
facilitate [fə'sɪlɪteɪt] facilitar; **facilities** instalaciones *fpl*
fact [fækt] hecho *m*; ***in ~, as a matter of ~*** de hecho
faction ['fækʃn] facción *f*
factor ['fæktər] factor *m*
faculty ['fækəltɪ] facultad *f*
fad [fæd] moda *f*
fade [feɪd] *of colors* desteñirse; *of memories* desvanecerse; **faded** *color* desteñido, descolorido
fag [fæg] F (*homosexual*) maricón *m* F
fail [feɪl] **1** *v/i* fracasar **2** *v/t exam* suspender; **failing** fallo *m*; **failure** fracaso *m*; *in exam* suspenso *m*
faint [feɪnt] **1** *adj line, smile* tenue; *smell, noise* casi imperceptible **2** *v/i* desmayarse; **faintly** levemente
fair[1] [fer] *n* COM feria *f*
fair[2] [fer] *adj hair* rubio; *complexion* claro; (*just*) justo
fairly ['ferlɪ] *treat* justamente, con justicia; (*quite*) bastante; **fairness** *of treatment* imparcialidad *f*
faith [feɪθ] fe *f*; **faithful** fiel; **faithfully** religiosamente
fake [feɪk] **1** *n* falsificación *f* **2** *adj* falso **3** *v/t* (*forge*) falsificar; (*feign*) fingir
fall[1] [fɒːl] *n season* otoño *m*
fall[2] [fɒːl] **1** *v/i* caer; *of person* caerse **2** *n* caída *f*
◆ **fall behind** retrasarse
◆ **fall for** *person* enamorarse de; (*be deceived by*) dejarse engañar por
◆ **fall through** *of plans* venirse abajo
fallible ['fæləbl] falible
false [fɑːls] falso; **false start** *in race* salida *f* nula; **false teeth** dentadura *f* postiza; **falsify** falsificar
fame [feɪm] fama *f*
familiar [fə'mɪljər] familiar; ***be ~ with sth*** estar familiarizado con algo; **familiarity** *with subject etc* familiaridad *f*; **familiarize: *~ o.s. with*** familiarizarse con
family ['fæməlɪ] familia *f*; **family doctor** médico *m/f* de familia; **family planning** planificación *f* familiar; **family tree** árbol *m* genealógico
famine ['fæmɪn] hambruna *f*
famous ['feɪməs] famoso

fan[1] [fæn] *n* (*supporter*) seguidor(a) *m(f)*; *of singer, band* admirador(a) *m(f)*, fan *m/f*
fan[2] [fæn] **1** *n electric* ventilador *m*; *handheld* abanico *m* **2** *v/t* abanicar
fanatical [fə'nætɪkl] fanático; **fanaticism** fanatismo *m*
fantasize ['fæntəsaɪz] fantasear (***about*** sobre); **fantastic** (*very good*) fantástico; (*very big*) inmenso; **fantasy** fantasía *f*
fanzine ['fænzi:n] fanzine *m*
far [fɑ:r] lejos; (*much*) mucho; ***~ bigger*** mucho más grande; ***how ~ is it to ...?*** ¿a cuánto está...?; ***as ~ as the corner*** hasta la esquina
farce [fɑ:rs] farsa *f*
fare [fer] (*price*) tarifa *f*; *actual money* dinero *m*
Far 'East Lejano Oriente *m*
farewell [fer'wel] despedida *f*
farfetched [fɑ:r'fetʃt] inverosímil, exagerado
farm [fɑ:rm] granja *f*; **farmer** granjero(-a) *m(f)*; **farming** agricultura *f*; **farmworker** trabajador(a) *m(f)* del campo; **farmyard** corral *m*
'far-off lejano; **farsighted** previsor; *optically* hipermétrope; **farther** más lejos; **farthest** más lejos
fascinate ['fæsɪneɪt] fascinar; **fascinating** fascinante; **fascination** fascinación *f*
fascism ['fæʃɪzm] fascismo *m*; **fascist** **1** *n* fascista *m/f* **2** *adj* fascista
fashion ['fæʃn] moda *f*; (*manner*) modo *m*, manera *f*; ***out of ~*** pasado de moda; **fashionable** de moda; **fashionably** *dressed* a la moda; **fashion-conscious** que sigue la moda; **fashion designer** modisto(-a) *m(f)*; **fashion show** desfile *f* de moda
fast[1] [fæst] **1** *adj* rápido; ***be ~*** *of clock* ir adelantado **2** *adv* rápido; ***~ asleep*** profundamente dormido
fast[2] [fæst] *n not eating* ayuno *m*
fasten ['fæsn] **1** *v/t lid* cerrar (*poniendo el cierre*); *dress* abrochar **2** *v/i of dress etc* abrocharse; **fastener** *for dress, lid* cierre *f*
'fast food comida *f* rápida; **fast lane** carril *f* rápido; **fast train** rápido *m*
fat [fæt] **1** *adj* gordo **2** *n on meat, for baking* grasa *f*
fatal ['feɪtl] *illness* mortal; *error* fatal; **fatality** víctima *f* mortal; **fatally** mortalmente
fate [feɪt] destino *m*
'fat-free sin grasas
father ['fɑ:ðər] padre *m*; **fatherhood** paternidad *f*; **father-in-law** suegro *m*; **fatherly** paternal
fatigue [fə'ti:g] fatiga *f*
fatten ['fætn] *animal* engordar; **fatty** **1** *adj* graso **2** *n* F (*person*) gordinflón (-ona) *m(f)* F
faucet ['fɒ:sɪt] *Span* grifo *m*, *L.Am.* llave *f*

fault [fɒ:lt] (*defect*) fallo *m*; ***it's your ~*** es culpa tuya; **faultless** impecable; **faulty** defectuoso

favor ['feɪvər] **1** *n* favor *m* **2** *v/t* (*prefer*) preferir; **favorable** favorable; **favorite 1** *n* favorito(-a) *m*(*f*); *food* comida *f* favorita **2** *adj* favorito; **favoritism** favoritismo *m*; **favour** *Br* ☞ **favor**

fax [fæks] **1** *n* fax *m* **2** *v/t* enviar por fax

fear [fɪr] **1** *n* miedo *m*, temor *m* **2** *v/t* temer; **fearless** valiente; **fearlessly** sin miedo

feasibility study [fi:zə'bɪlətɪ] estudio *m* de viabilidad; **feasible** factible, viable

feast [fi:st] banquete *m*

feat [fi:t] hazaña *f*, proeza *f*

feather ['feðər] pluma *f*

feature ['fi:ʧər] *on face* rasgo *m*, facción *f*; *of city, building, style* característica *f*; *article in paper* reportaje *m*; **feature film** largometraje *m*

February ['februeri] febrero *m*

federal ['fedərəl] federal; **federation** federación *f*

'fed up F harto, hasta las narices F

fee [fi:] honorarios *mpl*; *for entrance* entrada *f*; *for membership* cuota *f*

feeble ['fi:bl] *person, laugh* débil; *attempt* flojo; *excuse* pobre

feed [fi:d] alimentar, dar de comer a; **feedback** reacción *f*

feel [fi:l] **1** *v/t* (*touch*) tocar; (*sense*) sentir; (*think*) creer, pensar **2** *v/i*: ***it ~s like silk*** tiene la textura de la seda; ***do you ~ like a drink?*** ¿te apetece una bebida?

◆ **feel up to** sentirse con fuerzas para

feeler ['fi:lər] *of insect* antena *f*; **feeling** sentimiento *m*; (*sensation*) sensación *f*

fellow 'citizen conciudadano(-a) *m*(*f*)

felony ['felənɪ] delito *m* grave

felt [felt] fieltro *m*; **felt tip** rotulador *m*

female ['fi:meɪl] **1** *adj* hembra; *relating to people* femenino **2** *n* hembra *f*; *person* mujer *f*

feminine ['femɪnɪn] **1** *adj* femenino **2** *n* GRAM femenino *m*; **feminism** feminismo *m*; **feminist 1** *n* feminista *m*/*f* **2** *adj* feminista

fence [fens] cerca *f*, valla *f*

fender ['fendər] MOT aleta *f*

fermentation [fɜ:rmen'teɪʃn] fermentación *f*

ferocious [fə'roʊʃəs] feroz

ferry ['ferɪ] ferry *m*, transbordador *m*

fertile ['fɜ:rtəl] fértil; **fertility** fertilidad *f*; **fertilize** fertilizar; **fertilizer** *for soil* fertilizante *m*

fervent ['fɜ:rvənt] ferviente

fester ['festər] *of wound* enconarse

festival ['festɪvl] festival *m*; **festive** festivo; **festivities** celebraciones *fpl*
fetal ['fi:tl] fetal
fetch [fetʃ] *person* recoger; *thing* traer, ir a buscar; *price* alcanzar
fetus ['fi:təs] feto *m*
feud [fju:d] enemistad *f*
fever ['fi:vər] fiebre *f*; **feverish** con fiebre; *excitement* febril
few [fju:] **1** *adj* pocos; ***a ~*** unos pocos **2** *pron* pocos(-as); ***quite a ~*** bastantes; **fewer** menos
fiancé [fɪ'ɑ:nseɪ] prometido *m*, novio *m*; **fiancée** prometida *f*, novia *f*
fiber ['faɪbər] fibra *f*; **fiberglass** fibra *f* de vidrio; **fiber optics** tecnología *f* de la fibra óptica
fibre *Br* ☞ ***fiber***
fickle ['fɪkl] inconstante
fiction ['fɪkʃn] literatura *f* de ficción; (*made-up story*) ficción *f*; **fictional** de ficción; **fictitious** ficticio
fiddle ['fɪdl] **1** *n* violín *m* **2** *v/i*: ***~ around with*** enredar con **3** *v/t accounts*, *result* amañar
fidgety ['fɪdʒɪtɪ] inquieto
field [fi:ld] campo *m*; *for sport* campo *m*, *L.Am.* cancha *f*; (*competitors in race*) participantes *mpl*; **fielder** *in baseball* fildeador(-a) *m(f)*
fierce [fɪrs] feroz; *storm* violento; **fiercely** ferozmente
fiery ['faɪrɪ] fogoso, ardiente
fifteen [fɪf'ti:n] quince; **fifteenth** decimoquinto; **fifth** quinto; **fiftieth** quincuagésimo; **fifty** cincuenta; **fifty-fifty** a medias
fight [faɪt] **1** *n* lucha *f*, pelea *f*; (*argument*) pelea *f*; *for survival etc* lucha *f*; *in boxing* combate *m* **2** *v/t enemy*, *person* luchar contra, pelear contra; *injustice* luchar contra **3** *v/i* luchar, pelear; (*argue*) pelearse; **fighter** combatiente *m/f*; *airplane* caza *m*; (*boxer*) púgil *m*; **fighting** peleas *fpl*; MIL luchas *fpl*
figure ['fɪgər] **1** *n* figura *f*; (*digit*) cifra *f* **2** *v/t* F (*think*) imaginarse, pensar
◆ **figure on** F (*plan*) pensar
◆ **figure out** entender; *calculation* resolver
file[1] [faɪl] **1** *n of documents* expediente *m*; COMPUT archivo *m*, fichero *m* **2** *v/t* archivar
file[2] [faɪl] *n for wood etc* lima *f*
'file cabinet archivador *m*
fill [fɪl] llenar; *tooth* empastar, *L.Am.* emplomar; *prescription* despachar
◆ **fill in** *form*, *hole* rellenar
◆ **fill out 1** *v/t form* rellenar **2** *v/i* (*get fatter*) engordar
fillet ['fɪlɪt] filete *m*
filling ['fɪlɪŋ] **1** *n in sandwich* relleno *m*; *in tooth* empaste *m*, *L.Am.* emplomadura *f* **2** *adj*: ***be ~*** *of food* llenar mucho; **filling station** estación *f* de servicio
film [fɪlm] **1** *n* carrete *m*;

(*movie*) película *f* **2** *v/t* filmar; **film-maker** cineasta *m/f*; **film star** estrella *f* de cine

filter ['fɪltər] **1** *n* filtro *m* **2** *v/t* filtrar

filth [fɪlθ] suciedad *f*; **filthy** sucio; *language etc* obsceno

final ['faɪnl] **1** *adj* último; *decision* final, definitivo **2** *n* SP final *f*; **finale** final *m*; **finalist** finalista *m/f*; **finalize** ultimar; **finally** finalmente

finance ['faɪnæns] **1** *n* finanzas *fpl* **2** *v/t* financiar; **financial** financiero; **financially** económicamente; **financier** financiero(-a) *m(f)*

find [faɪnd] encontrar

◆ **find out** descubrir

findings ['faɪndɪŋz] *of report* conclusiones *fpl*

fine[1] [faɪn] *adj day* bueno; *wine, performance, city* excelente; *distinction, line* fino

fine[2] [faɪn] **1** *n* multa *f* **2** *v/t* multar, poner una multa a

finger ['fɪŋgər] **1** *n* dedo *m* **2** *v/t* tocar; **fingerprint** huella *f* digital *or* dactilar

finicky ['fɪnɪkɪ] *person* quisquilloso; *design* enrevesado

finish ['fɪnɪʃ] **1** *v/t & v/i* acabar, terminar **2** *n of product* acabado *m*; *of race* final *f*

◆ **finish with** *boyfriend etc* cortar con

Finland ['fɪnlənd] Finlandia; **Finn** finlandés(-esa) *m(f)*; **Finnish 1** *adj* finlandés **2** *n language* finés *m*

fire [faɪr] **1** *n* fuego *m*; *electric, gas* estufa *f*; (*blaze*) incendio *m*; (*bonfire, campfire etc*) hoguera *f*; ***be on ~*** estar ardiendo; ***set ~ to sth*** prender fuego a algo **2** *v/i* (*shoot*) disparar (***at*** a) **3** *v/t* F (*dismiss*) despedir; **fire alarm** alarma *f* contra incendios; **firearm** arma *f* de fuego; **firecracker** petardo *m*; **fire department** (cuerpo *m* de) bomberos *mpl*; **fire engine** coche *m* de bomberos; **fire escape** salida *f* de incendios; **fire extinguisher** extintor *m*; **fire fighter** bombero (-a) *m(f)*; **fireplace** chimenea *f*, hogar *m*; **fire station** parque *m* de bomberos; **fire truck** coche *m* de bomberos; **fireworks** fuegos *mpl* artificiales

firm[1] [fɜːrm] *adj* firme

firm[2] [fɜːrm] *n com* empresa *f*

first [fɜːrst] **1** *adj & adv* primero; ***at ~*** al principio **2** *n* primero(-a) *m(f)*; **first aid** primeros *mpl* auxilios; **first class 1** *adj ticket, seat* de primera (clase); (*very good*) excelente **2** *adv travel* en primera (clase); **first floor** planta *f* baja, *Br* primer piso *m*; **First Lady** primera dama *f*; **firstly** en primer lugar; **first name** nombre *m* (de pila); **first night** estreno *m*; **first-rate** excelente

fiscal ['fɪskl] fiscal; **fiscal year** año *m* fiscal

fish [fɪʃ] **1** *n* pez *m*; *to eat* pescado *m* **2** *v/i* pescar; **fisherman** pescador *m*; **fishing** pesca *f*; **fishing boat** (barco *m*) pesquero *m*; **fish stick** palito *m* de pescado; **fishy** F (*suspicious*) sospechoso

fist [fɪst] puño *m*

fit[1] [fɪt] *n* MED ataque *m*

fit[2] [fɪt] *adj* en forma; *morally* adecuado

fit[3] [fɪt] **1** *v/t* (*attach*) colocar; ***these pants don't ~ me any more*** estos pantalones ya no me entran **2** *v/i of clothes* quedar bien

fitness ['fɪtnɪs] *physical* buena forma *f*; **fitting** apropiado; **fittings** equipamiento *m*

five [faɪv] cinco

fix [fɪks] **1** *n* (*solution*) solución *f* **2** *v/t* (*attach*) fijar; (*repair*) reparar; *meeting etc* organizar; *lunch* preparar; *dishonestly*: *match etc* amañar; **fixed** fijo; **fixings** guarnición *f*

flab [flæb] *on body* grasa *f*; **flabby** *muscles etc* fofo

flag[1] [flæg] *n* bandera *f*

flag[2] [flæg] *v/i* (*tire*) desfallecer

'flagpole asta *f* (de bandera)

flagrant ['fleɪgrənt] flagrante

flair [fler] (*talent*) don *m*

flake [fleɪk] *of snow* copo *m*; *of skin* escama *f*; *of plaster* desconchón *m*

flamboyant [flæm'bɔɪənt] extravagante; **flamboyantly** extravagantemente

flame [fleɪm] llama *f*

flamenco [flə'meŋkoʊ] flamenco *m*; **flamenco dancer** bailaor(a) *m*(*f*)

flammable ['flæməbl] inflamable

flank [flæŋk] **1** *n of horse etc* costado *m*; MIL flanco *m* **2** *v/t* flanquear

flap [flæp] **1** *n of envelope, pocket* solapa *f*; *of table* hoja *f* **2** *v/t wings* batir **3** *v/i of flag etc* ondear

◆ **flare up** [fler] *of violence* estallar; *of illness* exacerbarse; *of fire* llamear; (*get very angry*) estallar

flash [flæʃ] **1** *n of light* destello *m*; PHOT flash *m*; ***in a ~*** F en un abrir y cerrar de ojos; ***a ~ of lightning*** un relámpago **2** *v/i of light* destellar; **flashback** flash-back *m*; **flashlight** linterna *f*; PHOT flash *m*; **flashy** *pej* ostentoso, chillón

flask [flæsk] (*hip ~*) petaca *f*

flat[1] [flæt] **1** *adj* llano, plano; *beer* sin gas; *battery* descargado; *tire* desinflado; *shoes* bajo; MUS bemol **2** *adv* MUS demasiado bajo **3** *n* (*~ tire*) pinchazo *m*

flat[2] [flæt] *n Br* apartamento *m*, *Span* piso *m*

flatly ['flætlɪ] *deny* rotundamente; **flat rate** tarifa *f* única; **flatten** *land, road* allanar, aplanar; *by bombing, demolition* arrasar

flatter ['flætər] halagar; **flatterer** adulador(a) *m*(*f*); **flattering** *comments* halagador;

color, clothes favorecedor; **flattery** halagos *mpl*
flavor ['fleɪvər] **1** *n* sabor *m* **2** *v/t food* condimentar; **flavoring** aromatizante *m*; **flavour** *Br* ☞ ***flavor***
flaw [flɒ:] defecto *m*, fallo *m*; **flawless** impecable
flee [fli:] escapar, huir
fleet [fli:t] NAUT, *of vehicles* flota *f*
fleeting ['fli:tɪŋ] *visit etc* fugaz
flesh [fleʃ] carne *f*; *of fruit* pulpa *f*
flex [fleks] *muscles* flexionar; **flexibility** flexibilidad *f*; **flexible** flexible; **flextime** horario *m* flexible
flicker ['flɪkər] parpadear
flier [flaɪr] (*circular*) folleto *m*
flight [flaɪt] *in airplane* vuelo *m*; (*fleeing*) huida *f*; **~** (***of stairs***) tramo *m* (de escaleras); **flight attendant** auxiliar *m/f* de vuelo; **flight path** ruta *f* de vuelo; **flight recorder** caja *f* negra; **flight time** *departure* hora *f* del vuelo; *duration* duración *f* del vuelo; **flighty** inconstante
flimsy ['flɪmzɪ] *furniture* endeble; *dress*, *material* débil; *excuse* pobre
flinch [flɪntʃ] encogerse
flipper ['flɪpər] aleta *f*
flirt [flɜ:rt] **1** *v/i* flirtear, coquetear **2** *n* ligón (-ona) *m(f)*; **flirtatious** coqueto
float [flout] *also* FIN flotar
flock [flɑ:k] **1** *n of sheep* rebaño *m* **2** *v/i* acudir en masa
flood [flʌd] **1** *n* inundación *f* **2** *v/t of river* inundar; **flooding** inundaciones *fpl*; **floodlight** foco *m*; **flood waters** crecida *f*
floor [flɔ:r] suelo *m*; (*story*) piso *m*
flop [flɑ:p] **1** *v/i* dejarse caer; F (*fail*) pinchar F **2** *n* F (*failure*) pinchazo *m* F; **floppy (disk)** disquete *m*
florist ['flɔ:rɪst] florista *m/f*
flour [flaʊr] harina *f*
flourish ['flʌrɪʃ] *of plant* crecer rápidamente; *fig* florecer; **flourishing** *business*, *trade* floreciente
flow [floʊ] **1** *v/i* fluir **2** *n* flujo *m*; **flowchart** diagrama *m* de flujo
flower [flaʊr] **1** *n* flor *f* **2** *v/i* florecer
flu [flu:] gripe *f*
fluctuate ['flʌktjʊeɪt] fluctuar; **fluctuation** fluctuación *f*
fluency ['flu:ənsɪ] *in a language* fluidez *f*; *fluent*: ***he speaks ~ Spanish*** habla español con soltura; **fluently** *speak*, *write* con soltura
fluid ['flu:ɪd] fluido *m*
flunk [flʌŋk] F *subject* suspender, *Span* catear F
flush [flʌʃ] **1** *v/t*: ***~ the toilet*** tirar de la cadena **2** *v/i* (*go red*) ruborizarse
flutter ['flʌtər] *of wings* aletear; *of flag* ondear; *of heart* latir con fuerza

fly[1] [flaɪ] *n insect* mosca *f*
fly[2] [flaɪ] *n on pants* bragueta *f*
fly[3] [flaɪ] **1** *v/i* volar; *of flag* ondear **2** *v/t airplane* pilotar; *airline* volar con; (*transport by air*) enviar por avión
◆ **fly past** *of time* volar
flying ['flaɪɪŋ] volar *m*
foam [foʊm] *on liquid* espuma *f*; **foam rubber** gomaespuma *f*
focus ['foʊkəs] foco *m*
◆ **focus on** concentrarse en; PHOT enfocar
fodder ['fɑːdər] forraje *m*
fog [fɑːg] niebla *f*; **foggy** neblinoso, con niebla
foil[1] [fɔɪl] *n* papel *m* de aluminio
foil[2] [fɔɪl] *v/t* (*thwart*) frustrar
fold [foʊld] **1** *v/t paper etc* doblar; **~ *one's arms*** cruzarse de brazos **2** *v/i of business* quebrar **3** *n in cloth etc* pliegue *m*
◆ **fold up 1** *v/t* plegar **2** *v/i of chair, table* plegarse
folder ['foʊldər] *for documents*, COMPUT carpeta *f*; **folding** plegable
foliage ['foʊlɪɪdʒ] follaje *m*
folk [foʊk] (*people*) gente *f*; **folk music** música *f* folk *or* popular; **folk singer** cantante *m/f* de folk
follow ['fɑːloʊ] **1** *v/t* seguir; (*understand*) entender **2** *v/i logically* deducirse
◆ **follow up** *inquiry* hacer el seguimiento de; **follower** seguidor(a) *m(f)*; **following 1** *adj* siguiente **2** *n people* seguidores(-as) *mpl* (*fpl*); ***the ~*** lo siguiente
fond [fɑːnd] cariñoso; *memory* entrañable; ***he's ~ of travel*** le gusta viajar; ***I'm very ~ of him*** le tengo mucho cariño
fondle ['fɑːndl] acariciar
fondness ['fɑːndnɪs] *for s.o.* cariño *m* (***for*** por); *for wine, food* afición *f*
font [fɑːnt] *for printing* tipo *m*; *in church* pila *f* bautismal
food [fuːd] comida *f*; **food poisoning** intoxicación *f* alimentaria
fool [fuːl] **1** *n* tonto(-a) *m(f)*, idiota *m/f* **2** *v/t* engañar; **foolhardy** temerario; **foolish** tonto; **foolproof** infalible
foot [fʊt] *also measurement* pie *m*; *of animal* pata *f*; ***put one's ~ in it*** F meter la pata F; **footage** secuencias *fpl*; **football** *Br* (*soccer*) fútbol *m*; *American* fútbol *m* americano; *ball* balón *m or* pelota *f* (de fútbol); **football player** *American style* jugador(a) *m(f)* de fútbol americano; *Br in soccer* jugador(a) *m(f)* de fútbol, futbolista *m/f*; **foothills** estribaciones *fpl*; **footnote** nota *f* a pie de página; **footpath** sendero *m*; **footprint** pisada *f*; **footstep** paso *m*
for [fər, fɔːr] *purpose, destination* para; (*in exchange for*)

por; ***what is this ~?*** ¿para qué sirve esto?; ***what ~?*** ¿para qué?; ***I bought it ~ $25*** lo compré por 5 dólares; ***~ three days*** durante tres días; ***please get it done ~ Monday*** por favor tenlo listo (para) el lunes; ***I walked ~ a mile*** caminé una milla; ***I am ~ the idea*** estoy a favor de la idea

forbid [fər'bɪd] prohibir; **forbidden** prohibido; **forbidding** *person, look* amenazador; *prospect* intimidador

force [fɔːrs] **1** *n* fuerza *f*; ***come into ~*** *of law etc* entrar en vigor **2** *v/t door, lock* forzar; ***~ s.o. to do sth*** forzar a alguien a hacer algo; **forced** forzado; **forced landing** aterrizaje *m* forzoso; **forceful** *argument* poderoso; *speaker* vigoroso; *character* enérgico

forceps ['fɔːrseps] MED fórceps *m inv*

forcibly ['fɔːrsəblɪ] por la fuerza

foreboding [fər'boudɪŋ] premonición *f*; **forecast 1** *n* pronóstico *m* **2** *v/t* pronosticar; **forefathers** ancestros *mpl*; **forefinger** (dedo *m*) índice *m*; **foreground** primer plano *m*; **forehead** frente *f*

foreign ['fɑːrən] extranjero; **foreign affairs** asuntos *mpl* exteriores; **foreign body** cuerpo *m* extraño; **foreign currency** divisa *f* extranjera; **foreigner** extranjero(-a) *m(f)*; **foreign exchange** divisas *fpl*

foreman capataz *m*; **foremost** principal

forensic medicine [fə'rensɪk] medicina *f* forense; **forensic scientist** forense *m/f*

'forerunner predecesor(a) *m(f)*; **foresee** prever; **foresight** previsión *f*

forest ['fɑːrɪst] bosque *m*; **forestry** silvicultura *f*

fore'tell predecir

forever [fə'revər] siempre

'foreword prólogo *m*

forfeit ['fɔːrfət] (*lose*) perder; (*give up*) renunciar a

forge [fɔːrdʒ] falsificar; **forgery** falsificación *f*

forget [fər'get] olvidar; **forgetful** olvidadizo

forgive [fər'gɪv] perdonar; **forgiveness** perdón *m*

fork [fɔːrk] *for eating* tenedor *m*; *for garden* horca *f*; *in road* bifurcación *f*

form [fɔːrm] **1** *n* (*shape*) forma *f*; *document* formulario *m*, impreso *m* **2** *v/t in clay etc* moldear; *friendship* establecer; *opinion* formarse; (*constitute*) formar **3** *v/i* (*take shape, develop*) formarse; **formal** formal; *recognition etc* oficial; *dress* de etiqueta; **formality** formalidad *f*; **formally** *speak* formalmente; *recognized* oficialmente

format ['fɔːrmæt] **1** *v/t text* formatear **2** *n of paper, program etc* formato *m*

formation [fɔːr'meɪʃn] formación *f*
former ['fɔːrmər] antiguo; ***the*** ~ el primero; **formerly** antiguamente
formidable ['fɔːrmɪdəbl] *personality* formidable; *opponent*, *task* terrible
formula ['fɔːrmjʊlə] fórmula *f*
fort [fɔːrt] MIL fuerte *m*
forthcoming ['fɔːrθkʌmɪŋ] (*future*) próximo; *personality* comunicativo
'forthright directo
fortieth ['fɔːrtɪɪθ] cuadragésimo
fortnight ['fɔːrtnaɪt] *Br* quincena *f*
fortress ['fɔːrtrɪs] MIL fortaleza *f*
fortunate ['fɔːrtʃnət] afortunado; **fortunately** afortunadamente; **fortune** fortuna *f*
forty ['fɔːrtɪ] cuarenta
forward ['fɔːrwərd] **1** *adv* hacia delante **2** *adj pej*: *person* atrevido **3** *n* SP delantero(-a) *m*(*f*) **4** *v/t letter* reexpedir; **forward-looking** con visión de futuro
fossil ['fɑːsəl] fósil *m*
foster ['fɑːstər] *child* acoger; *attitude*, *belief* fomentar
foul [faʊl] **1** *n* SP falta *f* **2** *adj smell* asqueroso; *weather* terrible **3** *v/t* SP hacer (una) falta a
found [faʊnd] *school etc* fundar; **foundation** *of theory etc* fundamento *m*; (*organization*) fundación *f*; **foundations** *of building* cimientos *mpl*; **founder** fundador(a) *m*(*f*)
fountain ['faʊntɪn] fuente *f*
four [fɔːr] cuatro; **four-star** *hotel etc* de cuatro estrellas;
fourteen catorce; **fourteenth** decimocuarto;
fourth cuarto; **four-wheel drive** MOT todoterreno *m*
fox [fɑːks] **1** *n* zorro *m* **2** *v/t* (*puzzle*) dejar perplejo
foyer ['fɔɪər] vestíbulo *m*
fraction ['frækʃn] fracción *f*; **fractionally** ligeramente
fracture ['fræktʃər] **1** *n* fractura *f* **2** *v/t* fracturar
fragile ['frædʒəl] frágil
fragment ['frægmənt] fragmento *m*
fragrance ['freɪgrəns] fragancia *f*; **fragrant** fragante
frail [freɪl] frágil, delicado
frame [freɪm] **1** *n of picture*, *window* marco *m*; *of eyeglasses* montura *f*; *of bicycle* cuadro *m* **2** *v/t picture* enmarcar; F *person* tender una trampa a; **framework** estructura *f*; *for agreement* marco *m*
France [fræns] Francia
franchise ['fræntʃaɪz] *for business* franquicia *f*
frank [fræŋk] franco; **frankly** francamente; **frankness** franqueza *f*
frantic ['fræntɪk] frenético
fraternal [frə'tɜːrnl] fraternal
fraud [frɒːd] fraude *m*; *person* impostor(a) *m*(*f*); **fraudu-**

lent fraudulento

frayed [freɪd] *cuffs* deshilachado

freak [fri:k] **1** *n event* fenómeno *m* anormal; *two-headed animal etc* monstruo *m*; F *strange person* bicho *m* raro F **2** *adj storm etc* anormal

free [fri:] **1** *adj* libre; *no cost* gratis, gratuito **2** *v/t prisoners* liberar; **freedom** libertad *f*; **free enterprise** empresa *f* libre; **free kick** golpe *m* franco; **freelance** autónomo, free-lance; **freely** *admit* libremente; **free speech** libertad *f* de expresión; **freeway** autopista *f*

freeze [fri:z] **1** *v/t food, wages, video* congelar **2** *v/i of water* congelarse; **freeze-dried** liofilizado; **freezer** congelador *m*; **freezing 1** *adj* muy frío **2** *n*: ***10 degrees below ~*** diez grados bajo cero

freight [freɪt] transporte *m*; *costs* flete *m*; **freighter** *ship* carguero *m*; *airplane* avión *m* de carga

French [frentʃ] **1** *adj* francés **2** *n language* francés *m*; ***the ~*** los franceses; **French fries** *Span* patatas *fpl or L.Am.* papas *fpl* fritas; **Frenchman** francés *m*; **Frenchwoman** francesa *f*

frenzied ['frenzɪd] frenético; *mob* desenfrenado; **frenzy** frenesí *m*

frequency ['fri:kwənsɪ] *also* RAD frecuencia *f*

frequent[1] ['fri:kwənt] *adj* frecuente

frequent[2] [frɪ'kwent] *v/t bar* frecuentar

frequently ['fri:kwəntlɪ] con frecuencia

fresh [freʃ] fresco; *start* nuevo; (*impertinent*) descarado; **fresh air** aire *m* fresco

◆ **freshen up 1** *v/i* refrescarse **2** *v/t paintwork etc* renovar

freshly ['freʃlɪ] recién; **freshman** estudiante *m/f* de primer año; **freshwater** de agua dulce

fret [fret] **1** *v/i* inquietarse **2** *n of guitar* traste *m*

friction ['frɪkʃn] PHYS rozamiento *m*; *between people* fricción *f*

Friday ['fraɪdeɪ] viernes *m inv*

fridge [frɪdʒ] nevera *f*, frigorífico *m*

friend [frend] amigo(-a) *m(f)*; **friendliness** simpatía *f*; **friendly** agradable; *person also* simpático; *argument, relations* amistoso; **friendship** amistad *f*

fries [fraɪz] *Span* patatas *fpl or L.Am.* papas *fpl* fritas

fright [fraɪt] susto *m*; **frighten** asustar; ***be ~ed of*** tener miedo de; **frightening** aterrador, espantoso

frill [frɪl] *on dress etc* volante *m*; (*fancy extra*) extra *m*

fringe [frɪndʒ] *on dress etc* flecos *mpl*; *Br in hair* flequillo *m*; (*edge*) margen *m*; **fringe benefits** ventajas *fpl* adicionales

frisk [frɪsk] cachear

◆ **fritter away** ['frɪtər] *time* desperdiciar; *fortune* despilfarrar

frivolity [frɪ'vɑːlətɪ] frivolidad *f*; **frivolous** frívolo

frizzy ['frɪzɪ] *hair* crespo

frog [frɑːg] rana *f*

'frogman hombre *m* rana

from [frɑːm] *in time* desde; *in space* de, desde; **~ *the 18th century*** desde el siglo XVIII; **~ *9 to 5*** de 9 a 5; **~ *today on*** a partir de hoy; **~ *here to there*** de *or* desde aquí hasta allí; ***we drove here* ~ *Las Vegas*** vinimos en coche desde Las Vegas; ***a letter* ~ *Jo*** una carta de Jo; ***I am* ~ *New Jersey*** soy de Nueva Jersey

front [frʌnt] **1** *n of building, book* portada *f*; (*cover organization*) tapadera *f*; MIL, *of weather* frente *m*; ***in* ~** delante; *in a race* en cabeza; ***in* ~ *of*** delante de **2** *adj wheel, seat* delantero **3** *v/t TV program* presentar; **front door** puerta *f* principal

frontier ['frʌntɪr] frontera *f*; *of science* límite *m*

front 'line MIL línea *f* del frente; **front page** *of newspaper* portada *f*; **front-wheel drive** tracción *f* delantera

frost [frɑːst] escarcha *f*; **frostbite** congelación *f*; **frosting** *on cake* glaseado *m*; **frosty** *weather* gélido; *welcome* glacial

froth [frɑːθ] espuma *f*

frown [fraʊn] fruncir el ceño

frozen ['froʊzn] *ground, food* congelado

fruit [fruːt] fruta *f*; **fruitful** *discussions etc* fructífero; **fruit juice** *Span* zumo *m or L.Am.* jugo *m* de fruta; **fruit salad** macedonia *f*

frustrate ['frʌstreɪt] frustrar; **frustrating** frustrante; **frustration** frustración *f*

fry [fraɪ] freír; **frypan** sartén *f*

fuck [fʌk] V *Span* follar con V, *L.Am.* coger V; ***~! ~!*** ¡joder! V

fuel ['fjuəl] **1** *n* combustible *m* **2** *v/t fig* avivar

fugitive ['fjuːdʒətɪv] fugitivo(-a) *m(f)*

fulfill, *Br* **fulfil** [fʊl'fɪl] *dream, task* realizar; *contract* cumplir; **fulfillment,** *Br* **fulfilment** *of contract etc* cumplimiento *m*; *moral, spiritual* satisfacción *f*

full [fʊl] lleno; *account, schedule* completo; *life* pleno; ***pay in* ~** pagar al contado; **full moon** luna *f* llena; **full stop** *Br* punto *m*; **full-time** *worker, job* a tiempo completo; **fully** completamente; *describe* en detalle

fumble ['fʌmbl] *ball* dejar caer

fumes [fjuːmz] humos *mpl*

fun [fʌn] **1** *n* diversión *f*; ***for* ~** para divertirse; ***it was great* ~** fue muy divertido **2** *adj* F

person, *game* divertido
function ['fʌŋkʃn] **1** *n* función *f*; (*reception etc*) acto *m* **2** *v/i* funcionar; **~ *as*** hacer de; **functional** funcional
fund [fʌnd] **1** *n* fondo *m* **2** *v/t project etc* financiar
fundamental [fʌndə'mentl] fundamental; (*crucial*) esencial; **fundamentalist** fundamentalista *m/f*; **fundamentally** fundamentalmente
funding ['fʌndɪŋ] (*money*) fondos *mpl*, financiación *f*
funeral ['fju:nərəl] funeral *m*; **funeral home** funeraria *f*
fungus ['fʌŋgəs] hongos *mpl*
funnies ['fʌnɪz] F *sección de humor*; **funnily** (*oddly*) de modo extraño; (*comically*) de forma divertida; **~ *enough*** curiosamente; **funny** (*comical*) divertido, gracioso; (*odd*) curioso, raro
fur [fɜ:r] piel *f*
furious ['fjʊrɪəs] furioso; *effort* febril
furnace ['fɜ:rnɪs] horno *m*
furnish ['fɜ:rnɪʃ] *room* amueblar; (*supply*) suministrar; **furniture** mobiliario *m*, muebles *mpl*
further ['fɜ:rðər] **1** *adj* adicional; (*more distant*) más lejano **2** *adv walk*, *drive* más lejos **3** *v/t cause etc* promover; **furthermore** es más
furtive ['fɜ:rtɪv] furtivo
fury ['fjʊrɪ] furia *f*, ira *f*
fuse [fju:z] **1** *n* ELEC fusible *m* **2** *v/i* ELEC fundirse **3** *v/t* ELEC fundir; **fusebox** caja *f* de fusibles
fusion ['fju:ʒn] fusión *f*
fuss [fʌs] escándalo *m*; **fussy** *person* quisquilloso; *design etc* recargado
futile ['fju:tl] inútil, vano; **futility** inutilidad *f*
future ['fju:ʧər] **1** *n* futuro *m* **2** *adj* futuro; **futuristic** *design* futurista
fuzzy ['fʌzɪ] *hair* crespo; (*out of focus*) borroso

G

gadget ['gædʒɪt] artilugio *m*, chisme *m*
gag [gæg] **1** *n over mouth* mordaza *f*; (*joke*) chiste *m* **2** *v/t also fig* amordazar
gain [geɪn] (*acquire*) ganar; *victory* obtener
gala ['gælə] gala *f*
galaxy ['gæləksɪ] galaxia *f*
gale [geɪl] vendaval *m*
gallery ['gælərɪ] *for art* museo *m*; *private* galería de arte; *in theater* galería *f*
gallon ['gælən] galón *m* (*0,785 litros*, *en GB 0,546*)
gallop ['gæləp] galopar
gamble ['gæmbl] jugar; **gambler** jugador(a) *m*(*f*); **gambling** juego *m*
game [geɪm] partido *m*; *child-*

ren's, *in tennis* juego *m*
gang [gæŋ] *of criminals* banda *f*; *of friends* cuadrilla *f*; **gangster** gángster *m*; **gangway** pasarela *f*
gap [gæp] *in wall* hueco *m*; *for parking*, *in figures* espacio *m*; *in time* intervalo *m*; *in conversation* interrupción *f*
gape [geɪp] *of person* mirar boquiabierto; **gaping** *hole* enorme
garage [gə'rɑːʒ] *for parking* garaje *m*; *for repairs* taller *m*; *Br for gas* gasolinera *f*
garbage ['gɑːrbɪdʒ] *also fig* basura *f*; *fig* (*nonsense*) tonterías *fpl*; **garbage can** cubo *m* de la basura; *in street* papelera *f*; **garbage truck** camión *m* de la basura
garbled ['gɑːrbld] *message* confuso
garden ['gɑːrdn] jardín *m*; **gardening** jardinería *f*
garish ['gerɪʃ] *color* chillón; *design* estridente
garlic ['gɑːrlɪk] ajo *m*
garment ['gɑːrmənt] prenda *f* (de vestir)
garnish ['gɑːrnɪʃ] guarnecer
gas [gæs] gas *m*; (*gasoline*) gasolina *f*, *Rpl* nafta *f*
gash [gæʃ] corte *m* profundo
gasket ['gæskɪt] junta *f*
gasoline ['gæsəliːn] gasolina *f*, *Rpl* nafta *f*
gasp [gæsp] **1** *n* grito *m* apagado **2** *v/i* lanzar un grito apagado
'gas pedal acelerador *m*; **gas pump** surtidor *m* (de gasolina); **gas station** gasolinera *f*, *S.Am.* bomba
gate [geɪt] *of house*, *at airport* puerta *f*; *made of iron* verja *f*; **gateway** *also fig* entrada *f*
gather ['gæðər] **1** *v/t facts* reunir; ~ ***speed*** ganar velocidad **2** *v/i of crowd* reunirse; **gathering** grupo *m* de personas
gaudy ['gɒːdɪ] chillón
gauge [geɪdʒ] **1** *n* indicador *m* **2** *v/t pressure* medir, calcular; *opinion* estimar
gaunt [gɒːnt] demacrado
gawky ['gɒːkɪ] desgarbado
gawp [gɒːp] F mirar boquiabierto
gay [geɪ] gay
gaze [geɪz] **1** *n* mirada *f* **2** *v/i* mirar fijamente
gear [gɪr] (*equipment*) equipo *m*; *in vehicle* marcha *f*; **gearbox** MOT caja *f* de cambios; **gear shift** MOT palanca *f* de cambios
gel [dʒel] *for hair* gomina *f*; *for shower* gel *m*
gem [dʒem] gema *f*; *fig* (*book etc*) joya *f*; (*person*) cielo *m*
gender ['dʒendər] género *m*
gene [dʒiːn] gen *m*
general ['dʒenrəl] **1** *n* MIL general *m* **2** *adj* general; **generalization** generalización *f*; **generalize** generalizar; **generally** generalmente, por lo general; ~ ***speaking*** en términos generales
generate ['dʒenəreɪt] generar; *feeling* provocar; **gene-**

ration generación *f*; **generator** generador *m*

generosity [dʒenə'rɑːsətɪ] generosidad *f*; **generous** generoso

genetic [dʒɪ'netɪk] genético; **genetically** genéticamente; **~ *modified*** transgénico; **~ *engineered*** transgénico; **genetic engineering** ingeniería *f* genética; **genetic fingerprint** identificación *f* genética; **genetics** genética *f*

genial ['dʒiːnjəl] afable

genitals ['dʒenɪtlz] genitales *mpl*

genius ['dʒiːnjəs] genio *m*

genocide ['dʒenəsaɪd] genocidio *m*

gentle ['dʒentl] *person* tierno, delicado; *touch, detergent, breeze* suave; *slope* poco inclinado; **gentleman** caballero *m*; **gentleness** *of person* ternura *f*, delicadeza; *of touch, detergent, breeze* suavidad *f*; *gently* con delicadeza

genuine ['dʒenuɪn] *antique* genuino, auténtico; (*sincere*) sincero; **genuinely** realmente, de verdad

geographical [dʒɪə'græfɪkl] geográfico; **geography** geografía *f*

geological [dʒɪə'lɑːdʒɪkl] geológico; **geologist** geólogo(-a) *m(f)*; **geology** geología *f*

geometric, geometrical [dʒɪə'metrɪk(l)] geométrico; **geometry** geometría *f*

geriatric [dʒerɪ'ætrɪk] **1** *adj* geriátrico **2** *n* anciano(-a) *m(f)*

germ [dʒɜːrm] *also fig* germen *m*

German ['dʒɜːrmən] **1** *adj* alemán **2** *n person* alemán (-ana) *m(f)*; *language* alemán *m*; **German shepherd** pastor *m* alemán; **Germany** Alemania

gesture ['dʒestʃər] *also fig* gesto *m*

get [get] (*obtain*) conseguir; (*buy*) comprar; (*fetch*) traer; (*receive*: *letter, knowledge, respect*) recibir; (*catch*: *bus, train etc*) tomar, *Span* coger; (*understand*) entender; **~ *home*** llegar a casa; **~ *tired*** cansarse; **~ *the TV fixed*** hacer que arreglen la televisión; **~ *one's hair cut*** cortarse el pelo; **~ *s.o. to do sth*** hacer que alguien haga algo; **~ *to do sth*** (*have opportunity*) llegar a hacer algo; **~ *sth ready*** preparar algo; **~ *going*** (*leave*) marcharse, irse; ***have got*** tener; ***have got to*** tener que; ***I have got to see him*** tengo que verlo; **~ *to know*** llegar a conocer

◆ **get at** (*criticize*) meterse con; (*mean*) querer decir

◆ **get by** (*pass*) pasar; *financially* arreglárselas

◆ **get down 1** *v/i from ladder etc* bajarse (***from*** de); (*duck* *etc*) agacharse **2** *v/t* (*depress*) desanimar

◆ **get in 1** *v/i* (*arrive*) llegar; *to car* subir(se) **2** *v/t to suitcase etc* meter

◆ **get into** *house* entrar en; *car* subir(se) a; *computer system* introducirse en

◆ **get off 1** *v/i from bus etc* bajarse; (*finish work*) salir; (*not be punished*) librarse **2** *v/t* (*remove*) quitar; *clothes* quitarse

◆ **get on 1** *v/i to bike, bus* montarse, subirse; (*be friendly*) llevarse bien; (*advance: of time*) hacerse tarde; (*become old*) hacerse mayor; (*make progress*) progresar **2** *v/t*: ***get on the bus*** montarse en el autobús

◆ **get out 1** *v/i of car, prison etc* salir; ***get out!*** ¡vete!, ¡fuera de aquí! **2** *v/t nail etc* sacar, extraer; *stain* quitar; *gun, pen* sacar

◆ **get through** *on telephone* conectarse

◆ **get up 1** *v/i* levantarse **2** *v/t* (*climb*) subir

'getaway *from robbery* fuga *f*; **get-together** reunión *f*

ghastly ['gæstlɪ] terrible

ghetto ['getoʊ] gueto *m*

ghost [goʊst] fantasma *m*; **ghostly** fantasmal

ghoul [gu:l] macabro(-a) *m*(*f*)

giant ['dʒaɪənt] **1** *n* gigante *m* **2** *adj* gigantesco, gigante

gibberish ['dʒɪbərɪʃ] F memeces *fpl* F

gibe [dʒaɪb] pulla *f*

giddiness ['gɪdɪnɪs] mareo *m*; **giddy** mareado

gift [gɪft] regalo *m*; *talent* don *m*; **gift certificate** vale *m* de regalo; **gifted** con talento; **giftwrap** envolver para regalo

gig [gɪg] F concierto *m*

gigabyte ['gɪgəbaɪt] COMPUT gigabyte *m*

gigantic [dʒaɪ'gæntɪk] gigantesco

giggle ['gɪgl] **1** *v/i* soltar risitas **2** *n* risita *f*

gimmick ['gɪmɪk] truco *m*

gin [dʒɪn] ginebra *f*; ***~ and tonic*** gin-tonic *m*

gipsy ['dʒɪpsɪ] gitano(-a) *m*(*f*)

girder ['gɜ:rdər] viga *f*

girl [gɜ:rl] chica *f*; (**young**) **~** niña *f*, chica *f*; **girlfriend** *of boy* novia *f*; *of girl* amiga *f*; **girlish** de niñas

gist [dʒɪst] esencia *f*

give [gɪv] dar; *as present* regalar; (*supply*: *electricity etc*) proporcionar; *cry, groan* soltar

◆ **give away** *as present* regalar; (*betray*) traicionar

◆ **give back** devolver

◆ **give in 1** *v/i* (*surrender*) rendirse **2** *v/t* (*hand in*) entregar

◆ **give onto** (*open onto*) dar a

◆ **give out 1** *v/t leaflets etc* repartir **2** *v/i of supplies, strength* agotarse

◆ **give up 1** *v/t smoking etc*

dejar de **2** *v/i* (*stop making effort*) rendirse
◆ **give way** *of bridge etc* hundirse
give-and-'take toma *m* y daca
gizmo ['gɪzmoʊ] F cacharro *m*
glad [glæd] contento; **gladly** con mucho gusto
glamor ['glæmər] atractivo *m*, glamour *m*; **glamorize** hacer atractivo; **glamorous** atractivo, glamoroso; **glamour** *Br* ☞ ***glamor***
glance [glæns] **1** *n* ojeada *f* **2** *v/i* echar una ojeada
gland [glænd] glándula *f*
glare [gler] **1** *n of sun, lights* resplandor *m* **2** *v/i of lights* resplandecer
◆ **glare at** mirar con furia a
glaring ['glerɪŋ] *mistake* garrafal
glass [glæs] vidrio *m*; *for drink* vaso *m*; **glasses** gafas *fpl*, *L.Am.* lentes *mpl*, *L.Am.* anteojos *mpl*
glazed [gleɪzd] *look* vidrioso
gleam [gli:m] **1** *n* resplandor *m* **2** *v/i* resplandecer
glee [gli:] júbilo *m*, regocijo *m*; **gleeful** jubiloso
glib [glɪb] fácil; **glibly** con labia
glide [glaɪd] *of bird, plane* planear; *of piece of furniture* deslizarse; **glider** planeador *m*; **gliding** *sport* vuelo *m* sin motor
glimpse [glɪmps] **1** *n* vistazo *m* **2** *v/t* vislumbrar
glint [glɪnt] **1** *n* destello *m*; *in eyes* centelleo *m* **2** *v/i of light* destellar; *of eyes* centellear
glisten ['glɪsn] relucir
glitter ['glɪtər] destellar
gloat [gloʊt] regodearse
◆ **gloat over** regodearse de
global ['gloʊbl] global; **globalization** COM globalización *f*; **global warming** calentamiento *m* global; **globe** globo *m*; (*model of earth*) globo *m* terráqueo
gloom [glu:m] (*darkness*) tinieblas *fpl*; *mood* abatimiento *m*; **gloomy** *room* tenebroso; *mood, person* abatido
glorious ['glɔ:rɪəs] *weather* espléndido; *victory* glorioso; **glory** gloria *f*
gloss [glɑ:s] (*shine*) lustre *m*; (*general explanation*) glosa *f*; **glossary** glosario *m*; **glossy 1** *adj paper* satinado **2** *n magazine* revista *f* en color
glove [glʌv] guante *m*; **glove compartment** guantera *f*
glow [gloʊ] **1** *n* resplandor *m*, brillo *m*; *in cheeks* rubor *m* **2** *v/i* resplandecer, brillar; *of cheeks* ruborizarse; **glowing** *description* entusiasta
glucose ['glu:koʊs] glucosa *f*
glue [glu:] **1** *n* pegamento *m*, cola *f* **2** *v/t* pegar, encolar
glum [glʌm] sombrío, triste
glut [glʌt] exceso *m*, superabundancia *f*
glutton ['glʌtən] glotón(-ona)

m(f)

gnaw [nɒː] *bone* roer

go [gou] ir (***to*** a); (*leave*) irse, marcharse; (*work*, *function*) funcionar; (*come out*: *of stain etc*) irse; (*cease*: *of pain etc*) pasarse; (*match*: *of colors etc*) ir bien, pegar; ~ ***shopping*** ir de compras; ***hamburger to*** ~ hamburguesa para llevar

◆ **go away** *of person* irse, marcharse; *of rain*, *pain*, *clouds* desaparecer

◆ **go back** (*return*) volver; (*date back*) remontarse

◆ **go by** *of car*, *time* pasar

◆ **go down** bajar; *of sun* ponerse

◆ **go in** *to room*, *house* entrar; *of sun* ocultarse; (*fit*: *of part etc*) ir, encajar

◆ **go off** (*leave*) marcharse; *of bomb* explotar; *of gun* dispararse; *of alarm* saltar; *Br of milk etc* echarse a perder

◆ **go on** (*continue*) continuar; (*happen*) pasar

◆ **go out** *of person* salir; *of light*, *fire* apagarse

◆ **go over** (*check*) examinar

◆ **go through** *illness*, *hard times* atravesar; (*check*) revisar; (*read through*) estudiar

◆ **go under** (*sink*) hundirse; *of company* ir a la quiebra

◆ **go up** subir

◆ **go without 1** *v/t food etc* pasar sin **2** *v/i* pasar privaciones

'go-ahead 1 *n* luz *f* verde **2** *adj* dinámico

goal [goul] SP *target* portería *f*, *L.Am.* arco *m*; SP *point* gol *m*; (*objective*) objetivo *m*, meta *f*; **goalkeeper** portero(-a) *m(f)*, *L.Am.* arquero(-a) *m(f)*; **goal kick** saque *m* de puerta; **goalpost** poste *m*

goat [gout] cabra *f*

gobble ['gɑːbl] engullir

gobbledygook ['gɑːbldɪguːk] F jerigonza *f* F

'go-between intermediario(-a) *m(f)*

god [gɑːd] dios *m*; ***thank God!*** ¡gracias a Dios!; **godchild** ahijado(-a) *m(f)*; **godfather** *also in mafia* padrino *m*; **godmother** madrina *f*

gofer ['goufər] F recadero(-a) *m(f)*

goggles ['gɑːglz] gafas *fpl*

goings-on [gouɪŋz'ɑːn] actividades *fpl*

gold [gould] **1** *n* oro *m* **2** *adj* de oro; **golden** dorado; **golden wedding** bodas *fpl* de oro; **gold medal** medalla *f* de oro; **gold mine** *fig* mina *f*

golf [gɑːlf] golf *m*; **golf ball** pelota *f* de golf; **golf club** *organization* club *m* de golf; *stick* palo *m* de golf; **golf course** campo *m* de golf; **golfer** golfista *m/f*

good [gud] bueno; **goodbye** adiós; **good-for-nothing** inútil *m/f*; **Good Friday** Viernes *m inv* Santo; **good-humored**, *Br* **good-hu-**

moured jovial, afable; **good-looking** guapo; **good-natured** bondadoso; **goodness** *moral* bondad *f*; *of fruit etc* valor *m* nutritivo; **goods** COM mercancías *fpl*; **goodwill** buena voluntad *f*

goof [gu:f] F meter la pata F

goose [gu:s] ganso *m*, oca *f*; **goose bumps** carne *f* de gallina

gorgeous ['gɔ:rdʒəs] *weather* maravilloso; *dress*, *hair* precioso; *woman*, *man* buenísimo; *smell* estupendo

gospel ['gɑ:spl] evangelio *m*

gossip ['gɑ:sɪp] **1** *n* cotilleo *m*; *person* cotilla *m/f* **2** *v/i* cotillear; **gossip column** ecos *mpl* de sociedad

gourmet ['gʊrmeɪ] gourmet *m/f*

govern ['gʌvərn] gobernar; **government** gobierno *m*; **governor** gobernador(a) *m(f)*

gown [gaʊn] *long dress* vestido *m*; *wedding dress* traje *m*; *of academic*, *judge* toga *f*; *of surgeon* bata *f*

grab [græb] agarrar; *food* tomar

grace [greɪs] *of dancer etc* gracia *f*; ***say ~*** bendecir la mesa; **graceful** elegante; **gracious** *person* amable; *style* elegante

grade [greɪd] **1** *n quality* grado *m*; EDU curso *m*; (*mark*) nota *f* **2** *v/t* clasificar; **grade crossing** paso *m* a nivel; **grade school** escuela *f* primaria

gradient ['greɪdɪənt] pendiente *f*

gradual ['grædʒʊəl] gradual; **gradually** gradualmente, poco a poco

graduate **1** ['grædʒʊət] *n* licenciado(-a) *m(f)*; *from high school* bachiller *m/f* **2** ['grædʒʊeɪt] *v/i from university* licenciarse, *L.Am.* egresarse; *from high school* sacar el bachillerato; **graduation** graduación *f*

graffiti [grə'fi:ti:] graffiti *m*

graft [græft] **1** *n* BOT, MED injerto *m*; *corruption* corrupción *f* **2** *v/t* BOT, MED injertar

grain [greɪn] grano *m*; *in wood* veta *f*

gram [græm] gramo *m*

grammar ['græmər] gramática *f*; **grammatical** gramatical

grand [grænd] **1** *adj* grandioso; F (*very good*) estupendo, genial **2** *n* F (*$1000*) mil dólares; **grandchild** nieto(-a) *m(f)*; **granddaughter** nieta *f*; **grandeur** grandiosidad *f*; **grandfather** abuelo *m*; **grand jury** jurado *m* de acusación, gran jurado; **grandmother** abuela *f*; **grandparents** abuelos *mpl*; **grand piano** piano *m* de cola; **grandson** nieto *m*

granite ['grænɪt] granito *m*

grant [grænt] **1** *n money* subvención *f* **2** *v/t* conceder

granule ['grænju:l] gránulo *m*
grape [greɪp] uva *f*; **grapefruit** pomelo *m*, *L.Am.* toronja *f*
graph [græf] gráfico *m*, gráfica *f*; **graphic 1** *adj* (*vivid*) gráfico **2** *n* COMPUT gráfico *m*
◆ **grapple with** ['græpl] *attacker* forcejear con; *problem etc* enfrentarse a
grasp [græsp] **1** *n physical* asimiento *m*; *mental* comprensión *f* **2** *v/t physically* agarrar; (*understand*) comprender
grass [græs] hierba *f*; **grasshopper** saltamontes *m inv*; **grass roots** *people* bases *fpl*; **grassy** lleno de hierba
grate[1] [greɪt] *n metal* parrilla *f*, reja *f*
grate[2] [greɪt] **1** *v/t in cooking* rallar **2** *v/i of sound* rechinar
grateful ['greɪtfəl] agradecido; **gratefully** con agradecimiento
gratify ['grætɪfaɪ] satisfacer
grating ['greɪtɪŋ] **1** *n* reja *f* **2** *adj sound*, *voice* chirriante
gratitude ['grætɪtu:d] gratitud *f*
grave[1] [greɪv] *n* tumba *f*
grave[2] [greɪv] *adj* grave
gravel ['grævl] gravilla *f*
'**gravestone** lápida *f*; **graveyard** cementerio *m*
gravity ['grævətɪ] PHYS gravedad *f*
gray [greɪ] gris; **gray-haired** canoso
graze[1] [greɪz] *v/i of cow etc* pastar, pacer
graze[2] [greɪz] **1** *v/t arm etc* rozar **2** *n* rozadura *f*
grease [gri:s] grasa *f*; **greasy** *food*, *hands*, *plate* grasiento; *hair*, *skin* graso
great [greɪt] grande, *before singular noun* gran; F (*very good*) estupendo, genial F; **Great Britain** Gran Bretaña; **greatly** muy; **greatness** grandeza *f*
Greece [gri:s] Grecia
greed [gri:d] *for money* codicia *f*; *for food* glotonería *f*; **greedily** con codicia; *eat* con glotonería; **greedy** *for food* glotón; *for money* codicioso
Greek [gri:k] **1** *adj* griego **2** *n* griego(-a) *m*(*f*); *language* griego *m*
green [gri:n] verde; *environmentally also* ecologista; **green beans** judías *fpl* verdes, *L.Am.* porotos *mpl* verdes, *Mex* ejotes *mpl*; **green belt** cinturón *m* verde; **green card** (*work permit*) permiso *m* de trabajo; **greenhouse effect** efecto *m* invernadero; **greens** verduras *f*
greet [gri:t] saludar; **greeting** saludo *m*
grenade [grɪ'neɪd] granada *f*
grey *Br* ☞ ***gray***
grid [grɪd] reja *f*, rejilla *f*; **gridiron** SP *campo de fútbol americano*; **gridlock** *in traffic* paralización *f* del tráfico

grief [griːf] dolor *m*, aflicción *f*; **grief-stricken** afligido; **grievance** queja *f*; **grieve** sufrir; ~ ***for s.o.*** llorar por alguien

grill [grɪl] **1** *n on window* reja *f* **2** *v/t (interrogate)* interrogar

grille [grɪl] reja *f*

grim [grɪm] *face* severo; *prospects* desolador; *surroundings* lúgubre

grimace ['grɪməs] gesto *m*, mueca *f*

grime [graɪm] mugre *f*; **grimy** mugriento

grin [grɪn] **1** *n* sonrisa *f* (amplia) **2** *v/i* sonreír abiertamente

grind [graɪnd] *coffee* moler; *meat* picar

grip [grɪp] agarrar; **gripping** apasionante

gristle ['grɪsl] cartílago *m*

grit [grɪt] **1** *n (dirt)* arenilla *f*; *for roads* gravilla *f* **2** *v/t*: ~ ***one's teeth*** apretar los dientes; **gritty** F *movie etc* duro F

groan [groʊn] **1** *n* gemido *m* **2** *v/i* gemir

groceries ['groʊsərɪz] comestibles *mpl*; **grocery store** tienda *f* de comestibles *or Mex* abarrotes

groggy ['grɑːgɪ] F grogui F

groin [grɔɪn] ANAT ingle *f*

groom [gruːm] **1** *n for bride* novio *m*; *for horse* mozo *m* de cuadra **2** *v/t horse* almohazar; *(train, prepare)* preparar

groove [gruːv] ranura *f*

grope [groʊp] **1** *v/i in the dark* caminar a tientas **2** *v/t sexually* manosear

gross [groʊs] *(coarse, vulgar)* grosero; *exaggeration* tremendo; *error* craso; FIN bruto

ground [graʊnd] **1** *n* suelo *m*; *(reason)* motivo *m*; ELEC tierra *f* **2** *v/t* ELEC conectar a tierra; **grounding** *in subject* fundamento *m*; **groundless** infundado; **ground meat** carne *f* picada; **groundwork** trabajos *mpl* preliminares

group [gruːp] **1** *n* grupo *m* **2** *v/t* agrupar; **groupie** F grupi *f* F

grouse [graʊs] **1** *n* F queja *f* **2** *v/i* F quejarse, refunfuñar

grovel ['grɑːvl] *fig* arrastrarse

grow [groʊ] **1** *v/i* crecer; ~ ***old / tired*** envejecer / cansarse **2** *v/t flowers* cultivar

◆ **grow up** crecer

growl [graʊl] **1** *n* gruñido *m* **2** *v/i* gruñir

'grown-up **1** *n* adulto(-a) *m(f)* **2** *adj* maduro

growth [groʊθ] crecimiento *m*; *(increase)* incremento *m*; MED bulto *m*

grudge [grʌdʒ] rencor *m*; **grudging** rencoroso; **grudgingly** de mala gana

grueling, *Br* **gruelling** ['gruːəlɪŋ] agotador

gruff [grʌf] seco, brusco

grumble ['grʌmbl] murmurar; **grumbler** quejica *m/f*

grunt [grʌnt] **1** *n* gruñido *m* **2**

v/i gruñir

guarantee [gærən'ti:] **1** *n* garantía *f* **2** *v/t* garantizar; **guarantor** garante *m/f*

guard [gɑ:rd] **1** *n* (*security* ~) guardia *m/f*, guarda *m/f*; MIL guardia *f*; *in prison* guardián (-ana) *m(f)* **2** *v/t* guardar; **guard dog** perro *m* guardián; **guarded** *reply* cauteloso; **guardian** LAW tutor(a) *m(f)*

Guatemala [gwætə'mɑ:lə] Guatemala; **Guatemalan 1** *adj* guatemalteco **2** *n* guatemalteco(-a) *m(f)*

guerrilla [gə'rɪlə] guerrillero(-a) *m(f)*; **guerrilla warfare** guerra *f* de guerrillas

guess [ges] **1** *n* conjetura *f*, suposición *f* **2** *v/t the answer* adivinar; ***I ~ so*** me imagino que sí **3** *v/i* adivinar; **guesswork** conjeturas *fpl*

guest [gest] invitado(-a) *m(f)*; **guestroom** habitación *f* para invitados

guidance ['gaɪdəns] orientación *f*; **guide 1** *n person* guía *m/f*; *book* guía *f* **2** *v/t* guiar; **guidebook** guía *f*; **guided missile** misil *m* teledirigido; **guided tour** visita *f* guiada; **guidelines** directrices *fpl*

guilt [gɪlt] culpa *f*, culpabilidad *f*; LAW culpabilidad *f*; **guilty** *also* LAW culpable

guinea pig ['gɪnɪpɪg] *also fig* conejillo *m* de Indias

guitar [gɪ'tɑ:r] guitarra *f*; **guitarist** guitarrista *m/f*

gulf [gʌlf] golfo *m*; *fig* abismo *m*; **Gulf of Mexico** Golfo *m* de México

gull [gʌl] *bird* gaviota *f*

gullet ['gʌlɪt] ANAT esófago *m*

gullible ['gʌlɪbl] crédulo

gulp [gʌlp] **1** *n of water etc* trago *m* **2** *v/i in surprise* tragar saliva

◆ **gulp down** *drink* tragar; *food* engullir

gum[1] [gʌm] *in mouth* encía *f*

gum[2] [gʌm] (*glue*) pegamento *m*, cola *f*; (*chewing* ~) chicle *m*

gun [gʌn] pistola *f*; *rifle* rifle *m*; *cannon* cañón *m*

◆ **gun down** matar a tiros

'gunfire disparos *mpl*; **gunman** hombre *m* armado; **gunshot** disparo *m*; **gunshot wound** herida *f* de bala

gurgle ['gɜ:rgl] *of baby* gorjear; *of drain* gorgotear

guru ['gu:ru:] *fig* gurú *m*

gush [gʌʃ] *of liquid* manar

gust [gʌst] ráfaga *f*

gusto ['gʌstoʊ] entusiasmo *m*

gusty ['gʌstɪ] con viento racheado

gut [gʌt] **1** *n* intestino *m*; F (*stomach*) tripa *f* F **2** *v/t* (*destroy*) destruir; **guts** F (*courage*) agallas *fpl* F; **gutsy** F (*brave*) valiente, con muchas agallas F

gutter ['gʌtər] *on sidewalk* cuneta *f*; *on roof* canal *m*

guy [gaɪ] F tipo *m* F, *Span* tío *m* F

guzzle ['gʌzl] tragar; *drink* engullir
gym [dʒɪm] gimnasio *m*; **gymnast** gimnasta *m/f*; **gymnastics** gimnasia *f*
gynecology, *Br* **gynaecology** [gaɪnɪ'kɑːlədʒɪ] ginecología *f*
gypsy ['dʒɪpsɪ] gitano(-a) *m(f)*

H

habit ['hæbɪt] hábito *m*, costumbre *m*
habitable ['hæbɪtəbl] habitable; **habitat** hábitat *m*
habitual [hə'bɪtʊəl] habitual
hacker ['hækər] COMPUT pirata *m/f* informático(-a)
hackneyed ['hæknɪd] manido
haemorrhage *Br* ☞ ***hemorrhage***
haggard ['hægərd] demacrado
haggle ['hægl] regatear
hail [heɪl] granizo *m*
hair [her] pelo *m*, cabello *m*; *single* pelo *m*; (*body* ~) vello *m*; **hairbrush** cepillo *m*; **haircut** corte *m* de pelo; ***have a*** ~ cortarse el pelo; **hairdo** peinado *m*; **hairdresser** peluquero(-a) *m(f)*; **hairdryer** secador *m* (de pelo); **hairpin** horquilla *f*; **hairpin curve** curva *f* muy cerrada; **hair-raising** espeluznante; **hair remover** depilatorio *m*; **hair-splitting** sutilezas *fpl*; **hairstyle** peinado *m*; **hairstylist** estilista *m/f*, peluquero(-a) *m(f)*; **hairy** *arm*, *animal* peludo; F (*frightening*) espeluznante
half [hæf] **1** *n* mitad *f*; ~ ***past ten***, ~ ***after ten*** las diez y media; ~ ***an hour*** media hora **2** *adj* medio **3** *adv* a medias; **half-hearted** desganado; **half time** SP descanso *m*; **halfway 1** *adj stage*, *point* intermedio **2** *adv* a mitad de camino
hall [hɒːl] *large room* sala *f*; (*hallway*) vestíbulo *m*
Halloween [hæloʊ'wiːn] *víspera de Todos los Santos*
halo ['heɪloʊ] halo *m*
halt [hɒːlt] **1** *v/i* detenerse **2** *v/t* detener **3** *n* alto *m*
halve [hæv] *input*, *costs* reducir a la mitad; *apple* partir por la mitad
ham [hæm] jamón *m*; **hamburger** hamburguesa *f*
hammer ['hæmər] **1** *n* martillo *m* **2** *v/i*: ~ ***at the door*** golpear la puerta
hammock ['hæmək] hamaca *f*
hamper[1] ['hæmpər] *n for food* cesta *f*
hamper[2] ['hæmpər] *v/t* (*obstruct*) estorbar, obstaculizar
hand [hænd] mano *f*; *of clock* manecilla *f*; (*worker*) brazo *m*; ***at*** ~, ***to*** ~ a mano; ***on***

the one ~ ..., on the other ~ por una parte..., por otra parte; ***on your right ~*** a mano derecha; ***give s.o. a ~*** echar una mano a alguien

◆ **hand down** transmitir

◆ **hand out** repartir

◆ **hand over** entregar

'handbag *Br* bolso *m*, *L.Am.* cartera *f*; **hand baggage** equipaje *m* de mano; **handcuff** esposar; **handcuffs** esposas *fpl*

handicap ['hændɪkæp] desventaja *f*; **handicapped** *physically* minusválido

handkerchief ['hæŋkərtʃɪf] pañuelo *m*

handle ['hændl] **1** *n of door* manilla *f*; *of suitcase* asa *f*; *of pan, knife* mango *m* **2** *v/t goods, person* manejar; *case, deal* llevar; **handlebars** manillar *m*, *L.Am.* manubrio *m*

'hand luggage equipaje *m* de mano; **handmade** hecho a mano; **hands-free** manos libres; **handshake** apretón *m* de manos

handsome ['hænsəm] guapo, atractivo

'handwriting caligrafía *f*; **handwritten** escrito a mano; **handy** *device* práctico

hang [hæŋ] colgar

◆ **hang on** (*wait*) esperar

◆ **hang up** TELEC colgar

hangar ['hæŋər] hangar *m*

hanger ['hæŋər] *for clothes* percha *f*

'hang glider *person* piloto *m* de ala delta; *device* ala *f* delta; **hang gliding** ala *f* delta;

hangover resaca *f*

hankie, hanky ['hæŋkɪ] F pañuelo *m*

haphazard [hæp'hæzərd] descuidado

happen ['hæpn] ocurrir, pasar

happily ['hæpɪlɪ] alegremente; (*luckily*) afortunadamente; **happiness** felicidad *f*; **happy** feliz, contento; *coincidence* afortunado; **happy-go-lucky** despreocupado

harass [hə'ræs] acosar; *enemy* asediar, hostigar; **harassed** agobiado; **harassment** acoso *m*

harbor, *Br* **harbour** ['hɑːrbər] **1** *n* puerto *m* **2** *v/t criminal* proteger; *grudge* albergar

hard [hɑːrd] **1** *adj* duro; (*difficult*) difícil; *facts, evidence* real **2** *adv hit, rain* fuerte; *work* duro; ***try ~*** esforzarse; **hardback** libro *m* de tapas duras; **hard-boiled** *egg* duro; **hard copy** copia *f* impresa; **hard core** (*pornography*) porno *m* duro; **hard currency** divisa *f* fuerte; **hard disk** disco *m* duro; **harden 1** *v/t* endurecer **2** *v/i of glue, attitude* endurecerse; **hard hat** casco *m*; (*construction worker*) obrero(-a) *m(f)* (de la construcción); **hardheaded** pragmático; **hardhearted** insensible; **hard line** línea *f* dura; **hardliner** partidario(-a) *m(f)* de la línea dura

hardly ['hɑːrdlɪ] apenas
hardness ['hɑːrdnɪs] dureza *f*; (*difficulty*) dificultad *f*; **hardship** penuria *f*, privación *f*; **hardware** ferretería *f*; COMPUT hardware *m*; **hardware store** ferretería *f*; **hard-working** trabajador; **hardy** resistente
harm [hɑːrm] **1** *n* daño *m* **2** *v/t* hacer daño a, dañar; **harmful** dañino, perjudicial; **harmless** inofensivo; *fun* inocente
harmonious [hɑːr'moʊnɪəs] armonioso; **harmonize** armonizar; **harmony** MUS, *fig* armonía *f*
harsh [hɑːʃ] *words* duro, severo; *color* chillón; *light* potente; **harshly** con dureza
harvest ['hɑːrvɪst] cosecha *f*
hash browns [hæʃ] *Span* patatas *fpl or L.Am.* papas *fpl* fritas; **hash mark** almohadilla *f*, *el signo* '#'
haste [heɪst] prisa *f*; **hastily** precipitadamente; **hasty** precipitado
hat [hæt] sombrero *m*
hatch [hætʃ] *for serving* trampilla *f*; *on ship* escotilla *f*
◆ **hatch out** *of eggs* romperse; *of chicks* salir del cascarón
hatchet ['hætʃɪt] hacha *f*
hate [heɪt] **1** *n* odio *m* **2** *v/t* odiar; **hatred** odio *m*
haul [hɒːl] **1** *n of fish* captura *f*; *from robbery* botín *m* **2** *v/t* (*pull*) arrastrar; **haulage** transporte *m*
haunch [hɒːntʃ] *of person* trasero *m*; *of animal* pierna *f*
haunt [hɒːnt] **1** *n* lugar *m* favorito **2** *v/t*: ***this place is ~ed*** en este lugar hay fantasmas
Havana [hə'vænə] La Habana
have [hæv] **1** *v/t* (*own*) tener; *breakfast*, *lunch* tomar; ***can I ~ a coffee?*** ¿me da un café?; ~ (***got***) ***to*** tener que; ***I'll ~ it repaired*** haré que lo arreglen; ***I had my hair cut*** me corté el pelo; **2** *v/aux* (*past tense*): ***I ~ eaten*** he comido
◆ **have on** (*wear*) llevar puesto
haven ['heɪvn] *fig* refugio *m*
hawk [hɒːk] *also fig* halcón *m*
hay [heɪ] heno *m*; **hay fever** fiebre *f* del heno
hazard ['hæzərd] peligro *m*; **hazard lights** MOT luces *fpl* de emergencia; **hazardous** peligroso
haze [heɪz] neblina *f*; **hazy** *image*, *memories* vago
he [hiː] él; ***~ is a doctor*** es médico
head [hed] **1** *n* cabeza *f*; (*boss*, *leader*) jefe(-a) *m*(*f*); *Br*: *of school* director(a) *m*(*f*); *on beer* espuma *f* **2** *v/t* (*lead*) estar a la cabeza de; *ball* cabecear
◆ **head for** dirigirse hacia
'**headache** dolor *m* de cabeza; **headband** cinta *f* para la cabeza; **header** *in soccer* cabezazo *m*; *in document* en-

cabezamiento *m*; **headhunter** COM cazatalentos *m/f inv*; **heading** *in list* encabezamiento *m*; **headlamp** faro *m*; **headline** *in newspaper* titular *m*; **head office** *of company* central *f*; **head-on 1** *adv crash* de frente **2** *adj crash* frontal; **headphones** auriculares *mpl*; **headquarters** sede *f*; *of army* cuartel *m* general; **headrest** reposacabezas *f inv*; **headroom** *under bridge* gálibo *m*; *in car* espacio *m* vertical; **headscarf** pañuelo *m* (para la cabeza); **headstrong** cabezudo; **head waiter** maître *m*; **heady** *wine etc* que se sube a la cabeza

heal [hi:l] curar

health [helθ] salud *f*; **health food store** tienda *f* de comida integral; **health insurance** seguro *m* de enfermedad; **healthy** *person* sano; *food*, *lifestyle* saludable; *economy* saneado

heap [hi:p] montón *m*

hear [hɪr] oír

◆ **hear from** (*have news from*) tener noticias de

hearing ['hɪrɪŋ] oído *m*; LAW vista *f*; **hearing aid** audífono *m*

hearse [hɜ:rs] coche *m* fúnebre

heart [hɑ:rt] *also fig* corazón *m*; *of problem* meollo *m*; ***know sth by ~*** saber algo de memoria; **heart attack** infarto *m*; **heartbreaking** desgarrador; **heartbroken** descorazonado; **heartburn** acidez *f* (de estómago)

hearth [hɑ:rθ] chimenea *f*

heartless ['hɑ:rtlɪs] despiadado; **hearty** *appetite* voraz; *meal* copioso; *person* cordial

heat [hi:t] calor *m*

◆ **heat up** calentar

heated ['hi:tɪd] *pool* climatizado; *discussion* acalorado; **heater** *in room* estufa *f*; **heating** calefacción *f*; **heatproof** resistente al calor; **heatwave** ola *f* de calor

heave [hi:v] (*lift*) subir

heaven ['hevn] cielo *m*; **heavenly** F divino F

heavy ['hevɪ] pesado; *cold*, *rain*, *accent* fuerte; *smoker* empedernido; *loss of life* grande; *bleeding* abundante; **heavy-duty** resistente; **heavyweight** SP de los pesos pesados

hectic ['hektɪk] frenético

hedge [hedʒ] seto *m*

heel [hi:l] talón *m*; *of shoe* tacón *m*; **heel bar** zapatería *f*

hefty ['heftɪ] *weight* pesado; *person* robusto

height [haɪt] altura *f*; **heighten** *tension* intensificar

heir [er] heredero *m*; **heiress** heredera *f*

helicopter ['helɪkɑ:ptər] helicóptero *m*

hell [hel] infierno *m*; ***what the ~ are you doing?*** F ¿qué demonios estás haciendo? F; ***go to ~!*** F ¡vete a paseo!

hello [hə'loʊ] hola; TELEC ¿sí?, *Span* ¿diga?, *S. Am.* ¿alo?, *Rpl* ¿oigo?, *Mex* ¿bueno?

helmet ['helmɪt] casco *m*

help [help] **1** *n* ayuda *f* **2** *v/t* ayudar; ***just ~ yourself*** *to food* toma lo que quieras; ***I can't ~ it*** no puedo evitarlo; **helper** ayudante *m/f*; **helpful** *advice* útil; *person* servicial; **helping** *of food* ración *f*; **helpless** (*unable to cope*) indefenso; (*powerless*) impotente; **helplessness** impotencia *f*

hem [hem] *of dress etc* dobladillo *m*

hemisphere ['hemɪsfɪr] hemisferio *m*

'hemline bajo *m*

hemorrhage ['hemərɪdʒ] **1** *n* hemorragia *f* **2** *v/i* sangrar

hen [hen] gallina *f*; **hen party** despedida *f* de soltera

hepatitis [hepə'taɪtɪs] hepatitis *f*

her [hɜːr] **1** *adj* su **2** *pron direct object* la; *indirect object* le; *after prep* ella; ***I know ~*** la conozco; ***I gave ~ the keys*** le di las llaves; ***I sold it to ~*** se lo vendí; ***this is for ~*** esto es para ella; ***it's ~*** es ella

herb [ɜːrb] hierba *f*; **herb(al) tea** infusión *f*

herd [hɜːrd] rebaño *m*

here [hɪr] aquí; ***over ~*** aquí; ***~'s to you!*** *as toast* ¡a tu salud!; ***~ you are*** *giving sth* ¡aquí tienes!

hereditary [hə'redɪterɪ] hereditario; **heredity** herencia *f*; **heritage** patrimonio *m*

hero ['hɪroʊ] héroe *m*; **heroic** heroico; **heroically** heroicamente

heroin ['heroʊɪn] heroína *f*

heroine ['heroʊɪn] heroína *f*

heroism ['heroʊɪzm] heroísmo *m*

herpes ['hɜːrpiːz] herpes *m*

hers [hɜːrz] el suyo, la suya; ***that ticket is ~*** esa entrada es suya; ***a cousin of ~*** un primo suyo

herself [hɜːr'self] *reflexive* se; *emphatic* ella misma; ***she hurt ~*** se hizo daño

hesitant ['hezɪtənt] indeciso; **hesitantly** con indecisión; **hesitate** dudar, vacilar; **hesitation** vacilación *f*

heterosexual [hetəroʊ'sekʃʊəl] heterosexual

hi [haɪ]¡hola!

hibernate ['haɪbərneɪt] hibernar

hiccup ['hɪkʌp] hipo *m*; (*minor problem*) tropiezo *m*

hidden ['hɪdn] oculto

hide[1] [haɪd] **1** *v/t* esconder **2** *v/i* esconderse

hide[2] [haɪd] *n of animal* piel *f*

'hide-and-seek escondite *m*; **hideaway** escondite *m*

hideous ['hɪdɪəs] horrendo; *person* repugnante

hiding ['haɪdɪŋ] (*beating*) paliza *f*; **hiding place** escondite *m*

hierarchy ['haɪrɑːrkɪ] jerarquía *f*

high [haɪ] **1** *adj* alto; *wind* fuerte; (*on drugs*) colocado P **2** *n* MOT directa *f*; *in statistics* máximo *m*; EDU escuela *f* secundaria, *Span* instituto *m*; **highbrow** intelectual; **highchair** trona *f*; **high-class** de categoría; **high-frequency** de alta frecuencia; **high-grade** de calidad superior; **high-handed** despótico; **high-heeled** de tacón alto; **high jump** salto *m* de altura; **high-level** de alto nivel; **highlight** **1** *n* (*main event*) momento *m* cumbre; *in hair* reflejo *m* **2** *v/t with pen* resaltar; COMPUT seleccionar, resaltar; **highlighter** *pen* fluorescente *m*; **highly** *desirable, likely* muy; ***think ~ of s.o.*** tener una buena opinión de alguien; **high performance** *drill, battery* de alto rendimiento; **high-pitched** agudo; **high point** *of career* punto *m* culminante; **high-powered** *engine* potente; *intellectual* de alto(s) vuelo(s); **high pressure** *weather* altas presiones *fpl*; **high-pressure** TECH a gran presión; *salesman* agresivo; *lifestyle* muy estresante; **high school** escuela *f* secundaria, *Span* instituto *m*; **high-strung** muy nervioso; **high tech** **1** *n* alta *f* tecnología **2** *adj* de alta tecnología; **highway** autopista *f*

hijack ['haɪdʒæk] **1** *v/t* secuestrar **2** *n* secuestro *m*; **hijacker** secuestrador(a) *m(f)*

hike[1] [haɪk] **1** *n* caminata *f* **2** *v/i* caminar

hike[2] [haɪk] *n in prices* subida *f*

hiker ['haɪkər] senderista *m/f*; **hiking** senderismo *m*

hilarious [hɪ'lerɪəs] divertidísimo, graciosísimo

hill [hɪl] colina *f*; (*slope*) cuesta *f*; **hillside** ladera *f*; **hilltop** cumbre *f*; **hilly** con colinas

hilt [hɪlt] puño *m*

him [hɪm] *direct object* lo; *indirect object* le; *after prep* él; ***I know ~*** lo conozco; ***I gave ~ the keys*** le di las llaves; ***I sold it to ~*** se lo vendí; ***this is for ~*** esto es para él; ***it's ~*** es él; **himself** *reflexive* se; *emphatic* él mismo; ***he hurt ~*** se hizo daño

hinder ['hɪndər] obstaculizar; ***~ s.o. from doing sth*** impedir a alguien hacer algo; **hindrance** obstáculo *m*

hinge [hɪndʒ] bisagra *f*

hint [hɪnt] (*clue*) pista *f*; (*piece of advice*) consejo *m*; (*suggestion*) indirecta *f*; *of red, sadness etc* rastro *m*

hip [hɪp] cadera *f*; **hip pocket** bolsillo *m* trasero

hire [haɪr] alquilar

his [hɪz] **1** *adj* su **2** *pron* el suyo, la suya; ***that ticket is ~*** esa entrada es suya; ***a cousin of ~*** un primo suyo

Hispanic [hɪ'spænɪk] **1** *n* hispano(-a) *m(f)* **2** *adj* hispano, hispánico
hiss [hɪs] silbar
historian [hɪ'stɔːrɪən] historiador(a) *m(f)*; **historic** histórico; **historical** histórico; **history** historia *f*
hit [hɪt] **1** *v/t* golpear; (*collide with*) chocar contra **2** *n* (*blow*) golpe *m*; MUS, (*success*) éxito *m*; *on website* acceso *m*
hitch [hɪʧ] **1** *n* (*problem*) contratiempo *m* **2** *v/t* (*fix*) enganchar; **hitchhike** hacer autoestop; **hitchhiker** autoestopista *m/f*
'hi-tech 1 *n* alta tecnología *f* **2** *adj* de alta tecnología
'hitman asesino *m* a sueldo; **hit-or-miss** a la buena ventura
HIV [eɪʧaɪ'viː] (= ***human immunodeficiency virus***) VIH *m* (= virus *m inv* de la inmunodeficiencia humana)
hive [haɪv] *for bees* colmena *f*
HIV-'positive seropositivo
hoard [hɔːrd] **1** *n* reserva *f* **2** *v/t* hacer acopio de; *money* acumular
hoarse [hɔːrs] ronco
hoax [hoʊks] bulo *m*, engaño *m*
hobble ['hɑːbl] cojear
hobby ['hɑːbɪ] hobby *m*
hobo ['hoʊboʊ] F vagabundo(-a) *m(f)*
hockey ['hɑːkɪ] (*ice* ~) hockey *m* sobre hielo
hog [hɑːg] (*pig*) cerdo *m*, *L.Am.* chancho *m*
hoist [hɔɪst] **1** *n* montacargas *m inv*; *manual* elevador *m* **2** *v/t* (*lift*) levantar; *flag* izar
hold [hoʊld] **1** *v/t in hand* llevar; (*support, keep in place*) sostener; *passport, license* tener; *prisoner* retener; (*contain*) contener; *post* ocupar; ***~ the line, please*** espere, por favor **2** *n in ship, plane* bodega *f*; ***take ~ of sth*** agarrar algo
◆ **hold back** *crowds* contener; *facts* guardar
◆ **hold out 1** *v/t hand* tender; *prospect* ofrecer **2** *v/i of supply* durar; (*survive*) resistir
◆ **hold up** *hand* levantar; *bank etc* atracar; (*make late*) retrasar
holder ['hoʊldər] (*container*) receptáculo *m*; *of passport, ticket etc* titular *m/f*; *of record* poseedor(a) *m(f)*; **holding company** holding *m*; **holdup** (*robbery*) atraco *m*; (*delay*) retraso *m*
hole [hoʊl] agujero *m*; *in ground* hoyo *m*
holiday ['hɑːlədeɪ] día *m* de fiesta; *Br*: *period* vacaciones *fpl*
Holland ['hɑːlənd] Holanda
hollow ['hɑːloʊ] hueco; *cheeks* hundido; *promise* vacío
holocaust ['hɑːləkɒːst] holocausto *m*
hologram ['hɑːləgræm] holo-

grama *m*
holster ['hoʊlstər] pistolera *f*
holy ['hoʊlɪ] santo; **Holy Spirit** Espíritu *m* Santo
home [hoʊm] **1** *n* casa *f*; (*native country*) tierra *f*; *for old people* residencia *f*; ***at ~*** *also* SP en casa; (*in country*) en mi / su / nuestra tierra; ***make yourself at ~*** ponte cómodo **2** *adv* a casa; ***go ~*** ir a casa; *to country* ir a mi / tu / su tierra; *to town, part of country* ir a mi / tu / su ciudad; **home address** domicilio *m*; **home banking** telebanca *f*, banca *f* electrónica; **homecoming** vuelta *f* a casa; **home computer** *Span* ordenador *m*, *L.Am.* computadora *f* doméstica; **home game** partido *m* en casa; **homeless 1** *adj* sin casa **2** *npl*: ***the ~*** los sin casa; **homeloving** hogareño; **homely** (*homeloving*) hogareño; (*not good-looking*) feúcho; **homemade** casero; **home page** página *f* inicial; **homesick** nostálgico; ***be ~*** tener morriña; **home town** ciudad *f* natal; **homeward** *to own house* a casa; *to own country* a mi / tu / su país; **homework** EDU deberes *mpl*
homicide ['hɑːmɪsaɪd] homicidio *m*; *department* brigada *f* de homicidios
homophobia [hɑːmə'foʊbɪə] homofobia *f*
homosexual [hɑːmə'sekʃʊəl] **1** *adj* homosexual **2** *n* homosexual *m/f*
Honduran [hɑːn'dʊrən] **1** *adj* hondureño **2** n hondureño(-a) *m(f)*; **Honduras** Honduras
honest ['ɑːnɪst] honrado; **honestly** honradamente; ***~!*** ¡desde luego!; **honesty** honradez *f*
honey ['hʌnɪ] miel *f*; F (*darling*) cariño *m*; **honeymoon** luna *f* de miel
honk [hɑːŋk] *horn* tocar
honor ['ɑːnər] **1** *n* honor *m* **2** *v/t* honrar; **honorable** honorable; **honour** *Br* ☞ ***honor***
hood [hʊd] *over head* capucha *f*; *over cooker* campana *f* extractora; MOT capó *m*; F (*gangster*) matón(-ona) *m(f)*
hook [hʊk] gancho *m*; *for coat etc* colgador *m*; *for fishing* anzuelo *m*; ***off the ~*** TELEC descolgado; **hooked** enganchado (***on*** a); **hooker** F fulana *f* F
hoot [huːt] **1** *v/t horn* tocar **2** *v/i of car* dar bocinazos; *of owl* ulular
hop [hɑːp] saltar
hope [hoʊp] **1** *n* esperanza *f* **2** *v/i* esperar; ***I ~ so*** eso espero **3** *v/t*: ***I ~ you like it*** espero que te guste; **hopeful** prometedor; **hopefully** *say, wait* esperanzadamente; ***~ …*** (*let's hope*) esperemos que…; **hopeless** *position* desesperado; (*useless: per-*

son) inútil
horizon [hə'raɪzn] horizonte *m*; **horizontal** horizontal
hormone ['hɔːrmoʊn] hormona *f*
horn [hɔːrn] *of animal* cuerno *m*; MOT bocina *f*
hornet ['hɔːrnɪt] avispón *m*
horny ['hɔːrnɪ] F *sexually* cachondo F
horrible ['hɑːrɪbl] horrible; *person* muy antipático; **horrify** horrorizar; **horrifying** horroroso; **horror** horror *m*
horse [hɔːrs] caballo *m*; **horse race** carrera *f* de caballos; **horseshoe** herradura *f*
horticulture ['hɔːrtɪkʌltʃər] horticultura *f*
hose [hoʊz] manguera *f*
hospitable [hɑː'spɪtəbl] hospitalario
hospital ['hɑːspɪtl] hospital *m*; **hospitality** hospitalidad *f*
host [hoʊst] *at party* anfitrión *m*; *of TV program* presentador(a) *m(f)*
hostage ['hɑːstɪdʒ] rehén *m*; **hostage taker** persona que toma rehenes
hostel ['hɑːstl] *for students* residencia *f*; (*youth* ~) albergue *m*
hostess ['hoʊstɪs] *at party* anfitriona *f*; *on airplane* azafata *f*; *in bar* cabaretera *f*
hostile ['hɑːstl] hostil; **hostility** hostilidad *f*; ***hostilities*** hostilidades
hot [hɑːt] caliente; *weather* caluroso; (*spicy*) picante; ***it's ~*** *of weather* hace calor; ***I'm ~*** tengo calor; **hot dog** perrito *m* caliente
hotel [hoʊ'tel] hotel *m*
hour [aʊr] hora *f*
house [haʊs] casa *f*; **housebreaking** allanamiento *m* de morada; **household** hogar *m*; **household name** nombre *m* conocido; **housekeeper** ama *f* de llaves; **House of Representatives** Cámara *f* de Representantes; **housewarming (party)** fiesta *f* de estreno de una casa; **housewife** ama *f* de casa; **housework** tareas *fpl* domésticas; **housing** vivienda *f*; TECH cubierta *f*
hovel ['hɑːvl] chabola *f*
hover ['hɑːvər] *of bird* cernerse; *of helicopter* permanecer inmóvil en el aire
how [haʊ] cómo; ***~ are you?*** ¿cómo estás?; ***~ about ...?*** ¿qué te parece...?; ***~ about a drink?*** ¿te apetece tomar algo?; ***~ much?*** ¿cuánto?; ***~ much is it?*** *cost* ¿cuánto vale *or* cuesta?; ***~ many?*** ¿cuántos?; ***~ often?*** ¿con qué frecuencia?; ***~ sad!*** ¡qué triste!; **however** sin embargo; ***~ big they are*** independientemente de lo grandes que sean
howl [haʊl] *of dog* aullido *m*; *of pain* alarido *m*; *with laughter* risotada *f*
hub [hʌb] *of wheel* cubo *m*; **hubcap** tapacubos *m inv*

◆ **huddle together** ['hʌdl] apiñarse, acurrucarse
hug [hʌg] abrazar
huge [hjuːdʒ] enorme
hull [hʌl] *of ship* casco *m*
hum [hʌm] tararear; *of machine* zumbar
human ['hjuːmən] **1** *n* humano *m* **2** *adj* humano; **human being** ser *m* humano
humane [hjuː'meɪn] humano
humanitarian [hjuːmænɪ'terɪən] humanitario
humanity [hjuː'mænətɪ] humanidad *f*; **human race** raza *f* humana; **human resources** recursos *mpl* humanos
humble ['hʌmbl] humilde
humdrum ['hʌmdrʌm] monótono, anodino
humid ['hjuːmɪd] húmedo; **humidifier** humidificador *m*; **humidity** humedad *f*
humiliate [hjuː'mɪlɪeɪt] humillar; **humiliating** humillante; **humiliation** humillación *f*; **humility** humildad *f*
humor ['hjuːmər] humor *m*; **humorous** gracioso; **humour** *Br* ☞ ***humor***
hunch [hʌntʃ] *(idea)* presentimiento *m*, corazonada *f*
hundred ['hʌndrəd] cien *m*; ***a ~ and one*** ciento uno; ***two ~*** doscientos; **hundredth** centésimo
hunger ['hʌŋgər] hambre *f*
hung-over: ***be ~*** tener resaca
hungry ['hʌŋgrɪ] hambriento; ***I'm ~*** tengo hambre
hunk [hʌŋk] cacho *m*; F *man* cachas *m inv* F
hunt [hʌnt] **1** *n* caza *f* **2** *v/t* cazar; **hunter** cazador(a) *m(f)*; **hunting** caza *f*
hurdle ['hɜːrdl] SP valla *f*; *fig* obstáculo *m*
hurl [hɜːrl] lanzar
hurray [hʊ'reɪ] ¡hurra!
hurricane ['hʌrɪkən] huracán *m*
hurried ['hʌrɪd] apresurado; **hurry 1** *n* prisa *f*; ***be in a ~*** tener prisa **2** *v/i* darse prisa
◆ **hurry up 1** *v/i* darse prisa; ***hurry up!*** ¡date prisa! **2** *v/t* meter prisa a
hurt [hɜːrt] **1** *v/i* doler **2** *v/t* hacer daño a; *emotionally* herir; ***I've ~ my hand*** me he hecho daño en la mano
husband ['hʌzbənd] marido *m*
hush [hʌʃ] silencio *m*
◆ **hush up** *scandal etc* acallar
husky ['hʌskɪ] *voice* áspero
hut [hʌt] cabaña *f*; *workman's* cobertizo *m*
hybrid ['haɪbrɪd] híbrido *m*
hydrant ['haɪdrənt] hidrante *m* de incendios
hydraulic [haɪ'drɒːlɪk] hidráulico
hydroelectric [haɪdroʊɪ'lektrɪk] hidroeléctrico
hydrogen ['haɪdrədʒən] hidrógeno *m*
hygiene ['haɪdʒiːn] higiene *f*; **hygienic** higiénico
hymn [hɪm] himno *m*
hype [haɪp] bombo *m*

hyperactive [haɪpər'æktɪv] hiperactivo; **hypersensitive** hipersensible; **hypertext** COMPUT hipertexto *m*
hypnosis [hɪp'noʊsɪs] hipnosis *f*; **hypnotize** hipnotizar
hypocrisy [hɪ'pɑːkrəsɪ] hipocresía *f*; **hypocrite** hipócrita *m/f*; **hypocritical** hipócrita
hypothesis [haɪ'pɑːθəsɪs] hipótesis *f inv*; **hypothetical** hipotético
hysterectomy [hɪstə'rektəmɪ] histerectomía *f*
hysteria [hɪ'stɪrɪə] histeria *f*; **hysterical** histérico; F (*very funny*) tronchante F; **hysterics** ataque *f* de histeria; (*laughter*) ataque *f* de risa

I

I [aɪ] yo; **~ *am a student*** soy estudiante
ice [aɪs] hielo *m*; **icebox** nevera *f*, *Rpl* heladera *f*; **ice cream** helado *m*; **ice cube** cubito *m* de hielo; **iced** *drink* helado; **ice hockey** hockey *m* sobre hielo; **ice rink** pista *f* de hielo; **ice skate** patín *m* de cuchilla; **ice skating** patinaje *m* sobre hielo
icon ['aɪkɑːn] *also* COMPUT icono *m*
icy ['aɪsɪ] *road* con hielo; *surface* helado; *welcome* frío
ID [aɪ'diː] (= ***identity***) documentación *f*
idea [aɪ'diːə] idea *f*; **ideal** ideal; **idealistic** idealista
identical [aɪ'dentɪkl] idéntico; **identification** identificación *f*; *papers etc* documentación *f*; **identify** identificar; **identity** identidad *f*; **~ *card*** carné *m* de identidad
ideological [aɪdɪə'lɑːdʒɪkl] ideológico; **ideology** ideología *f*
idiomatic [ɪdɪə'mætɪk] *natural* natural
idiot ['ɪdɪət] idiota *m/f*; **idiotic** idiota
idle ['aɪdl] **1** *adj not working* desocupado; (*lazy*) vago; *threat* vano; *machinery* inactivo **2** *v/i of engine* funcionar al ralentí
idol ['aɪdl] ídolo *m*; **idolize** idolatrar
if [ɪf] si
ignite [ɪg'naɪt] inflamar; **ignition** *in car* encendido *m*; ***~ key*** llave *m* de contacto
ignorance ['ɪgnərəns] ignorancia *f*; **ignorant** ignorante; (*rude*) maleducado; **ignore** ignorar; COMPUT omitir
ill [ɪl] enfermo; ***fall ~, be taken ~*** caer enfermo
illegal [ɪ'liːgl] ilegal
illegible [ɪ'ledʒəbl] ilegible
illegitimate [ɪlɪ'dʒɪtɪmət] *child* ilegítimo
illicit [ɪ'lɪsɪt] ilícito

illiterate [ɪ'lɪtərət] analfabeto
illness ['ɪlnɪs] enfermedad *f*
illogical [ɪ'lɑːdʒɪkl] ilógico
illtreat maltratar
illuminating [ɪ'luːmɪneɪtɪŋ] *remarks* iluminador
illusion [ɪ'luːʒn] ilusión *f*
illustrate ['ɪləstreɪt] ilustrar; **illustration** ilustración *f*; **illustrator** ilustrador(a) *m(f)*
image ['ɪmɪdʒ] imagen *f*
imaginary [ɪ'mædʒɪnərɪ] imaginario; **imagination** imaginación *f*; **imaginative** imaginativo; **imagine** imaginar, imaginarse; ***you're imagining things*** son imaginaciones tuyas
IMF [aɪem'ef] (= ***International Monetary Fund***) FMI *m* (= Fondo *m* Monetario Internacional)
imitate ['ɪmɪteɪt] imitar; **imitation** imitación *f*
immaculate [ɪ'mækjʊlət] inmaculado
immature [ɪmə'ʧʊər] inmaduro
immediate [ɪ'miːdɪət] inmediato; **immediately** inmediatamente
immense [ɪ'mens] inmenso
immerse [ɪ'mɜːrs] sumergir
immigrant ['ɪmɪgrənt] inmigrante *m/f*; **immigrate** inmigrar; **immigration** inmigración *f*
imminent ['ɪmɪnənt] inminente
immobilize [ɪ'moʊbɪlaɪz] *factory* paralizar; *person, car* inmovilizar
immoderate [ɪ'mɑːdərət] desmedido, exagerado
immoral [ɪ'mɔːrəl] inmoral; **immorality** inmoralidad *f*
immortal [ɪ'mɔːrtl] inmortal; **immortality** inmortalidad *f*
immune [ɪ'mjuːn] *to illness* inmune; *from ruling* con inmunidad; **immune system** MED sistema *m* inmunológico; **immunity** inmunidad *f*
impact ['ɪmpækt] impacto *m*
impair [ɪm'per] dañar
impartial [ɪm'pɑːrʃl] imparcial
impassable [ɪm'pæsəbl] *road* intransitable
impassioned [ɪm'pæʃnd] *speech, plea* apasionado
impatience [ɪm'peɪʃəns] impaciencia *f*; **impatient** impaciente; **impatiently** impacientemente
impeccable [ɪm'pekəbl] impecable
impede [ɪm'piːd] dificultar; **impediment** *in speech* defecto *m* del habla
impending [ɪm'pendɪŋ] inminente
imperative [ɪm'perətɪv] **1** *adj* imprescindible **2** *n* GRAM imperativo *m*
imperfect [ɪm'pɜːrfekt] **1** *adj* imperfecto **2** *n* GRAM imperfecto *m*
impersonal [ɪm'pɜːrsənl] impersonal; **impersonate** *as a joke* imitar; *illegally* hacerse pasar por

impertinence [ɪm'pɜːrtɪnəns] impertinencia *f*; **impertinent** impertinente

impervious [ɪm'pɜːrvɪəs]: **~ *to*** inmune a

impetuous [ɪm'petʃʊəs] impetuoso

impetus ['ɪmpɪtəs] *of campaign etc* ímpetu *m*

implement 1 ['ɪmplɪmənt] *n* utensilio *m* **2** ['ɪmplɪment] *v/t* poner en práctica

implicate ['ɪmplɪkeɪt] implicar; **implication** consecuencia *f*

implore [ɪm'plɔːr] implorar

imply [ɪm'plaɪ] implicar

impolite [ɪmpə'laɪt] maleducado

import ['ɪmpɔːrt] **1** *n* importación *f* **2** *v/t* importar

importance [ɪm'pɔːrtəns] importancia *f*; **important** importante

importer [ɪm'pɔːrtər] importador(a) *m(f)*

impose [ɪm'poʊz] *tax* imponer; **imposing** imponente

impossibility [ɪmpɑːsɪ'bɪlɪtɪ] imposibilidad *f*; **impossible** imposible

impotence ['ɪmpətəns] impotencia *f*; **impotent** impotente

impractical [ɪm'præktɪkəl] poco práctico

impress [ɪm'pres] impresionar; **impression** impresión *f*; (*impersonation*) imitación *f*; **impressive** impresionante

imprint ['ɪmprɪnt] *of credit card* impresión *f*

imprison [ɪm'prɪzn] encarcelar; **imprisonment** encarcelamiento *m*

improbable [ɪm'prɑːbəbəl] improbable

improve [ɪm'pruːv] mejorar; **improvement** mejora *f*, mejoría *f*

improvise ['ɪmprəvaɪz] improvisar

impudent ['ɪmpjʊdənt] insolente, desvergonzado

impulse ['ɪmpʌls] impulso *m*; **impulsive** impulsivo

in [ɪn] **1** *prep* en; **~ *two hours from now*** dentro de dos horas; (*over period of*) en dos horas; **~ *the morning*** por la mañana; **~ *yellow*** de amarillo; **~ *crossing the road*** (*while*) al cruzar la calle; **~ *agreeing to this*** (*by virtue of*) al expresar acuerdo con esto; ***one* ~ *ten*** uno de cada diez **2** *adv* dentro; ***is he* ~?** *at home* ¿está en casa?; **~ *here*** aquí dentro **3** *adj* (*fashionable*) de moda

inability [ɪnə'bɪlɪtɪ] incapacidad *f*

inaccurate [ɪn'ækjʊrət] inexacto

inadequate [ɪn'ædɪkwət] insuficiente

inadvisable [ɪnəd'vaɪzəbl] poco aconsejable

inanimate [ɪn'ænɪmət] inanimado

inappropriate [ɪnə'proʊprɪət]

inadecuado, improcedente; *choice* inapropiado
inaudible [ɪn'ɒ:dəbl] inaudible
inaugural [ɪ'nɒ:gjʊrəl] *speech* inaugural; **inaugurate** inaugurar
inborn ['ɪnbɔ:rn] innato
Inc. (= ***Incorporated***) S.A. (= sociedad *f* anónima)
incalculable [ɪn'kælkjʊləbl] *damage* incalculable
incapable [ɪn'keɪpəbl]] incapaz
incentive [ɪn'sentɪv] incentivo *m*
incessant [ɪn'sesnt] incesante; **incessantly** incesantemente
incest ['ɪnsest] incesto *m*
inch [ɪntʃ] pulgada *f*
incident ['ɪnsɪdənt] incidente *m*; **incidental** sin importancia; ~ ***expenses*** gastos *mpl* varios; **incidentally** a propósito
incision [ɪn'sɪʒn] incisión *f*; **incisive** incisivo
incite [ɪn'saɪt] incitar
inclination [ɪnklɪ'neɪʃn] inclinación *f*
inclose ☞ ***enclose***
include [ɪn'klu:d] incluir; **including** incluyendo; **inclusive 1** *adj price* total, global **2** *prep*: ~ ***of*** incluyendo, incluido **3** *adv*: ***from Monday to Thursday*** ~ de lunes al jueves, ambos inclusive; ***$1000*** ~ 1.000 dólares todo incluido
incoherent [ɪnkoʊ'hɪrənt] incoherente
income ['ɪnkəm] ingresos *mpl*; **income tax** impuesto *m* sobre la renta
incomparable [ɪn'kɑ:mpərəbl] incomparable
incompatibility [ɪnkəmpætɪ'bɪlɪtɪ] incompatibilidad *f*; **incompatible** incompatible
incompetence [ɪn'kɑ:mpɪtəns] incompetencia *f*; **incompetent** incompetente
incomplete [ɪnkəm'pli:t] incompleto
incomprehensible [ɪnkɑ:mprɪ'hensɪbl] incomprensible
inconceivable [ɪnkən'si:vəbl] inconcebible
inconsiderate [ɪnkən'sɪdərət] desconsiderado
inconsistent [ɪnkən'sɪstənt] incoherente, inconsecuente; *player* irregular
inconspicuous [ɪnkən'spɪkjʊəs] discreto
inconvenience [ɪnkən'vi:nɪəns] inconveniencia *f*; **inconvenient** inconveniente
incorporate [ɪn'kɔ:rpəreɪt] incorporar
incorrect [ɪnkə'rekt] incorrecto
increase 1 [ɪn'kri:s] *v/t & v/i* aumentar **2** ['ɪnkri:s] *n* aumento *m*; **increasing** creciente; **increasingly** cada vez más
incredible [ɪn'kredɪbl] increíble

incur [ɪn'kɜːr] *costs* incurrir en; *debts* contraer; *anger* provocar
incurable [ɪn'kjʊrəbl] incurable
indecent [ɪn'diːsnt] indecente
indecisive [ɪndɪ'saɪsɪv] indeciso; **indecisiveness** indecisión *f*
indeed [ɪn'diːd] (*in fact*) ciertamente, efectivamente; *yes, agreeing* ciertamente, en efecto
indefinable [ɪndɪ'faɪnəbl] indefinible
indefinite [ɪn'defɪnɪt] indefinido; **indefinitely** indefinidamente
indelicate [ɪn'delɪkət] poco delicado
independence [ɪndɪ'pendəns] independencia *f*; **Independence Day** Día *m* de la Independencia; **independent** independiente
indescribable [ɪndɪ'skraɪbəbl] indescriptible
index ['ɪndeks] *for book* índice *m*
India ['ɪndɪə] (la) India; **Indian 1** *adj* indio **2** *n from India* indio(-a) *m(f)*, hindú *m/f*; *American* indio(-a) *m(f)*
indicate ['ɪndɪkeɪt] **1** *v/t* indicar **2** *v/i Br when driving* poner el intermitente; **indication** indicio *m*
indict [ɪn'daɪt] acusar
indifference [ɪn'dɪfrəns] indiferencia *f*; **indifferent** indiferente; (*mediocre*) mediocre
indigestion [ɪndɪ'dʒestʃn] indigestión *f*
indignant [ɪn'dɪgnənt] indignado; **indignation** indignación *f*
indirect [ɪndɪ'rekt] indirecto; **indirectly** indirectamente
indiscreet [ɪndɪ'skriːt] indiscreto
indiscriminate [ɪndɪ'skrɪmɪnət] indiscriminado
indispensable [ɪndɪ'spensəbl] indispensable
indisposed [ɪndɪ'spoʊzd] (*not well*) indispuesto
indisputable [ɪndɪ'spjuːtəbl] indiscutible
indistinct [ɪndɪ'stɪŋkt] indistinto, impreciso
indistinguishable [ɪndɪ'stɪŋgwɪʃəbl] indistinguible
individual [ɪndɪ'vɪdʒʊəl] **1** *n* individuo *m* **2** *adj* individual; **individually** individualmente
indoctrinate [ɪn'dɑːktrɪneɪt] adoctrinar
Indonesia [ɪndə'niːʒə] Indonesia; **Indonesian 1** *adj* indonesio **2** *n person* indonesio(-a) *m(f)*
indoor ['ɪndɔːr] *activities* de interior; *sport* de pista cubierta; *arena* cubierto; **indoors** dentro
indorse ☞ ***endorse***
indulgent [ɪn'dʌldʒənt] indulgente

industrial [ɪn'dʌstrɪəl] industrial; **industrial dispute** conflicto *m* laboral; **industrialist** industrial *m/f*; **industrious** trabajador, aplicado; **industry** industria *f*
ineffective [ɪnɪ'fektɪv] ineficaz
inefficient [ɪnɪ'fɪʃənt] ineficiente
inept [ɪ'nept] inepto
inequality [ɪnɪ'kwɑːlɪtɪ] desigualdad *f*
inescapable [ɪnɪ'skeɪpəbl] inevitable
inevitable [ɪn'evɪtəbl] inevitable; **inevitably** inevitablemente
inexcusable [ɪnɪkskjuːzəbl] inexcusable
inexhaustible [ɪnɪgzɒːstəbl] *supply* inagotable
inexpensive [ɪnɪk'spensɪv] barato, económico
inexperienced [ɪnɪkspɪrɪənst] inexperto
inexplicable [ɪnɪk'splɪkəbl] inexplicable
infallible [ɪn'fælɪbl] infalible
infamous ['ɪnfəməs] infame
infancy ['ɪnfənsɪ] infancia *f*; **infant** bebé *m*; **infantile** *pej* infantil
infantry ['ɪnfəntrɪ] infantería *f*
infect [ɪn'fekt] infectar; **infection** infección *f*; **infectious** infeccioso; *laughter* contagioso
infer [ɪn'fɜːr] inferir (***from*** de)
inferior [ɪn'fɪrɪər] inferior (***to*** a); **inferiority** inferioridad *f*; **inferiority complex** complejo *m* de inferioridad
infertile [ɪn'fɜːrtl] *woman, plant* estéril; *soil* estéril, yermo; **infertility** esterilidad *f*
infidelity [ɪnfɪ'delɪtɪ] infidelidad *f*
infinite ['ɪnfɪnət] infinito; **infinitive** infinitivo *m*; **infinity** infinidad *f*
inflammable [ɪn'flæməbl] inflamable; **inflammation** MED inflamación *f*
inflatable [ɪn'fleɪtəbl] *dinghy* hinchable, inflable; **inflate** *tire, dinghy* hinchar, inflar; *economy* inflar; **inflation** inflación *f*; **inflationary** inflacionario, inflacionista
inflexible [ɪn'fleksɪbl] inflexible
inflict [ɪn'flɪkt] infligir (***on*** a)
influence ['ɪnflʊəns] **1** *n* influencia *f* **2** *v/t* influir en, influenciar; **influential** influyente
inform [ɪn'fɔːrm] **1** *v/t* informar **2** *v/i*: ~ ***on s.o.*** delatar a alguien
informal [ɪn'fɔːrməl] informal; **informality** informalidad *f*
informant [ɪn'fɔːrmənt] confidente *m/f*; **information** información *f*; **information technology** tecnologías *fpl* de la información; **informative** informativo; **informer** confidente *m/f*
infra-red [ɪnfrə'red] infrarro-

jo
infrastructure ['ɪnfrətrʌktʃər] infraestructura *f*
infrequent [ɪn'fri:kwənt] poco frecuente
infuriate [ɪn'fjʊrɪeɪt] enfurecer, exasperar; **infuriating** exasperante
ingenious [ɪn'dʒi:nɪəs] ingenioso
ingot ['ɪŋgət] lingote *m*
ingratitude [ɪn'grætɪtu:d] ingratitud *f*
ingredient [ɪn'gri:dɪənt] *also fig* ingrediente *m*
inhabit [ɪn'hæbɪt] habitar; **inhabitant** habitante *m/f*
inhale [ɪn'heɪl] **1** *v/t* inhalar **2** *v/i when smoking* tragarse el humo
inherit [ɪn'herɪt] heredar; **inheritance** herencia *f*
inhibited [ɪn'hɪbɪtɪd] inhibido, cohibido; **inhibition** inhibición *f*
inhospitable [ɪnhɑ:'spɪtəbl] *person* inhospitalario; *city, climate* inhóspito
inhuman [ɪn'hju:mən] inhumano
initial [ɪ'nɪʃl] **1** *adj* inicial **2** *n* inicial *f* **3** *v/t* (*write ~s on*) poner las iniciales en; **initially** inicialmente; **initiate** iniciar; **initiation** iniciación *f*, inicio *m*; **initiative** iniciativa *f*
inject [ɪn'dʒekt] inyectar; **injection** inyección *f*
injure ['ɪndʒər] lesionar; **injury** lesión *f*; *wound* herida *f*
injustice [ɪn'dʒʌstɪs] injusticia *f*
ink [ɪŋk] tinta *f*
inland ['ɪnlənd] interior; *mail* nacional
in-laws ['ɪnlɒ:z] familia *f* política
inmate ['ɪnmeɪt] *of prison* recluso(-a) *m(f)*; *of mental hospital* paciente *m/f*
inn [ɪn] posada *f*, mesón *m*
innate [ɪ'neɪt] innato
inner ['ɪnər] interior
innocence ['ɪnəsəns] inocencia *f*; **innocent** inocente
innocuous [ɪ'nɑ:kjʊəs] inocuo
innovation [ɪnə'veɪʃn] innovación *f*; **innovative** innovador; **innovator** innovador(a) *m(f)*
inoculate [ɪ'nɑ:kjʊleɪt] inocular; **inoculation** inoculación *f*
inoffensive [ɪnə'fensɪv] inofensivo
'in-patient paciente *m/f* interno(-a)
input ['ɪnpʊt] **1** *n into project etc* contribución *f*; COMPUT entrada *f* **2** *v/t into project* contribuir; COMPUT introducir
inquest ['ɪnkwest] investigación *f* (***into*** sobre)
inquire [ɪn'kwaɪr] preguntar; **inquiry** consulta *f*, pregunta *f*; *into rail crash etc* investigación *f*
inquisitive [ɪn'kwɪzətɪv] curioso, inquisitivo
insane [ɪn'seɪn] *person* loco,

demente; *idea* descabellado

insanitary [ɪn'sænɪterɪ] antihigiénico

insanity [ɪn'sænɪtɪ] locura *f*, demencia *f*

inscription [ɪn'skrɪpʃn] inscripción *f*

insect ['ɪnsekt] insecto *m*; **insecticide** insecticida *f*

insecure [ɪnsɪ'kjʊr] inseguro; **insecurity** inseguridad *f*

insensitive [ɪn'sensɪtɪv] insensible

insert 1 ['ɪnsɜːrt] *n in magazine etc* encarte *m* **2** [ɪn'sɜːrt] *v/t* introducir, meter; *extra text* insertar

inside [ɪn'saɪd] **1** *n* interior *m*; ~ ***out*** del revés **2** *prep* dentro de; ~ ***of 2 hours*** dentro de 2 horas **3** *adv stay*, *remain* dentro; *go*, *carry* adentro; ***we went*** ~ entramos **4** *adj*: ~ ***information*** información *f* confidencial; ~ ***lane*** SP calle *f* de dentro; ***inside pocket*** bolsillo *m* interior; **insider** *persona con acceso a información confidencial*; **insider trading** FIN uso *m* de información privilegiada; **insides** (*stomach*) tripas *fpl*

insignificant [ɪnsɪg'nɪfɪkənt] insignificante

insincere [ɪnsɪn'sɪr] poco sincero, falso; **insincerity** falta *f* de sinceridad

insinuate [ɪn'sɪnʊeɪt] (*imply*) insinuar

insist [ɪn'sɪst] insistir (***on*** en); **insistent** insistente

insolent ['ɪnsələnt] insolente

insolvent [ɪn'sɑːlvənt] insolvente

insomnia [ɪn'sɑːmnɪə] insomnio *m*

inspect [ɪn'spekt] inspeccionar; **inspection** inspección *f*; **inspector** *in factory* inspector(a) *m(f)*

inspiration [ɪnspə'reɪʃn] inspiración *f*; **inspire** *respect etc* inspirar

instability [ɪnstə'bɪlɪtɪ] inestabilidad *f*

install [ɪn'stɒːl] instalar; **installation** instalación *f*; **installment**, *Br* **instalment** *of story etc* episodio *m*; *payment* plazo *m*; **installment plan** compra *f* a plazos

instance ['ɪnstəns] ejemplo *m*; ***for*** ~ por ejemplo

instant ['ɪnstənt] **1** *adj* instantáneo **2** *n* instante *m*; **instantaneous** instantáneo; **instant coffee** café *m* instantáneo; **instantly** al instante

instead [ɪn'sted]: ***would you like coffee*** ~***?*** ¿preferiría mejor café?; ~ ***of me*** en mi lugar; ~ ***of going*** en vez de ir, en lugar de ir

instinct ['ɪnstɪŋkt] instinto *m*; **instinctive** instintivo

institute ['ɪnstɪtuːt] **1** *n* instituto *m* **2** *v/t new law* establecer; *inquiry* iniciar; **institution** institución *f*; (*setting up*) iniciación *f*

instruct [ɪn'strʌkt] (*order*) dar

instrucciones a; (*teach*) instruir; **instruction** instrucción *f*; **instructive** instructivo; **instructor** instructor(a) *m(f)*
instrument ['ɪnstrumənt] instrumento *m*
insubordinate [ɪnsə'bɔːrdɪnət] insubordinado
insufficient [ɪnsə'fɪʃnt] insuficiente
insulate ['ɪnsəleɪt] aislar; **insulation** aislamiento *m*
insulin ['ɪnsəlɪn] insulina *f*
insult 1 ['ɪnsʌlt] *n* insulto *m* **2** [ɪn'sʌlt] *v/t* insultar
insurance [ɪn'ʃurəns] seguro *m*; **insurance company** compañía *f* de seguros, aseguradora *f*; **insurance policy** póliza *f* de seguros; **insurance premium** prima *f* (del seguro); **insure** asegurar
insurmountable [ɪnsər'maʊntəbl] insuperable
intact [ɪn'tækt] intacto
integrate ['ɪntɪgreɪt] integrar (***into*** en); **integrity** (*honesty*) integridad *f*; ***a man of ~*** un hombre íntegro
intellect ['ɪntəlekt] intelecto *m*; **intellectual 1** *adj* intelectual **2** *n* intelectual *m/f*
intelligence [ɪn'telɪdʒəns] inteligencia *f*; (*information*) información *f* secreta; **intelligent** inteligente
intelligible [ɪn'telɪdʒəbl] inteligible
intend [ɪn'tend]: ***~ to do sth*** tener la intención de hacer algo
intense [ɪn'tens] intenso; *personality* serio; **intensify 1** *v/t* intensificar **2** *v/i* intensificarse; **intensity** intensidad *f*; **intensive** intensivo; **intensive care** cuidados *mpl* intensivos
intention [ɪn'tenʃn] intención *f*; **intentional** intencionado; **intentionally** a propósito, adrede
interaction [ɪntər'ækʃn] interacción *f*; **interactive** interactivo
intercept [ɪntər'sept] interceptar
interchange ['ɪntərtʃeɪndʒ] *of highways* nudo *m* vial; **interchangeable** intercambiable
intercom ['ɪntərkɑːm] interfono *m*; *for front door* portero *m* automático
intercourse ['ɪntərkɔːrs] *sexual* coito *m*
interdependent [ɪntərdɪ'pendənt] interdependiente
interest ['ɪntrəst] **1** *n also* FIN interés *m* **2** *v/t* interesar; **interested** interesado; **interesting** interesante; **interest rate** tipo *m* de interés
interface ['ɪntərfeɪs] **1** *n* interface *m*, interfaz *f* **2** *v/i* relacionarse
interfere [ɪntər'fɪr] interferir; **interference** intromisión *f*; *on radio* interferencia *f*
interior [ɪn'tɪrɪər] **1** *adj* inte-

rior **2** *n* interior *m*; **interior design** interiorismo *m*; **interior designer** interiorista *m/f*

interlude ['ɪntərlu:d] *at theater, concert* intermedio *m*; (*period*) intervalo *m*

intermediary [ɪntər'mi:dɪərɪ] intermediario; **intermediate** intermedio *m*

intermission [ɪntər'mɪʃn] *in theater* intermedio *m*

internal [ɪn'tɜ:rnl] interno; **internally** internamente; **Internal Revenue (Service)** Hacienda *f*, *Span* Agencia *f* Tributaria

international [ɪntər'næʃnl] internacional; **internationally** internacionalmente

Internet ['ɪntərnet] Internet *f*; ***on the ~*** en Internet

interpret [ɪn'tɜ:rprɪt] interpretar; **interpretation** interpretación *f*; **interpreter** intérprete *m/f*

interrogate [ɪn'terəgeɪt] interrogar; **interrogation** interrogatorio *m*; **interrogator** interrogador(a) *m(f)*

interrupt [ɪntər'rʌpt] interrumpir; **interruption** interrupción *f*

intersect [ɪntər'sekt] **1** *v/t* cruzar **2** *v/i* cruzarse; **intersection** *of roads* intersección *f*

interstate ['ɪntərsteɪt] autopista *f* interestatal

interval ['ɪntərvl] intervalo *m*; *in theater* intermedio *m*

intervene [ɪntər'vi:n] intervenir; **intervention** intervención *f*

interview ['ɪntərvju:] **1** *n* entrevista *f* **2** *v/t* entrevistar; **interviewer** entrevistador(a) *m(f)*

intimate ['ɪntɪmət] íntimo

intimidate [ɪn'tɪmɪdeɪt] intimidar; **intimidation** intimidación *f*

into ['ɪntʊ] en; ***translate ~ English*** traducir al inglés; ***he's ~ classical music*** F (*likes*) le gusta *or Span* le va mucho la música clásica; ***he's ~ local politics*** F (*is involved with*) está muy metido en el mundillo de la política local

intolerable [ɪn'tɑ:lərəbl] intolerable; **intolerant** intolerante

intoxicated [ɪn'tɑ:ksɪkeɪtɪd] ebrio, embriagado

intravenous [ɪntrə'vi:nəs] intravenoso

intricate ['ɪntrɪkət] intrincado

intrigue 1 ['ɪntri:g] *n* intriga *f* **2** [ɪn'tri:g] *v/t* intrigar; **intriguing** intrigante

introduce [ɪntrə'du:s] presentar; *new technique etc* introducir; **introduction** *to person* presentación *f*; *to a new food, sport etc* iniciación *f*; *in book, of new techniques etc* introducción *f*

intrude [ɪn'tru:d] molestar; **intruder** intruso(-a) *m(f)*; **intrusion** intromisión *f*

intuition [ɪntuːˈɪʃn] intuición *f*
invade [ɪnˈveɪd] invadir
invalid[1] [ɪnˈvælɪd] *adj* nulo
invalid[2] [ˈɪnvəlɪd] *n* MED minusválido(-a) *m(f)*
invalidate [ɪnˈvælɪdeɪt] invalidar
invaluable [ɪnˈvæljubl] inestimable
invariably [ɪnˈveɪrɪəblɪ] (*always*) invariablemente
invasion [ɪnˈveɪʒn] invasión *f*
invent [ɪnˈvent] inventar; **invention** *action* invención *f*; *thing invented* invento *m*; **inventive** inventivo; **inventor** inventor(a) *m(f)*
inventory [ˈɪnvəntɔːrɪ] inventario *m*
invert [ɪnˈvɜːrt] invertir
invest [ɪnˈvest] invertir
investigate [ɪnˈvestɪgeɪt] investigar; **investigation** investigación *f*
investment [ɪnˈvestmənt] inversión *f*; **investor** inversor(a) *m(f)*
invincible [ɪnˈvɪnsəbl] invencible
invisible [ɪnˈvɪzɪbl] invisible
invitation [ɪnvɪˈteɪʃn] invitación *f*; **invite** invitar
invoice [ˈɪnvɔɪs] **1** *n* factura *f* **2** *v/t customer* enviar la factura a
involuntary [ɪnˈvɑːlənterɪ] involuntario
involve [ɪnˈvɑːlv] *work, expense* involucrar, entrañar; ***what does it ~?*** ¿en qué consiste?; **involved** (*complex*) complicado; **involvement** *in project, crime* participación *f*, intervención *f*
invulnerable [ɪnˈvʌlnərəbl] invulnerable
inward [ˈɪnwərd] **1** *adj feeling, smile* interior **2** *adv* hacia dentro; **inwardly** por dentro
IQ [aɪˈkjuː] (= ***intelligence quotient***) cociente *m* intelectual
Iran [ɪˈrɑːn] Irán; **Iranian 1** *adj* iraní **2** *n* iraní *m/f*
Iraq [ɪˈræːk] Iraq, Irak; **Iraqi 1** *adj* iraquí **2** *n* iraquí *m/f*
Ireland [ˈaɪrlənd] Irlanda; **Irish** irlandés
iron [ˈaɪərn] **1** *n* hierro *m*; *for clothes* plancha *f* **2** *v/t* planchar
ironic(al) [aɪˈrɑːnɪk(l)] irónico
ˈironing board tabla *f* de planchar
irony [ˈaɪrənɪ] ironía *f*
irrational [ɪˈræʃənl] irracional
irreconcilable [ɪrekənˈsaɪləbl] irreconciliable
irregular [ɪˈregjʊlər] irregular
irrelevant [ɪˈreləvənt] irrelevante
irreplaceable [ɪrɪˈpleɪsəbl] irreemplazable
irrepressible [ɪrɪˈpresəbl] *sense of humor* incontenible; *person* irreprimible
irresistible [ɪrɪˈzɪstəbl] irresistible
irresponsible [ɪrɪˈspɑːnsəbl] irresponsable
irreverent [ɪˈrevərənt] irreve-

rente

irrevocable [ɪ'revəkəbl] irrevocable

irrigate ['ɪrɪgeɪt] regar; **irrigation** riego *m*

irritable ['ɪrɪtəbl] irritable; **irritate** irritar; **irritating** irritante; **irritation** irritación *f*

Islam ['ɪzlɑːm] (el) Islam; **Islamic** islámico

island ['aɪlənd] isla *f*

isolate ['aɪsəleɪt] aislar; **isolated** aislado; **isolation** aislamiento *m*

ISP [aɪes'piː] (= ***Internet service provider***) proveedor *m* de (acceso a) Internet

Israel ['ɪzreɪl] Israel; **Israeli 1** *adj* israelí **2** *n person* israelí *m/f*

issue ['ɪʃuː] **1** *n* (*matter*) tema *m*, asunto *m*; *of magazine* número *m* **2** *v/t coins* emitir; *passport etc* expedir; *warning* dar

IT [aɪ'tiː] (= ***information technology***) tecnologías *fpl* de la información

it [ɪt] *as object* lo *m*, la *f*; ***what color is ~? – ~ is red*** ¿de qué color es? - es rojo; ***~'s raining*** llueve; ***~'s me / him*** soy yo / es él; ***that's ~!*** (*that's right*) ¡eso es!; (*finished*) ¡ya está!

Italian [ɪ'tæljən] **1** *adj* italiano **2** *n person* italiano(-a) *m(f)*; *language* italiano *m*

italics [ɪ'tælɪks] cursiva *f*

Italy ['ɪtəlɪ] Italia

itch [ɪʧ] **1** *n* picor *m* **2** *v/i* picar

item ['aɪtəm] artículo *m*; *on agenda* punto *m*; *of news* noticia *f*; **itemize** *invoice* detallar

itinerary [aɪ'tɪnərerɪ] itinerario *m*

its [ɪts] su

it's [ɪts] ☞ ***it is***; ***it has***

itself [ɪt'self] *reflexive* se; ***by ~*** (*alone, automatically*) solo

J

jab [dʒæb] clavar

jack [dʒæk] MOT gato *m*; *in cards* jota *f*

jacket ['dʒækɪt] chaqueta *f*; *of book* sobrecubierta *f*

'jackpot gordo *m*

jagged ['dʒægɪd] accidentado

jaguar ['dʒægʊər] jaguar *m*

jail [dʒeɪl] cárcel *f*

jam¹ [dʒæm] *n for bread* mermelada *f*

jam² [dʒæm] **1** *n* mot atasco *m*; F (*difficulty*) aprieto *m* **2** *v/t* (*ram*) meter, embutir; (*cause to stick*) atascar **3** *v/i* (*stick*) atascarse

janitor ['dʒænɪtər] portero(-a) *m(f)*

January ['dʒænʊerɪ] enero *m*

Japan [dʒə'pæn] Japón; **Japanese 1** *adj* japonés **2** *n* japonés(-esa) *m(f)*; *language*

japonés *m*; ***the ~*** los japoneses
jar [dʒɑːr] *container* tarro *m*
jargon ['dʒɑːrgən] jerga *f*
jaw [dʒɒː] mandíbula *f*
jaywalker ['dʒeɪwɒːkər] peatón(-ona) *m(f)* imprudente
jazz [dʒæz] jazz *m*
jealous ['dʒeləs] celoso; **jealousy** celos *mpl*; *of possessions* envidia *f*
jeans [dʒiːnz] vaqueros *mpl*, jeans *mpl*
jeep [dʒiːp] jeep *m*
jeer [dʒɪr] **1** *n* abucheo *m* **2** *v/i* abuchear
Jello® ['dʒeloʊ] gelatina *f*
jelly ['dʒelɪ] mermelada *f*; **jellyfish** medusa *f*
jeopardize ['dʒepərdaɪz] poner en peligro
jerk¹ [dʒɜːrk] **1** *n* sacudida *f* **2** *v/t* dar un tirón a
jerk² [dʒɜːrk] *n* F imbécil *m/f*, *Span* gilipollas *m/f inv* F
jerky ['dʒɜːrkɪ] brusco
Jesus ['dʒiːzəs] Jesús
jet [dʒet] (*airplane*) reactor *m*; *of water* chorro *m*; (*nozzle*) boquilla *f*; **jetlag** desfase *m* horario, jet lag *m*
jettison ['dʒetɪsn] tirar por la borda
jetty ['dʒetɪ] malecón *m*
Jew [dʒuː] judío(-a) *m(f)*
jewel ['dʒuːəl] *also fig* joya *f*; **jeweler**, *Br* **jeweller** joyero(-a) *m(f)*; **jewellery** *Br*, **jewelry** joyas *fpl*
Jewish ['dʒuːɪʃ] judío
jigsaw ['dʒɪgsɒː] rompecabezas *m inv*, puzzle *m*
jilt [dʒɪlt] dejar plantado
jingle ['dʒɪŋgl] **1** *n song* melodía *f* publicitaria **2** *v/i of keys, coins* tintinear
jinx [dʒɪŋks] gafe *m*; ***there's a ~ on this project*** este proyecto está gafado
jittery ['dʒɪtərɪ] F nervioso
job [dʒɑːb] trabajo *m*; **jobless** desempleado, *Span* parado
jockey ['dʒɑːkɪ] jockey *m/f*
jog [dʒɑːg] *as exercise* hacer jogging *or* footing; **jogger** persona *f* que hace jogging *or* footing; **jogging:** ***go ~*** ir a hacer jogging *or* footing
john [dʒɑːn] P (*toilet*) baño *m*, váter *m*
join [dʒɔɪn] **1** *n* juntura *f* **2** *v/i of roads, rivers* juntarse; (*become a member*) hacerse socio **3** *v/t* (*connect*) unir; *person* unirse a; *club* hacerse socio de; *of road* desembocar en
◆ **join in** participar
joint [dʒɔɪnt] ANAT articulación *f*; *in woodwork* junta *f*; *of meat* pieza *f*; **joint account** cuenta *f* conjunta; **joint venture** empresa *f* conjunta
joke [dʒoʊk] **1** *n* chiste *m*; (*practical ~*) broma *f* **2** *v/i* bromear; **joker** bromista *m/f*; *in cards* comodín *m*; **jokingly** en broma
jostle ['dʒɑːsl] empujar
journal ['dʒɜːrnl] (*magazine*)

revista *f*; (*diary*) diario *m*; **journalism** periodismo *m*; **journalist** periodista *m/f*

journey ['dʒɜːrnɪ] viaje *m*

joy [dʒɔɪ] alegría *f*, gozo *m*

jubilant ['dʒuːbɪlənt] jubiloso; **jubilation** júbilo *m*

judge [dʒʌdʒ] **1** *n* juez *m/f* **2** *v/t* juzgar; (*estimate*) calcular **3** *v/i* juzgar; **judg(e)ment** LAW fallo *m*; (*opinion*) juicio *m*; **Judg(e)ment Day** Día *m* del Juicio Final

judicial [dʒuː'dɪʃl] judicial

juggle [dʒʌgl] *also fig* hacer malabarismos con

juice [dʒuːs] *Span* zumo *m*, *L.Am.* jugo *m*; **juicy** *also fig* jugoso

July [dʒʊ'laɪ] julio *m*

jumbo (jet) ['dʒʌmboʊ] jumbo *m*; **jumbo(-sized)** gigante

jump [dʒʌmp] **1** *n* salto *m*; (*increase*) incremento *m*, subida *f* **2** *v/i* saltar; (*increase*) dispararse **3** *v/t fence etc* saltar; F (*attack*) asaltar; **~ *the lights*** saltarse el semáforo

◆ **jump at** *opportunity* no dejar escapar

jumper ['dʒʌmpər] *dress* pichi *m*; **jumpy** nervioso

June [dʒuːn] junio *m*

jungle ['dʒʌŋgl] selva *f*, jungla *f*

junior ['dʒuːnjər] **1** *adj* de rango inferior; (*younger*) más joven **2** *n in rank* subalterno(-a) *m*(*f*); **junior high** escuela *f* secundaria (*para alumnos de entre 12 y 14 años*)

junk [dʒʌŋk] trastos *mpl*; **junk food** comida *f* basura; **junkie** F drogota *m/f* F; **junk mail** propaganda *f* postal

jurisdiction [dʒʊrɪs'dɪkʃn] jurisdicción *f*

juror ['dʒʊrər] miembro *m* del jurado; **jury** jurado *m*

just [dʒʌst] **1** *adj cause* justo **2** *adv* (*barely*) justo; (*exactly*) justo, justamente; (*only*) sólo, solamente; ***have ~ done sth*** acabar de hacer algo; **~ *about*** (*almost*) casi; ***I was ~ about to leave when …*** estaba a punto de salir cuando…; **~ *now*** (*at the moment*) ahora mismo; ***I saw her ~ now*** *a few moments ago* la acabo de ver

justice ['dʒʌstɪs] justicia *f*

justifiable [dʒʌstɪ'faɪəbl] justificable; **justifiably** justificadamente; **justification** justificación *f*; **justify** *also text* justificar

justly ['dʒʌstlɪ] (*fairly*) con justicia; (*rightly*) con razón

◆ **jut out** [dʒʌt] sobresalir

juvenile ['dʒuːvənl] *crime* juvenil; *court* de menores; *pej* infantil; **juvenile delinquent** delincuente *m/f* juvenil

K

k [keɪ] (= ***kilobyte***) k (= kilobyte *m*); (= ***thousand***) mil
keel [kiːl] NAUT quilla *f*
keen [kiːn] *interest* gran
keep [kiːp] **1** *v/t* guardar; (*not lose*) conservar; (*detain*) entretener; *family* mantener; *animals* tener, criar; ***~ trying!*** ¡sigue intentándolo!; ***don't ~ interrupting!*** ¡deja de interrumpirme!; ***~ sth from s.o.*** ocultar algo a alguien **2** *v/i of food, milk* aguantar; ***~ calm!*** ¡tranquilízate!
◆ **keep back** (*hold in check*) contener; *information* ocultar
◆ **keep down** *voice* bajar; *costs etc* reducir; *food* retener
◆ **keep to** *path* seguir; *rules* cumplir, respetar
◆ **keep up 1** *v/i when walking, running etc* seguir el ritmo (***with*** de) **2** *v/t pace* seguir, mantener; *payments* estar al corriente de; *bridge, pants* sujetar
'keepsake recuerdo *m*
kennel ['kenl] caseta *f* del perro; **kennels** residencia *f* canina
kerosene ['kerəsiːn] queroseno *m*
ketchup ['ketʃʌp] ketchup *m*
kettle ['ketl] hervidor *m*
key [kiː] **1** *n* llave *f*; *on keyboard, piano* tecla *f*; *of piece of music* clave *f*; *on map* leyenda *f* **2** *adj* (*vital*) clave **3** *v/t & v/i* COMPUT teclear
◆ **key in** *data* teclear
'keyboard COMPUT, MUS teclado *m*; **keyboarder** COMPUT operador(a) *m(f)*, teclista *m/f*; **keycard** tarjeta *f* (de hotel); **keyed-up** nervioso; **keyring** llavero *m*
kick [kɪk] **1** *n* patada *f* **2** *v/t* dar una patada a; F *habit* dejar **3** *v/i of horse* cocear
◆ **kick around** *ball* dar patadas a; F (*discuss*) comentar
◆ **kick off** comenzar, sacar de centro; F (*start*) empezar
◆ **kick out** *of bar, company* echar; *of country* expulsar
'kickback F (*bribe*) soborno *m*; **kickoff** SP saque *m*
kid [kɪd] F **1** *n* (*child*) crío *m* F, niño *m* **2** *v/t* tomar el pelo a F **3** *v/i* bromear
kidnap ['kɪdnæp] secuestrar; **kidnapper** secuestrador *m*; **kidnapping** secuestro *m*
kidney ['kɪdnɪ] ANAT riñón *m*; *in cooking* riñones *mpl*
kill [kɪl] matar; **killer** (*murderer*) asesino *m*; **killing** asesinato *m*
kiln [kɪln] horno *m*
kilo ['kiːlou] kilo *m*; **kilobyte** kilobyte *m*; **kilogram** kilo-

gramo *m*; **kilometer**, *Br* **kilometre** kilómetro *m*
kind[1] [kaɪnd] *adj* amable
kind[2] [kaɪnd] *n* (*sort*) tipo *m*; (*make, brand*) marca *f*; **~ of** ... *sad, lonely etc* un poco...
kind-hearted [kaɪnd'hɑːrtɪd] agradable, amable; **kindly** amable, agradable; **kindness** amabilidad *f*
king [kɪŋ] rey *m*; **kingdom** reino *m*
kinky ['kɪŋkɪ] F vicioso
kiosk ['kiːɑːsk] quiosco *m*
kiss [kɪs] **1** *n* beso *m* **2** *v/t* besar **3** *v/i* besarse
kit [kɪt] (*equipment*) equipo *m*
kitchen ['kɪtʃɪn] cocina *f*
kitten ['kɪtn] gatito *m*
kitty ['kɪtɪ] *money* fondo *m*
klutz [klʌts] F (*clumsy person*) manazas *m* F
knack [næk] habilidad *f*
knee [niː] rodilla *f*; **kneecap** rótula *f*
kneel [niːl] arrodillarse
knee-length hasta la rodilla
knife [naɪf] *for food* cuchillo *m*; *carried outside* navaja *f*
knit [nɪt] **1** *v/t* tejer **2** *v/i* tricotar; **knitwear** prendas *fpl* de punto
knob [nɑːb] *on door* pomo *m*; *on drawer* tirador *m*; *of butter* nuez *f*
knock [nɑːk] **1** *n* golpe *m* **2** *v/t* (*hit*) golpear; F (*criticize*) criticar **3** *v/i on door* llamar
◆ **knock down** *of car* atropellar; *building* tirar; *object* tirar al suelo; F (*reduce price of*) rebajar
◆ **knock out** dejar K.O.; *of medicine* dejar para el arrastre F; *power lines etc* destruir; (*eliminate*) eliminar
◆ **knock over** tirar; *of car* atropellar
knockout ['nɑːkaʊt] K.O. *m*
knot [nɑːt] **1** *n* nudo *m* **2** *v/t* anudar
know [noʊ] **1** *v/t* saber; *person, place* conocer; (*recognize*) reconocer **2** *v/i* saber; ***I don't ~*** no (lo) sé; **knowhow** pericia *f*; **knowing** cómplice; **knowingly** deliberadamente; *smile etc* con complicidad; **know-it-all** F sabiondo F; **knowledge** conocimiento *m*; ***to the best of my ~*** por lo que sé
knuckle ['nʌkl] nudillo *m*
Koran [kə'ræn] Corán *m*
Korea [kə'riːə] Corea; **Korean** **1** *adj* coreano **2** *n* coreano(a) *m*(*f*); *language* coreano *m*
kosher ['koʊʃər] REL kosher; F legal F
kudos ['kjuːdɑːs] prestigio *m*

L

lab [læb] laboratorio *m*
label ['leɪbl] **1** *n* etiqueta *f* **2** *v/t* etiquetar
labor ['leɪbər] trabajo *m*; *in pregnancy* parto *m*
laboratory ['læbrətɔurɪ] laboratorio *m*
labored ['leɪbərd] *style, speech* elaborado; **laborer** obrero(-a) *m(f)*; **laborious** laborioso; **labor union** sindicato *m*; **labour** *Br* ☞ ***labor***
lace [leɪs] encaje *m*; *for shoe* cordón *m*
lack [læk] **1** *n* falta *f*, carencia *f* **2** *v/t* carecer de; ***he ~s confidence*** le falta confianza
lacquer ['lækər] laca *f*
ladder ['lædər] escalera *f* (de mano)
laden ['leɪdn] cargado (***with*** de)
ladies room ['leɪdi:z] servicio *m* de señoras
lady ['leɪdɪ] señora *f*; **ladybug** mariquita *f*; **ladylike** femenino
lager ['lɑ:gər] *Br* cerveza *f* rubia
laidback [leɪd'bæk] tranquilo, despreocupado
lake [leɪk] lago *m*
lamb [læm] cordero *m*
lame [leɪm] cojo; *excuse* pobre
laminated ['læmɪneɪtɪd] laminado; *paper* plastificado
lamp [læmp] lámpara *f*; **lamppost** farola *f*; **lampshade** pantalla *f* (*de lámpara*)
land [lænd] **1** *n* tierra *f*; ***by ~*** por tierra **2** *v/t airplane* aterrizar; *job* conseguir **3** *v/i of airplane* aterrizar; *of ball* caer; **landing** *of airplane* aterrizaje *m*; *of staircase* rellano *m*; **landing strip** pista *f* de aterrizaje; **landlady** *of hostel etc* dueña *f*; *of rented room* casera *f*; *Br*: *of bar* patrona *f*; **landlord** *of hostel etc* dueño *m*; *of rented room* casero *m*; *Br*: *of bar* patrón *m*; **landmark** punto *m* de referencia; *fig* hito *m*; **land owner** terrateniente *m/f*; **landscape 1** *n* (*also painting*) paisaje *m* **2** *adv print* en formato apaisado; **landslide** corrimiento *m* de tierras; **landslide victory** victoria *f* arrolladora
lane [leɪn] *in country* camino *m*; (*alley*) callejón *m*; MOT carril *m*
language ['læŋgwɪdʒ] lenguaje *m*; *of nation* idioma *f*, lengua *f*; **language lab** laboratorio *m* de idiomas
lap[1] [læp] *of track* vuelta *f*
lap[2] [læp] *of water* chapoteo *m*
lap[3] [læp] *of person* regazo *m*
lapel [lə'pel] solapa *f*
lapse [læps] **1** *n* (*mistake*) desliz *m*; *of time* lapso *m* **2** *v/i of membership* vencer

laptop ['læptɑːp] COMPUT ordenador *m* portátil, *L.Am.* computadora *f* portátil
larceny ['lɑːrsənɪ] latrocinio *m*
larder ['lɑːrdər] despensa *f*
large [lɑːrdʒ] grande; **largely** (*mainly*) en gran parte, principalmente
laryngitis [lærɪn'dʒaɪtɪs] laringitis *f*
laser ['leɪzər] láser *m*; **laser printer** impresora *f* láser
lash[1] [læʃ] *v/t with whip* azotar
lash[2] [læʃ] *n* (*eyelash*) pestaña *f*
last[1] [læst] **1** *adj in series* último; (*preceding*) anterior; **~ *Friday*** el viernes pasado; **~ *night*** anoche **2** *adv* ***at ~*** por fin, al fin
last[2] [læst] *v/i* durar; **lasting** duradero; **lastly** por último
late [leɪt] **1** *adj*: ***be ~ of person, bus etc*** llegar tarde; ***it's ~*** *at night* es tarde **2** *adv arrive, leave* tarde; **lately** últimamente, recientemente; **later** más tarde; **latest** último
Latin A'merica Latinoamérica, América Latina; **Latin American 1** *n* latinoamericano(-a) *m(f)* **2** *adj* latinoamericano
Latino [læ'tiːnoʊ] **1** *adj* latino **2** n latino(-a)
latitude ['lætɪtuːd] latitud *f*; (*freedom*) libertad *f*
latter ['lætər] último
laugh [læf] **1** *n* risa *f* **2** *v/i* reírse
◆ **laugh at** reírse de
laughter ['læftər] risas *fpl*
launch [lɒːntʃ] **1** *n small boat* lancha *f*; *of ship* botadura *f*; *of rocket, product* lanzamiento *m* **2** *v/t rocket, product* lanzar; *ship* botar
launder ['lɒːndər] *clothes* lavar (y planchar); *money* blanquear; **laundromat** lavandería *f*; **laundry** *place* lavadero *m*; *dirty clothes* ropa *f* sucia; *clean clothes* ropa *f* lavada
lavatory ['lævətɔːrɪ] *place* cuarto *m* de baño, lavabo *m*; *equipment* retrete *m*
lavish ['lævɪʃ] espléndido
law [lɒː] ley *f*; *subject* derecho *m*; ***be against the ~*** estar prohibido; **law-abiding** respetuoso con la ley; **law court** juzgado *m*; **lawful** legal; *wife* legítimo; **lawless** sin ley
lawn [lɒːn] césped *m*; **lawn mower** cortacésped *m*
'lawsuit pleito *m*; **lawyer** abogado(-a) *m(f)*
lax [læks] poco estricto
laxative ['læksətɪv] laxante *m*
lay [leɪ] (*put down*) dejar, poner; *eggs* poner; V *sexually* tirarse a V
◆ **lay off** *workers* despedir
◆ **lay out** *objects* colocar; *page* diseñar, maquetar
layer ['leɪər] estrato *m*; *of soil, paint* capa *f*
'layman laico *m*
'lay-out diseño *m*

lazy ['leɪzɪ] *person* holgazán, perezoso; *day* ocioso
lb (= ***pound***) libra *f* (*de peso*)
lead¹ [li:d] **1** *v/t procession* ir al frente de; *company* dirigir; (*guide, take*) conducir **2** *v/i in race, competition* ir en cabeza; (*provide leadership*) tener el mando
lead² [li:d] *n for dog* correa *f*
lead³ [led] *n substance* plomo *m*; **leaded** *gas* con plomo
leader ['li:dər] líder *m*; **leadership** liderazgo *m*
lead-free ['ledfri:] *gas* sin plomo
leading ['li:dɪŋ] *runner* en cabeza; *company, product* puntero; **leading-edge** *company* en la vanguardia; *technology* de vanguardia
leaf [li:f] hoja *f*
◆ **leaf through** hojear
leaflet ['li:flət] folleto *m*
league [li:g] liga *f*
leak [li:k] **1** *n in roof* gotera *f*; *in pipe* agujero *m*; *of air, gas* fuga *f*; *of information* filtración *f* **2** *v/i of boat* hacer agua; *of pipe* tener un agujero; *of liquid, gas* fugarse
lean¹ [li:n] **1** *v/i* estar inclinado; ~ ***against sth*** apoyarse en algo **2** *v/t* apoyar
lean² [li:n] *adj meat* magro
leap [li:p] **1** *n* salto *m* **2** *v/i* saltar; **leap year** año *m* bisiesto
learn [lɜ:rn] **1** *v/t* aprender **2** *v/i* aprender; ~ ***about*** (*hear about*) enterarse de; **learner** estudiante *m/f*; **learning** (*knowledge*) conocimientos *mpl*; *act* aprendizaje *m*
lease [li:s] **1** *n* arrendamiento *m* **2** *v/t* arrendar
◆ **lease out** arrendar
leash [li:ʃ] *for dog* correa *f*
least [li:st] **1** *adj* (*slightest*) menor **2** *adv* menos **3** *n* lo menos; ***at*** ~ por lo menos
leather ['leðər] **1** *n* piel *f*, cuero **2** *adj* de piel, de cuero
leave [li:v] **1** *n* (*vacation*) permiso *m* **2** *v/t city, place* marcharse de, irse de; *person, food, memory,* (*forget*) dejar; ~ ***s.o.*** / ***sth alone*** dejar a alguien / algo en paz; ***be left*** quedar **3** *v/i of person* marcharse, irse; *of plane, train, bus* salir
◆ **leave behind** *intentionally* dejar; (*forget*) dejarse
◆ **leave out** omitir; (*not put away*) no guardar
leaving party ['li:vɪŋ] fiesta *f* de despedida
lecture ['lektʃər] **1** *n* clase *f*; *to general public* conferencia *f* **2** *v/i at university* dar clases (***in*** de); **lecturer** profesor(a) *m*(*f*)
ledge [ledʒ] *of window* alféizar *f*; *on rock face* saliente *m*; **ledger** COM libro *m* mayor
left [left] **1** *adj* izquierdo **2** *n also* POL izquierda *f*; ***on*** / ***to the*** ~ a la izquierda **3** *adv turn, look* a la izquierda; **left-hand** de la izquierda; **left-handed** zurdo; **left lug-**

gage (office) *Br* consigna *f*; **left-overs** *food* sobras *fpl*; **left-wing** POL izquierdista, de izquierdas
leg [leg] *of person* pierna *f*; *of animal*, *table* pata *f*
legacy ['legəsɪ] legado *m*
legal ['liːgl] legal; **legal adviser** asesor(a) *m(f)* jurídico(-a); **legality** legalidad *f*; **legalize** legalizar
legend ['ledʒənd] leyenda *f*; **legendary** legendario
legible ['ledʒəbl] legible
legislate ['ledʒɪsleɪt] legislar; **legislation** legislación *f*; **legislative** legislativo; **legislature** POL legislativo *m*
legitimate [lɪ'dʒɪtɪmət] legítimo
'leg room espacio *m* para las piernas
leisure ['liːʒər] ocio *m*; **leisurely** tranquilo, relajado
lemon ['lemən] limón *m*; **lemonade** limonada *f*
lend [lend] prestar
length [leŋθ] longitud *f*; (*piece*: *of material etc*) pedazo *m*; ***at ~ describe*** detalladamente; (*finally*) finalmente; **lengthen** alargar; **lengthy** largo
lenient ['liːnɪənt] indulgente, poco severo
lens [lenz] *of camera* objetivo *m*, lente *f*; *of eyeglasses* cristal *m*; *of eye* cristalino *m*; (*contact ~*) lente *m* de contacto, *Span* lentilla *f*
Lent [lent] REL Cuaresma *f*
leotard ['liːoʊtɑːrd] malla *f*
lesbian ['lezbɪən] **1** *n* lesbiana *f* **2** *adj* lésbico, lesbiano
less [les] menos; ***~ than $200*** menos de 200 dólares; **lessen** disminuir
lesson ['lesn] lección *f*
let [let] (*allow*) dejar, permitir; *Br house* alquilar; ***~ me go!*** ¡déjame!; ***~'s go*** vamos; ***~'s stay*** vaquedémonos; ***~ go of sth*** soltar algo
◆ **let down** *hair* soltarse; *blinds* bajar; (*disappoint*) decepcionar
◆ **let in** *to house* dejar pasar
◆ **let out** *from room*, *building* dejar salir; *jacket etc* agrandar; *groan* soltar; *Br room* alquilar, *Mex* rentar
◆ **let up** (*stop*) amainar
lethal ['liːθl] letal
lethargic [lɪ'θɑːrdʒɪk] aletargado; **lethargy** sopor *m*
letter ['letər] *of alphabet* letra *f*; *in mail* carta *f*; **letterbox** *Br* buzón *m*; **letterhead** (*heading*) membrete *m*; (*headed paper*) papel *m* con membrete
lettuce ['letɪs] lechuga *f*
leukemia [luː'kiːmɪə] leucemia *f*
level ['levl] **1** *adj surface* nivelado, llano; *in competition* igualado **2** *n* nivel *m*; ***on the ~*** F (*honest*) honrado; **level-headed** ecuánime
lever ['levər] palanca *f*; **leverage** apalancamiento *m*; (*influence*) influencia *f*

levy ['levɪ] *taxes* imponer
liability [laɪə'bɪlətɪ] responsabilidad *f*; (*likeliness*) propensión *f* (***to*** a); **liable** responsable (***for*** de); ***be ~ to*** (*likely*) ser propenso a
◆ **liaise with** [lɪ'eɪz] actuar de enlace con
liaison [lɪ'eɪzɑːn] (*contacts*) contacto *m*, enlace *m*
liar [laɪr] mentiroso(-a) *m(f)*
libel ['laɪbl] **1** *n* calumnia *f* **2** *v/t* calumniar
liberal ['lɪbərəl] liberal; *portion etc* abundante
liberate ['lɪbəreɪt] liberar; **liberated** liberado; **liberation** liberación *f*; **liberty** libertad *f*
librarian [laɪ'brerɪən] bibliotecario(-a) *m(f)*; **library** biblioteca *f*
Libya ['lɪbɪə] Libia; **Libyan 1** *adj* libio **2** n libio(-a) *m(f)*
licence *Br* ☞ ***license n***
license ['laɪsns] **1** *n* permiso *m*, licencia *f* **2** *v/t* autorizar; **license number** (número *m* de) matrícula *f*; **license plate** *of car* (placa *f* de) matrícula *f*
lick [lɪk] lamer
lid [lɪd] (*top*) tapa *f*
lie[1] [laɪ] **1** *n* (*untruth*) mentira *f* **2** *v/i* mentir
lie[2] [laɪ] *v/i of person* estar tumbado; *of object* estar; (*be situated*) estar, encontrarse
◆ **lie down** tumbarse
lieutenant [lʊ'tenənt] teniente *m/f*
life [laɪf] vida *f*; **life expectancy** esperanza *f* de vida; **lifeguard** socorrista *m/f*; **life imprisonment** cadena *f* perpetua; **life insurance** seguro *m* de vida; **life jacket** chaleco *m* salvavidas; **lifeless** sin vida; **lifelike** realista; **lifelong** de toda la vida; **life-sized** de tamaño natural; **life support** máquina *f* de respiración asistida; **life-threatening** que puede ser mortal; **lifetime** vida *f*; ***in my ~*** durante mi vida
lift [lɪft] **1** *v/t* levantar **2** *v/i of fog* disiparse **3** *n Br* (*elevator*) ascensor *m*; ***give s.o. a ~*** llevar a alguien (en coche); **lift-off** *of rocket* despegue *m*
ligament ['lɪgəmənt] ligamento *m*
light[1] [laɪt] **1** *n* luz *f*; ***do you have a ~?*** ¿tienes fuego? **2** *v/t fire, cigarette* encender; (*illuminate*) iluminar **3** *adj color, sky* claro; *room* luminoso
light[2] [laɪt] *adj* (*not heavy*) ligero
◆ **light up 1** *v/t* iluminar **2** *v/i* (*start to smoke*) encender un cigarrillo
'light bulb bombilla *f*
lighten[1] ['laɪtn] *color* aclarar
lighten[2] ['laɪtn] *load* aligerar
lighter ['laɪtər] *for cigarettes* encendedor *m*, *Span* mechero *m*; **light-headed** mareado; **lighting** iluminación *f*; **lightness** *of room, color* cla-

ridad *f*; *in weight* ligereza *f*; **lightning: *a flash of ~*** un relámpago; **lightweight** *in boxing* peso *m* ligero; **light year** año *m* luz

like¹ [laɪk] **1** *prep* como; ***what is she ~?*** ¿cómo es?; ***it's not ~ him*** (*not his character*) no es su estilo **2** *conj* como; ***~ I said*** como dije

like² [laɪk] *v/t*: ***I ~ it / her*** me gusta; ***I would ~ ...*** querría ...; ***I would ~ to ...*** me gustaría...; ***would you ~ ...?*** ¿querrías...?; ***she ~s to swim*** le gusta nadar; ***if you ~*** si quieres

likeable ['laɪkəbl] simpático; **likelihood** probabilidad *f*; **likely** probable; **likeness** (*resemblance*) parecido *m*; **likewise** igualmente; **liking** afición *f* (***for*** a)

limb [lɪm] miembro *m*

lime¹ [laɪm] *fruit, tree* lima *f*

lime² [laɪm] *substance* cal *f*

limit ['lɪmɪt] **1** *n* límite *m* **2** *v/t* limitar; **limitation** limitación *f*; **limited company** *Br* sociedad *f* limitada

limousine ['lɪməziːn] limusina *f*

limp¹ [lɪmp] *adj* flojo

limp² [lɪmp] *n*: ***he has a ~*** cojea

line¹ [laɪn] *n* línea *f*; *of trees* fila *f*; *of people* fila *f*, cola *f*; ***the ~ is busy*** está ocupado, *Span* está comunicando; ***stand in ~*** hacer cola

line² [laɪn] *v/t with lining* forrar

linear ['lɪnɪər] lineal

linen ['lɪnɪn] *material* lino *m*; (*sheets etc*) ropa *f* blanca

liner ['laɪnər] *ship* transatlántico *m*

linesman ['laɪnzmən] SP juez *m* de línea, linier *m*

linger ['lɪŋgər] *of person* entretenerse; *of pain* persistir

lingerie ['lænʒəriː] lencería *f*

linguist ['lɪŋgwɪst] lingüista *m/f*; **linguistic** lingüístico

lining ['laɪnɪŋ] *of clothes* forro *m*; *of brakes, pipe* revestimiento *m*

link [lɪŋk] **1** *n* conexión *f*; *between countries* vínculo *m*; *in chain* eslabón *m*; *in Internet* enlace *m* **2** *v/t* conectar

lion ['laɪən] león *m*

lip [lɪp] labio *m*

liposuction ['lɪpoʊsʌkʃn] liposucción *f*

'lipread leer los labios; **lipstick** barra *f* de labios

liqueur [lɪ'kjʊr] licor *m*

liquid ['lɪkwɪd] **1** *n* líquido *m* **2** *adj* líquido; **liquidate** *assets* liquidar; F (*kill*) cepillarse a F; **liquidation** liquidación *f*; ***go into ~*** ir a la quiebra; **liquidity** FIN liquidez *f*; **liquidize** licuar; **liquidizer** licuadora *f*

liquor ['lɪkər] bebida *f* alcohólica; **liquor store** tienda *f* de bebidas alcohólicas

lisp [lɪsp] **1** *n* ceceo *m* **2** *v/i* cecear

list [lɪst] **1** *n* lista *f* **2** *v/t* enume-

rar
listen ['lɪsn] escuchar
◆ **listen to** escuchar
listener ['lɪsnər] *to radio* oyente *m/f*
listless ['lɪstlɪs] apático
liter ['li:tər] litro *m*
literal ['lɪtərəl] literal; **literally** literalmente
literary ['lɪtərerɪ] literario; **literature** literatura *f*; *about product* folletos *mpl*
litre *Br* ☞ ***liter***
litter ['lɪtər] basura *f*; *of animal* camada *f*
little ['lɪtl] **1** *adj* pequeño **2** *n* poco *m*; ***a ~ wine*** un poco de vino **3** *adv* poco; ***a ~ bigger*** un poco más grande
live[1] [lɪv] *v/i* vivir
◆ **live up to** *expectations* responder a; *reputation* estar a la altura de
live[2] [laɪv] *adj broadcast* en directo; *ammunition* real; *wire* con corriente
livelihood ['laɪvlɪhʊd] vida *f*, sustento *m*; **liveliness** vivacidad *f*; *of debate* lo animado; **lively** animado
liver ['lɪvər] hígado *m*
livestock ['laɪvstɑ:k] ganado *m*
livid ['lɪvɪd] (*angry*) enfurecido, furioso
living ['lɪvɪŋ] **1** *adj* vivo **2** *n* vida *f*; **living room** sala *f* de estar, salón *m*
lizard ['lɪzərd] lagarto *m*
load [loʊd] **1** *n* carga *f* **2** *v/t car, truck, gun* cargar; *camera* poner el carrete a; *software* cargar (en memoria)
loaf [loʊf] pan *m*
◆ **loaf around** F gandulear F
loafer ['loʊfər] *shoe* mocasín *m*
loan [loʊn] **1** *n* préstamo *m*; ***on ~*** prestado **2** *v/t* prestar
loathe [loʊð] detestar, aborrecer; **loathing** odio *m*, aborrecimiento *m*
lobby ['lɑ:bɪ] *in hotel, theater* vestíbulo *m*; POL lobby *m*
lobe [loʊb] *of ear* lóbulo *m*
lobster ['lɑ:bstər] langosta *f*
local ['loʊkl] **1** *adj* local **2** *n* ***are you a ~?*** ¿eres de aquí?; **local call** TELEC llamada *f* local; **local elections** elecciones *fpl* municipales; **local government** administración *f* municipal; **locality** localidad *f*; **localize** localizar; **locally** *live, work* cerca, en la zona; **local time** hora *f* local
locate [loʊ'keɪt] *new factory etc* emplazar, ubicar; (*identify position of*) situar; ***be ~d*** encontrarse; **location** (*siting*) emplazamiento *m*; (*identifying position of*) localización *f*; ***on ~*** *movie* en exteriores
lock[1] [lɑ:k] *n of hair* mechón *m*
lock[2] [lɑ:k] **1** *n on door* cerradura *f* **2** *v/t door* cerrar (con llave)
◆ **lock up** *in prison* encerrar
locker ['lɑ:kər] taquilla *f*; **locker room** vestuario *m*

locust ['loʊkəst] langosta *f*
lodge [lɑːdʒ] **1** *v/t complaint* presentar **2** *v/i of bullet* alojarse
lofty ['lɑːftɪ] elevado
log [lɑːg] *wood* tronco *m*; *written record* registro *m*
◆ **log in** entrar
◆ **log off** salir
◆ **log on** entrar (***to*** a)
◆ **log off** salir
'**log cabin** cabaña *f*
logic ['lɑːdʒɪk] lógica *f*; **logical** lógico; **logically** lógicamente
logistics [lə'dʒɪstɪks] logística *f*
logo ['loʊgoʊ] logotipo *m*
loiter ['lɔɪtər] holgazanear
lollipop ['lɑːlɪpɑːp] piruleta *f*
London ['lʌndən] Londres
loneliness ['loʊnlɪnɪs] soledad *f*; **lonely** *person* solo; *place* solitario; **loner** solitario(-a) *m*(*f*)
long[1] [lɒːŋ] **1** *adj* largo **2** *adv* mucho tiempo; ***that was ~ ago*** eso fue hace mucho tiempo; ***how ~ will it take?*** ¿cuánto se tarda?; ***we can't wait any~er*** no podemos esperar más tiempo; ***so ~ as*** (*provided*) siempre que ; ***so ~!*** ¡hasta la vista!
long[2] [lɒːŋ] *v/i*: ***~ for sth*** *home* echar en falta algo; *change* anhelar algo; ***be ~ing to do sth*** anhelar hacer algo;
long-distance *race* de fondo; *flight*, *call* de larga distancia; **longevity** longevidad *f*; **longing** anhelo *m*; **longitude** longitud *f*; **long jump** salto *m* de longitud; **long-range** *missile* de largo alcance; *forecast* a largo plazo; **long-sleeved** de manga larga; **long-standing** antiguo; **long-term** a largo plazo
loo [luː] *Br* F baño *m*
look [lʊk] **1** *n* (*appearance*) aspecto *m*; (*glance*) mirada *f*; ***~s*** (*beauty*) atractivo *m*, guapura *f* **2** *v/i* mirar; (*search*) buscar; (*seem*) parecer
◆ **look after** *children* cuidar (de); *property* proteger
◆ **look ahead** *fig* mirar hacia el futuro
◆ **look around 1** *v/i* mirar **2** *v/t museum*, *city* dar una vuelta por
◆ **look at** mirar; (*examine*) estudiar; (*consider*) considerar
◆ **look back** mirar atrás
◆ **look down on** mirar por encima del hombro a
◆ **look for** buscar
◆ **look into** (*investigate*) investigar
◆ **look onto** *garden etc* dar a
◆ **look out** *through window etc* mirar; (*pay attention*) tener cuidado
◆ **look over** *translation* revisar; *house* inspeccionar
◆ **look through** *magazine*, *notes* echar un vistazo a
◆ **look up 1** *v/i from paper etc* levantar la mirada; (*improve*) mejorar **2** *v/t word*, *phone number* buscar; (*visit*) visitar

◆ **look up to** (*respect*) admirar
'**lookout** *person* centinela *m*
loop [lu:p] bucle *m*; **loophole** *in law etc* vacío *m* legal
loose [lu:s] *connection, clothes* suelto; *morals* disoluto; *wording* impreciso; **loosely** *worded* vagamente; **loosen** aflojar
loot [lu:t] **1** *n* botín *m* **2** *v/i* saquear; **looter** saqueador(a) *m(f)*
lop-sided [lɑ:p'saɪdɪd] torcido
Lord [lɔ:rd] (*God*) Señor *m*
lorry ['lɑ:rɪ] *Br* camión *m*
lose [lu:z] **1** *v/t* perder **2** *v/i* SP perder; *of clock* retrasarse; **loser** perdedor(-a) *m(f)*; F *in life* fracasado(-a) *m(f)*
loss [lɑ:s] pérdida *f*
lost [lɑ:st] perdido; **lost-and--found**, *Br* **lost property (office)** oficina *f* de objetos perdidos
lot [lɑ:t]: ***a ~* (*of*), *~s* (*of*)** mucho, muchos; ***a ~ easier*** mucho más fácil
lotion ['loʊʃn] loción *f*
lottery ['lɑ:tərɪ] lotería *f*
loud [laʊd] fuerte; *color* chillón; **loudspeaker** altavoz *m*, *L.Am.* altoparlante *m*
louse [laʊs] piojo *m*; *lousy* F asqueroso F
lout [laʊt] gamberro *m*
lovable ['lʌvəbl] adorable, encantador; **love 1** *n* amor *m*; *in tennis* nada *f*; ***fall in ~*** enamorarse (***with*** de); ***make ~*** hacer el amor **2** *v/t* amar; **love affair** aventura *f* amorosa; **lovely** *face, hair, color, tune* precioso, lindo; *person, character* encantador; *holiday, weather, meal* estupendo; **lover** amante *m/f*; **loving** cariñoso; **lovingly** con cariño
low [loʊ] **1** *adj* bajo **2** *n in weather* zona *f* de bajas presiones; *in statistics* mínimo *m*; **lowbrow** poco intelectual; **low-calorie** bajo en calorías; **low-cut** escotado; **lower** *to the ground, hemline, price* bajar; *flag* arriar; *pressure* reducir; **low-fat** de bajo contenido graso; **lowkey** discreto
loyal ['lɔɪəl] leal (***to*** a); **loyally** lealmente; **loyalty** lealtad *f* (***to*** a)
lozenge ['lɑ:zɪndʒ] *shape* rombo *m*; *tablet* pastilla *f*
Ltd (= ***limited***) S.L. (= sociedad *f* limitada)
lubricant ['lu:brɪkənt] lubricante *m*; **lubricate** lubricar; **lubrication** lubricación *f*
lucid ['lu:sɪd] lúcido
luck [lʌk] suerte *f*; ***good ~!*** ¡buena suerte!; **luckily** por suerte; **lucky** *person, coincidence* afortunado; *day, number* de la suerte; ***you were ~*** ¡tuviste suerte!
lucrative ['lu:krətɪv] lucrativo
ludicrous ['lu:dɪkrəs] ridículo
lug [lʌg] arrastrar
luggage ['lʌgɪdʒ] equipaje *m*

lukewarm ['lu:kwɔ:rm] tibio; *reception* indiferente
lull [lʌl] *in storm, fighting* tregua *f*; *in conversation* pausa *f*
lumber ['lʌmbər] (*timber*) madera *f*
luminous ['lu:mɪnəs] luminoso
lump [lʌmp] *of sugar, earth* terrón *m*; (*swelling*) bulto *m*; **lump sum** pago *m* único; **lumpy** *liquid, sauce* grumoso; *mattress* lleno de bultos
lunacy ['lu:nəsɪ] locura *f*
lunar ['lu:nər] lunar
lunatic ['lu:nətɪk] lunático(-a) *m(f)*
lunch [lʌntʃ] almuerzo *m*, comida *f*; ***have*** ~ almorzar, comer; **lunch box** fiambrera *f*; **lunch break** pausa *f* para el almuerzo; **lunchtime** hora *f* del almuerzo
lung [lʌŋ] pulmón *m*
lurch [lɜ:rtʃ] *of drunk* tambalearse; *of ship* dar sacudidas
lure [lʊr] **1** *n* atractivo *m* **2** *v/t* atraer
lurid ['lʊrɪd] *color* chillón; *details* espeluznante
lurk [lɜ:rk] *of person* estar oculto
lush [lʌʃ] *vegetation* exuberante
lust [lʌst] lujuria *f*
luxurious [lʌg'ʒʊrɪəs] lujoso; **luxuriously** lujosamente; **luxury 1** *n* lujo *m* **2** *adj* de lujo
lynch [lɪntʃ] linchar
lyrics ['lɪrɪks] letra *f*

M

ma'am [mæm] señora *f*
machine [mə'ʃi:n] máquina *f*; **machine gun** ametralladora *f*; **machinery** maquinaria *f*
machismo [mə'kɪzmoʊ] machismo *m*
macho ['mætʃoʊ] macho
macro ['mækroʊ] COMPUT macro *m*
mad [mæd] (*insane*) loco; F (*angry*) enfadado; **madden** (*infuriate*) sacar de quici; **maddening** exasperante; **madhouse** *fig* casa *f* de locos; **madman** loco *m*; **madness** locura *f*
Madonna [mə'dɑ:nə] madona *f*
Mafia ['mɑ:fɪə]: ***the*** ~ la mafia
magazine [mægə'zi:n] *printed* revista *f*
Magi ['meɪdʒaɪ] REL: ***the*** ~ los Reyes Magos
magic ['mædʒɪk] **1** *n* magia *f* **2** *adj* mágico; **magical** mágico; **magician** *performer* mago(-a) *m(f)*
magnanimous [mæg'nænɪməs] magnánimo
magnet ['mægnɪt] imán *m*; **magnetic** magnético; *fig: personality* cautivador; **mag-**

netism *of person* magnetismo *m*
magnificence [mæg'nɪfɪsəns] magnificencia *f*; **magnificent** magnífico
magnify ['mægnɪfaɪ] aumentar; *difficulties* magnificar; **magnifying glass** lupa *f*
magnitude ['mægnɪtu:d] magnitud *f*
maid [meɪd] (*servant*) criada *f*; *in hotel* camarera *f*
maiden name ['meɪdn] apellido *m* de soltera
mail [meɪl] **1** *n* correo *m* **2** *v/t letter* enviar (por correo); **mailbox** *also* COMPUT buzón *m*; **mailing list** lista *f* de direcciones; **mailman** cartero *m*; **mailshot** mailing *m*
maim [meɪm] mutilar
main [meɪn] principal; **main course** plato *m* principal; **mainframe** *Span* ordenador *m* central, *L.Am.* computadora *f* central; **mainly** principalmente; **main road** carretera *f* general; **main street** calle *f* principal
maintain [meɪn'teɪn] mantener; **maintenance** mantenimiento *m*
majestic [mə'dʒestɪk] majestuoso
major ['meɪdʒər] **1** *adj* (*significant*) importante, principal **2** *n* MIL comandante *m*
◆ **major in** especializarse en
majority [mə'dʒɑ:rətɪ] *also* POL mayoría *f*
make [meɪk] **1** *n* (*brand*) marca *f* **2** *v/t* hacer; *cars* fabricar, producir; *movie* rodar; *speech* pronunciar; *decision* tomar; (*earn*) ganar; MATH hacer; ***two and two ~ four*** dos y dos son cuatro; ***~ s.o. do sth*** (*force to*) obligar a alguien a hacer algo; (*cause to*) hacer que alguien haga algo; ***~ s.o. happy / angry*** hacer feliz / enfadar a alguien; ***~ it*** (*catch bus, train*) llegar a tiempo; (*come*) ir; (*succeed*) tener éxito; (*survive*) sobrevivir; ***what time do you ~ it?*** ¿qué hora llevas?; ***~ do with*** conformarse con; ***what do you ~ of it?*** ¿qué piensas?
◆ **make out** *list* hacer, elaborar; *check* extender; (*see*) distinguir; (*imply*) pretender
◆ **make up 1** *v/i of woman, actor* maquillarse; *after quarrel* reconciliarse **2** *v/t story* inventar; *face* maquillar; (*constitute*) suponer, formar
◆ **make up for** compensar por
'make-believe ficción *f*, fantasía *f*
maker ['meɪkər] (*manufacturer*) fabricante *m*; **makeshift** improvisado; **make-up** (*cosmetics*) maquillaje *m*
maladjusted [mælə'dʒʌstɪd] inadaptado
male [meɪl] **1** *adj* masculino; *animal* macho **2** *n man* hombre *m*, varón *m*; *animal, bird* macho *m*; **male chauvinism**

machismo *m*; **male chauvinist pig** machista *m*

malevolent [mə'levələnt] malévolo

malfunction [mæl'fʌŋkʃn] **1** *n* fallo *m* (***in*** de) **2** *v/i* fallar

malice ['mælɪs] malicia *f*; **malicious** malicioso

malignant [mə'lɪgnənt] *tumor* maligno

mall [mɒːl] (*shopping* **~**) centro *m* comercial

malnutrition [mælnuː'trɪʃn] desnutrición *f*

maltreat [mæl'triːt] maltratar; **maltreatment** maltrato *m*

mammal ['mæml] mamífero *m*

man [mæn] **1** *n* hombre *m*; (*humanity*) el hombre; *in checkers* ficha *f* **2** *v/t telephones*, *front desk* atender; *spacecraft* tripular

manage ['mænɪdʒ] **1** *v/t business* dirigir; *money* gestionar; *suitcase* poder con; **~ *to* ...** conseguir... **2** *v/i* (*cope*) arreglárselas; **manageable** (*easy to handle*) manejable; (*feasible*) factible; **management** (*managing*) gestión *f*, administración *f*; (*managers*) dirección *f*; **management consultant** consultor(a) *m(f)* en administración de empresas; **manager** *of hotel*, *company* director(a) *m(f)*; *of shop*, *restaurant* encargado(a) *m(f)*; **managerial** de gestión; **managing director** director(a) *m(f)* gerente

mandate ['mændeɪt] (*authority*) mandato *m*; (*task*) tarea *f*; **mandatory** obligatorio

maneuver [mə'nuːvər] **1** *n* maniobra *f* **2** *v/t* maniobrar

mangle ['mæŋgl] (*crush*) destrozar

manhandle ['mænhændl] mover a la fuerza

manhood ['mænhʊd] madurez *f*; (*virility*) virilidad *f*; **manhunt** persecución *f*

mania ['meɪnɪə] (*craze*) pasión *f*; **maniac** F chiflado(-a) *m(f)* F

manicure ['mænɪkjʊr] manicura *f*

manifest ['mænɪfest] **1** *adj* manifiesto **2** *v/t* manifestar

manipulate [mə'nɪpjəleɪt] *person*, *bones* manipular; **manipulation** *of person*, *bones* manipulación *f*; **manipulative** manipulador

man'kind la humanidad; **manly** (*brave*) de hombres; (*strong*) varonil; **man-made** *materials* sintético; *structure* artificial

manner ['mænər] *of doing sth* manera *f*, modo *m*; (*attitude*) actitud *f*; **manners** modales *mpl*; ***good*** / ***bad* ~** buena / mala educación

manoeuvre *Br* ☞ ***maneuver***

'manpower (*workers*) mano *f* de obra; *for other tasks* recursos *mpl* humanos

manual ['mænjʊəl] **1** *adj* manual **2** *n* manual *m*; **manu-**

ally a mano

manufacture [mænjʊ'fæktʃər] **1** *n* fabricación *f* **2** *v/t equipment* fabricar; **manufacturer** fabricante *m*; **manufacturing** *industry* manufacturero

manure [mə'nʊr] estiércol *m*

manuscript ['mænjʊskrɪpt] manuscrito *m*

many ['menɪ] **1** *adj* muchos; ***take as ~ apples as you like*** toma todas las manzanas que quieras; ***too ~ problems*** demasiados problemas **2** *pron* muchos; ***a great ~, a good ~*** muchos; ***how ~ do you need?*** ¿cuántos necesitas?; ***as ~ as 200*** hasta 200

map [mæp] mapa *m*

maple ['meɪpl] arce *m*

mar [mɑːr] empañar

marathon ['mærəθɑːn] *race* maratón *m or f*

marble ['mɑːrbl] *material* mármol *m*

March [mɑːrtʃ] marzo *m*

march [mɑːrtʃ] **1** *n* marcha *f* **2** *v/i* marchar; **marcher** manifestante *m/f*

Mardi Gras ['mɑːrdɪgrɑː] martes *m inv* de Carnaval

margin ['mɑːrdʒɪn] *also* COM margen *m*; **marginal** (*slight*) marginal; **marginally** (*slightly*) ligeramente

marihuana, marijuana [mærɪ'hwɑːnə] marihuana *f*

marina [mə'riːnə] puerto *m* deportivo

marine [mə'riːn] **1** *adj* marino **2** *n* MIL marine *m/f*, infante *m/f* de marina

marital ['mærɪtl] marital; **marital status** estado *m* civil

maritime ['mærɪtaɪm] marítimo

mark [mɑːrk] **1** *n* señal *f*, marca *f*; (*stain*) marca *f*, mancha *f*; (*sign, token*) signo *m*, señal *f*; (*trace*) señal *f*; *Br* EDU nota *f* **2** *v/t* (*stain*) manchar; *Br* EDU calificar; (*indicate, commemorate*) marcar **3** *v/i of fabric* mancharse; **marked** (*definite*) marcado, notable; **marker** (*highlighter*) rotulador *m*

market ['mɑːrkɪt] **1** *n* mercado *m*; (*stock ~*) bolsa *f* **2** *v/t* comercializar; **marketable** comercializable; **market economy** economía *f* de mercado; **marketing** marketing *m*; **market leader** líder *m* del mercado; **marketplace** *in town* plaza *f* del mercado; *for commodities* mercado *m*; **market research** investigación *f* de mercado; **market share** cuota *f* de mercado

mark-up ['mɑːrkʌp] margen *m*

marriage ['mærɪdʒ] matrimonio *m*; *event* boda *f*; **marriage certificate** certificado *m* de matrimonio; **married** casado; ***be ~ to ...*** estar casado con...; **married life** vida *f* matrimonial; **marry** casarse con; *of priest* casar; ***get mar-***

ried casarse
marsh [mɑːrʃ] *Br* pantano *m*, ciénaga *f*
marshal ['mɑːrʃl] *in police* jefe(-a) *m(f)* de policía; *in security service* miembro *m* del servicio de seguridad
martial 'law ley *f* marcial
martyr ['mɑːrtər] mártir *m/f*
marvel ['mɑːrvl] maravilla *f*; **marvelous,** *Br* **marvellous** maravilloso
Marxism ['mɑːrksɪzm] marxismo *m*; **Marxist 1** *adj* marxista **2** *n* marxista *m/f*
mascara [mæ'skærə] rímel *m*
mascot ['mæskət] mascota *f*
masculine ['mæskjʊlɪn] masculino; **masculinity** (*virility*) masculinidad *f*
mash [mæʃ] hacer puré de, majar
mask [mæsk] **1** *n* máscara *f*; *to cover mouth, nose* mascarilla *f* **2** *v/t feelings* enmascarar
masochism ['mæsəkɪzm] masoquismo *m*; **masochist** masoquista *m/f*
mass[1] [mæs] **1** *n* (*great amount*) gran cantidad *f*; (*body*) masa *f*; ***~es of*** F un montón de F **2** *v/i* concentrarse
mass[2] [mæs] *n* REL misa *f*
massacre ['mæsəkər] **1** *n* masacre *f*, matanza *f*; F *in sport* paliza *f* **2** *v/t* masacrar; F *in sport* dar una paliza a
massage ['mæsɑːʒ] **1** *n* masaje *m* **2** *v/t* dar un masaje en; *figures* maquillar
massive ['mæsɪv] enorme; *heart attack* muy grave
mass 'media medios *mpl* de comunicación; **mass-produce** fabricar en serie; **mass production** fabricación *f* en serie
mast [mæst] *of ship* mástil *m*; *for radio signal* torre *f*
master ['mæstər] **1** *n of dog* dueño *m*, amo *m*; *of ship* patrón *m* **2** *v/t skill* dominar; **master bedroom** dormitorio *m* principal; **master key** llave *f* maestra; **masterly** magistral; **mastermind 1** *n* cerebro *m* **2** *v/t* dirigir, organizar; **masterpiece** obra *f* maestra; **master's (degree)** máster *m*; **mastery** dominio *m*
mat [mæt] *for floor* estera *f*; *for table* salvamanteles *m inv*
match[1] [mætʃ] *n for cigarette* cerilla *f*, fósforo *m*
match[2] [mætʃ] **1** *n* SP partido *m*; *in chess* partida *f* **2** *v/t* (*be the same as*) coincidir con; (*be in harmony with*) hacer juego con; (*equal*) igualar **3** *v/i of colors* hacer juego; **matching** a juego; **matchstick** cerilla *f*, fósforo *m*
mate [meɪt] **1** *n of animal* pareja *f*; NAUT oficial *m/f* **2** *v/i* aparearse
material [mə'tɪrɪəl] **1** *n* (*fabric*) tejido *m*; (*substance*) material *m* **2** *adj* material; **materialism** materialismo *m*; **materialist** materialista

m/f; **materialistic** materialista; **materialize** (*appear*) aparecer; (*come into existence*) hacerse realidad

maternal [mə'tɜːrnl] maternal; **maternity** maternidad *f*; **maternity leave** baja *f* por maternidad

math [mæθ] matemáticas *fpl*; **mathematical** matemático; **mathematician** matemático(-a) *m(f)*

maths *Br* ☞ **math**

matinée ['mætɪneɪ] sesión *f* de tarde

matriarch ['meɪtrɪɑːrk] matriarca *f*

matrimony ['mætrəmounɪ] matrimonio *m*

matt [mæt] mate

matter ['mætər] **1** *n* (*affair*) asunto *m*; PHYS materia *f*; ***what's the ~?*** ¿qué pasa? **2** *v/i* importar; ***it doesn't ~*** no importa; **matter-of-fact** tranquilo

mattress ['mætrɪs] colchón *m*

mature [mə'ʧʊr] **1** *adj* maduro **2** *v/i of person* madurar; *of insurance policy* vencer; **maturity** madurez *f*

maximize ['mæksɪmaɪz] maximizar; **maximum 1** *adj* máximo **2** *n* máximo *m*

May [meɪ] mayo *m*

may [meɪ] *v/aux* ◇ *possibility*: ***it ~ rain*** puede que llueva; ***you ~ be right*** puede que tengas razón; ***it ~ not happen*** puede que no ocurra ◇ *permission* poder; ***~ I help?*** ¿puedo ayudar

maybe ['meɪbiː] quizás, tal vez

mayo, mayonnaise ['meɪou, meɪə'neɪz] mayonesa *f*

mayor [mer] alcalde *m*

maze [meɪz] laberinto *m*

MB (= ***megabyte***) MB (= megabyte *m*)

MBA [embiː'eɪ] (= ***Master of Business Administration***) MBA *m* (= Máster *m* en Administración de Empresas)

MD [em'diː] (= ***Doctor of Medicine***) Doctor(a) *m(f)* en Medicina; (= ***managing director***) director(a) *m(f)* gerente

me [miː] *object* me; *after prep* mí; ***he knows ~*** me conoce; ***he sold it to ~*** me lo vendió; ***this is for ~*** esto es para mí; ***with ~*** conmigo; ***it's ~*** soy yo; ***taller than ~*** más alto que yo

meadow ['medou] prado *m*

meager, *Br* **meagre** ['miːgər] escaso, exiguo

meal [miːl] comida *f*

mean[1] [miːn] *adj with money* tacaño; (*nasty*) malo, cruel

mean[2] [miːn] *v/t* (*intend to say*) querer decir; (*signify*) querer decir, significar; ***be ~t for*** ser para; *of remark* ir dirigido a; **meaning** *of word* significado *m*; **meaningful** (*comprehensible*) con sentido; (*constructive*), *glance* significativo; **meaningless** sin sentido

means [miːnz] *financial* medios *mpl*; (*way*) medio *m*;

by all ~ (*certainly*) por supuesto; ***by ~ of*** mediante
meantime ['miːntaɪm] mientras tanto
measles ['miːzlz] sarampión *m*
measure ['meʒər] **1** *n* (*step*) medida *f* **2** *v/t & v/i* medir
◆ **measure up** estar a la altura (***to*** de)
measurement ['meʒərmənt] medida *f*; **measuring tape** cinta *f* métrica
meat [miːt] carne *f*; **meatball** albóndiga *f*
mechanic [mɪ'kænɪk] mecánico(-a) *m*(*f*); **mechanical** *also fig* mecánico; **mechanical engineer** ingeniero(-a) *m*(*f*) industrial; **mechanically** *also fig* mecánicamente; **mechanism** mecanismo *m*; **mechanize** mecanizar
medal ['medl] medalla *f*; **medalist**, *Br* **medallist** medallista *m/f*
meddle ['medl] entrometerse
media ['miːdɪə]: ***the ~*** los medios de comunicación; **media coverage** cobertura *f* informativa
median strip [miːdɪən'strɪp] mediana *f*
'**media studies** ciencias *fpl* de la información
mediate ['miːdɪeɪt] mediar; **mediation** mediación *f*; **mediator** mediador(a) *m*(*f*)
medical ['medɪkl] **1** *adj* médico **2** *n* reconocimiento *m* médico; **medicated** medicinal; **medication** medicamento *m*, medicina *f*; **medicinal** medicinal; **medicine** *science* medicina *f*; (*medication*) medicina *f*, medicamento *m*
medieval [medɪ'iːvl] medieval
mediocre [miːdɪ'oʊkər] mediocre; **mediocrity** *of work etc*, *person* mediocridad *f*
meditate ['medɪteɪt] meditar; **meditation** meditación *f*
Mediterranean [medɪtə'reɪnɪən] **1** *adj* mediterráneo **2** *n*: ***the ~*** el Mediterráneo
medium ['miːdɪəm] **1** *adj* (*average*) medio; *steak* a punto **2** *n size* talla *f* media; (*means*) medio *m*; (*spiritualist*) médium *m/f*
medley ['medlɪ] (*assortment*) mezcla *f*
meet [miːt] **1** *v/t by appointment* encontrarse con, reunirse con; *by chance*, *of eyes* encontrarse con; (*get to know*) conocer; (*collect*) ir a buscar; *in competition* enfrentarse con; (*satisfy*) satisfacer **2** *v/i* encontrarse; *in competition* enfrentarse; *of committee etc* reunirse **3** *n* SP reunión *f*; **meeting** *by chance* encuentro *m*; *in business* reunión *f*
megabyte ['megəbaɪt] COMPUT megabyte *m*
mellow ['meloʊ] **1** *adj* suave **2** *v/i of person* suavizarse, sosegarse

melodious [mɪ'loudɪəs] melodioso
melodramatic [melədrə'mætɪk] melodramático
melody ['melədɪ] melodía *f*
melon ['melən] melón *m*
melt [melt] **1** *v/i* fundirse, derretirse **2** *v/t* fundir, derretir; **melting pot** *fig* crisol *m*
member ['membər] miembro *m*; **Member of Congress** diputado(-a) *m(f)*; **membership** afiliación *f*; *number of members* número *m* de miembros
membrane ['membreɪn] membrana *f*
memento [me'mentou] recuerdo *m*
memo ['memou] nota *f*
memoirs ['memwɑːrz] memorias *fpl*
memorable ['memərəbl] memorable
memorial [mɪ'mɔːrɪəl] **1** *adj* conmemorativo **2** *n* monumento *m* conmemorativo; **Memorial Day** Día *m* de los Caídos
memorize ['meməraɪz] memorizar; **memory** (*recollection*) recuerdo *m*; (*power of recollection*), COMPUT memoria *f*
men [men] *pl* ☞ ***man***
menace ['menɪs] **1** *n* amenaza *f*; *person* peligro *m* **2** *v/t* amenazar; **menacing** amenazador
mend [mend] reparar; *clothes* coser, remendar; *shoes* remendar
menial ['miːnɪəl] ingrato, penoso
menopause ['menəpɒːz] menopausia *f*
'men's room servicio *m* de caballeros
menstruate ['menstrueɪt] menstruar
mental ['mentl] mental; F (*crazy*) chiflado F, pirado F; **mental hospital** hospital *m* psiquiátrico; **mental illness** enfermedad *f* mental; **mentality** mentalidad *f*; **mentally** mentalmente
mention ['menʃn] **1** *n* mención *f* **2** *v/t* mencionar; ***don't ~ it*** (*you're welcome*) no hay de qué
mentor ['mentɔːr] mentor(a) *m(f)*
menu ['menuː] *for food*, COMPUT menú *m*
mercenary ['mɜːrsɪnərɪ] **1** *adj* mercenario **2** *n* MIL mercenario(-a) *m(f)*
merchandise ['mɜːrtʃəndaɪz] mercancías *fpl*, *L.Am.* mercadería *f*
merchant ['mɜːrtʃənt] comerciante *m/f*
merciful ['mɜːrsɪfəl] compasivo, piadoso; **mercifully** (*thankfully*) afortunadamente; **merciless** despiadado; **mercy** clemencia *f*, compasión *f*
mere [mɪr] mero, simple; **merely** meramente, simplemente

merge [mɜːrdʒ] *of two lines etc* juntarse, unirse; *of companies* fusionarse; **merger** COM fusión *f*
merit ['merɪt] **1** *n* (*worth*) mérito *m*; (*advantage*) ventaja *f* **2** *v/t* merecer
mesh [meʃ] malla *f*
mess [mes] (*untidiness*) desorden *m*; (*trouble*) lío *m*
message ['mesɪdʒ] *also of movie etc* mensaje *m*
messenger ['mesɪndʒər] (*courier*) mensajero(-a) *m*(*f*)
messy ['mesɪ] *room, person* desordenado; *job* sucio; *divorce* desagradable
metabolism [mə'tæbəlɪzm] metabolismo *m*
metal ['metl] **1** *n* metal *m* **2** *adj* metálico; **metallic** metálico
metaphor ['metəfər] metáfora *f*
meteor ['miːtɪər] meteoro *m*; **meteoric** *fig* meteórico; **meteorite** meteorito *m*
meteorological [miːtɪrə'lɑːdʒɪkl] meteorológico; **meteorologist** meteorólogo(-a) *m*(*f*); **meteorology** meteorología *f*
meter[1] ['miːtər] *for gas, electricity* contador *m*; (*parking* ~) parquímetro *m*
meter[2] ['miːtər] *unit of length* metro *m*
method ['meθəd] método *m*; **methodical** metódico
meticulous [mə'tɪkjʊləs] meticuloso, minucioso
metre *Br* ☞ ***meter***[2]
metropolis [mɪ'trɑːpəlɪs] metrópolis *f inv*; **metropolitan** metropolitano
mew [mjuː] ☞ ***miaow***
Mexican ['meksɪkən] **1** *adj* mexicano, mejicano **2** *n* mexicano(-a) *m*(*f*), mejicano(-a) *m*(*f*); **Mexico** México, Méjico; **Mexico City** Ciudad *f* de México, *Mex* México, *Mex* el Distrito Federal, *Mex* el D.F.
miaow [mɪaʊ] **1** *n* maullido *m* **2** *v/i* maullar
mice [maɪs] *pl* ☞ ***mouse***
'**microchip** microchip *m*; **microclimate** microclima *m*; **microcosm** microcosmos *m inv*; **microorganism** microorganismo *m*; **microphone** micrófono *m*; **microprocessor** microprocesador *m*; **microscope** microscopio *m*; **microscopic** microscópico; **microwave** *oven* microondas *m inv*
midday [mɪd'deɪ] mediodía *m*
middle ['mɪdl] **1** *adj* del medio **2** *n* medio *m*; ***be in the ~ of doing sth*** estar ocupado haciendo algo; **middle-aged** de mediana edad; **middle-class** de clase media; ***middle class(es)*** clases *fpl* medias; **Middle East** Oriente *m* Medio; **middleman** intermediario *m*; **middle name** segundo nombre *m*; **middleweight** *boxer* peso *m* medio
midfielder [mɪd'fiːldər] centrocampista *m/f*

midget ['mɪdʒɪt] en miniatura
midnight ['mɪdnaɪt] medianoche *f*; **midsummer** pleno verano *m*; **midweek** a mitad de semana; **Midwest** Medio Oeste *m* (de Estados Unidos); **midwife** comadrona *f*; **midwinter** pleno invierno *m*
might[1] [maɪt] *v/aux* poder, ser posible que; ***I ~ be late*** puede *or* es posible que llegue tarde; ***you ~ have told me!*** ¡me lo podías haber dicho!
might[2] [maɪt] *n* (*power*) poder *m*, fuerza *f*
mighty ['maɪtɪ] **1** *adj* poderoso **2** *adv* F (*extremely*) muy, cantidad de F
migraine ['mi:greɪn] migraña *f*
migrant worker ['maɪgrənt] trabajador(a) *m(f)* itinerante; **migrate** emigrar; **migration** emigración *f*
mike [maɪk] F micro *m* F
mild [maɪld] *weather* apacible; *cheese, voice* suave; *curry etc* no muy picante; **mildly** *say sth* con suavidad; *spicy* ligeramente; **mildness** *of weather, voice* suavidad *f*
mile [maɪl] milla *f*; **milestone** *fig* hito *m*
militant ['mɪlɪtənt] **1** *adj* militante **2** *n* militante *m/f*
military ['mɪlɪterɪ] **1** *adj* militar **2** *n*: ***the ~*** el ejército, las fuerzas armadas
militia [mɪ'lɪʃə] milicia *f*
milk [mɪlk] **1** *n* leche *f* **2** *v/t* ordeñar; **milk chocolate** chocolate *m* con leche; **milkshake** batido *m*
mill [mɪl] *for grain* molino *m*; *for textiles* fábrica *f* de tejidos
millennium [mɪ'lenɪəm] milenio *m*
milligram ['mɪlɪgræm] miligramo *m*
millimeter, *Br* **millimetre** ['mɪlɪmi:tər] milímetro *m*
million ['mɪljən] millón *m*; **millionaire** millonario(-a) *m(f)*
mime [maɪm] representar con gestos
mimic ['mɪmɪk] **1** *n* imitador(a) *m(f)* **2** *v/t* imitar
mince [mɪns] picar
mind [maɪnd] **1** *n* mente *f*; ***bear*** *or* ***keep sth in ~*** recordar algo; ***change one's ~*** cambiar de opinión; ***make up one's ~*** decidirse; ***have something on one's ~*** tener algo en la cabeza; ***keep one's ~ on sth*** concentrarse en algo **2** *v/t* (*look after*) cuidar (de); (*heed*) prestar atención a; ***I don't ~ what we do*** no me importa lo que hagamos; ***do you ~ if I smoke?*** ¿le importa que fume? **3** *v/i*: ***never ~!*** ¡no importa!; ***I don't ~*** no me importa, me da igual; **mind-boggling** increíble; **mindless** *violence* gratuito
mine[1] [maɪn] *pron* el mío, la mía; ***that book is ~*** eso libro es mío; ***a cousin of ~*** un primo mío

mine[2] [maɪn] *n for coal etc* mina *f*
mine[3] [maɪn] **1** *n* (*explosive*) mina *f* **2** *v/t* minar
'minefield MIL campo *m* de minas; *fig* campo *m* minado; **miner** minero(-a) *m(f)*
mineral ['mɪnərəl] mineral *m*; **mineral water** agua *f* mineral
'minesweeper NAUT dragaminas *m inv*
mingle ['mɪŋgl] *of sounds etc* mezclarse; *at party* alternar
mini ['mɪnɪ] *skirt* minifalda *f*
miniature ['mɪnɪʧər] en miniatura
minimal ['mɪnɪməl] mínimo; **minimalism** minimalismo *m*; **minimize** minimizar; **minimum** **1** *adj* mínimo **2** *n* mínimo *m*
mining ['maɪnɪŋ] minería *f*
'miniskirt minifalda *f*
minister ['mɪnɪstər] POL ministro(-a) *m(f)*; REL ministro(-a) *m(f)*, pastor(a) *m(f)*; **ministerial** ministerial
'minivan monovolumen *m*
mink [mɪŋk] visón *m*; *coat* abrigo *m* de visón
minor ['maɪnər] **1** *adj problem, setback* menor, pequeño; *operation, argument* de poca importancia; *aches and pains* leve **2** *n* LAW menor *m/f* de edad; **minority** minoría *f*
mint [mɪnt] *herb* menta *f*; *chocolate* pastilla *f* de chocolate con sabor a menta; *hard candy* caramelo *m* de menta
minus ['maɪnəs] **1** *n* (~ *sign*) (signo *m* de) menos *m* **2** *prep* menos
minuscule ['mɪnəskju:l] minúsculo
minute[1] ['mɪnɪt] *n of time* minuto *m*
minute[2] [maɪ'nu:t] *adj* (*tiny*) diminuto, minúsculo; (*detailed*) minucioso
'minute hand ['mɪnɪt] minutero *m*
minutely [maɪ'nu:tlɪ] *in detail* minuciosamente; (*very slightly*) mínimamente
minutes ['mɪnɪts] *of meeting* acta(s) *f(pl)*
miracle ['mɪrəkl] milagro *m*; **miraculous** milagroso; **miraculously** milagrosamente
mirror ['mɪrər] **1** *n* espejo *m*; MOT (espejo *m*) retrovisor *m* **2** *v/t* reflejar
misanthropist [mɪ'zænθrəpɪst] misántropo(-a) *m(f)*
misbehave [mɪsbə'heɪv] portarse mal; **misbehavior**, *Br* **misbehaviour** mal comportamiento *m*
miscalculate [mɪs'kælkjʊleɪt] calcular mal; **miscalculation** error *m* de cálculo
miscarriage ['mɪskærɪdʒ] MED aborto *m* (espontáneo)
miscellaneous [mɪsə'leɪnɪəs] diverso
mischief ['mɪsʧɪf] (*naughtiness*) travesura *f*, trastada *f*; **mischievous** (*naughty*) travieso; (*malicious*) malicioso
misconception [mɪs-

kən'sepʃn] idea *f* equivocada
misconduct [mɪs'kɑːndʌkt] mala conducta *f*
misconstrue [mɪskən'struː] malinterpretar
misdemeanor, *Br* **misdemeanour** [mɪsdə'miːnər] falta *f*, delito *m* menor
miser ['maɪzər] avaro(-a) *m*(*f*)
miserable ['mɪzrəbl] (*unhappy*) triste, infeliz; *weather, performance* horroroso
miserly ['maɪzərlɪ] *person* avaro
misery ['mɪzərɪ] (*unhappiness*) tristeza *f*, infelicidad *f*; (*wretchedness*) miseria *f*
misfire [mɪs'faɪr] *of joke, scheme* salir mal
misfit ['mɪsfɪt] *in society* inadaptado(-a) *m*(*f*)
misfortune [mɪs'fɔːrʧən] desgracia *f*
misguided [mɪs'gaɪdɪd] *person* equivocado; *attempt, plan* desacertado
mishandle [mɪs'hændl] *situation* llevar mal
misinform [mɪsɪn'fɔːrm] informar mal
misinterpret [mɪsɪn'tɜːrprɪt] malinterpretar; **misinterpretation** mala interpretación *f*
misjudge [mɪs'dʒʌdʒ] *person, situation* juzgar mal
mislay [mɪs'leɪ] perder
mislead [mɪs'liːd] engañar; **misleading** engañoso
mismanage [mɪs'mænɪdʒ] gestionar mal; **mismanagement** mala gestión *f*
misprint ['mɪsprɪnt] errata *f*
mispronounce [mɪsprə'naʊns] pronunciar mal; **mispronunciation** pronunciación *f* incorrecta
misread [mɪs'riːd] *word, figures* leer mal; *situation* malinterpretar
misrepresent [mɪsreprɪ'zent] deformar, tergiversar
miss[1] [mɪs]: ***Miss Smith*** la señorita Smith; ***~!*** ¡señorita!
miss[2] [mɪs] **1** *n* SP fallo *m* **2** *v/t target* no dar en; *emotionally* echar de menos; *bus, train* perder; (*not notice*) pasar por alto; (*not be present at*) perderse; ***~ a class*** faltar a una clase **3** *v/i* fallar
misshapen [mɪs'ʃeɪpən] deforme
missile ['mɪsəl] misil *m*; (*sth thrown*) arma *f* arrojadiza
missing ['mɪsɪŋ] desaparecido; ***be ~*** *of person, plane* haber desaparecido
mission ['mɪʃn] *task* misión *f*; *people* delegación *f*
misspell [mɪs'spel] escribir incorrectamente
mist [mɪst] neblina *f*
mistake [mɪ'steɪk] **1** *n* error *m*, equivocación *f*; ***make a ~*** cometer un error, equivocarse; *v/t* confundir; ***~ X for Y*** confundir X con Y; **mistaken** erróneo, equivocado; ***be ~*** estar equivocado
mister ['mɪstər] ☞ ***Mr***

mistress ['mɪstrɪs] *lover* amante *f*, querida *f*; *of servant* ama *f*; *of dog* dueña *f*, ama *f*
mistrust [mɪs'trʌst] **1** *n* desconfianza *f* (***of*** en) **2** *v/t* desconfiar de
misunderstand [mɪsʌndər'stænd] entender mal; **misunderstanding** (*mistake*) malentendido *m*; (*argument*) desacuerdo *m*
misuse 1 [mɪs'ju:s] *n* uso *m* indebido **2** [mɪs'ju:z] *v/t* usar indebidamente
mitigating circumstances ['mɪtɪgeɪtɪŋ] circunstancias *fpl* atenuantes
mitt [mɪt] *in baseball* guante *m* de béisbol; **mitten** mitón *m*
mix [mɪks] **1** *n* (*mixture*) mezcla *f*; *cooking*: *ready to use* preparado *m* **2** *v/t* mezclar; *cement* preparar **3** *v/i socially* relacionarse
◆ **mix up** (*confuse*) confundir (***with*** con); (*put in wrong order*) revolver, desordenar; ***be mixed up in*** estar metido en
mixed [mɪkst] *feelings* contradictorio; *reviews* variado; **mixer** *for food* batidora *f*; *drink* refresco *m* (*para mezclar con bebida alcohólica*); **mixture** mezcla *f*; *medicine* preparado *m*; **mix-up** confusión *f*
moan [moʊn] **1** *n of pain* gemido *m* **2** *v/i in pain* gemir
mob [mɑ:b] **1** *n* muchedumbre *f* **2** *v/t* asediar, acosar
mobile ['moʊbəl] **1** *adj person* con movilidad; (*that can be moved*) móvil **2** *n* móvil *m*; **mobile home** casa *f* caravana; **mobile phone** *Br* teléfono *m* móvil; **mobility** movilidad *f*
mobster ['mɑ:bstər] gángster *m*
mock [mɑ:k] **1** *adj* fingido, simulado **2** *v/t* burlarse de; **mockery** (*derision*) burlas *fpl*; (*travesty*) farsa *f*
mode [moʊd] (*form*), COMPUT modo *m*
model ['mɑ:dl] **1** *adj employee, husband* modélico, modelo **2** *n miniature* maqueta *f*, modelo *m*; (*pattern*) modelo *m*; (*fashion* ~) modelo *m/f* **3** *v/i for designer* trabajar de modelo; *for artist, photographer* posar
modem ['moʊdem] módem *m*
moderate 1 ['mɑ:dərət] *adj* moderado **2** ['mɑ:dərət] *n* POL moderado(-a) *m*(*f*) **3** ['mɑ:dəreɪt] *v/t* moderar; **moderately** medianamente, razonablemente; **moderation** moderación *f*
modern ['mɑ:dn] moderno; **modernization** modernización *f*; **modernize 1** *v/t* modernizar **2** *v/i of business, country* modernizarse
modest ['mɑ:dɪst] modesto; **modesty** modestia *f*
modification [mɑ:dɪfɪ'keɪʃn] modificación *f*; **modify** modificar
module ['mɑ:du:l] módulo *m*

moist [mɔɪst] húmedo; **moisten** humedecer; **moisture** humedad *f*; **moisturizer** *for skin* crema *f* hidratante

molasses [mə'læsɪz] melaza *f*

mold[1] [mould] *n on food* moho *m*

mold[2] [mould] **1** *n* molde *m* **2** *v/t clay, character* moldear

moldy ['mouldɪ] *food* mohoso

molecule ['mɑːlɪkjuːl] molécula *f*

molest [mə'lest] *child, woman* abusar sexualmente de

mollycoddle ['mɑːlɪkɑːdl] F mimar, consentir

molten ['moultən] fundido

mom [mɑːm] F mamá *f*

moment ['moumənt] momento *m*; ***at the ~*** en estos momentos, ahora mismo; **momentarily** (*for a moment*) momentáneamente; (*in a moment*) de un momento a otro; **momentary** momentáneo; **momentous** trascendental, muy importante

momentum [mə'mentəm] impulso *m*

monarch ['mɑːnərk] monarca *m/f*

monastery ['mɑːnəsterɪ] monasterio *m*; **monastic** monástico

Monday ['mʌndeɪ] lunes *m inv*

monetary ['mɑːnɪterɪ] monetario

money ['mʌnɪ] dinero *m*; **money belt** faltriquera *f*; **money market** mercado *m* monetario; **money order** giro *m* postal

mongrel ['mʌŋgrəl] perro *m* cruzado

monitor ['mɑːnɪtər] **1** *n* COMPUT monitor *m* **2** *v/t* controlar

monk [mʌŋk] monje *m*

monkey ['mʌŋkɪ] mono *m*; F *child* diablillo *m* F; **monkey wrench** llave *f* inglesa

monolog, *Br* **monologue** ['mɑːnəlɑːg] monólogo *m*

monopolize [mə'nɑːpəlaɪz] monopolizar; **monopoly** monopolio *m*

monotonous [mə'nɑːtənəs] monótono; **monotony** monotonía *f*

monster ['mɑːnstər] monstruo *m*; **monstrosity** monstruosidad *f*

month [mʌnθ] mes *m*; **monthly 1** *adj* mensual **2** *adv* mensualmente **3** *n magazine* revista *f* mensual

monument ['mɑːnumənt] monumento *m*

mood [muːd] (*frame of mind*) humor *m*; (*bad ~*) mal humor *m*; *of meeting, country* atmósfera *f*; **moody** temperamental; (*bad-tempered*) malhumorado

moon [muːn] luna *f*; **moonlight** luz *f* de luna; **moonlit** iluminado por la luna

moor [mur] *boat* atracar

moose [muːs] alce *m* americano

mop [mɑːp] **1** *n for floor* fregona *f*; *for dishes* estropajo *m* (*con mango*) **2** *v/t floor* fregar; *face* limpiar
◆ **mop up** limpiar; MIL acabar con
moral ['mɔːrəl] **1** *adj* moral; *person, behavior* moralista **2** *n of story* moraleja *f*; **~s** moral *f*, moralidad *f*
morale [mə'ræl] moral *f*
morality [mə'rælətɪ] moralidad *f*
morbid ['mɔːrbɪd] morboso
more [mɔːr] **1** *adj* más; ***there are no ~ eggs*** no quedan huevos; ***some ~ tea?*** ¿más té?; ***~ and ~ students*** cada vez más estudiantes **2** *adv* más; ***~ important*** más importante; ***~ and ~*** cada vez más; ***~ or less*** más o menos; ***once ~*** una vez más; ***~ than $100*** más de 100 dólares; ***he earns ~ than I do*** gana más que yo; ***I don't live there any ~*** ya no vivo allí **3** *pron* más; ***a little ~*** un poco más; **moreover** además
morgue [mɔːrg] depósito *m* de cadáveres
morning ['mɔːrnɪŋ] mañana *f*; ***in the ~*** por la mañana; ***tomorrow ~*** mañana por la mañana; ***good ~*** buenos días
moron ['mɔːrɑːn] F imbécil *m/f* F, subnormal *m/f* F
morphine ['mɔːrfiːn] morfina *f*
mortal ['mɔːrtl] **1** *adj* mortal **2** *n* mortal *m/f*; **mortality** mortalidad *f*
mortar ['mɔːrtər] MIL, *cement* mortero *m*
mortgage ['mɔːrgɪdʒ] **1** *n* hipoteca *f* **2** *v/t* hipotecar
mosaic [moʊ'zeɪɪk] mosaico *m*
Moscow ['mɑːskaʊ] Moscú
Moslem ['mʊzlɪm] **1** *adj* musulmán **2** *n* musulmán(-ana) *m*(*f*)
mosque [mɑːsk] mezquita *f*
mosquito [mɑːs'kiːtoʊ] mosquito *m*
moss [mɑːs] musgo *m*
most [moʊst] **1** *adj* la mayoría de **2** *adv* (*very*) muy, sumamente; ***the ~ beautiful*** el más hermoso; ***that's the one I like ~*** ése es el que más me gusta; ***~ of all*** sobre todo **3** *pron* la mayoría de; ***~ of her novels*** la mayoría de sus novelas; ***at (the) ~*** como mucho; ***make the ~ of*** aprovechar al máximo; **mostly** principalmente, sobre todo
motel [moʊ'tel] motel *m*
moth [mɑːθ] mariposa *f* nocturna; (*clothes ~*) polilla *f*
mother ['mʌðər] **1** *n* madre *f* **2** *v/t* mimar; **motherhood** maternidad *f*; **Mothering Sunday** ☞ ***Mother's Day***; **mother-in-law** suegra *f*; **motherly** maternal; **Mother's Day** Día *m* de la Madre; **mother tongue** lengua *f* materna
motif [moʊ'tiːf] motivo *m*
motion ['moʊʃn] (*movement*) movimiento *m*; (*proposal*)

moción *f*; **motionless** inmóvil

motivate ['moutɪveɪt] *person* motivar; **motivation** motivación *f*; **motive** motivo *m*

motor ['moutər] motor *m*; **motorbike** moto *f*; **motorcycle** motocicleta *f*; **motorcyclist** motociclista *m/f*; **motor home** autocaravana *f*; **motor mechanic** mecánico(-a) *m(f)* (de automóviles); **motor racing** carreras *fpl* de coches; **motor vehicle** vehículo *m* de motor

motto ['mɑːtou] lema *m*

mould *etc Br* ☞ ***mold*** *etc*

mound [maund] montículo *m*

mount [maunt] **1** *n* (*mountain*) monte *m*; (*horse*) montura *f* **2** *v/t steps* subir; *horse, bicycle* montar en; *campaign, photo* montar **3** *v/i* aumentar, crecer

◆ **mount up** acumularse

mountain ['mauntɪn] montaña *f*; **mountaineer** montañero(-a) *m(f)*, alpinista *m/f*, *L.Am.* andinista *m/f*; **mountaineering** montañismo *m*, alpinismo *m*, *L.Am.* andinismo *m*; **mountainous** montañoso

mourn [mɔːrn] llorar; **mourner** doliente *m/f*; **mournful** *voice, face* triste

mouse [maus] (*pl* ***mice*** [maɪs]) *also* COMPUT ratón *m*; **mouse mat** alfombrilla *f*

moustache ☞ ***mustache***

mouth [mauθ] boca *f*; *of river* desembocadura *f*; **mouthful** *of food* bocado *m*; *of drink* trago *m*; **mouthpiece** *of instrument* boquilla *f*; (*spokesperson*) portavoz *m/f*; **mouthwash** enjuague *m* bucal; **mouthwatering** apetitoso

move [muːv] **1** *n in chess, checkers* movimiento *m*; (*step, action*) paso *m*; (*change of house*) mudanza *f* **2** *v/t object* mover; (*transfer*) trasladar; *emotionally* conmover; ***~ house*** mudarse de casa **3** *v/i* moverse; (*transfer*) trasladarse

◆ **move around** *in room* andar; *from place to place* trasladarse, mudarse

◆ **move in** *to house, neighborhood* mudarse; *to office* trasladarse

movement ['muːvmənt] *also organization*, MUS movimiento *m*; **movers** *firm* empresa *f* de mudanzas; (*men*) empleados *mpl* de una empresa de mudanzas

movie ['muːvɪ] película *f*; ***go to a ~ / the ~s*** ir al cine; **moviegoer** aficionado(a) *m/f* al cine; **movie theater** cine *m*, sala *f* de cine

moving ['muːvɪŋ] movible; *emotionally* conmovedor

mow [mou] *grass* cortar; **mower** cortacésped *m*

mph [empiː'eɪtʃ] (= ***miles per hour***) millas *fpl* por hora

Mr ['mɪstər] Sr.

Mrs ['mɪsɪz] Sra.
Ms [mɪz] Sra. (*casada o no casada*)
much [mʌtʃ] **1** *adj* mucho; ***so ~ money*** tanto dinero; ***as ~ ... as ...*** tanto… como **2** *adv* mucho; ***~ too large*** demasiado grande; ***very ~*** mucho; ***thank you very ~*** muchas gracias; ***I love you very ~*** te quiero muchísimo; ***too ~*** demasiado **3** *pron* mucho; ***what did she say? – nothing ~*** ¿qué dijo? – no demasiado; ***as ~ as ...*** tanto… como…
mud [mʌd] barro *m*
muddle ['mʌdl] **1** *n* lío *m* **2** *v/t person* liar
muddy ['mʌdɪ] embarrado
muffin ['mʌfɪn] magdalena *f*
muffle ['mʌfl] ahogar, amortiguar; **muffler** MOT silenciador *m*
mug[1] [mʌg] *n* taza *f*; F (*face*) jeta *f* F, *Span* careto *m* F
mug[2] [mʌg] *v/t* (*attack*) atracar
mugger ['mʌgər] atracador(a) *m*(*f*); **mugging** atraco *m*; **muggy** bochornoso
mule [mju:l] *animal* mulo(-a) *m*(*f*); (*slipper*) pantufla *f*
multicultural [mʌltɪ'kʌltʃərəl] multicultural; **multilateral** POL multilateral; **multimedia** **1** *n* multimedia *f* **2** *adj* multimedia; **multinational** **1** *adj* multinacional **2** *n* COM multinacional *f*
multiple ['mʌltɪpl] múltiple;
multiple sclerosis esclerosis *f* múltiple
multiplex ['mʌltɪpleks] *movie theater* (cine *m*) multisalas *m inv*, multicine *m*
multiplication [mʌltɪplɪ'keɪʃn] multiplicación *f*; **multiply** **1** *v/t* multiplicar **2** *v/i* multiplicarse
multi-tasking ['mʌltɪtæskɪŋ] multitarea *f*
mumble ['mʌmbl] **1** *n* murmullo *m* **2** *v/t* farfullar **3** *v/i* hablar entre dientes
munch [mʌntʃ] mascar
municipal [mju:'nɪsɪpl] municipal
mural ['mjʊrəl] mural *m*
murder ['mɜ:rdər] **1** *n* asesinato *m* **2** *v/t person* asesinar, matar; *song* destrozar; **murderer** asesino(-a) *m*(*f*)
murky ['mɜ:rkɪ] *water* turbio, oscuro; *fig* turbio
murmur ['mɜ:rmər] **1** *n* murmullo *m* **2** *v/t* murmurar
muscle ['mʌsl] músculo *m*; **muscular** *pain* muscular; *person* musculoso
museum [mju:'zɪəm] museo *m*
mushroom ['mʌʃrʊm] **1** *n* seta *f*, hongo *m*; (*button ~*) champiñón *m* **2** *v/i* crecer rápidamente
music ['mju:zɪk] música *f*; *in written form* partitura *f*; **musical** **1** *adj* musical; *person* con talento para la música **2** *n* musical *m*; **musician** músico(-a) *m*(*f*)

mussel ['mʌsl] mejillón *m*
must [mʌst] *v/aux* ◇ *necessity* tener que, deber; ***I ~ be on time*** tengo que *or* debo llegar a la hora; ***I ~n't be late*** no tengo que llegar tarde, no debo llegar tarde ◇ *probability* deber de; ***it ~ be about 6 o'clock*** deben de ser las seis
mustache [mə'stæʃ] bigote *m*
mustard ['mʌstərd] mostaza *f*
musty ['mʌstɪ] *room* que huele a humedad; *smell* a humedad
mutilate ['mju:tɪleɪt] mutilar
mutiny ['mju:tɪnɪ] **1** *n* motín *m* **2** *v/i* amotinarse
mutter ['mʌtər] murmurar
mutual ['mju:ʧʊəl] mutuo
muzzle ['mʌzl] **1** *n of animal* hocico *m*; *for dog* bozal *m* **2** *v/t* poner un bozal a; ***~ the press*** amordazar a la prensa
my [maɪ] mi; **myself** *reflexive* me; *emphatic* yo mismo(-a); ***I hurt ~*** me hizo daño
mysterious [mɪ'stɪrɪəs] misterioso; **mysteriously** misteriosamente; **mystery** misterio *m*; **mystify** dejar perplejo
myth [mɪθ] *also fig* mito *m*; **mythical** mítico

N

nag [næg] *of person* dar la lata; **nagging** *person* quejica; *doubt* persistente; *pain* continuo
nail [neɪl] *for wood* clavo *m*; *on finger, toe* uña *f*; **nail polish** esmalte *m* de uñas; **nail polish remover** quitaesmaltes *m inv*
naive [naɪ'i:v] ingenuo
naked ['neɪkɪd] desnudo
name [neɪm] **1** *n* nombre *m*; ***what's your ~?*** ¿cómo te llamas? **2** *v/t* llamar; **namely** a saber; **namesake** tocayo(-a) *m(f)*, homónimo(-a) *m(f)*
nanny ['nænɪ] niñera *f*
nap [næp] cabezada *f*
napkin ['næpkɪn] (*table ~*) servilleta *f*; (*sanitary ~*) compresa *f*
narcotic [nɑ:r'kɑ:tɪk] narcótico *m*, estupefaciente *m*
narrate [nə'reɪt] narrar; **narrative** **1** *n* (*story*) narración *f* **2** *adj poem, style* narrativo; **narrator** narrador(a) *m(f)*
narrow ['næroʊ] estrecho; *views, mind* cerrado; **narrowly** *win* por poco; **narrow-minded** cerrado
nasty ['næstɪ] *person, smell* desagradable; *thing to say* malintencionado; *weather* horrible; *cut, wound* feo; *disease* serio
nation ['neɪʃn] nación *f*; **national** **1** *adj* nacional **2** *n* ciu-

dadano(-a) *m(f)*; **national anthem** himno *m* nacional; **national debt** deuda *f* pública; **nationalism** nacionalismo *m*; **nationality** nacionalidad *f*; **nationalize** *industry etc* nacionalizar

native ['neɪtɪv] **1** *adj* nativo **2** *n* nativo(-a) *m(f)*, natural *m/f*; *tribesman* nativo(-a) *m(f)*, indígena *m/f*; **Native American** indio(-a) *m (f)* americano(-a)

NATO ['neɪtoʊ] (= ***North Atlantic Treaty Organization***) OTAN *f* (= Organización *f* del Tratado del Atlántico Norte)

natural ['nætʃrəl] natural; **naturalist** naturalista *m/f*; **naturalize:** ***become ~d*** naturalizarse, nacionalizarse; **naturally** (*of course*) naturalmente; *behave, speak* con naturalidad; (*by nature*) por naturaleza

nature naturaleza *f*; **nature reserve** reserva *f* natural

naughty ['nɒːtɪ] travieso, malo; *photograph, word etc* picante

nausea ['nɒːzɪə] náusea *f*; **nauseate** dar náuseas a; **nauseating** *smell, taste* nauseabundo; *person* repugnante; **nauseous** nauseabundo; ***feel ~*** tener náuseas

nautical ['nɒːtɪkl] náutico

naval ['neɪvl] naval

navel ['neɪvl] ombligo *m*

navigate ['nævɪgeɪt] navegar; *in car* hacer de copiloto; **navigation** navegación *f*; *in car* direcciónes *fpl*; **navigator** *on ship* oficial *m* de derrota; *in airplane* navegante *m/f*; *in car* copiloto *m/f*

navy ['neɪvɪ] armada *f*, marina *f* (de guerra); **navy blue** **1** *n* azul *m* marino **2** *adj* azul marino

near [nɪr] **1** *adv* cerca **2** *prep* cerca de **3** *adj* cercano, próximo; **nearby** cerca; **nearly** casi; **near-sighted** miope

neat [niːt] ordenado; *whiskey* solo, seco; *solution* ingenioso; F (*terrific*) genial F

necessarily ['nesəserəlɪ] necesariamente; **necessary** necesario, preciso; **necessity** necesidad *f*

neck [nek] cuello *m*; **necklace** collar *m*; **neckline** *of dress* escote *m*; **necktie** corbata *f*

née [neɪ] de soltera

need [niːd] **1** *n* necesidad *f*; ***if ~ be*** si fuera necesario **2** *v/t* necesitar; ***you don't ~ to wait*** no hace falta que esperes; ***I ~ to talk to you*** necesito hablar contigo

needle ['niːdl] aguja *f*; **needlework** costura *f*

needy ['niːdɪ] necesitado

negative ['negətɪv] negativo

neglect [nɪ'glekt] **1** *n* abandono *m*, descuido *m* **2** *v/t garden, health* descuidar, desatender; **neglected** *garden* abandonado, descuidado;

author olvidado
negligence ['neglɪdʒəns] negligencia *f*; **negligent** negligente; **negligible** *amount* insignificante
negotiable [nɪ'goʊʃəbl] negociable; **negotiate 1** *v/i* negociar **2** *v/t deal* negociar; *obstacles* franquear, salvar; *bend in road* tomar; **negotiation** negociación *f*; **negotiator** negociador(a) *m(f)*
neighbor ['neɪbər] vecino(-a) *m(f)*; **neighborhood** vecindario *m*, barrio *m*; **neighboring** *house, state* vecino, colindante; **neighborly** amable
neighbour *etc Br* ☞ ***neighbor*** *etc*
neither ['ni:ðər] **1** *adj* ninguno; ~ ***applicant*** ninguno de los candidatos **2** *pron* ninguno(-a) *m(f)*; **3** *adv*: ~ ... ***nor*** ... ni... ni... **4** *conj*: ~ ***do I*** yo tampoco; ~ ***can I*** yo tampoco
neon light ['ni:ɑ:n] luz *f* de neón
nephew ['nefju:] sobrino *m*
nerve [nɜ:rv] nervio *m*; (*courage*) valor *m*; (*impudence*) descaro *m*; **nerve-racking** angustioso, exasperante; **nervous** nervioso; **nervous breakdown** crisis *f inv* nerviosa; **nervousness** nerviosismo *m*; **nervy** (*fresh*) descarado
nest [nest] nido *m*
net[1] [net] *n* red *f*; ***the*** ~ COMPUT la Red; ***on the*** ~ en Internet
net[2] [net] *adj price, weight* neto
nettle ['netl] ortiga *f*
'network *of contacts, cells*, COMPUT red *f*
neurologist [nu:'rɑ:lədʒɪst] neurólogo(-a) *m(f)*
neurosis [nu:'roʊsɪs] neurosis *f inv*; **neurotic** neurótico
neuter ['nu:tər] *animal* castrar; **neutral 1** *adj country* neutral; *color* neutro **2** *n gear* punto *m* muerto; **neutrality** neutralidad *f*; **neutralize** neutralizar
never ['nevər] nunca; ***you're*** ~ ***going to believe this*** no te vas a creer esto; **nevertheless** sin embargo, no obstante
new [nu:] nuevo; **newborn** recién nacido; **newcomer** recién llegado(-a) *m(f)*; **newly** (*recently*) recientemente, recién; **newly-weds** recién casados *mpl*
news [nu:z] *also* RAD noticias *fpl*; *on TV* noticias *fpl*, telediario *m*; **newscast** TV noticias *fpl*, telediario *m*; *on radio* noticias *fpl*; **newscaster** TV presentador(a) *m(f)* de informativos; **news flash** flash *m* informativo; **newspaper** periódico *m*; **newsreader** TV *etc* presentador(a) *m(f)* de informativos; **news report** reportaje *m*; **newsstand** quiosco *m*; **newsvendor** vendedor(a) *m(f)* de pe-

riódicos

'New Year año *m* nuevo; ***Happy ~!*** ¡Feliz Año Nuevo!; **New Year's Day** Día *m* de Año Nuevo; **New Year's Eve** Nochevieja *f*; **New York 1** *n*: **~ (*City*)** Nueva York **2** *adj* neoyorquino; **New Yorker** neoyorquino(-a) *m*(*f*); **New Zealand** ['zi:lənd] Nueva Zelanda; **New Zealander** neozelandés(-esa) *m*(*f*)

next [nekst] **1** *adj in time* próximo, siguiente; *in space* siguiente **2** *adv* luego, después; **~ *to*** (*beside*) al lado de; (*in comparison with*) en comparación con; **next-door 1** *adj neighbor* de al lado **2** *adv live* al lado; **next of kin** pariente *m* más cercano

nibble ['nɪbl] mordisquear

Nicaragua [nɪkə'rɑ:gwə] Nicaragua; **Nicaraguan 1** *adj* nicaragüense **2** *n* nicaragüense *m/f*

nice [naɪs] *trip, house, hair* bonito, *L.Am.* lindo; *person* agradable, simpático; *weather* bueno, agradable; *meal, food* bueno, rico; **nicely** *written, presented* bien; (*pleasantly*) amablemente

niche [ni:ʃ] *in market* hueco *m*, nicho *m*; (*special position*) hueco *m*

nick [nɪk] (*cut*) muesca *f*, mella *f*

nickel ['nɪkl] níquel *m*; (*coin*) *moneda de cinco centavos*

'nickname apodo *m*, mote *m*

niece [ni:s] sobrina *f*

night [naɪt] noche *f*; ***tomorrow ~*** mañana por la noche; ***11 o'clock at ~*** las 11 de la noche; ***during the ~*** por la noche; ***good ~*** buenas noches; **nightcap** *drink* copa *f* (*tomada antes de ir a dormir*); **nightclub** club *m* nocturno, discoteca *f*; **nightdress** camisón *m*; **night flight** vuelo *m* nocturno; **nightlife** vida *f* nocturna; **nightly** todas las noches; **nightmare** *also fig* pesadilla *f*; **night porter** portero *m* de noche; **night school** escuela *f* nocturna; **night shift** turno *m* de noche; **nightshirt** camisa *f* de dormir; **nightspot** local *m* nocturno; **nighttime: *at ~*, *in the ~*** por la noche

nimble ['nɪmbl] ágil

nine [naɪn] nueve; **nineteen** diecinueve; **nineteenth** decimonoveno; **ninetieth** nonagésimo; **ninety** noventa; **ninth** noveno

nip [nɪp] (*pinch*) pellizco *m*; (*bite*) mordisco *m*

nipple ['nɪpl] pezón *m*

nitrogen ['naɪtrədʒn] nitrógeno *m*

no [noʊ] **1** *adv* no **2** *adj*: ***there's ~ coffee left*** no queda café; ***I have ~ money*** no tengo dinero; ***I'm ~ expert*** no soy un experto; ***~ smoking*** prohibido fumar

noble ['noʊbl] noble

nobody ['noʊbədɪ] nadie

no-brainer [noʊ'breɪnər] juego *m* de niños; ***the math test was a ~*** la prueba de matemáticas estaba chupada
nod [nɑːd] **1** *n* movimiento *m* de la cabeza **2** *v/i* asentir con la cabeza
noise [nɔɪz] ruido *m*; **noisy** ruidoso
nominal ['nɑːmɪnl] simbólico
nominate ['nɑːmɪneɪt] (*appoint*) nombrar; **nomination** nombramiento *m*; (*proposal*) nominación *f*; **nominee** candidato(-a) *m*(*f*)
nonalco'holic sin alcohol
noncommissioned officer ['nɑːnkəmɪʃnd] suboficial *m*/*f*
noncommittal [nɑːnkə'mɪtl] evasivo
nondescript ['nɑːndɪskrɪpt] anodino
none [nʌn]: ***~ of the students*** ninguno de los estudiantes; ***~ of the water*** nada del agua; ***there are ~ left*** no queda ninguno; ***there is ~ left*** no queda nada
nonentity [nɑːn'entətɪ] nulidad *f*
none'xistent inexistente
non'fiction no ficción *f*
noninter'ference no intervención *f*
noninter'vention no intervención *f*
no-'nonsense *approach* directo
non'payment impago *m*
nonpol'luting que no contamina
non'resident no residente *m*/*f*
nonsense ['nɑːnsəns] disparate *m*, tontería *f*
non'smoker no fumador(a) *m*(*f*)
non'standard no estándar
non'stop **1** *adj flight* directo, sin escalas; *chatter* ininterrumpido **2** *adv travel* directamente; *chatter* sin parar
non'union no sindicado
non'violence no violencia *f*; **nonviolent** no violento
noodles ['nuːdlz] tallarines *mpl* (chinos)
noon [nuːn] mediodía *m*
'no-one ☞ ***nobody***
noose [nuːs] lazo *m* corredizo
nor [nɔːr] ni; ***~ do I*** yo tampoco, ni yo
norm [nɔːrm] norma *f*; **normal** normal; **normality** normalidad *f*; **normally** normalmente
north [nɔːrθ] **1** *n* norte *m* **2** *adj* norte **3** *adv travel* al norte; **North America** América del Norte, Norteamérica; **North American 1** *n* norteamericano(-a) *m*(*f*) **2** *adj* norteamericano; **northeast** nordeste *m*, noreste *m*; **northerly** norte, del norte; **northern** norteño, del norte; **northerner** norteño(-a) *m*(*f*); **North Korea** Corea del Norte; **North Korean 1** *adj* norcoreano **2** *n* norcoreano(-a) *m*(*f*); **North Pole**

Polo *m* Norte; **northward** *travel* hacia el norte; **northwest** noroeste *m*

Norway ['nɔːrweɪ] Noruega; **Norwegian** **1** *adj* noruego **2** *n person* noruego(-a) *m(f)*; *language* noruego *m*

nose [noʊz] nariz *m*; *of animal* hocico *m*

◆ **nose around** F husmear

nostalgia [nɑː'stældʒə] nostalgia *f*; **nostalgic** nostálgico

nostril ['nɑːstrəl] ventana *f* de la nariz

nosy ['noʊzɪ] F entrometido

not [nɑːt] no; ~ ***this one, that one*** éste no, ése; ~ ***now*** ahora no; ~ ***for me, thanks*** para mí no, gracias; ***I don't know*** no lo sé; ***he didn't help*** no ayudó

notable ['noʊtəbl] notable

notch [nɑːtʃ] muesca *f*, mella *f*

note [noʊt] *written*, MUS nota *f*; **notebook** cuaderno *m*, libreta *f*; COMPUT *Span* ordenador *m* portátil, *L.Am.* computadora *f* portátil; **noted** destacado; **notepad** bloc *m* de notas; **notepaper** papel *m* de carta

nothing ['nʌθɪŋ] nada; ~ ***but*** sólo; ~ ***much*** no mucho; ***for*** ~ (*for free*) gratis; (*for no reason*) por nada

notice ['noʊtɪs] **1** *n on bulletin board* cartel *m*, letrero *m*; (*advance warning*) aviso *m*; *in newspaper* anuncio *m*; ***at short*** ~ con poca antelación; ***until further*** ~ hasta nuevo aviso; ***hand in one's*** ~ *to employer* presentar la dimisión; ***take no*** ~ ***of*** no hacer caso de **2** *v/t* notar, fijarse en; **noticeable** apreciable, evidente

notify ['noʊtɪfaɪ] notificar, informar

notion ['noʊʃn] noción *f*, idea *f*

notorious [noʊ'tɔːrɪəs] de mala fama

noun [naʊn] nombre *m*, sustantivo *m*

nourishing ['nʌrɪʃɪŋ] nutritivo; **nourishment** alimento *m*, alimentación *f*

novel ['nɑːvl] novela *f*; **novelist** novelista *m/f*; **novelty** (*being new*) lo novedoso; (*sth new*) novedad *f*

November [noʊ'vembər] noviembre *m*

novice ['nɑːvɪs] principiante *m/f*

now [naʊ] ahora; ~ ***and again***, ~ ***and then*** de vez en cuando; ***by*** ~ ya; **nowadays** hoy en día

nowhere ['noʊwer] en ningún lugar; ***it's*** ~ ***near finished*** no está acabado ni mucho menos; ***he was*** ~ ***to be seen*** no se le veía en ninguna parte

nuclear ['nuːklɪər] nuclear; **nuclear energy** energía *f* nuclear; **nuclear power** energía *f* nuclear; POL po-

tencia *f* nuclear; **nuclear power station** central *f* nuclear; **nuclear reactor** reactor *m* nuclear
nude [nu:d] **1** *adj* desnudo **2** *n painting* desnudo *m*
nudge [nʌdʒ] dar un toque con el codo a; *parked car* dar un empujoncito a
nudist ['nu:dɪst] nudista *m/f*
nuisance ['nu:sns] incordio *m*, molestia *f*; ***make a ~ of o.s.*** dar la lata
null and 'void [nʌl] nulo y sin efecto
numb [nʌm] entumecido; *emotionally* insensible
number ['nʌmbər] **1** *n* número *m* **2** *v/t* (*put a ~ on*) numerar
numeral ['nu:mərəl] número *m*
numerous ['nu:mərəs] numeroso
nun [nʌn] monja *f*
nurse [nɜ:rs] enfermero(-a) *m*(*f*); **nursery** guardería *f*; *for plants* vivero *m*; **nursery rhyme** canción *f* infantil; **nursery school** parvulario *m*, jardín *m* de infancia; **nursing** enfermería *f*; **nursing home** *for old people* residencia *f*
nut [nʌt] nuez *f*; *for bolt* tuerca *f*; **nutcrackers** cascanueces *m inv*
nutrient ['nu:trɪənt] nutriente *m*; **nutrition** nutrición *f*; **nutritious** nutritivo
nuts [nʌts] F (*crazy*) chalado F, pirado F

O

oar [ɔ:r] remo *m*
oasis [oʊ'eɪsɪs] *also fig* oasis *m inv*
oath [oʊθ] LAW, (*swearword*) juramento *m*
'oatmeal harina *f* de avena
obedience [oʊ'bi:dɪəns] obediencia *f*; **obedient** obediente; **obediently** obedientemente
obese [oʊ'bi:s] obeso; **obesity** obesidad *f*
obey [oʊ'beɪ] obedecer
obituary [ə'bɪtʊerɪ] necrología *f*, obituario *m*
object[1] ['ɑ:bdʒɪkt] *n also gram* objeto *m*; (*aim*) objetivo *m*
object[2] [əb'dʒekt] *v/i* oponerse
objection [əb'dʒekʃn] objeción *f*; **objectionable** (*unpleasant*) desagradable; **objective 1** *adj* objetivo **2** *n* objetivo *m*; **objectively** objetivamente; **objectivity** objetividad *f*
obligation [ɑ:blɪ'geɪʃn] obligación *f*; **obligatory** obligatorio; **obliging** atento, servicial
oblique [ə'bli:k] **1** *adj refer-*

ence indirecto **2** *n in punctuation* barra *f* inclinada
obliterate [ə'blɪtəreɪt] *city* arrasar; *memory* borrar
oblivion [ə'blɪvɪən] olvido *m*
oblong ['ɑːblɒːŋ] rectangular
obscene [ɑːb'siːn] obsceno; *salary, poverty* escandaloso; **obscenity** obscenidad *f*
obscure [əb'skjʊr] oscuro; **obscurity** oscuridad *f*
observant [əb'zɜːrvnt] observador; **observation** observación *f*; **observe** observar; **observer** observador(a) *m(f)*
obsess [ɑːb'ses] obsesionar; **obsession** obsesión *f*
obsolete ['ɑːbsəliːt] obsoleto
obstacle ['ɑːbstəkl] obstáculo *m*
obstetrician [ɑːbstə'trɪʃn] obstetra *m/f*, tocólogo(-a) *m(f)*; **obstetrics** obstetricia *f*, tocología *f*
obstinacy ['ɑːbstɪnəsɪ] obstinación *f*; **obstinate** obstinado
obstruct [ɑːb'strʌkt] *road* obstruir; *investigation, police* obstaculizar; **obstruction** *on road etc* obstrucción *f*; **obstructive** *behavior* obstruccionista
obtain [əb'teɪn] obtener, lograr; **obtainable** *products* disponible
obtuse [əb'tuːs] *fig* duro de mollera
obvious ['ɑːbvɪəs] obvio, evidente; **obviously** obviamente
occasion [ə'keɪʒn] ocasión *f*; **occasional** ocasional, esporádico; **occasionally** ocasionalmente
occupant ['ɑːkjʊpənt] ocupante *m/f*; **occupation** ocupación *f*; **occupy** ocupar
occur [ə'kɜːr] ocurrir, suceder; **occurrence** acontecimiento *m*
ocean ['oʊʃn] océano *m*
o'clock [ə'klɑːk]: ***at five ~*** a las cinco
October [ɑːk'toʊbər] octubre *m*
odd [ɑːd] (*strange*) raro, extraño; (*not even*) impar; **oddball** F bicho *m* raro F; **odds and ends** *objects* cacharros *mpl*; *things to do* cosillas *fpl*; **odds-on** *favorite* indiscutible
odometer [oʊ'dɑːmətər] cuentakilómetros *m inv*
odor, *Br* **odour** ['oʊdər] olor *m*
of [ɑːv] de; ***the name ~ the street / hotel*** el nombre de la calle / del hotel; ***five minutes ~ twelve*** las doce menos cinco, *L.Am* cinco para los doce; ***die ~ cancer*** morir de cáncer; ***love ~ money*** amor por el dinero
off [ɑːf] **1** *prep*: ***~ the main road*** (*away from*) apartado de la carretera principal; (*leading off*) saliendo de la carretera principal; ***$20 ~ the price*** una rebaja en el

precio de 20 dólares; ***he's ~ his food*** no come nada, está desganado **2** *adv*: **be ~** *of light, TV, machine* estar apagado; *of brake, lid, top* no estar puesto; *not at work* faltar; *on vacation* estar de vacaciones; *canceled* estar cancelado; ***we're ~ tomorrow*** *leaving* nos vamos mañana; ***take a day ~*** tomarse un día de fiesta; ***it's 3 miles ~*** está a tres millas de distancia; ***it's a long way ~*** *in distance* está muy lejos; *in future* todavía queda mucho tiempo **3** *adj*: ***the ~ switch*** el interruptor de apagado

offence *Br* ☞ ***offense***

offend [ə'fend] (*insult*) ofender; **offender** LAW delincuente *m/f*; **offense** LAW delito *m*; ***take ~ at sth*** ofenderse por algo; **offensive 1** *adj behavior, remark* ofensivo; *smell* repugnante **2** *n* (MIL: *attack*) ofensiva *f*

offer ['ɑːfər] **1** *n* oferta *f* **2** *v/t* ofrecer

off'hand *attitude* brusco

office ['ɑːfɪs] *building* oficina *f*; *room* oficina *f*, despacho *m*; *position* cargo *m*; **officer** MIL oficial *m/f*; *in police* agente *m/f*; **official 1** *adj* oficial **2** *n* funcionario(-a) *m(f)*; **officially** oficialmente; **officious** entrometido

'off-line *work* fuera de línea; ***go ~*** desconectarse

'offpeak *rates* en horas valle, fuera de las horas punta

'off-season temporada *f* baja

'offset *losses* compensar

'offshore *drilling rig* cercano a la costa; *investment* en el exterior

'offside SP fuera de juego

'offspring *of person* vástagos *mpl*, hijos *mpl*; *of animal* crías *fpl*

off-the-'record confidencial

often ['ɑːfn] a menudo, frecuentemente

oil [ɔɪl] **1** *n* aceite *m*; *petroleum* petróleo *m* **2** *v/t hinges, bearings* engrasar; **oil change** cambio *m* del aceite; **oil company** compañía *f* petrolera; **oilfield** yacimiento *m* petrolífero; **oil painting** óleo *m*; **oil refinery** refinería *f* de petróleo; **oil rig** plataforma *f* petrolífera; **oil slick** marea *f* negra; **oil tanker** petrolero *m*; **oil well** pozo *m* petrolífero; **oily** grasiento

ointment ['ɔɪntmənt] ungüento *m*, pomada *f*

ok [oʊ'keɪ]: ***can I? – ~*** ¿puedo? - de acuerdo *or Span* vale; ***is it ~ with you if …?*** ¿te parecería bien si…?; ***are you ~?*** (*well, not hurt*) ¿estás bien?

old [oʊld] viejo; (*previous*) anterior, antiguo; ***how ~ is he?*** ¿cuántos años tiene?; **old age** vejez *f*; **old-fashioned** anticuado

olive ['ɑːlɪv] aceituna *f*, oliva *f*; **olive oil** aceite *m* de oliva

Olympic 'Games [ə'lɪmpɪk] Juegos *mpl* Olímpicos
omelet, *Br* **omelette** ['ɑːmlɪt] tortilla *f* (francesa)
ominous ['ɑːmɪnəs] siniestro
omission [oʊ'mɪʃn] omisión *f*; **omit** omitir
on [ɑːn] **1** *prep* en; **~ the table** en la mesa; **~ TV** en la televisión; **~ Sunday** el domingo; **~ the 1st of ...** el uno de...; **this is ~ me** (*I'm paying*) invito yo; **have you any money ~ you?** ¿llevas dinero encima?; **~ his arrival** cuando llegue; **~ hearing this** al escuchar esto **2** *adv*: **be ~** *of light, TV, computer etc* estar encendido *or L.Am.* prendido; *of brake, lid* estar puesto; *of meeting etc: be scheduled to happen* haber sido acordado; **what's ~ tonight?** *on TV etc* ¿qué dan *or Span* ponen esta noche?; (*what's planned?*) ¿qué planes hay para esta noche?; **with his hat ~** con el sombrero puesto; **you're ~** (*I accept*) trato hecho; **~ you go** (*go ahead*) adelante; **talk ~** seguir hablando; **and so ~** etcétera; **~ and ~** *talk etc* sin parar **3** *adj*: **the ~ switch** el interruptor de encendido
once [wʌns] **1** *adv* (*one time, formerly*) una vez; **~ again**, **~ more** una vez más; **at ~** (*immediately*) de inmediato **2** *conj* una vez que; **~ you have finished** una vez que hayas acabado
one [wʌn] **1** *n number* uno *m* **2** *adj* un(a); **~ day** un día **3** *pron* uno(-a); **which ~?** ¿cuál?; **~ by ~** uno por uno; **we help ~ another** nos ayudamos mutuamente; **what can ~ say?** ¿qué puede uno decir?; **the little ~s** los pequeños; **I for ~** yo personalmente; **what can ~ say?** ¿qué puede uno decir?; **one-parent family** familia *f* monoparental; **oneself** uno(-a) mismo(-a) *m(f)*; **do sth by ~** hacer algo sin ayuda; **look after ~** cuidarse; **be by ~** estar solo; **one-way street** calle *f* de sentido único; **one-way ticket** billete *m* de ida
onion ['ʌnjən] cebolla *f*
'on-line en línea; **go ~ to** conectarse a; **on-line banking** banca *f* electrónica; **on-line dating** encuentros *mpl* online; **on-line shopping** compras *fpl* online
onlooker ['ɑːnlʊkər] espectador(a) *m(f)*, curioso(-a) *m(f)*
only ['oʊnlɪ] **1** *adv* sólo, solamente; **not ~ ... but ...** *also* no sólo... sino también... **2** *adj* único
'onset comienzo *m*
on-the-job 'training formación *f* continua
opaque [oʊ'peɪk] opaco
open ['oʊpən] **1** *adj also honest* abierto; **in the ~ air** al aire

libre **2** *v/t* abrir **3** *v/i of door, shop* abrir; *of flower* abrirse; **open-air** *meeting, concert* al aire libre; *pool* descubierto; **open day** jornada *f* de puertas abiertas; **open-ended** *contract etc* abierto; **opening** *in wall etc* abertura *f*; *of film, novel etc* comienzo *m*; (*job*) puesto *m* vacante; **openly** (*honestly, frankly*) abiertamente; **open-minded** de mentalidad abierta; **open ticket** billete *m* abierto

opera ['ɑːpərə] ópera *f*; **opera house** (teatro *m* de la) ópera *f*; **opera singer** cantante *m/f* de ópera

operate ['ɑːpəreɪt] **1** *v/i* operar; *of machine* funcionar (***on*** con) **2** *v/t machine* manejar

◆ **operate on** MED operar

'**operating room** MED quirófano *m*; **operating system** COMPUT sistema *m* operativo; **operation** MED operación *f*; *of machine* manejo *m*; **operator** TELEC operador(a) *m(f)*; *of machine* operario(-a) *m(f)*; (*tour* ~) operador *m* turístico

opinion [ə'pɪnjən] opinión *f*; **opinion poll** encuesta *f* de opinión

opponent [ə'pounənt] oponente *m/f*, adversario(-a) *m(f)*

opportunist [ɑːpər'tuːnɪst] oportunista *m/f*; **opportunity** oportunidad *f*

oppose [ə'pouz] oponerse a; ***be ~d to …*** estar en contra de…

opposite ['ɑːpəzɪt] **1** *adj* contrario; *views, meaning* opuesto **2** *adv* enfrente; ***the house ~*** la casa de enfrente **3** *prep* enfrente de; **opposite number** homólogo(-a) *m(f)*

opposition [ɑːpə'zɪʃn] *to plan*, POL oposición *f*

oppress [ə'pres] *the people* oprimir; **oppressive** *rule* opresor; *weather* agobiante

optician [ɑːp'tɪʃn] óptico(-a) *m(f)*

optimism ['ɑːptɪmɪzm] optimismo *m*; **optimist** optimista *m/f*; **optimistic** optimista; **optimistically** con optimismo

optimum ['ɑːptɪməm] óptimo

option ['ɑːpʃn] opción *f*; **optional** optativo

or [ɔːr] o; *before a word beginning with the letter o* u

oral ['ɔːrəl] oral; *hygiene* bucal

orange ['ɔːrɪndʒ] **1** *adj* naranja **2** *n fruit* naranja *f*; *color* naranja *m*; **orange juice** *Span* zumo *m or L.Am.* jugo *m* de naranja

orator ['ɔːrətər] orador(a) *m(f)*

orbit ['ɔːrbɪt] **1** *n of earth* órbita *f* **2** *v/t the earth* girar alrededor de

orchard ['ɔːrtʃərd] huerta *f* (de frutales)

orchestra ['ɔːrkɪstrə] orquesta *f*

orchid ['ɔːrkɪd] orquídea *f*
ordain [ɔːr'deɪn] ordenar
ordeal [ɔːr'diːl] calvario *m*, experiencia *f* penosa
order ['ɔːrdər] **1** *n* (*command*, *sequence*) orden *m*; *for goods* pedido *m*; ***an ~ of fries*** unas patatas fritas; ***in ~ to*** para; ***out of ~*** (*not functioning*) estropeado; (*not in sequence*) desordenado **2** *v/t* (*put in sequence, proper layout*) ordenar; *goods, meal* pedir; ***~ s.o. to do sth*** ordenar a alguien hacer algo *or* que haga algo **3** *v/i in restaurant* pedir; **orderly 1** *adj lifestyle* ordenado, metódico **2** *n in hospital* celador(a) *m*(*f*)
ordinarily [ɔːrdɪ'nerɪlɪ] (*as a rule*) normalmente; **ordinary** común, normal
ore [ɔːr] mineral *m*, mena *f*
organ ['ɔːrgən] ANAT, MUS órgano *m*; **organic** *food* ecológico, biológico; *fertilizer* orgánico; **organically** *grown* ecológicamente, biológicamente; **organism** organismo *m*
organization [ɔːrgənaɪ'zeɪʃn] organización *f*; **organize** organizar; **organizer** *person* organizador(a) *m*(*f*)
orient ['ɔːrɪənt] (*direct*) orientar; **Oriental** oriental
origin ['ɑːrɪdʒɪn] origen *m*; **original 1** *adj* original **2** *n painting etc* original *m*; **originality** originalidad *f*; **originally** originalmente; **originate 1** *v/t idea* crear **2** *v/i of idea, belief* originarse; *of family* proceder
ornamental [ɔːrnə'mentl] ornamental
ornate [ɔːr'neɪt] recargado
orphan ['ɔːrfn] huérfano(-a) *m*(*f*)
orthodox ['ɔːrθədɑːks] ortodoxo
orthopedic [ɔːrθə'piːdɪk] ortopédico
ostensibly [ɑː'stensəblɪ] aparentemente
ostentatious [ɑːsten'teɪʃəs] ostentoso
ostracize ['ɑːstrəsaɪz] condenar al ostracismo
other ['ʌðər] **1** *adj* otro; ***the ~ day*** (*recently*) el otro día; ***every ~ day*** cada dos días **2** *n*: ***the ~*** el otro; ***the ~s*** los otros
otherwise ['ʌðərwaɪz] **1** *conj* si no **2** *adv* (*differently*) de manera diferente
ought [ɒːt]: ***I / you ~ to know*** debo / debes saberlo; ***you ~ to have done it*** deberías haberlo hecho
ounce [aʊns] onza *f*
our [aʊr] nuestro(-a)
ours [aʊrz] el nuestro, la nuestra; ***that book is ~*** ese libro es nuestro; ***a friend of ~*** un amigo nuestro; **ourselves** *reflexive* nos; *emphatic* nosotros mismos *mpl*, nosotras mismas *fpl*; ***we hurt ~*** nos hicimos daño
oust [aʊst] *from office* derrocar

out [aʊt]: ***be ~*** *of light, fire* estar apagado; *of flower* estar en flor; (*not at home*), *of sun* haber salido; *of calculations* estar equivocado; (*be published*) haber sido publicado; (*no longer in competition*) estar eliminado; (*no longer in fashion*) estar pasado de moda; ***~ here in Dallas*** aquí en Dallas; (***get***) ***~!*** ¡vete!; (***get***) ***~ of my room!*** ¡fuera de mi habitación!; ***that's ~!*** (*out of the question*) ¡eso es imposible!; ***he's ~ to win*** (*fully intends to*) va a por la victoria

'outbreak estallido *m*

'outcast paria *m/f*

'outcome resultado *m*

'outcry protesta *f*

out'dated anticuado

out'do superar

out'door *toilet, life* al aire libre; **out'doors** fuera

outer ['aʊtər] *wall etc* exterior

'outfit (*clothes*) traje *m*, conjunto *m*; (*company, organization*) grupo *m*

out'last durar más que

'outlet *of pipe* desagüe *m*; *for sales* punto *m* de venta; ELEC enchufe *m*

'outline 1 *n of person, building etc* perfil *m*, contorno *m*; *of plan, novel* resumen *m* **2** *v/t plans etc* resumir

out'live sobrevivir a

'outlook (*prospects*) perspectivas *fpl*

out'number superar en número

out of ◇ *motion* fuera de; ***run ~ the house*** salir corriendo de la casa; ◇ *position*: ***100 miles ~ Detroit*** a 100 millas de Detroit ◇ *cause* por; ***~ curiosity*** por curiosidad ◇ *without*: ***we're ~ gas*** no nos queda gasolina ◇ *from a group* de cada **2 ~ *10*** 2 de cada 10

out-of-'date anticuado, desfasado

'output 1 *n of factory* producción *f*; COMPUT salida *f* **2** *v/t* (*produce*) producir

'outrage 1 *n feeling* indignación *f*; *act* ultraje *m* **2** *v/t* indignar, ultrajar; **outrageous** *acts* atroz; *prices* escandaloso

'outright 1 *adj winner* absoluto **2** *adv win* completamente; *kill* en el acto

'outset principio *m*

out'shine eclipsar

'outside 1 *adj wall* exterior; *lane* de fuera **2** *adv sit, go* fuera **3** *prep* fuera de; (*apart from*) aparte de **4** *n of building, case etc* exterior *m*

'outsize *clothing* de talla especial

'outskirts afueras *fpl*

out'smart ☞ ***outwit***

'outsource subcontratar

out'standing *quality* destacado; *writer, athlete* excepcional; FIN pendiente

outstretched ['aʊtstretʃt] *hands* extendido

outward ['aʊtwərd] *appearance* externo; ~ ***journey*** viaje *m* de ida; **outwardly** aparentemente
out'weigh pesar más que
out'wit mostrarse más listo que
oval ['oʊvl] oval, ovalado
oven ['ʌvn] horno *m*
over ['oʊvər] **1** *prep* (*above*) sobre, encima de; (*across*) al otro lado de; (*more than*) más de; (*during*) durante; ***she walked ~ the street*** cruzó la calle; ***travel all ~ Brazil*** viajar por todo Brasil; ***we're ~ the worst*** lo peor ya ha pasado; ***~ and above*** además de **2** *adv*: ***be ~*** (*finished*) haber acabado; ***there were just 6 ~*** sólo quedaban seis; ***~ in Japan*** allá en Japón; ***~ here / there*** por aquí / allá; ***it hurts all ~*** me duele por todas partes; ***painted white all ~*** pintado todo de blanco; ***it's all ~*** se ha acabado; ***~ and ~ again*** una y otra vez; ***do sth ~*** (***again***) volver a hacer algo; **overall** (*in general*) en general; **overalls** *Span* mono *m*, *L.Am.* overol *m*
over'awe intimidar
over'balance perder el equilibrio
over'bearing dominante
'overcast *day* nublado; *sky* cubierto
over'charge *customer* cobrar de más a
'overcoat abrigo *m*
over'come *difficulties* superar, vencer
over'crowded *train* atestado; *city* superpoblado
over'do (*exaggerate*) exagerar; *in cooking* recocer, cocinar demasiado; **over'done** *meat* demasiado hecho
'overdose sobredosis *f inv*
'overdraft descubierto *m*; **overdraw** *account* dejar al descubierto
over'dressed demasiado trajeado
over'estimate sobreestimar
over'expose sobreexponer
'overflow[1] *n pipe* desagüe *m*, rebosadero *m*
over'flow[2] *v/i of water* desbordarse
over'haul revisar
'overhead 1 *adj lights*, *railway* elevado **2** *n* FIN gastos *mpl* generales
over'hear oír por casualidad
over'heated recalentado
overjoyed [oʊvər'dʒɔɪd] contentísimo, encantado
'overland 1 *adj route* terrestre **2** *adv travel* por tierra
over'lap *of tiles etc* solaparse; *of periods of time* coincidir; *of theories* tener puntos en común
over'load sobrecargar
over'look *of tall building etc* dominar; (*not see*) pasar por alto
overly ['oʊvərlɪ] excesivamente, demasiado

'overnight *travel* por la noche; *fig change etc* de la noche a la mañana
'overpass paso *m* elevado
over'power *physically* dominar
overpriced [oʊvər'praɪst] demasiado caro
overrated [oʊvə'reɪtɪd] sobrevalorado
over'ride anular; **overriding** *concern* primordial
over'rule *decision* anular
over'seas 1 *adv live, work* en el extranjero; *go* al extranjero **2** *adj* extranjero
over'see supervisar
over'shadow *fig* eclipsar
'oversight descuido *m*
over'sleep quedarse dormido
over'state exagerar; **overstatement** exageración *f*
over'take *in work, development* adelantarse a; *Br* MOT adelantar
over'throw[1] *v/t* derrocar
'overthrow[2] *n* derrocamiento *m*
'overtime 1 *n* SP: ***in ~*** en la prórroga **2** *adv*: ***work ~*** hacer horas extras
over'turn 1 *v/t vehicle* volcar; *object* dar la vuelta a; *government* derribar **2** *v/i of vehicle* volcar
'overview visión *f* general
overwhelming [oʊvər'welmɪŋ] *feeling* abrumador; *majority* aplastante
over'work 1 *n* exceso *m* de trabajo **2** *v/i* trabajar en exceso
owe [oʊ] deber; **owing to** debido a
owl [aʊl] búho *m*
own[1] [oʊn] *v/t* poseer
own[2] [oʊn] **1** *adj* propio; **2** *pron*: ***an apartment of my ~*** mi propio apartamento; ***on my ~*** yo solo
◆ **own up** confesar
owner ['oʊnər] dueño(-a) *m(f)*, propietario(-a) *m(f)*; **ownership** propiedad *f*
oxygen ['ɑːksɪdʒən] oxígeno *m*
oyster ['ɔɪstər] ostra *f*
ozone ['oʊzoʊn] ozono *m*; **ozone layer** capa *f* de ozono

P

PA [piː'eɪ] (= ***personal assistant***) secretario(-a) *m(f)* personal
pace [peɪs] (*step*) paso *m*; (*speed*) ritmo *m*; **pacemaker** MED marcapasos *m inv*; SP liebre *f*
Pacific [pə'sɪfɪk]: ***the ~*** (***Ocean***) el (Océano) Pacífico
pacifier ['pæsɪfaɪər] *for baby* chupete *m*; **pacifism** pacifismo *m*; **pacifist** pacifista *m/f*; **pacify** tranquilizar; *country*

pacificar

pack [pæk] **1** *n* (*back~*) mochila *f*; *of food, cigarettes* paquete *m* **2** *v/t item of clothing etc* meter en la maleta; *goods* empaquetar; *groceries* meter en una bolsa; ***~ one's bag*** hacer la bolsa **3** *v/i* hacer la maleta; **package 1** *n* paquete *m* **2** *v/t in packs* embalar; *idea* presentar; **packaging** *of product* embalaje *m*; *of idea* presentación *f*; **packet** paquete *m*

pact [pækt] pacto *m*

pad[1] [pæd] **1** *n for protection* almohadilla *f*; *for absorbing liquid* compresa *f*; *for writing* bloc *m* **2** *v/t with material* acolchar; *speech, report* meter paja en

pad[2] [pæd] *v/i* (*move quietly*) caminar silenciosamente

padding ['pædɪŋ] *material* relleno *m*; *in speech etc* paja *f*

paddle ['pædəl] **1** *n for canoe* canalete *m*, remo *m* **2** *v/i in canoe* remar; *in water* chapotear

paddock ['pædək] potrero *m*

padlock ['pædlɑːk] candado *m*

page[1] [peɪdʒ] *n of book etc* página *f*

page[2] [peɪdʒ] *v/t* (*call*) llamar; *by PA* llamar por megafonía; *by beeper* llamar por el buscapersonas *or Span* busca

pager ['peɪdʒər] buscapersonas *m inv*, *Span* busca *m*

paid employment [peɪd] empleo *m* remunerado

pain [peɪn] dolor *m*; ***be in ~*** sentir dolor; **painful** dolorido; *blow, condition, subject* doloroso; (*laborious*) difícil; **painfully** (*extremely, acutely*) extremadamente; **painkiller** analgésico *m*; **painless** indoloro; **painstaking** meticuloso

paint [peɪnt] **1** *n* pintura *f* **2** *v/t* pintar; **paintbrush** *large* brocha *f*; *small* pincel *m*; **painter** *decorator* pintor(a) *m*(*f*) (de brocha gorda); *artist* pintor(a) *m*(*f*); **painting** *activity* pintura *f*; *picture* cuadro *m*; **paintwork** pintura *f*

pair [per] *of shoes etc* par *m*; *of people, animals* pareja *f* ; ***a ~ of pants*** unos pantalones

pajamas [pə'dʒɑːməz] pijama *m*

Pakistan [pɑːkɪ'stɑːn] Paquistán, Pakistán; **Pakistani 1** *n* paquistaní *m/f*, pakistaní *m/f* **2** *adj* paquistaní, pakistaní

pal [pæl] F (*friend*) amigo(-a) *m*(*f*), *Span* colega *m/f* F

palace ['pælɪs] palacio *m*

palate ['pælət] paladar *m*

palatial [pə'leɪʃl] palaciego

pale [peɪl] *person* pálido; ***she went ~*** palideció

Palestine ['pæləstaɪn] Palestina; **Palestinian 1** *n* palestino(-a) *m*(*f*) **2** *adj* palestino

pallet ['pælɪt] palé *m*

pallor ['pælər] palidez *f*

palm [pɑːm] *of hand* palma *f*;

palm tree palmera *f*
paltry ['pɒːltrɪ] miserable
pamper ['pæmpər] mimar
pamphlet ['pæmflɪt] *for information* folleto *m*; *political* panfleto *m*
pan [pæn] *for cooking* cacerola *f*; *for frying* sartén *f*
Panama ['pænəmɑː] Panamá; **Panama Canal:** ***the ~*** el Canal de Panamá; **Panama City** Ciudad *f* de Panamá; **Panamanian 1** *adj* panameño **2** *n* panameño(-a) *m(f)*
pancake ['pænkeɪk] crepe *m*, *L.Am.* panqueque *m*
pandemonium [pændɪ'moʊnɪəm] pandemónium *m*
pane [peɪn] *of glass* hoja *f*
panel ['pænl] panel *m*; *people* grupo *m*, panel *m*; **paneling,** *Br* **panelling** paneles *mpl*
panic ['pænɪk] **1** *n* pánico *m* **2** *v/i* ser preso del pánico; **panic-stricken** preso del pánico
panorama [pænə'rɑːmə] panorama *m*; **panoramic** panorámico
pant [pænt] jadear
panties ['pæntɪz] *Span* bragas *fpl*, *L.Am.* calzones *mpl*
pantihose ☞ ***pantyhose***
pants [pænts] pantalones *mpl*
pantyhose ['pæntɪhoʊz] medias *fpl*, pantis *mpl*
papal ['peɪpəl] papal
paparazzi [pæpə'rætsiː] paparazzi *mfpl*
paper ['peɪpər] **1** *n* papel *m*; (*news~*) periódico *m*; *academic* estudio *m*; *at conference* ponencia *f*; (*examination ~*) examen *m*; ***~s*** (*documents*) documentos *mpl*; *of vehicle*, (*identity ~s*) papeles *mpl*, documentación *f* **2** *adj* de papel **3** *v/t room* empapelar; **paperback** libro *m* en rústica; **paper clip** clip *m*; **paperwork** papeleo *m*
parachute ['pærəʃuːt] **1** *n* paracaídas *m inv* **2** *v/i* saltar en paracaídas **3** *v/t troops*, *supplies* lanzar en paracaídas
parade [pə'reɪd] **1** *n procession* desfile *m* **2** *v/i* desfilar; (*walk about*) pasearse
paradise ['pærədaɪs] paraíso *m*
paradox ['pærədɑːks] paradoja *f*; **paradoxical** paradójico; **paradoxically** paradójicamente
paragraph ['pærəgræf] párrafo *m*
Paraguay ['pærəgwaɪ] Paraguay; **Paraguayan 1** *adj* paraguayo **2** *n* paraguayo(-a) *m(f)*
parallel ['pærəlel] **1** *n* paralela *f*; GEOG paralelo *m*; *fig* paralelismo *m* **2** *adj also fig* paralelo **3** *v/t* (*match*) equipararse a
paralysis [pə'ræləsɪs] parálisis *f*; **paralyze** *also fig* paralizar
paramedic [pærə'medɪk] auxiliar *m/f* sanitario(-a)
parameter [pə'ræmɪtər] parámetro *m*
paramilitary [pærə'mɪlɪterɪ] **1**

adj paramilitar **2** *n* paramilitar *m/f*

paranoia [pærə'nɔɪə] paranoia *f*; **paranoid** paranoico

paraphrase ['pærəfreɪz] parafrasear

parasite ['pærəsaɪt] *also fig* parásito *m*

parasol ['pærəsɑːl] sombrilla *f*

paratrooper ['pærətruːpər] paracaidista *m/f* (*militar*)

parcel ['pɑːrsl] paquete *m*

pardon ['pɑːrdn] **1** *n* LAW indulto *m*; ***I beg your ~?*** (*what did you say?*) ¿cómo ha dicho?; ***I beg your ~*** (*I'm sorry*) discúlpeme **2** *v/t* perdonar; LAW indultar; ***~ me?*** ¿perdón?

parent ['perənt] *father* padre *m*; *mother* madre *f*; ***my ~s*** mis padres; **parental** de los padres; **parent company** empresa *f* matriz; **parent-teacher association** asociación *f* de padres y profesores

parish ['pærɪʃ] parroquia *f*

park[1] [pɑːrk] *n* parque *m*

park[2] [pɑːrk] *v/t & v/i* MOT estacionar, *Span* aparcar; **parking** MOT estacionamiento *m*, *Span* aparcamiento *m*; **parking brake** freno *m* de mano; **parking garage** párking *m*, *Span* aparcamiento *m*; **parking lot** estacionamiento *m*, *Span* aparcamiento *m* (*al aire libre*); **parking meter** parquímetro *m*; **parking ticket** multa *f* de estacionamiento

parliament ['pɑːrləmənt] parlamento *m*

parole [pə'roʊl] **1** *n* libertad *f* condicional **2** *v/t* poner en libertad condicional

parrot ['pærət] loro *m*

part [pɑːrt] **1** *n* parte *f*; *of machine* pieza *f* (de repuesto); *in movie* papel *m*; *in hair* raya *f*; ***take ~ in*** tomar parte en **2** *adv* (*partly*) en parte **3** *v/i* separarse; **partial** (*incomplete*) parcial; **partially** parcialmente

participant [pɑːr'tɪsɪpənt] participante *m/f*; **participate** participar; **participation** participación *f*

particular [pər'tɪkjələr] (*specific*) particular, concreto; (*demanding*) exigente; *about friends etc* selectivo; *pej* especial, quisiquilloso; **particularly** particularmente

partition [pɑːr'tɪʃn] (*screen*) tabique *m*; *of country* partición *f*, división *f*

partly ['pɑːrtlɪ] en parte

partner ['pɑːrtnər] COM socio(-a) *m*(*f*); *in relationship* compañero(-a) *m*(*f*); *in tennis, dancing* pareja *f*; **partnership** COM sociedad *f*; *in particular activity* colaboración *f*

'part-time a tiempo parcial

party ['pɑːrtɪ] **1** *n* (*celebration*) fiesta *f*; POL partido *m*; (*group of people*) grupo *m* **2** *v/i* F salir de marcha F

pass [pæs] **1** *n for entry*, SP pase *m*; *in mountains* desfiladero *m* **2** *v/t* (*hand*) pasar; (*go past*) pasar por delante de; (*overtake*) adelantar; (*go beyond*) sobrepasar; (*approve*) aprobar **3** *v/i of time* pasar; *in exam* aprobar; (*go away*) pasarse

◆ **pass away** *euph* fallecer, pasar a mejor vida

◆ **pass on** **1** *v/t information, book* pasar **2** *v/i* (*euph: die*) fallecer, pasar a mejor vida

◆ **pass out** (*faint*) desmayarse

◆ **pass up** *opportunity* dejar pasar

passable ['pæsəbl] *road* transitable; (*acceptable*) aceptable

passage ['pæsɪdʒ] (*corridor*) pasillo *m*; *from book* pasaje *m*; *of time* paso *m*

passenger ['pæsɪndʒər] pasajero(-a) *m*(*f*)

passer-by [pæsər'baɪ] transeúnte *m*/*f*

passion ['pæʃn] pasión *f*; **passionate** *lover* apasionado; (*fervent*) fervoroso

passive ['pæsɪv] **1** *adj* pasivo **2** *n* GRAM (voz *f*) pasiva *f*; **passive smoking** (el) fumar pasivamente

'**passport** pasaporte *m*; **passport control** control *m* de pasaportes; **password** contraseña *f*

past [pæst] **1** *adj* (*former*) pasado; ***the ~ few days*** los últimos días **2** *n* pasado **3** *prep in position* después de; ***it's half ~ two*** son las dos y media **4** *adv*: ***run / walk ~*** pasar

pasta ['pæstə] pasta *f*

paste [peɪst] **1** *n* (*adhesive*) cola *f* **2** *v/t* (*stick*) pegar

pastime ['pæstaɪm] pasatiempo *m*

past par'ticiple GRAM participio *m* pasado

pastry ['peɪstrɪ] *for pie* masa *f*; *small cake* pastel *m*

'**past tense** GRAM (tiempo *m*) pasado *m*

pasty ['peɪstɪ] *face* pálido

pat [pæt] **1** *n* palmadita *f* **2** *v/t* dar palmaditas a

patch [pætʃ] **1** *n on clothing* parche *m*; (*area*) mancha *f*; ***a bad ~*** *of time* un mal momento, una mala racha **2** *v/t clothing* remendar

◆ **patch up** (*repair*) hacer un remiendo a, arreglar a medias; *quarrel* solucionar

patchy ['pætʃɪ] *quality* desigual; *work* irregular

patent ['peɪtnt] **1** *adj* patente, evidente **2** *n for invention* patente *f* **3** *v/t invention* patentar

paternal [pə'tɜːrnl] *relative* paterno; *pride, love* paternal; **paternalism** paternalismo *m*; **paternalistic** paternalista; **paternity** paternidad *f*

path [pæθ] *also fig* camino *m*

pathetic [pə'θetɪk] *invoking pity* patético; F (*very bad*) lamentable F

pathological [pæθə'lɑːdʒɪkl] patológico
patience ['peɪʃns] paciencia *f*; **patient 1** *n* paciente *m/f* **2** *adj* paciente; **patiently** pacientemente
patio ['pætɪoʊ] *Br* patio *m*
patriot ['peɪtrɪət] patriota *m/f*; **patriotic** patriótico; **patriotism** patriotismo *m*
patrol [pə'troʊl] **1** *n* patrulla *f* **2** *v/t streets, border* patrullar; **patrol car** coche *m* patrulla; **patrolman** policía *m*, patrullero *m*; **patrol wagon** furgón *m* policial
patron ['peɪtrən] *of store, movie theater* cliente *m/f*; *of artist, charity etc* patrocinador(a) *m(f)*; **patronize** *person* tratar con condescendencia; **patronizing** condescendiente; **patron saint** santo(-a) *m(f)* patrón(-ona), patrón(-ona) *m(f)*
pattern ['pætərn] *on fabric* estampado *m*; *for sewing* diseño *m*; (*model*) modelo *m*; *in behavior, events* pauta *f*
paunch [pɒːntʃ] barriga *f*
pause [pɒːz] **1** *n* pausa *f* **2** *v/i* parar; *when speaking* hacer una pausa **3** *v/t tape* poner en pausa
pave [peɪv] *with concrete* pavimentar; *with slabs* adoquinar; **pavement** (*roadway*) calzada *f*; *Br* (*sidewalk*) acera *f*
paw [pɒː] **1** *n of animal* pata *f*; F (*hand*) pezuña *f* F **2** *v/t* F sobar F
pawn [pɒːn] *in chess* peón *m*; *fig* títere *m*
pay [peɪ] **1** *n* paga *f*, sueldo *m* **2** *v/t* pagar; *~ **attention*** prestar atención **3** *v/i* pagar; (*be profitable*) ser rentable; *~ **for** purchase* pagar
◆ **pay back** *person* devolver el dinero a; *loan* devolver
◆ **pay off 1** *v/t debt* liquidar; (*bribe*) sobornar **2** *v/i* (*be profitable*) valer la pena
◆ **pay up** pagar
payable ['peɪəbl] pagadero; **pay check**, *Br* **pay cheque** cheque *m* del sueldo; **payday** día *m* de paga; **payee** beneficiario(-a) *m(f)*; **payment** pago *m*; **pay phone** teléfono *m* público
PC [piː'siː] (= ***personal computer***) PC *m*, *Span* ordenador *m or L.Am.* computadora personal; (= ***politically correct***) políticamente correcto
pea [piː] *Span* guisante *m*, *L.Am.* arveja *f*, *Mex* chícharo *m*
peace [piːs] paz *f*; (*quietness*) tranquilidad; **peaceful** tranquilo; *demonstration* pacífico; **peacefully** pacíficamente
peach [piːtʃ] *fruit* melocotón *m*, *L.Am.* durazno *m*; *tree* melocotonero *m*, *L.Am.* duraznero *m*
peak [piːk] **1** *n of mountain* cima *f*; *mountain* pico *m*; *fig*

climax *m* **2** *v/i* alcanzar el máximo; **peak hours** horas *fpl* punta
peanut ['pi:nʌt] cacahuete *m*, *L.Am.* maní *m*, *Mex* cacahuate *m*; ***get paid ~s*** F cobrar una miseria F; **peanut butter** crema *f* de cacahuete
pear [per] pera *f*
pearl [pɜ:rl] perla *f*
pecan ['pi:kən] pacana *f*
peck [pek] **1** *n bite* picotazo *m*; *kiss* besito *m* **2** *v/t bite* picotear; *kiss* dar un besito a
peculiar [pɪ'kju:ljər] (*strange*) raro; **peculiarity** rareza *f*; (*special feature*) peculiaridad *f*
pedal ['pedl] **1** *n of bike* pedal *m* **2** *v/i* pedalear; (*cycle*) recorrer en bicicleta
peddle ['pedl] *drugs* traficar con
pedestrian [pɪ'destrɪən] peatón(-ona) *m(f)*
pediatric [pi:dɪ'ætrɪk] pediátrico; **pediatrician** pediatra *m/f*; **pediatrics** pediatría *f*
pedicure ['pedɪkjʊr] pedicura *f*
pedigree ['pedɪgri:] **1** *n of animal* pedigrí; *of person* linaje *m* **2** *adj* con pedigrí
pee [pi:] F hacer pis F
peek [pi:k] **1** *n* ojeada *f* **2** *v/i* echar una ojeada
peel [pi:l] **1** *n* piel *f* **2** *v/t fruit, vegetables* pelar **3** *v/i of nose, shoulders* pelarse; *of paint* levantarse
peep [pi:p] ☞ ***peek***; **peephole** mirilla *f*
peer¹ [pɪr] *n* (*equal*) igual *m*
peer² [pɪr] *v/i* mirar
peg [peg] *for hat, coat* percha *f*; *for tent* clavija *f*; ***off the ~*** de confección
pejorative [pɪ'dʒɑ:rətɪv] peyorativo
pellet ['pelɪt] pelotita *f*; (*bullet*) perdigón *m*
pen¹ [pen] (*ballpoint ~*) bolígrafo *m*
pen² [pen] (*enclosure*) corral *m*
pen³ [pen] ☞ ***penitentiary***
penalize ['pi:nəlaɪz] penalizar
penalty ['penəltɪ] sanción *f*; SP penalti *m*; **penalty area** SP área *f* de castigo; **penalty clause** LAW cláusula *f* de penalización; **penalty kick** (lanzamiento *m* de) penalti *m*
pencil ['pensɪl] lápiz *m*; **pencil sharpener** sacapuntas *m inv*
pendant ['pendənt] *necklace* colgante *m*
penetrate ['penɪtreɪt] (*pierce*) penetrar; *market* penetrar en; **penetration** penetración *f*; *of defenses* incursión *f*; *of market* entrada *f*
penguin ['peŋgwɪn] pingüino *m*
penicillin [penɪ'sɪlɪn] penicilina *f*
peninsula [pə'nɪnsʊlə] península *f*
penitence ['penɪtəns] (*re-*

morse) arrepentimiento *m*; **penitentiary** prisión *f*, cárcel *f*

'pen name seudónimo *m*

pennant ['penənt] banderín *f*

penniless ['penɪlɪs] sin un centavo

'pen pal amigo(-a) *m*(*f*) por correspondencia

pension ['penʃn] pensión *f*
◆ **pension off** jubilar

pensive ['pensɪv] pensativo

Pentagon ['pentəgɑːn]: ***the ~*** el Pentágono

pentathlon [pen'tæθlən] pentatlón *m*

penthouse ['penthaʊs] ático *m* (*de lujo*)

pent-up ['pentʌp] reprimido

penultimate [pe'nʌltɪmət] penúltimo

people ['piːpl] gente *f*; (*individuals*) personas *fpl*; (*race, tribe*) pueblo *m*; ***the ~*** (*citizens*) el pueblo, los ciudadanos; ***~ say ...*** se dice que…

pepper ['pepər] *spice* pimienta *f*; *vegetable* pimiento *m*; **peppermint** *candy* caramelo *m* de menta

per [pɜːr] por; ***~ annum*** al año, por año

perceive [pər'siːv] percibir; (*view, interpret*) interpretar

percent [pər'sent] por ciento; **percentage** porcentaje *m*, tanto *m* por ciento

perceptible [pər'septəbl] perceptible; **perceptibly** visiblemente; **perception** *through senses* percepción *f*; *of situation* apreciación *f*; (*insight*) perspicacia *f*; **perceptive** perceptivo

percolate ['pɜːrkəleɪt] *of coffee* filtrarse; **percolator** cafetera *f* de filtro

perfect 1 ['pɜːrfɪkt] *n* GRAM pretérito *m* perfecto **2** ['pɜːrfɪkt] *adj* perfecto **3** [pər'fekt] *v/t* perfeccionar; **perfection** perfección *f*; **perfectionist** perfeccionista *m/f*; **perfectly** perfectamente; (*totally*) completamente

perforated ['pɜːrfəreɪtɪd] *line* perforado

perform [pər'fɔːrm] **1** *v/t* (*carry out*) realizar; *of actors etc* interpretar **2** *v/i of actor, musician, dancer* actuar; *of machine* funcionar; **performance** *by actor etc* actuación *f*, interpretación *f*; *of play* representación *f*; *of employee* rendimiento *m*; *of official, company, in sport* actuación *f*; *of machine* rendimiento *m*; **performer** intérprete *m/f*

perfume ['pɜːrfjuːm] perfume *m*

perfunctory [pər'fʌŋktərɪ] superficial

perhaps [pər'hæps] quizá(s), tal vez

peril ['perəl] peligro *m*

perimeter [pə'rɪmɪtər] perímetro *m*

period ['pɪrɪəd] periodo *m*, período *m*; (*menstruation*) periodo *m*, regla *f*; *punctuation mark* punto *m*; **periodic**

periódico; **periodical** publicación *f* periódica
peripheral [pə'rɪfərəl] **1** *adj* (*not crucial*) secundario **2** *n* COMPUT periférico *m*; **periphery** periferia *f*
perish ['perɪʃ] *of rubber* estropearse; *of person* perecer; **perishable** *food* perecedero
perjure ['pɜːrdʒər]: **~ *o.s.*** perjurar; **perjury** perjurio *m*
perm [pɜːrm] **1** *n* permanente *f* **2** *v/t* hacer la permanente
permanent ['pɜːrmənənt] permanente; **permanently** permanentemente
permeate ['pɜːrmɪeɪt] impregnar
permissible [pər'mɪsəbl] permisible; **permission** permiso *m*; **permissive** permisivo; **permit 1** *n* licencia *f* **2** *v/t* permitir
perpendicular [pɜːrpən'dɪkjʊlər] perpendicular
perpetual [pər'petʃʊəl] perpetuo; *interruptions* continuo; **perpetually** constantemente
perplex [pər'pleks] dejar perplejo; **perplexity** perplejidad *f*
persecute ['pɜːrsɪkjuːt] perseguir; (*hound*) acosar; **persecution** persecución *f*; (*harassment*) acoso *m*; **persecutor** perseguidor(a) *m*(*f*)
perseverance [pɜːrsɪ'vɪrəns] perseverancia *f*; **persevere** perseverar
persist [pər'sɪst] persistir; **persistent** *person*, *questions* perseverante; *rain*, *unemployment etc* persistente; **persistently** (*continually*) constantemente
person ['pɜːrsn] persona *f*; **personal** (*private*) personal; *life* privado; **personal computer** *Span* ordenador *m* personal, *L.Am.* computadora *f* personal; **personality** personalidad *f*; **personally** (*for my part*) personalmente; (*in person*) en persona; **personal organizer** organizador *m* personal; **personal stereo** walkman *m* ®; **personify** *of person* personificar
personnel [pɜːrsə'nel] personal *m*
perspective [pər'spektɪv] *in art* perspectiva *f*; ***get sth into ~*** poner algo en perspectiva
perspiration [pɜːrspɪ'reɪʃn] sudor *m*, transpiración *f*; **perspire** sudar, transpirar
persuade [pər'sweɪd] persuadir; **persuasion** persuasión *f*; **persuasive** persuasivo
perturb [pər'tɜːrb] perturbar; **perturbing** perturbador
Peru [pə'ruː] Perú; **Peruvian 1** *adj* peruano **2** *n* peruano(-a) *m*(*f*)
pervasive [pər'veɪsɪv] *influence*, *ideas* dominante
perversion [pər'vɜːrʃn] *sexual* perversión *f*; **pervert** *sexual* pervertido(-a) *m*(*f*)
pessimism ['pesɪmɪzm] pesi-

mismo *m*; **pessimist** pesimista *m/f*; **pessimistic** pesimista
pest [pest] plaga *f*; F *person* tostón *m* F
pester ['pestər] acosar; **~ *s.o. to do sth*** dar la lata a alguien para que haga algo
pesticide ['pestɪsaɪd] pesticida *f*
pet [pet] **1** *n* animal *m* doméstico; (*favorite*) preferido(-a) *m(f)* **2** *adj* preferido **3** *v/t animal* acariciar **4** *v/i of couple* magrearse F
petite [pə'tiːt] chiquito(-a); *size* menudo
petition [pə'tɪʃn] petición *f*
petrify ['petrɪfaɪ] dejar petrificado
petrochemical [petroʊ'kemɪkl] petroquímico
petrol ['petrl] *Br* gasolina *f*, *Arg* nafta *f*
petroleum [pɪ'troʊlɪəm] petróleo *m*
petting ['petɪŋ] magreo *m* F
petty ['petɪ] *person, behavior* mezquino; *details* sin importancia
pew [pjuː] banco *m* (*de iglesia*)
pharmaceutical [fɑːrmə'suːtɪkl] farmaceútico; **pharmaceuticals** fármacos *mpl*
pharmacist ['fɑːrməsɪst] *in store* farmaceútico(-a) *m(f)*; **pharmacy** *store* farmacia *f*
phase [feɪz] fase *f*
phenomenal [fɪ'nɑːmɪnl] fenomenal; **phenomenon** fenómeno *m*
philanthropic [fɪlən'θrɑːpɪk] filantrópico; **philanthropist** filántropo(-a) *m(f)*; **philanthropy** filantropía *f*
Philippines ['fɪlɪpiːnz]: ***the ~*** las Filipinas
philosopher [fɪ'lɑːsəfər] filósofo(-a) *m(f)*; **philosophical** filosófico; **philosophy** filosofía *f*
phobia ['foʊbɪə] fobia *f*
phone [foʊn] **1** *n* teléfono *m* **2** *v/t* llamar (por teléfono) a **3** *v/i* llamar (por teléfono); **phone book** guía *f* (de teléfonos); **phone booth** cabina *f* (de teléfonos); **phonecall** llamada *f* (telefónica); **phone card** tarjeta *f* telefónica; **phone number** número *m* de teléfono
phon(e)y ['foʊnɪ] F falso
photo ['foʊtoʊ] foto *f*; **photocopier** fotocopiadora *f*; **photocopy** **1** *n* fotocopia *f* **2** *v/t* fotocopiar; **photogenic** fotogénico; **photograph** **1** *n* fotografía *f* **2** *v/t* fotografiar; **photographer** fotógrafo(-a) *m(f)*; **photography** fotografía *f*
phrase [freɪz] **1** *n* frase *f* **2** *v/t* expresar
physical ['fɪzɪkl] **1** *adj* físico **2** *n* MED reconocimiento *m* médico; **physically** físicamente
physician [fɪ'zɪʃn] médico(-a) *m(f)*
physicist ['fɪzɪsɪst] físico(-a) *m(f)*; **physics** física *f*

physiotherapist [fɪzɪoʊ'θerəpɪst] fisioterapeuta *m/f*; **physiotherapy** fisioterapia *f*
physique [fɪ'ziːk] físico *m*
pianist ['pɪənɪst] pianista *m/f*; **piano** piano *m*
pick [pɪk] (*choose*) escoger, elegir; *flowers, fruit* recoger
◆ **pick up 1** *v/t* recoger, *Span* coger; *habit* adquirir, *Span* coger; *illness* contraer, *Span* coger; *telephone* descolgar; *language, skill* aprender; (*buy*) comprar; *sexually* ligar con **2** *v/i* (*improve*) mejorar
picket ['pɪkɪt] **1** *n of strikers* piquete *m* **2** *v/t* hacer piquete delante de
'**pickpocket** carterista *m/f*
pick-up (truck) ['pɪkʌp] camioneta *f*
picky ['pɪkɪ] F tiquismiquis F
picnic ['pɪknɪk] **1** *n* picnic *m* **2** *v/i* ir de picnic
picture ['pɪktʃər] **1** *n* (*photo*) fotografía *f*; (*painting*) cuadro *m*; (*illustration*) dibujo *m*; (*movie*) película *f*; *on TV* imagen *f* **2** *v/t* imaginar
picturesque [pɪktʃə'resk] pintoresco
pie [paɪ] pastel *m*
piece [piːs] (*fragment*) fragmento *m*; *component, in game* pieza *f*; ***a ~ of advice*** un consejo; ***take to ~s*** desmontar
◆ **piece together** *broken plate* recomponer; *evidence* reconstruir
piecemeal ['piːsmiːl] poco a poco
pier [pɪr] *Br at seaside* malecón *m*
pierce [pɪrs] (*penetrate*) perforar; *ears* agujerear; **piercing** *scream* desgarrador; *gaze* penetrante; *wind* cortante
pig [pɪg] *also fig* cerdo *m*; *greedy* glotón(-a) *m*(*f*)
pigeon ['pɪdʒɪn] paloma *f*; **pigeonhole** casillero *m*
pigheaded [pɪg'hedɪd] F cabezota F; **pigpen** *also fig* pocilga *f*
pile [paɪl] montón *m*, pila *f*
◆ **pile up 1** *v/i of work, bills* acumularse **2** *v/t* amontonar
pile-up ['paɪlʌp] MOT choque *m* múltiple
pilfering ['pɪlfərɪŋ] hurtos *mpl*
pill [pɪl] pastilla *f*; ***be on the ~*** tomar la píldora
pillar ['pɪlər] pilar *m*
pillow ['pɪloʊ] almohada *f*; **pillowcase** funda *f* de almohada
pilot ['paɪlət] **1** *n of airplane* piloto *m/f*; *for ship* práctico *m* **2** *v/t airplane* pilotar
pimp [pɪmp] proxeneta *m*, *Span* chulo *m* F
pimple ['pɪmpl] grano *m*
PIN [pɪn] (= ***personal identification number***) PIN *m* (= número *m* de identificación personal)
pin [pɪn] **1** *n for sewing* alfiler *m*; *in bowling* bolo *m*; (*badge*) pin *m*; ELEC clavija *f* **2** *v/t* (*hold down*) mantener;

(*attach*) sujetar
◆ **pin up** *notice* sujetar con chinchetas
pincers ['pɪnsərz] *of crab* pinzas *fpl*; *tool* tenazas *fpl*
pinch [pɪntʃ] **1** *n* pellizco *m*; *of salt etc* pizca *f* **2** *v/t* pellizcar **3** *v/i of shoes* apretar
pine [paɪn] *tree*, *wood* pino *m*; **pineapple** piña *f*, *L.Am.* ananá(s) *f*
pink [pɪŋk] rosa
pinnacle ['pɪnəkl] *fig* cima *f*
'pinpoint determinar; **pins and needles** hormigueo *m*; **pin-up** modelo *m/f* de revista
pioneer [paɪə'nɪr] **1** *n* pionero(-a) *m*(*f*) **2** *v/t* ser pionero en; **pioneering** *work* pionero
pious ['paɪəs] piadoso
pip [pɪp] *Br of fruit* pepita *f*
pipe [paɪp] **1** *n* tubería *f*; *for smoking* pipa *f*; **2** *v/t* conducir por tuberías; **pipeline** *for oil* oleoducto *m*; *for gas* gasoducto *m*
pirate ['paɪrət] **1** *n* pirata *m/f* **2** *v/t software* piratear
pissed [pɪst] P (*annoyed*) cabreado P; *Br* P (*drunk*) borracho, pedo F
pistol ['pɪstl] pistola *f*
piston ['pɪstən] pistón *m*
pit [pɪt] (*hole*) hoyo *m*; (*coal mine*) mina *f*; *in fruit* hueso *m*
pitch[1] [pɪtʃ] *n* MUS tono *m*
pitch[2] [pɪtʃ] **1** *v/i in baseball* lanzar la pelota **2** *v/t tent* montar; *ball* lanzar
pitcher[1] ['pɪtʃər] *baseball player* lanzador(a) *m*(*f*), pítcher *m/f*
pitcher[2] ['pɪtʃər] *container* jarra *f*
pitfall ['pɪtfɒːl] dificultad *f*
pitiful ['pɪtɪfəl] *sight* lastimoso; *excuse*, *attempt* lamentable; **pitiless** despiadado
pittance ['pɪtns] miseria *f*
pity ['pɪtɪ] **1** *n* pena *f*, lástima *f*; ***what a ~!*** ¡qué pena! **2** *v/t person* compadecerse de
pizza ['piːtsə] pizza *f*
placard ['plækɑːrd] pancarta *f*
place [pleɪs] **1** *n* sitio *m*, lugar *m*; *in race*, *competition* puesto *m*; (*seat*) sitio *m*; ***at my / his ~*** en mi / su casa; ***in ~ of*** en lugar de; ***take ~*** tener lugar **2** *v/t* (*put*) poner, colocar; *order* hacer
placid ['plæsɪd] apacible
plagiarism ['pleɪdʒərɪzm] plagio *m*; **plagiarize** plagiar
plain[1] [pleɪn] *n* llanura *f*
plain[2] [pleɪn] **1** *adj* (*clear*, *obvious*) claro; (*not fancy*) simple; (*not pretty*) feíllo; (*not patterned*) liso; (*blunt*) directo **2** *adv* verdaderamente; **plainly** (*clearly*) evidentemente; (*bluntly*) directamente; (*simply*) con sencillez; **plain spoken** directo
plaintive ['pleɪntɪv] quejumbroso
plan [plæn] **1** *n* plan *m*; (*drawing*) plano *m* **2** *v/t* planear; (*design*) hacer los planos de **3** *v/i* hacer planes

plane[1] [pleɪn] (*airplane*) avión *m*

plane[2] [pleɪn] *tool* cepillo *m*

planet ['plænɪt] planeta *f*

plank [plæŋk] *of wood* tablón *m*; *fig*: *of policy* punto *m*

planning ['plænɪŋ] planificación *f*

plant[1] [plænt] **1** *n* planta *f* **2** *v/t* plantar

plant[2] [plænt] *n* (*factory*) fábrica *f*, planta *f*; (*equipment*) maquinaria *f*

plantation [plæn'teɪʃn] plantación *f*

plaque [plæk] *on wall*, *teeth* placa *f*

plaster ['plæstər] **1** *n* yeso *m* **2** *v/t* enyesar

plastic ['plæstɪk] **1** *n* plástico *m* **2** *adj* (*made of* ~) de plástico; **plastic (money)** plástico *m*, tarjetas *fpl* de pago; **plastic surgeon** cirujano(-a) *m*(*f*) plástico(-a); **plastic surgery** cirugía *f* estética

plate [pleɪt] plato *m*; *of metal* chapa *f*

plateau ['plætoʊ] meseta *f*

platform ['plætfɔːrm] (*stage*) plataforma *f*; *of railroad station* andén *m*; *fig*: *political* programa *m*

platinum ['plætɪnəm] **1** *n* platino *m* **2** *adj* de platino

platonic [plə'tɑːnɪk] platónico

platoon [plə'tuːn] *of soldiers* sección *f*

plausible ['plɒːzəbl] plausible

play [pleɪ] **1** *n* juego *m*; *in theater*, *on TV* obra *f* (de teatro) **2** *v/i* jugar; *of musician* tocar **3** *v/t* MUS tocar; *game* jugar; *tennis*, *football* jugar a; *opponent* jugar contra; (*perform*: *Macbeth etc*) representar; *particular role* interpretar

◆ **play around** F (*be unfaithful*) acostarse con otras personas

◆ **play down** quitar importancia a

player ['pleɪər] SP jugador(a) *m*(*f*); (*musician*) intérprete *m*/*f*; (*actor*) actor *m*, actriz *f*; **playful** *punch etc* de broma; **playground** zona *f* de juegos; **playing card** carta *f*; **playwright** autor(a) *m*(*f*)

plaza ['plɑːzə] *for shopping* centro *m* comercial

plc [piːel'siː] *Br* (= ***public limited company***) S.A. *f* (= sociedad *f* anónima)

plea [pliː] súplica *f*

plead [pliːd]: ~ ***guilty*** / ***not guilty*** declararse culpable / inocente; ~ ***with*** suplicar

pleasant ['pleznt] agradable

please [pliːz] **1** *adv* por favor; ~ ***do*** claro que sí, por supuesto **2** *v/t* complacer; ~ ***yourself!*** ¡haz lo que quieras!; **pleased** contento; (*satisfied*) satisfecho; ~ ***to meet you*** encantado de conocerle; **pleasing** agradable; **pleasure** satisfacción *f*; *as opposed to work* placer *m*; ***with*** ~ faltaría más

pleat [pliːt] *in skirt* tabla *f*
pledge [pledʒ] **1** *n* (*promise*) promesa *f*; (*guarantee*) compromiso *m*; (*money*) donación *f*; ***Pledge of Allegiance*** *juramento de lealtad a la bandera estadounidense* **2** *v/t* (*promise*) prometer; (*guarantee*) comprometerse; *money* donar
plentiful ['plentɪfəl] abundante; **plenty** abundancia *f*; **~ *of books / food*** muchos libros / mucha comida
pliable ['plaɪəbl] flexible
pliers ['plaɪərz] alicates *mpl*
plight [plaɪt] situación *f* difícil
plod [plɑːd] (*walk*) arrastrarse
plot[1] [plɑːt] *n* (*land*) terreno *m*
plot[2] [plɑːt] **1** *n* (*conspiracy*) complot *m*; *of novel* argumento *m* **2** *v/t* tramar **3** *v/i* conspirar
plotter ['plɑːtər] conspirador(a) *m(f)*; COMPUT plóter *m*
plow, *Br* **plough** [plaʊ] **1** *n* arado *m* **2** *v/t & v/i* arar
◆ **plow back** *profits* reinvertir
pluck [plʌk] *eyebrows* depilar; *chicken* desplumar
plug [plʌg] **1** *n for sink, bath* tapón *m*; *electrical* enchufe *m*; (*spark* ~) bujía *f* **2** *v/t hole* tapar; *new book etc* hacer publicidad de
◆ **plug in** enchufar
plumage ['pluːmɪdʒ] plumaje *m*
plumber ['plʌmər] *Span* fontanero(-a) *m(f)*, *L.Am.* plomero(-a) *m(f)*; **plumbing** *pipes* tuberías *fpl*
plummet ['plʌmɪt] caer en picado
plump [plʌmp] rellenito
plunge [plʌndʒ] **1** *n* salto *m*; *in prices* caída *f* **2** *v/i* precipitarse; *of prices* caer en picado **3** *v/t* hundir; (*into water*) sumergir; **plunging** *neckline* escotado
plural ['plʊərəl] plural *m*
plus [plʌs] **1** *prep* más **2** *adj* más de **3** *n symbol* signo *m* más; (*advantage*) ventaja *f* **4** *conj* (*moreover, in addition*) además
plush [plʌʃ] lujoso
plywood ['plaɪwʊd] madera *f* contrachapada
PM [piː'em] *Br* (= ***Prime Minister***) Primer(a) *m(f)* Ministro(a)
p.m. [piː'em] (= ***post meridiem***) p.m.; ***at 2*** **~** a las 2 de la tarde; ***at 11*** **~** a las 11 de la noche
pneumonia [nuː'moʊnɪə] pulmonía *f*, neumonía *f*
poach[1] [poʊʧ] *cook* hervir
poach[2] [poʊʧ] (*hunt*) cazar furtivamente; *fish* pescar furtivamente
poached egg [poʊʧt'eg] huevo *m* escalfado
P.O. Box [piː'oʊbɑːks] apartado *m* de correos
pocket ['pɑːkɪt] **1** *n* bolsillo *m* **2** *adj radio, dictionary* de bol-

sillo **3** *v/t* meter en el bolsillo; **pocketbook** (*purse*) bolso *m*; (*billfold*) cartera *f*; *book* libro *m* de bolsillo; **pocket calculator** calculadora *f* de bolsillo

podium ['poʊdɪəm] podio *m*

poem ['poʊɪm] poema *m*; **poet** poeta *m/f*, poetisa *f*; **poetic** poético; **poetry** poesía *f*

poignant ['pɔɪnjənt] conmovedor

point [pɔɪnt] **1** *n of pencil, knife* punta *f*; *in competition* punto *m*; (*purpose*) objetivo *m*; (*moment*) momento *m*; *in decimals* coma *f*; ***what's the ~ of telling him?*** ¿qué se consigue diciéndoselo?; ***that's beside the ~*** eso no viene a cuento; ***be on the ~ of*** estar a punto de; ***get to the ~*** ir al grano **2** *v/i* señalar con el dedo

◆ **point out** *sights* indicar; *advantages etc* destacar

◆ **point to** señalar con el dedo; *fig* (*indicate*) indicar

pointed ['pɔɪntɪd] *remark* mordaz; **pointer** *for teacher* puntero *m*; (*hint*) consejo *m*; (*sign, indication*) indicador *m*; **pointless** inútil; **point of view** punto *m* de vista

poise [pɔɪz] confianza *f*; **poised** *person* con aplomo

poison ['pɔɪzn] **1** *n* veneno *m* **2** *v/t* envenenar; **poisonous** venenoso

poke [poʊk] **1** *n* empujón *m* **2** *v/t* (*prod*) empujar; (*stick*) clavar

◆ **poke around** F husmear

poker ['poʊkər] *game* póquer *m*

polar ['poʊlər] polar

pole[1] [poʊl] *for support* poste *m*; *for tent, pushing things* palo *m*

pole[2] [poʊl] *of earth* polo *m*

police [pə'liːs] policía *f*; **police car** coche *m* de policía; **policeman** policía *m*; **police state** estado *m* policial; **police station** comisaría *f* (de policía); **policewoman** (mujer *f*) policía *f*

policy[1] ['pɑːlɪsɪ] política *f*

policy[2] ['pɑːlɪsɪ] (*insurance ~*) póliza *f*

polio ['poʊlɪoʊ] polio *f*

polish ['pɑːlɪʃ] **1** *n* abrillantador *m*; (*nail ~*) esmalte *m* de uñas **2** *v/t* dar brillo a; *speech* pulir; **polished** *performance* brillante

polite [pə'laɪt] educado; **politely** educadamente; **politeness** educación *f*

political [pə'lɪtɪkl] político; **politically correct** políticamente correcto; **politician** político(-a) *m*(*f*); **politics** política *f*

poll [poʊl] **1** *n* (*survey*) encuesta *f*, sondeo *m*; ***go to the ~s*** (*vote*) acudir a las urnas **2** *v/t people* sondear; *votes* obtener

pollen ['pɑːlən] polen *m*

pollster ['pɑːlstər] encues-

tador(a) *m(f)*
pollutant [pə'lu:tənt] contaminante *m*; **pollute** contaminar; **pollution** contaminación *f*
'**polo shirt** polo *m*
polyester [pɑ:lɪ'estər] poliéster *m*
polystyrene [pɑ:lɪ'staɪri:n] poliestireno *m*
polyunsaturated [pɑ:lɪʌn'sætjəreɪtɪd] poliinsaturado
pond [pɑ:nd] estanque *m*
pontiff ['pɑ:ntɪf] pontífice *m*
pony ['pouni] poni *m*; **ponytail** coleta *f*
pool¹ [pu:l] *n* (*swimming* ~) piscina *f*, *L.Am.* pileta *f*, *Mex* alberca *f*; *of water, blood* charco *m*
pool² [pu:l] *n game* billar *m* americano
pool³ [pu:l] **1** *n* (*common fund*) bote *m*, fondo *m* común **2** *v/t resources* juntar
'**pool hall** sala *f* de billares
'**pool table** mesa *f* de billar americano
poop [pu:p] F caca *f* F
pooped [pu:pt] F hecho polvo F
poor [pʊr] **1** *adj* pobre; (*not good*) mediocre, malo **2** *npl*: ***the*** ~ los pobres; **poorly** mal
pop¹ [pɑ:p] MUS pop *m*
pop² [pɑ:p] F (*father*) papá *m* F
'**popcorn** palomitas *fpl* de maíz
pope [poʊp] papa *m*
Popsicle® ['pɑ:psɪkl] polo *m* (*helado*)
popular ['pɑ:pjʊlər] popular; **popularity** popularidad *f*
populate ['pɑ:pjʊleɪt] poblar; **population** población *f*
porch [pɔ:rʧ] porche *m*
pork [pɔ:rk] cerdo *m*
porn [pɔ:rn] F porno *m* F; **pornographic** pornográfico; **pornography** pornografía *f*
port¹ [pɔ:rt] *n* puerto *m*
port² [pɔ:rt] *adj* (*left-hand*) a babor
portable ['pɔ:rtəbl] **1** *adj* portátil **2** *n* COMPUT portátil *m*; *TV* televisión *f* portátil
porter ['pɔ:rtər] *for luggage* mozo(-a) *m(f)*
portion ['pɔ:rʃn] parte *f*; *of food* ración *f*
portrait ['pɔ:rtreɪt] **1** *n* retrato *m* **2** *adv print* en formato vertical; **portray** *of artist* retratar; *of actor* interpretar; *of author* describir
Portugal ['pɔ:rʧʊgl] Portugal; **Portuguese 1** *adj* portugués **2** *n person* portugués(-esa) *m(f)*; *language* portugués *m*
pose [pouz] **1** *n* (*pretense*) pose *f* **2** *v/i for artist* posar **3** *v/t problem, threat* representar
position [pə'zɪʃn] **1** *n* posición *f*; (*stance, point of view*) postura *f*; (*job*) puesto *m* **2** *v/t* situar, colocar
positive ['pɑ:zətɪv] positivo; **positively** (*decidedly*) verda-

deramente; (*definitely*) claramente
possess [pə'zes] poseer; **possession** posesión *f*; **possessive** posesivo
possibility [pɑːsə'bɪlətɪ] posibilidad *f*; **possible** posible; **possibly** (*perhaps*) puede ser, quizás
post¹ [poʊst] **1** *n of wood, metal* poste *m* **2** *v/t notice* pegar; *on bulletin board* poner; *profits* presentar
post² [poʊst] **1** *n* (*place of duty*) puesto *m* **2** *v/t soldier, employee* destinar; *guards* apostar
post³ [poʊst] *Br* **1** *n* (*mail*) correo *m* **2** *v/t letter* echar al correo
postage ['poʊstɪdʒ] franqueo *m*; **postage stamp** *fml* sello *m*, *L.Am.* estampilla *f*, *Mex* timbre *m*; **postal** postal; **postcard** (tarjeta *f*) postal *f*; **postdate** posfechar
poster ['poʊstər] póster *m*, *L.Am.* afiche *m*
postgraduate ['poʊstgrædʒʊət] posgraduado(-a) *m*(*f*)
posthumous ['pɑːstʊməs] póstumo
posting ['poʊstɪŋ] (*assignment*) destino *m*
'postmark matasellos *m inv*
post-mortem [poʊst'mɔːrtəm] autopsia *f*
'post office oficina *f* de correos
postpone [poʊst'poʊn] posponer, aplazar; **postponement** aplazamiento *m*
pot¹ [pɑːt] *for cooking* olla *f*; *for coffee* cafetera *f*; *for tea* tetera *f*; *for plant* maceta *f*
pot² [pɑːt] F (*marijuana*) maría *f* F
potato [pə'teɪtoʊ] *Span* patata *f*, *L.Am.* papa *f*; **potato chips**, *Br* **potato crisps** *Span* patatas *fpl* fritas, *L.Am.* papas *fpl* fritas
potent ['poʊtənt] potente
potential [pə'tenʃl] **1** *adj* potencial **2** *n* potencial *m*; **potentially** potencialmente
pothole ['pɑːthoʊl] *in road* bache *m*
potter ['pɑːtər] alfarero(-a) *m*(*f*); **pottery** alfarería *f*
pouch [paʊtʃ] *bag* bolsa *f*; *for mail* saca *f*
poultry ['poʊltrɪ] *birds* aves *fpl* de corral; *meat* carne *f* de ave
pound¹ [paʊnd] *n weight* libra *f* (*453,6 gr*)
pound² [paʊnd] *n for strays* perrera *f*; *for cars* depósito *m*
pound³ [paʊnd] *v/i of heart* palpitar con fuerza
pour [pɔːr] **1** *v/t into a container* verter; (*spill*) derramar **2** *v/i*: ***it's ~ing*** (***with rain***) está lloviendo a cántaros
◆ **pour out** *liquid* servir; *troubles* contar
poverty ['pɑːvərtɪ] pobreza *f*
powder ['paʊdər] **1** *n* polvo *m*; *for face* polvos *mpl* **2** *v/t face* empolvarse
power ['paʊər] (*strength*) fuer-

za *f*; *of engine* potencia; (*authority*) poder *m*; (*energy*) energía *f*; (*electricity*) electricidad *f*; **power cut** apagón *m*; **power failure** apagón *m*; **powerful** poderoso; *car* potente; *drug* fuerte; **powerless** impotente; **power line** línea *f* de conducción eléctrica; **power outage** apagón *m*; **power station** central *f* eléctrica; **power steering** dirección *f* asistida

PR [piː'ɑːr] (= ***public relations***) relaciones *fpl* públicas

practical ['præktɪkl] práctico; *layout* funcional; **practically** de manera práctica; (*almost*) prácticamente

practice ['præktɪs] **1** *n* práctica *f*; (*rehearsal*) ensayo *m*; (*custom*) costumbre *f* **2** *v/i* practicar; *of musician* ensayar; *of footballer* entrenarse **3** *v/t* practicar; *law, medicine* ejercer

practise *Br* ☞ ***practice*** *v/i & v/t*

prairie ['preri] pradera *f*

praise [preɪz] **1** *n* elogio *m*, alabanza *f* **2** *v/t* elogiar; **praiseworthy** elogiable

pray [preɪ] rezar; **prayer** oración *f*

preach [priːʧ] **1** *v/i* predicar; (*moralize*) sermonear **2** *v/t sermon* predicar; **preacher** predicador(a) *m(f)*

precaution [prɪ'kɒːʃn] precaución *f*; **precautionary** *measure* preventivo

precede [prɪ'siːd] preceder; (*walk in front of*) ir delante de; **precedent** precedente *m*; **preceding** anterior

precious ['preʃəs] preciado; *gem* precioso

precise [prɪ'saɪs] preciso; **precisely** exactamente; **precision** precisión *f*

preconceived ['priːkənsiːvd] *idea* preconcebido

precondition [priːkən'dɪʃn] condición *f* previa

predator ['predətər] *animal* depredador(a) *m(f)*; **predatory** depredador

predecessor ['priːdɪsesər] *in job* predecesor(a) *m(f)*; *machine* modelo *m* anterior

predicament [prɪ'dɪkəmənt] apuro *m*

predict [prɪ'dɪkt] predecir, pronosticar; **prediction** predicción *f*, pronóstico *m*

predominant [prɪ'dɑːmɪnənt] predominante; **predominantly** predominantemente

prefabricated [priː'fæbrɪkeɪtɪd] prefabricado

preface ['prefɪs] prólogo *m*, prefacio *m*

prefer [prɪ'fɜːr] preferir; **preferable** preferible; **preferably** preferentemente; **preference** preferencia *f*; **preferential** preferente

pregnancy ['pregnənsɪ] embarazo *m*; **pregnant** embarazada; *animal* preñada

prehistoric [priːhɪs'tɑːrɪk]

prehistórico
prejudice ['predʒʊdɪs] **1** *n* prejuicio *m* **2** *v/t person* predisponer, influir; *chances* perjudicar; **prejudiced** parcial, predispuesto
preliminary [prɪ'lɪmɪnerɪ] preliminar
premarital [priː'mærɪtl] prematrimonial
premature ['priːmətʊr] prematuro
premier ['premɪr] (*Prime Minister*) primer(a) ministro(-a) *m*(*f*)
première ['premɪer] estreno *m*
premises ['premɪsɪz] local *m*
premium ['priːmɪəm] *in insurance* prima *f*
prenatal [priː'neɪtl] prenatal
preoccupied [prɪ'ɑːkjʊpaɪd] preocupado
preparation [prepə'reɪʃn] preparación *f*; **~s** preparativos *mpl*; **prepare 1** *v/t* preparar; ***be ~d to do sth*** *be willing* estar dispuesto a hacer algo **2** *v/i* prepararse
preposition [prepə'zɪʃn] preposición *f*
prerequisite [priː'rekwɪzɪt] requisito *m* previo
prescribe [prɪ'skraɪb] MED recetar; **prescription** MED receta *f*
presence ['prezns] presencia *f*
present[1] ['preznt] **1** *adj* (*current*) actual; ***be ~*** estar presente **2** *n*: ***the ~*** *also gram* el presente
present[2] ['preznt] *n* (*gift*) regalo *m*
present[3] [prɪ'zent] *v/t* presentar; *award* entregar
presentation [prezn'teɪʃn] presentación *f*; **present-day** actual; **presenter** presentador(a) *m*(*f*); **presently** (*at the moment*) actualmente; (*soon*) pronto
preservative [prɪ'zɜːrvətɪv] conservante *m*; **preserve 1** *n* (*domain*) dominio *m* **2** *v/t standards, peace etc* mantener; *food, wood* conservar
preside [prɪ'zaɪd] presidir; **presidency** presidencia *f*; **president** presidente(-a) *m*(*f*); **presidential** presidencial
press [pres] **1** *n*: ***the ~*** la prensa **2** *v/t button* pulsar, presionar; (*urge*) presionar; (*squeeze*) apretar; *clothes* planchar; **pressing** urgente; **pressure 1** *n* presión *f* **2** *v/t* presionar
prestige [pre'stiːʒ] prestigio *m*; **prestigious** prestigioso
presumably [prɪ'zuːməblɪ] presumiblemente; **presume** suponer; **presumption** *of innocence, guilt* presunción *f*
presuppose [priːsə'poʊs] presuponer
pre-tax ['priːtæks] antes de impuestos
pretence *Br* ☞ ***pretense***
pretend [prɪ'tend] **1** *v/t* fingir, hacer como si; *claim* preten-

der **2** *v/i* fingir; **pretense** farsa *f*; **pretentious** pretencioso

pretext ['pri:tekst] pretexto *m*

pretty ['prɪtɪ] **1** *adj village, house, fabric etc* bonito, lindo; *child, woman* guapo, lindo **2** *adv* (*quite*) bastante

prevail [prɪ'veɪl] (*triumph*) prevalecer; **prevailing** predominante

prevent [prɪ'vent] impedir, evitar; **prevention** prevención *f*; **preventive** preventivo

preview ['pri:vju:] **1** *n of movie etc* preestreno *m* **2** *v/t* hacer la presentación previa de

previous ['pri:vɪəs] anterior, previo; **previously** anteriormente, antes

prey [preɪ] presa *f*

price [praɪs] **1** *n* precio *m* **2** *v/t* COM poner precio a; **priceless** que no tiene precio

prick[1] [prɪk] **1** *n pain* punzada *f* **2** *v/t* (*jab*) pinchar

prick[2] [prɪk] *n* V (*penis*) polla *f* V, carajo *m* V; V *person Span* gilipollas *m inv* V, *L.Am.* pendejo *m* V

prickle ['prɪkl] *on plant* espina *f*; **prickly** *beard, plant* que pincha; (*irritable*) irritable

pride [praɪd] *in person, achievement* orgullo *m*; (*self-respect*) amor *m* propio

priest [pri:st] sacerdote *m*; (*parish* ~) cura *m*

primarily [praɪ'merɪlɪ] principalmente; **primary** **1** *adj* principal **2** *n* POL elecciones *fpl* primarias

prime 'minister primer(a) ministro *m*(*f*)

primitive ['prɪmɪtɪv] primitivo

prince [prɪns] príncipe *m*; **princess** princesa *f*

principal ['prɪnsəpl] **1** *adj* principal **2** *n of school* director(a) *m*(*f*); *of university* rector(a) *m*(*f*); **principally** principalmente

principle ['prɪnsəpl] principio *m*; ***on*** ~ por principios; ***in*** ~ en principio

print [prɪnt] **1** *n in book etc* letra *f*; (*photograph*) grabado *m*; ***out of*** ~ agotado **2** *v/t* imprimir; (*use block capitals*) escribir en mayúsculas; **printer** *person* impresor(a) *m*(*f*); *machine* impresora *f*; *company* imprenta *f*; **print-out** copia *f* impresa

prior [praɪr] **1** *adj* previo **2** *prep*: ~ ***to*** antes de

prioritize [praɪ'ɔ:rətaɪz] (*put in order of priority*) ordenar atendiendo a las prioridades; (*give priority to*) dar prioridad a; **priority** prioridad *f*

prison ['prɪzn] prisión *f*, cárcel *f*; **prisoner** prisionero(-a) *m*(*f*); ***take s.o.*** ~ hacer prisionero a alguien; **prisoner of war** prisionero(-a) *m*(*f*) de guerra

privacy ['prɪvəsɪ] intimidad *f*; **private** **1** *adj* privado **2** *n* MIL soldado *m/f* raso; **privately** (*in private*) en privado; *with one other* a solas; (*inwardly*) para sí

privilege ['prɪvəlɪdʒ] (*special treatment*) privilegio *m*; (*honor*) honor *m*; **privileged** privilegiado

prize [praɪz] **1** *n* premio *m* **2** *v/t* apreciar, valorar; **prizewinner** premiado(-a) *m(f)*; **prizewinning** premiado

probability [prɑːbə'bɪlətɪ] probabilidad *f*; **probable** probable; **probably** probablemente

probation [prə'beɪʃn] *in job* período *m* de prueba; LAW libertad *f* condicional

probe [proʊb] **1** *n* (*investigation*) investigación *f*; *scientific* sonda *f* **2** *v/t* examinar; (*investigate*) investigar

problem ['prɑːbləm] problema *m*; ***no ~!*** ¡claro!

procedure [prə'siːdʒər] procedimiento *m*; **proceed** (*go: of people*) dirigirse; *of work etc* proseguir, avanzar; **proceedings** (*events*) actos *mpl*; **proceeds** recaudación *f*

process ['prɑːses] **1** *n* proceso *m* **2** *v/t food* tratar; *raw materials, data* procesar; *application* tramitar; **procession** desfile *m*; *religious* procesión *f*; **processor** procesador *m*

prod [prɑːd] **1** *n* empujoncito *m* **2** *v/t* dar un empujoncito a; *with elbow* dar un codazo a

prodigy ['prɑːdɪdʒɪ]: (***child***) ~ niño(-a) *m(f)* prodigio

produce[1] ['prɑːduːs] *n* productos *mpl* del campo

produce[2] [prə'duːs] *v/t* producir; (*manufacture*) fabricar; (*bring out*) sacar

producer [prə'duːsər] productor(a) *m(f)*; (*manufacturer*) fabricante *m/f*; **product** producto *m*; **production** producción *f*; **productive** productivo; **productivity** productividad *f*

profess [prə'fes] manifestar; **profession** profesión *f*; **professional 1** *adj* profesional **2** *n* profesional *m/f*; **professionally** *play sport* profesionalmente; (*well, skillfully*) con profesionalidad

professor [prə'fesər] catedrático(-a) *m(f)*

proficient [prə'fɪʃnt] competente; (*skillful*) hábil

profile ['proʊfaɪl] *of face* perfil *m*; *biographical* reseña *f*

profit ['prɑːfɪt] **1** *n* beneficio *m* **2** *v/i*: ***~ from*** beneficiarse de; **profitability** rentabilidad *f*; **profitable** rentable

profound [prə'faʊnd] profundo

prognosis [prɑːg'noʊsɪs] pronóstico *m*

program ['proʊgræm] **1** *n* programa *m* **2** *v/t* COMPUT programar; **programme** *Br* ☞ ***program***; **programmer**

programador(a) *m(f)*
progress 1 ['prɑːgres] *n* progreso *m* **2** [prə'gres] *v/i* (*advance in time*) avanzar; (*move on*) pasar; (*make* ~) progresar; **progressive** (*enlightened*) progresista; (*which progresses*) progresivo; **progressively** progresivamente
prohibit [prə'hɪbɪt] prohibir; **prohibitive** *prices* prohibitivo
project[1] ['prɑːdʒekt] *n* proyecto *m*; edu trabajo *m*; (*housing area*) barriada *f* de viviendas sociales
project[2] [prə'dʒekt] **1** *v/t movie* proyectar; *figures, sales* calcular **2** *v/i* (*stick out*) sobresalir
projection [prə'dʒekʃn] (*forecast*) previsión *f*; **projector** *for slides* proyector *m*
prolog, *Br* **prologue** ['proʊlɑːg] prólogo *m*
prolong [prə'lɒːŋ] prolongar
prominent ['prɑːmɪnənt] *nose, chin* prominente; (*significant*) destacado
promiscuity [prɑːmɪ'skjuːətɪ] promiscuidad *f*; **promiscuous** promiscuo
promise ['prɑːmɪs] **1** *n* promesa *f* **2** *v/t* prometer; **promising** prometedor
promote [prə'moʊt] *employee* ascender; (*encourage, foster*) promover; COM promocionar; **promoter** *of sports event* promotor(a) *m(f)*; **promotion** *of employee* ascenso *m*; *of scheme, idea*, COM promoción *f*
prompt [prɑːmpt] **1** *adj* (*on time*) puntual; (*speedy*) rápido **2** *v/t* (*cause*) provocar; *actor* apuntar; **promptly** (*on time*) puntualmente; (*immediately*) inmediatamente
prone [proʊn]: ***be ~ to*** ser propenso a
pronoun ['proʊnaʊn] pronombre *m*
pronounce [prə'naʊns] *word* pronunciar; (*declare*) declarar
pronto ['prɑːntoʊ] F ya, en seguida
pronunciation [prənʌnsɪ'eɪʃn] pronunciación *f*
proof [pruːf] prueba(s) *f(pl)*
prop [prɑːp] THEA accesorio *m*
◆ **prop up** apoyar
propaganda [prɑːpə'gændə] propaganda *f*
propel [prə'pel] propulsar; **propeller** hélice *f*
proper ['prɑːpər] (*real*) de verdad; (*correct, fitting*) adecuado; **properly** (*correctly*) bien; (*fittingly*) adecuadamente; **property** propiedad *f*; (*land*) propiedad(es) *f(pl)*
proportion [prə'pɔːrʃn] proporción *f*; **proportional** proporcional
proposal [prə'poʊzl] propuesta *f*; *of marriage* proposición *f*; **propose 1** *v/t* sugerir, proponer; (*plan*) proponerse **2** *v/i* (*make offer of*

marriage) pedir la mano (***to*** a); **proposition 1** *n* propuesta *f* **2** *v/t woman* hacer proposiciones a
proprietor [prə'praɪətər] propietario(-a) *m*(*f*)
prosecute ['prɑːsɪkjuːt] LAW procesar; **prosecution** LAW procesamiento *m*; *lawyers* acusación *f*
prospect ['prɑːspekt] (*chance, likelihood*) probabilidad *f*; (*thought of something in the future*) perspectiva *f*; ***~s*** perspectivas *fpl* (de futuro); **prospective** potencial
prosper ['prɑːspər] prosperar; **prosperity** prosperidad *f*; **prosperous** próspero
prostitute ['prɑːstɪtuːt] prostituta *f*; ***male ~*** prostituto *m*; **prostitution** prostitución *f*
protect [prə'tekt] proteger; **protection** protección *f*; **protective** protector; **protector** protector(a) *m*(*f*)
protein ['proutiːn] proteína *f*
protest 1 ['proutest] *n* protesta *f* **2** [prə'test] *v/t* protestar, quejarse de; (*object to*) protestar contra **3** [prə'test] *v/i* protestar
Protestant ['prɑːtɪstənt] **1** *n* protestante *m/f* **2** *adj* protestante
protester [prə'testər] manifestante *m/f*
prototype ['proutətaɪp] prototipo *m*
protrude [prə'truːd] sobresalir; **protruding** saliente; *ears, teeth* prominente
proud [praud] orgulloso; **proudly** con orgullo, orgullosamente
prove [pruːv] demostrar, probar
proverb ['prɑːvɜːrb] proverbio *m*, refrán *m*
provide [prə'vaɪd] proporcionar; ***~d*** (***that***) (*on condition that*) con la condición de que, siempre que
province ['prɑːvɪns] provincia *f*; **provincial** *city* provincial; *pej*: *attitude* de pueblo, provinciano
provision [prə'vɪʒn] (*supply*) suministro *m*; *of law, contract* disposición *f*; **provisional** provisional
provocation [prɑːvə'keɪʃn] provocación *f*; **provocative** provocador; *sexually* provocativo; **provoke** provocar
prowl [praul] merodear; **prowler** merodeador(a) *m*(*f*)
proximity [prɑːk'sɪmətɪ] proximidad *f*
proxy ['prɑːksɪ] (*authority*) poder *m*; *person* apoderado(-a) *m*(*f*)
prudence ['pruːdns] prudencia *f*; **prudent** prudente
pry [praɪ] entrometerse
PS ['piːes] (= ***postscript***) PD (= posdata *f*)
pseudonym ['suːdənɪm] pseudónimo *m*
psychiatric [saɪkɪ'ætrɪk] psi-

quiátrico; **psychiatrist** psiquiatra *m/f*; **psychiatry** psiquiatría *f*
psychoanalysis [saɪkouən'æləsɪs] psicoanálisis *m*; **psychoanalyst** psicoanalista *m/f*; **psychoanalyze** psicoanalizar
psychological [saɪkə'lɑːdʒɪkl] psicológico; **psychologist** psicólogo(-a) *m(f)*; **psychology** psicología *f*
psychopath ['saɪkoupæθ] psicópata *m/f*
psychosomatic [saɪkousə'mætɪk] psicosomático
pub [pʌb] *Br* bar *m*
public ['pʌblɪk] **1** *adj* público **2** *n*: ***the ~*** el público
publication [pʌblɪ'keɪʃn] publicación *f*
public 'holiday día *m* festivo
publicity [pʌb'lɪsətɪ] publicidad *f*; **publicize** (*make known*) publicar, hacer público; COM dar publicidad a
publicly ['pʌblɪklɪ] públicamente
'public school colegio *m* público; *Br* colegio *m* privado
publish ['pʌblɪʃ] publicar; **publisher** *person* editor(a) *m(f)*; *company* editorial *f*; **publishing** industria *f* editorial; **publishing company** editorial *f*
Puerto Rican [pwertou'riːkən] **1** *adj* portorriqueño, puertorriqueño **2** *n* portorriqueño(-a) *m(f)*, puertorriqueño(-a) *m(f)*; **Puerto Rico** Puerto Rico
puff [pʌf] **1** *n of wind* racha *f*; *from cigarette* calada *f*; *of smoke* bocanada *f* **2** *v/i* (*pant*) resoplar; **puffy** *eyes, face* hinchado
pull [pʊl] **1** *n on rope* tirón *m*; F (*appeal*) gancho *m* F; F (*influence*) enchufe *m* F **2** *v/t* (*drag*) arrastrar; (*tug*) tirar de; *tooth* sacar **3** *v/i* tirar
◆ **pull ahead** *in race* adelantarse
◆ **pull down** (*lower*) bajar; (*demolish*) derribar
◆ **pull in** *of bus, train* llegar
◆ **pull up 1** *v/t* (*raise*) subir; *item of clothing* subirse; *weeds* arrancar **2** *v/i of car etc* parar
pulley ['pʊlɪ] polea *f*
pulsate [pʌl'seɪt] *of heart* palpitar; *of music* vibrar
pulse [pʌls] pulso *m*
pulverize ['pʌlvəraɪz] pulverizar
pump [pʌmp] **1** *n* bomba *f*; (*gas ~*) surtidor *m* **2** *v/t* bombear
pumpkin ['pʌmpkɪn] calabaza *f*
pun [pʌn] juego *m* de palabras
punch [pʌntʃ] **1** *n blow* puñetazo *m*; *implement* perforadora *f* **2** *v/t with fist* dar un puñetazo a; *hole, ticket* agujerear
punctual ['pʌŋktʃuəl] puntual; **punctuality** puntualidad *f*
punctuation [pʌŋktʃu'eɪʃn]

puntuación *f*
puncture ['pʌŋktʃər] **1** *n* perforación *f* **2** *v/t* perforar
punish ['pʌnɪʃ] castigar; **punishing** *schedule* exigente; *pace* fuerte; **punishment** castigo *m*
puny ['pju:nɪ] *person* enclenque
pup [pʌp] cachorro *m*
pupil[1] ['pju:pl] *of eye* pupila *f*
pupil[2] ['pju:pl] (*student*) alumno(-a) *m*(*f*)
puppet ['pʌpɪt] *also fig* marioneta *f*
purchase[1] ['pɜ:rtʃəs] **1** *n* adquisición *f*, compra *f* **2** *v/t* adquirir, comprar
purchase[2] ['pɜ:rtʃəs] *n* (*grip*) agarre *m*
purchaser ['pɜ:rtʃəsər] comprador(a) *m*(*f*)
pure [pjʊr] puro; **purely** puramente
purge [pɜ:rdʒ] **1** *n of political party* purga *f* **2** *v/t* purgar *f*
purify ['pjʊrɪfaɪ] *water* depurar
puritan ['pjʊrɪtən] puritano(-a) *m*(*f*)
purity ['pjʊrɪtɪ] pureza *f*
purpose ['pɜ:rpəs] (*aim, object*) próposito *m*, objeto *m*; ***on** ~* a propósito; **purposely** decididamente
purr [pɜ:r] *of cat* ronronear
purse [pɜ:rs] (*pocket book*) bolso *m*; *Br for money* monedero *m*
pursue [pər'su:] *person* perseguir; *career* ejercer; *course of action* proseguir; **pursuer** perseguidor(a) *m*(*f*); **pursuit** (*chase*) persecución *f*; *of happiness etc* búsqueda *f*; (*activity*) actividad *f*
push [pʊʃ] **1** *n* empujón *m* **2** *v/t* (*shove*) empujar; *button* apretar, pulsar; (*pressurize*) presionar; F *drugs* pasar F **3** *v/i* empujar; **pusher** F *of drugs* camello *m* F; **push-up** flexión *f* (de brazos); **pushy** F avasallador, agresivo
puss, pussy (cat) [pʊs, 'pʊsɪ (kæt)] F minino *m* F
put [pʊt] poner; *question* hacer; ***~ the cost at*** estimar el costo en
◆ **put across** *idea etc* hacer llegar
◆ **put aside** *money* apartar; *work* dejar a un lado
◆ **put away** *in closet etc* guardar; *in institution* encerrar; F (*consume*) cepillarse F; *money* apartar; *animal* sacrificar
◆ **put back** (*replace*) volver a poner
◆ **put down** dejar; *deposit* entregar; *rebellion* reprimir; (*belittle*) dejar en mal lugar
◆ **put forward** *idea etc* proponer, presentar
◆ **put in** meter; *time* dedicar; *request, claim* presentar
◆ **put off** *light, TV* apagar; (*postpone*) posponer, aplazar; (*deter*) desalentar; (*repel*) desagradar
◆ **put on** *light, TV* encender,

L.Am. prender; *tape*, *music* poner; *jacket*, *eye glasses* ponerse; (*perform*) representar; (*assume*) fingir

◆ **put out** *hand* extender; *fire*, *light* apagar

◆ **put together** (*assemble*, *organize*) montar

◆ **put up** *hand*, *building* levantar; *person for the night* alojar; *prices* subir; *poster* colocar; *money* aportar

◆ **put up with** aguantar

putty ['pʌtɪ] masilla *f*

puzzle ['pʌzl] **1** *n* (*mystery*) enigma *m*; *game* pasatiempos *mpl*; (*jigsaw*) puzzle *m*; (*crossword*) crucigrama *m* **2** *v/t* desconcertar; **puzzling** desconcertante

PVC [piːviː'siː] (= ***polyvinyl chloride***) PVC *m* (= cloruro *m* de polivinilo)

pyjamas *Br* ☞ ***pajamas***

pylon ['paɪlən] torre *f* de alta tensión

Pyrenees [pɪrə'niːz]: ***the*** ~ los Pirieos

Q

quadrangle ['kwɑːdræŋgl] cuadrángulo *m*; *courtyard* patio *m*

quadruped ['kwɑːdrʊped] cuadrúpedo *m*

quail [kweɪl] temblar (***at*** ante)

quaint [kweɪnt] *cottage* pintoresco; *ideas etc* extraño

quake [kweɪk] **1** *n* (*earthquake*) terremoto *m* **2** *v/i of earth*, *with fear* temblar

qualification [kwɑːlfɪ'keɪʃn] *from university etc* título *m*; **qualified** titulado; (*restricted*) limitado; **qualify 1** *v/t of degree*, *course etc* habilitar; *remark etc* matizar **2** *v/i* (*get degree etc*) titularse, *L.Am.* egresar; *in competition* calificarse

quality ['kwɑːlətɪ] calidad *f*; (*characteristic*) cualidad *f*; **quality control** control *m* de calidad

quandary ['kwɑːndərɪ] dilema *m*

quantify ['kwɑːntɪfaɪ] cuantificar

quantity ['kwɑːntətɪ] cantidad *f*

quarantine ['kwɑːrəntiːn] cuarentena *f*

quarrel ['kwɑːrəl] **1** *n* pelea *f* **2** *v/i* pelearse

quarry[1] ['kwɑːrɪ] *in hunt* presa *f*

quarry[2] ['kwɑːrɪ] *for mining* cantera *f*

quart [kwɔːrt] cuarto *m* de galón (*0,946 litre*)

quarter ['kwɔːrtər] cuarto *m* *25 cents* cuarto *m* de dólar; *part of town* barrio *m*; ***a*** ~ ***of an hour*** un cuarto de hora; ***a*** ~ ***of 5*** las cinco menos cuarto, *L.Am.* un cuarto para las cinco; ***a ~ after 5*** las cinco y cuarto; **quarter-final** cuarto *m* de final; **quarter-finalist** cuartofinalista *m/f*; **quarterly 1** *adj* trimestral **2** *adv* trimestralmente; **quarters** MIL alojamiento *m*; **quartet** MUS cuarteto *m*

quartz [kwɔːrts] cuarzo *m*

quash [kwɑːʃ] *rebellion* aplastar, sofocar; *court decision* revocar

quaver ['kweɪvər] **1** *n in voice* temblor *m* **2** *v/i of voice* temblar

queasy ['kwiːzɪ] mareado

queen [kwiːn] reina *f*

queer [kwɪr] (*peculiar*) raro, extraño

quell [kwel] *protest* acallar; *riot* aplastar, sofocar

quench [kwentʃ] *thirst* apagar, saciar; *flames* apagar

query ['kwɪrɪ] **1** *n* duda *f*, pregunta *f* **2** *v/t* (*express doubt about*) cuestionar; (*check*) comprobar

quest [kwest] busca *f*

question ['kwestʃn] **1** *n* pregunta *f*; (*matter*) cuestión *f*, asunto *m* **2** *v/t person* preguntar a; LAW interrogar; (*doubt*) cuestionar; **questionable** cuestionable; **questioning 1** *adj look* inquisitivo **2** *n* interrogatorio *m*; **question mark** signo *m* de interrogación; **questionnaire** cuestionario *m*

queue [kjuː] **1** *n Br* cola *f* **2** *v/i* hacer cola

quibble ['kwɪbl] discutir (*por algo insignificante*)

quick [kwɪk] rápido; ***be ~!*** ¡date prisa!; **quickly** rápidamente, rápido, deprisa; **quickwitted** agudo

quiet ['kwaɪət] tranquilo; *engine* silencioso; ***~!*** ¡silencio!; **quietly** (*not loudly*) silenciosamente; (*without fuss*) discretamente; (*peacefully*) tranquilamente; ***speak ~*** hablar en voz baja; **quietness** *of voice* suavidad *f*; *of night, street* silencio *m*, calma *f*

quilt [kwɪlt] *on bed* edredón *m*

quinine ['kwɪniːn] quinina *f*

quip [kwɪp] **1** *n joke* broma *f*; *remark* salida *f* **2** *v/i* bromear

quirk [kwɜːrk] peculiaridad *f*, rareza *f*; **quirky** peculiar, raro

quit [kwɪt] **1** *v/t job* dejar, abandonar **2** *v/i* (*leave job*) dimitir; COMPUT salir

quite [kwaɪt] (*fairly*) bastante; (*completely*) completamente; ***~ a lot*** bastante

quiver ['kwɪvər] estremecerse

quiz [kwɪz] **1** *n* concurso *m* (*de preguntas y respuestas*) **2** *v/t* interrogar (***about*** sobre)

quota ['kwoʊtə] cuota *f*

quotation [kwoʊ'teɪʃn] *from author* cita *f*; (*price*) presupuesto *m*; **quotation marks** comillas *fpl*; **quote 1** *n from author* cita *f*; (*price*) presupuesto *m*; (*quotation mark*) comilla *f*; ***in ~s*** entre comillas **2** *v/t text* citar; *price* dar

R

rabbit ['ræbɪt] conejo *m*
rabble ['ræbl] chusma *f*, multitud *f*; **rabble-rouser** agitador(a) *m(f)*
rabies ['reɪbiːz] rabia *f*
raccoon [rə'kuːn] mapache *m*
race[1] [reɪs] *n of people* raza *f*
race[2] [reɪs] **1** *n* SP carrera *f* **2** *v/i (run fast)* correr **3** *v/t* correr contra; ***I'll ~ you*** te echo una carrera
'racecourse hipódromo *m*; **racehorse** caballo *m* de carreras; **race riot** disturbios *mpl* raciales; **racetrack** circuito *m*; *for horses* hipódromo *m*
racial ['reɪʃl] racial
racing ['reɪsɪŋ] carreras *fpl*
racism ['reɪsɪzm] racismo *m*; **racist 1** *n* racista *m/f* **2** *adj* racista
rack [ræk] **1** *n for bags on train* portaequipajes *m inv*; *for CDs* mueble *m* **2** *v/t*: ***~ one's brains*** devanarse los sesos
racket[1] ['rækɪt] SP raqueta *f*
racket[2] ['rækɪt] *(noise)* jaleo *m*; *(criminal activity)* negocio *m* sucio
radar ['reɪdɑːr] radar *m*
radiance ['reɪdɪəns] esplendor *m*; **radiant** *smile* resplandeciente; **radiate** *of heat, light* irradiar; **radiation** PHYS radiación *f*; **radiator** radiador *m*
radical ['rædɪkl] **1** *adj* radical **2** *n* POL radical *m/f*; **radicalism** POL radicalismo *m*; **radically** radicalmente
radio ['reɪdɪoʊ] radio *f*; **radioactive** radiactivo; **radioactivity** radiactividad *f*; **radio alarm** radio *m* despertador; **radiographer** técnico(-a) *m(f)* de rayos X; **radiography** radiografía *f*; **radio station** emisora *f* de radio
radius ['reɪdɪəs] radio *m*
raft [ræft] balsa *f*
rafter ['ræftər] viga *f*
rag [ræg] *for cleaning etc* trapo *m*
rage [reɪdʒ] **1** *n* ira *f*, cólera *f* **2** *v/i of storm* bramar
ragged ['rægɪd] andrajoso
raid [reɪd] **1** *n by troops*, FIN incursión *f*; *by police* redada *f*; *by robbers* atraco *m* **2** *v/t of troops* realizar una incursión en; *of police* realizar una redada en; *of robbers* atracar; *fridge* saquear; **raider** *on bank etc* atracador(a) *m(f)*
rail [reɪl] *on track* riel *m*, carril *m*; *(hand~)* pasamanos *m inv*, baranda *f*; *for towel* barra *f*; ***by ~*** en tren; **railings** *around park etc* verja *f*; **railroad** ferrocarril *m*; *track* vía *f* férrea; **railroad station** estación *f* de ferrocarril *or* de tren; **railway** *Br* ferrocarril

m; *track* vía *f* férrea

rain [reɪn] **1** *n* lluvia *f* **2** *v/i* llover; ***it's ~ing*** llueve; **rainbow** arco *m* iris; **raincheck**: ***can I take a ~ on that?*** F ¿lo podríamos aplazar para algún otro momento?; **raincoat** impermeable *m*; **raindrop** gota *f* de lluvia; **rainfall** pluviosidad *f*; **rain forest** selva *f*; **rainproof** *fabric* impermeable; **rainstorm** tormenta *f*, aguacero *m*; **rainy** lluvioso

raise [reɪz] **1** *n in salary* aumento *m* de sueldo **2** *v/t shelf etc* levantar; *offer* incrementar; *children* criar; *question* plantear; *money* reunir

rake [reɪk] *for garden* rastrillo *m*

rally ['rælɪ] (*meeting*, *reunion*) concentración *f*; *political* mitin *m*; MOT rally *m*; *in tennis* peloteo *m*

RAM [ræm] COMPUT (= ***random access memory***) RAM *f* (= memoria *f* de acceso aleatorio)

ram [ræm] **1** *n* carnero *m* **2** *v/t ship*, *car* embestir

ramble ['ræmbl] **1** *n walk* caminata *f* **2** *v/i walk* caminar; *in speaking* divagar; (*talk incoherently*) *hablar sin decir nada coherente*; **rambling** *speech* inconexo

ramp [ræmp] rampa *f*; *for raising vehicle* elevador *m*

rampant ['ræmpənt] *inflation* galopante

rampart ['ræmpɑːrt] muralla *f*

ramshackle ['ræmʃækl] destartalado, desvencijado

ranch [ræntʃ] rancho *m*; **rancher** ranchero(-a) *m*(*f*); **ranchhand** peón(-ona) *m*(*f*)

rancid ['rænsɪd] rancio

rancor, *Br* **rancour** ['rænkər] rencor *m*

R & D [ɑːrən'diː] (= ***research and development***) I+D *f* (= investigación *f* y desarrollo)

random ['rændəm] **1** *adj* al azar; ***~ sample*** muestra *f* aleatoria;**2** *n*: ***at ~*** al azar

range [reɪndʒ] **1** *n of products* gama *f*; *of gun*, *airplane* alcance *m*; *of voice* registro *m*; *of mountains* cordillera *f*; ***at close ~*** de cerca **2** *v/i*: ***~ from X to Y*** ir desde X a Y; **ranger** guardabosques *m/f inv*

rank [ræŋk] **1** *n* MIL, *in society* rango *m* **2** *v/t* clasificar

◆ **rank among** figurar entre

ransack ['rænsæk] saquear

ransom ['rænsəm] rescate *m*

rap [ræp] **1** *n at door etc* golpe *m*; MUS rap *m* **2** *v/t table etc* golpear

rape[1] [reɪp] **1** *n* violación *f* **2** *v/t* violar

rape[2] [reɪp] *n* BOT colza *f*

rapid ['ræpɪd] rápido; **rapidity** rapidez *f*; **rapidly** rápidamente; **rapids** rápidos *mpl*

rapist ['reɪpɪst] violador(a) *m*(*f*)

rare [rer] raro; *steak* poco hecho; **rarely** raramente, raras

veces; **rarity** rareza *f*
rash¹ [ræʃ] *n* MED sarpullido *m*, erupción *f* cutánea
rash² [ræʃ] *adj act* precipitado; **rashly** precipitadamente
rat [ræt] rata *f*
rate [reɪt] *of exchange* tipo *m*; *of pay* tarifa *f*; (*price*) tarifa *f*, precio *m*; (*speed*) ritmo *m*; ***at this ~*** (*at this speed*) a este ritmo; (*if we carry on like this*) si seguimos así; ***at any ~*** (*anyway*) en todo caso; (*at least*) por lo menos
rather ['ræðər] (*fairly, quite*) bastante; ***I would ~ stay here*** preferiría quedarme aquí
ratification [rætɪfɪ'keɪʃn] ratificación *f*; **ratify** ratificar
ratings ['reɪtɪŋz] índice *m* de audiencia
ratio ['reɪʃɪoʊ] proporción *f*
ration ['ræʃn] **1** *n* ración *f* **2** *v/t supplies* racionar
rational ['ræʃənl] racional; **rationality** racionalidad *f*; **rationalization** racionalización *f*; **rationalize 1** *v/t* racionalizar **2** *v/i* buscar una explicación racional; **rationally** racionalmente
rattle ['rætl] **1** *n noise* traqueteo *m*; *toy* sonajero *m* **2** *v/t chains etc* entrechocar **3** *v/i of chains etc* entrechocarse; *of crates* traquetear; **rattlesnake** serpiente *f* de cascabel
raucous ['rɒːkəs] estridente
rave [reɪv] **1** *v/i* (*talk deliriously*) delirar; (*talk wildly*) desvariar; ***~ about sth*** (*be very enthusiastic*) estar muy entusiasmado con algo **2** *n party* fiesta *f* tecno
ravenous ['rævənəs] famélico
ravine [rə'viːn] barranco *m*
raw [rɒː] *meat, vegetable* crudo; *sugar* sin refinar; *iron* sin tratar; **raw materials** materias *fpl* primas
ray [reɪ] rayo *m*
razor ['reɪzər] maquinilla *f* de afeitar; **razor blade** cuchilla *f* de afeitar
re [riː] COM con referencia a
reach [riːʧ] **1** *n*: ***within ~*** al alcance; ***out of ~*** fuera del alcance **2** *v/t* llegar a; *decision, agreement* alcanzar
react [rɪ'ækt] reaccionar; **reaction** reacción *f*; **reactionary 1** *n* POL reaccionario(-a) *m(f)* **2** *adj* POL reaccionario; **reactor** *nuclear* reactor *m*
read [riːd] leer
◆ **read out** *aloud* leer en voz alta
readable ['riːdəbl] *writing* legible; *book* ameno; **reader** *person* lector(a) *m(f)*
readily ['redɪlɪ] *admit, agree* de buena gana
reading ['riːdɪŋ] lectura *f*
readjust [riːə'dʒʌst] **1** *v/t* reajustar **2** *v/i to conditions* volver a adaptarse
ready ['redɪ] (*prepared*) listo, preparado; (*willing*) dispuesto; ***get sth ~*** preparar algo;

ready cash dinero *m* contante y sonante; **ready-made** *stew etc* precocinado; *solution* ya hecho; **ready-to-wear** de confección

real [ri:l] real; *surprise, genius* auténtico; **real estate** bienes *mpl* inmuebles; **real estate agent** agente *m/f* inmobiliario(-a); **realism** realismo *m*; **realist** realista *m/f*; **realistic** realista; **realistically** realísticamente; **reality** realidad *f*; **realize** darse cuenta de; FIN (*yield*) producir; (*sell*) realizar, liquidar; **really** *in truth* de verdad; *big, small* muy; ***I am ~ sorry*** lo siento en el alma; **real time** COMPUT tiempo *m* real; **real-time** COMPUT en tiempo real

realtor ['ri:ltər] agente *m/f* inmobiliario(-a); **realty** bienes *mpl* inmuebles

reappear [ri:ə'pɪr] reaparecer; **reappearance** reaparición *f*

rear [rɪr] **1** *n* parte *f* de atrás **2** *adj legs* de atrás; *seats, wheels, lights* trasero

rearm [ri:'ɑ:rm] **1** *v/t* rearmar **2** *v/i* rearmarse

rearrange [ri:ə'reɪnʒ] *flowers* volver a colocar; *furniture* reordenar; *schedule* cambiar

rear-view 'mirror espejo *m* retrovisor

reason ['ri:zn] razón *f*; **reasonable** razonable; **reasonably** *act* razonablemente; (*quite*) bastante; **reasoning** razonamiento *m*

reassure [ri:ə'ʃʊr] tranquilizar; **reassuring** tranquilizador

rebate ['ri:beɪt] *money back* reembolso *m*

rebel 1 ['rebl] *n* rebelde *m/f* **2** [rɪ'bel] *v/i* rebelarse; **rebellion** rebelión *f*; **rebellious** rebelde; **rebelliousness** rebeldía *f*

rebound [rɪ'baʊnd] *of ball etc* rebotar

rebuild ['ri:bɪld] reconstruir

recall [rɪ'kɒ:l] *goods* retirar del mercado; (*remember*) recordar

recap ['ri:kæp] recapitular

recapture [ri:'kæptʃər] MIL reconquistar; *criminal* volver a detener

recede [rɪ'si:d] *of flood waters* retroceder

receipt [rɪ'si:t] *for purchase* recibo *m*; ***~s*** FIN ingresos *mpl*; **receive** recibir; **receiver** *of letter* destinatario(-a) *m(f)*; TELEC auricular *m*; *for radio* receptor *m*; **receivership:** ***be in ~*** estar en suspensión de pagos

recent ['ri:snt] reciente; **recently** recientemente

reception [rɪ'sepʃn] recepción *f*; (*welcome*) recibimiento *m*; **reception desk** recepción *f*; **receptionist** recepcionista *m/f*; **receptive:** ***be ~ to sth*** ser receptivo a algo

recess ['ri:ses] *in wall etc* hue-

co *m*; EDU recreo *m*; *of legislature* periodo *m* vacacional; **recession** *economic* recesión *f*
recharge [riː'ʧɑːrdʒ] *battery* recargar
recipe ['resəpɪ] receta *f*
recipient [rɪ'sɪpɪənt] *of parcel etc* destinatario(-a) *m(f)*; *of payment* receptor(a) *m(f)*
reciprocal [rɪ'sɪprəkl] recíproco
recite [rɪ'saɪt] *poem* recitar; *details, facts* enumerar
reckless ['reklɪs] imprudente; *driving* temerario; **recklessly** con imprudencia; *drive* con temeridad
reckon ['rekən] (*think, consider*) estimar, considerar
◆ **reckon on** contar con
reclaim [rɪ'kleɪm] *land from sea* ganar, recuperar; *lost property, rights* reclamar
recline [rɪ'klaɪn] reclinarse; **recliner** *chair* sillón *m* reclinable
recluse [rɪ'kluːs] solitario(-a) *m(f)*
recognition [rekəg'nɪʃn] *of state, achievements* reconocimiento *m*; **recognizable** reconocible; **recognize** reconocer
recoil [rɪ'kɔɪl] echarse atrás
recollect [rekə'lekt] recordar; **recollection** recuerdo *m*
recommend [rekə'mend] recomendar; **recommendation** recomendación *f*
recompense ['rekəmpens] recompensa *f*
reconcile ['rekənsaɪl] *people* reconciliar; *differences, facts* conciliar; **reconciliation** *of people* reconciliación *f*; *of differences, facts* conciliación *f*
recondition [riːkən'dɪʃn] reacondicionar
reconnaissance [rɪ'kɑːnɪsns] MIL reconocimiento *m*
reconsider [riːkən'sɪdər] reconsiderar
reconstruct [riːkən'strʌkt] reconstruir
record[1] ['rekɔːrd] *n* MUS disco *m*; SP *etc* récord *m*; *written document, in database* registro *m*; **~s** archivos *mpl*; ***have a criminal ~*** tener antecedentes penales
record[2] [rɪ'kɔːrd] *v/t electronically* grabar; *in writing* anotar
'**record-breaking** récord *inv*; **record holder** plusmarquista *m/f*
recording [rɪ'kɔːrdɪŋ] grabación *f*
recount [rɪ'kaʊnt] (*tell*) relatar
re-count ['riːkaʊnt] **1** *n of votes* segundo recuento *m* **2** *v/t* (*count again*) volver a contar
recoup [rɪ'kuːp] *financial losses* resarcirse de
recover [rɪ'kʌvər] **1** *v/t sth lost* recuperar; *composure* recobrar **2** *v/i from illness* recupe-

rarse; **recovery** recuperación *f*
recreation [rekrɪ'eɪʃn] ocio *m*; **recreational** *done for pleasure* recreativo
recruit [rɪ'kru:t] **1** *n* MIL recluta *m/f*; *to company* nuevo(-a) trabajador(a) **2** *v/t new staff* contratar; **recruitment** MIL reclutamiento *m*; *to company* contratación *f*
rectangle ['rektæŋgl] rectángulo *m*; **rectangular** rectangular
rectify ['rektɪfaɪ] rectificar
recuperate [rɪ'ku:pəreɪt] recuperarse
recur [rɪ'kɜ:r] *of event* repetirse; *of symptoms* reaparecer; **recurrent** recurrente
recycle [ri:'saɪkl] reciclar; **recycling** reciclado *m*
red [red] rojo; ***in the ~*** en números rojos; **Red Cross** Cruz *f* Roja
redecorate [ri:'dekəreɪt] *paint* volver a pintar; *paper* volver a empapelar
redeem [rɪ'di:m] *debt* amortizar; REL redimir
redevelop [ri:dɪ'veləp] *part of town* reedificar
'**redhead** pelirrojo(-a) *m(f)*; **red light** *at traffic light* semáforo *m* (en) rojo; **red light district** zona *f* de prostitución; **red meat** carne *f* roja; **redneck** F *individuo racista y reaccionario, normalmente de clase trabajadora*; **red tape** F burocracia *f*, papeleo *m*
reduce [rɪ'du:s] reducir; *price* rebajar; **reduction** reducción *f*; *in price* rebaja *f*
reek [ri:k] apestar (***of*** a)
reel [ri:l] *of film* rollo *m*; *of thread* carrete *m*
re-e'lect reelegir; **re-election** reelección *f*
re-'entry *of spacecraft* reentrada *f*
ref [ref] F árbitro(-a) *m(f)*
◆ **refer to** referirse a; *dictionary etc* consultar
referee [refə'ri:] SP árbitro(-a) *m(f)*; *for job*: *persona que pueda dar referencias*; **reference** referencia *f*; **reference book** libro *m* de consulta; **reference number** número *m* de referencia
referendum [refə'rendəm] referéndum *m*
refill ['ri:fɪl] volver a llenar
refine [rɪ'faɪn] refinar; *technique* perfeccionar; **refinement** *to process, machine* mejora *f*; **refinery** refinería *f*
reflect [rɪ'flekt] **1** *v/t light* reflejar **2** *v/i* (*think*) reflexionar; **reflection** *in water, glass etc* reflejo *m*; (*consideration*) reflexión *f*
reflex ['ri:fleks] *in body* reflejo *m*
reform [rɪ'fɔ:rm] **1** *n* reforma *f* **2** *v/t* reformar; **reformer** reformador(a) *m(f)*
refresh [rɪ'freʃ] refrescar; **refreshing** *drink* refrescante; *experience* reconfortante; **refreshments** refrigerio *m*

refrigerate [rɪ'frɪdʒəreɪt] refrigerar; **refrigerator** frigorífico *m*, refrigerador *m*
refuel [riːf'juəl] **1** *v/t airplane* reabastecer de combustible a **2** *v/i of airplane* repostar
refuge ['refjuːdʒ] refugio *m*; ***take ~*** *from storm etc* refugiarse; **refugee** refugiado(-a) *m(f)*
refund 1 ['riːfʌnd] *n* reembolso *m* **2** [rɪ'fʌnd] *v/t* reembolsar
refusal [rɪ'fjuːzl] negativa *f*; **refuse 1** *v/i* negarse **2** *v/t help, food* rechazar; ***~ to do sth*** negarse a hacer algo
regain [rɪ'geɪn] recuperar
regard [rɪ'gɑːrd] **1** *n*: ***with ~ to*** con respecto a; (***kind***) ***~s*** saludos; ***with no ~ for*** sin tener en cuenta **2** *v/t*: ***~ as*** con respecto a; **regarding** con respecto a; **regardless** a pesar de todo; ***~ of*** sin tener en cuenta
regime [reɪ'ʒiːm] (*government*) régimen *m*
regiment ['redʒɪmənt] regimiento *m*
region ['riːdʒən] región *f*; **regional** regional
register ['redʒɪstər] **1** *n* registro *m*; *at school* lista *f* **2** *v/t birth, death* registrar; *vehicle* matricular; *letter* certificar; *emotion* mostrar **3** *v/i at university* matricularse; *with police* registrarse; **registered letter** carta *f* certificada; **registration** registro *m*; *at university* matriculación *f*
regret [rɪ'gret] **1** *v/t* lamentar, sentir **2** *n* arrepentimiento *m*, pesar *m*; **regretful** arrepentido; **regrettable** lamentable
regular ['regjulər] **1** *adj* regular; (*normal*) normal **2** *n at bar etc* habitual *m/f*; **regularity** regularidad *f*; **regularly** regularmente
regulate ['reguleɪt] regular; **regulation** (*rule*) regla *f*, norma *f*
rehabilitate [riːhə'bɪlɪteɪt] *ex-criminal* rehabilitar
rehearsal [rɪ'hɜːrsl] ensayo *m*; **rehearse** ensayar
reign [reɪn] **1** *n* reinado *m* **2** *v/i* reinar
reimburse [riːɪm'bɜːrs] reembolsar
reinforce [riːɪn'fɔːrs] *structure* reforzar; *beliefs* reafirmar; **reinforced concrete** hormigón *m* armado; **reinforcements** MIL refuerzos *mpl*
reinstate [riːɪn'steɪt] *in office* reincorporar; *in text* volver a colocar
reject [rɪ'dʒekt] rechazar; **rejection** rechazo *m*
relapse ['riːlæps] MED recaída *f*
related [rɪ'leɪtɪd] *by family* emparentado; *events, ideas etc* relacionado; **relation** *in family* pariente *m/f*; (*connection*) relación *f*; **relationship** relación *f*; **relative 1** *n* pariente *m/f* **2** *adj* relativo; **rel-**

atively relativamente

relax [rɪ'læks] **1** *v/i* relajarse **2** *v/t muscle, pace* relajar; **~!** ¡tranquilízate!; **relaxation** relajación *f*; **relaxed** relajado; **relaxing** relajante

relay 1 [riː'leɪ] *v/t message* pasar; *radio, TV signals* retransmitir **2** ['riːleɪ] *n*: **~ (*race*)** carrera *f* de relevos

release [rɪ'liːs] **1** *n from prison* liberación *f*; *of CD etc* lanzamiento *m*; *CD, record* trabajo *m* **2** *v/t prisoner* liberar; *parking brake* soltar; *information* hacer público

relegate ['relɪgeɪt] relegar

relent [rɪ'lent] ablandarse; **relentless** (*determined*) implacable; *rain etc* que no cesa

relevance ['reləvəns] pertinencia *f*; **relevant** pertinente

reliability [rɪlaɪə'bɪlətɪ] fiabilidad *f*; **reliable** fiable; **reliance** confianza *f*, dependencia *f*

relic ['relɪk] reliquia *f*

relief [rɪ'liːf] alivio *m*; **relieve** *pain* aliviar; (*take over from*) relevar

religion [rɪ'lɪdʒən] religión *f*; **religious** religioso

relinquish [rɪ'lɪŋkwɪʃ] renunciar a

relish ['relɪʃ] **1** *n sauce* salsa *f*; (*enjoyment*) goce *m* **2** *v/t idea, prospect* gozar con

relive [riː'lɪv] *event* revivir

relocate [riːlə'keɪt] *of business, employee* trasladarse

reluctance [rɪ'lʌktəns] reticencia *f*; **reluctant** reticente, reacio

◆ **rely on** [rɪ'laɪ] depender de; ***rely on s.o. to do sth*** contar con alguien para hacer algo

remain [rɪ'meɪn] (*be left*) quedar; (*stay*) permanecer; **remainder** *also* MATH resto *m*; **remaining** restante; **remains** *of body* restos *mpl* (mortales)

remake ['riːmeɪk] *of movie* nueva versión *f*

remark [rɪ'mɑːrk] **1** *n* comentario *m*, observación *f* **2** *v/t* comentar, observar; **remarkable** extraordinario; **remarkably** extraordinariamente

remarry [riː'mærɪ] volver a casarse

remedy ['remədɪ] MED, *fig* remedio *m*

remember [rɪ'membər] **1** *v/t* recordar, acordarse de **2** *v/i* recordar, acordarse

remind [rɪ'maɪnd]: ***~ s.o. of sth*** recordar algo a alguien; ***~ s.o. of s.o.*** recordar alguien a alguien; ***~ s.o. to do sth*** recordar a alguien que haga algo; **reminder** recordatorio *m*

reminisce [remɪ'nɪs] contar recuerdos

remission [rɪ'mɪʃn] remisión *f*; ***go into ~*** MED remitir

remnant ['remnənt] resto *m*

remorse [rɪ'mɔːrs] remordimientos *mpl*; **remorseless** *person* despiadado; *pace, de-*

mands implacable

remote [rɪ'moʊt] *village, possibility* remoto; (*aloof*) distante; *ancestor* lejano; **remote control** control *m* remoto; *for TV* mando *m* a distancia; **remotely** remotamente

removable [rɪ'mu:vəbl] de quita y pon; **removal** eliminación *f*; **remove** eliminar; *lid* quitar; *coat etc* quitarse; *doubt*, *suspicion* despejar; *growth*, *organ* extirpar

rename [ri:'neɪm] cambiar el nombre a

rendez-vous ['rɑ:ndeɪvu:] *romantic* cita *f*; MIL encuentro *m*

renew [rɪ'nu:] *contract* renovar; *discussions* reanudar; **renewal** *of contract etc* renovación *f*; *of discussions* reanudación *f*

renounce [rɪ'naʊns] renunciar a

renovate ['renəveɪt] renovar; **renovation** renovación *f*

rent [rent] **1** *n* alquiler *m*; ***for*** **~** se alquila **2** *v/t* alquilar, *Mex* rentar; **rental** *for apartment, TV* alquiler *m*, *Mex* renta *f*; **rental car** coche *m* de alquiler; **rent-free** sin pagar alquiler

reopen [ri:'oʊpn] **1** *v/t* reabrir; *negotiations* reanudar **2** *v/i of theater etc* volver a abrir

reorganization [ri:ɔ:rgənaɪz'eɪʃn] reorganización *f*; **reorganize** reorganizar

repaint [ri:'peɪnt] repintar

repair [rɪ'per] **1** *v/t* reparar; *shoes* arreglar **2** *n* reparación *f*; *of shoes* arreglo *m*; **repairman** técnico *m*

repatriate [ri:'pætrɪeɪt] repatriar; **repatriation** repatriación *f*

repay [ri:'peɪ] *money* devolver; *person* pagar; **repayment** devolución *f*; *installment* plazo *m*

repeal [rɪ'pi:l] *law* revocar

repeat [rɪ'pi:t] **1** *v/t* repetir **2** *n TV program* repetición *f*; **repeatedly** repetidamente, repetidas veces

repel [rɪ'pel] *attack* rechazar; *insects* repeler, ahuyentar; (*disgust*) repeler, repugnar; **repellent 1** *n* (*insect* **~**) repelente *m* **2** *adj* repelente

repercussions [ri:pər'kʌʃnz] repercusiones *fpl*

repertoire ['repərtwɑ:r] repertorio *m*

repetition [repɪ'tɪʃn] repetición *f*; **repetitive** repetitivo

replace [rɪ'pleɪs] (*put back*) volver a poner; (*take place of*) reemplazar, sustituir; **replacement** *person* sustituto(-a) *m*(*f*); *thing* recambio *m*, reemplazo *m*; **replacement part** (pieza *f* de) recambio *m*

replay ['ri:pleɪ] **1** *n recording* repetición *f* (de la jugada); *match* repetición *f* (del partido) **2** *v/t match* repetir

replenish [rɪ'plenɪʃ] *container*

rellenar; *supplies* reaprovisionar

replica ['replıkə] réplica *f*

reply [rı'plaı] **1** *n* respuesta *f*, contestación *f* **2** *v/t & v/i* responder, contestar

report [rı'pɔːrt] **1** *n* (*account*) informe *m*; *by journalist* reportaje *m* **2** *v/t facts* informar; *to authorities* informar de **3** *v/i of journalist* informar; (*present o.s.*) presentarse (*to* ante); **reporter** reportero(-a) *m*(*f*)

repossess [riːpə'zes] COM embargar

represent [reprı'zent] representar; **representative 1** *n* representante *m/f*; POL representante *m/f*, diputado(-a) *m*(*f*) **2** *adj* (*typical*) representativo

repress [rı'pres] *revolt* reprimir; *feelings, laughter* reprimir, controlar; **repression** POL represión *f*; **repressive** POL represivo

reprieve [rı'priːv] **1** *n* LAW indulto *m*; *fig* aplazamiento *m* **2** *v/t prisoner* indultar

reprimand ['reprımænd] reprender

reprint ['riːprınt] **1** *n* reimpresión *f* **2** *v/t* reimprimir

reprisal [rı'praızl] represalia *f*

reproach [rı'proʊtʃ] **1** *n* reproche *m* **2** *v/t*: **~ s.o. for sth** reprochar algo a alguien; **reproachful** de reproche

reproduce [riːprə'duːs] **1** *v/t atmosphere, mood* reproducir **2** *v/i* BIO reproducirse; **reproduction** reproducción *f*; **reproductive** reproductivo

reptile ['reptaıl] reptil *m*

republic [rı'pʌblık] república *f*; **republican** *n* republicano(-a) *m*(*f*)

repulsive [rı'pʌlsıv] repulsivo

reputable ['repjʊtəbl] reputado, acreditado; **reputation** reputación *f*

request [rı'kwest] **1** *n* petición *f*, solicitud *f*; ***on* ~** por encargo **2** *v/t* pedir, solicitar

require [rı'kwaır] (*need*) requerir, necesitar; **required** (*necessary*) necesario; **requirement** (*need*) necesidad *f*; (*condition*) requisito *m*

requisition [rekwı'zıʃn] requisar

re-route [riː'ruːt] desviar

rerun ['riːrʌn] **1** *n of TV program* reposición *f* **2** *v/t tape* volver a poner

reschedule [riː'ʃeduːl] volver a programar

rescue ['reskjuː] **1** *n* rescate *m* **2** *v/t* rescatar

research [rı'sɜːrtʃ] investigación *f*; **research and development** investigación *f* y desarrollo; **researcher** investigador(a) *m*(*f*)

resemblance [rı'zembləns] parecido *m*, semejanza *f*; **resemble** parecerse a

resent [rı'zent] estar molesto por; **resentful** resentido; **resentment** resentimiento *m*

reservation [rezər'veıʃn] reserva *f*; **reserve 1** *n* reserva *f*; SP reserva *m/f* **2** *v/t* reservar; *judgment* reservarse; **reserved** *table, manner* reservado

reservoir ['rezərvwɑːr] *for water* embalse *m*

residence ['rezɪdəns] *fml: house etc* residencia *f*; (*stay*) estancia *f*; **resident** residente *m/f*; **residential** residencial

residue ['rezɪduː] residuo *m*

resign [rɪ'zaɪn] **1** *v/t position* dimitir de; ~ ***o.s. to*** resignarse a **2** *v/i from job* dimitir; **resignation** *from job* dimisión *f*; *mental* resignación *f*

resilient [rɪ'zɪlɪənt] *personality* fuerte; *material* resistente

resist [rɪ'zɪst] **1** *v/t* resistir; *new measures* oponer resistencia a **2** *v/i* resistir; **resistance** resistencia *f*; **resistant** *material* resistente

resolution [rezə'luːʃn] resolución *f*; *at New Year etc* propósito *m*

resort [rɪ'zɔːrt] *place* centro *m* turístico; ***as a last*** ~ como último recurso

◆ **resort to** recurrir a

◆ **resound with** [rɪ'zaʊnd] resonar con

resounding [rɪ'zaʊndɪŋ] *success, victory* clamoroso

resource [rɪ'sɔːrs] recurso *m*; **resourceful** *person* lleno de recursos; *approach* ingenioso

respect [rɪ'spekt] **1** *n* respeto *m*; ***in this / that*** ~ en cuanto a esto / eso; ***in many*** ~***s*** en muchos aspectos **2** *v/t* respetar; **respectability** respetabilidad *f*; **respectable** respetable; **respectful** respetuoso; **respective** respectivo; **respectively** respectivamente

respiration [respɪ'reɪʃn] respiración *f*; **respirator** MED respirador *m*

respond [rɪ'spɑːnd] responder; **response** respuesta *f*

responsibility [rɪspɑːnsɪ'bɪlətɪ] responsabilidad *f*; **responsible** reponsable (***for*** de); *job* de responsabilidad

rest[1] [rest] **1** *n* descanso *m* **2** *v/i* descansar **3** *v/t* (*lean, balance*) apoyar

rest[2] [rest]: ***the*** ~ el resto

restaurant ['restrɑːnt] restaurante *m*

restful ['restfəl] tranquilo; **rest home** residencia *f* de ancianos; **restless** inquieto; **restlessly** sin descanso

restoration [restə'reɪʃn] restauración *f*; **restore** *building etc* restaurar; (*bring back*) devolver

restrain [rɪ'streɪn] contener; **restraint** (*moderation*) moderación *f*

restrict [rɪ'strɪkt] restringir; **restricted** *view* limitado; **restriction** restricción *f*

'rest room aseo *m*, servicios *mpl*

result [rɪ'zʌlt] resultado *m*; ***as a ~ of this*** como resultado de esto
resume [rɪ'zu:m] **1** *v/t* reanudar **2** *v/i* continuar
résumé ['rezʊmeɪ] currículum *m* (vitae)
resumption [rɪ'zʌmpʃn] reanudación *f*
resurface [ri:'sɜ:fɪs] **1** *v/t roads* volver a asfaltar **2** *v/i* (*reappear*) reaparecer
resurrection [rezə'rekʃn] REL resurrección *f*
retail ['ri:teɪl] **1** *adv*: ***sell sth ~*** vender algo al por menor **2** *v/i*: ***it ~s at*** su precio de venta al público es de; **retailer** minorista *m/f*
retain [rɪ'teɪn] conservar; *heat* retener; **retainer** FIN anticipo *m*
retaliate [rɪ'tælɪeɪt] tomar represalias; **retaliation** represalias *fpl*
rethink [ri:'θɪŋk] replantear
reticence ['retɪsns] reserva *f*; **reticent** reservado
retire [rɪ'taɪr] *from work* jubilarse; **retired** jubilado; **retirement** jubilación *f*; **retiring** retraído
retort [rɪ'tɔ:rt] **1** *n* réplica *f* **2** *v/t* replicar
retract [rɪ'trækt] *claws* retraer; *undercarriage* replegar; *statement* retirar
're-train reciclarse
retreat [rɪ'tri:t] **1** *v/i* retirarse **2** *n* MIL retirada *f*; *place* retiro *m*
retrieve [rɪ'tri:v] recuperar
retroactive [retroʊ'æktɪv] retroactivo; **retroactively** con retroactividad
retrograde ['retrəgreɪd] retrógrado
retrospective [retrə'spektɪv] retrospectiva *f*
return [rɪ'tɜ:rn] **1** *n to a place* vuelta *f*, regreso *m*; (*giving back*) devolución *f*; COMPUT retorno *m*; *in tennis* resto *m*; (*profit*) rendimiento *m*; *Br ticket* billete *m or L.Am.* boleto *m* de ida y vuelta; ***many happy ~s*** (***of the day***) feliz cumpleaños; ***in ~ for*** a cambio de **2** *v/t* devolver; (*put back*) volver a colocar **3** *v/i* (*go back, come back*) volver, regresar; *of good times, doubts* volver
reunification [ri:ju:nɪfɪ'keɪʃn] reunificación *f*
reunion [ri:'ju:njən] reunión *f*; **reunite** reunir
reusable [ri:'ju:zəbl] reutilizable; **reuse** reutilizar
◆ **rev up** [rev] *engine* revolucionar
revaluation [ri:væljʊ'eɪʃn] revaluación *f*
reveal [rɪ'vi:l] revelar; **revealing** *remark* revelador; *dress* insinuante, atrevido; **revelation** revelación *f*
revenge [rɪ'vendʒ] venganza *f*; ***take one's ~*** vengarse
revenue ['revənu:] ingresos *mpl*
reverberate [rɪ'vɜ:rbəreɪt] *of*

sound reverberar

revere [rɪ'vɪr] reverenciar; **reverence** reverencia *f*; **reverent** reverente

reverse [rɪ'vɜːrs] **1** *adj sequence* inverso **2** *n* (*back*) dorso *m*; MOT marcha *f* atrás; ***the*** ~ (*the opposite*) lo contrario **3** *v/i* MOT hacer marcha atrás

review [rɪ'vjuː] **1** *n of book, movie* reseña *f*; *of troops* revista *f*; *of situation etc* revisión *f* **2** *v/t book, movie* reseñar; *troops* pasar revista a; *situation etc* revisar; EDU repasar; **reviewer** *of book, movie* crítico(-a) *m(f)*

revise [rɪ'vaɪz] *opinion, text* revisar; **revision** revisión *f*

revival [rɪ'vaɪvl] *of custom, old style* resurgimiento *m*; *of patient* reanimación *f*; **revive 1** *v/t custom, old style* hacer resurgir; *patient* reanimar **2** *v/i of business, exchange rate etc* reactivarse

revoke [rɪ'vouk] *law* derogar; *license* revocar

revolt [rɪ'voult] **1** *n* rebelión *f* **2** *v/i* rebelarse; **revolting** repugnante; **revolution** POL, (*turn*) revolución *f*; **revolutionary 1** *n* POL revolucionario(-a) *m(f)* **2** *adj* revolucionario; **revolutionize** revolucionar

revolve [rɪ'vɑːlv] girar (***around*** en torno a); **revolver** revólver *m*

revulsion [rɪ'vʌlʃn] repugnancia *f*

reward [rɪ'wɔːrd] **1** *n* recompensa *f* **2** *v/t financially* recompensar; **rewarding** *experience* gratificante

rewind [riː'waɪnd] *film, tape* rebobinar

rewrite [riː'raɪt] reescribir

rhetoric ['retərɪk] retórica *f*

rhyme [raɪm] **1** *n* rima *f* **2** *v/i* rimar

rhythm ['rɪðm] ritmo *m*

rib [rɪb] ANAT costilla *f*

ribbon ['rɪbən] cinta *f*

rice [raɪs] arroz *m*

rich [rɪʧ] **1** *adj* rico; *food* sabroso **2** *npl*: ***the*** ~ los ricos

ricochet ['rɪkəʃeɪ] rebotar

rid [rɪd]: ***get*** ~ ***of*** deshacerse de

ride [raɪd] **1** *n on horse, in vehicle* paseo *m*, vuelta *f*; (*journey*) viaje *m*; ***do you want a*** ~ ***into town?*** ¿quieres que te lleve al centro? **2** *v/t horse* montar a; *bike* montar en **3** *v/i on horse* montar; **rider** *on horse* jinete *m*, amazona *f*; *on bicycle* ciclista *m/f*; *on motorbike* motorista *m/f*

ridge [rɪdʒ] borde *m*; *of mountain* cresta *f*; *of roof* caballete *m*

ridicule ['rɪdɪkjuːl] **1** *n* burlas *fpl* **2** *v/t* ridiculizar; **ridiculous** ridículo; **ridiculously** *expensive, difficult* terriblemente

riding ['raɪdɪŋ] *on horseback* equitación *f*

rifle ['raɪfl] rifle *m*

rift [rɪft] *in earth* grieta *f*; *in party etc* escisión *f*
rig [rɪg] **1** *n* (*oil* ~) plataforma *f* petrolífera; (*truck*) camión *m* **2** *v/t elections* amañar
right [raɪt] **1** *adj* (*correct*) correcto; (*suitable*) adecuado, apropiado; (*not left*) derecho; ***be ~*** *of answer* estar correcto; *of person* tener razón; *of clock* ir bien; ***put things ~*** arreglar las cosas; ***that's all ~*** *doesn't matter* no te preocupes; *when s.o. says thank you* de nada; *is quite good* está bastante bien; ***I'm all ~*** *not hurt* estoy bien; *have got enough* no, gracias **2** *adv* (*directly*) justo; (*correctly*) correctamente; (*not left*) a la derecha; ***~ now*** ahora mismo **3** *n civil, legal etc* derecho *m*; *not left*, POL derecha *f*; ***be in the ~*** tener razón
right-'angle ángulo *m* recto; **rightful** *owner etc* legítimo; **right-handed** *person* diestro; **right-hand man** mano *f* derecha; **right of way** *in traffic* preferencia *f*; *across land* derecho *m* de paso; **right wing** POL derecha *f*; SP banda *f* derecha; **right-wing** POL de derechas
rigid ['rɪdʒɪd] rígido
rigor ['rɪgər] rigor *m*; **rigorous** riguroso; **rigorously** *check* rigurosamente
rigour *Br* ☞ ***rigor***
rile [raɪl] F fastidiar, *Span* mosquear F
rim [rɪm] *of wheel* llanta *f*; *of cup* borde *m*; *of eye glasses* montura *f*
ring[1] [rɪŋ] *n* (*circle*) círculo *m*; *on finger* anillo *m*; *in boxing* cuadrilátero *m*, ring *m*; *at circus* pista *f*
ring[2] [rɪŋ] **1** *n of bell* timbrazo *m*; *of voice* tono *m* **2** *v/t bell* hacer sonar; *Br* TELEC llamar **3** *v/i of bell* sonar
'ringleader cabecilla *m* / *f*; **ring-pull** anilla *f*
rink [rɪŋk] pista *f* de patinaje
rinse [rɪns] **1** *n for hair color* reflejo *m* **2** *v/t* aclarar
riot ['raɪət] **1** *n* disturbio *m* **2** *v/i* causar disturbios; **rioter** alborotador(a) *m*(*f*); **riot police** policía *f* antidisturbios
rip [rɪp] **1** *n in cloth etc* rasgadura *f* **2** *v/t cloth* rasgar
◆ **rip off** F *customers* robar F
ripe [raɪp] *fruit* maduro; **ripen** *of fruit* madurar; **ripeness** madurez *f*
'rip-off F robo *m* F
ripple ['rɪpl] *on water* onda *f*
rise [raɪz] **1** *v/i from chair etc* levantarse; *of sun* salir; *of rocket* ascender, subir; *of price, temperature, water* subir **2** *n in price, temperature* subida *f*, aumento *m*; *in water level* subida *f*; *in salary* aumento *m*
risk [rɪsk] **1** *n* riesgo *m*; ***take a ~*** arriesgarse **2** *v/t* arriesgar; **risky** arriesgado
ritual ['rɪtʊəl] **1** *n* ritual *m* **2** *adj* ritual

rival ['raɪvl] **1** *n* rival *m/f* **2** *v/t* rivalizar con; **rivalry** rivalidad *f*

river ['rɪvər] río *m*; **riverbank** ribera *f*; **riverbed** lecho *m*; **River Plate:** ***the ~*** el Río de la Plata; **riverside 1** *adj* a la orilla del río **2** *n* ribera *f*, orilla *f* del río

riveting ['rɪvɪtɪŋ] fascinante

road [roʊd] *in country* carretera *f*; *in city* calle *f*; **roadblock** control *m* de carretera; **road-holding** *of vehicle* adherencia *f*; **road map** mapa *m* de carreteras; **road safety** seguridad *f* vial; **roadsign** señal *f* de tráfico; **roadway** calzada *f*; **roadworthy** en condiciones de circular

roam [roʊm] vagar

roar [rɔːr] **1** *n of traffic* estruendo *m*; *of lion* rugido *m*; *of person* grito *m*, bramido *m* **2** *v/i of engine*, *lion* rugir; *of person* gritar, bramar

roast [roʊst] **1** *n of beef etc* asado *m* **2** *v/t* asar **3** *v/i of food* asarse; **roast beef** rosbif *m*

rob [rɑːb] *person* robar a; *bank* atracar, robar; **robber** atracador(a) *m(f)*; **robbery** atraco *m*, robo *m*

robe [roʊb] *of judge* toga *f*; *of priest* sotana *f*; (*bath~*) bata *f*

robot ['roʊbɑːt] robot *m*

robust [roʊ'bʌst] robusto; *material* resistente

rock [rɑːk] **1** *n* roca *f*; MUS rock *m* **2** *v/t baby* acunar; *cradle* mecer; (*surprise*) impactar **3** *v/i on chair* mecerse; *of boat* balancearse; **rock-bottom** *prices* mínimo; **rock climber** escalador(a) *m(f)*; **rock climbing** escalada *f* (en roca)

rocket ['rɑːkɪt] **1** *n* cohete *m* **2** *v/i of prices etc* dispararse

rocking chair ['rɑːkɪŋ] mecedora *f*; **rock 'n' roll** rock and roll *m*; **rocky** *beach* pedregoso

rod [rɑːd] vara *f*; *for fishing* caña *f*

rodent ['roʊdnt] roedor *m*

rogue [roʊg] granuja *m/f*

role [roʊl] papel *m*; **role model** ejemplo *m*

roll [roʊl] **1** *n* (*bread ~*) panecillo *m*; *of film* rollo *m*; (*list*, *register*) lista *f* **2** *v/i of ball etc* rodar

◆ **roll over 1** *v/i* darse la vuelta **2** *v/t person*, *object* dar la vuelta a; (*renew*) renovar; (*extend*) refinanciar

'roll-call lista *f*; **roller** *for hair* rulo *m*; **roller blade®** patín *m* en línea; **roller coaster** montaña *f* rusa; **roller skate** patín *m* (de ruedas)

ROM [rɑːm] COMPUT (= ***read only memory***) ROM *f* (= memoria *f* de sólo lectura)

Roman 'Catholic 1 *n* REL católico(-a) *m(f)* romano(-a) **2** *adj* católico romano

romance [rə'mæns] (*affair*) aventura *f* (amorosa); *novel* novela *f* rosa; *movie* película *f* romántica; **romantic** romántico

roof [ruːf] techo *m*, tejado *m*; **roof-rack** MOT baca *f*

rookie ['rʊkɪ] F novato(-a) *m(f)*

room [ruːm] habitación *f*; (*space*) espacio *m*, sitio *m*; **room clerk** recepcionista *m/f*; **roommate** compañero(-a) *m(f)* de habitación; *sharing apartment* compañero(-a) *m(f)* de piso; **room service** servicio *m* de habitaciones; **room temperature** temperatura *f* ambiente; **roomy** *car etc* espacioso; *clothes* holgado

root [ruːt] raíz *f*

rope [roʊp] cuerda *f*; *thick* soga *f*

rosary ['roʊzərɪ] REL rosario *m*

rose [roʊz] BOT rosa *f*

roster ['rɑːstər] turnos *mpl*; *actual document* calendario *m* con los turnos

rostrum ['rɑːstrəm] estrado *m*

rosy ['roʊzɪ] *cheeks* sonrosado; *future* de color de rosa

rot [rɑːt] **1** *n in wood* putrefacción *f* **2** *v/i of food, wood* pudrirse; *of teeth* cariarse

rotate [roʊ'teɪt] **1** *v/i* girar **2** *v/t* hacer girar; *crops* rotar; **rotation** rotación *f*

rotten ['rɑːtn] *food, wood etc* podrido; F *weather, luck* horrible

rough [rʌf] **1** *adj surface, ground* accidentado; *hands, skin* áspero; *voice* ronco; (*violent*) bruto; *crossing* movido; *seas* bravo; (*approximate*) aproximado **2** *n in golf* rough *m*; **roughage** *in food* fibra *f*; **roughly** (*approximately*) aproximadamente; (*harshly*) brutalmente

roulette [ruː'let] ruleta *f*

round [raʊnd] **1** *adj* redondo **2** *n of mailman, drinks, competition* ronda *f*; *in boxing* round *m*, asalto *m* **3** *v/t corner* doblar **4** *adv & prep* ☞ ***around***

◆ **round up** *figure* redondear (hacia la cifra más alta); *suspects, criminals* detener

roundabout ['raʊndəbaʊt] **1** *adj* indirecto **2** *n Br on road* rotonda *f*, *Span* glorieta *f*; **round-the-world** alrededor del mundo; **round trip** viaje *m* de ida y vuelta; **round-up** *of cattle* rodeo *m*; *of suspects* redada *f*; *of news* resumen *m*

rouse [raʊz] *from sleep* despertar; *emotions* excitar; **rousing** emocionante

route [raʊt] ruta *f*, recorrido *m*

routine [ruː'tiːn] **1** *adj* habitual **2** *n* rutina *f*

row[1] [roʊ] *n* (*line*) hilera *f* **3** ***days in a ~*** 3 días seguidos

row[2] [roʊ] *v/i in boat* remar

rowboat bote *m* de remos

rowdy ['raʊdɪ] alborotador, *Span* follonero

royal ['rɔɪəl] real; **royalty** realeza *f*; *on book etc* derechos

mpl de autor
rub [rʌb] frotar
rubber ['rʌbər] **1** *n material* goma *f*, caucho *m* **2** *adj* de goma *or* caucho; **rubber band** goma *f* elástica
rubble ['rʌbl] escombros *mpl*
ruby ['ru:bɪ] *jewel* rubí *m*
rudder ['rʌdər] timón *m*
ruddy ['rʌdɪ] *face* rubicundo
rude [ru:d] *person*, *behavior* maleducado, grosero; *language* grosero; **rudely** (*impolitely*) groseramente; **rudeness** mala *f* educación, grosería *f*
rudimentary [ru:dɪ'mentərɪ] rudimentario; **rudiments** rudimentos *mpl*
rueful ['ru:fl] arrepentido; **ruefully** con arrepentimiento
ruffian ['rʌfɪən] rufián *m*
ruffle ['rʌfl] **1** *n on dress* volante *m* **2** *v/t hair* despeinar; *clothes* arrugar; *person* alterar
rug [rʌg] alfombra *f*; (*blanket*) manta *f* (de viaje)
rugby ['rʌgbɪ] rugby *m*
rugged ['rʌgɪd] *scenery* escabroso; *face* de rasgos duros; *resistance* decidido
ruin ['ru:ɪn] **1** *n* ruina *f* **2** *v/t* arruinar
rule [ru:l] **1** *n* regla *f*; *of monarch* reinado *m*; ***as a ~*** por regla general **2** *v/t country* gobernar **3** *v/i of monarch* reinar; **ruler** *for measuring* regla *f*; *of state* gobernante *m/f*; **ruling 1** *n* fallo *m*, decisión *f* **2** *adj party* gobernante, en el poder
rum [rʌm] *drink* ron *m*
rumble ['rʌmbl] *of stomach* gruñir; *of thunder* retumbar
rumor, *Br* **rumour** ['ru:mər] **1** *n* rumor *m* **2** *v/t*: ***it is ~ed that …*** se rumorea que…
rump [rʌmp] *of animal* cuartos *mpl* traseros
rumple ['rʌmpl] arrugar
rump 'steak filete *m* de lomo
run [rʌn] **1** *n on foot*, *in pantyhose* carrera *f*; *Br*: *in car* viaje *m*; THEA: *of play* temporada *f*; ***in the short / long ~*** a corto / largo plazo **2** *v/i* correr; *of river* correr, discurrir; *of paint*, *make-up* correrse; *of play* estar en cartel; *of engine*, *software* funcionar; *in election* presentarse; ***~ for President*** presentarse a las elecciones presidenciales **3** *v/t race* correr; *business etc* dirigir; *software* usar; *car* tener; (*use*) usar
◆ **run away** salir corriendo, huir; *from home* escaparse
◆ **run down 1** *v/t* (*knock down*) atropellar; (*criticize*) criticar; *stocks* reducir **2** *v/i of battery* agotarse
◆ **run off 1** *v/i* salir corriendo **2** *v/t* (*print off*) tirar
◆ **run out** *of contract* vencer; *of supplies* agotarse
◆ **run out of** quedarse sin
◆ **run over 1** *v/t* (*knock down*) atropellar **2** *v/i of water etc*

desbordarse
◆ **run up** *debts* acumular
runaway ['rʌnəweɪ] *persona que se ha fugado de casa*; **run-down** *person* débil; *part of town* ruinoso
rung [rʌŋ] *of ladder* peldaño *m*
runner ['rʌnər] *athlete* corredor(a) *m(f)*; **runner beans** judías *fpl* verdes, *L.Am.* porotos *mpl* verdes, *Mex* ejotes *mpl*; **runner-up** subcampeón(-ona) *m(f)*; **running 1** *n* SP el correr; (*jogging*) footing *m*; *of business* gestión *f* **2** *adj*: ***for two days ~*** durante dos días seguidos; **running water** agua *f* corriente; **runny** *mixture* fluido; *nose* que moquea; **run-up** SP élan *m*; ***in the ~ to*** en el periodo previo a; **runway** pista *f* (de aterrizaje / despegue)
rupture ['rʌptʃər] **1** *n* ruptura *f* **2** *v/i of pipe etc* romperse
rural ['rʊrəl] rural
ruse [ru:z] artimaña *f*
rush [rʌʃ] **1** *n* prisa *f* **2** *v/t person* meter prisa a; *meal* comer a toda prisa **3** *v/i* darse prisa; **rush hour** hora *f* punta
Russia ['rʌʃə] Rusia; **Russian 1** *adj* ruso **2** *n* ruso(-a) *m(f)*; *language* ruso *m*
rust [rʌst] **1** *n* óxido *m* **2** *v/i* oxidarse; **rust-proof** inoxidable; **rusty** oxidado
rut [rʌt] *in road* rodada *f*; ***be in a ~*** *fig* estar estancado
ruthless ['ru:θlɪs] implacable, despiadado; **ruthlessly** sin compasión, despiadadamente; **ruthlessness** falta *f* de compasión
rye [raɪ] centeno *m*; **rye bread** pan *m* de centeno

S

sabotage ['sæbətɑ:ʒ] **1** *n* sabotaje *m* **2** *v/t* sabotear; **saboteur** saboteador(a) *m(f)*
sachet ['sæʃeɪ] sobrecito *m*
sack [sæk] **1** *n bag* saco *m*; *for groceries* bolsa *f* **2** *v/t* F echar
sacred ['seɪkrɪd] sagrado
sacrifice ['sækrɪfaɪs] **1** *n* sacrificio *m* **2** *v/t* sacrificar
sacrilege ['sækrɪlɪdʒ] sacrilegio *m*
sad [sæd] triste; *state of affairs* lamentable
saddle ['sædl] **1** *n* silla *f* de montar **2** *v/t horse* ensillar
sadism ['seɪdɪzm] sadismo *m*; **sadist** sádico(-a) *m(f)*; **sadistic** sádico
sadly ['sædlɪ] con tristeza; (*regrettably*) lamentablemente; **sadness** tristeza *f*
safe [seɪf] **1** *adj* seguro; *driver* prudente; (*not in danger*) a salvo **2** *n* caja *f* fuerte; **safeguard 1** *n* garantía *f* **2** *v/t* salvaguardar; **safely** *arrive* sin

percances; *drive* prudentemente; *assume* con certeza; **safety** seguridad *f*; **safety pin** imperdible *m*
sag [sæg] *of ceiling* combarse; *of rope* destensarse; *of tempo* disminuir
saga ['sægə] saga *f*
sage [seɪdʒ] *herb* salvia *f*
sail [seɪl] **1** *n of boat* vela *f*; *trip* viaje *m* (en barco) **2** *v/i* navegar; (*depart*) zarpar; **sailboard 1** *n* tabla *f* de windsurf **2** *v/i* hacer windsurf; **sailboarding** windsurf *m*; **sailboat** barco *m* de vela, velero *m*; **sailing** SP vela *f*; **sailor** marinero(-a) *m*(*f*); *in the navy* marino *m*/*f*
saint [seɪnt] santo *m*
sake [seɪk]: ***for my ~*** por mí
salad ['sæləd] ensalada *f*
salary ['sælərɪ] sueldo *m*, salario *m*
sale [seɪl] venta *f*; *reduced prices* rebajas *fpl*; ***be on ~*** estar a la venta; *at reduced prices* estar de rebajas; **sales department** ventas *fpl*; **sales clerk** dependiente(-a) *m*(*f*); **sales figures** cifras *fpl* de ventas; **salesman** vendedor *m*; **saleswoman** vendedora *f*
salient ['seɪlɪənt] sobresaliente, destacado
saliva [sə'laɪvə] saliva *f*
salmon ['sæmən] salmón *m*
saloon [sə'lu:n] (*bar*) bar *m*; *Br* MOT turismo *m*
salt [sɒ:lt] sal *f*; **salty** salado
salute [sə'lu:t] **1** *n* MIL saludo **2** *v/t & v/i* MIL saludar
Salvador(e)an [sælvə'dɔ:rən] **1** *adj* salvadoreño **2** *n* salvadoreño(-a) *m*(*f*)
salvage ['sælvɪdʒ] *from wreck* rescatar
salvation [sæl'veɪʃn] *also fig* salvación *f*
same [seɪm] **1** *adj* mismo **2** *pron*: ***the ~*** lo mismo; ***Happy New Year – the ~ to you*** Feliz Año Nuevo - igualmente; ***all the ~*** (*even so*) aun así **3** *adv*: ***the ~*** igual
sample ['sæmpl] muestra *f*
sanction ['sæŋkʃn] **1** *n* (*approval*) consentimiento *m*; (*penalty*) sanción *f* **2** *v/t* (*approve*) sancionar
sand [sænd] **1** *n* arena *f* **2** *v/t with sandpaper* lijar
sandal ['sændl] sandalia *f*
'**sandbag** saco *m* de arena; **sand dune** duna *f*; **sander** *tool* lijadora *f*; **sandpaper 1** *n* lija *f* **2** *v/t* lijar
sandwich ['sænwɪtʃ] *Span* bocadillo *m*, *L.Am.* sandwich *m*
sandy ['sændɪ] *soil* arenoso; *feet, towel etc* lleno de arena; *hair* rubio oscuro; ***~ beach*** playa *f* de arena
sane [seɪn] cuerdo
sanitarium [sænɪ'terɪəm] sanatorio *m*
sanitary ['sænɪterɪ] salubre, higiénico; **sanitary napkin** compresa *f*; **sanitation** instalaciones *fpl* sanitarias; (*re-*

moval of waste) saneamiento *m*

sanity ['sænətɪ] razón *f*, juicio *m*

Santa Claus ['sæntəklɒːz] Papá Noel *m*, Santa Claus *m*

sap [sæp] **1** *n in tree* savia *f* **2** *v/t s.o.'s energy* consumir

sapphire ['sæfaɪr] zafiro *m*

sarcasm ['sɑːrkæzm] sarcasmo *m*; **sarcastic** sarcástico; **sarcastically** sarcásticamente

sardine [sɑːr'diːn] sardina *f*

sardonic [sɑːr'dɑːnɪk] sardónico

satellite ['sætəlaɪt] satélite *m*; **satellite dish** antena *f* parabólica; **satellite TV** televisión *f* por satélite

satin ['sætɪn] satín *m*

satire ['sætaɪr] sátira *f*; **satirical** satírico; **satirize** satirizar

satisfaction [sætɪs'fækʃn] satisfacción *f*; **satisfactory** satisfactorio; (*just good enough*) suficiente; **satisfy** satisfacer; *conditions* cumplir

Saturday ['sætərdeɪ] sábado *m*

sauce [sɒːs] salsa *f*; **saucepan** cacerola *f*; **saucer** plato *m* (*de taza*)

Saudi Arabia [saudɪə'reɪbɪə] Arabia Saudí *or* Saudita; **Saudi Arabian 1** *adj* saudita, saudí **2** *n* saudita *m/f*, saudí *m/f*

sausage ['sɒːsɪdʒ] salchicha *f*

savage ['sævɪdʒ] **1** *adj* salvaje; *criticism* feroz **2** *n* salvaje *m/f*; **savagery** crueldad *f*

save [seɪv] **1** *v/t* (*rescue*) rescatar, salvar; *money, time* ahorrar; (*collect*), COMPUT guardar; *goal* parar; REL salvar **2** *v/i* (*put money aside*) ahorrar; SP hacer una parada **3** *n* SP parada *f*; **saver** *person* ahorrador(a) *m*(*f*); **savings** ahorros *mpl*; **savings account** cuenta *f* de ahorros; **savings and loan** caja *f* de ahorros; **savings bank** caja *f* de ahorros

savior, *Br* **saviour** ['seɪvjər] REL salvador *m*

savor ['seɪvər] saborear; **savory** *not sweet* salado

savour *etc Br* ☞ ***savor*** *etc*

saw [sɒː] **1** *n tool* serrucho *m*, sierra *f* **2** *v/t* aserrar; **sawdust** serrín *m*, aserrín *m*

saxophone ['sæksəfoun] saxofón *m*

say [seɪ] decir; ***that is to ~*** es decir; **saying** dicho *m*

scab [skæb] *on skin* costra *f*

scaffolding ['skæfəldɪŋ] *on building* andamiaje *m*

scald [skɒːld] escaldar

scale[1] [skeɪl] *n on fish* escama *f*

scale[2] [skeɪl] **1** *n* (*size*) escala *f*, tamaño *m*; *on thermometer, map*, MUS escala *f* **2** *v/t cliffs etc* escalar

scales [skeɪlz] *for weighing* báscula *f*, peso *m*

scallop ['skæləp] *shellfish* vieira *f*

scalp [skælp] cuero *m* cabelludo
scalpel ['skælpl] bisturí *m*
scam [skæm] F chanchullo *m* F
scampi ['skæmpɪ] gambas *fpl* rebozadas
scan [skæn] **1** *v/t horizon* otear; *page* ojear; COMPUT escanear **2** *n of brain* escáner *m*; *of fetus* ecografía *f*
◆ **scan in** COMPUT escanear
scandal ['skændl] escándalo *m*; **scandalize** escandalizar; **scandalous** escandaloso
scanner ['skænər] MED, COMPUT escáner *m*; *for fetus* ecógrafo *m*
scanty ['skæntɪ] *skirt* cortísimo; *bikini* mínimo
scapegoat ['skeɪpgout] cabeza *f* de turco
scar [skɑːr] **1** *n* cicatriz *f* **2** *v/t* cicatrizar
scarce [skers] *in short supply* escaso; **scarcely**: **~ *anything*** casi nada; ***I ~ know her*** apenas la conozco; **scarcity** escasez *f*
scare [sker] **1** *v/t* asustar, ***be ~d of*** tener miedo de **2** *n* (*panic, alarm*) miedo *m*, temor *m*; **scaremonger** alarmista *m/f*
scarf [skɑːrf] pañuelo *m*; *woollen* bufanda *f*
scarlet ['skɑːrlət] escarlata
scary ['skerɪ] espeluznante
scathing ['skeɪðɪŋ] feroz
scatter ['skætər] **1** *v/t leaflets* esparcir; *seeds* diseminar **2** *v/i of people* dispersarse; **scattered** disperso
scavenge ['skævɪndʒ] rebuscar; **scavenger** carroñero *m*; (*person*) *persona que busca comida entre la basura*
scenario [sɪ'nɑːrɪou] situación *f*
scene [siːn] escena *f*; *of accident, crime etc* lugar *m*; (*argument*) escena *f*, número *m*; ***behind the ~s*** entre bastidores; **scenery** paisaje *m*; THEA escenario *m*
scent [sent] olor *m*; *Br* (*perfume*) perfume *m*, fragancia *f*
sceptic *etc Br* ☞ ***skeptic*** *etc*
schedule ['skedjuːl] **1** *n of events, work* programa *m*; *of exams* calendario *m*; *for train, work, of lessons* horario *m*; ***be on ~*** *of work* ir según lo previsto; *of train* ir a la hora prevista; ***be behind ~*** ir con retraso **2** *v/t* (*put on ~*) programar; **scheduled flight** vuelo *m* regular
scheme [skiːm] **1** *n* (*plan*) plan *m*; (*plot*) confabulación *f* **2** *v/i* (*plot*) confabularse; **scheming** maquinador
schizophrenia [skɪtsə'friːnɪə] esquizofrenia *f*; **schizophrenic** **1** *n* esquizofrénico(-a) *m*(*f*) **2** *adj* esquizofrénico
scholar ['skɑːlər] erudito(-a) *m*(*f*); **scholarly** erudito; **scholarship** *work* estudios *mpl*; *financial award* beca *f*

school [skuːl] escuela *f*, colegio *m*; (*university*) universidad *f*; **school bag** cartera *f*; **schoolchildren** escolares *mpl*

science ['saɪəns] ciencia *f*; **scientific** científico; **scientist** científico(-a) *m*(*f*)

scissors ['sɪzərz] tijeras *fpl*

scoff[1] [skɑːf] F (*eat fast*) zamparse F

scoff[2] [skɑːf] (*mock*) burlarse, mofarse

scold [skoʊld] regañar

scoop [skuːp] *implement* cuchara *f*; *story* exclusiva *f*

scooter ['skuːtər] *with motor* escúter *m*; *child's* patinete *m*

scope [skoʊp] alcance *m*; (*freedom, opportunity*) oportunidad *f*

scorch [skɔːrʧ] quemar; **scorching** abrasador

score [skɔːr] **1** *n* SP resultado *m*; *in competition* puntuación *f*; (*written music*) partitura *f*; *of movie etc* banda *f* sonora **2** *v/t goal, line* marcar; *point* anotar **3** *v/i* marcar; (*keep the* ~) llevar el tanteo; **scoreboard** marcador *m*; **scorer** *of goal* goleador(a) *m*(*f*); *of point* anotador(a) *m*(*f*)

scorn [skɔːrn] **1** *n* desprecio *m* **2** *v/t idea* despreciar; **scornful** despreciativo; **scornfully** con desprecio

Scot [skɑːt] escocés(-esa) *m*(*f*); **Scotch** (*whiskey*) whisky *m* escocés; **Scotch tape®** celo *m*, *L.Am.* Durex® *m*; **Scotland** Escocia; **Scottish** escocés

scoundrel ['skaʊndrəl] canalla *m* / *f*

scour ['skaʊər] (*search*) rastrear, peinar

scowl [skaʊl] **1** *n* ceño *m* **2** *v/i* fruncir el ceño

scramble ['skræmbl] **1** *n* (*rush*) prisa *f* **2** *v/t message* cifrar **3** *v/i* (*climb*) trepar; **scrambled eggs** huevos *mpl* revueltos

scrap [skræp] **1** *n metal* chatarra *f*; (*fight*) pelea *f*; *of food* trocito *m*; *of common sense* pizca *f* **2** *v/t plan* abandonar; *paragraph* borrar

scrape [skreɪp] **1** *n on paintwork etc* arañazo *m* **2** *v/t paintwork* rayar

'scrap metal chatarra *f*

scrappy ['skræpɪ] *work, play* desorganizado

scratch [skræʧ] **1** *n mark* marca *f*; ***start from*** ~ empezar desde cero; ***not up to*** ~ insuficiente **2** *v/t* (*mark: skin*) arañar; (*mark: paint*) rayar; *because of itch* rascarse **3** *v/i of cat etc* arañar; *because of itch* rascarse

scrawl [skrɒːl] **1** *n* garabato *m* **2** *v/t* garabatear

scrawny ['skrɒːnɪ] escuálido

scream [skriːm] **1** *n* grito *m* **2** *v/i* gritar

screech [skriːʧ] **1** *n of tires* chirrido *m*; (*scream*) chillido *m* **2** *v/i of tires* chirriar;

(*scream*) chillar

screen [skri:n] **1** *n in room, hospital* mampara *f*; *protective* cortina *f*; *in movie theater*, COMPUT pantalla *f* **2** *v/t* (*protect, hide*) ocultar; *movie* proyectar; *for security reasons* investigar; **screenplay** guión *m*; **screen saver** COMPUT salvapantallas *m inv*; **screen test** prueba *f*

screw [skru:] **1** *n* tornillo *m* **2** *v/t* atornillar (***to*** a); V (*have sex with*) echar un polvo con V; F (*cheat*) timar F; **screwdriver** destornillador *m*; **screwed up** F acomplejado; **screwy** F chiflado F; *idea, film* descabellado F

scribble ['skrɪbl] **1** *n* garabato *m* **2** *v/t & v/i* garabatear

script [skrɪpt] *for play* guión *m*; *form of writing* caligrafía *f*; **scripture: *the* (*Holy*) *Scriptures*** las Sagradas Escrituras; **scriptwriter** guionista *m / f*

◆ **scroll down** [skroul] COMPUT avanzar

◆ **scroll up** COMPUT retroceder

scrounge [skraundʒ] gorronear; **scrounger** gorrón (-ona) *m*(*f*)

scrub [skrʌb] *floors* fregar; *hands* frotar

scruples ['skru:plz] escrúpulos *mpl*; **scrupulous** *with moral principles* escrupuloso; (*thorough*) meticuloso; *attention to detail* minucioso; **scrupulously** (*meticulously*) minuciosamente

scrutinize ['skru:tɪnaɪz] estudiar, examinar; **scrutiny** escrutinio *m*

scuba diving ['sku:bə] submarinismo *m*

scuffle ['skʌfl] riña *f*

sculptor ['skʌlptər] escultor(a) *m*(*f*); **sculpture** escultura *f*

scum [skʌm] *on liquid* película *f* de suciedad; *pej*: *people* escoria *f*

sea [si:] mar *m*; **seabird** ave *f* marina; **seafood** marisco *m*; **seagull** gaviota *f*

seal[1] [si:l] *n animal* foca *f*

seal[2] [si:l] **1** *n on document*, tech sello *m* **2** *v/t container* sellar

'sea level: *above* ~ sobre el nivel del mar; ***below* ~** bajo el nivel del mar

seam [si:m] *on garment* costura *f*; *of ore* filón *m*

'seaman marinero *m*; **seaport** puerto *m* marítimo

search [sɜ:rʧ] **1** *n* búsqueda *f* **2** *v/t* registrar

◆ **search for** buscar

searching ['sɜ:rʧɪŋ] *look* escrutador; *question* difícil; **searchlight** reflector *m*

'seashore orilla *f*; **seasick** mareado; ***get* ~** marearse; **seaside** costa *f*, playa *f*

season ['si:zn] estación *f*; *for tourism etc* temporada *f*; **seasonal** *fruit, vegetables* del tiempo; *employment* temporal; **seasoned** *wood* seco; *traveler, campaigner* experimentado; **seasoning** condimento *m*; **season ticket** abono *m*

seat [siːt] asiento *m*; *in theater* butaca *f*; *of pants* culera *f*; ***please take a ~*** por favor, siéntese; **seat belt** cinturón *m* de seguridad

'seaweed alga(s) *f(pl)*

secluded [sɪ'kluːdɪd] apartado

second ['sekənd] **1** *n of time* segundo *m* **2** *adj* segundo **3** *adv come in* en segundo lugar **4** *v/t motion* apoyar; **secondary** secundario; **second floor** primer piso *m*, *Br* segundo piso *m*; **second-hand** de segunda mano; **secondly** en segundo lugar; **second-rate** inferior

secrecy ['siːkrəsɪ] secretismo *m*; **secret 1** *n* secreto *m* **2** *adj* secreto

secretarial [sekrə'terɪəl] de secretario; **secretary** secretario(-a) *m(f)*; POL ministro(-a) *m(f)*; **Secretary of State** *in USA* Secretario(-a) *m(f)* de Estado

secretive ['siːkrətɪv] reservado; **secretly** en secreto

sect [sekt] secta *f*

section ['sekʃn] sección *f*; *of building* zona *f*; *of apple* parte *f*

sector ['sektər] sector *m*

secular ['sekjələr] laico

secure [sɪ'kjʊr] **1** *adj shelf etc* seguro; *job, contract* fijo **2** *v/t shelf etc* asegurar; *help* conseguir; **se'curities market** FIN mercado *m* de valores; **security** seguridad *f*; *for investment* garantía *f*; **security alert** alerta *f*; **security forces** fuerzas *fpl* de seguridad; **security guard** guardia *m/f* de seguridad; **security risk** *person* peligro *m* (para la seguridad)

sedan [sɪ'dæn] MOT turismo *m*

sedate [sɪ'deɪt] sedar

sedative ['sedətɪv] sedante *m*

sedentary ['sedənterɪ] *job* sedentario

sediment ['sedɪmənt] sedimento *m*

seduce [sɪ'duːs] seducir; **seduction** seducción *f*; **seductive** *dress* seductor; *offer* tentador

see [siː] ver; ***~ you!*** F ¡hasta la vista!, ¡chao! F

◆ **see off** *at airport etc* despedir; (*chase away*) espantar

seed [siːd] semilla *f*; *in tennis* cabeza *f* de serie; **seedy** *bar, district* de mala calaña

seeing 'eye dog ['siːɪŋ] perro *m* lazarillo; **seeing (that)** dado que, ya que

seek [siːk] buscar

seem [siːm] parecer; **seemingly** aparentemente

seesaw ['siːsɒː] subibaja *m*

'see-through transparente

segment ['segmənt] segmento *m*

segregate ['segrɪgeɪt] segregar; **segregation** segregación *f*
seismology [saɪz'mɑːlədʒɪ] sismología *f*
seize [siːz] *s.o., s.o.'s arm* agarrar; *opportunity* aprovechar; *of Customs, police etc* incautarse de; **seizure** MED ataque *m*; *of drugs etc* incautación *f*; *amount seized* alijo *m*
seldom ['seldəm] raramente, casi nunca
select [sɪ'lekt] **1** *v/t* seleccionar **2** *adj* (*exclusive*) selecto; **selection** selección *f*; (*choosing*) elección *f*; **selective** selectivo
self [self] ego *m*; **self-assurance** confianza *f* en sí mismo; **self-assured** seguro de sí mismo; **self-centered,** *Br* **self-centred** egoísta; **self-confidence** confianza *f* en sí mismo; **self-confident** seguro de sí mismo; **self-conscious** tímido; **self-consciousness** timidez *f*; **self-control** autocontrol *m*; **self-defence** *Br*, **self-defense** autodefensa *f*; ***in ~*** en defensa propia; **self-employed** autónomo; **self-evident** obvio; **self-expression** autoexpresión *f*; **self-government** autogobierno *m*; **self-interest** interés *m* propio; **selfish** egoísta; **selfless** desinteresado; **self-made man** hombre *m* hecho a sí mismo; **self-pity** autocompasión *f*; **self-portrait** autorretrato *m*; **self-reliant** autosuficiente; **self-respect** amor *m* propio; **self-satisfied** *pej* pagado de sí mismo; **self-service** de autoservicio; **self-service restaurant** (restaurante *m*) autoservicio *m*; **self-taught** autodidacta
sell [sel] **1** *v/t* vender **2** *v/i of products* venderse; **sell-by date** fecha *f* límite de venta; **seller** vendedor(a) *m*(*f*); **selling** COM ventas *fpl*; **selling point** COM ventaja *f*
Sellotape® ['selәteɪp] *Br* celo *m*, *L.Am.* Durex**®** *m*
semester [sɪ'mestər] semestre *m*
semi ['semɪ] *truck* camión *m* semirremolque; **semicircle** semicírculo *m*; **semiconductor** ELEC semiconductor *m*; **semifinal** semifinal *f*; **semifinalist** semifinalista *m*/*f*
seminar ['semɪnɑːr] seminario *m*
semi'skilled semicualificado
senate ['senət] senado *m*; **senator** senador(a) *m*(*f*)
send [send] enviar, mandar
◆ **send back** devolver
◆ **send for** mandar buscar
sender ['sendər] *of letter* remitente *m* / *f*
senile ['siːnaɪl] senil; **senility** senilidad *f*
senior ['siːnjər] (*older*) mayor; *in rank* superior; **senior citizen** persona *f* de la tercera

edad; **seniority** *in job* antigüedad *f*

sensation [sen'seɪʃn] sensación *f*; **sensational** sensacional

sense [sens] **1** *n* (*meaning*, *point*, *hearing etc*) sentido *m*; (*feeling*) sentimiento *m*; (*common sense*) sentido *m* común, sensatez *f*; ***come to one's ~s*** entrar en razón; ***it doesn't make ~*** no tiene sentido **2** *v/t s.o.'s presence* sentir, notar; **senseless** (*pointless*) absurdo

sensible ['sensəbl] sensato; *shoes etc* práctico, apropiado; **sensibly** con sensatez

sensitive ['sensətɪv] sensible; **sensitivity** sensibilidad *f*

sensor ['sensər] sensor *m*

sensual ['senʃʊəl] sensual; **sensuality** sensualidad *f*

sensuous ['senʃʊəs] sensual

sentence ['sentəns] **1** *n* GRAM oración *f*; LAW sentencia *f* **2** *v/t* LAW sentenciar, condenar

sentiment ['sentɪmənt] (*sentimentality*) sentimentalismo *m*; (*opinion*) opinión *f*; **sentimental** sentimental; **sentimentality** sentimentalismo *m*

sentry ['sentrɪ] centinela *m*

separate **1** ['sepərət] *adj* separado **2** ['sepəreɪt] *v/t* separar **3** ['sepəreɪt] *v/i of couple* separarse; **separated** *couple* separado; **separately** *pay*, *treat* por separado; **separation** separación *f*

September [sep'tembər] septiembre *m*

septic ['septɪk] séptico

sequel ['si:kwəl] continuación *f*

sequence ['si:kwəns] secuencia *f*

serene [sɪ'ri:n] sereno

sergeant ['sɑ:rdʒənt] sargento *m* / *f*

serial ['sɪrɪəl] serie *f*, serial *m*; *in magazine* novela *f* por entregas; **serialize** *novel on TV* emitir en forma de serie; *in newspaper* publicar por entregas; **serial number** *of product* número *m* de serie

series ['sɪri:z] serie *f*

serious ['sɪrɪəs] *situation*, *damage*, *illness* grave; (*person: earnest*) serio; *company* serio; **seriously** *injured* gravemente; ***take s.o. ~*** tomar a alguien en serio; **seriousness** *of person* seriedad *f*; *of situation* seriedad *f*, gravedad *f*; *of illness* gravedad *f*

sermon ['sɜ:rmən] sermón *m*

servant ['sɜ:rvənt] sirviente(-a) *m*(*f*)

serve [sɜ:rv] **1** *n in tennis* servicio *m*, saque *m* **2** *v/t food*, *meal* servir; *customer in shop* atender; *one's country* servir a **3** *v/i* servir; *in tennis* servir, sacar; **server** *in tennis* jugador(a) *m*(*f*) al servicio; COMPUT servidor *m*; **service** **1** *n to customers*, *community* servicio *m*; *for vehicle*, *machine* revisión *f*; *in tennis* servicio *m*, saque *m*; **~s** (~ *sector*) el sector servicios **2** *v/t vehicle, machine* revisar; **service charge** servicio *m* (*tarifa*); **serviceman** MIL militar *m*; **service station** estación *f* de servicio; **serving** *of food* ración *f*

session ['seʃn] sesión *f*; *with boss etc* reunión *f*

set [set] **1** *n of tools* juego *m*; *of books* colección *f*; (*group of people*) grupo *m*; MATH conjunto *m*; (THEA: *scenery*) decorado *m*; *where a movie is made* plató *m*; *in tennis* set *m* **2** *v/t* (*place*) colocar; *movie, novel etc* ambientar; *date, time, limit* fijar; *alarm* poner; *clock* poner en hora; *broken limb* recomponer; *jewel* engastar; ~ ***the table*** poner la mesa **3** *v/i of sun* ponerse; *of glue* solidificarse **4** *adj ideas* fijo; (*ready*) preparado

◆ **set off 1** *v/i on journey* salir **2** *v/t bomb* hacer explotar; *chain reaction* desencadenar; *alarm* activar

◆ **set out 1** *v/i on journey* salir (***for*** hacia) **2** *v/t ideas, goods* exponer

◆ **set up 1** *v/t company* establecer; *equipment, machine* instalar; *market stall* montar; *meeting* organizar; F (*frame*) tender una trampa a **2** *v/i in business* emprender un negocio

'setback contratiempo *m*

settee [se'ti:] *Br* sofá *m*

setting ['setɪŋ] *of novel etc* escenario *m*; *of house* ubicación *f*

settle ['setl] **1** *v/i of bird, dust* posarse; *of building* hundirse; *to live* establecerse **2** *v/t dispute, uncertainty* resolver; *debts* saldar; *nerves, stomach* calmar

◆ **settle down** (*stop being noisy*) tranquilizarse; (*stop wild living*) sentar la cabeza; *in an area* establecerse

◆ **settle for** (*accept*) conformarse con

settled ['setld] *weather* estable; **settlement** *of claim* resolución *f*; *of debt* liquidación *f*; *of dispute* acuerdo *m*; (*payment*) suma *f*; *of building* hundimiento *m*; **settler** *in new country* colono *m*

'set-up (*structure*) estructura *f*; (*relationship*) relación *f*; F (*frame-up*) trampa *f*

seven ['sevn] siete; **seventeen** diecisiete; **seventeenth** décimoséptimo; **seventh** séptimo; **seventieth** septuagésimo; **seventy** setenta

sever ['sevər] cortar; *relations* romper

several ['sevrl] **1** *adj* varios **2** *pron* varios(-as) *mpl* (*fpl*)

severe [sɪ'vɪr] *illness* grave; *penalty, winter, weather* severo; *teacher* estricto; **severely** *punish, speak* con severidad; *injured, disrupted* gravemen-

te; **severity** severidad *f*; *of illness* gravedad *f*
Seville [sə'vɪl] Sevilla
sew [soʊ] coser
sewage ['suːɪdʒ] aguas *fpl* residuales; **sewer** alcantarilla *f*, cloaca *f*
sewing ['soʊɪŋ] *skill* costura *f*; *that being sewn* labor *f*
sex [seks] sexo *m*; ***have ~ with*** tener relaciones sexuales con; **sexist 1** *adj* sexista **2** *n* sexista *m / f*; **sexual** sexual; **sexuality** sexualidad *f*; **sexually** sexualmente; ***~ transmitted disease*** enfermedad *f* de transmisión sexual; **sexy** sexy *inv*
shabbily ['ʃæbɪlɪ] *dressed* con desaliño; *treat* muy mal; **shabby** *coat etc* desgastado; *treatment* malo
shack [ʃæk] choza *f*
shade [ʃeɪd] **1** *n for lamp* pantalla *f*; *of color* tonalidad *f*; *on window* persiana *f*; ***in the ~*** a la sombra **2** *v/t from sun, light* proteger de la luz
shadow ['ʃædoʊ] sombra *f*
shady ['ʃeɪdɪ] *spot* umbrío; *character* sospechoso
shaft [ʃæft] TECH eje *m*, árbol *m*; *of mine* pozo *m*
shake [ʃeɪk] **1** *n* sacudida *f* **2** *v/t* agitar; *emotionally* conmocionar; ***he shook his head*** negó con la cabeza; ***~ hands with s.o.*** estrechar *or* dar la mano a alguien **3** *v/i of voice, building* temblar; **shaken** *emotionally* conmocionado; **shake-up** reestructuración *f*; **shaky** *table etc* inestable; *after illness* débil; *after shock* conmocionado; *grasp of sth* flojo; *voice, hand* tembloroso
shall [ʃæl] ◇ *future*: ***I ~ do my best*** haré todo lo que pueda ◇ *suggesting*: ***~ we go?*** ¿nos vamos?
shallow ['ʃæloʊ] *water* poco profundo; *person* superficial
shame [ʃeɪm] **1** *n* vergüenza *f*, *Col, Mex, Ven* pena *f*; ***what a ~!*** ¡qué pena *or* lástima! **2** *v/t* avergonzar, *Col, Mex, Ven* apenar; **shameful** vergonzoso; **shameless** desvergonzado
shampoo [ʃæm'puː] champú *m*
shanty town ['ʃæntɪ] *Span* barrio *m* de chabolas, *L.Am.* barriada *f*, *Arg* villa *f* miseria, *Chi* callampa *f*, *Mex* ciudad *f* perdida, *Urug* cantegril *m*
shape [ʃeɪp] **1** *n* forma *f* **2** *v/t clay* modelar; *character* determinar; *the future* dar forma a; **shapeless** *dress etc* amorfo; **shapely** *figure* esbelto
share [ʃer] **1** *n* parte *f*; FIN acción *f* **2** *v/t & v/i* compartir; **shareholder** accionista *m / f*
shark [ʃɑːrk] tiburón *m*
sharp [ʃɑːrp] **1** *adj knife* afilado; *mind* vivo; *pain* agudo; *taste* ácido **2** *adv* MUS dema-

siado alto; ***at 3 o'clock ~*** a las tres en punto; **sharpen** *knife* afilar; *skills* perfeccionar

shatter ['ʃætər] **1** *v/t glass* hacer añicos; *illusions* destrozar **2** *v/i of glass* hacerse añicos; **shattered** F destrozado F; **shattering** *news* demoledor

shave [ʃeɪv] **1** *v/t* afeitar **2** *v/i* afeitarse **3** *n* afeitado *m*; **shaven** *head* afeitado; **shaver** *electric* máquinilla *f* de afeitar (eléctrica)

shawl [ʃɒ:l] chal *m*

she [ʃi:] ella; ***~ is a student*** es estudiante

sheath [ʃi:θ] *for knife* funda *f*; *contraceptive* condón *m*

shed[1] [ʃed] *v/t blood, tears* derramar; *leaves* perder

shed[2] [ʃed] *n* cobertizo *m*

sheep [ʃi:p] oveja *f*; **sheepdog** perro *m* pastor; **sheep-herder** pastor *m*; **sheepish** avergonzado

sheer [ʃɪr] verdadero; *cliffs* escarpado

sheet [ʃi:t] sábana *f*; *of paper, glass* hoja *f*; *of metal* chapa *f*

shelf [ʃelf] estante *m*; **shelves** estanterías *fpl*

shell [ʃel] **1** *n of mussel etc* concha *f*; *of egg* cáscara *f*; *of tortoise* caparazón *m*; MIL proyectil *m* **2** *v/t peas* pelar; MIL bombardear (*con artillería*); **shellfire** fuego *m* de artillería; **shellfish** marisco *m*

shelter ['ʃeltər] **1** *n* refugio *m*; (*bus ~*) marquesina *f* **2** *v/i* refugiarse **3** *v/t* (*protect*) proteger; **sheltered** *place* resguardado; ***lead a ~ life*** llevar una vida protegida

shelve [ʃelv] *fig* posponer

shepherd ['ʃepərd] pastor *m*

sheriff ['ʃerɪf] sheriff *m/f*

shield [ʃi:ld] **1** *n* escudo *m*; TECH placa *f* protectora; *of policeman* placa *f* **2** *v/t* (*protect*) proteger

shift [ʃɪft] **1** *n* cambio *m*; *at work* turno *m* **2** *v/t* (*move*) mover; *stains etc* eliminar **3** *v/i* (*move*) moverse; (*change*) trasladarse; *of wind* cambiar; **shifty** *pej* sospechoso

shin [ʃɪn] espinilla *f*

shine [ʃaɪn] **1** *v/i* brillar; *fig*: *of student etc* destacar (***at*** en) **2** *n on shoes etc* brillo *m*; **shiny** brillante

ship [ʃɪp] **1** *n* barco *m*, buque *m* **2** *v/t* (*send*) enviar; **3** *v/i of new product* distribuirse; **shipment** envío *m*; **shipowner** naviero(-a) *m*(*f*), armador(a) *m*(*f*); **shipping** (*sea traffic*) navíos *mpl*, buques *mpl*; (*sending*) envío *m*; **shipwreck** naufragio *m*; **shipyard** astillero *m*

shirt [ʃɜ:rt] camisa *f*

shit [ʃɪt] **1** *n* P mierda *f* P **2** *v/i* P cagar P **3** *int* P mierda P; **shitty** F asqueroso F

shiver ['ʃɪvər] tiritar

shock [ʃɑ:k] **1** *n* shock *m*, impresión *f*; ELEC descarga *f*;

be in ~ MED estar en estado de shock **2** *v/t* impresionar, dejar boquiabierto; **shock absorber** MOT amortiguador *m*; **shocking** escandaloso; F *weather, spelling* terrible

shoddy ['ʃɑːdɪ] *goods* de mala calidad; *behavior* vergonzoso

shoe [ʃuː] zapato *m*; **shoe-lace** cordón *m*; **shoemaker** zapatero(-a) *m(f)*; **shoe mender** zapatero(-a) *m(f)* remendón(-ona); **shoestore** zapatería *f*

shoot [ʃuːt] **1** *n* BOT brote *m* **2** *v/t* disparar; *and kill* matar de un tiro; *movie* rodar

◆ **shoot down** *airplane* derribar; *fig*: *suggestion* echar por tierra

◆ **shoot up** *of prices* dispararse; *of children* crecer mucho; *of new buildings etc* aparecer de repente

shooting star ['ʃuːtɪŋ] estrella *f* fugaz

shop [ʃɑːp] **1** *n* tienda *f* **2** *v/i* comprar; ***go ~ping*** ir de compras; **shopkeeper** tendero(-a) *m(f)*; **shoplifter** ladrón(-ona) *m(f)* (*en tienda*); **shoplifting** hurtos *mpl* (*en tiendas*); **shopper** comprador(a) *m(f)*; **shopping** *items* compra *f*; **shopping bag** bolsa *f* de la compra; **shopping list** lista *f* de la compra; **shopping mall** centro *m* comercial

shore [ʃɔːr] orilla *f*

short [ʃɔːrt] **1** *adj* corto; *in height* bajo; ***we're ~ of fuel*** nos queda poco combustible **2** *adv*: ***cut ~*** interrumpir; ***go ~ of*** pasar sin; ***in ~*** en resumen; **shortage** escasez *f*, falta *f*; **shortcoming** defecto *m*; **shortcut** atajo *m*; **shorten** *dress, hair, vacation* acortar; *chapter, article* abreviar; *work day* reducir; **shortfall** déficit *m*; **short-lived** efímero; **shortly** (*soon*) pronto; ***~ before / after*** justo antes / después; **shortness** *of visit* brevedad *f*; *in height* baja *f* estatura; **shorts** pantalones *mpl* cortos, shorts *mpl*; *underwear* calzoncillos *mpl*; **shortsighted** miope; *fig* corto de miras; **short-sleeved** de manga corta; **short-tempered** irascible; **short-term** a corto plazo

shot [ʃɑːt] *from gun* disparo *m*; (*photo*) fotografía *f*; (*injection*) inyección *f*; **shotgun** escopeta *f*

should [ʃʊd]: ***what ~ I do?*** ¿qué debería hacer?; ***you ~n't do that*** no deberías hacer eso; ***you ~ have heard him!*** ¡tendrías que haberle oído!

shoulder ['ʃoʊldər] ANAT hombro *m*

shout [ʃaʊt] **1** *n* grito *m* **2** *v/t & v/i* gritar; **shouting** griterío *m*

shove [ʃʌv] **1** *n* empujón *m* **2**

v/t & v/i empujar

shovel [ˈʃʌvl] pala *f*

show [ʃoʊ] **1** *n* THEA espectáculo *m*; *TV* programa *m*; *of emotion* muestra *f* **2** *v/t* mostrar; *at exhibition* exponer; *movie* proyectar **3** *v/i* (*be visible*) verse

◆ **show in** hacer pasar a

◆ **show off 1** *v/t skills* mostrar **2** *v/i pej* presumir, alardear

◆ **show up 1** *v/t shortcomings etc* poner de manifiesto **2** *v/i* (*be visible*) verse; F (*arrive*) aparecer

ˈ**show business** el mundo del espectáculo; **showcase** vitrina *f*; *fig* escaparate *m*; **showdown** enfrentamiento *m*

shower [ˈʃaʊər] **1** *n of rain* chaparrón *m*; *to wash* ducha *f*, *Mex* regadera *f*; (*party*) *fiesta con motivo de un bautizo, una boda etc., en la que los invitados llevan obsequios*; ***take a ~*** ducharse **2** *v/i* ducharse

ˈ**show-off** *pej* fanfarrón(-ona) *m*(*f*); **showroom** sala *f* de exposición *f*; **showy** llamativo

shred [ʃred] **1** *n of paper etc* trozo *m*; *of fabric* jirón *m* **2** *v/t paper* hacer trizas; *in cooking* cortar en tiras; **shredder** *for documents* trituradora *f* (de documentos)

shrewd [ʃru:d] *person* astuto; *investment* inteligente; **shrewdness** *of person* astucia *f*; *of decision* inteligencia *f*

shriek [ʃri:k] **1** *n* alarido *m*, chillido *m* **2** *v/i* chillar

shrill [ʃrɪl] estridente, agudo

shrimp [ʃrɪmp] gamba *f*; *larger Span* langostino *m*, *L.Am.* camarón *m*

shrine [ʃraɪn] santuario *m*

shrink[1] [ʃrɪŋk] *v/i of material* encoger(se); *of support etc* reducirse

shrink[2] [ʃrɪŋk] *n* F (*psychiatrist*) psiquiatra *m/f*

shrivel [ˈʃrɪvl] *of skin* arrugarse; *of leaves* marchitarse

shrub [ʃrʌb] arbusto *m*; **shrubbery** arbustos *mpl*

shrug [ʃrʌg]: *~* (***one's shoulders***) encoger los hombros

shudder [ˈʃʌdər] **1** *n of fear, disgust* escalofrío *m*; *of earth* temblor *m* **2** *v/i with fear, disgust* estremecerse; *of earth* temblar

shuffle [ˈʃʌfl] **1** *v/t cards* barajar **2** *v/i in walking* arrastrar los pies

shun [ʃʌn] rechazar

shut [ʃʌt] cerrar

◆ **shut down 1** *v/t business* cerrar; *computer* apagar **2** *v/i of business* cerrarse; *of computer* apagarse

◆ **shut up** F (*be quiet*) callarse; **shut up!** ¡cállate!

shutter [ˈʃʌtər] *on window* contraventana *f*; PHOT obturador *m*

'shuttlebus *at airport* autobús *m* de conexión
shy [ʃaɪ] tímido; **shyness** timidez *f*
sick [sɪk] enfermo; *sense of humor* morboso, macabro; **be ~** *Br* (*vomit*) vomitar; **sicken 1** *v/t* (*disgust*) poner enfermo; (*make ill*) hacer enfermar **2** *v/i*: ***be ~ing for sth*** estar incubando algo; **sickening** *stench* nauseabundo; *crime* repugnante; **sick leave** baja *f* (por enfermedad); **sickness** enfermedad *f*; (*vomiting*) vómitos *mpl*
side [saɪd] lado *m*; *of mountain* ladera *f*; *of person* costado *m*; SP equipo *m*; ***take ~s*** (*favor one ~*) tomar partido (***with*** por); ***~ by ~*** uno al lado del otro; **side effect** efecto *m* secundario; **sidestep** *fig* evadir; **side street** bocacalle *f*; **sidewalk** acera *f*, *Rpl* vereda *f*, *Mex* banqueta *f*; **sideways** de lado
siege [si:dʒ] sitio *m*
sieve [sɪv] tamiz *m*
sift [sɪft] tamizar; *data* examinar a fondo
sigh [saɪ] **1** *n* suspiro *m* **2** *v/i* suspirar
sight [saɪt] vista *f*; ***~s*** *of city* lugares *mpl* de interés; ***know by ~*** conocer de vista; **sightseeing**: ***go ~*** hacer turismo; **sightseer** turista *m/f*
sign [saɪn] **1** *n* señal *f*; *outside shop* cartel *m*, letrero *m* **2** *v/t* & *v/i* firmar
signal ['sɪgnl] **1** *n* señal *f* **2** *v/i of driver* poner el intermitente
signatory ['sɪgnətɔːrɪ] signatario(-a) *m(f)*, firmante *m/f*
signature ['sɪgnətʃər] firma *f*
significance [sɪg'nɪfɪkəns] importancia *f*, relevancia *f*; **significant** *event etc* importante, relevante; (*quite large*) considerable; **significantly** *larger, more expensive* considerablemente
signify ['sɪgnɪfaɪ] significar, suponer
'sign language lenguaje *m* por señas; **signpost** señal *f*
silence ['saɪləns] **1** *n* silencio *m* **2** *v/t* hacer callar; **silent** silencioso
silhouette [sɪlu:'et] silueta *f*
silicon ['sɪlɪkən] silicio *m*
silicone ['sɪlɪkoʊn] silicona *f*
silk [sɪlk] **1** *n* seda *f* **2** *adj shirt etc* de seda; **silky** sedoso
silliness ['sɪlɪnɪs] tontería *f*; **silly** tonto
silo ['saɪloʊ] silo *m*
silver ['sɪlvər] **1** *n* plata *f* **2** *adj ring* de plata; *hair* canoso; **silverware** plata *f*
similar ['sɪmɪlər] parecido, similar; **similarity** parecido *m*, similitud *f*; **similarly** de la misma manera
simple ['sɪmpl] sencillo; *person* simple; **simple-minded** *pej* simplón; **simplicity** sencillez *f*, simplicidad *f*; **simplify** simplificar; **simplistic**

simplista; **simply** sencillamente
simultaneous [saɪml'teɪnɪəs] simultáneo; **simultaneously** simultáneamente
sin [sɪn] **1** *n* pecado *m* **2** *v/i* pecar
since [sɪns] **1** *prep* desde **2** *adv* desde entonces **3** *conj in expressions of time* desde que; (*seeing that*) ya que, dado que
sincere [sɪn'sɪr] sincero; **sincerely** sinceramente; ***Sincerely Yours ~*** atentamente; **sincerity** sinceridad *f*
sinful ['sɪnfəl] *person* pecador; *things* pecaminoso
sing [sɪŋ] cantar
singe [sɪndʒ] chamuscar
singer ['sɪŋər] cantante *m/f*
single ['sɪŋgl] **1** *adj* único; (*not married*) soltero *m* **2** *n* MUS sencillo *m*; (*~ room*) habitación *f* individual; *person* soltero(-a) *m(f)*; *Br ticket* billete *m or L.Am.* boleto *m* de ida; ***~s*** *in tennis* individuales *mpl*; **single-handed** en solitario; **single-minded** determinado, resuelto; **single parent** padre *m* / madre *f* soltero(-a); **single parent family** familia *f* monoparental; **single room** habitación *f* individual
singular ['sɪŋgjʊlər] GRAM **1** *adj* singular **2** *n* singular *m*
sinister ['sɪnɪstər] siniestro; *sky* amenazador
sink [sɪŋk] **1** *n in kitchen* fregadero *m*; *in bathroom* lavabo *m* **2** *v/i of ship*, *object* hundirse; *of sun* ponerse; *of interest rates etc* descender, bajar **3** *v/t ship* hundir; *funds* investir
sinner ['sɪnər] pecador(a) *m(f)*
sip [sɪp] **1** *n* sorbo *m* **2** *v/t* sorber
sir [sɜːr] señor *m*; ***excuse me***, ~ perdone, caballero
siren ['saɪrən] sirena *f*
sirloin ['sɜːrlɔɪn] solomillo *m*
sister ['sɪstər] hermana *f*; **sister-in-law** cuñada *f*
sit [sɪt] estar sentado; (*~ down*) sentarse
◆ **sit down** sentarse
sitcom ['sɪtkɑːm] telecomedia *f*, comedia *f* de situación
site [saɪt] **1** *n* emplazamiento *m*; *of battle* lugar *m* **2** *v/t new offices etc* situar
sitting ['sɪtɪŋ] *of committee*, *for artist* sesión *f*; *for meals* turno *m*; **sitting room** sala *f* de estar, salón *m*
situated ['sɪtʊeɪtɪd] situado; **situation** situación *f*
six [sɪks] seis; **sixteen** dieciséis; **sixteenth** decimosexto; **sixth** sexto; **sixtieth** sexagésimo; **sixty** sesenta
size [saɪz] tamaño *m*; *of loan* importe *m*; *of jacket* talla *f*; *of shoes* número *m*; **sizeable** *house*, *order* considerable; *meal* copioso
skate [skeɪt] **1** *n* patín *m* **2** *v/i* patinar; **skateboard** monopatín *m*; **skateboarding** pa-

tinaje *m* en monopatín; **skater** patinador(a) *m(f)*; **skating** patinaje *m*; **skating rink** pista *f* de patinaje

skeleton ['skelɪtn] esqueleto *m*

skeptic ['skeptɪk] escéptico(-a) *m(f)*; **skeptical** escéptico; **skepticism** escepticismo *m*

sketch [sketʃ] **1** *n* boceto *m*, esbozo *m*; THEA sketch *m* **2** *v/t* bosquejar; **sketchy** *knowledge etc* básico, superficial

ski [ski:] **1** *n* esquí *m* **2** *v/i* esquiar

skid [skɪd] **1** *n of car* patinazo *m*; *of person* resbalón *m* **2** *v/i of car* patinar; *of person* resbalar

skier ['ski:ər] esquiador(a) *m(f)*; **skiing** esquí *m*

skilful *etc Br* ☞ ***skillful*** *etc*

skill [skɪl] destreza *f*, habilidad *f*; **skilled** capacitado; **skillful** hábil, habilidoso; **skillfully** con habilidad *or* destreza

skim [skɪm] *surface* rozar; *milk* desnatar, descremar

skimpy ['skɪmpɪ] *account etc* superficial; *dress* cortísimo; *bikini* mínimo

skin [skɪn] **1** *n* piel *f* **2** *v/t* despellejar, desollar; **skin diving** buceo *m*; **skinny** escuálido; **skin-tight** ajustado

skip [skɪp] **1** *n* (*little jump*) brinco *m*, saltito *m* **2** *v/i* brincar **3** *v/t* (*omit*) pasar por alto; **skipper** capitán(-ana) *m(f)*

skirt [skɜ:rt] falda *f*

skull [skʌl] cráneo *m*

skunk [skʌŋk] mofeta *f*

sky [skaɪ] cielo *m*; **skylight** claraboya *f*; **skyline** horizonte *m*; **skyscraper** rascacielos *m inv*

slab [slæb] *of stone* losa *f*; *of cake etc* trozo *m* grande

slack [slæk] *rope* flojo; *work* descuidado; *period* tranquilo; **slacken** *rope*, *pace* aflojar; **slacks** pantalones *mpl*

slam [slæm] **1** *v/t door* cerrar de un golpe **2** *v/i of door* cerrarse de golpe

slander ['slændər] **1** *n* difamación *f* **2** *v/t* difamar; **slanderous** difamatorio

slang [slæŋ] argot *m*, jerga *f*; *of a specific group* jerga *f*

slant [slænt] **1** *v/i* inclinarse **2** *n* inclinación *f*; *given to a story* enfoque *m*; **slanting** *roof* inclinado; *eyes* rasgado

slap [slæp] **1** *n* (*blow*) bofetada *f* **2** *v/t* dar una bofetada a

slash [slæʃ] **1** *n cut* corte *m*, raja *f*; *in punctuation* barra *f* **2** *v/t skin etc* cortar; *prices* recortar drásticamente

slaughter ['slɒ:tər] **1** *n of animals* sacrificio *m*; *of people*, *troops* matanza *f* **2** *v/t animals* sacrificar; *people*, *troops* masacrar; **slaughterhouse** matadero *m*

slave [sleɪv] esclavo(-a) *m(f)*

slay [sleɪ] asesinar; **slaying**

(*murder*) asesinato *m*

sleaze [sli:z] POL corrupción *f*; **sleazy** *bar* sórdido; *person* de mala calaña

sleep [sli:p] **1** *n* sueño *m*; ***go to ~*** dormirse **2** *v/i* dormir

◆ **sleep with** (*have sex with*) acostarse con

sleeping bag ['sli:pɪŋ] saco *m* de dormir; **sleeping car** RAIL coche *m* cama; **sleeping pill** somnífero *m*, pastilla *f* para dormir; **sleepwalker** sonámbulo(-a) *m(f)*; **sleepwalking** sonambulismo *m*; **sleepy** adormilado, somnoliento; *town* tranquilo; ***I'm ~*** tengo sueño

sleet [sli:t] aguanieve *f*

sleeve [sli:v] manga *f*; **sleeveless** sin mangas

slender ['slendər] *figure, arms* esbelto; *margin* escaso; *chance* remoto

slice [slaɪs] **1** *n of bread* rebanada *f*; *of cake* trozo *m*; *of salami, cheese* loncha *f*; *fig*: *of profits etc* parte *f* **2** *v/t loaf etc* cortar (en rebanadas)

slick [slɪk] **1** *adj performance* muy logrado; (*pej*: *cunning*) con mucha labia **2** *n of oil* marea *f* negra

slide [slaɪd] **1** *n for kids* tobogán *m*; PHOT diapositiva *f* **2** *v/i* deslizarse; *of exchange rate etc* descender **3** *v/t* deslizar

slight [slaɪt] *person, figure* menudo; (*small*) pequeño; *accent* ligero; ***no, not in the ~est*** no, en absoluto; **slightly** un poco

slim [slɪm] delgado; *chance* remoto

slime [slaɪm] (*mud*) lodo *m*; *of slug etc* baba *f*; **slimy** *liquid* viscoso; *river bed* lleno de lodo

sling [slɪŋ] **1** *n for arm* cabestrillo *m* **2** *v/t* F (*throw*) tirar

slip [slɪp] **1** *n* (*mistake*) desliz *m* **2** *v/i on ice etc* resbalar; *of quality etc* empeorar

◆ **slip up** (*make mistake*) equivocarse

slipped 'disc [slɪpt] hernia *f* discal

slipper ['slɪpər] zapatilla *f* (*de estar por casa*)

slippery ['slɪpərɪ] *surface, road* resbaladizo; *fish* escurridizo

'slip-up (*mistake*) error *m*

slit [slɪt] **1** *n* (*tear*) raja *f*; (*hole*) rendija *f*; *in skirt* corte *m* **2** *v/t* abrir

sliver ['slɪvər] trocito *m*; *of wood, glass* astilla *f*

slob [slɑ:b] *pej* dejado(-a) *m/f*, guarro(-a) *m/f*

slog [slɑ:g] paliza *f*

slogan ['sloʊgən] eslogan *m*

slop [slɑ:p] derramar

slope [sloʊp] **1** *n of roof* inclinación *f*; *of mountain* ladera *f* **2** *v/i* inclinarse

sloppy ['slɑ:pɪ] descuidado; *too sentimental* sensiblero

slot [slɑ:t] ranura *f*; *in schedule* hueco *m*; **slot machine** *for cigarettes, food* máquina

f expendedora; *for gambling* máquina *f* tragaperras
slovenly ['slʌvnlɪ] descuidado
slow [sloʊ] lento; ***be ~ of clock*** ir retrasado
◆ **slow down 1** *v/t work, progress* restrasar; *traffic, production* ralentizar **2** *v/i in walking, driving* reducir la velocidad; *of production etc* relantizarse
'slowdown *in production* ralentización *f*; **slowly** despacio, lentamente; **slowness** lentitud *f*
sluggish ['slʌgɪʃ] lento
slum [slʌm] suburbio *m*, arrabal
slump [slʌmp] **1** *n in trade* desplome *m* **2** *v/i economically, of person* desplomarse
slur [slɜːr] **1** *n on character* difamación *f* **2** *v/t words* arrastrar
slush [slʌʃ] nieve *f* derretida; (*pej*: *sentimental stuff*) sensiblería *f*; **slush fund** fondo *m* para corruptelas
slut [slʌt] *pej* fulana *f*
sly [slaɪ] ladino
small [smɒːl] pequeño, *L.Am.* chico
smart¹ [smɑːrt] *adj* elegante; (*intelligent*) inteligente; *pace* rápido
smart² [smɑːrt] *v/i* (*hurt*) escocer
'smart card tarjeta *f* inteligente; **smartly** *dressed* con elegancia
smash [smæʃ] **1** *n noise* estruendo *m*; (*car crash*) choque *m*; *in tennis* smash *m* **2** *v/t break* hacer pedazos *or* añicos **3** *v/i break* romperse
smattering ['smætərɪŋ] *of a language* nociones *fpl*
smear [smɪr] **1** *n of ink* borrón *m*; *of paint* mancha *f*; *Br* MED citología *f*; *on character* difamación *f* **2** *v/t character* difamar
smell [smel] **1** *n* olor *m*; ***sense of ~*** sentido *m* del olfato **2** *v/t* oler **3** *v/i unpleasantly* oler (mal); (*sniff*) olfatear; **smelly** apestoso
smile [smaɪl] **1** *n* sonrisa *f* **2** *v/i* sonreír
smirk [smɜːrk] sonrisa *f* maligna
smoke [smoʊk] **1** *n* humo *m* **2** *v/t cigarettes* fumar; *bacon* ahumar **3** *v/i of person* fumar; **smoke-free** *zone* de no fumadores; **smoker** fumador(-a) *m*(*f*); **smoking**: ***no ~*** prohibido fumar; **smoky** lleno de humo
smolder, *Br* **smoulder** ['smoʊldər] *of fire* arder
smooth [smuːð] **1** *adj surface, skin* liso, suave; *sea* en calma; (*peaceful*) tranquilo; *ride, drive* sin vibraciones; *transition* sin problemas; *pej*: *person* meloso **2** *v/t hair* alisar; **smoothly** *without problems* sin incidentes
smother ['smʌðər] *flames* sofocar; *person* asfixiar

smudge [smʌdʒ] **1** *n of paint* mancha *f*; *of ink* borrón *m* **2** *v/t ink* emborronar; *paint* difuminar
smug [smʌg] engreído
smuggle ['smʌgl] pasar de contrabando; **smuggler** contrabandista *m/f*; **smuggling** contrabando *m*
smutty ['smʌtɪ] *joke* obsceno
snack [snæk] tentempié *m*, aperitivo *m*
snag [snæg] (*problem*) inconveniente *m*, pega *f*
snake [sneɪk] serpiente *f*
snap [snæp] **1** *n* chasquido *m*; PHOT foto *f* **2** *v/t break* romper **3** *v/i break* romperse **4** *adj decision, judgment* rápido, súbito; **snappy** *person, mood* irascible; *decision* rápido; (*elegant*) elegante; **snapshot** foto *f*
snarl [snɑːrl] **1** *n of dog* gruñido *m* **2** *v/i* gruñir
snatch [snætʃ] arrebatar; (*steal*) robar; (*kidnap*) secuestrar
snazzy ['snæzɪ] F vistoso, *Span* chulo F
sneakers ['sniːkərz] zapatillas *fpl* de deporte
sneaky ['sniːkɪ] F (*crafty*) ladino, cuco F
sneer [sniːr] **1** *n* mueca *f* desdeñosa **2** *v/i* burlarse (***at*** de)
sneeze [sniːz] **1** *n* estornudo *m* **2** *v/i* estornudar
snicker ['snɪkər] reírse (*en voz baja*)
sniff [snɪf] **1** *v/i to clear nose* sorberse los mocos; *of dog* olfatear **2** *v/t* (*smell*) oler; *of dog* olfatear
sniper ['snaɪpər] francotirador(a) *m(f)*
snitch [snɪtʃ] F **1** *n* (*telltale*) chivato(-a) *m(f)* **2** *v/i* chivarse
snivel ['snɪvl] gimotear
snob [snɑːb] presuntuoso(-a) *m(f)*; **snobbery** presuntuosidad *f*; **snobbish** presuntuoso
snoop [snuːp] fisgón(-ona) *m(f)*
snooty ['snuːtɪ] presuntuoso
snooze [snuːz] **1** *n* cabezada *f* **2** *v/i* echar una cabezada
snore [snɔːr] roncar; **snoring** ronquidos *mpl*
snorkel ['snɔːrkl] snorkel *m*, tubo *m* para buceo
snort [snɔːrt] *of bull, person* bufar, resoplar
snow [snoʊ] **1** *n* nieve *f* **2** *v/i* nevar; **snowball** bola *f* de nieve; **snowdrift** nevero *m*; **snowman** muñeco *m* de nieve; **snowplow** quitanieves *f inv*; **snowstorm** tormenta *f* de nieve; **snowy** *weather* de nieve; *hills* nevado
snub [snʌb] **1** *n* desaire **2** *v/t* desairar; **snub-nosed** con la nariz respingona
snug [snʌg] (*tight-fitting*) ajustado
so [soʊ] **1** *adv* tan; ***it was ~ easy*** fue tan fácil; ***I'm ~ cold*** tengo tanto frío; ***that was ~***

kind of you fue muy amable de tu parte; ***not ~ much*** no tanto; ***~ much easier*** mucho más fácil; ***you shouldn't drink ~ much*** no deberías beber tanto; ***I miss you ~*** te echo tanto de menos; ***~ am / do I*** yo también; ***~ is she / does she*** ella también; ***and ~ on*** etcétera **2** *pron*: ***I hope / think ~*** eso espero / creo; ***you didn't tell me – I did ~*** no me lo dijiste – sí que lo hice; ***15 or ~*** unos 15 **3** *conj for that reason* así que; *in order that* para que; ***~ (that) I could come too*** para que yo también pudiera venir; ***~ what?*** F ¿y qué? F

soak [souk] (*steep*) poner en remojo; *of water* empapar; **soaked** empapado

soap [soup] *for washing* jabón *m*; **soap (opera)** telenovela *f*; **soapy** jabonoso

soar [sɔːr] *of rocket etc* elevarse; *of prices* dispararse

sob [sɑːb] **1** *n* sollozo *m* **2** *v/i* sollozar

sober ['soubər] sobrio; (*serious*) serio

so-'called (*referred to as*) así llamado; (*incorrectly referred to as*) mal llamado

soccer ['sɑːkər] fútbol *m*

sociable ['souʃəbl] sociable

social ['souʃl] social; **social democrat** socialdemócrata *m/f*; **socialism** socialismo *m*; **socialist 1** *adj* socialista **2** *n* socialista *m/f*; **socialize** socializar; **social worker** asistente(-a) *m(f)* social

society [sə'saɪətɪ] sociedad *f*

sociologist [sousɪ'ɑːlədʒɪst] sociólogo(-a) *m(f)*; **sociology** sociología *f*

sock¹ [sɑːk] *n for wearing* calcetín *m*

sock² [sɑːk] *v/t* (*punch*) dar un puñetazo a

socket ['sɑːkɪt] *for light bulb* casquillo *m*; *of arm* cavidad *f*; *of eye* cuenca *f*; *Br* ELEC enchufe *m*

soda ['soudə] (*~ water*) soda *f*; (*soft drink*) refresco *m*; (*ice-cream ~*) *refresco de soda con helado*

sofa ['soufə] sofá *m*

soft [sɑːft] *voice, light, skin* suave; *pillow, attitude* blando; **soften** *position* ablandar; *impact, blow* amortiguar; **softly** suavemente; **software** software *m*

soggy ['sɑːgɪ] empapado

soil [sɔɪl] **1** *n* (*earth*) tierra *f* **2** *v/t* ensuciar

solar 'energy ['soulər] energía *f* solar

soldier ['souldʒər] soldado *m*

sole¹ [soul] *n of foot* planta *f*; *of shoe* suela *f*

sole² [soul] *adj* único

solely ['soulɪ] únicamente

solemn ['sɑːləm] solemne; **solemnity** solemnidad *f*; **solemnly** solemnemente

solicit [sə'lɪsɪt] *of prostitute* abordar clientes

solid ['sɑːlɪd] sólido; (*without*

holes) compacto; *gold, silver* macizo; **solidarity** solidaridad *f*; **solidify** solidificarse; **solidly** *built* sólidamente; *in favor of* unánimente
solitaire [sɑːlɪ'ter] *card game* solitario *m*
solitary ['sɑːlɪterɪ] *life* solitario; (*single*) único; **solitude** soledad *f*
solo ['soulou] **1** *n* MUS solo *m* **2** *adj* en solitario; **soloist** solista *m/f*
soluble ['sɑːljubl] *substance, problem* soluble; **solution** *also mixture* solución *f*
solve [sɑːlv] *problem* solucionar, resolver; *mystery* resolver; **solvent** *financially* solvente
somber, *Br* **sombre** ['sɑːmbər] (*dark*) oscuro; (*serious*) sombrío
some [sʌm] **1** *adj*: ***would you like ~ water / cookies?*** ¿quieres agua / galletas?; ***~ countries*** algunos países; ***I gave him ~ money*** le di (algo de) dinero; ***~ people say that …*** hay quien dice… **2** *pron*: ***~ of the group*** parte del grupo; ***would you like ~?*** ¿quieres? **3** *adv* (*a bit*): ***we'll have to wait ~*** tendremos que esperar algo *or* un poco; **somebody** alguien; **someday** algún día; **somehow** (*by one means or another*) de alguna manera; (*for some unknown reason*) por alguna razón; **someone** ☞ ***somebody***; **someplace** ☞ ***somewhere***
somersault ['sʌmərsɒːlt] **1** *n* voltereta *f* **2** *v/i of vehicle* dar una vuelta de campana
'something algo; **sometime**: ***~ last year*** en algún momento del año pasado; **sometimes** a veces; **somewhat** un tanto; **somewhere 1** *adv* en alguna parte *or* algún lugar **2** *pron*: ***let's go ~ quiet*** vamos a algún sitio tranquilo; ***~ to park*** un sitio donde aparcar
son [sʌn] hijo *m*
song [sɒːŋ] canción *f*
'son-in-law yerno *m*; **son of a bitch** V hijo *m* de puta P
soon [suːn] pronto; ***as ~ as*** tan pronto como; ***as ~ as possible*** lo antes posible; ***~er or later*** tarde o temprano; ***the ~er the better*** cuanto antes mejor
soothe [suːð] calmar
sophisticated [sə'fɪstɪkeɪtɪd] sofisticado; **sophistication** sofisticación *f*
sophomore ['sɑːfəmɔːr] estudiante *m/f* de segundo año
soprano [sə'prænou] *singer* soprano *m/f*; *voice* voz *f* de soprano
sordid ['sɔːrdɪd] sórdido
sore [sɔːr] **1** *adj* (*painful*) dolorido; F (*angry*) enojado, *Span* mosqueado F; ***is it ~?*** ¿duele? **2** *n* llaga *f*
sorrow ['sɑːrou] pena *f*
sorry ['sɑːrɪ] *day, sight*, (*sad*)

triste; ***(I'm) ~!*** *apologizing* ¡lo siento!

sort [sɔːrt] **1** *n* clase *f*, tipo *m*; ***~ of*** F un poco, algo **2** *v/t* ordenar, clasificar; COMPUT ordenar

SOS [esoʊ'es] SOS *m*; *fig* llamada *f* de auxilio

so-'so F así así F

soul [soʊl] REL, *fig* alma *f*; *character* personalidad *f*

sound[1] [saʊnd] **1** *adj* (*sensible*) sensato; (*healthy*) sano; *sleep* profundo **2** *adv*: ***be ~ asleep*** estar profundamente dormido

sound[2] [saʊnd] **1** *n* sonido *m*; (*noise*) ruido *m* **2** *v/i* parecer; ***that ~s interesting*** parece interesante

soundly ['saʊndlɪ] *sleep* profundamente; *beaten* rotundamente; **soundproof** insonorizado; **soundtrack** banda *f* sonora

soup [suːp] sopa *f*

sour [saʊr] agrio

source [sɔːrs] fuente *f*; *of river* nacimiento *m*

south [saʊθ] **1** *adj* sur, del sur **2** *n* sur *m* **3** *adv* al sur; **South Africa** Sudáfrica; **South African** **1** *adj* sudafricano **2** *n* sudafricano(-a) *m*(*f*); **South America** Sudamérica, América del Sur; **South American** **1** *adj* sudamericano **2** *n* sudamericano(-a) *m*(*f*); **south-east** **1** *n* sudeste *m*, sureste *m* **2** *adj* sudeste, sureste **3** *adv* al sudeste *or* sureste; **southeastern** del sudeste; **southerly** *wind* sur, del sur; *direction* sur; **southern** sureño; **southerner** sureño(-a) *m*(*f*); **southernmost** más al sur; **South Pole** Polo *m* Sur; **southward** hacia el sur; **southwest** **1** *n* sudoeste *m*, suroeste *m* **2** *adj* sudoeste, suroeste **3** *adv* al sudoeste *or* suroeste; **southwestern** del sudoeste *or* suroeste

souvenir [suːvə'nɪr] recuerdo *m*

sovereign ['sɑːvrɪn] *state* soberano; **sovereignty** *of state* soberanía *f*

sow[1] [saʊ] *n* (*female pig*) cerda *f*, puerca *f*

sow[2] [soʊ] *v/t seeds* sembrar

space [speɪs] espacio *m*; **space shuttle** transbordador *m* espacial; **space station** estación *f* espacial; **spacious** espacioso

spade [speɪd] pala *f*; ***~s*** *in card game* picas *fpl*

spaghetti [spə'getɪ] espaguetis *mpl*

Spain [speɪn] España

spam [spæm] COMPUT propaganda *f* electrónica

span [spæn] abarcar; *of bridge* cruzar

Spaniard ['spænjərd] español(a) *m*(*f*); **Spanish** **1** *adj* español **2** *n language* español *m*; ***the ~*** los españoles

spanner ['spænər] *Br* llave *f*

spare [sper] **1** *v/t*: ***can you ~***

me $50? ¿me podrías dejar 50 dólares?; ***can you ~ the time?*** ¿tienes tiempo? **2** *adj pair of glasses, set of keys* de repuesto **3** *n* recambio *m*, repuesto *m*; **spare part** pieza *f* de recambio *or* repuesto; **spare ribs** costillas *fpl* de cerdo; **spare room** habitación *f* de invitados; **spare time** tiempo *m* libre; **spare wheel** MOT rueda *f* de recambio; **sparing** moderado; **sparingly** con moderación

spark [spɑːrk] chispa *f*

sparkle ['spɑːrkl] destellar; **sparkling wine** vino *m* espumoso; **spark plug** bujía *f*

sparse [spɑːrs] *vegetation* escaso

spartan ['spɑːrtn] *room* espartano

spasmodic [spæz'mɑːdɪk] intermitente

spate [speɪt] *fig* oleada *f*

spatial ['speɪʃl] espacial

speak [spiːk] **1** *v/i* hablar (***to, with*** con); (*make a speech*) dar una charla; ***~ing*** TELEC al habla **2** *v/t foreign language* hablar; **speaker** *at conference* conferenciante *m/f*; (*orator*) orador(a) *m(f)*; *of sound system* altavoz *m*, *L.Am.* altoparlante *m*; *of language* hablante *m/f*

special ['speʃl] especial; **specialist** especialista *m/f*; **specialize** especializarse (***in*** en); **specially** ☞ ***especially***; **specialty** especialidad *f*

species ['spiːʃiːz] especie *f*

specific [spə'sɪfɪk] específico; **specifically** específicamente; **specifications** *of machine etc* especificaciones *fpl*; **specify** especificar

specimen ['spesɪmən] muestra *f*

spectacular [spek'tækjʊlər] espectacular

spectator [spek'teɪtər] espectador(a) *m(f)*

spectrum ['spektrəm] *fig* espectro *m*

speculate ['spekjʊleɪt] *also* FIN especular; **speculation** *also* FIN especulación *f*; **speculator** FIN especulador(a) *m(f)*

speech [spiːtʃ] (*address*) discurso *m*; *in play* parlamento *m*; (*ability to speak*) habla *f*, dicción *f*; (*way of speaking*) forma *f* de hablar; **speechless** sin habla

speed [spiːd] **1** *n* velocidad *f*; (*promptness*) rapidez *f* **2** *v/i run* correr; *drive too quickly* sobrepasar el límite de velocidad; **speedboat** motora *f*, planeadora *f*; **speed bump** resalto *m* (*para reducir la velocidad del tráfico*), *Arg* despertador *m*, *Mex* tope *m*; **speed-dial button** botón *m* de marcado rápido; **speedily** con rapidez; **speeding: *fined for ~*** multado por exceso de velocidad; **speed limit** límite *m* de velocidad; **speedometer** velocímetro *m*; **speedy** rápido

spell[1] [spel] **1** *v/t word* deletrear; ***how do you ~ ...?*** ¿cómo se escribe... ? **2** *v/i* deletrear

spell[2] [spel] *n of time* periodo *m*, temporada *f*

spelling ['spelɪŋ] ortografía *f*

spend [spend] *money* gastar; *time* pasar; **spendthrift** *pej* derrochador(a) *m*(*f*)

sperm [spɜːrm] espermatozoide *m*; (*semen*) esperma *f*

sphere [sfɪr] *also fig* esfera *f*

spice [spaɪs] (*seasoning*) especia *f*; **spicy** *food* con especias; (*hot*) picante

spider ['spaɪdər] araña *f*; **spiderweb** telaraña *f*

spike [spaɪk] pincho *m*; *on running shoe* clavo *m*

spill [spɪl] **1** *v/t* derramar **2** *v/i* derramarse **3** *n* derrame *m*

spin[1] [spɪn] **1** *n* (*turn*) giro *m* **2** *v/t* hacer girar **3** *v/i of wheel* girar

spin[2] [spɪn] *v/t cotton* hilar; *web* tejer

spinach ['spɪnɪdz] espinacas *fpl*

spinal ['spaɪnl] de la columna vertebral; **spinal column** columna *f* vertebral; **spinal cord** médula *f* espinal; **spine** *of person, animal* columna *f* vertebral; *of book* lomo *m*; *on plant, hedgehog* espina *f*; **spineless** (*cowardly*) débil

'spin-off producto *m* derivade

spiny ['spaɪnɪ] espinoso

spiral ['spaɪrəl] **1** *n* espiral **2** *v/i* (*rise quickly*) subir vertiginosamente

spire [spaɪr] aguja *f*

spirit ['spɪrɪt] espíritu *m*; (*courage*) valor *m*; **spirited** (*energetic*) enérgico; **spirits** (*morale*) la moral; ***be in good / poor ~*** tener la moral alta / baja; **spiritual** espiritual

spit [spɪt] *of person* escupir

spite [spaɪt] rencor *m*; ***in ~ of*** a pesar de; **spiteful** malo, malicioso; **spitefully** con maldad *or* malicia

splash [splæʃ] **1** *n small amount of liquid* chorrito *m*; *of color* mancha *f* **2** *v/t person* salpicar **3** *v/i* chapotear; *of water* salpicar

◆ **splash down** *of spacecraft* amerizar

splendid ['splendɪd] espléndido; **splendor**, *Br* **splendour** esplendor *m*

splint [splɪnt] MED tablilla *f*

splinter ['splɪntər] **1** *n* astilla *f* **2** *v/i* astillarse

split [splɪt] **1** *n damage* raja *f*; (*disagreement*) escisión *f*; (*division, share*) reparto *m* **2** *v/t damage* rajar; *logs* partir en dos; (*cause disagreement in*) escindir; (*share*) repartir **3** *v/i* (*tear*) rajarse; (*disagree*) escindirse

◆ **split up** *of couple* separarse

spoil [spɔɪl] estropear, arruinar; **spoilsport** F aguafiestas *m/f inv* F; **spoilt** *child* consentido, mimado

spoke [spoʊk] *of wheel* radio *m*

spokesperson ['spoʊkspɜːrsən] portavoz *m/f*

sponge [spʌndʒ] esponja *f*; **sponger** F gorrón(-ona) *m(f)* F

sponsor ['spɑːnsər] **1** *n* patrocinador *m* **2** *v/t* patrocinar; **sponsorship** patrocinio *m*

spontaneous [spɑːn'teɪnɪəs] espontáneo; **spontaneously** espontáneamente

spool [spuːl] carrete *m*

spoon [spuːn] cuchara *f*; **spoonful** cucharada *f*

sporadic [spə'rædɪk] esporádico

sport [spɔːrt] deporte *m*; **sporting** deportivo; **sports car** (coche *m*) deportivo *m*; **sportsman** deportista *m*; **sportswoman** deportista *f*; **sporty** *person* deportista; *clothes* deportivo

spot[1] [spɑːt] *n* (*pimple etc*) grano *m*; (*in pattern*) lunar *m*

spot[2] [spɑːt] *n* (*place*) lugar *m*, sitio *m*

spot[3] [spɑːt] *v/t* (*notice*) ver

'spot check control *m* al azar; **spotless** inmaculado; **spotlight** foco *m*; **spotty** *with pimples* con granos

spouse [spaʊs] *fml* cónyuge *m/f*

spout [spaʊt] **1** *n* pitorro *m* **2** *v/i of liquid* chorrear **3** *v/t* F soltar F

sprain [spreɪn] **1** *n* esguince *m* **2** *v/t* hacerse un esguince en

sprawl [sprɒːl] despatarrarse; *of city* expandirse; **sprawling** *city* extendido

spray [spreɪ] **1** *n of sea water* rociada *f*; *for hair* spray *m*; *container* aerosol *m*, spray *m* **2** *v/t* rociar; **spraygun** pistola *f* pulverizadora

spread [spred] **1** *n of disease, religion etc* propagación *f*; F (*big meal*) comilona *f* F **2** *v/t* (*lay*) extender; *butter* untar; *rumor* difundir; *disease* propagar; *arms, legs* extender **3** *v/i of disease, fire* propagarse; *of rumor, news* difundirse; **spreadsheet** COMPUT hoja *f* de cálculo

sprightly ['spraɪtlɪ] lleno de energía

spring[1] [sprɪŋ] *n season* primavera *f*

spring[2] [sprɪŋ] *n device* muelle *m*

spring[3] [sprɪŋ] **1** *n* (*jump*) salto *m*; (*stream*) manantial *m* **2** *v/i* saltar

'springboard trampolín *m*; **springtime** primavera *f*

sprinkle ['sprɪŋkl] espolvorear; **sprinkler** *for garden* aspersor *m*; *in ceiling* rociador *m* contra incendios

sprint [sprɪnt] **1** *n* esprint *m*; SP carrera *f* de velocidad **2** *v/i* (*run fast*) correr a toda velocidad; *of runner* esprintar; **sprinter** SP esprínter *m/f*, ve-

locista *m/f*
spy [spaɪ] **1** *n* espía *m/f* **2** *v/i* espiar **3** *v/t* (*see*) ver
◆ **spy on** espiar
squabble ['skwɑːbl] **1** *n* riña *f* **2** *v/i* reñir
squalid ['skwɒːlɪd] inmundo, miserable; **squalor** inmundicia *f*
squander ['skwɒːndər] *money* despilfarrar
square [skwer] **1** *adj in shape* cuadrado; ~ ***miles*** millas cuadradas **2** *n also* MATH cuadrado *m*; *in town* plaza *f*; *in board game* casilla *f*
squash¹ [skwɑːʃ] *n vegetable* calabacera *f*
squash² [skwɑːʃ] *n game* squash *m*
squash³ [skwɑːʃ] *v/t* (*crush*) aplastar
squat [skwɑːt] **1** *adj person* chaparro; *figure*, *buildings* bajo **2** *v/i sit* agacharse
squeak [skwiːk] **1** *n of mouse* chillido *m*; *of hinge* chirrido *m* **2** *v/i of mouse* chillar; *of hinge* chirriar
squeal [skwiːl] **1** *n* chillido **2** *v/i* chillar; *of brakes* armar un estruendo
squeamish ['skwiːmɪʃ] aprensivo
squeeze [skwiːz] (*press*) apretar; (*remove juice from*) exprimir
squid [skwɪd] calamar *m*
squirm [skwɜːrm] retorcerse
St (= ***saint***) Sto; Sta (= santo *m*; santa *f*); (= ***street***) c/ (= calle *f*)
stab [stæb] apuñalar
stability [stə'bɪlətɪ] estabilidad *f*; **stabilize 1** *v/t prices*, *boat* estabilizar **2** *v/i of prices etc* estabilizarse; **stable 1** *adj* estable; *patient's condition* estacionario **2** *n for horses* establo *m*
stack [stæk] **1** *n* (*pile*) pila *f* **2** *v/t* apilar
stadium ['steɪdɪəm] estadio *m*
staff [stæf] (*employees*) personal *m*; (*teachers*) profesorado *m*
stage¹ [steɪdʒ] *n in project etc* etapa *f*
stage² [steɪdʒ] **1** *n* THEA escenario *m* **2** *v/t play* escenificar; *demonstration* llevar a cabo
stagger ['stægər] **1** *v/i* tambalearse **2** *v/t* (*amaze*) dejar anonadado; *coffee breaks etc* escalonar; **staggering** asombroso
stagnant ['stægnənt] *also fig* estancado; **stagnate** *fig* estancarse
'stag party despedida *f* de soltero
stain [steɪn] **1** *n* (*dirty mark*) mancha *f*; *for wood* tinte *m* **2** *v/t* (*dirty*) manchar; *wood* teñir; **stained-glass window** vidriera *f*; **stainless steel** acero *m* inoxidable
stair [ster] escalón *m*; ***the ~s*** la(s) escalera(s); **staircase** escalera(s) *f*(/*pl*)
stake [steɪk] **1** *n of wood* esta-

ca *f*; *when gambling* apuesta *f*; (*investment*) participación *f*; ***be at ~*** estar en juego **2** *v/t money* apostar; *reputation* jugarse; *person* ayudar (*económicamente*)

stale [steɪl] *bread* rancio; *air* viciado; *fig*: *news* viejo

stalk[1] [stɒːk] *n of fruit, plant* tallo *m*

stalk[2] [stɒːk] *v/t* (*follow*) acechar; *person* seguir

stall[1] [stɒːl] *n at market* puesto *m*; *for cow, horse* casilla *f*

stall[2] [stɒːl] **1** *v/i of engine* calarse; (*play for time*) intentar ganar tiempo **2** *v/t engine* calar; *person* retener

stalls [stɒːlz] patio *m* de butacas

stalwart ['stɒːlwərt] *support* incondicional

stamina ['stæmɪnə] resistencia *f*

stammer ['stæmər] **1** *n* tartamudeo *m* **2** *v/i* tartamudear

stamp[1] [stæmp] **1** *n for letter* sello *m*, *L.Am.* estampilla *f*, *Mex* timbre *m*; *device* tampón *m*; *mark made with device* sello *m* **2** *v/t* sellar

stamp[2] [stæmp] *v/t*: ***~ one's feet*** patear

stance [stæns] (*position*) postura *f*

stand [stænd] **1** *n at exhibition* puesto *m*, stand *m*; (*witness ~*) estrado *m*; (*support, base*) soporte *m*; ***take the ~*** LAW subir al estrado **2** *v/i of building* encontrarse, hallarse; *as opposed to sit* estar de pie; (*rise*) ponerse de pie **3** *v/t* (*tolerate*) soportar; (*put*) colocar

◆ **stand by 1** *v/i* (*not take action*) quedarse sin hacer nada; (*be ready*) estar preparado **2** *v/t person* apoyar; *decision* atenerse a

◆ **stand down** (*withdraw*) retirarse

◆ **stand for** (*tolerate*) aguantar; (*represent*) significar

◆ **stand out** destacar

◆ **stand up 1** *v/i* levantarse **2** *v/t* F plantar F

◆ **stand up for** defender

◆ **stand up to** hacer frente a

standard ['stændərd] **1** *adj* (*usual*) habitual **2** *n* (*level*) nivel *m*; TECH estándar *m*; **standardize** normalizar; **standard of living** nivel *m* de vida

'**standby** *fly* con un billete stand-by; **standing** *in society etc* posición *f*; (*repute*) reputación *f*; **standoffish** distante; **standpoint** punto *m* de vista; **standstill**: ***be at a ~*** estar paralizado; ***bring to a ~*** paralizar

staple[1] ['steɪpl] *n foodstuff* alimento *m* básico

staple[2] ['steɪpl] **1** *n* (*fastener*) grapa *f* **2** *v/t* grapar

stapler ['steɪplər] grapadora *f*

star [stɑːr] **1** *n also person* estrella *f* **2** *v/t of movie* estar protagonizado por; **starboard** de estribor

stare [ster] mirar fijamente; **~ *at*** mirar fijamente

stark [stɑːrk] **1** *adj landscape* desolado; *reminder, picture etc* desolador **2** *adv*: **~ *naked*** completamente desnudo

starry ['stɑːrɪ] *night* estrellado; **Stars and Stripes** *la bandera estadounidense*

start [stɑːrt] **1** *n* comienzo *m*, principio *m*; *of race* salida *f* **2** *v/t & v/i* empezar, comenzar; *of engine* arrancar; ***~ing from tomorrow*** a partir de mañana **3** *v/t business* montar; **starter** (*of meal*) entrada *f*; *of car* motor *m* de arranque

startle ['stɑːrtl] sobresaltar; **startling** sorprendente

starvation [stɑːr'veɪʃn] inanición *f*, hambre *f*; **starve** pasar hambre; ***I'm starving*** F me muero de hambre F

state[1] [steɪt] **1** *n* (*condition, country*) estado *m*; ***the States*** (los) Estados Unidos **2** *adj capital etc* estatal; *banquet etc* de estado

state[2] [steɪt] *v/t* declarar

'State Department Departamento *m* de Estado, *Ministerio de Asuntos Exteriores*; **statement** declaración *f*; (*bank* **~**) extracto *m*; **state of emergency** estado *m* de emergencia; **state-of-the--art** modernísimo; **statesman** hombre *m* de estado

static (elec'tricity) ['stætɪk] electricidad *f* estática

station ['steɪʃn] **1** *n* RAIL estación *f*; RAD emisora *f*; TV canal *m* **2** *v/t guard etc* apostar; **stationary** parado

stationery ['steɪʃənerɪ] artículos *mpl* de papelería

'station wagon ranchera *f*

statistical [stə'tɪstɪkl] estadístico; **statistically** estadísticamente; **statistician** estadístico(-a) *m(f)*; **statistics** *science* estadística *f*; *figures* estadísticas *fpl*

statue ['stætʃuː] estatua *f*; **Statue of Liberty** Estatua *f* de la Libertad

status ['stætəs] categoría *f*, posición *f*; **status symbol** símbolo *m* de estatus

statute ['stætuːt] estatuto *m*

staunch [stɒːntʃ] *supporter* incondicional; *friend* fiel

stay [steɪ] **1** *n* estancia *f*, *L.Am.* estadía *f* **2** *v/i in a place* quedarse; *in a condition* permanecer; **~ *in a hotel*** alojarse en un hotel

◆ **stay behind** quedarse

◆ **stay up** (*not go to bed*) quedarse levantado

steadily ['stedɪlɪ] *improve etc* constantemente; **steady 1** *adj* (*not shaking*) firme; (*continuous*) continuo; *beat* regular; *boyfriend* estable **2** *adv*: ***they've been going ~ for two years*** llevan saliendo dos años **3** *v/t* afianzar; *voice* calmar

steak [steɪk] filete *m*

steal [stiːl] **1** *v/t* robar **2** *v/i* (*be*

a thief) robar; ~ **in / out** entrar / salir furtivamente

stealthy ['stelθɪ] sigiloso

steam [sti:m] **1** *n* vapor *m* **2** *v/t food* cocinar al vapor; **steamed up** F (*angry*) enojado, *Span* mosqueado F; **steamer** *for cooking* olla *f* para cocinar al vapor

steel [sti:l] **1** *n* acero *m* **2** *adj* (*made of* ~) de acero; **steelworker** trabajador(a) *m(f)* del acero

steep[1] [sti:p] *adj hill etc* empinado; F *prices* caro

steep[2] [sti:p] *v/t* (*soak*) poner en remojo

steer[1] [stɪr] *n animal* buey *m*

steer[2] [stɪr] *v/t car* conducir, *L.Am.* manejar; *boat* gobernar; *person* guiar; *conversation* llevar; **steering** MOT dirección *f*; **steering wheel** volante *m*, *S.Am.* timón *m*

stem[1] [stem] *n of plant* tallo *m*; *of glass* pie *m*; *of word* raíz *f*

stem[2] [stem] *v/t* (*block*) contener

stench [stentʃ] peste *f*

stencil ['stensɪl] **1** *n* plantilla *f* **2** *v/t pattern* estarcir

step [step] **1** *n* (*pace*) paso *m*; (*stair*) escalón *m*; (*measure*) medida *f* **2** *v/i*: ~ **on sth** pisar algo

◆ **step down** *from post etc* dimitir

◆ **step up** (*increase*) incrementar

'**stepbrother** hermanastro *m*; **stepdaughter** hijastra *f*; **stepfather** padrastro *m*; **stepladder** escalera *f* de tijera; **stepmother** madrastra *f*; **stepsister** hermanastra *f*; **stepson** hijastro *m*

stereo ['sterɪoʊ] (*sound system*) equipo *m* de música; **stereotype** estereotipo *m*

sterile ['sterəl] estéril; **sterilize** esterilizar

sterling ['stɜ:rlɪŋ] FIN libra *f* esterlina

stern[1] [stɜ:rn] *adj* severo

stern[2] [stɜ:rn] *n* NAUT popa *f*

sternly con severidad

steroids ['sterɔɪdz] esteroides *mpl*

stew [stu:] guiso *m*

steward ['stu:ərd] *on plane* auxiliar *m* de vuelo; *on ship* camarero *m*; *at demonstration* miembro *m* de la organización; **stewardess** *on plane* auxiliar *f* de vuelo; *on ship* camarera *f*

stick[1] [stɪk] *n* palo *m*; *of policeman* porra *f*; (*walking* ~) bastón *m*

stick[2] [stɪk] **1** *v/t with adhesive* pegar; F (*put*) meter **2** *v/i* (*jam*) atascarse; (*adhere*) pegarse

◆ **stick by** F apoyar, no abandonar

◆ **stick to** *of sth sticky* pegarse a; F *plan etc* seguir; F (*trail, follow*) pegarse a F

◆ **stick up for** F defender

sticker ['stɪkər] pegatina *f*;

stick-in-the-mud F aburrido(-a) *m(f)* F; **sticky** pegajoso; *label* adhesivo

stiff [stɪf] *board, manner* rígido; *brush, penalty, competition* duro; *muscle* agarrotado; *drink* cargado; **stiffness** *of muscles* agarrotamiento *m*; *of manner* rigidez *f*

stifle ['staɪfl] reprimir; **stifling** sofocante

stigma ['stɪgmə] estigma *m*

still[1] [stɪl] **1** *adj* (*not moving*) quieto; *with no wind* sin viento **2** *adv*: ***keep ~!*** ¡estáte quieto!

still[2] [stɪl] *adv* (*yet*) todavía, aún; (*nevertheless*) de todas formas

'stillborn: ***be ~*** nacer muerto; **still life** naturaleza *f* muerta

stilted ['stɪltɪd] forzado

stimulant ['stɪmjʊlənt] estimulante *m*; **stimulate** estimular; **stimulating** estimulante; **stimulation** estimulación *f*; **stimulus** (*incentive*) estímulo *m*

sting [stɪŋ] **1** *n from bee, jellyfish* picadura *f* **2** *v/t of bee, jellyfish* picar **3** *v/i of eyes, scratch* escocer; **stinging** *criticism* punzante

stink [stɪŋk] **1** *n* (*bad smell*) peste *f*; F (*fuss*) escándalo F **2** *v/i* (*smell bad*) apestar; F (*be very bad*) dar asco

stipulate ['stɪpjʊleɪt] estipular; **stipulation** estipulación *f*

stir [stɜːr] **1** *v/t* remover, dar vueltas a **2** *v/i of sleeping person* moverse; **stirring** *music, speech* conmovedor

stitch [stɪʧ] **1** *n in sewing* puntada *f*; *in knitting* punto *m*; ***~es*** MED puntos *mpl* **2** *v/t sew* coser; **stitching** (*stitches*) cosido *m*

stock [stɑːk] **1** *n* (*reserves*) reservas *fpl*; COM *of store* existencias *fpl*; (*animals*) ganado *m*; FIN acciones *fpl*; *for soup etc* caldo *m*; ***in ~*** en existencias; ***out of ~*** agotado **2** *v/t* COM (*have*) tener en existencias; COM (*sell*) vender; **stockbreeder** ganadero(-a) *m(f)*; **stockbroker** corredor(a) *m(f)* de bolsa; **stock exchange** bolsa *f* (de valores); **stockholder** accionista *m/f*; **stockist** distribuidor(a) *m(f)*; **stock market** mercado *m* de valores; **stockpile 1** *n of food, weapons* reservas *fpl* **2** *v/t* acumular

stocky ['stɑːkɪ] bajo y robusto

stodgy ['stɑːdʒɪ] *food* pesado

stoical ['stoʊɪkl] estoico; **stoicism** estoicismo *m*

stomach ['stʌmək] **1** *n* estómago *m*, tripa *f* **2** *v/t* (*tolerate*) soportar

stone [stoʊn] piedra *f*; **stoned** F (*on drugs*) colocado F

stool [stuːl] (*seat*) taburete *m*

stoop[1] [stuːp] *v/i* (*bend down*) agacharse

stoop[2] [stuːp] *n* (*porch*) porche *m*

stop [stɑːp] **1** *n for train, bus*

parada *f* **2** *v/t* (*put an end to*) poner fin a; (*prevent*) impedir; (*cease*), *person in street* parar; *car, bus, train: of driver* detener; *check* bloquear; **~ *doing sth*** dejar de hacer algo **3** *v/i* (*come to a halt*) pararse, detenerse; *in a particular place: of bus, train* parar

◆ **stop over** hacer escala

'stopgap solución *f* intermedia; **stoplight** (*traffic light*) semáforo *m*; (*brake light*) luz *m* de freno; **stopover** parada *f*; *in air travel* escala *f*; **stopper** *for bottle* tapón *m*; **stop sign** (señal *f* de) stop *m*; **stopwatch** cronómetro *m*

storage ['stɔːrɪdʒ] almacenamiento *m*; **store 1** *n* tienda *f*; (*stock*) reserva *f*; (*storehouse*) almacén *m* **2** *v/t* almacenar; COMPUT guardar; **storefront** fachada *f* de tienda; **storekeeper** tendero(-a) *m*(*f*); **store window** escaparate *m*, *L.Am.* vidriera *f*, *Mex* aparador *m*

storey *Br* ☞ ***story²***

storm [stɔːrm] tormenta *f*; **stormy** tormentoso

story¹ ['stɔːrɪ] (*tale*) cuento *m*; (*account*) historia *f*; (*newspaper article*) artículo *m*; F (*lie*) cuento *m*

story² ['stɔːrɪ] *of building* piso *m*, planta *f*

stout [staʊt] *person* relleno, corpulento

stove [stoʊv] *for cooking* cocina *f*, *Col, Mex, Ven* estufa *f*; *for heating* estufa *f*

stow [stoʊ] guardar

◆ **stow away** viajar de polizón

'stowaway polizón *m*

straight [streɪt] **1** *adj line, back* recto; *hair* liso; (*honest, direct*) franco; *whiskey* solo; (*tidy*) en orden; (*conservative*) serio; (*not homosexual*) heterosexual **2** *adv* (*in a straight line*) recto; (*directly, immediately*) directamente; (*clearly*) con claridad; ***go ~*** F *of criminal* reformarse; ***~away, ~ off*** en seguida; ***~ out*** directamente; ***~ up*** *without ice* solo; ***~ ahead*** *be situated* todo derecho; *walk, drive* todo recto; *look* hacia delante; **straighten** enderezar; **straightforward** (*honest, direct*) franco; (*simple*) simple

strain¹ [streɪn] **1** *n on rope* tensión *f*; *on engine, heart* esfuerzo *m*; *on person* agobio *m* **2** *v/t finances* crear presión en; ***~ one's back*** hacerse daño en la espalda

strain² [streɪn] *v/t vegetables* escurrir; *oil, fat etc* colar

strained [streɪnd] *relations* tirante; **strainer** *for vegetables etc* colador *m*

strait [streɪt] estrecho *m*; **straitlaced** mojigato

strange [streɪndʒ] (*odd, curious*) extraño, raro; (*unknown, foreign*) extraño;

strangely (*oddly*) de manera extraña; **~ *enough*** aunque parezca extraño; **stranger** (*person you don't know*) extraño(-a) *m*(*f*), desconocido(-a) *m*(*f*) ; ***I'm a ~ here myself*** yo tampoco soy de aquí

strangle ['stræŋgl] strangular

strap [stræp] *of purse, watch* correa *f*; *of bra, dress* tirante *m*; *of shoe* tira *f*; **strapless** sin tirantes

strategic [strə'ti:dʒɪk] estratégico; **strategy** estrategia *f*

straw [strɒ:] paja *f*; *for drink* pajita *f*; **strawberry** fresa *f*, *S.Am.* frutilla *f*

stray [streɪ] **1** *adj animal* callejero; *bullet* perdido **2** *n dog* perro *m* callejero; *cat* gato *m* callejero **3** *v/i* extraviarse, perderse; *fig*: *of eyes, thoughts* desviarse

streak [stri:k] **1** *n of dirt, paint* raya *f*; *in hair* mechón *m*; *fig*: *of nastiness etc* vena *f* **2** *v/i move quickly* pasar disparado

stream [stri:m] riachuelo *m*; *fig*: *of people* oleada *f*; **streamline** *fig* racionalizar; **streamlined** *car, plane* aerodinámico; *organization* racionalizado

street [stri:t] calle *f*; **streetcar** tranvía *m*; **streetlight** farola *f*; **street people** los sin techo; **street value** *of drugs* valor *m* en la calle

strength [streŋθ] fuerza *f*; *fig* (*strong point*) punto *m* fuerte; *of friendship etc* solidez *f*; *of emotion* intensidad *f*; *of currency* fortaleza *f*; **strengthen 1** *v/t muscles, currency* fortalecer; *bridge* reforzar; *country, relationship* consolidar **2** *v/i of bonds, ties* consolidarse; *of currency* fortalecerse

strenuous ['strenjʊəs] agotador; **strenuously** *deny* tajantemente

stress [stres] **1** *n* (*emphasis*) énfasis *m*; (*tension*) estrés *m*; *on syllable* acento *m* **2** *v/t syllable* acentuar; *importance etc* hacer hincapié en; **stressed out** F estresado; **stressful** estresante

stretch [stretʃ] **1** *n of land, water* extensión *f*; *of road* tramo *m* **2** *adj fabric* elástico **3** *v/t material, income* estirar; F *rules* ser flexible con **4** *v/i to relax, reach* estirarse; (*spread*) extenderse; **stretcher** camilla *f*

strict [strɪkt] estricto; **strictly** con rigor; ***it is ~ forbidden*** está terminantemente prohibido

stride [straɪd] **1** *n* zancada *f* **2** *v/i* caminar dando zancadas

strident ['straɪdnt] estridente

strike [straɪk] **1** *n of workers* huelga *f*; *in baseball* strike *m*; *of oil* descubrimiento *m*; ***be on ~*** estar en huelga **2** *v/i of workers* hacer huelga; (*attack*) atacar; *of disaster* sobrevenir; *of clock* dar las horas **3** *v/t* (*hit*) golpear; *of disaster* sacudir; *match* encender; *oil* descubrir

◆ **strike out** (*delete*) tachar; *in baseball* eliminar a, *L.Am.* ponchar

'strikebreaker esquirol(a) *m(f)*; **striker** (*person on strike*) huelguista *m / f*; *in soccer* delantero(-a) *m(f)*; **striking** (*marked*) sorprendente, llamativo; (*eye-catching*) deslumbrante

string [strɪŋ] cuerda *f*; **stringed instrument** instrumento *m* de cuerda

stringent ['strɪndʒnt] riguroso

strip [strɪp] **1** *n of land* franja *f*; (*comic* ~) tira *f* cómica **2** *v/t* (*remove*) quitar; (*undress*) desnudar **3** *v/i* (*undress*) desnudarse; *of stripper* hacer striptease; **strip club** club *m* de striptease

stripe [straɪp] raya *f*; *indicating rank* galón *m*; **striped** a rayas

stripper ['strɪpər] artista *m/f* de striptease; **striptease** striptease *m*

stroke [stroʊk] **1** *n* MED derrame *m* cerebral; *in painting* pincelada *f*; (*style of swimming*) estilo *m* **2** *v/t* acariciar

stroll [stroʊl] **1** *n* paseo *m* **2** *v/i* caminar; **stroller** *for baby* silla *f* de paseo

strong [strɒːŋ] fuerte; *structure* resistente; *candidate* claro, con muchos posibilidades; *support, supporter, views, objection* firme; **strongly** fuertemente; **strong-minded** decidido; **strong point** (punto *m*) fuerte *m*; **strongroom** cámar *f* acorazada; **strong-willed** tenaz

structural ['strʌktʃərl] estructural; **structure 1** *n* (*something built*) construcción *f*; *of novel, society etc* estructura *f* **2** *v/t* estructurar

struggle ['strʌgl] **1** *n* lucha *f* **2** *v/i with a person* forcejear; (*have a hard time*) luchar

strut [strʌt] pavonearse

stub [stʌb] *of cigarette* colilla *f*; *of check* matriz *f*; *of ticket* resguardo *m*

stubborn ['stʌbərn] *person* testarudo, terco; *defense, refusal* tenaz, pertinaz

stubby ['stʌbɪ] regordete

stuck [stʌk] F: ***be ~ on s.o.*** estar colado por alguien F

student ['stuːdnt] estudiante *m/f*; *at high school* alumno(-a) *m(f)*

studio ['stuːdɪoʊ] estudio *m*

studious ['stuːdɪəs] estudioso; **study 1** *n* estudio *m* **2** *v/t & v/i* estudiar

stuff [stʌf] **1** *n* (*things*) cosas *fpl*; ***what's that ~?*** ¿qué es eso? **2** *v/t turkey* rellenar; ***~ sth into sth*** meter algo dentro de algo; **stuffing** relleno *m*; **stuffy** *room* cargado; *person* estirado

stumble ['stʌmbl] tropezar;

stumbling-block escollo *m*
stump [stʌmp] **1** *n of tree* tocón *m* **2** *v/t of question* dejar perplejo
stun [stʌn] *of blow* dejar sin sentido; *of news* dejar atonito; **stunning** (*amazing*) increíble; (*very beautiful*) imponente
stunt [stʌnt] *for publicity* truco *m*; *in movie* escena *f* peligrosa; **stuntman** *in movie* doble *m*, especialista *m*
stupefy ['stu:pɪfaɪ] dejar perplejo
stupendous [stu:'pendəs] extraordinario
stupid ['stu:pɪd] estúpido; **stupidity** estupidez *f*
sturdy ['stɜ:rdɪ] *person* robusto; *table, plant* resistente
stutter ['stʌtər] tartamudear
style [staɪl] estilo *m*; (*fashion*) moda *f*; **stylish** elegante; **stylist** (*hair* ~) estilista *m/f*
subcommittee ['sʌbkəmɪtɪ] subcomité *m*
subconscious [sʌb'kɑ:nʃəs] subconsciente; **subconsciously** inconscientemente
subcontract [sʌbkɑ:n'trækt] subcontratar; **subcontractor** subcontratista *m/f*
subdivide [sʌbdɪ'vaɪd] subdividir
subdue [səb'du:] someter
subheading ['sʌbhedɪŋ] subtítulo *m*
subhuman [sʌb'hju:mən] inhumano
subject 1 ['sʌbdʒɪkt] *n* (*topic*) tema *m*; (*branch of learning*) asignatura *f*, materia *f*; GRAM sujeto *m*; *of monarch* súbdito(-a) *m(f)* **2** ['sʌbdʒɪkt] *adj*: ***be ~ to*** *have tendency to* ser propenso a; *be regulated by* estar sujeto a **3** [səb'dʒekt] *v/t* someter; **subjective** subjetivo
sublet ['sʌblet] realquilar
submachine gun [sʌbmə'ʃi:ngʌn] metralleta *f*
submarine ['sʌbməri:n] submarino *m*
submission [səb'mɪʃn] (*surrender*) sumisión *f*; *to committee etc* propuesta *f*; **submissive** sumiso; **submit 1** *v/t plan* presentar **2** *v/i* someterse
subordinate [sə'bɔ:rdɪneɪt] **1** *adj position* subordinado **2** *n* subordinado(-a) *m(f)*
subpoena [sə'pi:nə] **1** *n* citación *f* **2** *v/t person* citar
◆ **subscribe to** [səb'skraɪb] *magazine etc* suscribirse a; *theory* suscribir
subscriber [səb'skraɪbər] *to magazine* suscriptor(a) *m(f)*; **subscription** suscripción *f*
subsequent ['sʌbsɪkwənt] posterior
subside [səb'saɪd] *of waters* bajar; *of winds* amainar; *of building* hundirse; *of fears* calmarse
subsidiary [səb'sɪdɪerɪ] filial *f*

subsidize ['sʌbsɪdaɪz] subvencionar; **subsidy** subvención *f*
substance ['sʌbstəns] sustancia *f*
substandard [sʌb'stændərd] deficiente
substantial [səb'stænʃl] sustancial, considerable; **substantially** (*considerably*) considerablemente; (*in essence*) sustancialmente
substantive [səb'stæntɪv] significativo
substitute ['sʌbstɪtuːt] **1** *n* sustituto *m*; SP suplente *m/f* **2** *v/t* sustituir; ***~ X for Y*** sustituir Y por X; **substitution** sustitución *f*
subtitle ['sʌbtaɪtl] subtítulo *m*
subtle ['sʌtl] sutil
subtract [səb'trækt] restar
suburb ['sʌbɜːrb] zona *f* residencial de la periferia; **suburban** de la periferia; *attitudes, lifestyle* aburguesado
subversive [səb'vɜːrsɪv] **1** *adj* subversivo **2** *n* subversivo(-a) *m(f)*
subway ['sʌbweɪ] metro *m*
succeed [sək'siːd] **1** *v/i* tener éxito; ***~ to the throne*** suceder en el trono; ***~ in doing sth*** conseguir hacer algo **2** *v/t* (*come after*) suceder; **success** éxito *m*; **successful** *person* con éxito; ***be ~ in doing sth*** lograr hacer algo; **successfully** con éxito; **successive** sucesivo; **successor** sucesor(a) *m(f)*
succinct [sək'sɪŋkt] sucinto
succumb [sə'kʌm] (*give in*) sucumbir
such [sʌʧ] **1** *adj* (*of that kind*) tal; ***~ men are dangerous*** los hombres así son peligrosos; ***don't make ~ a fuss*** no armes tanto alboroto; ***~ as*** como; ***there is no ~ word as …*** no existe la palabra… **2** *adv* tan; ***as ~*** como tal; ***~ a nice day*** un día tan bueno;
suck [sʌk] **1** *v/t candy etc* chupar **2** *v/i* P: ***it ~s*** es una mierda P; **sucker** F (*person*) primo(-a) *m/f* F; F (*lollipop*) piruleta *f*; **suction** succión *f*
sudden ['sʌdn] repentino; **suddenly** de repente
sue [suː] demandar
suede [sweɪd] ante *m*
suffer ['sʌfər] **1** *v/i* sufrir; (*deteriorate*) deteriorarse **2** *v/t loss, setback* sufrir; **suffering** sufrimiento *m*
sufficient [sə'fɪʃnt] suficiente; **sufficiently** suficientemente
suffocate ['sʌfəkeɪt] **1** *v/i* asfixiarse **2** *v/t* asfixiar; **suffocation** asfixia *f*
sugar ['ʃugər] **1** *n* azúcar *m or f* **2** *v/t* echar azúcar a
suggest [sə'dʒest] sugerir; **suggestion** sugerencia *f*
suicide ['suːɪsaɪd] suicidio *m*
suit [suːt] **1** *n* traje *m*; *in cards* palo *m* **2** *v/t of clothes, color* sentar bien a; **suitable** apropiado; **suitably** apropiada-

mente; **suitcase** maleta *f*, *L.Am.* valija *f*
suite [swi:t] *of rooms*, MUS suite *f*; *furniture* tresillo *m*
sulk [sʌlk] enfurruñarse; **sulky** enfurruñado
sullen ['sʌlən] malhumorado, huraño
sultry ['sʌltrɪ] sofocante, bochornoso; *sexually* sensual
sum [sʌm] *(total)*, *in arithmetic* suma *f*; *(amount)* cantidad *f*
◆ **sum up 1** *v/t (summarize)* resumir; *(assess)* catalogar **2** *v/i* LAW recapitular
summarize ['sʌməraɪz] resumir; **summary** resumen *m*
summer ['sʌmər] verano *m*
summit ['sʌmɪt] *also* POL cumbre *f*
summon ['sʌmən] llamar; *meeting* convocar; **summons** LAW citación *f*
sun [sʌn] sol *m*; **sunbathe** tomar el sol; **sunbed** cama *f* de rayos UVA; **sunblock** crema *f* solar de alta protección; **sunburn** quemadura *f* (del sol); **sunburnt** quemado (por el sol); **Sunday** domingo *m*; **sunglasses** gafas *fpl or L.Am.* anteojos *mpl* de sol; **sunny** soleado; *disposition* radiante; ***it's ~*** hace sol; **sunrise** amanecer *m*; **sunset** atardecer *m*, puesta *f* de sol; **sunshade** sombrilla *f*; **sunshine** sol *m*; **sunstroke** insolación *f*; **suntan** bronceado *m*
super ['su:pər] **1** *adj* F genial F, estupendo F **2** *n (janitor)* portero(-a) *m(f)*
superb [sʊ'pɜ:rb] excelente
superficial [su:pər'fɪʃl] superficial
superfluous [sʊ'pɜ:rflʊəs] superfluo
superintendent [su:pərɪn'tendənt] *of apartment block* portero(-a) *m(f)*
superior [su:'pɪrɪər] **1** *adj (better)* superior; *pej: attitude* arrogante **2** *n in organization* superior *m*
superlative [su:'pɜ:rlətɪv] **1** *adj* excelente **2** *n* GRAM superlativo *m*
'supermarket supermercado *m*
'superpower POL superpotencia *f*
supersonic [su:pər'sɑ:nɪk] supersónico
superstition [su:pər'stɪʃn] superstición *f*; **superstitious** supersticioso
supervise ['su:pərvaɪz] *class* vigilar; *workers* supervisar; *activities* dirigir; **supervisor** *at work* supervisor(a) *m(f)*
supper ['sʌpər] cena *f*, *L.Am.* comida *f*
supplement ['sʌplɪmənt] *(extra payment)* suplemento *m*
supplier [sə'plaɪər] COM proveedor *m*; **supply** *n* suministro *m*, abastecimiento *m*; **supplies** *of food* provisiones *fpl*; ***~ and demand*** la oferta y la demanda **2** *v/t goods* suministrar

support [sə'pɔːrt] **1** *n for structure* soporte *m*; (*backing*) apoyo *m* **2** *v/t structure* soportar; *financially* mantener; (*back*) apoyar; **supporter** partidario(-a) *m(f)*; *of football team etc* seguidor(a) *m(f)*; **supportive** comprensivo; ***be ~*** apoyar (***toward, of*** a)

suppose [sə'pouz] (*imagine*) suponer; ***you are not ~d to ...*** (*not allowed to*) no deberías...; **supposing ...** y si...; **supposedly** supuestamente

suppress [sə'pres] reprimir, sofocar; **suppression** represión *f*

supremacy [suː'preməsɪ] supremacía *f*; **supreme** supremo; **Supreme Court** Tribunal *m* Supremo, *L.Am.*Corte *f* Suprema

surcharge ['sɜːrtʃɑːrdʒ] recargo *m*

sure [ʃur] **1** *adj* seguro; ***make ~ that ...*** asegurarse de que... **2** *adv*: ***~ enough*** efectivamente; ***it ~ is hot today*** F vaya calor que hace F; ***~!*** F ¡claro!; **surety** *for loan* fianza *f*

surf [sɜːrf] **1** *n* surf *m* **2** *v/t*: ***~ the Net*** navegar por Internet

surface ['sɜːrfɪs] **1** *n* superficie *f* **2** *v/i from water* salir a la superficie; (*appear*) aparecer; **surface mail** correo *m* terrestre

'surfboard tabla *f* de surf; **surfer** surfista *m/f*; **surfing** surf *m*; ***go ~*** ir a hacer surf

surge [sɜːrdʒ] *in electric current* sobrecarga *f*; *in demand etc* incremento *m* repentino

surgeon ['sɜːrdʒən] cirujano(-a) *m(f)*; **surgery** cirugía *f*; **surgical** quirúrgico; **surgically** quirúrgicamente

surly ['sɜːrlɪ] arisco, hosco

surmount [sər'maʊnt] *difficulties* superar

surname ['sɜːrneɪm] apellido *m*

surpass [sər'pæs] superar

surplus ['sɜːrpləs] **1** *n* excedente *m* **2** *adj* excedente

surprise [sər'praɪz] **1** *n* sorpresa *f* **2** *v/t* sorprender; ***be / look ~d*** quedarse / parecer sorprendido; **surprising** sorprendente; **surprisingly** sorprendentemente

surrender [sə'rendər] **1** *v/i of army* rendirse **2** *v/t weapons etc* entregar **3** *n* rendición *f*; (*handing in*) entrega *f*

surrogate 'mother ['sʌrəgət] madre *f* de alquiler

surround [sə'raʊnd] **1** *v/t* rodear **2** *n of picture etc* marco *m*; **surrounding** circundante; **surroundings** *of village etc* alrededores *mpl*; (*environment*) entorno *m*

survey **1** ['sɜːrveɪ] *n of modern literature etc* estudio *m*; *Br*: *of building* tasación *f*, peritaje; *poll* encuesta *f* **2** [sər'veɪ] *v/t* (*look at*) contemplar; *Br*: *building* tasar, peritar; **surveyor** *Br* tasador(a)

m(f) or perito (-a) *m(f)* de la propiedad
survival [sər'vaɪvl] supervivencia *f*; **survive 1** *v/i* sobrevivir **2** *v/t accident etc* sobrevivir a; *(outlive)* sobrevivir; **survivor** superviviente *m/f*
suspect 1 ['sʌspekt] *n* sospechoso(-a) *m(f)* **2** [sə'spekt] *v/t person* sospechar de; *(suppose)* sospechar; **suspected** *murderer* presunto; *cause, heart attack etc* supuesto
suspend [sə'spend] colgar; *from office* suspender; **suspenders** *for pants* tirantes *mpl*, *S.Am.* suspensores *mpl*; *Br: for stockings* liga *f*
suspense [sə'spens] *Span* suspense *m*, *L.Am.* suspenso *m*; **suspension** MOT, *from duty* suspensión *f*
suspicion [sə'spɪʃn] sospecha *f*; **suspicious** *(causing suspicion)* sospechoso; *(feeling suspicion)* receloso; **suspiciously** *behave* de manera sospechosa; *ask* con recelo
sustain [sə'steɪn] sostener; **sustainable** sostenible
SUV [esju:'vi:] (= ***sport utility vehicle***) SUV *m*, todoterreno *m* ligero
swab [swɑ:b] *material* torunda *f*; *test* muestra *f*
swallow[1] ['swɑ:loʊ] *v/t & v/i* tragar
swallow[2] ['swɑ:loʊ] *n bird* golondrina *f*
swamp [swɑ:mp] **1** *n* pantano *m* **2** *v/t*: ***be ~ed with*** estar inundado de; **swampy** pantanoso
swap [swɑ:p] **1** *v/t* cambiar **2** *v/i* hacer un cambio
swarm [swɔ:rm] **1** *n of bees* enjambre *m* **2** *v/i*: ***the town was ~ing with …*** la ciudad estaba abarrotada de…
swarthy ['swɔ:rðɪ] moreno
swat [swɑ:t] *insect* aplastar
sway [sweɪ] **1** *n (influence)* dominio *m* **2** *v/i* tambalearse
swear [swer] **1** *v/i (use swearword)* decir palabrotas *or* tacos **2** *v/t (promise)*, LAW jurar
◆ **swear in** *witnesses etc* tomar juramento a
'swearword palabrota *f*, taco *m*
sweat [swet] **1** *n* sudor *m* **2** *v/i* sudar; **sweatband** banda *f* (en la frente); *on wrist* muñequera *f*; **sweater** suéter *m*, *Span* jersey *m*; **sweatshirt** sudadera *f*; **sweaty** sudoroso
Swede [swi:d] sueco(-a) *m(f)*; **Sweden** Suecia; **Swedish 1** *adj* sueco **2** *n* sueco *m*
sweep [swi:p] **1** *v/t floor, leaves* barrer **2** *n (long curve)* curva *f*; **sweeping** *statement* demasiado generalizado; *changes* radical
sweet [swi:t] dulce; F *(kind)* amable; F *(cute)* mono; **sweetcorn** maíz *m*, *S.Am.* choclo *m*; **sweeten** endulzar; **sweetheart** novio(-a) *m(f)*
swell [swel] **1** *v/i of wound,*

limb hincharse **2** *adj* F (*good*) genial F **3** *n of the sea* oleaje *m*; **swelling** MED hinchazón *f*
swerve [swɜːrv] *of driver, car* girar bruscamente
swift [swɪft] rápido
swim [swɪm] **1** *v/i* nadar **2** *n* baño *m*; ***go for a ~*** ir a darse un baño; **swimmer** nadador(a) *m*(*f*); **swimming** natación *f*; **swimming pool** piscina *f*, *Mex* alberca *f*, *Rpl* pileta *f*; **swimsuit** traje *m* de baño, bañador *m*
swindle ['swɪndl] **1** *n* estafa *f* **2** *v/t* estafar; ***~ s.o. out of sth*** estafar algo a alguien
swing [swɪŋ] **1** *n* oscilación *f*; *for child* columpio *m* **2** *v/t* balancear; *hips* menear **3** *v/i* balancearse; (*turn*) girar; *of opinion etc* cambiar
Swiss [swɪs] **1** *adj* suizo **2** *n person* suizo(-a) *m*(*f*); ***the ~*** los suizos
switch [swɪʧ] **1** *n for light* interruptor *m*; (*change*) cambio *m* **2** *v/t* (*change*) cambiar de **3** *v/i* (*change*) cambiar
◆ **switch off** apagar
◆ **switch on** encender, *L.Am.* prender
Switzerland ['swɪtsərlənd] Suiza
swivel ['swɪvl] girar
swollen ['swoʊlən] hinchado
'swordfish pez *f* espada
syllabus ['sɪləbəs] plan *m* de estudios
symbol ['sɪmbəl] símbolo *m*; **symbolic** simbólico; **symbolism** simbolismo *m*; **symbolist** simbolista *m/f*; **symbolize** simbolizar
symmetrical [sɪ'metrɪkl] simétrico; **symmetry** simetría *f*
sympathetic [sɪmpə'θetɪk] (*showing pity*) compasivo; (*understanding*) comprensivo
◆ **sympathize with** ['sɪmpəθaɪz] comprender
sympathizer ['sɪmpəθaɪzər] POL simpatizante *m/f*; **sympathy** (*pity*) compasión *f*; (*understanding*) comprensión *f*
symphony ['sɪmfənɪ] sinfonía *f*
symptom ['sɪmptəm] *also fig* síntoma *f*
synchronize ['sɪŋkrənaɪz] sincronizar
synonym ['sɪnənɪm] sinónimo *m*; **synonymous** sinónimo
synthesizer ['sɪnθəsaɪzər] MUS sintetizador *m*; **synthetic** sintético
syphilis ['sɪfɪlɪs] sífilis *f*
Syria ['sɪrɪə] Siria; **Syrian 1** *adj* sirio **2** *n* sirio(-a) *m*(*f*)
syringe [sɪ'rɪndʒ] jeringuilla *f*
syrup ['sɪrəp] almíbar *m*
system ['sɪstəm] sistema *m*; **systematic** sistemático; **systematically** sistemáticamente; **systems analyst** COMPUT analista *m/f* de sistemas

T

table ['teɪbl] mesa *f*; *of figures* cuadro *m*; **tablecloth** mantel *m*; **table lamp** lámpara *f* de mesa; **table of contents** índice *m* (de contenidos); **tablespoon** *object* cuchara *f* grande; *quantity* cucharada *f* grande
tablet ['tæblɪt] MED pastilla *f*
tabloid ['tæblɔɪd] *newspaper* periódico *m* sensacionalista (*de tamaño tabloide*)
taboo [tə'buː] tabú *inv*
tacit ['tæsɪt] tácito
tack [tæk] **1** *n* (*nail*) tachuela *f* **2** *v/t* (*sew*) hilvanar **3** *v/i of yacht* dar bordadas
tackle ['tækl] **1** *n* (*equipment*) equipo *m*; SP entrada *f* **2** *v/t* SP entrar a; *problem* abordar; *intruder* hacer frente a
tacky ['tækɪ] *glue* pegajoso; F (*poor quality*) chabacano, *Span* hortera F; *behavior* impresentable
tact [tækt] tacto *m*; **tactful** diplomático; **tactfully** diplomáticamente
tactical ['tæktɪkl] táctico; **tactics** táctica *f*
tactless ['tæktlɪs] indiscreto
tag [tæg] (*label*) etiqueta *f*
tail [teɪl] cola *f*; **tail light** luz *f* trasera
tailor ['teɪlər] sastre *m*; **tailor-made** *also fig* hecho a medida
'tailpipe *of car* tubo *m* de escape
take [teɪk] (*remove*) llevarse, *Span* coger; (*steal*) llevarse; (*transport, accompany*) llevar; (*accept*: *money, credit cards*) aceptar; (*study*: *math, French*) hacer, estudiar; *photograph, photocopy* hacer, sacar; *exam, degree* hacer; *shower* darse; *stroll* dar; *medicine, s.o.'s temperature, taxi* tomar; (*endure*) aguantar
◆ **take after** parecerse a
◆ **take away** *pain* hacer desaparecer; *object* quitar; MATH restar
◆ **take back** (*return*: *object*) devolver; *person* llevar de vuelta; (*accept back*: *husband etc*) dejar volver
◆ **take down** *from shelf* bajar; *scaffolding* desmontar; *trousers* bajarse; (*write down*) anotar, apuntar
◆ **take in** (*take indoors*) recoger; (*give accommodation to*) acoger; (*make narrower*) meter; (*deceive*) engañar; (*include*) incluir
◆ **take off 1** *v/t clothes, hat* quitarse; *10% etc* descontar; (*mimic*) imitar; (*cut off*) cortar **2** *v/i of airplane* despegar, *L.Am.* decolar; (*become popular*) empezar a cuajar
◆ **take on** *job* aceptar; *staff*

contratar

◆ **take out** *from bag*, *from bank*, *tooth* sacar; *word from text* quitar; *insurance policy* suscribir; ***he took her out to dinner*** la llevó a cenar

◆ **take over 1** *v/t company etc* adquirir **2** *v/i of new management etc* asumir el cargo; *of new government* asumir el poder; (*do sth in s.o.'s place*) tomar el relevo

◆ **take up** *carpet etc* levantar; (*carry up*) subir; (*shorten: dress etc*) acortar; *hobby* empezar a hacer; *subject* empezar a estudiar; *offer* aceptar; *new job* comenzar; *space, time* ocupar

'takeoff *of airplane* despegue *m*, *L.Am.* decolaje *m*; (*impersonation*) imitación *f*; **takeover** COM adquisición *f*; **takeover bid** oferta *f* pública de adquisición, OPA *f*; **takings** recaudación *f*

tale [teɪl] cuento *m*, historia *f*

talent ['tælənt] talento *m*; **talented** con talento; **talent scout** cazatalentos *m inv*

talk [tɒːk] **1** *v/t & v/i* hablar; **~ *business*** hablar de negocios **2** *n* (*conversation*) charla *f*, *C.Am.*, *Mex* plática *f*; (*lecture*) conferencia *f*, **~s** negociaciones *fpl*

◆ **talk back** responder, contestar

talkative ['tɒːkətɪv] hablador; **talk show** programa *m* de entrevistas

tall [tɒːl] alto

tally ['tælɪ] **1** *n* cuenta *f* **2** *v/i* cuadrar, encajar

tame [teɪm] *animal* manso, domesticado; *joke etc* soso

◆ **tamper with** ['tæmpər] *lock* intentar forzar; *brakes* tocar

tampon ['tæmpɑːn] tampón *m*

tan [tæn] **1** *n from sun* bronceado *m*; (*color*) marrón *m* claro **2** *v/i in sun* broncearse **3** *v/t leather* curtir

tangent ['tændʒənt] MATH tangente *f*

tangible ['tændʒɪbl] tangible

tangle ['tæŋgl] lío *m*

tango ['tæŋgoʊ] tango *m*

tank [tæŋk] *for water* depósito *m*, tanque *m*; *for fish* pecera *f*; MOT depósito *m*; MIL, *for skin diver* tanque *m*; **tanker** *truck* camión *m* cisterna; *ship* buque *m* cisterna; *for oil* petrolero *m*

tanned [tænd] moreno, bronceado

tantalizing ['tæntəlaɪzɪŋ] sugerente

tantrum ['tæntrəm] rabieta *f*

tap [tæp] **1** *n Br* (*faucet*) grifo *m*, *L.Am.* llave *f* **2** *v/t* (*knock*) dar un golpecito en; *phone* intervenir

tape [teɪp] **1** *n* cinta *f* **2** *v/t conversation etc* grabar; *with sticky tape* pegar con cinta adhesiva; **tape deck** pletina *f*; **tape drive** COMPUT unidad *f* de cinta; **tape meas-**

ure cinta *f* métrica

taper ['teɪpər] estrecharse

'tape recorder magnetofón *m*, *L.Am.* grabador *m*; **tape recording** grabación *f* (magnetofónica)

tar [tɑːr] alquitrán *m*

tardy ['tɑːrdɪ] tardío

target ['tɑːrgɪt] **1** *n in shooting* blanco *m*; *for sales, production* objetivo *m* **2** *v/t market* apuntar a; **target audience** audiencia *f* objetivo; **target date** fecha *f* fijada; **target market** mercado *m* objetivo

tariff ['tærɪf] (*price*) tarifa *f*; (*tax*) arancel *m*

tarmac ['tɑːrmæk] *for road surface* asfalto *m*; *at airport* pista *f*

tarnish ['tɑːrnɪʃ] *metal* deslucir; *reputation* empañar

tarpaulin [tɑːr'pɒːlɪn] lona *f* (*impermeable*)

tart [tɑːrt] tarta *f*, pastel *m*

task [tæsk] tarea *f*; **task force** *for a special job* equipo *m* de trabajo; MIL destacamento *m*

taste [teɪst] **1** *n* gusto *m*; *of food etc* sabor *m* **2** *v/t also fig* probar **3** *v/i*: ***it ~s like ...*** sabe a...; **tasteful** de buen gusto; **tastefully** con buen gusto; **tasteless** *food* insípido; *remark* de mal gusto; **tasting** *of wine* cata *f*, degustación *f*; **tasty** sabroso, rico

tattered ['tætərd] *clothes* andrajoso; *book* destrozado

tattoo [tə'tuː] tatuaje *m*

taunt [tɒːnt] **1** *n* pulla *f* **2** *v/t* mofarse de

taut [tɒːt] tenso

tax [tæks] **1** *n* impuesto *m* **2** *v/t people* cobrar impuestos a; *product* gravar; **taxable income** ingresos *mpl* gravables; **taxation** (*act of taxing*) imposición *f* de impuestos; (*taxes*) fiscalidad *f*, impuestos *mpl*; **tax bracket** banda *f* impositiva; **tax-deductible** desgravable; **tax evasion** evasión *f* fiscal; **tax-free** libre de impuestos; **tax haven** paraíso *m* fiscal

taxi ['tæksɪ] taxi *m*; **taxi driver** taxista *m/f*

taxing ['tæksɪŋ] difícil

'taxi stand, *Br* **'taxi rank** parada *f* de taxis

'taxpayer contribuyente *m/f*; **tax return** declaración *f* de la renta; **tax year** año *m* fiscal

TB [tiː'biː] (= ***tuberculosis***) tuberculosis *f*

tea [tiː] *drink* té *m*; *meal* merienda *f*; **teabag** bolsita *f* de té

teach [tiːtʃ] **1** *v/t* enseñar **2** *v/i*: ***he always wanted to ~*** siempre quiso ser profesor; **teacher** *at primary school* maestro(-a) *m*(*f*); *at secondary school, university* profesor(a) *m*(*f*); **teaching** *profession* enseñanza *f*, docencia *f*

'tea-cup taza *f* de té

teak [tiːk] teca *f*

team [tiːm] equipo *m*; **team spirit** espíritu *m* de equipo; **teamster** camionero(-a) *m(f)*; **teamwork** trabajo *m* en equipo

'teapot tetera *f*

tear[1] [ter] **1** *n in cloth etc* desgarrón *m*, rotura *f* **2** *v/t paper, cloth* rasgar **3** *v/i* (*run fast, drive fast*) ir a toda velocidad

◆ **tear down** *poster* arrancar; *building* derribar

◆ **tear out** *page* arrancar

◆ **tear up** romper

tear[2] [tɪr] *n in eye* lágrima *f*; ***be in ~s*** estar llorando; **tearful** lloroso; **tear gas** gas *m* lacrimógeno

tease [tiːz] tomar el pelo a; *animal* hacer rabiar

'teaspoon *object* cucharilla *f*; *quantity* cucharadita *f*

technical ['teknɪkl] técnico; **technically** técnicamente; **technician** técnico(-a) *m(f)*; **technique** técnica *f*

technological [teknə'lɑːdʒɪkl] tecnológico; **technology** tecnología *f*; **technophobia** rechazo *m* de las nuevas tecnologías

teddy bear ['tedɪber] osito *m* de peluche

tedious ['tiːdɪəs] tedioso

tee [tiː] *in golf* tee *m*

teenage ['tiːneɪdʒ] *fashions* adolescente, juvenil; **teenager** adolescente *m/f*

teens [tiːnz] adolescencia *f*

teeny ['tiːnɪ] F chiquitín F

teeth [tiːθ] *pl* ☞ ***tooth***

teethe [tiːð] echar los dientes

telecommunications [telɪkəmjuːnɪ'keɪʃnz] telecomunicaciones *fpl*

telegraph pole ['telɪgræf] *Br* poste *m* telegráfico

telepathic [telɪ'pæθɪk] telepático; **telepathy** telepatía *f*

telephone ['telɪfoʊn] **1** *n* teléfono *m* **2** *v/t & v/i* telefonear; **telephone book** guía *f* telefónica, listín *m* telefónico; **telephone booth** cabina *f* telefónica; **telephone call** llamada *f* telefónica; **telephone conversation** conversación *f* por teléfono *or* telefónica; **telephone directory** guía *f* telefónica, listín *m* telefónico; **telephone number** número *m* de teléfono

telephoto lens [telɪ'foʊtoʊlenz] teleobjetivo *m*

telesales ['telɪseɪlz] televentas *fpl*

telescope ['telɪskoʊp] telescopio *m*

televise ['telɪvaɪz] televisar

television ['telɪvɪʒn] televisión *f*; ***on ~*** en la televisión; **television program**, *Br* **television programme** programa *m* televisivo; **television studio** estudio *m* de televisión

tell [tel] **1** *v/t* contar; ***I can't ~ the difference*** no veo la diferencia; ***~ s.o. sth*** decir algo a alguien; ***~ s.o. to do sth*** decir a alguien que haga algo **2** *v/i* (*have effect*) hacerse notar; **teller** *in bank* cajero(-a) *m(f)*; **telling off** regañina *f*; **telltale 1** *adj signs* revelador **2** *n* chivato(-a) *m(f)*

temp [temp] **1** *n employee* trabajador(a) *m(f)* temporal **2** *v/i* hacer trabajo temporal

temper ['tempər] (*bad* ~) mal humor *m*; ***lose one's ~*** perder los estribos

temperament ['temprəmənt] temperamento *m*; **temperamental** (*moody*) temperamental

temperate ['tempərət] templado

temperature ['temprətʃər] temperatura *f*; (*fever*) fiebre *f*

temple¹ ['templ] REL templo *m*

temple² ['templ] ANAT sien *f*

tempo ['tempou] tempo *m*

temporarily [tempə'rerılı] temporalmente; **temporary** temporal

tempt [tempt] tentar; **temptation** tentación *f*; **tempting** tentador

ten [ten] diez

tenacious [tı'neıʃəs] tenaz; **tenacity** tenacidad *f*

tenant ['tenənt] *of building* inquilino(-a) *m(f)*; *of land* arrendatario(-a) *m(f)*

tend¹ [tend] *v/t* (*look after*) cuidar (de)

tend² [tend] *v/i*: ***~ to do sth*** soler hacer algo

tendency ['tendənsı] tendencia *f*

tender¹ ['tendər] *adj* (*sore*) sensibleo; (*affectionate*) cariñoso, tierno; *steak* tierno

tender² ['tendər] *n* COM oferta *f*

tenderness ['tendərnıs] (*soreness*) dolor *m*; *of kiss etc* cariño *m*, ternura *f*

tendon ['tendən] tendón *m*

tennis ['tenıs] tenis *m*; **tennis ball** pelota *f* de tenis; **tennis court** pista *f* de tenis, cancha *f* de tenis; **tennis player** tenista *m/f*

tenor ['tenər] MUS tenor *m*

tense¹ [tens] *n* gram tiempo *m*

tense² [tens] *adj muscle, voice* tenso

tension ['tenʃn] tensión *f*

tent [tent] tienda *f*

tentative ['tentətıv] *move, offer* provisional

tenth [tenθ] **1** *adj* décimo **2** *n* décimo *m*; *of second, degree* décima *f*

tepid ['tepıd] tibio

term [tɜːrm] *in office etc* mandato *m*; *Br* EDU trimestre *m*; (*condition, word*) término *m*; ***be on good / bad ~s with s.o.*** llevarse bien / mal con alguien; ***in the long / short ~*** a largo / corto plazo

terminal ['tɜːrmınl] **1** *n at airport, for buses* terminal *f*; ELEC, COMPUT terminal *m*; *of battery* polo *m* **2** *adj illness* terminal; **terminally: *~ ill*** en la fase terminal de una enfermedad; **terminate 1** *v/t contract* rescindir; *pregnancy* interrumpir **2** *v/i* finalizar; **termination** *of contract* rescisión *f*; *of pregnancy* interrupción *f*

terminus ['tɜːrmɪnəs] *for buses* final *m* de trayecto; *for trains* estación *f* terminal

terrace ['terəs] terraza *f*

terrain [te'reɪn] terreno *m*

terrible ['terəbl] terrible; **terribly** (*very*) tremendamente

terrific [tə'rɪfɪk] estupendo; **terrifically** (*very*) tremendamente

terrify ['terɪfaɪ] aterrorizar; **terrifying** aterrador

territorial [terɪ'tɔːrɪəl] territorial; **territory** territorio *m*

terror ['terər] terror *m*; **terrorism** terrorismo *m*; **terrorist** terrorista *m/f*; **terrorist attack** atentado *m* terrorista; **terrorize** aterrorizar

terse [tɜːrs] tajante, seco

test [test] **1** *n* prueba *f*; *academic, for driving* examen *m* **2** *v/t* probar; **test-drive** *car* probar en carretera

testicle ['testɪkl] testículo *m*

testify ['testɪfaɪ] LAW testificar, prestar declaración

testimony ['testɪmənɪ] LAW testimonio *m*

testy ['testɪ] irritable

tetanus ['tetənəs] tétanos *m*

text [tekst] **1** *n* texto *m*; (~ *message*) mensaje *m* **2** *v/t* mandar un mensaje a; **textbook** libro *m* de texto

textile ['tekstəl] textil *m*

text message mensaje *m* de texto

texture ['tekstʃər] textura *f*

than [ðæn] que; *with numbers* de; ***bigger ~ me*** más grande que yo

thank [θæŋk] dar las gracias a; ***~ you*** gracias; **thankful** agradecido; **thankfully** (*luckily*) afortunadamente; **thankless** *task* ingrato; **thanks** gracias *fpl*; **Thanksgiving (Day)** Día *m* de Acción de Gracias

that [ðæt] **1** *adj* ese *m*, esa *f*; *more remote* aquel *m*, aquella; ***~ one*** ése **2** *pron* ése *m*, ésa; *more remote* aquél *m*, aquella *f*; ***what is ~?*** ¿qué es eso?; ***who is ~?*** ¿quién es ése?; ***~'s tea*** es té; ***~'s very kind*** qué amable; **3** *rel pron* que; ***the car ~ you see*** el coche que ves **4** *conj* que; ***I think ~ ...*** creo que… **5** *adv* (*so*) tan; ***~ expensive*** tan caro

thaw [θɒː] *of snow* derretirse, fundirse; *of frozen food* descongelarse

the [ðə] el, la; *plural* los, las; ***~ sooner ~ better*** cuanto antes, mejor

theater, *Br* **theatre** ['θɪətər] teatro *m*; **theatrical** *also fig* teatral

theft [θeft] robo *m*

their [ðer] su; **theirs** el suyo, la suya; ***that book is ~*** ese libro es suyo; ***a friend of ~*** un ami-

go suyo
them [ðem] *direct object* los *mpl*, las *fpl*; *indirect object* les; *after prep* ellos *mpl*, ellas *fpl*; ***I know ~*** los / las conozco; ***I gave ~ the keys*** les di las llaves; ***I sold it to ~*** se lo vendí; ***with ~*** con ellos / ellas; ***it's ~*** son ellos / ellas; ***if a person asks for help, you should help ~*** si una persona pide ayuda, hay que ayudarla
theme [θi:m] tema *m*; **theme park** parque *m* temático
themselves [ðem'selvz] *reflexive* se; *emphatic* ellos mismos *mpl*, ellas mismas *fpl*; ***they hurt ~*** se hicieron daño
then [ðen] (*at that time, deducing*) entonces; (*after that*) luego, después; ***by ~*** para entonces
theoretical [θɪə'retɪkl] teórico; **theoretically** en teoría; **theory** teoría *f*
therapeutic [θerə'pju:tɪk] terapéutico; **therapist** terapeuta *m/f*; **therapy** terapia *f*
there [ðer] allí, ahí, allá; ***down ~*** allí *or* ahí *or* allá abajo; ***~ is / are …*** hay…; ***~ is / are not …*** no hay…; ***~ you are*** *giving sth* aquí tienes; *finding sth* aquí está; *completing sth* ya está; ***~ and back*** ida y vuelta; ***it's 5 miles ~ and back*** entre ida y vuelta hay cinco millas; ***~ he is!*** ¡ahí está!; **~, ~!** ¡venga!; **thereabouts** aproximadamente; **therefore** por (lo) tanto
thermometer [θər'mɑ:mɪtər] termómetro *m*
thermos flask ['θɜ:rməs] termo *m*
these [ði:z] **1** *adj* estos(-as) **2** *pron* éstos *mpl*, éstas *fpl*
thesis ['θi:sɪs] tesis *f inv*
they [ðeɪ] ellos *mpl*, ellas *fpl*; ***~ are Mexican*** son mexicanos; ***if anyone looks at this, ~ will see that …*** si alguien mira esto, verá que…; ***~ say that …*** dicen que…
thick [θɪk] *soup* espeso; *fog* denso; *wall*, *book* grueso; *hair* poblado; F (*stupid*) corto; **thicken** *sauce* espesar; **thickskinned** *fig* insensible
thief [θi:f] ladrón(-ona) *m(f)*
thigh [θaɪ] muslo *m*
thin [θɪn] *person* delgado; *hair* ralo, escaso; *soup* claro; *coat*, *line* fino
thing [θɪŋ] cosa *f*
think [θɪŋk] pensar; *hold an opinion* pensar, creer; ***I ~ so*** creo que sí; ***I don't ~ so*** creo que no; ***what do you ~ of it?*** ¿qué te parece
◆ **think over** reflexionar sobre
◆ **think through** pensar bien
◆ **think up** *plan* idear
'think tank grupo *m* de expertos
thin-skinned [θɪn'skɪnd] sensible
third [θɜ:rd] **1** *adj* tercero **2** *n* tercero(a) *m(f)*; *fraction* tercio *m*, tercera parte *f*; **thirdly**

en tercer lugar; **third party** tercero *m*; **third-party insurance** seguro *m* a terceros; **Third World** Tercer Mundo *m*

thirst [θɜːrst] sed *f*; **thirsty** sediento; ***be ~*** tener sed

thirteen [θɜːr'tiːn] trece; **thirteenth** decimotercero; **thirtieth** trigésimo; **thirty** treinta

this [ðɪs] **1** *adj* este *m*, esta *f*; ***~ one*** éste **2** *pron* esto *m*, esta *f*; ***~ is good*** esto es bueno; ***~ is ...*** *introducing s.o.* éste / ésta es…; TELEC soy… **3** *adv*: ***~ high*** así de alto

thorn [θɔːrn] espina *f*; **thorny** *also fig* espinoso

thorough ['θɜːroʊ] *search* minucioso; *knowledge* profundo; *person* concienzudo; **thoroughbred** *horse* purasangre *m*; **thoroughly** completamente; *clean up* a fondo; *search* minuciosamente

those [ðoʊz] **1** *adj* esos *mpl*, esas *fpl*; *more remote* aquellos *mpl*, aquellas *fpl* **2** *pron* ésos *mpl*, ésas *fpl*; *more remote* aquéllos *mpl*, aquéllas *mpl*

though [ðoʊ] **1** *conj* (*although*) aunque; ***as ~*** como si **2** *adv* sin embargo

thought [θɒːt] *single* idea *f*; *collective* pensamiento *m*; **thoughtful** pensativo; *book* serio; (*considerate*) atento; **thoughtless** desconsiderado

thousand ['θaʊznd] mil *m*; **thousandth** milésimo

thrash [θræʃ] *also* SP dar una paliza a

◆ **thrash out** *solution* alcanzar

thrashing ['θræʃɪŋ] *also* SP paliza *f*

thread [θred] **1** *n* hilo *m*; *of screw* rosca *f* **2** *v/t needle* enhebrar; *beads* ensartar; **threadbare** raído

threat [θret] amenaza *f*; **threaten** amenazar; **threatening** amenazador

three [θriː] tres; **three-quarters** tres cuartos *mpl*

threshold ['θreʃhoʊld] *of house*, *new age* umbral *m*

thrifty ['θrɪftɪ] ahorrativo

thrill [θrɪl] **1** *n* emoción *f*, estremecimiento *m* **2** *v/t*: ***be ~ed*** estar entusiasmado; **thriller** *movie* película *f* de *Span* suspense *or L.Am.* suspenso; *novel* novela *f* de *Span* suspense *or L.Am.* suspenso; **thrilling** emocionante

thrive [θraɪv] *of plant* medrar; *of business* prosperar

throat [θroʊt] garganta *f*; **throat lozenge** pastilla *f* para la garganta

throb [θrɑːb] **1** *n of heart* latido *m*; *of music* zumbido *m* **2** *v/i of heart* latir; *of music* zumbar

throne [θroʊn] trono *m*

throttle ['θrɑːtl] **1** *n on motorbike* acelerador *m*; *on boat*

palanca *f* del gas **2** *v/t* (*strangle*) estrangular
through [θruː] **1** *prep* ◇ (*across*) a través de; ***go ~ the city*** atravesar la ciudad ◇ (during) durante; ***Monday ~ Friday*** de lunes a viernes ◇ (*by means of*) por medio de; ***arranged ~ him*** acordado por él **2** *adv*: ***wet ~*** completamente mojado **3** *adj*: ***be ~*** *of couple* haber terminado; ***I'm ~ with ...*** (*finished with*) he terminado con...; **throughout 1** *prep* durante, a lo largo de **2** *adv* (*in all parts*) en su totalidad
throw [θroʊ] **1** *v/t* tirar; (*disconcert*) desconcertar; *party* dar **2** *n* lanzamiento *m*
◆ **throw away** tirar, *L.Am.* botar
◆ **throw out** *old things* tirar, *L.Am.* botar; *from bar, job, home* echar; *from country* expulsar; *plan* rechazar
◆ **throw up 1** *v/t ball* lanzar hacia arriba **2** *v/i* (*vomit*) vomitar
'throw-away *remark* insustancial, pasajero; (*disposable*) desechable; **throw-in** SP saque *m* de banda
thru [θruː] ☞ ***through***
thrust [θrʌst] (*push hard*) empujar; *knife* hundir
thud [θʌd] golpe *m* sordo
thug [θʌg] matón *m*
thumb [θʌm] **1** *n* pulgar *m* **2** *v/t*: ***~ a ride*** hacer autoestop;
thumbtack chincheta *f*
thunder ['θʌndər] truenos *mpl*; **thunderous** *applause* tormenta *f*; **thunderstorm** tormenta *f* (*con truenos*); **thunderstruck** atónito; **thundery** *weather* tormentoso
Thursday ['θɜːrzdeɪ] jueves *m inv*
thus [ðʌs] (*in this way*) así
thwart [θwɔːrt] frustrar
tick [tɪk] **1** *n of clock* tictac *m*; Br (*checkmark*) señal *f* de visto bueno **2** *v/i of clock* hacer tictac
ticket ['tɪkɪt] *for bus, train, lottery* billete *m*, *L.Am.* boleto *m*; *for airplane* billete *m*, *L.Am.* pasaje *m*; *for theater, museum* entrada *f*, *L.Am.* boleto *m*; *for speeding etc* multa *f*; **ticket machine** máquina *f* expendedora de billetes; **ticket office** *at station* ostrador *m* de venta de billetes; THEA taquilla *f*, *L.Am.* boletería *f*
ticking ['tɪkɪŋ] *noise* tictac *m*
tickle ['tɪkl] **1** *v/t person* hacer cosquillas a **2** *v/i of material* hacer cosquillas
tidal wave ['taɪdlweɪv] maremoto *m* (*ola*)
tide [taɪd] marea *f*
tidiness ['taɪdɪnɪs] orden *m*; **tidy** ordenado
◆ **tidy up 1** *v/t* ordenar; ***tidy o.s. up*** arreglarse **2** *v/i* recoger
tie [taɪ] **1** *n* (*necktie*) corbata *f*;

SP (*even result*) empate *m*; ***he doesn't have any ~s*** no está atado a nada **2** *v/t knot, hands* atar **3** *v/i* SP empatar

◆ **tie down** *also fig* atar

◆ **tie up** *person, laces* atar; *boat* amarrar; *hair* recoger

tier [tɪr] *of hierarchy* nivel *m*; *in stadium* grada *f*

tight [taɪt] **1** *adj clothes* ajustado, estrecho; *security* estricto; (*hard to move*) apretado; (*properly shut*) cerrado; (*not leaving much time*) justo de tiempo; F (*drunk*) como una cuba F **2** *adv hold* fuerte; *shut* bien; **tighten** *screw* apretar; *control* endurecer; *security* intensificar; **tight-fisted** agarrado; **tightly** ☞ ***tight***; **tightrope** cuerda *f* floja; **tights** *Br* medias *fpl*, pantis *mpl*

tile [taɪl] *on floor* baldosa *f*; *on wall* azulejo *m*; *on roof* teja *f*

till[1] [tɪl] ☞ ***until***

till[2] [tɪl] (*cash register*) caja *f* (registradora)

tilt [tɪlt] **1** *v/t* inclinar **2** *v/i* inclinarse

timber ['tɪmbər] madera *f* (de construcción)

time [taɪm] **1** *n* tiempo *m*; (*occasion*) vez *f*; ***have a good ~*** pasarlo bien; ***what's the ~?*** ¿qué hora es?; ***the first ~*** la primera vez; ***all the ~*** todo el rato; ***at the same ~*** *speak, reply etc* a la vez; (*however*) al mismo tiempo; ***on ~*** puntual; ***in ~*** con tiempo **2** *v/t* cronometrar; **time bomb** bomba *f* de relojería; **time difference** diferencia *f* horaria; **time-lag** intervalo *m*; **time limit** plazo *m*; **timely** oportuno; **time out** SP tiempo *m* muerto; **timer** *device* temporizador *m*; **timesaving** ahorro *m* de tiempo; **timescale** *of project* plazo *m* (de tiempo); **time switch** temporizador *m*; **time zone** huso *m* horario

timid ['tɪmɪd] tímido

tin [tɪn] *metal* estaño *m*; *Br* (*can*) lata *f*; **tinfoil** papel *m* de aluminio

tinge [tɪndʒ] matiz *m*

tingle ['tɪŋgl] hormigueo *m*

tinkle ['tɪŋkl] *of bell* tintineo *m*

tinsel ['tɪnsl] espumillón *m*

tint [tɪnt] **1** *n of color* matiz *m*; *in hair* tinte *m* **2** *v/t hair* teñir; **tinted** *glasses* con un tinte; *paper* coloreado

tiny ['taɪnɪ] diminuto, minúsculo

tip[1] [tɪp] *n of stick, finger* punta *f*; *of mountain* cumbre *f*; *of cigarette* filtro *m*

tip[2] [tɪp] **1** *n advice* consejo *m*; *money* propina *f* **2** *v/t waiter etc* dar propina a

◆ **tip off** avisar

'tip-off soplo *m*

tipped [tɪpt] *cigarettes* con filtro

tippy-toe ['tɪpɪtoʊ]: ***on ~*** de puntillas

tipsy ['tɪpsɪ] achispado

tire¹ [taɪr] *n* neumático *m*, *L.Am.* llanta *f*

tire² [taɪr] **1** *v/t* cansar, fatigar **2** *v/i* cansarse, fatigarse

tired [taɪrd] cansado, fatigado; **tiredness** cansancio *m*, fatiga *f*; **tireless** *efforts* incansable, infatigable; **tiresome** (*annoying*) pesado; **tiring** agotador

tissue ['tɪʃuː] ANAT tejido *m*; (*handkerchief*) pañuelo *m* de papel, Kleenex® *m*; **tissue paper** papel *m* de seda

title ['taɪtl] título *m*; LAW título *m* de propiedad; **titleholder** SP campeón(-ona) *m(f)*

to [tuː] **1** *prep* a; ***~ Japan / Chicago*** a Japón / Chicago; ***~ the north of ...*** al norte de...; ***give sth ~ s.o.*** dar algo a alguien; ***from Monday ~ Wednesday*** de lunes a miércoles; ***from 10 ~ 15 people*** de 10 a 15 personas; *with verbs*: ***~ speak*** hablar; ***learn ~ swim*** aprender a nadar; ***too heavy ~ carry*** demasiado pesado para llevarlo **2** *adv*: ***~ and fro*** de un lado para otro

toast [toʊst] **1** *n* pan *m* tostado; *when drinking* brindis *m inv* **2** *v/t when drinking* brindar por; **toaster** tostador(a) *m(f)*

tobacco [tə'bækoʊ] tabaco *m*

today [tə'deɪ] hoy

toddler ['tɑːdlər] niño *m* pequeño

to-do [tə'duː] F revuelo *m*

toe [toʊ] dedo *m* del pie; *of shoe* puntera *f*; **toenail** uña *f* del pie

together [tə'geðər] juntos (-as); (*at the same time*) a la vez

toilet ['tɔɪlɪt] *place* cuarto *m* de baño, servicio *m*; *equipment* retrete *m*; **toilet paper** papel *m* higiénico; **toiletries** artículos *mpl* de tocador

token ['toʊkən] (*sign*) muestra *f*; *Br* (*gift ~*) vale *m*; (*disk*) ficha *f*

tolerable ['tɑːlərəbl] *pain etc* soportable; (*quite good*) aceptable; **tolerance** tolerancia *f*; **tolerant** tolerante; **tolerate** tolerar

toll¹ [toʊl] *v/i of bell* tañer

toll² [toʊl] *n* (*deaths*) mortandad *f*

toll³ [toʊl] *n for bridge, road* peaje *m*; telec tarifa *f*

'toll booth cabina *f* de peaje; **toll-free** TELEC gratuito

tomato [tə'meɪtoʊ] tomate *m*, *Mex* jitomate *m*; **tomato ketchup** ketchup *m*

tomb [tuːm] tumba *f*; **tombstone** lápida *f*

tomcat ['tɑːmkæt] gato *m*

tomorrow [tə'mɔːroʊ] mañana; ***the day after ~*** pasado mañana; ***~ morning*** mañana por la mañana

ton [tʌn] tonelada *f* (*907 kg*)

tone [toʊn] *of color, conversation* tono *m*; *of musical instrument* timbre *m*; *of neigh-*

borhood nivel *m*; **toner** tóner *m*
tongue [tʌŋ] lengua *f*
tonic ['tɑːnɪk] MED tónico *m*; **tonic (water)** (agua *f*) tónica *f*
tonight [tə'naɪt] esta noche
too [tuː] (*also*) también; (*excessively*) demasiado; ***me ~*** yo también; ***~ much rice*** demasiado arroz
tool [tuːl] herramienta *f*
tooth [tuːθ] diente *m*; **toothache** dolor *m* de muelas; **toothbrush** cepillo *m* de dientes; **toothpaste** pasta *f* de dientes, dentífrico *m*; **toothpick** palillo *m*
top [tɑːp] **1** *n of mountain* cima *f*; *of tree* copa *f*; *of wall, screen, page* parte *f* superior; (*lid: of bottle etc*) tapón *m*; *of pen* capucha *f*; *clothing* camiseta *f*, top *m*; (MOT: *gear*) directa *f*; ***on ~ of*** encima de, sobre; ***be ~ of the league*** ser el primero de la liga; ***get to the ~*** *of company, mountain* llegar a la cumbre **2** *adj branches* superior; *floor* de arriba, último; *management, official* alto; *player* mejor; *speed, note* máximo
topic ['tɑːpɪk] tema *m*; **topical** de actualidad
topless ['tɑːplɪs] en topless; **topmost** superior; **topping** *on pizza* ingrediente *m*
topple ['tɑːpl] **1** *v/i* derrumbarse **2** *v/t government* derrocar
top 'secret altamente confidencial
topsy-turvy [tɑːpsɪ'tɜːrvɪ] (*in disorder*) desordenado; *world* al revés
torment 1 ['tɔːrment] *n* tormento *m* **2** [tɔːr'ment] *v/t* atormentar
tornado [tɔːr'neɪdoʊ] tornado *m*
torpedo [tɔːr'piːdoʊ] **1** *n* torpedo *m* **2** *v/t also fig* torpedear
torrent ['tɑːrənt] *also fig* torrente *m*; *of lava* colada *f*
torture ['tɔːrtʃər] **1** *n* tortura *f* **2** *v/t* torturar
toss [tɑːs] *ball* lanzar; *rider* desmontar; *salad* remover
total ['toʊtl] **1** *n* total *m* **2** *adj amount* total; *disaster, stranger* completo; *idiot* de tomo y lomo; **totalitarian** totalitario; **totally** totalmente
totter ['tɑːtər] tambalearse
touch [tʌtʃ] **1** *n* toque *m*; *sense* tacto *m*; ***lose ~ with s.o.*** perder el contacto con alguien; ***in ~*** SP fuera **2** *v/t* tocar; *emotionally* conmover **3** *v/i* tocar; *of two lines etc* tocarse
◆ **touch down** *of airplane* aterrizar; SP marcar un ensayo
'touchdown *of airplane* aterrizaje *m*; SP touchdown *m*, ensayo *m*; **touching** conmovedor; **touchline** SP línea *f* de banda; **touch screen** pantalla *f* tactíl; **touchy** *person* susceptible

tough [tʌf] *person, meat, punishment* duro; *question, exam* difícil; *material* resistente, fuerte

tour [tʊr] **1** *n of museum etc* recorrido *m*; *of area* viaje *m* (**of** por); *of band etc* gira *f* **2** *v/t area* recorrer **3** *v/i of band etc* estar de gira; **tour guide** guía *m/f* turístico(-a); **tourism** turismo *m*; **tourist** turista *m/f*; **tourist industry** industria *f* turística; **tourist (information) office** oficina *f* de turismo

tournament ['tʊrnəmənt] torneo *m*

'tour operator operador *m* turístico

tow [toʊ] remolcar

◆ **tow away** *car* llevarse

toward [tɔːrd] hacia

towel ['taʊəl] toalla *f*

tower ['taʊər] torre *m*

town [taʊn] ciudad *f*; *small* pueblo *m*; **town center**, *Br* **town centre** centro *m* de la ciudad / del pueblo; **town council** ayuntamiento *m*; **town hall** ayuntamiento *m*

toxic ['tɑːksɪk] tóxico; **toxin** toxina *f*

toy [tɔɪ] juguete *m*

trace [treɪs] **1** *n of substance* resto *m* **2** *v/t* (*find*) localizar; (*follow: footsteps of*) seguir el rastro a; (*draw*) trazar

track [træk] (*path*) senda *f*, camino; *for horses* hipódromo *m*; *for cars* circuito *m*; *for athletics* pista *f*; *on CD* canción *f*, corte *m*; RAIL vía *f*; ***keep ~ of sth*** llevar la cuenta de algo

◆ **track down** localizar

'tracksuit *Br* chándal *m*

tractor ['træktər] tractor *m*

trade [treɪd] **1** *n* (*commerce*) comercio *m*; (*profession, craft*) oficio *m* **2** *v/i* (*do business*) comerciar **3** *v/t* (*exchange*) intercambiar; **trade fair** feria *f* de muestras; **trademark** marca *f* registrada; **trade mission** misión *f* comercial; **trader** comerciante *m*

tradition [trə'dɪʃn] tradición *f*; **traditional** tradicional; **traditionally** tradicionalmente

traffic ['træfɪk] tráfico *m*

◆ **traffic in** *drugs* traficar con

'traffic circle rotonda *f*, *Span* glorieta; **traffic cop** F poli *m* de tráfico F; **traffic jam** atasco *m*; **traffic light** semáforo *m*; **traffic sign** señal *f* de tráfico

tragedy ['trædʒədɪ] tragedia *f*; **tragic** tragico

trail [treɪl] **1** *n* (*path*) camino *m*, senda *f*; *of blood* rastro *m* **2** *v/t* (*follow*) seguir la pista de; (*tow*) arrastrar **3** *v/i* (*lag behind*) ir a la zaga; **trailer** *pulled by vehicle* remolque *m*; (*mobile home*) caravana *f*; *of movie* avance *m*, tráiler *m*

train[1] [treɪn] *n* tren *m*

train[2] [treɪn] **1** *v/t team, athlete* entrenar; *employee* formar;

dog adiestrar **2** *v/i of team, athlete* entrenarse; *of teacher etc* formarse

trainee aprendiz(a) *m(f)*; **trainer** SP entrenador(a) *m(f)*; *of dog* adiestrador(a) *m(f)*; **~s** *Br*: *shoes* zapatillas *fpl* de deporte; **training** *of staff* formación *f*; SP entrenamiento *m*

'train station estación *f* de tren

traitor ['treɪtər] traidor(a) *m(f)*

◆ **trample on** pisotear

trampoline ['træmpəliːn] cama *f* elástica

tranquil ['træŋkwɪl] tranquilo; **tranquility,** *Br* **tranquillity** tranquilidad *f*; **tranquilizer,** *Br* **tranquillizer** tranquilizante *m*

transaction [træn'zækʃn] *action* transacción *f*; *deal* negociación *f*

transatlantic [trænzət'læntɪk] transatlántico

transcript ['trænskrɪpt] transcripción *f*

transfer 1 [træns'fɜːr] *v/t* transferir **2** [træns'fɜːr] *v/i in traveling* hacer transbordo **3** ['trænsfɜːr] *n also of money* transferencia *f*; *in travel* transbordo *m*; **transferable** *ticket* transferible; **transfer fee** *for football player* traspaso *m*

transform [træns'fɔːrm] transformar; **transformation** transformación *f*; **transformer** ELEC transformador *m*

transfusion [træns'fjuːʒn] transfusión *f*

transit ['trænzɪt]: *in* **~** en tránsito; **transition** transición *f*; **transitional** de transición; **transit lounge** *at airport* sala *f* de tránsito; **transit passenger** pasajero *m* en tránsito

translate [træns'leɪt] traducir; **translation** traducción *f*; **translator** traductor(a) *m(f)*

transmission [trænz'mɪʃn] *of news, program* emisión *f*; *of disease*, MOT transmisión *f*; **transmit** *program* emitir; *disease* transmitir; **transmitte** *for radio, TV* emisora *f*

transparency [træns'pærənsɪ] PHOT diapositiva *f*; **transparent** transparente; *(obvious)* obvio

transplant MED **1** [træns'plænt] *v/t* trasplantar **2** ['trænsplænt] *n* trasplante *m*

transport 1 [træn'spɔːrt] *v/t* transportar **2** ['trænspɔːrt] *n* transporte *m*; **transportation** transporte *m*

transvestite [træns'vestaɪt] travestí *m*, travestido *m*

trap [træp] **1** *n* trampa *f* **2** *v/t* atrapar; **trappings** *of power* parafernalia *f*

trash [træʃ] *(garbage)* basura *f*; *(poor product)* bazofia *f*; *(despicable person)* escoria *f*; **trashcan** cubo *m* de la ba-

sura; **trashy** *goods* barato
traumatic [trəˈmætɪk] traumático; **traumatize** traumatizar
travel [ˈtrævl] **1** *n* viajes *mpl* **2** *v/t & v/i* viajar; **travel agency** agencia *f* de viajes; **travel agent** agente *m* de viajes; **traveler,** *Br* **traveller** viajero(-a) *m(f)*; **traveler's check,** *Br* **traveller's cheque** cheque *m* de viaje; **travel expenses** gastos *mpl* de viaje; **travel insurance** seguro *m* de asistencia en viaje
trawler [ˈtrɒːlər] (barco *m*) arrastrero *m*
tray [treɪ] bandeja *f*
treacherous [ˈtretʃərəs] traicionero; **treachery** traición *f*
tread [tred] **1** *n* pasos *mpl*; *of staircase* huella *f* (del peldaño); *of tire* dibujo *m* **2** *v/i* andar
treason [ˈtriːzn] traición *f*
treasure [ˈtreʒər] **1** *n also person* tesoro *m* **2** *v/t gift etc* apreciar mucho; **treasurer** tesorero(-a) *m(f)*; **Treasury Department** Ministerio *m* de Hacienda
treat [triːt] **1** *n* placer; ***it's my ~*** (*I'm paying*) yo invito **2** *v/t* tratar; ***~ s.o. to sth*** invitar a alguien a algo; **treatment** tratamiento *m*
treaty [ˈtriːtɪ] tratado *m*
treble [ˈtrebl] **1** *adv*: ***~ the price*** el triple del precio **2** *v/i* triplicarse
tree [triː] árbol *m*
tremble [ˈtrembl] temblar
tremendous [trɪˈmendəs] (*very good*) estupendo; (*enormous*) enorme; **tremendously** (*very*) tremendamente; (*a lot*) enormemente
tremor [ˈtremər] *of earth* temblor *m*
trench [trentʃ] trinchera *f*
trend [trend] tendencia *f*; (*fashion*) moda *f*; **trendy** de moda; *views* moderno
trespass [ˈtrespæs] entrar sin autorización; ***no ~ing*** prohibido el paso; **trespasser** intruso(-a) *m(f)*
trial [ˈtraɪəl] LAW juicio *m*; *of equipment* prueba *f*; ***be on ~*** LAW estar siendo juzgado
triangle [ˈtraɪæŋgl] triángulo *m*; **triangular** triangular
tribe [traɪb] tribu *f*
tribunal [traɪˈbjuːnl] tribunal *m*
tributary [ˈtrɪbjəterɪ] *of river* afluente *m*
trick [trɪk] **1** *n* (*to deceive, knack*) truco *m* **2** *v/t* engañar; **trickery** engaños *mpl*
trickle [ˈtrɪkl] **1** *n* hilo *m*, reguero *m*; *fig*: *of money* goteo *m* **2** *v/i* gotear
tricky [ˈtrɪkɪ] (*difficult*) difícil
trifling [ˈtraɪflɪŋ] insignificante
trigger [ˈtrɪgər] *on gun* gatillo *m*
◆ **trigger off** desencadenar
trim [trɪm] **1** *adj* (*neat*) muy

cuidado; *figure* delgado **2** *v/t hair, costs* recortar; (*decorate: dress*) adornar **3** *n* (*light cut*) recorte *m*

trinket ['trɪŋkɪt] baratija *f*

trip [trɪp] **1** *n* (*journey*) viaje *m* **2** *v/i* (*stumble*) tropezar **3** *v/t* (*make fall*) poner la zancadilla a

◆ **trip up 1** *v/t* (*make fall*) poner la zancadilla a; (*cause to go wrong*) confundir **2** *v/i* (*stumble*) tropezar; (*make a mistake*) equivocarse

triple ['trɪpl] ☞ ***treble***

trite [traɪt] manido

triumph ['traɪʌmf] triunfo *m*

trivial ['trɪvɪəl] trivial; **triviality** trivialidad *f*

trolley ['trɑːlɪ] (*streetcar*) tranvía *m*

troops [truːps] tropas *fpl*

trophy ['troʊfɪ] trofeo *m*

tropic ['trɑːpɪk] trópico *m*; **tropical** tropical; **tropics** trópicos *mpl*

trot [trɑːt] trotar

trouble ['trʌbl] **1** *n* (*difficulties*) problema *m*, problemas *mpl*; (*inconvenience*) molestia *f*; (*disturbance*) conflicto *m*; ***get into*** ~ meterse en líos **2** *v/t* (*worry*) preocupar; (*bother, disturb*) molestar; **troublemaker** alborotador(a) *m*(*f*); **troubleshooting** resolución *f* de problemas; **troublesome** problemático

trousers ['traʊzərz] *Br* pantalones *mpl*

trout [traʊt] trucha *f*

truant ['truːənt]: ***play*** ~ hacer novillos, *Mex* irse de pinta, *S.Am.* hacerse la rabona

truce [truːs] tregua *f*

truck [trʌk] camión *m*; **truck driver** camionero(-a) *m*(*f*); **truck stop** restaurante *m* de carretera

trudge [trʌdʒ] **1** *v/i* caminar fatigosamente **2** *n* caminata *f*

true [truː] verdadero, cierto; *friend, American* auténtico; ***come*** ~ *of hopes, dream* hacerse realidad; **truly** verdaderamente; ***Yours*** ~ le saluda muy atentamente

trumpet ['trʌmpɪt] trompeta *f*

trunk [trʌŋk] *of tree, body* tronco *m*; *of elephant* trompa *f*; (*large case*) baúl *m*; *of car* maletero *m*, *C.Am.*, *Mex* cajuela *f*, *Rpl* baúl *m*

trust [trʌst] **1** *n* confianza *f*; FIN fondo *m* de inversión **2** *v/t* confiar en; **trusted** de confianza; **trustee** fideicomisario(-a) *m*(*f*); **trustful, trusting** confiado; **trustworthy** de confianza

truth [truːθ] verdad *f*; **truthful** sincero; *account* verdadero

try [traɪ] probar; LAW juzgar; ~ ***to do sth*** intentar hacer algo, tratar de hacer algo; **trying** (*annoying*) molesto

T-shirt ['tiːʃɜːrt] camiseta *f*

tub [tʌb] (*bath*) bañera *f*, *L.Am.* tina *f*; *for liquid* cuba *f*; *of yoghurt* envase *m*; **tubby**

rechoncho
tube [tuːb] tubo *m*; **tubeless tire** sin cámara de aire
Tuesday ['tuːzdeɪ] martes *m inv*
tuft [tʌft] *of hair* mechón *m*; *of grass* mata *f*
tug [tʌg] **1** *n* (*pull*) tirón *m*; NAUT remolcador *m* **2** *v/t* (*pull*) tirar de
tuition [tuː'ɪʃn] clases *fpl*
tumble ['tʌmbl] caer, caerse; **tumbledown** destartalado; **tumbler** *for drink* vaso *m*; *in circus* acróbata *m / f*
tummy ['tʌmɪ] F tripa *f* F, barriga *f* F; **tummy ache** dolor *m* de tripa *or* barriga
tumor, *Br* **tumour** ['tuːmər] tumor *m*
tumult ['tuːmʌlt] tumulto *m*; **tumultuous** tumultuoso
tuna ['tuːnə] atún *m*
tune [tuːn] **1** *n* melodía *f* **2** *v/t instrument* afinar
◆ **tune up 1** *v/i of orchestra* afinar **2** *v/t engine* poner a punto
tuneful ['tuːnfəl] melodioso; **tune-up** *of engine* puesta *f* a punto
tunnel ['tʌnl] túnel *m*
turbine ['tɜːrbaɪn] turbina *f*
turbulence ['tɜːrbjələns] *in air travel* turbulencia *f*; **turbulent** turbulento
turf [tɜːrf] césped *m*; *piece* tepe *m*
turkey ['tɜːrkɪ] pavo *m*
turmoil ['tɜːrmɔɪl] desorden *m*, agitación *f*
turn [tɜːrn] **1** *n* (*rotation*) vuelta *f*; *in road* curva *f*; *junction* giro *m*; *in vaudeville* número *m*; ***take ~s in doing sth*** turnarse para hacer algo; ***it's my ~*** me toca a mí **2** *v/t wheel* girar; *corner* dar la vuelta a **3** *v/i of driver, car, wheel* girar; *of person*: *turn around* volverse; ***it has ~ed cold*** se ha enfriado
◆ **turn around 1** *v/t object* dar la vuelta a; *company* dar un vuelco a; COM (*deal with*) procesar **2** *v/i of person* volverse; *of driver* dar la vuelta
◆ **turn away 1** *v/t* (*send away*) rechazar **2** *v/i* (*walk away*) marcharse; (*look away*) desviar la mirada
◆ **turn back 1** *v/t edges* doblar **2** *v/i of walkers etc* volver; *in course of action* echarse atrás
◆ **turn down** *offer* rechazar; *volume, heating* bajar; *edge* doblar
◆ **turn off 1** *v/t TV, engine* apagar; *faucet* cerrar; *heater* apagar **2** *v/i of car, driver* doblar
◆ **turn on 1** *v/t TV, engine, heating* encender, *L.Am.* prender; *faucet* abrir; F *sexually* excitar F **2** *v/i of machine* encenderse, *L.Am.* prenderse
◆ **turn over 1** *v/i in bed* darse la vuelta; *of vehicle* volcar **2** *v/t* (*put upside down*) dar la

vuelta a; *page* pasar; FIN facturar

◆ **turn up 1** *v/t collar* subirse; *volume, heating* subir **2** *v/i* (*arrive*) aparecer

turning ['tɜːrnɪŋ] giro *m*; **turning point** punto *m* de inflexión; **turnout** *of people* asistencia *f*; **turnover** FIN facturación *f*; **turnpike** autopista *f* de peaje; **turn signal** *on car* intermitente *m*

turquoise ['tɜːrkwɔɪz] turquesa

turtle ['tɜːrtl] tortuga *f* (marina); **turtleneck sweater** suéter *m* de cuello alto

tusk [tʌsk] colmillo *m*

tutor ['tuːtər] *Br: at university* tutor *m*; (***private***) ~ profesor(a) *m(f)* particular

tuxedo [tʌk'siːdoʊ] esmoquin *m*

TV [tiː'viː] televisión *f*; ***on*** ~ en la televisión; **TV dinner** menú *m* precocinado; **TV guide** guía *f* televisiva; **TV program**, *Br* **TV programme** programa *m* de televisión

twang [twæŋ] **1** *n in voice* entonación *f* nasal **2** *v/t guitar string* puntear

tweezers ['twiːzərz] pinzas *fpl*

twelfth [twelfθ] duodécimo; **twelve** doce

twentieth ['twentɪɪθ] vigésimo; **twenty** veinte

twice [twaɪs] dos veces; ~ ***as much*** el doble

twig [twɪg] ramita *f*

twilight ['twaɪlaɪt] crepúsculo *m*

twin [twɪn] gemelo *m*; **twin beds** camas *fpl* gemelas

twinge [twɪndʒ] *of pain* punzada *f*

twinkle ['twɪŋkl] *of stars* parpadeo *m*; *of eyes* brillo *m*

twin 'room habitación *f* con camas gemelas

twirl [twɜːrl] **1** *v/t* hacer girar **2** *n of cream etc* voluta *f*

twist [twɪst] **1** *v/t* retorcer; ~ ***one's ankle*** torcerse el tobillo **2** *v/i of road, river* serpentear **3** *n in rope, road* vuelta *f*; *in plot* giro *m* inesperado; **twisty** *road* serpenteante

twitch [twɪʧ] *nervous* tic *m*

twitter ['twɪtər] gorjear

two [tuː] dos; ***the*** ~ ***of them*** los dos, ambos

tycoon [taɪ'kuːn] magnate *m*

type [taɪp] **1** *n* (*sort*) tipo *m*, clase *f* **2** *v/i* (*use a keyboard*) escribir a máquina **3** *v/t with a typewriter* escribir a máquina

typhoon [taɪ'fuːn] tifón *m*

typhus ['taɪfəs] tifus *m*

typical ['tɪpɪkl] típico; **typically** típicamente

typist ['taɪpɪst] mecanógrafo(-a) *m(f)*

tyrannical [tɪ'rænɪkl] tiránico; **tyrannize** tiranizar; **tyranny** tiranía *f*; **tyrant** tirano(-a) *m(f)*

tyre *Br* ☞ ***tire***[1]

U

ugly ['ʌglɪ] feo

UK [juː'keɪ] (= ***United Kingdom***) RU *m* (= Reino *m* Unido)

ulcer ['ʌlsər] úlcera *f*; *in mouth* llaga *f*

ultimate ['ʌltɪmət] (*final*) final; (*fundamental*) esencial; **ultimately** (*in the end*) en última instancia

ultimatum [ʌltɪ'meɪtəm] ultimátum *m*

ultrasound ['ʌltrəsaʊnd] MED ultrasonido *m*; (*scan*) ecografía *f*

ultraviolet [ʌltrə'vaɪələt] ultravioleta

umbrella [ʌm'brelə] paraguas *m inv*

umpire ['ʌmpaɪr] árbitro *m*; *in tennis* juez *m/f* de silla

UN [juː'en] (= ***United Nations***) ONU *f* (= Organización *f* de las Naciones Unidas)

unable [ʌn'eɪbl]: ***be ~ to do sth*** *not know how* no saber hacer algo; *not be in a position* no poder hacer algo

unacceptable [ʌnək'septəbl] inaceptable

unaccountable [ʌnə'kaʊntəbl] inexplicable

un-American [ʌnə'merɪkən] poco americano; *activities* antiamericano

unanimous [juː'nænɪməs] *verdict* unánime; **unanimously** unánimemente

unapproachable [ʌnə'proʊtʃəbl] *person* inaccesible

unarmed [ʌn'ɑːrmd] *person* desarmado

unassuming [ʌnə'suːmɪŋ] sin pretensiones

unattached [ʌnə'tætʃt] *without a partner* sin compromiso, sin pareja

unattended [ʌnə'tendɪd] desatendido

unauthorized [ʌn'ɒːθəraɪzd] no autorizado

unavoidable [ʌnə'vɔɪdəbl] inevitable

unbalanced [ʌn'bælənst] *also* PSYCH desequilibrado

unbearable [ʌn'berəbl] insoportable

unbeatable [ʌn'biːtəbl] *team* invencible; *quality* insuperable

unbeaten [ʌn'biːtn] *team* invicto

unbelievable [ʌnbɪ'liːvəbl] *also* F increíble

unbias(s)ed [ʌn'baɪəst] imparcial

unblock [ʌn'blɑːk] *pipe* desatascar

unbreakable [ʌn'breɪkəbl] *plates* irrompible; *world record* inalcanzable

unbutton [ʌn'bʌtn] desabotonar

uncanny [ʌn'kænɪ] *resemblance* increíble; *skill* inexplicable; (*worrying*: *feeling*) extraño, raro
unceasing [ʌn'si:sɪŋ] incesante
uncertain [ʌn'sɜ:rtn] *future*, *origins* incierto; **uncertainty** incertidumbre *f*
uncle ['ʌŋkl] tío *m*
uncomfortable [ʌn'kʌmftəbl] *chair* incómodo
uncommon [ʌn'kɑ:mən] poco corriente, raro
uncompromising [ʌn'kɑ:mprəmaɪzɪŋ] inflexible
unconditional [ʌnkən'dɪʃnl] incondicional
unconscious [ʌn'kɑ:nʃəs] MED, PSYCH inconsciente
uncontrollable [ʌnkən'troʊləbl] incontrolable
unconventional [ʌnkən'venʃnl] poco convencional
uncooperative [ʌnkoʊ'ɑ:pərətɪv]: ***be ~*** no estar dispuesto a colaborar
uncover [ʌn'kʌvər] *remove cover from* destapar; *plot*, *remains* descubrir
undamaged [ʌn'dæmɪdʒd] intacto
undecided [ʌndɪ'saɪdɪd] *question* sin resolver; ***be ~ about*** estar indeciso sobre
undeniable [ʌndɪ'naɪəbl] innegable
under ['ʌndər] debajo de, bajo; (*less than*) menos de; ***it is ~ investigation*** está siendo investigado
'undercarriage tren *m* de aterrizaje
'undercover *agent* secreto
under'cut COM vender más barato que
under'done *meat* poco hecho
under'estimate subestimar
under'fed malnutrido
under'go *surgery* ser sometido a; *experiences* sufrir
under'graduate estudiante *m/f* universitario(-a) (*todavía no licenciado*(*a*))
'underground 1 *adj* subterráneo; POL clandestino **2** *adv work* bajo tierra
under'hand (*devious*) poco honrado
under'line *text* subrayar
under'lying subyacente
under'mine *position* minar
underneath [ʌndər'ni:θ] **1** *prep* debajo de, bajo **2** *adv* debajo
'underpants calzoncillos *mpl*
'underpass *for pedestrians* paso *m* subterráneo
underprivileged [ʌndər'prɪvɪlɪdʒd] desfavorecido
under'rate subestimar
understaffed [ʌndər'stæft] sin suficiente personal
under'stand entender, comprender; *language* entender; **understandable** comprensible; **understandably** comprensiblemente; **understanding 1** *adj person* com-

prensivo **2** *n* interpretación *f*; (*agreement*) acuerdo *m*
under'take *task* emprender; **~ to do sth** (*agree to*) encargarse de hacer algo; **undertaking** (*enterprise*) proyecto *m*, empresa *f*
under'value infravalorar
'underwear ropa *f* interior
'underworld *criminal* hampa *f*; *in mythology* Hades *m*
under'write FIN asegurar
undeserved [ʌndɪ'zɜːrvd] inmerecido
undesirable [ʌndɪ'zaɪrəbl] *features* no deseado; *person* indeseable
undisputed [ʌndɪ'spjuːtɪd] *champion* indiscutible
undo [ʌn'duː] *parcel* abrir; *buttons*, *shirt* desabrochar; *shoelaces* desatar; *s.o.'s work* deshacer
undoubtedly [ʌn'daʊtɪdlɪ] indudablemente
undress [ʌn'dres] **1** *v/t* desvestir; ***get ~ed*** desvestirse **2** *v/i* desvestirse
undue [ʌn'duː] (*excessive*) excesivo; **unduly** injustamente; (*excessively*) excesivamente
unearth [ʌn'ɜːrθ] descubrir; *remains* desenterrar
uneasy [ʌn'iːzɪ] *relationship*, *peace* tenso
uneatable [ʌn'iːtəbl] incomible
uneconomic [ʌniːkə'nɑːmɪk] antieconómico
uneducated [ʌn'edʒəkeɪtɪd] inculto, sin educación
unemployed [ʌnɪm'plɔɪd] desempleado, *Span* parado; **unemployment** desempleo *m*, *Span* paro *m*
unequal [ʌn'iːkwəl] desigual
unerring [ʌn'erɪŋ] *judgement*, *instinct* infalible
uneven [ʌn'iːvn] *quality* desigual; *surface* irregular
uneventful [ʌnɪ'ventfəl] *day*, *journey* sin incidentes
unexpected [ʌnɪk'spektɪd] inesperado; **unexpectedly** inesperadamente
unfair [ʌn'fer] injusto
unfaithful [ʌn'feɪθfəl] *husband*, *wife* infiel; ***be ~ to s.o.*** ser infiel a alguien
unfamiliar [ʌnfə'mɪljər] desconocido, extraño
unfasten [ʌn'fæsn] *belt* desabrochar
unfavorable, *Br* **unfavourable** [ʌn'feɪvərəbl] desfavorable
unfinished [ʌn'fɪnɪʃt] inacabado
unfold [ʌn'foʊld] **1** *v/t letter* desdoblar; *arms* descruzar **2** *v/i of story etc* desarrollarse; *of view* abrirse
unforeseen [ʌnfɔːr'siːn] imprevisto
unforgettable [ʌnfər'getəbl] inolvidable
unforgivable [ʌnfər'gɪvəbl] imperdonable
unfortunate [ʌn'fɔːrtʃənət] desafortunado; *event* desgraciado; **unfortunately** des-

graciadamente
unfounded [ʌn'faʊndɪd] infundado
unfriendly [ʌn'frendlɪ] *person* antipático; *place* desagradable; *welcome* hostil
ungrateful [ʌn'greɪtfəl] desagradecido
unhappiness [ʌn'hæpɪnɪs] infelicidad *f*; **unhappy** infeliz; *day* triste; *customer etc* descontento
unharmed [ʌn'hɑːrmd] ileso
unhealthy [ʌn'helθɪ] enfermizo; *food*, *economy* poco saludable
unheard-of [ʌn'hɜːrdəv] inaudito
unhygienic [ʌnhaɪ'dʒiːnɪk] antihigiénico
unification [juːnɪfɪ'keɪʃn] unificación *f*
uniform ['juːnɪfɔːrm] **1** *n* uniforme *m* **2** *adj* uniforme
unify ['juːnɪfaɪ] unificar
unilateral [juːnɪ'lætərəl] unilateral
unimaginable [ʌnɪ'mædʒɪnəbl] inimaginable
unimaginative [ʌnɪ'mædʒɪnətɪv] sin imaginación
unimportant [ʌnɪm'pɔːrtənt] poco importante
uninhabitable [ʌnɪn'hæbɪtəbl] inhabitable; **uninhabited** *building* deshabitado; *region* desierto
unintentional [ʌnɪn'tenʃnl] no intencionado; **unintentionally** sin querer
uninteresting [ʌn'ɪntrəstɪŋ] sin interés
uninterrupted [ʌnɪntə'rʌptɪd] ininterrumpido
union ['juːnjən] POL unión *f*; (*labor* ~) sindicato *m*
unique [juː'niːk] único
unit ['juːnɪt] unidad *f*
unite [juː'naɪt] **1** *v/t* unir **2** *v/i* unirse; **united** unido; **United Kingdom** Reino *m* Unido; **United Nations** Naciones *fpl* Unidas; **United States (of America)** Estados *mpl* Unidos (de América)
unity ['juːnətɪ] unidad *f*
universal [juːnɪ'vɜːrsl] universal; **universe** universo *m*
university [juːnɪ'vɜːrsətɪ] universidad *f*
unjust [ʌn'dʒʌst] injusto
unkind [ʌn'kaɪnd] desagradable, cruel
unknown [ʌn'noʊn] desconocido
unleaded [ʌn'ledɪd] sin plomo
unless [ən'les] a menos que, a no ser que
unlikely [ʌn'laɪklɪ] improbable; *explanation* inverosímil
unlimited [ʌn'lɪmɪtɪd] ilimitado
unload [ʌn'loʊd] descargar
unlock [ʌn'lɑːk] abrir
unluckily [ʌn'lʌkɪlɪ] desgraciadamente, por desgracia; **unlucky** *day* aciago, funesto; *person* sin suerte; ***that was so ~ for you!*** ¡qué mala suerte tuviste!
unmanned [ʌn'mænd] *space-*

craft no tripulado
unmarried [ʌn'mærɪd] soltero
unmistakable [ʌnmɪ'steɪkəbl] inconfundible
unnatural [ʌn'nætʃrəl] anormal
unnecessary [ʌn'nesəserɪ] innecesario
unnerving [ʌn'nɜːrvɪŋ] desconcertante
unobtainable [ʌnəb'teɪnəbl] *goods* no disponible; TELEC desconectado
unobtrusive [ʌnəb'truːsɪv] discreto
unoccupied [ʌn'ɑːkjʊpaɪd] *building* desocupado; *post* vacante
unofficial [ʌnə'fɪʃl] no oficial; **unofficially** extraoficialmente
unorthodox [ʌn'ɔːrθədɑːks] poco ortodoxo
unpack [ʌn'pæk] **1** *v/t* deshacer **2** *v/i* deshacer el equipaje
unpaid [ʌn'peɪd] *work* no remunerado
unpleasant [ʌn'pleznt] desagradable
unplug [ʌn'plʌg] *TV, computer* desenchufar
unpopular [ʌn'pɑːpjələr] impopular
unprecedented [ʌn'presɪdentɪd] sin precedentes
unpredictable [ʌnprɪ'dɪktəbl] imprevisible, impredecible
unpretentious [ʌnprɪ'tenʃəs] modesto, sin pretensiones
unproductive [ʌnprə'dʌktɪv] *meeting* infructuoso; *soil* improductivo
unprofessional [ʌnprə'feʃnl] poco profesional
unprofitable [ʌn'prɑːfɪtəbl] no rentable
unprovoked [ʌnprə'voʊkt] *attack* no provocado
unqualified [ʌn'kwɑːlɪfaɪd] sin titulación
unquestionably [ʌn'kwestʃnəblɪ] indiscutiblemente; **unquestioning** *attitude* incondicional
unreadable [ʌn'riːdəbl] *book* ilegible
unrealistic [ʌnrɪə'lɪstɪk] poco realista
unreasonable [ʌn'riːznəbl] irrazonable
unrelated [ʌnrɪ'leɪtɪd] *issues* no relacionado; *people* no emparentado
unrelenting [ʌnrɪ'lentɪŋ] implacable
unreliable [ʌnrɪ'laɪəbl] *machine* poco fiable; *person* informal
unrest [ʌn'rest] malestar *m*; (*rioting*) disturbios *mpl*
unrestrained [ʌnrɪ'streɪnd] *emotions* incontrolado
unroll [ʌn'roʊl] desenrollar
unruly [ʌn'ruːlɪ] revoltoso
unsanitary [ʌn'sænɪterɪ] insalubre
unsatisfactory [ʌnsætɪs'fæktərɪ] insatisfactorio
unscathed [ʌn'skeɪðd] (*not injured*) ileso; (*not damaged*) intacto

unscrew [ʌn'skru:] *top* desenroscar; *hooks* desatornillar
unscrupulous [ʌn'skru:pjələs] sin escrúpulos
unselfish [ʌn'selfɪʃ] generoso
unsettled [ʌn'setld] *issue* sin decidir; *weather*, *lifestyle* inestable; *bills* sin pagar
unshaven [ʌn'ʃeɪvn] sin afeitar
unskilled [ʌn'skɪld] no cualificado
unsophisticated [ʌnsə'fɪstɪkeɪtɪd] sencillo; *equipment* simple
unstable [ʌn'steɪbl] inestable
unsteady [ʌn'stedɪ] *hand* tembloroso; *ladder* inestable
unsuccessful [ʌnsək'sesfəl] *writer etc* fracasado; *candidate* perdedor; *party*, *attempt* fallido; **unsuccessfully** sin éxito
unsuitable [ʌn'su:təbl] inadecuado; *thing to say* inoportuno
unswerving [ʌn'swɜ:rvɪŋ] *loyalty* inquebrantable
unthinkable [ʌn'θɪŋkəbl] impensable
untidy [ʌn'taɪdɪ] *room*, *desk* desordenado; *hair* revuelto
untie [ʌn'taɪ] desatar
until [ən'tɪl] **1** *prep* hasta; ***not ~ Friday*** no antes del viernes **2** *conj* hasta que; ***can you wait ~ I'm ready?*** ¿puedes esperar hasta que esté listo?
untiring [ʌn'taɪrɪŋ] *efforts* incansable
untold [ʌn'tould] *suffering* indecible; *riches* inconmensurable; *story* nunca contado
untrue [ʌn'tru:] falso
unused [ʌn'ju:zd] *goods* sin usar
unusual [ʌn'ju:ʒl] poco corriente; ***it is ~ …*** es raro *or* extraño…; **unusually** inusitadamente
unveil [ʌn'veɪl] *statue etc* desvelar
unwell [ʌn'wel] indispuesto, mal
unwilling [ʌn'wɪlɪŋ] poco dispuesto, reacio; **unwillingly** de mala gana
unwind [ʌn'waɪnd] *of story* irse desarrollando; (*relax*) relajarse
unwise [ʌn'waɪz] imprudente
unwrap [ʌn'ræp] desenvolver
unzip [ʌn'zɪp] abrir la cremallera de; COMPUT descomprimir
up [ʌp] **1** *adv position* arriba; *movement* hacia arriba; ***~ here / there*** aquí / allí arriba; ***be ~*** (*out of bed*) estar levantado; *of sun* haber salido; *of temperature* haber subido; (*have expired*) haberse acabado; ***what's ~?*** F ¿qué pasa?; ***~ to 1989*** hasta el año 1989; ***he came ~ to me*** se me acercó; ***what are you ~ to these days?*** ¿qué es de tu vida?; ***be ~ to something*** (***bad***) estar tramando algo; ***I don't feel ~ to it*** no me sien-

to en condiciones de hacerlo; ***it's ~ to you*** tú decides; ***it is ~ to them to solve it*** (*their duty*) les corresponde a ellos resolverlo **2** *prep*: ***further ~ the mountain*** más arriba de la montaña; ***they ran ~ the street*** corrieron por la calle; ***we traveled ~ to Chicago*** subimos hasta Chicago **3** *n*: ***~s and downs*** altibajos *mpl*

'upbringing educación *f*

up'date *file* actualizar

up'grade modernizar; ***~ s.o. to business class*** cambiar a alguien a clase ejecutiva

upheaval [ʌp'hiːvl] *emotional* conmoción *f*; *physical* trastorno *m*; *political, social* sacudida *f*

up'hold *rights* defender, conservar; (*vindicate*) confirmar

'upkeep mantenimiento *m*

'upload COMPUT cargar

up'market *Br restaurant, hotel* de categoría

upon [ə'pɑːn] ☞ ***on***

upper ['ʌpər] superior

'upright 1 *adj citizen* honrado **2** *adv sit* derecho; **upright (piano)** piano *m* vertical

'uprising levantamiento *m*

'uproar alboroto *m*; (*protest*) tumulto *m*

up'set 1 *v/t* tirar; *emotionally* disgustar **2** *adj emotionally* disgustado; **upsetting** triste

upside 'down boca abajo

up'stairs 1 *adv* arriba **2** *adj room* de arriba

up'stream río arriba

up'tight F (*nervous*) tenso; (*inhibited*) estrecho

up-to-'date *information* actualizado

'upturn *in economy* mejora *f*

upward ['ʌpwərd] hacia arriba; ***~ of 100*** más de 100

uranium [jʊ'reɪnɪəm] uranio *m*

urban ['ɜːrbən] urbano

urge [ɜːrdʒ] **1** *n* impulso *m* **2** *v/t*: ***~ s.o. to do sth*** rogar a alguien que haga algo; **urgency** urgencia *f*; **urgent** urgente

urinate ['jʊrəneɪt] orinar; **urine** orina *f*

Uruguay ['jʊrəgwaɪ] Uruguay; **Uruguayan 1** *adj* uruguayo **2** *n* uruguayo(-a) *m(f)*

US [juː'es] (= ***United States***) EE.UU. *mpl* (= Estados *mpl* Unidos)

us [ʌs] nos; *after prep* nosotros (-as); ***that's for ~*** eso es para nosotros; ***who's that? – it's ~*** ¿quién es? - ¡somos nosotros!

USA [juːes'eɪ] (= ***United States of America***) EE.UU. *mpl* (= Estados *mpl* Unidos)

usage ['juːzɪdʒ] uso *m*

use 1 [juːz] *v/t tool, word* utilizar, usar; *skills, car* usar; *a lot of gas* consumir; *pej*: *person* utilizar **2** [juːs] *n* uso *m*, utilización *f*; ***it's no ~ waiting*** no sirve de nada esperar

◆ **use up** agotar

used[1] [juːzd] *adj car etc* de se-

gunda mano
used[2] [juːst]: ***be ~ to*** estar acostumbrado a; ***get ~ to*** acostumbrarse a
used[3] [juːst]: ***I ~ to like him*** antes me gustaba; ***they ~ to meet every Saturday*** solían verse todos los sábados
useful ['juːsfʊl] útil; **usefulness** utilidad *f*; **useless** inútil; *machine* inservible; **user** usuario(-a) *m(f)*; **user-friendly** de fácil manejo
usual ['juːʒl] habitual; ***as ~*** como de costumbre; **usually** normalmente
utensil [juː'tensl] utensilio *m*
utilize ['juːtɪlaɪz] utilizar
utter ['ʌtər] **1** *adj* completo **2** *v/t sound* decir; **utterly** completamente

V

vacant ['veɪkənt] *building* vacío; *position* vacante; *look* vago, distraído; **vacantly** distraídamente; **vacate** *room* desalojar
vacation [veɪ'keɪʃn] vacaciones *fpl*; ***be on ~*** estar de vacaciones
vaccinate ['væksɪneɪt] vacunar; **vaccination** *action* vacunación *f*; (*vaccine*) vacuna *f*; **vaccine** vacuna *f*
vacuum ['vækjʊəm] **1** *n* vacío *m* **2** *v/t floors* aspirar
vagrant ['veɪgrənt] vagabundo(-a) *m(f)*
vague [veɪg] vago; **vaguely** vagamente
vain [veɪn] **1** *adj* vanidoso; *hope* vano **2** *n*: ***in ~*** en vano
valiant ['væljənt] valiente
valid ['vælɪd] válido; **validate** *with official stamp* sellar; *alibi* dar validez a; **validity** validez *f*
valley ['vælɪ] valle *m*
valuable ['væljʊbl] **1** *adj* valioso **2** *n*: ***~s*** objetos *mpl* de valor; **valuation** tasación *f*, valoración *f*; **value 1** *n* valor *m* **2** *v/t* valorar
valve [vælv] válvula *f*
van [væn] camioneta *f*, furgoneta *f*
vandal ['vændl] vándalo *m*; **vandalism** vandalismo *m*; **vandalize** destrozar (*intencionadamente*)
vanilla [və'nɪlə] **1** *n* vainilla *f* **2** *adj* de vainilla
vanish ['vænɪʃ] desaparecer
vanity ['vænətɪ] vanidad *f*
vapor ['veɪpər] vapor *m*; **vaporize** vaporizar; **vapour** *Br* ☞ ***vapor***
variable ['verɪəbl] **1** *adj* variable **2** *n* variable *f*; **variant** variante *f*; **variation** variación *f*; **varied** variado; **variety** variedad *f*; **various** (*several*) varios; (*different*) diversos
varnish ['vɑːrnɪʃ] **1** *n for*

wood barniz *m*; *for fingernails* esmalte *m* **2** *v/t wood* barnizar
vary ['verɪ] variar; ***it varies*** depende
vase [veɪz] jarrón *m*
vast [væst] vasto; *number, improvement* enorme; **vastly** enormemente
Vatican ['vætɪkən]: ***the ~*** el Vaticano
vault[1] [vɒːlt] *n in roof* bóveda *f*; ***~s*** (*cellar*) sótano *m*; *of bank* cámara *f* acorazada
vault[2] [vɒːlt] **1** *n* SP salto *m* **2** *v/t beam etc* saltar
VCR [viːsiː'ɑːr] (= ***video cassette recorder***) aparato *m* de *Span* vídeo *or L.Am.* video
veal [viːl] ternera *f*
veer [vɪr] girar, torcer
vegetable ['vedʒtəbl] hortaliza *f*; ***~s*** verduras *fpl*; **vegetarian 1** *n* vegetariano(-a) *m(f)* **2** *adj* vegetariano; **vegetation** vegetación *f*
vehement ['viːəmənt] vehemente
vehicle ['viːɪkl] vehículo *m*
veil [veɪl] velo *m*
vein [veɪn] ANAT vena *f*
velocity [vɪ'lɑːsətɪ] velocidad *f*
velvet ['velvɪt] terciopelo *m*
vendetta [ven'detə] vendetta *f*
vending machine ['vendɪŋ] máquina *f* expendedora; **vendor** LAW parte *f* vendedora
veneer [və'nɪr] *on wood* chapa *f*; *of politeness etc* apariencia *f*
venerable ['venərəbl] venerable; **veneration** veneración *f*
venereal disease [vɪ'nɪrɪəl] enfermedad *f* venérea
venetian 'blind [və'niːʃn] persiana *f* veneciana
Venezuela [venɪz'weɪlə] Venezuela; **Venezuelan 1** *adj* venezolano **2** *n* venezolano(-a) *m(f)*
venom ['venəm] veneno *m*
ventilate ['ventɪleɪt] ventilar; **ventilation** ventilación *f*; **ventilator** ventilador *m*; MED respirador *m*
venture ['ventʃər] **1** *n* (*undertaking*) iniciativa *f*; COM empresa *f* **2** *v/i* aventurarse
venue ['venjuː] *for meeting* lugar *m*; *for concert* local *m*, sala *f*
veranda [və'rændə] porche *m*
verb [vɜːrb] verbo *m*; **verbal** (*spoken*) verbal; **verbally** de palabra
verdict ['vɜːrdɪkt] veredicto *m*
verge [vɜːrdʒ] *of road* arcén *m*; ***be on the ~ of** ruin* estar al borde de; *tears* estar a punto de
verification [verɪfɪ'keɪʃn] (*checking*) verificación *f*; (*confirmation*) confirmación *f*; **verify** (*check*) verificar; (*confirm*) confirmar
vermin ['vɜːrmɪn] bichos *mpl*, alimañas *fpl*

vermouth [vɜːr'muːθ] vermut *m*
versatile ['vɜːrsətəl] polifacético, versátil; **versatility** polivalencia *f*, versatilidad *f*
verse [vɜːrs] verso *m*
version ['vɜːrʃn] versión *f*
versus ['vɜːrsəs] contra
vertical ['vɜːrtɪkl] vertical
vertigo ['vɜːrtɪgoʊ] vértigo *m*
very ['verɪ] **1** *adv* muy; ***the ~ best*** el mejor de todos **2** *adj*: ***at that ~ moment*** en ese mismo momento; ***that's the ~ thing I need*** eso es precisamente lo que necesito
vessel ['vesl] NAUT buque *m*
vest [vest] chaleco *m*; *Br* camiseta *f* interior
vestige ['vestɪdʒ] vestigio *m*
vet[1] [vet] *n* (*veterinary surgeon*) veterinario(-a) *m(f)*
vet[2] [vet] *v/t applicants etc* examinar, investigar
vet[3] [vet] *n* mil veterano(-a) *m(f)*
veteran ['vetərən] **1** *n* veterano(-a) *m(f)* **2** *adj* veterano
veterinarian [vetərə'nerɪən] veterinario(-a) *m(f)*
veto ['viːtoʊ] **1** *n* veto *m* **2** *v/t* vetar
via ['vaɪə] vía
viable ['vaɪəbl] viable
vibrate [vaɪ'breɪt] vibrar; **vibration** vibración *f*
vice[1] [vaɪs] *n* vicio *m*
vice[2] [vaɪs] *Br* ☞ ***vise***
vice 'president vicepresidente(-a) *m(f)*
vice versa [vaɪs'vɜːrsə] viceversa
vicious ['vɪʃəs] *dog* fiero; *attack*, *temper* feroz; **viciously** con brutalidad
victim ['vɪktɪm] víctima *f*; **victimize** tratar injustamente
victorious [vɪk'tɔːrɪəs] victorioso; **victory** victoria *f*
video ['vɪdɪoʊ] **1** *n Span* vídeo *m*, *L.Am.* video *m* **2** *v/t* grabar en *Span* vídeo *or L.Am.* video; **video camera** videocámara *f*; **video cassette** videocasete *m*; **video recorder** aparato *m* de *Span* vídeo *or L.Am.* video; **videotape** cinta *f* de *Span* vídeo *or L.Am.* video
vie [vaɪ] competir
Vietnam [vɪet'nɑːm] Vietnam; **Vietnamese 1** *adj* vietnamita **2** *n* vietnamita *m/f*; *language* vietnamita *m*
view [vjuː] **1** *n* vista *f*; *of situation* opinión *f*; ***in ~ of*** teniendo en cuenta **2** *v/t* ver **3** *v/i* (*watch TV*) ver la televisión; **viewer** TV telespectador(a) *m(f)*; **viewpoint** punto *m* de vista
vigor ['vɪgər] vigor *m*; **vigorous** vigoroso; *person* enérgico; *denial* rotundo; **vigorously** con vigor; *deny*, *defend* rotundamente; **vigour** *Br* ☞ ***vigor***
village ['vɪlɪdʒ] pueblo *m*; **villager** aldeano(-a) *m(f)*
villain ['vɪlən] malo(a) *m(f)*
vindicate ['vɪndɪkeɪt] (*show*

to be correct) dar la razón a; (*show to be innocent*) vindicar

vindictive [vɪn'dɪktɪv] vengativo

vine [vaɪn] vid *f*

vinegar ['vɪnɪgər] vinagre *m*

vineyard ['vɪnjɑːrd] viñedo *m*

vintage ['vɪntɪdʒ] **1** *n of wine* cosecha *f* **2** *adj* clásico *m*

violate ['vaɪəleɪt] violar; **violation** violación *f*; (*traffic ~*) infracción *f*

violence ['vaɪələns] violencia *f*; **violent** violento

violin [vaɪə'lɪn] violín *m*; **violinist** violinista *m/f*

VIP [viːaɪ'piː] (= ***very important person***) VIP *m*

viral ['vaɪrəl] vírico, viral

virgin ['vɜːrdʒɪn] virgen *m/f*; **virginity** virginidad *f*

virile ['vɪrəl] viril; **virility** virilidad *f*

virtual ['vɜːrtʃuəl] virtual; **virtually** (*almost*) virtualmente

virtue ['vɜːrʃtuː] virtud *f*; **virtuous** virtuoso

virus ['vaɪrəs] virus *m inv*

visa ['viːzə] visa *f*, visado *m*

vise [vaɪs] torno *m* de banco

visibility [vɪzə'bɪlətɪ] visibilidad *f*; **visible** visible; *anger* evidente

vision ['vɪʒn] visión *f*

visit ['vɪzɪt] **1** *n* visita *f* **2** *v/t* visitar; **visitor** visita *f*; (*tourist*), *to museum etc* visitante *m/f*

visor ['vaɪzər] visera *f*

visual ['vɪʒʊəl] visual; **visualize** visualizar; (*foresee*) prever; **visually** visualmente

vital ['vaɪtl] (*essential*) vital; **vitality** vitalidad *f*; **vitally**: *~* ***important*** de importancia vital

vitamin ['vaɪtəmɪn] vitamina *f*; **vitamin pill** pastilla *f* vitamínica

vivacious [vɪ'veɪʃəs] vivaz; **vivacity** vivacidad *f*

vivid ['vɪvɪd] *color* vivo; *imagination* vívido; **vividly** (*brightly*) vivamente; (*clearly*) vívidamente

V-neck ['viːnek] cuello *m* de pico

vocabulary [voʊ'kæbjʊlərɪ] vocabulario *m*

vocal ['voʊkl] vocal; *expressing opinions* ruidoso; **vocalist** MUS vocalista *m/f*

vocation [və'keɪʃn] vocación *f*; (*profession*) profesión *f*; **vocational** *guidance* profesional

vodka ['vɑːdkə] vodka *m*

vogue [voʊg] moda *f*; ***be in ~*** estar en boga

voice [vɔɪs] **1** *n* voz *f* **2** *v/t opinions* expresar; **voicemail** correo *m* de voz

volcano [vɑːl'keɪnoʊ] volcán *m*

volley ['vɑːlɪ] *of shots* ráfaga *f*; *in tennis* volea *f*

volt [voʊlt] voltio *m*; **voltage** voltaje *m*

volume ['vɑːljəm] volumen *m*; *of container* capacidad *f*

voluntarily [vɑːlən'terɪlɪ] voluntariamente; **voluntary**

voluntario; **volunteer 1** *n* voluntario(-a) *m(f)* **2** *v/i* ofrecerse voluntariamente
vomit ['vɑːmət] **1** *n* vómito *m* **2** *v/i* vomitar
voracious [və'reɪʃəs] voraz
vote [voʊt] **1** *n* voto *m* **2** *v/i* POL votar; **~ *for* / *against*** votar a favor / en contra; **voter** POL votante *m/f*; **voting** POL votación *f*
◆ **vouch for** [vaʊʧ] *truth* dar fe de; *person* responder por
vow [vaʊ] **1** *n* voto *m* **2** *v/t*: **~ *to do*** prometer hacer
vowel [vaʊl] vocal *f*
voyage ['vɔɪɪdʒ] viaje *m*
vulgar ['vʌlgər] vulgar, grosero
vulnerable ['vʌlnərəbl] vulnerable
vulture ['vʌlʧər] buitre *m*

W

waddle ['wɑːdl] *of duck* caminar; *of person* anadear
wade [weɪd] caminar en el agua
wafer ['weɪfər] *cookie* barquillo *m*; REL hostia *f*
waffle ['wɑːfl] *to eat* gofre *m*
wag [wæg] **1** *v/t* menear **2** *v/i* *of tail* menearse
wages ['weɪdʒɪz] salario *m*, sueldo *m*
waggle ['wægl] *hips* menear; *loose screw etc* mover
wail [weɪl] *of person* gemir; *of siren* sonar, aullar
waist [weɪst] cintura *f*
wait [weɪt] **1** *n* espera *f* **2** *v/i* esperar
◆ **wait for** esperar
◆ **wait on** (*serve*) servir; (*wait for*) esperar
◆ **wait up** esperar levantado
waiter ['weɪtər] camarero *m*; **waiting list** lista *f* de espera; **waiting room** sala *f* de espera; **waitress** camarera *f*
waive [weɪv] *right* renunciar; *requirement* no aplicar
wake [weɪk] **1** *v/i*: **~ (*up*)** despertarse **2** *v/t*: **~ (*up*)** despertar
walk [wɒːk] **1** *n* paseo *m*; *longer* caminata *f*; (*path*) camino *m*; ***go for a ~*** salir a dar un paseo **2** *v/i* caminar, andar; *as opposed to driving* ir a pie **3** *v/t dog* sacar a pasear
◆ **walk out** *of spouse* marcharse; *from theater etc* salir; (*go on strike*) declararse en huelga
walker ['wɒːkər] (*hiker*) excursionista *m/f*; *for baby, old person* andador *m*; **walking** (*hiking*) excursionismo *m*; **walkout** (*strike*) huelga *f*; **walkover** (*easy win*) paseo *m*
wall [wɒːl] muro *m*; *inside* pared *f*
wallet ['wɑːlɪt] (*billfold*) cartera *f*

'wallpaper 1 *n* papel *m* pintado **2** *v/t* empapelar; **wall-to--wall carpet** *Span* moqueta *f*, *L.Am.* alfombra *f*
waltz [wɒːlts] vals *m*
wan [wɑːn] *face* pálido *m*
wander ['wɑːndər] *(roam)* vagar, deambular; *(stray)* extraviarse
wangle ['wæŋgl] F agenciarse F
want [wɑːnt] **1** *n*: ***for ~ of*** por falta de **2** *v/t* querer; *(need)* necesitar; ***~ to do sth*** querer hacer algo; ***I ~ to stay here*** quiero quedarme aquí; ***she ~s you to go back*** quiere que vuelvas **3** *v/i*: ***he ~s for nothing*** no le falta nada; **wanted** *by police* buscado por la policía
war [wɔːr] *also fig* guerra *f*
ward [wɔːrd] *in hospital* sala *f*; *child* pupilo(-a) *m(f)*
◆ **ward off** *blow* parar; *attacker* rechazar; *cold* evitar
warden ['wɔːrdn] *of prison* director(-a) *m(f)*; *Br of hostel* vigilante *m/f*
'wardrobe *for clothes* armario *m*; *(clothes)* guardarropa *m*
warehouse ['werhaʊs] almacén *m*
'warfare guerra *f*; **warhead** ojiva *f*
warily ['werılı] cautelosamente
warm [wɔːrm] *hands, room, water* caliente; *weather, welcome* cálido; *coat* de abrigo
◆ **warm up 1** *v/t* calentar **2** *v/i* calentarse; *of athlete etc* calentar
warmly ['wɔːrmlı] calurosamente; **warmth** calor *m*; **warm-up** SP calentamiento *m*
warn [wɔːrn] advertir, avisar; **warning** advertencia *f*, aviso *m*
warp [wɔːrp] *of wood* combarse; **warped** *fig* retorcido
warrant ['wɔːrənt] **1** *n* orden *f* judicial **2** *v/t* justificar; **warranty** garantía *f*
warrior ['wɔːrıər] guerrero(-a) *m(f)*
wart [wɔːrt] verruga *f*
wary ['werı] cauto
wash [wɑːʃ] **1** *n* lavado *m*; ***have a ~*** lavarse **2** *v/t* lavar **3** *v/i* lavarse
◆ **wash up** *(wash one's hands and face)* lavarse
washable ['wɑːʃəbl] lavable; **washbasin, washbowl** lavabo *m*; **washcloth** toallita *f*; **washed out** agotado; **washer** *for faucet etc* arandela *f*; **washing** *(clothes washed)* ropa *f* limpia; *(dirty clothes)* ropa *f* sucia; ***do the ~*** lavar la ropa; **washing machine** lavadora *f*; **washroom** lavabo *m*, aseo *m*
wasp [wɑːsp] avispa *f*
waste [weıst] **1** *n* desperdicio *m*; *from industrial process* desechos *mpl*; ***it's a ~ of time / money*** es una pérdida de tiempo / dinero **2** *adj* residual **3** *v/t* derrochar;

money gastar; *time* perder; **waste basket** papelera *f*; **waste disposal (unit)** trituradora *f* de basuras; **wasteful** derrochador; **wasteland** erial *m*; **wastepaper** papel *m* usado

watch [wɑːtʃ] **1** *n timepiece* reloj *m*; ***keep ~*** hacer la guardia, vigilar **2** *v/t film*, *TV* ver; (*look after*) vigilar **3** *v/i* mirar, observar; **watchful** vigilante

water ['wɒːtər] **1** *n* agua *f* **2** *v/t plant* regar **3** *v/i*: ***my mouth is ~ing*** se me hace la boca agua; **watercolor,** *Br* **watercolour** acuarela *f*; **watered down** *fig* dulcificado; **waterfall** cascada *f*; **waterline** línea *f* de flotación; **waterlogged** anegado; *boat* lleno de agua; **watermelon** sandía *f*; **waterproof** impermeable; **waterside** orilla *f*; **waterskiing** esquí *m* acuático; **watertight** *compartment* estanco; *fig* irrefutable; **waterway** curso *m* de agua navegable; **watery** aguado

watt [wɑːt] vatio *m*

wave[1] [weɪv] *n in sea* ola *f*

wave[2] [weɪv] **1** *n of hand* saludo *m* **2** *v/i with hand* saludar con la mano **3** *v/t flag etc* agitar

'**wavelength** RAD longitud *f* de onda; ***be on the same ~*** *fig* estar en la misma onda

waver ['weɪvər] vacilar

wavy ['weɪvɪ] ondulado

wax [wæks] cera *f*

way [weɪ] (*method*) manera *f*; (*manner also*) modo *m*; (*route*) camino *m*; ***this ~*** (*like this*) así; (*in this direction*) por aquí; ***by the ~*** (*incidentally*) a propósito; ***in a ~*** (*in certain respects*) en cierto sentido; ***lose one's ~*** perderse; ***be in the ~*** (*be an obstruction*) estar en medio; ***no ~!*** ¡ni hablar!; **way in** entrada *f*; **way of life** modo *m* de vida; **way out** salida *f*

we [wiː] nosotros *mpl*, nosotras *fpl*; ***~ are the best*** somos los mejores

weak [wiːk] débil; *tea*, *coffee* poco cargado; **weaken 1** *v/t* debilitar **2** *v/i* debilitarse; **weakness** debilidad *f*

wealth [welθ] riqueza *f*; **wealthy** rico

weapon ['wepən] arma *f*

wear [wer] **1** *n*: ***~ (and tear)*** desgaste *m* **2** *v/t* (*have on*) llevar; (*damage*) desgastar **3** *v/i* (*wear out*) desgastarse; (*last*) durar

◆ **wear down** agotar

◆ **wear off** *of effect* pasar

◆ **wear out 1** *v/t* (*tire*) agotar; *shoes* desgastar **2** *v/i of shoes*, *carpet* desgastarse

wearily ['wɪrɪlɪ] cansinamente; **weary** cansado

weather ['weðər] **1** *n* tiempo *m* **2** *v/t crisis* capear, superar; **weather-beaten** curtido; **weather forecast** pronóstico *m* del tiempo; **weather-**

man hombre *m* del tiempo
weave [wiːv] **1** *v/t* tejer **2** *v/i* *move* zigzaguear
web [web] *of spider* tela *f*; ***the Web*** COMPUT la Web; **web page** página *f* web; **web site** sitio *m* web
wedding ['wedɪŋ] boda *f*; **wedding anniversary** aniversario *m* de boda; **wedding day** día *m* de la boda; **wedding dress** vestido *m* de boda *or* novia; **wedding ring** anillo *m* de boda
wedge [wedʒ] cuña *f*; *of cheese etc* trozo *m*
Wednesday ['wenzdeɪ] miércoles *m inv*
weed [wiːd] **1** *n* mala hierba **2** *v/t* escardar; **weed-killer** herbicida *m*; **weedy** F esmirriado, enclenque
week [wiːk] semana *f*; ***a ~ tomorrow*** de mañana en una semana; **weekday** día *m* de la semana; **weekend** fin *m* de semana; ***on the ~*** el fin de semana; **weekly 1** *adj* semanal **2** *n magazine* semanario *m* **3** *adv* semanalmente
weep [wiːp] llorar
wee-wee ['wiːwiː] F pipí *m*; ***do a ~*** hacer pipí
weigh [weɪ] pesar
◆ **weigh up** (*assess*) sopesar
weight [weɪt] peso *m*; **weightlessness** ingravidez *f*; **weightlifter** levantador(a) *m*(*f*) de pesas; **weightlifting** halterofilia *f*, levantamiento *m* de pesas; **weighty** *fig* (*important*) serio
weir [wɪr] presa *f* (*rebasadero*)
weird [wɪrd] extraño, raro; **weirdo** F bicho *m* raro F
welcome ['welkəm] **1** *adj* bienvenido; ***you're ~!*** ¡de nada! **2** *n* bienvenida *f* **3** *v/t guests etc* dar la bienvenida a; *decision etc* acoger positivamente
weld [weld] soldar
welfare ['welfer] bienestar *m*; *financial assistance* subsidio *m* estatal; **welfare check** *cheque con el importe del subsidio estatal*; **welfare state** estado *m* del bienestar; **welfare worker** asistente *m*/*f* social
well[1] [wel] *n for water, oil* pozo *m*
well[2] [wel] **1** *adv* bien; ***as ~*** (*too*) también; ***as ~ as*** (*in addition to*) así como; ***very ~*** muy bien; ***~, ~ !*** *surprise* ¡caramba!; ***~ ...*** *uncertainty* bueno… **2** *adj*: ***be ~*** estar bien; **well-balanced** equilibrado; **well-behaved** educado; **well-being** bienestar *m*; **well-done** *meat* muy hecho; **well-dressed** bien vestido; **well-earned** merecido; **well-heeled** F adinerado, *Span* con pasta F; **well-informed** bien informado; **well-known** conocido; **well-meaning** bienintencionado; **well-off** acomodado; **well-timed** oportuno; **well-wisher** admirador(a) *m*(*f*)

west [west] **1** *n* oeste *m*; ***the West*** (*Western nations*) el Occidente; (*western part of a country*) el oeste **2** *adj* del oeste **3** *adv travel* hacia el oeste; **westerly** *wind* del oeste; *direction* hacia el oeste; **western 1** *adj* occidental **2** *n movie* western *m*, película *f* del oeste; **Westerner** occidental *m/f*; **westernized** occidentalizado; **West Indian 1** *adj* antillano **2** *n* antillano(-a) *m*(*f*); **West Indies:** ***the ~*** las Antillas; **westward** hacia el oeste

wet [wet] mojado; (*damp*) húmedo; (*rainy*) lluvioso; **wet suit** traje *m* de neopreno

whack [wæk] F (*blow*) porrazo *m* F

whale [weɪl] ballena *f*

what [wɑːt] **1** *pron* qué; ***~ is it?*** (*what do you want*) ¿qué quieres?; ***~ about heading home?*** ¿y si nos fuéramos a casa?; ***~ for?*** (*why*) ¿para qué?; ***so ~?*** ¿y qué?; ***take ~ you need*** toma lo que te haga falta **2** *adj* qué; ***~ color is the car?*** ¿de qué color es el coche?; **whatever:** ***~ the season*** en cualquier estación; ***ok ~*** vale, lo que tú digas

wheat [wiːt] trigo *m*

wheel [wiːl] rueda *f*; (*steering ~*) volante *m*; **wheelchair** silla *f* de ruedas; **wheel clamp** *Br* cepo *m*

wheeze [wiːz] resoplido *m*

when [wen] **1** *adv* cuándo; ***~ do you open?*** ¿a qué hora abren? **2** *conj* cuando; ***~ I was a child*** cuando era niño; **whenever** (*each time*) cada vez que; ***~ you like*** cuando quieras

where [wer] **1** *adv* dónde; ***~ from?*** ¿de dónde?; ***~ to?*** ¿a dónde? **2** *conj* donde; ***this is ~ I used to live*** aquí es donde vivía antes; **whereas** mientras que; **wherever 1** *conj* dondequiera que; ***sit ~ you like*** siéntate donde prefieras **2** *adv* dónde; ***~ can it be?*** ¿dónde puede estar?

whet [wet] *appetite* abrir

whether ['weðər] si; ***~ you approve or not*** te parezca bien o no

which [wɪʧ] **1** *adj* qué; ***~ one is yours?*** ¿cuál es tuyo? **2** *pron interrogative* cuál; *relative* que; ***take one, it doesn't matter ~*** toma uno, no importa cuál

whiff [wɪf] (*smell*) olorcillo *m*

while [waɪl] **1** *conj* mientras; (*although*) si bien **2** *n* rato *m*

whim [wɪm] capricho *m*

whimper ['wɪmpər] gimotear

whine [waɪn] *of dog* gimotear; F (*complain*) quejarse

whip [wɪp] **1** *n* látigo *m* **2** *v/t* (*beat*) azotar; *cream* batir; F (*defeat*) dar una paliza a F

whirlpool ['wɜːrlpuːl] *in river* remolino *m*; *for relaxation* bañera *f* de hidromasaje

whisk [wɪsk] **1** *n kitchen implement* batidora *f* **2** *v/t eggs* batir
whiskey ['wɪskɪ] whisky *m*
whisper ['wɪspər] susurrar
whistle ['wɪsl] **1** *n sound* silbido *m*; *device* silbato *m* **2** *v/t & v/i* silbar
white [waɪt] **1** *n* blanco *m*; *of egg* clara *f*; *person* blanco(-a) *m(f)* **2** *adj* blanco; **white-collar worker** *persona que trabaja en una oficina*; **White House** Casa *f* Blanca; **white lie** mentira *f* piadosa; **whitewash 1** *n* cal *f*; *fig* encubrimiento *m* **2** *v/t* encalar; **white wine** vino *m* blanco
whittle ['wɪtl] *wood* tallar
◆ **whittle down** reducir
whizzkid ['wɪzkɪd] F joven *m/f* prodigio
who [huː] *interrogative* ¿quién?; *relative* que; *~ do you want to speak to?* ¿con quién quieres hablar?; **whoever** quienquiera
whole [houl] **1** *adj* entero; *the ~ country* todo el país **2** *n* totalidad *f*; *on the ~* en general; **whole-hearted** incondicional; **wholesale** al por mayor; *fig* indiscriminado; **wholesaler** mayorista *m/f*; **wholesome** saludable, sano; **wholly** completamente
whom [huːm] *fml* quién
whore [hɔːr] prostituta *f*
whose [huːz] *interrogative* de quién; *relative* cuyo(-a); *~ is this?* ¿de quién es esto?; *a country ~ economy ...* un país cuya economía…
why [waɪ] por qué
wicked ['wɪkɪd] malvado
wicker ['wɪkər] de mimbre
wicket ['wɪkɪt] *in station, bank etc* ventanilla *f*
wide [waɪd] ancho; *experience, range* amplio; *be 12 feet ~* tener 12 pies de ancho; **widely** ampliamente; **widen 1** *v/t* ensanchar **2** *v/i* ensancharse; **wide-open** abierto de par en par; **wide-ranging** amplio; **widespread** extendido
widow ['wɪdou] viuda *f*; **widower** viudo *m*
width [wɪdθ] anchura *f*, ancho *m*
wield [wiːld] *weapon* empuñar; *power* detentar
wife [waɪf] mujer *f*, esposa *f*
wig [wɪg] peluca *f*
wiggle ['wɪgl] menear
wild [waɪld] *animal* salvaje; *flower* silvestre; *teenager, party* descontrolado; (*crazy: scheme*) descabellado; *applause* arrebatado
wilderness ['wɪldərnɪs] desierto *m*, yermo *m*
'wildlife flora *f* y fauna *f*
wilful *Br* ☞ ***willful***
will[1] [wɪl] *n law* testamento *m*
will[2] [wɪl] *n* (*willpower*) voluntad *f*
will[3] [wɪl] *v/aux*: *I ~ let you know tomorrow* te lo diré mañana; *the car won't start* el coche no arranca; *~ you*

tell her that ...? ¿le quieres decir que...?; **~ *you stop that!*** ¡basta ya!

willful ['wɪlfəl] *person* tozudo, obstinado; *action* deliberado, intencionado; **willing** dispuesto; **willingly** gustosamente; **willingness** buena disposición *f*; **willpower** fuerza *f* de voluntad

willy-nilly [wɪlɪ'nɪlɪ] (*at random*) a la buena de Dios

wilt [wɪlt] *of plant* marchitarse

wily ['waɪlɪ] astuto

wimp [wɪmp] F enclenque *m/f* F, blandengue *m/f* F

win [wɪn] **1** *n* victoria *f*, triunfo *m* **2** *v/t* & *v/i* ganar

wince [wɪns] hacer una mueca de dolor

wind[1] [wɪnd] *n* viento *m*; (*flatulence*) gases *mpl*

wind[2] [waɪnd] **1** *v/i* serpentear **2** *v/t* enrollar

◆ **wind up 1** *v/t clock* dar cuerda a; *car window* subir, cerrar; *speech* finalizar; *business* concluir; *company* cerrar **2** *v/i* (*finish*) concluir

'wind-bag F cotorra *f* F; **windfall** *fig* dinero *m* inesperado

winding ['waɪndɪŋ] serpenteante

window ['wɪndoʊ] *also* COMPUT ventana *f*; ***in the ~*** *of store* en el escaparate *or L.Am.* la vidriera; **window seat** asiento *m* de ventana; **window-shop:** ***go ~ping*** ir de escaparates *or L.Am.* vidrieras; **windowsill** alféizar *m*; **windshield**, *Br* **windscreen** parabrisas *m inv*; **windshield wiper** limpiaparabrisas *m inv*; **windsurfer** windsurfista *m/f*; *board* tabla *f* de windsurf; **windsurfing** el windsurf; **windy** ventoso

wine [waɪn] vino *m*; **wine cellar** bodega *f*; **wine list** lista *f* de vinos; **winery** bodega *f*

wing [wɪŋ] ala *f*; SP lateral *m/f*, extremo *m/f*; **wingspan** envergadura *f*

wink [wɪŋk] *of person* guiñar, hacer un guiño

winner ['wɪnər] ganador(a) *m*(*f*), vencedor(a) *m*(*f*); *of lottery* acertante *m/f*; **winning** ganador; **winning post** meta *f*; **winnings** ganancias *fpl*

winter ['wɪntər] invierno *m*; **winter sports** deportes *mpl* de invierno; **wintry** invernal

wipe [waɪp] limpiar; *tape* borrar

wiper ['waɪpər] ☞ ***windshield wiper***

wire [waɪr] alambre *m*; ELEC cable *m*; **wireless phone** teléfono *m* inalámbrico; **wiring** ELEC cableado *m*; **wiry** *person* fibroso

wisdom ['wɪzdəm] *of person* sabiduría *f*; *of action* prudencia *f*, sensatez *f*

wise [waɪz] sabio; *action, decision* prudente, sensato; **wisecrack** F chiste *m*; **wise-**

ly *act* prudentemente, sensatamente

wish [wɪʃ] **1** *n* deseo *m*; ***best ~es*** un saludo cordial **2** *v/t* desear

◆ **wish for** desear

wisp [wɪsp] *of hair* mechón *m*; *of smoke* voluta *f*

wistful ['wɪstfəl] nostálgico; **wistfully** con nostalgia

wit [wɪt] ingenio *m*; *person* ingenioso(-a) *m(f)*

witch [wɪʧ] bruja *f*; **witchhunt** *fig* caza *f* de brujas

with [wɪð] con; ***shivering ~ fear*** temblando de miedo; ***a girl ~ brown eyes*** una chica de ojos castaños; ***are you ~ me?*** (*do you understand*) ¿me sigues?; ***~ no money*** sin dinero

withdraw [wɪð'drɒ:] **1** *v/t* retirar **2** *v/i* retirarse; **withdrawal** retirada *f*; *of money* reintegro *m*; **withdrawal symptoms** síndrome *m* de abstinencia; **withdrawn** *person* retraído

wither ['wɪðər] marchitarse

with'hold *information* ocultar; *payment* retener; *consent* negar

with'in dentro de; *in expressions of time* en menos de

with'out sin

with'stand resistir, soportar

witness ['wɪtnɪs] **1** *n* testigo *m/f* **2** *v/t* ser testigo de

witticism ['wɪtɪsɪzm] comentario *m* gracioso; **witty** ingenioso, agudo

wobble ['wɑ:bl] tambalearse; **wobbly** tambaleante

wolf [wʊlf] **1** *n* lobo *m* **2** *v/t*: ~ (***down***) engullir

woman ['wʊmən] mujer *f*; **womanizer** mujeriego(-a) *m(f)*; **womanly** femenino

womb [wu:m] matriz *f*, útero *m*

women ['wɪmɪn] *pl* ☞ ***woman***; **women's lib** la liberación de la mujer

wonder ['wʌndər] **1** *n* (*amazement*) asombro *m*; ***no ~!*** ¡no me sorprende! **2** *v/i* preguntarse; ***I ~ if you could help*** ¿le importaría ayudarme?; **wonderful** maravilloso; **wonderfully** maravillosamente

won't [woʊnt] ☞ ***will not***

wood [wʊd] madera *f*; *for fire* leña *f*; (*forest*) bosque *m*; **wooded** arbolado; **wooden** (*made of wood*) de madera; **woodpecker** pájaro *m* carpintero; **woodwork** carpintería *f*

wool [wʊl] lana *f*; **woolen,** *Br* **woollen 1** *adj* de lana **2** *n* prenda *f* de lana

word [wɜ:rd] **1** *n* palabra *f* **2** *v/t letter* redactar; **word processor** procesador *m* de textos

work [wɜ:rk] **1** *n* trabajo *m*; ***out of ~*** desempleado, *Span* en el paro **2** *v/i of person* trabajar; *of machine*, (*succeed*) funcionar

◆ **work out 1** *v/t problem* resolver; *solution* encontrar **2** *v/i at gym* hacer ejercicios; *of relationship etc* funcionar, ir bien

workable ['wɜːrkəbl] *solution* viable; **workaholic F** *persona adicta al trabajo*; **workday** (*hours of work*) jornada *f* laboral; (*not a holiday*) día *m* de trabajo; **worker** trabajador(a) *m*(*f*); **workforce** trabajadores *mpl*; **work hours** horas *fpl* de trabajo; **working class** clase *f* trabajadora; **working-class** de clase trabajadora; **working hours** ☞ ***workhours***; **workload** cantidad *f* de trabajo; **workman** obrero *m*; **workmanlike** competente; **workmanship** factura *f*, confección *f*; **work of art** obra *f* de arte; **workout** sesión *f* de ejercicios; **work permit** permiso *m* de trabajo; **workshop** *also seminar* taller *m*

world [wɜːrld] mundo *m*; **world-class** de categoría mundial; **World Cup** Mundial *m*, Copa *f* del Mundo; **world-famous** mundialmente famoso; **worldly** mundano; **world record** récord *m* mundial *or* del mundo; **world war** guerra *f* mundial; **worldwide 1** *adj* mundial **2** *adv* en todo el mundo

worn-'out gastado; *person* agotado

worried ['wʌrɪd] preocupado; **worry 1** *n* preocupación *f* **2** *v/t* preocupar **3** *v/i* preocuparse; **worrying** preocupante

worse [wɜːrs] peor; ***get ~*** empeorar; **worsen** empeorar

worship ['wɜːrʃɪp] **1** *n* culto *m* **2** *v/t* adorar

worst [wɜːrst] peor

worth [wɜːrθ]: ***be ~ ...*** valer…; ***be ~ it*** valer la pena; **worthwhile** que vale la pena

worthy ['wɜːrðɪ] digno; *cause* justo

would [wʊd]: ***I ~ help if I could*** te ayudaría si pudiera; ***~ you like to go to the movies?*** ¿te gustaría ir al cine?; ***~ you close the door?*** ¿podrías cerrar la puerta?

wound [wuːnd] **1** *n* herida *f* **2** *v/t* herir

wow [waʊ] ¡hala!

wrap [ræp] envolver; **wrapping** envoltorio *m*; **wrapping paper** papel *m* de envolver

wrath [ræθ] ira *f*

wreath [riːθ] corona *f* de flores

wreck [rek] **1** *n* restos *mpl* **2** *v/t ship* hundir; *car* destrozar; *plans*, *marriage* arruinar; **wreckage** *of car, plane* restos *mpl*; *of marriage, career* ruina *f*; **wrecker** grúa *f*

wrench [rentʃ] **1** *n tool* llave *f* **2** *v/t* (*pull*) arrebatar

wrestle ['resl] luchar; **wrestler** luchador(a) *m*(*f*) (de lucha libre); **wrestling** lucha *f* libre

wriggle ['rɪgl] *(squirm)* menearse; *along the ground* arrastrarse; *into small space* escurrirse
wrinkle ['rɪŋkl] arruga *f*
wrist [rɪst] muñeca *f*; **wristwatch** reloj *m* de pulsera
write [raɪt] escribir; *check* extender
◆ **write off** *debt* cancelar; *car* destrozar
writer ['raɪtər] escritor(a) *m(f)*; *of book, song* autor(a) *m(f)*; **write-up** reseña *f*
writhe [raɪð] retorcerse
writing ['raɪtɪŋ] *words, text* escritura *f*; *(hand-~)* letra *f*; ***in ~*** por escrito; **writing paper** papel *m* de escribir
wrong [rɒːŋ] **1** *adj answer* equivocado; *decision* erróneo; ***be ~*** *of person* estar equivocado; *of answer* ser incorrecto; *morally* ser injusto; ***what's ~?*** ¿qué pasa?; ***you have the ~ number*** TELEC se ha equivocado **2** *adv* mal **3** *n* mal *m*; **wrongful** ilegal; **wrongly** erróneamente
wry [raɪ] socarrón

X

xenophobia [zenoʊ'foʊbɪə] xenofobia *f*
X-ray ['eksreɪ] **1** *n picture* radiografía *f* **2** *v/t* radiografiar

Y

yacht [jɑːt] yate *m*; **yachting** vela *f*
Yank [jæŋk] F yanqui *m/f*
yank [jæŋk] tirar de
yard[1] [jɑːrd] *of prison etc* patio *m*; *behind house* jardín *m*; *for storage* almacén *m* (*al aire libre*)
yard[2] [jɑːrd] *measurement* yarda *f*
'yardstick patrón *m*
yarn [jɑːrn] *(thread)* hilo *m*; F *(story)* batallita *f* F
yawn [jɒːn] **1** *n* bostezo *m* **2** *v/i* bostezar
year [jɪr] año *m*; ***be six ~s old*** tener seis años (de edad); **yearly 1** *adj* anual **2** *adv* anualmente
yeast [jiːst] levadura *f*
yell [jel] **1** *n* grito *m* **2** *v/t & v/i* gritar
yellow ['jeloʊ] amarillo
yelp [jelp] **1** *n* aullido *m* **2** *v/i* aullar
yes [jes] sí; **yes man** *pej* pelotillero *m*
yesterday ['jestərdeɪ] ayer; ***the day before ~*** anteayer
yet [jet] **1** *adv* todavía, aún; ***have you finished ~?*** ¿has acabado ya?; ***he hasn't ar-***

rived ~ todavía *or* aún no ha llegado **2** *conj* (*however*) sin embargo

yield [ji:ld] **1** *n from fields etc* cosecha *f*; *from investment* rendimiento *m* **2** *v/t fruit, good harvest* proporcionar; *interest* rendir **3** *v/i* (*give way*) ceder; *of driver* ceder el paso

yoga ['jougə] yoga *m*

yoghurt ['jougərt] yogur *m*

yolk [jouk] yema *f*

you [ju:] ◇ *as subject, singular* tú, *L.Am.* usted, *Rpl, C.Am.* vos; *formal* usted; *plural*: *Span* vosotros, vosotras, *L.Am.* ustedes; *formal* ustedes; ***do ~ know him?*** ¿lo conoces / conoce?

◇ *as object, singular* te, *L.Am.* le; *formal* le; *plural*: *Span* os, *L.Am.* les; *formal* les

◇ *with preps, singular* ti (*other forms as subject*)

◇ *people, one*: ***~ never know*** nunca se sabe; ***~ have to pay*** hay que pagar; ***exercise is good for ~*** es bueno hacer ejercicio

young [jʌŋ] joven; **youngster** joven *m/f*

your [jʊr] *singular* tu, *L.Am.* su; *formal* su; *plural*: *Span* vuestro, *L.Am.* su; *formal* su

yours [jʊrz] *singular* el tuyo, la tuya, *L.Am.* el suyo, la suya; *formal* el suyo, la suya; *plural* el vuestro, la vuestra, *L.Am.* el suyo, la suya; *formal* el suyo, la suya; ***it's ~*** es tuyo etc; ***a friend of ~*** un amigo tuyo / suyo / vuestro; ***~*** *at end of letter* un saludo

yourself [jʊr'self] *reflexive* te, *L.Am.* se; *formal* se; *emphatic* tú mismo *m*, tú misma *f*, *L.Am.* usted mismo, usted misma; *Rpl, C.Am.* vos mismo, vos misma; *formal* usted mismo, usted misma; ***did you hurt ~?*** ¿te hiciste / se hizo daño?; **yourselves** *reflexive* os, *L.Am.* se; *formal* se; *emphatic* vosotros mismos *mpl*, vosotras mismas *fpl*, *L.Am.* ustedes mismos, ustedes mismas; *formal* ustedes mismos, ustedes mismas; ***did you hurt ~?*** ¿os hicisteis / se hicieron daño?

youth [ju:θ] juventud *f*; (*young man*) joven *m/f*; **youth club** club *m* juvenil; **youthful** joven; *fashion, idealism* juvenil

yuppie ['jʌpɪ] F yupi *m/f*

Z

zap [zæp] F (COMPUT: *delete*) borrar; (*kill*) liquidar F; (*hit*) golpear; (*send*) enviar

zeal [ziːl] celo *m*

zero ['zɪroʊ] cero *m*

zest [zest] entusiasmo *m*

zigzag ['zɪgzæg] **1** *n* zigzag *m* **2** *v/i* zigzaguear

zilch [zɪltʃ] F nada de nada

zip [zɪp] *Br* cremallera *f*

◆ **zip up** *dress, jacket* cerrar la cremallera de; COMPUT compactar

'zip code código *m* postal;

zipper cremallera *f*

zit [zɪt] F *on face* grano *m*

zone [zoʊn] zona *f*

zonked [zɑːŋkt] P (*exhausted*) molido P

zoo [zuː] zoo *m*

zoology [zuː'ɑːlədʒɪ] zoología *f*

'zoom lens zoom *m*

zucchini [zuː'kiːnɪ] calabacín *m*

Los verbos irregulares ingleses

Se citan las tres partes principales de cada verbo: infinitivo, pretérito, participio del pasado.

arise - arose - arisen
awake - awoke - awoken, awaked
be (am, is, are) - was (were) - been
bear - bore - borne
beat - beat - beaten
become - became - become
begin - began - begun
bend - bent - bent
bet - bet, betted - bet, betted
bid - bid - bid
bind - bound - bound
bite - bit - bitten
bleed - bled - bled
blow - blew - blown
break - broke - broken
breed - bred - bred
bring - brought - brought
broadcast - broadcast - broadcast
build - built - built
burn - burnt, burned - burnt, burned
burst - burst - burst
buy - bought - bought
cast - cast - cast
catch - caught - caught
choose - chose - chosen
cling - clung - clung
come - came - come
cost (*v/i*) - cost - cost
creep - crept - crept
cut - cut - cut
deal - dealt - dealt
dig - dug - dug
dive - dived, dove [doʊv] (1) - dived
do - did - done
draw - drew - drawn
dream - dreamt, dreamed - dreamt, dreamed
drink - drank - drunk
drive - drove - driven
eat - ate - eaten
fall - fell - fallen
feed - fed - fed
feel - felt - felt
fight - fought - fought
find - found - found
flee - fled - fled
fling - flung - flung
fly - flew - flown
forbid - forbad(e) - forbidden
forecast - forecast(ed) - forecast(ed)
forget - forgot - forgotten
forgive - forgave - forgiven
freeze - froze - frozen
get - got - got, gotten (2)
give - gave - given

go - went - gone
grind - ground - ground
grow - grew - grown
hang - hung, hanged - hung, hanged (3)
have - had - had
hear - heard - heard
hide - hid - hidden
hit - hit - hit
hold - held - held
hurt - hurt - hurt
keep - kept - kept
kneel - knelt, kneeled - knelt, kneeled
know - knew - known
lay - laid - laid
lead - led - led
lean - leaned, leant - leaned, leant (4)
leap - leaped, leapt - leaped, leapt (4)
learn - learned, learnt - learned, learnt (4)
leave - left - left
lend - lent - lent
let - let - let
lie - lay - lain
light - lighted, lit - lighted, lit
lose - lost - lost
make - made - made
mean - meant - meant
meet - met - met
mow - mowed - mowed, mown
pay - paid - paid
plead - pleaded, pled - pleaded, pled (5)
prove - proved - proved, proven
put - put - put
quit - quit(ted) - quit(ted)
read - read [red] - read [red]
ride - rode - ridden
ring - rang - rung
rise - rose - risen
run - ran - run
saw - sawed - sawn, sawed
say - said - said
see - saw - seen
seek - sought - sought
sell - sold - sold
send - sent - sent
set - set - set
sew - sewed - sewed, sewn
shake - shook - shaken
shed - shed - shed
shine - shone - shone
shit - shit(ted), shat - shit(ted), shat
shoot - shot - shot
show - showed - shown
shrink - shrank - shrunk
shut - shut - shut
sing - sang - sung
sink - sank - sunk
sit - sat - sat
slay - slew - slain
sleep - slept - slept
slide - slid - slid

sling - slung - slung
slit - slit - slit
smell - smelt, smelled - smelt, smelled
sow - sowed - sown, sowed
speak - spoke - spoken
speed - sped, speeded - sped, speeded
spell - spelt, spelled - spelt, spelled (4)
spend - spent - spent
spill - spilt, spilled - spilt, spilled
spin - spun - spun
spit - spat - spat
split - split - split
spoil - spoiled, spoilt - spoiled, spoilt
spread - spread - spread
spring - sprang, sprung - sprung
stand - stood - stood
steal - stole - stolen
stick - stuck - stuck
sting - stung - stung
stink - stunk, stank - stunk
stride - strode - stridden
strike - struck - struck
swear - swore - sworn
sweep - swept - swept
swell - swelled - swollen
swim - swam - swum
swing - swung - swung
take - took - taken
teach - taught - taught
tear - tore - torn
tell - told - told
think - thought - thought
thrive - throve - thriven, thrived (6)
throw - threw - thrown
thrust - thrust - thrust
tread - trod - trodden
wake - woke, waked - woken, waked
wear - wore - worn
weave - wove - woven (7)
weep - wept - wept
win - won - won
wind - wound - wound
write - wrote - written

(1) **dove** no se usa en inglés británico
(2) **gotten** no se usa en inglés británico
(3) **hung** para un cuadro; **hanged** para un ajusticiado
(4) en inglés americano se suele emplear la forma terminada en **-ed**
(5) **pled** se usa en inglés americano y escocés
(6) **thrived** es la forma más común
(7) aunque **weaved** en la acepción *zigzaguear*

Numbers – Numerales

Cardinal Numbers – Números cardinales

0 cero *zero, Br tb nought*
1 uno, una *one*
2 dos *two*
3 tres *three*
4 cuatro *four*
5 cinco *five*
6 seis *six*
7 siete *seven*
8 ocho *eight*
9 nueve *nine*
10 diez *ten*
11 once *eleven*
12 doce *twelve*
13 trece *thirteen*
14 catorce *fourteen*
15 quince *fifteen*
16 dieciséis *sixteen*
17 diecisiete *seventeen*
18 dieciocho *eighteen*
19 diecinueve *nineteen*
20 veinte *twenty*
21 veintiuno *twenty-one*
22 veintidós *twenty-two*
30 treinta *thirty*
31 treinta y uno *thirty-one*
40 cuarenta *forty*
50 cincuenta *fifty*
60 sesenta *sixty*
70 setenta *seventy*

80	ochenta *eighty*
90	noventa *ninety*
100	cien(to) *a hundred, one hundred*
101	ciento uno *a hundred and one*
110	ciento diez *a hundred and ten*
200	doscientos, -as *two hundred*
300	trescientos, -as *three hundred*
324	trescientos, -as venticuatro *three hundred and twenty-four*
400	cuatrocientos, -as *four hundred*
500	quinientos, -as *five hundred*
600	seiscientos, -as *six hundred*
700	setecientos, -as *seven hundred*
800	ochocientos, -as *eight hundred*
900	novecientos, -as *nine hundred*
1000	mil *a thousand, one thousand*
1959	mil novecientos cincuenta y nueve *one thousand nine hundred and fifty-nine*
2000	dos mil *two thousand*
1 000 000	un millón *a million, one million*
2 000 000	dos millones *two million*

Notes:

i) In Spanish numbers a comma is used for decimals:
1,25 **one point two five** uno coma veinticinco

ii) A period is used where, in English, we would use a comma:
1.000.000 = 1,000,000

Numbers like this can also be written using a space instead of a comma:
1 000 000 = 1,000,000

Ordinal Numbers – Números ordinales

Español		English	
1°	primero	**1st**	*first*
2°	segundo	**2nd**	*second*
3°	tercero	**3rd**	*third*
4°	cuarto	**4th**	*fourth*
5°	quinto	**5th**	*fifth*
6°	sexto	**6th**	*sixth*
7°	séptimo	**7th**	*seventh*
8°	octavo	**8th**	*eighth*
9°	noveno, nono	**9th**	*ninth*
10°	décimo	**10th**	*tenth*
11°	undécimo	**11th**	*eleventh*
12°	duodécimo	**12th**	*twelfth*
13°	decimotercero	**13th**	*thirteenth*
14°	decimocuarto	**14th**	*fourteenth*
15°	decimoquinto	**15th**	*fifteenth*
16°	decimosexto	**16th**	*sixteenth*
17°	decimoséptimo	**17th**	*seventeenth*
18°	decimoctavo	**18th**	*eighteenth*
19°	decimonoveno, decimonono	**19th**	*nineteenth*
20°	vigésimo	**20th**	*twentieth*
21°	vigésimo prim(er)o	**21st**	*twenty-first*
22°	vigésimo segundo	**22nd**	*twenty-second*
30°	trigésimo	**30th**	*thirtieth*
31°	trigésimo prim(er)o	**31st**	*thirty-first*
40°	cuadragésimo	**40th**	*fortieth*
50°	quincuagésimo	**50th**	*fiftieth*
60°	sexagésimo	**60th**	*sixtieth*
70°	septuagésimo	**70th**	*seventieth*
80°	octogésimo	**80th**	*eightieth*
90°	nonagésimo	**90th**	*ninetieth*

100˚	centésimo	**100th**	*hundredth*
101˚	centésimo primero	**101st**	*hundred and first*
110˚	centésimo décimo	**110th**	*hundred and tenth*
200˚	ducentésimo	**200th**	*two hundredth*
300˚	tricentésimo	**300th**	*three hundredth*
400˚	cuadringentésimo	**400th**	*four hundredth*
500˚	quingentésimo	**500th**	*five hundredth*
600˚	sexcentésimo	**600th**	*six hundredth*
700˚	septingentésimo	**700th**	*seven hundredth*
800˚	octingentésimo	**800th**	*eight hundredth*
900˚	noningentésimo	**900th**	*nine hundredth*
1000˚	milésimo	**1000th**	*thousandth*
2000˚	dos milésimo	**2000th**	*two thousandth*
1 000 000˚	millonésimo	**1,000,000th**	*millionth*
2 000 000˚	dos millonésimo	**2,000,000th**	*two millionth*

Note:
Spanish ordinal numbers are ordinary adjectives and consequently must agree:

her 13th granddaughter
su decimotercera nieta

Dates – Fechas

1996	mil novecientos noventa y seis	*nineteen ninety-six*
2005	dos mil cinco	*two thousand (and) five*

el diez de noviembre, el 10 de noviembre
(on) November 10, *Br* (on) the 10th of November

el uno de marzo, *L.Am.* **el primero de marzo, el 1˚ de marzo**
(on) March 1, *Br* (on) the 1st of March

pronóstico . forecast